2019

Airline Transport Pilot

TEST PREP

Study & Prepare

Pass your test and know what is essential to become a safe, competent pilot—from the most trusted source in aviation training

Aviation Supplies & Academics, Inc.
Newcastle, Washington

Airline Transport Pilot Test Prep
2019 Edition

Aviation Supplies & Academics, Inc.
7005 132nd Place SE
Newcastle, Washington 98059-3153
425.235.1500
www.asa2fly.com

FAA Questions herein are from United States government sources and contain current information as of: June 2018

None of the material in this publication supersedes any documents, procedures or regulations issued by the Federal Aviation Administration.

ASA assumes no responsibility for any errors or omissions. Neither is any liability assumed for damages resulting from the use of the information contained herein.

Important: This Test Prep should be sold with and used in conjunction with *Computer Testing Supplement for Airline Transport Pilot and Aircraft Dispatcher* (FAA-CT-8080-7C + Addendums A, B, C).

ASA reprints the FAA test figures and legends contained within this government document, and it is also sold separately and available from aviation retailers nationwide. Order #ASA-CT-8080-7CY.

ASA-TP-ATP-19
ISBN   978-1-61954-658-5

Printed in the United States of America

2019   2018   5   4   3   2   1

About the Contributors

Jackie Spanitz
General Manager
Aviation Supplies & Academics, Inc.

As General Manager of Aviation Supplies & Academics, Jackie Spanitz oversees maintenance and development of more than 750 titles and pilot supplies in the ASA product line. Ms. Spanitz has worked with airman training and testing for more than 20 years, including participation in the ACS development committees. Jackie holds a Bachelor of Science degree in aviation technology from Western Michigan University, a Masters degree from Embry Riddle Aeronautical University, and Instructor and Commercial Pilot certificates. She is the author of *Guide to the Flight Review*, and the technical editor for ASA's *Test Prep* and *FAR/AIM* series.

Jim Higgins
Associate Professor of Aviation
University of North Dakota

Jim Higgins is an Associate Professor of Aviation at the University of North Dakota (UND) where he teaches Advanced Aircraft Operations, Transport Category Operations, and Crew Resource Management. Prior to joining the faculty at UND, he was a line pilot and check airman at American Eagle Airlines. Professor Higgins has accumulated over 4,000 hours of flight time primarily in part Part 121 operations.

About ASA: Aviation Supplies & Academics, Inc. (ASA) has been providing trusted aviation training products for more than 75 years to flight instructors, aviation maintenance technicians, air traffic controllers, career aviators, students, remote pilots and drone operators. ASA's pilot supplies, software, and publications are supported with integrity, consistency, superior quality, and the best customer service in the industry. Aviators are invited to visit **www.asa2fly.com** for a free copy of our catalog.

Stay informed of aviation industry happenings

Website www.asa2fly.com
Updates www.asa2fly.com/testupdate
Twitter www.twitter.com/asa2fly
Facebook www.facebook.com/asa2fly
Blog www.learntoflyblog.com

Contents

Continued

Preface

Welcome to ASA's Test Prep Series. ASA's test books have been helping pilots prepare for the FAA Knowledge Tests for more than 60 years with great success. We are confident that with proper use of this book, you will score very well on any of the Airline Transport Pilot tests.

Begin your studies with a classroom or home-study ground school course, which will involve reading a comprehensive textbook (see the FAA Knowledge Exam References list on page x). Conclude your studies with this Test Prep or comparable software. Read the question, select your choice for the correct answer, then read the explanation. Use the Learning Statement Codes and references that conclude each explanation to identify additional resources if you need further study of a subject. Upon completion of your studies, take practice tests at www.prepware.com (see inside front cover for your free account).

The FAA Airline Transport Pilot questions have been arranged into chapters based on subject matter. Topical study, in which similar material is covered under a common subject heading, promotes better understanding, aids recall, and thus provides a more efficient study guide. Study and place emphasis on those questions most likely to be included in your test (identified by the aircraft and test category above each question). For example: a pilot preparing for the ATP Multi-engine test would focus on the questions marked "ALL" and "ATM"; a pilot preparing for the ATP Single-engine test would focus on the questions marked "ALL" and "ATS"; a pilot preparing for the ATP Helicopter (135) test would focus on the questions marked "ALL" and "RTC"; and candidates for the Dispatcher certificate would focus on the questions marked "ALL" and "DSP."

It is important to answer every question assigned on your FAA Knowledge Test. If in their ongoing review, the FAA authors decide a question has no correct answer, is no longer applicable, or is otherwise defective, your answer will be marked correct no matter which one you chose. However, you will not be given the automatic credit unless you have marked an answer. Unlike some other exams you may have taken, there is no penalty for "guessing" in this instance.

The FAA exams are "closed tests" which means the exact database of questions is not available to the public. The question and answer choices in this book are based on our extensive history and experience with the FAA testing process. You might see similar although not exactly the same questions on your official FAA exam. Answer stems may be rearranged from the A, B, C order you see in this book. Therefore, be careful to fully understand the intent of each question and corresponding answer while studying, rather than memorize the A, B, C answer. You may be asked a question that has unfamiliar wording; studying and understanding the information in this book and the associated references will give you the tools to answer question variations with confidence.

If your study leads you to question an answer choice, we recommend you seek the assistance of a local instructor. We welcome your questions, recommendations or concerns:

Aviation Supplies & Academics, Inc.
7005 132nd Place SE   Voice: 425.235.1500   Fax: 425.235.0128
Newcastle, WA 98059-3153   Email: cfi@asa2fly.com Website: www.asa2fly.com

The FAA appreciates testing experience feedback. You can contact the branch responsible for the FAA Knowledge Exams at:

Federal Aviation Administration
AFS-630, Airman Testing Standards Branch
PO Box 25082
Oklahoma City, OK 73125   Email: afs630comments@faa.gov

Updates and Practice Tests

Free Test Updates for the One-Year Life Cycle of Test Prep Books

The FAA rolls out new tests as needed throughout the year; this typically happens in June, October, and February. The FAA exams are "closed tests" which means the exact database of questions is not available to the public. ASA combines more than 60 years of experience with expertise in airman training and certification tests to prepare the most effective test preparation materials available in the industry.

You can feel confident you will be prepared for your FAA Knowledge Exam by using the ASA Test Preps. ASA publishes test books each June and keeps abreast of changes to the tests. These changes are then posted on the ASA website as a Test Update.

Visit the ASA website before taking your test to be certain you have the most current information. While there, sign up for ASA's free email Update service. We will then send you an email notification if there is a change to the test you are preparing for so you can review the Update for revised and/or new test information.

www.asa2fly.com/testupdate

We invite your feedback. After you take your official FAA exam, let us know how you did. Were you prepared? Did the ASA products meet your needs and exceed your expectations? We want to continue to improve these products to ensure applicants are prepared, and become safe aviators. Send feedback to: **cfi@asa2fly.com**

Description of the Tests

All test questions are the objective, multiple-choice type, with three answer choices. Each question can be answered by the selection of a single response. The answer to some questions depend on the response to a previous question to calculate the correct answer.

The FAA Knowledge Exams are designed to test your knowledge in many subject areas. If you are pursuing an airline transport pilot certificate or added rating, you should review the appropriate sections of 14 CFR Part 61 for the specific knowledge areas on each test. Those taking the ATM or "ATP–Airline Transport Pilot Multi-engine" exam will be tested on Part 121 as one of the knowledge areas. Those taking the ATS or "ATP–Airline Transport Pilot Single-engine" exam will be tested on Part 135 as one of the knowledge areas.

An applicant for an aircraft dispatcher certificate should review the appropriate sections of 14 CFR Part 65 for the specific knowledge areas on the test. The applicant will be tested on Part 121 as one of the knowledge areas. If Part 135 commuter operators (as defined in DOT Part 298) are required to have aircraft dispatchers in the future, Part 135 questions will be added to the test. The aircraft dispatcher applicant is not required to have the flying skills of an airline transport pilot but is expected to have the same knowledge.

For the most efficient and effective study program, begin by reading the book cover to cover. Study **all** *the questions first,* **then** *refer to the following table, placing emphasis on those questions most likely to be included on your test (identified by the aircraft category above each question number).*

Test Code	Test Name	Test Prep Study	Number of Questions	Min. Age	Allotted Time (hrs)
ADX	Aircraft Dispatcher	ALL, DSP	80	21	3.5
ATM	ATP Multi-engine Airplane	ALL, ATM	125	18 or 21	4.0
ATS	ATP Single-engine Airplane (Part 135)	ALL, ATS	90	21	3.0
ATH	ATP–Helicopter (Part 135)	ALL, RTC	80	21	3.0
ARH	ATP–Helicopter–Added Rating (Part 135)*	ALL, RTC	50	21	2.5
ACM	ATP Canadian Conversion ME**	ALL, ATM	60	23	2.5
ASC	ATP Canadian Conversion SE**	ALL, ATS	40	23	2.0
ACH	ATP Canadian Conversion– Helicopter**	ALL, ATH	40	23	2.0

*Expert Study Tip
If it's been more than 24 months since you took the initial ATP FAA Knowledge Exam, we recommend that you prepare for the Add-On test using the "ATP Single-engine" or "ATP–Helictoper (Part 135)" test. This will better prepare you for all questions that may be included on your add-on test.

**This test focuses on U.S. regulations, procedures and operations.

A score of 70 percent must be attained to successfully pass each test.

Note: All applicants transitioning from ATP airplane and/or helicopter need to take the additional knowledge test. For example, an applicant adding a helicopter rating to an existing ATP–Airplane certificate **will** need to take the 50-question add-on test.

Knowledge Test Eligibility Requirements

If you are pursuing an airline transport or aircraft dispatcher certificate, you should review Title 14 of the Code of Federal Regulations (14 CFR) Part 61, §61.23 "Medical Certificates: Requirement and Duration," 14 CFR §61.35 "Knowledge Test: Prerequisites and Passing Grades," and 14 CFR Part 61 (ATP) or Part 65 (ADX) for certificate requirements.

Process for Taking a Knowledge Test

The FAA has designated holders of airman knowledge testing (AKT) organization designation authorization (ODA). These AKT-ODAs sponsor hundreds of knowledge testing center locations. The testing centers offer a full range of airman knowledge tests including: Aircraft Dispatcher, Airline Transport Pilot, Aviation Maintenance Technician, Commercial Pilot, Flight Engineer, Flight Instructor, Flight Navigator, Ground Instructor, Inspection Authorization, Instrument Rating, Parachute Rigger, Private Pilot, Recreational Pilot, Sport Pilot, Remote Pilot, and Military Competence. Contact information for the AKT-ODA holders is provided at the end of this section.

The first step in taking a knowledge test is the registration process. You may either call the testing centers' 1-800 numbers or simply take the test on a walk-in basis. If you choose to use the 1-800 number to register, you will need to select a testing center, schedule a test date, and make financial arrangements for test payment. You may register for tests several weeks in advance, and you may cancel your appointment according to the AKT-ODA holder's cancellation policy. If you do not follow the AKT-ODA holder's cancellation policies, you could be subject to a cancellation fee.

The next step in taking a knowledge test is providing proper identification. Although no prior authorization is necessary, except in the case of failure (see "Acceptable Forms of Authorization" below), proper identification is required to take any airline transport pilot, aircraft dispatcher, or flight navigator knowledge test. Testing center personnel will not begin the test until your identification is verified. For U.S. citizens, an acceptable form of photo I.D. includes, but is not limited to: driver's license, government-issued I.D. card, passport, alien residency card, and/or military I.D. card. For non-U.S. citizens, a passport is required, along with one or more of the following forms of photo I.D.: driver's license, government-issued I.D. card, and/or military I.D. card.

Proper identification contains your photograph, signature, date of birth (must show that you will meet the age requirement for the certificate sought before the expiration date of the Airman Test Report), and actual residential address, if different from your mailing address.

Acceptable Forms of Authorization

1. Requires *no* instructor endorsements or other form of written authorization.
2. Failed, passing or expired Airman Knowledge Test Report, provided the applicant still has the *original* test report in his/her possession. (*See* Retesting explanation.)

An applicant taking the ATM test must present a graduation certificate that shows completion of an ATP Certification Training Program (CTP) described in §61.156. A graduation certificate must contain the following information in order to be considered valid:

1. The full name, address, and FAA certificate number of the training provider authorized to conduct the course.
2. The full name, FAA pilot certificate number, and address of the graduate.

3. The following statement: "The applicant named above has successfully completed the airline transport pilot Certification Training Program as required by §61.156, and therefore has met the prerequisite required by §61.35(a)(2) for the airline transport pilot airplane knowledge test."

4. The date of issuance.

5. The signature of the authorized instructor who completed the academic portion of the course.

6. A sequential number on the certificate starting with the first four identifiers of the training provider's certificate number.

Test-Taking Tips

Prior to launching the actual test, the AKT-ODA holder's testing software will provide you with an opportunity to practice navigating through the test. This practice (or tutorial) session may include a "sample" question(s). These sample questions have no relation to the content of the test, but are meant to familiarize you with the look and feel of the system screens, including selecting an answer, marking a question for later review, time remaining for the test, and other features of the testing software.

Follow these time-proven tips, which will help you develop a skillful, smooth approach to test-taking:

1. Be careful to fully understand the intent of each question and corresponding answer while studying, rather than memorize the A, B, C answer choice — answer stems may appear in a different order than you studied.

2. Take with you to the testing center proof of eligibility for this certificate, photo I.D., the testing fee, calculator, flight computer (ASA's E6-B, Micro E6-B which has the high-speed wind correction slide, or CX-3 Flight Computer), plotter, magnifying glass, and a sharp pointer, such as a safety pin.

3. Your first action when you sit down should be to write on the scratch paper the weight and balance and any other formulas and information you can remember from your study. Remember, some of the formulas may be on your E6-B.

4. Answer each question in accordance with the latest regulations and guidance publications.

5. Read each question carefully before looking at the possible answers. You should clearly understand the problem before attempting to solve it.

6. After formulating an answer, determine which answer choice corresponds the closest with your answer. The answer chosen should completely resolve the problem.

7. From the answer choices given, it may appear that there is more than one possible answer. However, there is only one answer that is correct and complete. The other answers are either incomplete, erroneous, or represent popular misconceptions.

8. If a certain question is difficult for you, it is best to mark it for REVIEW and proceed to the other questions. After you answer the less difficult questions, return to those which you marked for review and answer them. Be sure to untag these questions once you've answered them. The review marking procedure will be explained to you prior to starting the test. Although the computer should alert you to unanswered questions, make sure every question has an answer recorded. This procedure will enable you to use the available time to the maximum advantage.

9. Perform each math calculation twice to confirm your answer. If adding or subtracting a column of numbers, reverse your direction the second time to reduce the possibility of errors.

10. When solving a calculation problem, select the answer nearest to your solution. The problem has been checked with various types of calculators; therefore, if you have solved it correctly, your answer will be closer to the correct answer than any of the other choices.

11. Remember that information is provided in the FAA Legends and FAA Figures.

12. Remember to answer every question, even the ones with no completely correct answer, to ensure the FAA gives you credit for a bad question.

13. Take your time and be thorough but relaxed. Take a minute off every half-hour or so to relax the brain and the body. Get a drink of water halfway through the test.

14. Your test will be graded immediately upon completion. You will be allowed 10 minutes to review any questions you missed. You will see the question only; you will not see the answer choices or your selected response. This allows you to review the missed areas with an instructor prior to taking the Practical exam.

Test Reports

Your test will be graded immediately upon completion. You will be allowed 10 minutes to review any questions you missed. You will see the question only; you will not see the answer choices or your selected response. This allows you to review the missed areas with an instructor prior to taking the Practical exam. After this review period you will receive your Airman Test Report, with the testing center's embossed seal, which reflects your score.

Validity of Airman Test Reports

For an Airman Test Report to be valid, it must be dated within the 24-calendar month period preceding the month you complete the practical test. If the Airman Test Report expires before completion of the practical test, you must retake the knowledge test.

The 24-month limitation does not apply if you:

1. are employed as a flight crewmember by a certificate holder under 14 CFR Parts 121, 125, or 135 at the time of the practical test and have satisfactorily accomplished that operator's approved:

   a. pilot in command aircraft qualification training program that is appropriate to the certificate and rating sought; and

   b. qualification training requirements appropriate to the certificate and ratings sought; or

2. are employed as a flight crewmember in scheduled U.S. military air transport operations at the time of the practical test, and have accomplished the pilot in command aircraft qualification training program that is appropriate to the certificate and rating sought.

3. Per 14 CFR 61.39(b), complete the airline transport pilot certification program in §61.156, then complete the practical within the 60-calendar month period preceding the month the applicant completes the practical.

Test Reports and Learning Statement Codes

The Airman Test Report lists the learning statement codes for questions answered incorrectly. The total number of learning statement codes shown on the Airman Test Report is not necessarily an indication of the total number of questions answered incorrectly. Study these knowledge areas to improve your understanding of the subject matter. See the *Learning Statement Code/Question Number Cross-Reference* in the back of this book for a complete list of which questions apply to each learning statement code.

Your instructor is required to provide instruction on each of these knowledge areas listed on your Airman Test Report and to complete an endorsement of this instruction. The Airman Test Report must be presented to the examiner prior to taking the practical test. During the oral portion of the practical test, the examiner is required to evaluate the noted areas of deficiency.

If you wish to have your test hand-scored (if you believe a question or your score are in error), you must submit a request, in the form of a signed letter, to the Airman Testing Standards Branch, AFS-630. The request must be accompanied by a copy of your Airman Knowledge Test Report and a legible photocopy of a government issued identification with your photograph and signature. Mail or fax this information to (e-mail requests are not accepted due to security issues): FAA, AFS-630, PO Box 25082, Oklahoma City, OK 73125 or fax to 405-954-4748.

Should you require a duplicate Airman Test Report due to loss or destruction of the original, send a signed request accompanied by a check or money order for $12 payable to the FAA. Your request should be sent to the Federal Aviation Administration, Airmen Certification Branch, AFS-760, P.O. Box 25082, Oklahoma City, OK 73125.

Airman Knowledge Testing Sites

The following airman knowledge testing (AKT) organization designation authorization (ODA) holders are authorized to give FAA knowledge tests. This list should be helpful in case you choose to register for a test or simply want more information. The latest listing of computer testing center locations is available on the FAA website at **http://www.faa.gov/pilots/testing**, under "Knowledge Testing" select "Commercial Testing Center List" and a PDF will download automatically.

Computer Assisted Testing Service (CATS)
Applicant inquiry and test registration: 800-947-4228 or 650-259-8550
www.catstest.com

PSI Computer Testing
Applicant inquiry and test registration: 800-211-2753 or 360-896-9111
www.psiexams.com

Use of Test Aids and Materials

Airman knowledge tests require applicants to analyze the relationship between variables needed to solve aviation problems, in addition to testing for accuracy of a mathematical calculation. The intent is that all applicants are tested on concepts rather than rote calculation ability. It is permissible to use certain calculating devices when taking airman knowledge tests, provided they are used within the following guidelines. The term "calculating devices" is interchangeable with such items as calculators, computers, or any similar devices designed for aviation-related activities.

Guidelines for Use of Test Aids and Materials

The applicant may use test aids and materials within the guidelines listed below, if actual test questions or answers are not revealed.

1. Applicants may use test aids, such as scales, straightedges, protractors, plotters, navigation computers, log sheets, and all models of aviation-oriented calculating devices that are directly related to the test. In addition, applicants may use any test materials provided with the test.

2. Manufacturer's permanently inscribed instructions on the front and back of such aids listed in 1(a), e.g., formulas, conversions, regulations, signals, weather data, holding pattern diagrams, frequencies, weight and balance formulas, and air traffic control procedures are permissible.

3. The test proctor may provide calculating devices to applicants and deny them use of their personal calculating devices if the applicant's device does not have a screen that indicates all memory has been erased. The test proctor must be able to determine the calculating device's erasure capability. The use of calculating devices incorporating permanent or continuous type memory circuits without erasure capability is prohibited.

4. The use of magnetic cards, magnetic tapes, modules, computer chips, or any other device upon which prewritten programs or information related to the test can be stored and retrieved is prohibited. Printouts of data will be surrendered at the completion of the test if the calculating device used incorporates this design feature.

5. The use of any booklet or manual containing instructions related to the use of the applicant's calculating device is not permitted.

6. Dictionaries are not allowed in the testing area.

7. The test proctor makes the final determination relating to test materials and personal possessions that the applicant may take into the testing area.

Testing Procedures For Applicants Requesting Special Accommodations

If you are an applicant with a learning or reading disability, you may request approval from the local FAA office to take an airman knowledge test, using the special accommodations procedures outlined in the most current version of FAA Order 8080.6 "Conduct of Airman Knowledge Tests."

Prior to approval of any option, the FAA Aviation Safety Inspector must advise you of the regulatory certification requirement of being able to read, write, speak, and understand the English language.

Retesting Procedures

ADX

Retests do not require a 30-day waiting period if the applicant presents a signed statement from an airman holding a certificate and rating sought by the applicant. This statement must certify that the airman has given the applicant additional instruction in each of the subjects failed, and that the airman considers the applicant ready for retesting. Requires a 30-day waiting period for retesting if the applicant presents a failed test report without a signed statement.

Applicants taking retests *after previous failure* are required to submit the applicable score report indicating failure to the testing center prior to retesting. The original failed test report shall be retained by the proctor and attached to the applicable sign-in/out log. The latest test taken will reflect the official score.

All Airline Transport Pilot Tests

Applicants retesting *after failure* are required to submit the applicable score report indicating failure, along with an endorsement (on the test report) from an authorized instructor who gave the applicant the additional training, and certifying the applicant is competent to pass the test. The original failed test report (with retest endorsement) presented as authorization shall be retained by the proctor and attached to the applicable sign-in/out log. The latest test taken will reflect the official score.

ADX and All Airline Transport Pilot Tests

Applicants retesting *in an attempt to achieve a higher passing score* may retake the same test for a better grade after 30 days. The latest test taken will reflect the official score. Applicants are required to submit the *original* applicable score report indicating previous passing score to the testing center prior to testing. Testing center personnel must collect and destroy this report prior to issuing the new test report.

Note: The testing centers require a wait period of 24 hours before any applicant may retest.

Cheating or Other Unauthorized Conduct

Computer testing centers must follow strict security procedures to avoid test compromise. These procedures are established by the FAA and are covered in FAA Order 8080.6, Conduct of Airman Knowledge Tests. The FAA has directed testing centers to terminate a test at any time a test proctor suspects a cheating incident has occurred. An FAA investigation will then be conducted. If the investigation determines that cheating or unauthorized conduct has occurred, then any airman certificate or rating that you hold may be revoked, and you will be prohibited for 1 year from applying for or taking any test for a certificate or rating under 14 CFR Part 61.

Eligibility Requirements for the Airline Transport Pilot Certificate

To be eligible for an Airline Transport Pilot Certificate, a person must:

1. Be at least 23 years old (or 21 if meeting 61.160 requirements).
2. Be of good moral character.
3. Read, write and understand English, and speak it without impediment that would interfere with radio conversation.
4. Have a current third-class medical certificate.
5. Pass a knowledge examination on the appropriate subjects with a score of at least 70 percent.
6. Pass an oral and flight check on the subjects and maneuvers in the Airline Transport Pilot and Type Rating Practical Test Standards (#ASA-8081-5).
7. Have a Commercial Pilot Certificate or foreign or military equivalent.
8. For an ATP–Airplane Multi-engine or an ATP obtained concurrently with an airplane type rating, receive a graduation certificate from an authorized training provider certifying completion of an ATP certification training program specified in §61.156 before applying for the knowledge test.
9. For an ATP certificate with an airplane category and class rating, have at least 1,500 hours of total time as a pilot that includes at least:
   a. 500 hours of cross-country flight time.
   b. 100 hours of night flight time.
   c. 50 hours of flight time in the class of airplane for the rating sought.
   d. 75 hours of instrument flight time, in actual or simulated instrument conditions,
   e. 250 hours of PIC time
10. For a rotorcraft category and helicopter class rating, have 1,200 hours pilot time including:
    a. 500 hours cross-country flight time
    b. 100 hours night time, at least 15 hours in helicopters
    c. 200 hours in helicopters including 75 hours PIC time
    d. 75 hours of actual or simulated instrument time with at least 50 hours in flight and 25 hours PIC time in helicopters.

Knowledge Exam References

The FAA references the following documents to write the FAA Knowledge Exam questions. You should be familiar with the latest revision for all of these as part of your ground school studies, which you should complete before starting test preparation:

FAA-G-8082-1 *Airline Transport Pilot, Aircraft Dispatcher and Flight Navigator Test Guide*

ANA *Aerodynamics for Naval Aviators*

CUG *Aeronautical Chart User's Guide*

Aeronautical Information Manual (AIM)

FAA-H-8083-25 *Pilot's Handbook of Aeronautical Knowledge*

FAA-H-8083-3 *Airplane Flying Handbook*, or FAA-H-8083-21 *Helicopter Flying Handbook*

FAA-H-8083-6 *Advanced Avionics Handbook*

FAA-H-8083-15 *Instrument Flying Handbook*

FAA-H-8083-1 *Aircraft Weight and Balance Handbook*

FAA-H-8083-2 *Risk Management Handbook*

FAA-H-8083-16 *Instrument Procedures Handbook*

FAA-S-8081-5 *ATP Practical Test Standards*

AC 00-6 *Aviation Weather*

AC 00-24 *Thunderstorms*

AC 00-30 *Atmospheric Turbulence Avoidance*

AC 00-45 *Aviation Weather Services*

AC 00-54 *Pilot Wind Shear Guide*

AC 20-117 *Hazards Following Ground Deicing & Ground Operations in Conditions Conducive to Aircraft Icing*

AC 91-6 *Water, Slush and Snow on the Runway*

AC 91-43 *Unreliable Airspeed Indication*

AC 91-51 *Effect of Icing on Aircraft Control and Airplane Deice and Anti-Ice Systems*

AC 91-74 *Pilot Guide Flight in Icing Conditions*

AC 135-17 *Pilot Guide-Small Aircraft Ground Deicing*

AC 120-51 *Crew Resource Management Training*

AC 120-58 *Pilot Guide for Large Aircraft Ground Deicing*

14 CFR Part 1, 25, 61, 63, 71, 91, 97, 117, 119, 121, 125, 135

49 CFR Part 830

Chart Supplements U.S. (previously Airport/Facility Directory or A/FD)

IFR Enroute High Altitude Chart

IFR Enroute Low Altitude Chart

STAR — Standard Terminal Arrival

U.S. Terminal Procedures

Visit the ASA website for these and many more titles and pilot supplies for your aviation endeavors: **www.asa2fly.com**

ASA Test Prep Layout

The sample FAA questions have been sorted into chapters according to subject matter. Within each chapter, the questions have been further classified and all similar questions grouped together with a concise discussion of the material covered in each group. This discussion material of "Chapter text" is printed in a larger font and spans the entire width of the page. Immediately following the sample FAA Question is ASA's Explanation in *italics*. The last line of the Explanation contains the Learning Statement Code and further reference (if applicable). *See* the EXAMPLE below.

Figures referenced by the Chapter text only are numbered with the appropriate chapter number, i.e., "Figure 1-1" is Chapter 1's first chapter-text figure.

Some Questions refer to Figures or Legends immediately following the question number, i.e., "**8201.** (Refer to Figure 14.)." These are FAA Figures and Legends which can be found in the separate booklet: *Computer Testing Supplement* (CT-8080-XX). This supplement is bundled with the Test Prep and is the exact material you will have access to when you take your computerized test. We provide it separately, so you will become accustomed to referring to the FAA Figures and Legends as you would during the test.

Figures referenced by the Explanation and pertinent to the understanding of that particular question are labeled by their corresponding Question number. For example: the caption "Questions 8245 and 8248" means the figure accompanies the Explanations for both Question 8245 and Question 8248.

Answers to each question are found at the bottom of each page.

EXAMPLE:

Chapter text

Four aerodynamic forces are considered to be basic because they act upon an aircraft during all flight maneuvers. There is the downward-acting force called WEIGHT which must be overcome by the upward-acting force called LIFT, and there is the rearward-acting force called DRAG, which must be overcome by the forward-acting force called THRUST.

Category rating. This question may be found on tests for these ratings.*

ALL, ATM, ATS, DSP, RTC ◄

8201. (Refer to Figure 14.) The four forces acting on an airplane in flight are

See separate book: *Computerized Testing Supplement* (CT-8080-XX)

A— lift, weight, thrust, and drag.
B— lift, weight, gravity, and thrust. ◄
C— lift, gravity, power, and friction.

Question and answer choices

Lift, weight, thrust, and drag are the four basic ◄
aerodynamic forces acting on an aircraft in flight.
(PLT235) — FAA-H-8083-25 ◄

Explanation

Answer (B) is incorrect because the force of gravity is always the same number and reacts with the airplane's mass to produce a different weight for almost every airplane. Answer (C) is incorrect because weight is the final product of gravity, thrust is the final product of power, and drag is the final product of friction. Power, gravity, and friction are only parts of the aerodynamic forces of flight.

Code line. FAA Learning Statement Code in parentheses, followed by references for further study.

Incorrect answer explanation. Reasons why answer choices are *incorrect* explained here.

* Note: The FAA does *not* identify which questions are on the different ratings' tests. Unless the wording of a question is pertinent to only one rating category, it may be found on *any* of the tests.

ALL = All operations   **ATM** = Multi-engine operations
ATS = Single-engine operations   **DSP** = Dispatcher   **RTC** = Rotorcraft

Chapter 1
Regulations

Applicable Regulations

Although "FAR" is used as the acronym for "Federal Aviation Regulations," and found throughout the regulations themselves and hundreds of other publications, the FAA is now actively discouraging its use. "FAR" also means "Federal Acquisition Regulations." To eliminate any possible confusion, the FAA is now citing the federal aviation regulations with reference to Title 14 of the Code of Federal Regulations. For example, "FAR Part 91.3" is now referenced as "14 CFR Part 91 Section 3." The regulations change frequently; answer all questions in compliance with the most current regulations.

Three different Federal Aviation Regulation Parts can apply to operations of aircraft covered by this chapter: Parts 91, 121, and 135. Part 91 encompasses the general operation and flight rules for all aircraft operating within the United States. Often the rules of Part 121 or 135 supplement or even supersede Part 91. When an airplane is not operated for compensation, only the Part 91 rules apply. For the test, assume Part 121 or 135 rules apply unless the question specifically states otherwise.

Part 121 applies to air carriers (airlines) engaged in interstate or overseas air transportation. Carriers which operate under Part 121 engage in **common carriage**. This means that they offer their services to the public and receive compensation for those services.

Part 121 operators are subdivided into three categories. Carriers authorized to conduct scheduled operations within the 48 contiguous states are **domestic air carriers**. **Flag air carriers** conduct scheduled operations inside and outside the 48 contiguous states. A **supplemental carrier** conducts its operations anywhere that its operations specifications permit but only on a nonscheduled basis. There is a fourth category, **commercial operators of large aircraft**, but they must comply with the rules covering supplemental carriers and the distinction is unimportant to this discussion.

Part 135 applies to air taxi operators. These operators are subdivided into two categories, commuter and on-demand operations.

Other parts of the regulations apply as well. Part 61 governs certification of pilots and flight instructors. Part 67 covers the issuing and standards for medical certificates. Part 1 contains definitions and abbreviations.

The ATP Certificate

All required flight crew of an air carrier flight must hold Airline Transport Pilot (ATP) certificates with the appropriate type rating.

The pilot-in-command of a large aircraft (gross weight over 12,500 pounds) or of a turbojet powered airplane must have a type rating from that aircraft issued under 14 CFR Part 61.

Any type rating(s) on the pilot certificate of an applicant who successfully completes an ATP checkride will be included on the ATP Certificate with the privileges and limitations of the ATP Certificate, provided the applicant passes the checkride in the same category and class of aircraft for which the applicant holds the type rating(s). However, if a type rating for that category and class of aircraft on the superseded pilot certificate is limited to VFR, that limitation will be carried forward to the person's ATP Certificate level.

An ATP certificate holder may give instruction in "air transportation service" in aircraft for which he/she holds category, class and type ratings as an ATP. An ATP may not instruct more than 8 hours a day and not more than 36 hours in any 7-day period.

If a person's pilot or medical certificate is lost or destroyed he/she can request the FAA to send a FAX confirming that they were issued. This FAX can be used as a temporary replacement for the certificates for up to 60 days.

Continued

If a pilot certificate holder is convicted of driving under the influence of alcohol or drugs, the pilot must report that conviction to the FAA, Civil Aviation Security Division within 60 days. Failure to do so is grounds for suspending or revoking any pilot or flight instructor certificates held by that person.

A **crewmember** is a person assigned to duty in the aircraft during flight. This includes pilots, flight engineers, navigators, flight attendants or anyone else assigned to duty in the airplane. A **flight crewmember** is a pilot, flight engineer or flight navigator assigned to duty in the aircraft during flight.

No one may serve as a pilot on an air carrier after that person has reached his/her 65th birthday. Note that this rule applies to any pilot position in the aircraft, but it does not apply to other flight crew positions such as flight engineer or navigator. This is known as the "Age 65 Rule."

To exercise **ATP privileges** (such as pilot-in-command of an air carrier flight), a pilot must hold a first-class medical certificate issued within the preceding (6 or 12) calendar months — depending on whether the applicant is over or under 40 years of age. To exercise commercial pilot privileges (e.g. flying a parachute jump operation) a pilot must hold either a first- or second-class medical certificate within the preceding (6 or 12) calendar months. For example, a first-class certificate issued in February to a pilot over 40 years of age would be good anytime in February for ATP privileges through August 31 and then good through the last day of February the next year for commercial pilot privileges.

A prerequisite for taking a practical test requires the applicant hold at least a current third-class medical certificate, if a medical certificate is required. If the practical test is scheduled in an aircraft, the applicant is required to have the third-class medical certificate. The applicant is not required to hold a medical certificate when taking a test or check for a certificate, rating, or authorization conducted in a flight simulator or flight training device.

ALL
9350. Unless otherwise authorized, when is the pilot-in-command required to hold a type rating?

A— When operating an aircraft that is certificated for more than one pilot.
B— When operating an aircraft having a gross weight of more than 12,500 pounds.
C— When operating a multiengine aircraft having a gross weight of more than 6,000 pounds.

A person must hold a type rating to act as pilot-in-command of a large aircraft (over 12,500 pounds gross takeoff weight), or of a turbojet-powered airplane. (PLT443) — 14 CFR §61.31

Answer (A) is incorrect because an aircraft requiring more than one pilot does not constitute the need for a type rating. Answer (C) is incorrect because it does not matter if the aircraft is single-engine or multi-engine, and the aircraft must weigh over 12,500 lbs., not 6,000.

ALL
9350-1. The second-in-command of an aircraft in domestic operation under 14 CFR 121 must hold

A— an airline transport pilot certificate and a first class medical.
B— an airline transport pilot certificate with an SIC aircraft type rating.
C— a commercial pilot certificate with instrument rating, a second-class medical, and a type rating appropriate for the aircraft being flown.

No certificate holder may use nor may any pilot act as second-in-command (SIC) unless the pilot holds an airline transport pilot certificate and an appropriate aircraft type rating for the aircraft being flown. A second-in-command type rating obtained under 61.55 does not satisfy these requirements. (PLT450) — 14 CFR §121.436

Answers

9350   [B]   9350-1   [B]

ALL

9328. A commercial pilot has a type rating in a B-727 and B-737. A flight test is completed in a B-747 for the Airline Transport Pilot Certificate. What pilot privileges may be exercised regarding these airplanes?

A— Commercial – B-737; ATP – B-727 and B-747.
B— ATP – B-747; Commercial – B-727 and B-737.
C— ATP – B-747, B-727, and B-737.

Any type rating(s) on the pilot certificate of an applicant who successfully completes an ATP checkride will be included on the ATP Certificate with the privileges and limitations of the ATP Certificate, provided the applicant passes the checkride in the same category and class of aircraft for which the applicant holds the type rating(s). However, if a type rating for that category and class of aircraft on the superseded pilot certificate is limited to VFR, that limitation shall be carried forward to the person's ATP Certificate level. (PLT443)—14 CFR §61.157

ALL

9329. A commercial pilot has DC-3 and DC-9 type ratings. A flight test is completed for an Airline Transport Pilot Certificate in a B-727. What pilot privileges may be exercised?

A— ATP – B-727 and DC-3; Commercial – DC-9.
B— ATP – B-727 only; Commercial – DC-9 and DC 3.
C— ATP – B-727, DC-3, and DC-9.

Any type rating(s) on the pilot certificate of an applicant who successfully completes an ATP checkride will be included on the ATP Certificate with the privileges and limitations of the ATP Certificate, provided the applicant passes the checkride in the same category and class of aircraft for which the applicant holds the type rating(s). However, if a type rating for that category and class of aircraft on the superseded pilot certificate is limited to VFR, that limitation shall be carried forward to the person's ATP Certificate level. (PLT442) — 14 CFR §61.157

ALL

9329-1. The lowest CAT II minimums are

A— DH 100 and RVR 1200.
B— DH 150 and RVR 1600.
C— DH 50 and RVR 1200.

A Category II or Category III pilot authorization is issued by a letter of authorization as part of an applicant's instrument rating or ATP certificate. Upon original issue, the authorization contains the following limitations: for Category II operations, the limitation is 1,600 feet RVR and a 150-foot decision height. (PLT442) — 14 CFR 61.13

ALL

9329-2. The lowest authorized ILS minimums associated with CAT II approaches are

A— Decision Height (DH) 200 feet and Runway Visual Range (RVR) 2,400 feet (with touchdown zone and centerline lighting, RVR 1,800 feet).
B— DH 100 feet and RVR 1,200 feet.
C— No DH or DH below 50 feet and RVR less than 700 feet but not less than 150 feet.

Category I (CAT I) operation is a precision instrument approach and landing with a decision altitude that is not lower than 200 feet (60 meters) above the threshold and with either a visibility of not less than 1/2 statute mile (800 meters), or a runway visual range of not less than 1,800 feet (550 meters). Category II (CAT II) operation is a precision instrument approach and landing with a decision height lower than 200 feet (60 meters), but not lower than 100 feet (30 meters), and with a runway visual range of not less than 1,200 feet (350 meters). Category III (CAT III) operation is a precision instrument approach and landing with a decision height lower than 100 feet (30 meters) or no DH, and with a runway visual range less than 1200 feet (350 meters). (PLT442) — FAA-H-8083-16

ALL

9330. In a 24-hour consecutive period, what is the maximum time, excluding briefing and debriefing, that an airline transport pilot may instruct other pilots in air transportation service?

A— 6 hours.
B— 8 hours.
C— 10 hours.

An airline transport pilot may instruct other pilots in air transportation service in aircraft of the category, class and type for which he/she is rated. However, the ATP may not instruct for more than 8 hours in one day nor more than 36 hours in any 7-day period. (PLT460) — 14 CFR §61.167

ALL

9331. The flight instruction of other pilots in air transportation service by an airline transport pilot is restricted to

A— 30 hours in any 7-consecutive-day period.
B— 7 hours in any 24-consecutive-hour period.
C— 36 hours in any 7-consecutive-day period.

The ATP may not instruct for more than 8 hours in one day nor more than 36 hours in any 7-day period. (PLT460) — 14 CFR §61.167

Answers

| 9328 [C] | 9329 [C] | 9329-1 [B] | 9329-2 [B] | 9330 [B] | 9331 [C] |

ALL
9351. When a facsimile replacement is received for an airman's medical certificate, for what maximum time is this document valid?

A— 30 days.
B— 60 days.
C— 90 days.

A person who has lost an Airman's Certificate or a Medical Certificate, or both, may obtain a FAX from the FAA confirming that it was issued. The FAX may be carried as temporary certificate(s) for a period not to exceed 60 days. (PLT447) — 14 CFR §61.29

ALL
9332. How soon after the conviction for driving while intoxicated by alcohol or drugs shall it be reported to the FAA, Civil Aviation Security Division?

A— No later than 30 working days after the motor vehicle action.
B— No later than 60 days after the motor vehicle action.
C— Required to be reported upon renewal of medical certificate.

Each person holding a certificate issued under this part shall provide a written report of each motor vehicle action to the FAA, Civil Aviation Security Division, no later than 60 days after the motor vehicle action. (PLT463) — 14 CFR §61.15

ALL
9325. Which is a definition of the term "crewmember"?

A— Only a pilot, flight engineer, or flight navigator assigned to duty in an aircraft during flight time.
B— A person assigned to perform duty in an aircraft during flight time.
C— Any person assigned to duty in an aircraft during flight except a pilot or flight engineer.

"Crewmember" means a person assigned to perform duty in an aircraft during flight time. (PLT395) — 14 CFR §1.1

Answer (A) is incorrect because "crewmember" pertains to anyone assigned duty in the aircraft during flight. Answer (C) is also incorrect because "crewmember" also includes the pilot and flight engineer.

ALL
9349. When a type rating is to be added to an airline transport pilot certificate, and the practical test is scheduled in an approved flight simulator and an aircraft, the applicant is

A— required to have a least a current third-class medical certificate.
B— required to have a current first-class medical certificate.
C— not required to hold a medical certificate.

A prerequisite for taking a practical test requires that the applicant hold at least a current third-class medical certificate, if a medical certificate is required. In this case, since part of the practical test is scheduled in an aircraft, the applicant is required to have at least a current third-class medical certificate. (PLT427) — 14 CFR §61.39

ALL
9335. An applicant who is taking a practical test for a type rating to be added to a commercial pilot certificate, in an approved simulator, is

A— required to have a first-class medical certificate.
B— required to have a second-class medical certificate.
C— not required to have a medical certificate.

A prerequisite for taking a practical test requires that the applicant hold at least a current third-class medical certificate, if a medical certificate is required. The applicant is not required to hold a medical certificate when taking a test or check for a certificate, rating, or authorization conducted in a flight simulator or flight training device. In this case, since the practical test is scheduled in an approved flight simulator, the applicant is not required to have a medical certificate. (PLT427) — 14 CFR §§61.39, 61.23

Answers

9351	[B]	9332	[B]	9325	[B]	9349	[A]	9335	[C]

ALL

9333. An applicant who is scheduled for a practical test for an airline transport pilot certificate, in an approved flight simulator, is

A— required to have at least a current third-class medical certificate.
B— not required to have a medical certificate.
C— required to have a first-class medical certificate.

A prerequisite for taking a practical test requires that the applicant hold at least a current third-class medical certificate, if a medical certificate is required. The applicant is not required to hold a medical certificate when taking a test or check for a certificate, rating, or authorization conducted in a flight simulator or flight training device. In this case, since the practical test is scheduled in an approved flight simulator, the applicant is not required to have a medical certificate. (PLT427) — 14 CFR §61.39 and §61.23

ALL

9343. When a type rating is to be added to an airline transport pilot certificate, and the practical test is scheduled in an approved flight training device and/or approved flight simulator, the applicant is

A— required to have at least a third-class medical certificate.
B— is not required to have a medical certificate.
C— required to have a first-class medical certificate.

A prerequisite for taking a practical test requires that the applicant hold at least a current third-class medical certificate, if a medical certificate is required. The applicant is not required to hold a medical certificate when taking a test or check for a certificate, rating, or authorization conducted in a flight simulator or flight training device. In this case, since the practical test is scheduled in an approved flight training device and/or approved flight simulator, the applicant is not required to have a medical certificate. (PLT427) — 14 CFR §§61.39, 61.23

ALL

9340. An applicant who is scheduled for a practical test for an airline transport pilot certificate, in an aircraft, needs

A— a first-class medical certificate.
B— at least a current third-class medical certificate.
C— a second-class medical certificate.

A prerequisite for taking a practical test requires that the applicant hold at least a current third-class medical certificate, if a medical certificate is required. In this case, since the practical test is scheduled in an aircraft, the applicant is required to have at least a current third-class medical certificate. (PLT427) — 14 CFR §61.39

ATM, DSP

8191. The "age 65 rule" of 14 CFR Part 121 applies to

A— any required pilot crewmember.
B— any flight crewmember.
C— the pilot in command only.

No person may serve as a pilot on an airplane engaged in operations under 14 CFR Part 121 if that person has reached his/her 65th birthday. (PLT443) — 14 CFR §121.383

Answer (B) is incorrect because the "age 65" rule excludes flight engineers and navigators. Answer (C) is incorrect because the "age 65" rule applies to every pilot crewmember.

Answers

9333   [B]   9343   [B]   9340   [B]   8191   [A]

Flight Engineer Requirements

Many air carrier aircraft have a **flight engineer** as a required flight crewmember. All older airplanes that have a maximum takeoff weight of more than 80,000 pounds must have a flight engineer. On aircraft types certified after 1963, the aircraft's "type certificate" states whether or not a flight engineer is required.

On each flight that requires a flight engineer, at least one other member of the flight crew must be qualified to provide emergency performance of the flight engineer's duties if he/she becomes ill or incapacitated. Either pilot can fulfill the function and they need not hold a Flight Engineer Certificate to be "qualified."

ATM, DSP

8189. Under which condition is a flight engineer required as a flight crewmember in 14 CFR Part 121 operations?

A— If the airplane is being flown on proving flights, with revenue cargo aboard.

B— If the airplane is powered by more than two turbine engines.

C— If required by the airplane's type certificate.

No certificate holder may operate an airplane for which a type certificate was issued before January 2, 1964, having a maximum certificated takeoff weight of more than 80,000 pounds without a flight crewmember holding a current Flight Engineer Certificate. For each airplane type certificated after January 1, 1964, the requirement for a flight engineer is determined under the type certification requirements of 14 CFR §25.1523. (PLT409) — 14 CFR §121.387

Answer (A) is incorrect because the type certificate is the determining factor for a flight engineer. Answer (B) is incorrect because the type certificate is the determining factor for a flight engineer.

ATM, DSP

8190. When the need for a flight engineer is determined by aircraft weight, what is the takeoff weight that requires a flight engineer?

A— 80,000 pounds.

B— more than 80,000 pounds.

C— 300,000 pounds.

No certificate holder may operate an airplane for which a type certificate was issued before January 2, 1964, having a maximum certificated takeoff weight of more than 80,000 pounds without a flight crewmember holding a current Flight Engineer Certificate. (PLT440) — 14 CFR §121.387

ATM, DSP

8212. An air carrier uses an airplane that is certified for operation with a flightcrew of two pilots and one flight engineer. In case the flight engineer becomes incapacitated,

A— at least one other flight crewmember must be qualified to perform the flight engineer duties.

B— one crewmember must be qualified to perform the duties of the flight engineer.

C— one pilot must be qualified and have a flight engineer certificate to perform the flight engineer duties.

On each flight requiring a flight engineer at least one flight crewmember, other than the flight engineer, must be qualified to provide emergency performance of the flight engineer's functions for the safe completion of the flight if the flight engineer becomes ill or is otherwise incapacitated. A pilot need not hold a Flight Engineer's Certificate to perform the flight engineer's functions in such a situation. (PLT440) — 14 CFR §121.385

ATM, DSP

8213. When a flight engineer is a required crewmember on a flight, it is necessary for

A— one pilot to hold a flight engineer certificate and be qualified to perform the flight engineer duties in an emergency.

B— the flight engineer to be properly certificated and qualified, but also at least one other flight crewmember must be qualified and certified to perform flight engineer duties.

C— at least one other flight crewmember to be qualified to perform flight engineer duties, but a certificate is not required.

On each flight requiring a flight engineer at least one flight crewmember, other than the flight engineer, must be qualified to provide emergency performance of the flight engineer's functions for the safe completion of the flight if the flight engineer becomes ill or is otherwise incapacitated. A pilot need not hold a Flight Engineer's Certificate to perform the flight engineer's functions in such a situation. (PLT440) — 14 CFR §121.385

Answers

8189   [C]   8190   [B]   8212   [A]   8213   [C]

ATM, DSP

8188. If a flight engineer becomes incapacitated during flight, who may perform the flight engineer's duties?

A— The second in command only.
B— Any flight crewmember, if qualified.
C— Either pilot, if they have a flight engineer certificate.

On each flight requiring a flight engineer at least one flight crewmember, other than the flight engineer, must be qualified to provide emergency performance of the flight engineer's functions for the safe completion of the flight if the flight engineer becomes ill or is otherwise incapacitated. A pilot need not hold a Flight Engineer's Certificate to perform the flight engineer's functions in such a situation. (PLT440) — 14 CFR §121.385

Flight Attendants

One or more **flight attendants** are required on each passenger carrying airplane operating under Part 121 that has more than nine passenger seats. The number of flight attendants is determined by the number of installed passenger seats — not by the actual number of passengers on board.

One flight attendant is required on airplanes that can seat from 10 through 50 passengers. Two flight attendants are required on airplanes having a seating capacity from 51 through 100 seats. After that, an additional flight attendant is required for each unit (or partial unit) of 50 seats above 100. For example, three flight attendants are required on airplanes having from 101 through 150 seats, and four flight attendants must be on aircraft with 151 through 200 seats.

ATM, DSP

8192. An airplane has seats for 149 passengers and eight crewmembers. What is the minimum number of flight attendants required with 97 passengers aboard?

A— Four.
B— Three.
C— Two.

For airplanes having a seating capacity of more than 100 passengers, each certificate holder shall provide at least two flight attendants plus one additional flight attendant for a unit (or partial unit) of 50 passenger seats above a seating capacity of 100 passengers. The number of flight attendants is determined by the number of installed passenger seats (not by the actual number of passengers on board). For an airplane with a seating capacity of 149 passengers, three flight attendants are required. (PLT389) — 14 CFR §121.391

ATM, DSP

8193. When an air carrier airplane with a seating capacity of 187 has 137 passengers on board, what is the minimum number of flight attendants required?

A— Five.
B— Four.
C— Three.

For airplanes having a seating capacity of more than 100 passengers, each certificate holder shall provide at least two flight attendants plus one additional flight attendant for a unit (or partial unit) of 50 passenger seats above a seating capacity of 100 passengers. The number of flight attendants is determined by the number of installed passenger seats (not by the actual number of passengers on board). For an airplane with a seating capacity of 187 passengers, four flight attendants are required. (PLT389) — 14 CFR §121.391

ATM, DSP

8201. What is the minimum number of flight attendants required on an airplane having a passenger seating capacity of 188 with only 117 passengers aboard?

A— Five.
B— Four.
C— Three.

For airplanes having a seating capacity of more than 100 passengers, each certificate holder shall provide at least two flight attendants plus one additional flight attendant for a unit (or partial unit) of 50 passenger seats above a seating capacity of 100 passengers. The number of flight attendants is determined by the number of installed passenger seats (not by the actual number of passengers on board). For an airplane with a seating capacity of 188 passengers, four flight attendants are required. (PLT389) — 14 CFR §121.391

Answers

8188   [B]   8192   [B]   8193   [B]   8201   [B]

ATM, DSP

8202. What is the minimum number of flight attendants required on an airplane with a passenger seating capacity of 333 when 296 passengers are aboard?

A— Seven.
B— Six.
C— Five.

For airplanes having a seating capacity of more than 100 passengers, each certificate holder shall provide at least two flight attendants plus one additional flight attendant for a unit (or partial unit) of 50 passenger seats above a seating capacity of 100 passengers. The number of flight attendants is determined by the number of installed passenger seats (not by the actual number of passengers on board). For an airplane with a seating capacity of 333 passengers, seven flight attendants are required. (PLT389) — 14 CFR §121.391

Experience and Training Requirements

For these definitions of training, aircraft are divided into two "groups." **Group I** aircraft are propeller driven. Turbojet aircraft are **Group II**. **Initial training** is the training required for crewmembers and dispatchers who have not qualified and served in the same capacity (i.e., flight engineer, co-pilot, pilot-in-command) on another aircraft of the same group. **Transition training** is the training required for crewmembers or dispatchers who have qualified and served in the same capacity on another aircraft of the same group. **Upgrade training** is the training required for crewmembers who have qualified and served as second-in-command or flight engineer on a particular airplane type (e.g., Boeing 727) before they can serve as pilot-in-command or second-in-command, respectively, on that airplane. **Differences training** is the training required for crewmembers or dispatchers who have qualified and served on a particular type of airplane before they can serve in the same capacity on a variation of that airplane. For example, a crewmember who is qualified on a Boeing 727-100 would need differences training to serve on a Boeing 727-200.

The pilot-in-command (PIC) of an air carrier flight must have had a proficiency check within the preceding 12 calendar months. In addition, within the preceding 6 calendar months the pilot-in-command must have either passed a proficiency check or completed an approved simulator training course. Pilots other than the PIC must have either passed a proficiency check or completed "line oriented" simulator training within the last 24 calendar months. In addition, the co-pilot must have had a **proficiency check** or any other kind of simulator training within the last 12 calendar months.

The pilot-in-command of an air carrier flight must have completed a **line check** in one of the aircraft types he/she is qualified to fly within the preceding 12 calendar months. If the PIC is qualified in more than one type aircraft, a line check in any of them satisfies this requirement.

Recurrent training and **checkrides** are always due during a calendar month rather than by a certain date. In addition, if recurrent training or a check is taken during, before, or after the month, it is considered to have been taken during the month it was due. For example, if a crewmember had a check due in December, he/she could take it November, December or January and it would be considered as having been done in December. Also, January would be considered a "grace month" in that the crewmember could fly, even though he/she had technically gone beyond the due date of the check.

Every pilot on an air carrier flight must have made at least 3 takeoffs and landings in the type of airplane flown within the preceding 90 days. If a pilot doesn't meet these requirements, he/she must re-establish the recency of experience by making 3 takeoffs and 3 landings under the supervision of a check airman. These takeoffs and landings must meet the following:

Answers

8202   [A]

- At least 1 takeoff must be made with a simulated failure of the most critical engine.
- At least 1 landing must be made from an ILS approach to the lowest ILS minimums authorized for the certificate holder.
- At least 1 landing must be made to a full stop.

Air Carriers' Operations Specifications are usually written so that the instrument experience requirements of 14 CFR Part 61 do not apply to their pilots. This test asks four questions on the Part 61 requirements: 9333, 9339, 9342, 9344.

The pilot-in-command of an airplane who has less than one hundred hours in the aircraft type has higher than published landing minimums at the destination airport. Such a pilot-in-command must add 100 feet to the published DH or MDA and add 1/2-mile (or 2,400 feet RVR) to the required visibility. If a flight diverts to an alternate airport, the pilot-in-command may use the published minimums for the approach there, but in no event may the landing minimums be less than 300 and 1. If a pilot has at least 100 hours PIC in another aircraft under Part 121 operations, he/she may reduce the current restriction by 1 hour for each landing, up to 50 hours maximum.

A Category II Instrument Approach is an ILS approach with a published minimum visibility of less than 1,800 RVR but equal to or greater than 1,200 RVR. Most CAT II approaches have published decision heights of 150 and 100 feet HAT. To fly a published CAT II approach, the aircraft must meet certain equipment and maintenance requirements and the pilots must be trained and qualified. Part 61 sets forth requirements for pilot qualification and an Air Carrier's Operations Specifications may modify or replace those requirements. The test limits its questions to Part 61 rules. To qualify for CAT II approach authorization, a pilot must take a CAT II checkride. To be eligible for the checkride he/she must meet all recent experience requirements of Part 61 and have certain recent experience with regard to ILS approaches. Within the previous 6 months the pilot must have made at least 6 ILS approaches down to minimums (CAT I minimums are OK). At least 3 of the approaches must have been hand flown. The other 3 may have been flown using an approach coupler. When issued an original CAT II certification, a pilot is restricted to a DH of 150 feet and a minimum RVR of 1,600. This restriction is lifted when the pilot logs 3 CAT II approaches to the 150-foot DH within the previous 6 months.

An aircraft dispatcher must have spent at least five hours observing flight deck operations within the preceding 12 calendar months. The dispatcher must have done this for at least one of the types for each group he/she is to dispatch.

ALL
9339. A pilot, acting as second-in-command, successfully completes the instrument competency check specified in 14 CFR Part 61. How long does this pilot remain current if no further IFR flights are made?

A— 12 months.
B— 90 days.
C— 6 months.

No pilot may act as pilot-in-command under IFR unless he/she has, within the preceding 6 calendar months in the aircraft category for the instrument privileges sought, logged at least 6 instrument approaches, performed holding procedures, and intercepted and tracked courses through the use of navigation systems, or passed an instrument competency check in the category of aircraft involved. (PLT442) — 14 CFR §61.57

Answer (A) is incorrect because, upon completion of an instrument competency check, a pilot will remain current for 6 months. Answer (B) is incorrect because ninety days defines the 3 takeoffs and landings experience required to carry passengers.

Answers
9339   [C]

ALL
9344. To satisfy the minimum required instrument experience for IFR operations, a pilot must accomplish during the past 6 months at least

A— six instrument approaches, holding, intercepting and tracking courses through the use of navigation systems in an approved flight training device/simulator or in the category of aircraft to be flown.
B— six instrument approaches, three of which must be in the same category and class of aircraft to be flown, plus holding, intercepting and tracking courses in any aircraft.
C— six instrument approaches and 6 hours of instrument time, three of which may be in a glider.

No pilot may act as pilot-in-command under IFR unless he/she has, within the preceding 6 calendar months in the aircraft category for the instrument approaches, performed holding procedures, and intercepted and tracked courses through the use of navigation systems. (PLT442) — 14 CFR §61.57

ALL
9342. What instrument flight time may be logged by a second-in-command of an aircraft requiring two pilots?

A— All of the time the second-in-command is controlling the airplane solely by reference to flight instruments.
B— One-half the time the flight is on an IFR flight plan.
C— One-half the time the airplane is in actual IFR conditions.

A pilot may log as instrument flight time only that time during which he/she operates the aircraft solely by reference to the instruments, under actual or simulated instrument flight conditions. (PLT409) — 14 CFR §61.51

Answers (B) and (C) are incorrect because only when the pilot is flying in actual or simulated instrument flying conditions and is the sole manipulator of the controls may he/she log instrument flight time.

ALL
9342-1. An example of air carrier experience a pilot may use towards the 1,000 hours required to serve as PIC in Part 121 is flight time as an SIC

A— in Part 121 operations.
B— in Part 91, subpart K operations.
C— in Part 135 operations.

ATP certificate holders may use the 1,000 hours required to serve as PIC in Part 121 operations, as SIC in Part 121 operations, or PIC in Part 91 and 135 operations. (PLT450) — 14 CFR §121.436

ALL
9342-2. The holder of an ATP certificate with restricted privileges or an ATP certificate who also holds an aircraft type rating for the aircraft to be flown may act as

A— a PIC for a Part 121 supplemental air carrier.
B— a PIC for a Part 121 air carrier with 500 hours as a Part 121 SIC.
C— an SIC for a Part 121 air carrier.

The holder of an ATP-Restricted certificate may serve as second-in-command (SIC) for Part 121 operations requiring less than three pilots. (PLT450) — 14 CFR §61.167

ALL
9334. What recent experience is required to be eligible for the practical test for the original issue of a Category II authorization?

A— Within the previous 6 months, six ILS approaches flown manually to the Category I DH.
B— Within the previous 12 calendar months, six ILS approaches flown by use of an approach coupler to the Category I or Category II DH.
C— Within the previous 6 months, six ILS approaches, three of which may be flown to the Category I DH by use of an approach coupler.

To be eligible for Category II authorization, a pilot must have made at least 6 ILS approaches since the beginning of the 6th month before the test. These approaches must be under actual or simulated instrument flight conditions down to the minimum landing altitude for the ILS approach in the type aircraft in which the flight test is to be conducted. However, the approaches need not be conducted down to the decision heights authorized for Category II operations. At least 3 of these approaches must have been conducted manually, without the use of an approach coupler. (PLT442) — 14 CFR §61.67

Answer (A) is incorrect because only 3 of the approaches must be flown manually to Category I DH. Answer (B) is incorrect because the 6 ILS approaches must be flown within the preceding 6 calendar months and 3 of the approaches must be flown without an approach coupler.

Answers

9344 [A]	9342 [A]	9342-1 [A]	9342-2 [C]	9334 [C]

ALL

9345. To be eligible for the practical test for the renewal of a Category II authorization, what recent instrument approach experience is required?

A— Within the previous 6 months, six ILS approaches, three of which may be flown to the Category I DH by use of an approach coupler.
B— Within the previous 6 months, six ILS approaches flown by use of an approach coupler to the Category I DH.
C— Within the previous 12 calendar months, three ILS approaches flown by use of an approach coupler to the Category II DH.

To be eligible for Category II authorization, a pilot must have made at least 6 ILS approaches since the beginning of the 6th month before the test. These approaches must be under actual or simulated instrument flight conditions down to the minimum landing altitude for the ILS approach in the type aircraft in which the flight test is to be conducted. However, the approaches need not be conducted down to the decision heights authorized for Category II operations. At least 3 of these approaches must have been conducted manually, without the use of an approach coupler. (PLT442) — 14 CFR §61.67

Answer (B) is incorrect because only 3 of the 6 approaches may be flown using an approach coupler. Answer (C) is incorrect because the requirement is for a total of 6 approaches, only 3 of which may be flown by the use of an approach coupler. The approaches are not required to be flown down to Category II DH. Also, they must have been flown within the preceding 6 calendar months.

ALL

9346. When may a Category II ILS limitation be removed?

A— When three Cat II ILS approaches have been completed to a 150-foot decision height and landing.
B— When six ILS approaches to Category II minimums and landing have been completed in the past 6 months.
C— 120 days after issue or renewal.

Upon original issue, a Category II authorization contains a limitation for Category II operations of 1,600 feet RVR and a 150-foot decision height. This limitation is removed when the holder shows that since the beginning of the 6th preceding month he/she has made 3 Category II ILS approaches to a landing under actual or simulated instrument conditions with a 150-foot decision height. (PLT407) — 14 CFR §61.13

ALL

9347. A Category II ILS pilot authorization, when originally issued, is normally limited to

A— Category II operations not less than 1600 RVR and a 150-foot DH.
B— pilots who have completed an FAA-approved Category II training program.
C— Category II operations not less than 1200 RVR and a 100-foot DH.

Upon original issue, a Category II authorization contains a limitation for Category II operations of 1,600 feet RVR and a 150-foot decision height. This limitation is removed when the holder shows that since the beginning of the 6th preceding month he/she has made 3 Category II ILS approaches to a landing under actual or simulated instrument conditions with a 150-foot decision height. (PLT407) — 14 CFR §61.13

Answer (B) is incorrect because all pilots must undergo FAA-approved training for a Category II authorization. The initial limitation is to RVR and DH for 6 months. Answer (C) is incorrect because a 1,200 RVR and a 100-foot DH are the Category II minimums after the initial limitation is removed by the pilot completing 3 ILS approaches to a 150-foot DH in the preceding 6 months.

ALL

9348. What is the lowest decision height for which a Category II applicant can be certified during the original issuance of the authorization?

A— 100 feet AGL.
B— 150 feet AGL.
C— 200 feet AGL.

Upon original issue, a Category II authorization contains a limitation for Category II operations of 1,600 feet RVR and a 150-foot decision height. (PLT420) — 14 CFR §61.13

Answer (A) is incorrect because a 100-foot DH is allowed only after completion of 3 Category II ILS approaches to a 150-foot DH. Answer (C) is incorrect because 200 feet is the standard Category I ILS DH.

Answers

9345 [A]   9346 [A]   9347 [A]   9348 [B]

ATM, DSP

8215. The training required by flight crewmembers who have not qualified and served in the same capacity on another airplane of the same group (e.g., turbojet powered) is

A— upgrade training.
B— transition training.
C— initial training.

Initial training is the training required for crewmembers and dispatchers who have not qualified and served in the same capacity on another airplane of the same group. (PLT407) — 14 CFR §121.400

Answer (A) is incorrect because upgrade training is required of a flight engineer or second-in-command when he/she trains for the next higher position in a particular airplane type. Answer (B) is incorrect because transition training is the training required for crewmembers and dispatchers who have qualified and served in the same capacity on another airplane of the same group.

ATM, DSP

8216. A crewmember who has served as second-in-command on a particular type airplane (e.g., B-727-100), may serve as pilot-in-command upon completing which training program?

A— Upgrade training.
B— Recurrent training.
C— Initial training.

Upgrade training is the training required for crewmembers who have qualified and served as second-in-command or flight engineer on a particular airplane type, before they serve as pilot-in-command or second-in-command respectively, on that airplane. (PLT407) — 14 CFR §121.400

Answer (B) is incorrect because recurrent training is a periodic requirement of crewmembers who are qualified in their positions. Answer (C) is incorrect because initial training is the first training received for crewmembers who have not previously qualified and served in the same airplane group (e.g., turboprop or turbojet).

ATM, DSP

8217. The training required for crewmembers or dispatchers who have been qualified and served in the same capacity on other airplanes of the same group is

A— difference training.
B— transition training.
C— upgrade training.

Transition training is the training required for crewmembers and dispatchers who have qualified and served in the same capacity on another airplane of the same group. (PLT407) — 14 CFR §121.400

Answer (A) is incorrect because difference training is required of a crewmember who is qualified on a particular type of airplane prior to becoming qualified in a variation of that same type. Answer (C) is incorrect because upgrade training is required of a crewmember who is qualified in a particular type of airplane and then desires to advance to the next higher position in that airplane, e.g., from copilot to pilot.

ATM, DSP

8205. A pilot in command must complete a proficiency check or simulator training within the preceding

A— 6 calendar months.
B— 12 calendar months.
C— 24 calendar months.

For a person to serve as pilot-in-command he/she must have completed a proficiency check within the preceding 12 calendar months and, in addition, within the preceding 6 calendar months, either a proficiency check or an approved simulator training course. (PLT407) — 14 CFR §121.441

Answer (B) is incorrect because a proficiency check is mandatory within the preceding 12 months. Additionally, a proficiency check or simulator training is required within the preceding 6 months. Answer (C) is incorrect because a 24-month time frame applies to pilots other than the pilot-in-command.

ATM, DSP

8207. A pilot flight crewmember, other than pilot in command, must have received a proficiency check or line-oriented simulator training within the preceding

A— 6 calendar months.
B— 12 calendar months.
C— 24 calendar months.

Pilots other than the pilot-in-command must have completed either a proficiency check or a line-oriented simulator training course within the preceding 24 calendar months. (PLT407) — 14 CFR §121.441

Answer (A) is incorrect because 6 months is the requirement for pilot-in-command to complete a proficiency check or simulator training. Answer (B) is incorrect because 12 months is the requirement for pilots other than pilot-in-command to receive a proficiency check or "any other kind of simulation training" (not necessarily line-oriented simulator training).

Answers

| 8215 [C] | 8216 [A] | 8217 [B] | 8205 [A] | 8207 [C] |

ATM, DSP

8210. What are the line check requirements for the pilot in command for a domestic air carrier?

A— The line check is required every 12 calendar months in one of the types of airplanes to be flown.

B— The line check is required only when the pilot is scheduled to fly into special areas and airports.

C— The line check is required every 12 months in each type aircraft in which the pilot may fly.

No certificate holder may use any person nor may any person serve as pilot-in-command of an airplane unless, within the preceding 12 calendar months that person has passed a line check in which he/she satisfactorily performs the duties and responsibilities of a pilot-in-command in one of the types of airplanes to be flown. (PLT442) — 14 CFR §121.440

ATM, DSP

8214. If a flight crewmember completes a required annual flight check in December 2010 and the required annual recurrent flight check in January 2012, the latter check is considered to have been taken in

A— November 2010.
B— December 2011.
C— January 2011.

Whenever a crewmember or aircraft dispatcher who is required to take recurrent training, a flight check, or a competency check, takes the check or completes the training in the calendar month before or after the month in which that training or check is required, he/she is considered to have taken or completed it in the calendar month in which it was required. (PLT449) — 14 CFR §121.401

ATM, DSP

8208. Which is one of the requirements that must be met by a required pilot flight crewmember in re-establishing recency of experience?

A— At least one landing must be made with a simulated failure of the most critical engine.

B— At least one ILS approach to the lowest ILS minimums authorized for the certificate holder and a landing from that approach.

C— At least three landings must be made to a complete stop.

When a pilot has not made 3 takeoffs and landings within the preceding 90 days, the pilot must make at least 3 takeoffs and landings in the type of airplane in which that person is to serve or in an advanced simulator. These takeoffs and landings must include:

1. *At least 1 takeoff with a simulated failure of the most critical powerplant;*

2. *At least 1 landing from an ILS approach to the lowest ILS minimum authorized for the certificate holder; and*

3. *At least 1 landing to a full stop.*

(PLT442) — 14 CFR §121.439

Answer (A) is incorrect because at least 1 takeoff is required with a simulated failure of the most critical powerplant. Answer (C) is incorrect because only 1 landing to a complete stop is required.

ATM, DSP

8209. What is one of the requirements that must be met by an airline pilot to re-establish recency of experience?

A— At least one landing must be made from a circling approach.

B— At least one full stop landing must be made.

C— At least one precision approach must be made to the lowest minimums authorized for the certificate holder.

When a pilot has not made 3 takeoffs and landings within the preceding 90 days, the pilot must make at least 3 takeoffs and landings in the type of airplane in which that pilot is to serve, or in an advanced simulator. These takeoffs and landings must include:

1. *At least 1 takeoff with a simulated failure of the most critical powerplant;*

2. *At least 1 landing from an ILS approach to the lowest ILS minimum authorized for the certificate holder; and*

3. *At least 1 landing to a full stop.*

(PLT442) — 14 CFR §121.439

Answers (A) and (C) are incorrect because the only instrument approach required is an ILS approach to the lowest minimums authorized for the certificate holder.

Answers

8210 [A]	8214 [B]	8208 [B]	8209 [B]

ATM, DSP

8289. When a pilot's flight time consists of 80 hours' pilot in command in a particular type airplane, how does this affect the minimums for the destination airport?

A— Has no effect on destination but alternate minimums are no less than 300 and 1.

B— Minimums are decreased by 100 feet and 1/2 mile.

C— Minimums are increased by 100 feet and 1/2 mile.

If the pilot-in-command has not served 100 hours as pilot-in-command in operations under Part 121 in the type of airplane he/she is operating, the MDA or DH and visibility landing minimums in the certificate holder's operations specifications for regular, provisional, or refueling airports are increased by 100 feet and 1/2 mile (or the RVR equivalent). (PLT443) — 14 CFR §121.652

ATM, DSP

9586. (Refer to Figures 115, 116, 117, 118, 118A, 118B, and 118C.) At ARLIN Intersection, PTL 130 is notified that the Phoenix Sky Harbor Airport is closed. PTL 130 is told to proceed to Tucson. PTL 130 is operating under 14 CFR Part 121. The PIC on PTL 130 has less than 100 hours as PIC in the B-727 (approach category C). What are the PICs minimums for the VOR RWY 11L approach at Tucson Intl Airport?

A— 2,860-1/2.

B— 2,900-1.

C— 2,960-1.

If the pilot-in-command has not served 100 hours as PIC under Part 121 operations in the airplane type, the MDA or DH visibility minimums are increased by 100 feet and 1/2 mile above the published minimums. If a flight goes to an alternate airport, the minimums do not have to be raised by 100-1/2, but they can't be less than 300-1. In this case, 36 feet had to be added to the MDA to comply with the 300-1 rule. (PLT083) — 14 CFR §121.652

ATM, DSP

9589. (Refer to Figure 118A.) Determine the 14 CFR Part 121 landing minimums for the LOC BC RWY 26L approach at Phoenix Sky Harbor Intl.

PIC time 94 hours
Airplane V_{S0} maximum certificated weight 105 knots
V_{REF} approach speed 140 knots
DME NOTAMed OTS

A— 1,800/1-3/4.

B— 1,900/2-1/4.

C— 1,900/2-1/2.

Compute the approach category by multiplying 1.3 times the V_{S0} at the airplane's maximum weight. See FAA Legend 7. In this case 105 x 1.3 = 136.5 knots, which is category C. The category C minimums for the LOC BC RWY 26L without Haden is 1800 and 1-3/4. If the pilot-in-command of the airplane has not served 100 hours as PIC in Part 121 operations in the airplane type, the MDA or DH visibility minimums are increased by 100 feet and 1/2 mile above the published minimums. OTS stands for out of service. (PLT083) — 14 CFR §121.652

ATM, DSP

9646. (Refer to Figures 190, 195, 195A, 196 and 196A.) The PIC of PIL 10 has 87.5 hours and 26 landings as PIC in the B-767, while operating under Part 121. The PIC has 1,876 hours and 298 landings, as PIC in the L-1011 while operating under Part 121. What are the minimums for the ILS/DME RWY 35R approach at DEN for the PIC?

A— 5567/18.

B— 5667/42.

C— 5631/20.

If the pilot-in-command has not served 100 hours as PIC under Part 121 operations in the airplane type, the MDA or DH visibility minimums are increased by 100 feet and 1/2 mile above the published minimums. However, if the pilot has at least 100 hours of PIC time in another airplane under Part 121 operations, he/she may reduce the current restriction by one hour for each landing. If the total of landings and hours in the current airplane add up to 100 or more, the PIC may fly approaches to the published minimums. The maximum allowable reduction is 50 hours. (PLT443) — 14 CFR §121.652

Answers

8289   [C]   9586   [B]   9589   [B]   9646   [A]

ATM, DSP

9663. (Refer to Figure 206.) The PIC of PTL 55 has 75 hours and 30 landings as PIC in the B-747, while operating under Part 121. The PIC has 759 hours and 312 landings, as PIC, in the B-767 while operating under Part 121. What are the minimums for the ILS RWY 19L approach at SFO, for the PIC?

A— 308/64.
B— 208/40.
C— 308-1.

If the pilot-in-command has not served 100 hours as PIC under Part 121 operations in the airplane type, the MDA or DH visibility minimums are increased by 100 feet and 1/2 mile above the published minimums. However, if the pilot has at least 100 hours of PIC time in another airplane under Part 121 operations, he/she may reduce the current restriction by one hour for each landing. If the total of landings and hours in the current airplane add up to 100 or more, the PIC may fly approaches to the published minimums. The maximum allowable reduction is 50 hours. (PLT443) — 14 CFR §121.652

Answer (A) is incorrect because the PIC is not required to increase landing weather minimums by the 100 feet and 1/2-mile visibility because he/she substituted one hour for each of the 30 landings made in the 747 while operating under Part 121 (since the pilot also has at least 100 hours as PIC in another type airplane). In this case, the pilot had 759 landings in the B-767 while operating under Part 121. Answer (C) is incorrect because the pilot does not need to adjust the landing minimums (also the visibility adjustment is incorrect).

ATM, DSP

8285. Category II ILS operations below 1600 RVR and a 150-foot DH may be approved after the pilot in command has

A— logged 90 hours' flight time, 10 takeoffs and landings in make and model airplane and three Category II ILS approaches in actual or simulated IFR conditions with 150-foot DH since the beginning of the sixth preceding month, in operations under 14 CFR parts 91 and 121.
B— made at least six Category II approaches in actual IFR conditions with 100-foot DH within the preceding 12 calendar months.
C— logged 100 hours' flight time in make and model airplane under 14 CFR part 121 and three Category II ILS approaches in actual or simulated IFR conditions with 150-foot DH since the beginning of the sixth preceding month.

If the pilot-in-command of an airplane has not served 100 hours as pilot-in-command in operations under 14 CFR Part 121 in the type of airplane he/she is operating, the MDA or DH and visibility landing minimums in the certificate holder's operations specifications for regular, provisional, or refueling airports are increased by 100 feet and 1/2 mile (or the RVR equivalent). In addition, CAT II minimums and the sliding scale do not apply. Upon original issue, a Category II authorization contains a limitation for Category II operations of 1,600 feet RVR and a 150-foot decision height. This limitation is removed when the holder shows that since the beginning of the 6th preceding month he/she has made 3 Category II ILS approaches to a landing under actual or simulated instrument conditions with a 150-foot decision height. (PLT444) — 14 CFR §121.652 and §61.13

DSP

8230. To remain current as an aircraft dispatcher, a person must, in addition to other requirements,

A— within the preceding 12 calendar months, spend 2.5 hours observing flight deck operations, plus two additional takeoff and landings, in one of the types of airplanes in each group he/she is to dispatch.
B— within the preceding 12 calendar months, spend at least 5 hours observing flight deck operations in one of the types of airplanes in each group he/she is to dispatch.
C— within the preceding 12 calendar months, spend at least 5 hours observing flight deck operations in each type of airplane, in each group that he/she is to dispatch.

No domestic or flag air carrier may use any person as an aircraft dispatcher unless, within the preceding 12 calendar months, he/she has satisfactorily completed operating familiarization consisting of at least 5 hours observing operations from the flight deck under 14 CFR Part 121 in one of the types of airplanes in each group he/she is to dispatch. (PLT450) — 14 CFR §121.463

Answers

9663   [B]   8285   [C]   8230   [B]

Part 135 Flight Crew Requirements

ATS

8082. What are the minimum certificate and rating requirements for the pilot in command of a multiengine airplane being operated by a commuter air carrier?

A— Airline transport pilot; airplane category; multiengine class.

B— Commercial pilot; airplane category; multiengine class; instrument rating; airplane type rating, if required.

C— Airline transport pilot; airplane category; multiengine class; airplane type rating, if required.

No certificate holder may use a person, nor may any person serve, as pilot-in-command in passenger-carrying operations of a turbojet airplane, or an airplane having a passenger seating configuration, excluding any crew-member seat, of 10 seats or more, or a multi-engine airplane being operated by "commuter operations," unless that person holds an Airline Transport Pilot Certificate with appropriate category and class ratings and, if required, an appropriate type rating for that aircraft. (PLT443) — 14 CFR §135.243

ATS

8083. What are the minimum certificate and rating requirements for the pilot-in-command of a multiengine airplane in commuter air carrier service under IFR?

A— Airline transport pilot of any category; multiengine class rating.

B— Airline transport pilot; airplane category; multiengine class rating; airplane type rating, if required.

C— Commercial pilot; airplane category; multiengine class and instrument rating.

No certificate holder may use a person, nor may any person serve, as pilot-in-command in passenger-carrying operations of a turbojet airplane, or an airplane having a passenger seating configuration, excluding any crew-member seat, of 10 seats or more, or a multi-engine airplane being operated by "commuter operations," unless that person holds an Airline Transport Pilot Certificate with appropriate category and class ratings and, if required, an appropriate type rating for that aircraft. (PLT443) — 14 CFR §135.243

ATS

8094. Which takeoff computation must not exceed the length of the runway plus the length of the stopway for a turbine-engine-powered small transport category airplane?

A— Takeoff distance.

B— Acceleration-stop distance.

C— Acceleration-climb distance.

The accelerate-stop distance, as defined in 14 CFR §25.109, must not exceed the length of the runway plus the length of any stopway. (PLT456) — 14 CFR §135.379 and §135.397

ATS

8100. A person is assigned as pilot in command to fly both single-engine and multiengine airplanes and has passed the initial instrument proficiency check in a multiengine airplane. Which requirement applies regarding each succeeding instrument check?

A— The instrument check must be taken every 6 calendar months in both a single-engine and a multiengine airplane.

B— The instrument check must be taken alternately in single-engine and multiengine airplanes every 6 calendar months.

C— The instrument check may be taken in either a single-engine or multiengine airplane if taken at intervals of 6 calendar months.

No certificate holder may use a pilot, nor may any person serve as a pilot-in-command of an aircraft under IFR unless, since the beginning of the 6th calendar month before that service, that pilot has passed an instrument proficiency check given by the FAA or authorized check pilot. If the pilot-in-command is assigned to both single-engine aircraft and multi-engine aircraft, that pilot must initially take the instrument proficiency check in a multi-engine aircraft and each succeeding check alternately in single-engine and multi-engine aircraft. (PLT442) — 14 CFR §135.297

Answers

8082 [C]	8083 [B]	8094 [B]	8100 [B]

ATS

8103. A person is acting as pilot in command of a multiengine, turboprop-powered airplane operated in passenger-carrying service by a commuter air carrier. If eight takeoffs and landings are accomplished in that make and basic model, which additional pilot-in-command experience meets the requirement for designation as pilot in command?

A— 7 hours, and two takeoffs and landing.
B— 10 hours, and three takeoffs and landings.
C— 10 hours, and two takeoffs and one landings.

No certificate holder may use any person, nor may any person serve, as a pilot-in-command of an aircraft operated by "commuter operations" in passenger-carrying operations, unless that person has completed, on that make and basic model aircraft and in that crewmember position the following operating experience:

1. *Aircraft, single engine—10 hours;*

2. *Aircraft, multi-engine, reciprocating engine-powered—15 hours;*

3. *Aircraft, multi-engine, turbine engine-powered—20 hours; or*

4. *Airplane, turbojet-powered—25 hours.*

The hours of operating experience may be reduced to not less than 50% of the hours required above by the substitution of one additional takeoff and landing for each hour of flight. (PLT407) — 14 CFR §135.244

ATS

8107. What are the minimum certificate and rating requirements for the pilot in command of a turbojet airplane with two engines being operated by a Commuter Air Carrier (as defined in part 298)?

A— Airline transport pilot; airplane category; multiengine class rating; airplane type rating, if required.
B— Airline transport pilot of any category; multiengine class rating; airplane type rating.
C— Commercial pilot; airplane category; multiengine class rating; instrument rating; airplane type rating.

No certificate holder may use a person, nor may any person serve, as pilot-in-command in passenger-carrying operations of a turbojet airplane, or an airplane having a passenger seating configuration, excluding any crewmember seat, of 10 seats or more, or a multi-engine airplane being operated by "commuter operations" unless that person holds an Airline Transport Pilot Certificate

with appropriate category and class ratings and, if required, an appropriate type rating for that aircraft. (PLT443) — 14 CFR §135.243

ATS

8108. A person is acting as pilot in command of a multi-engine, reciprocating engine powered airplane operated in passenger-carrying service by a commuter air carrier. If five takeoffs and landings have been accomplished in that make and basic model, which additional pilot-in-command experience meets the requirement for designation as the pilot in command?

A— Two takeoffs and landings, and 8 hours.
B— Five takeoffs and landings, and 5 hours.
C— Three takeoffs and landings, and 7 hours.

No certificate holder may use any person, nor may any person serve, as a pilot-in-command of an aircraft operated by "commuter operations" in passenger-carrying operations, unless that person has completed, on that make and basic model aircraft and in that crewmember position the following operating experience:

1. *Aircraft, single engine—10 hours;*

2. *Aircraft, multi-engine, reciprocating engine-powered—15 hours;*

3. *Aircraft, multi-engine, turbine engine-powered—20 hours; or*

4. *Airplane, turbojet-powered — 25 hours.*

The hours of operating experience may be reduced to not less than 50% of the hours required above by the substitution of one additional takeoff and landing for each hour of flight. (PLT407) — 14 CFR §135.244

Answers
8103 [B]   8107 [A]   8108 [A]

ATS
8109. A person is acting as pilot in command of a turbojet powered airplane operated in passenger-carrying service by a commuter air carrier. If 10 takeoffs and landings have been accomplished in that make and basic model, which additional pilot-in-command experience meets the requirement for designation as pilot in command?

A— 10 hours.
B— 15 hours.
C— 10 hours, and five takeoffs and landings.

No certificate holder may use any person, nor may any person serve, as a pilot-in-command of an aircraft operated by "commuter operations" in passenger-carrying operations, unless that person has completed, on that make and basic model aircraft and in that crewmember position the following operating experience:

1. Aircraft, single engine—10 hours;

2. Aircraft, multi-engine, reciprocating engine-powered—15 hours;

3. Aircraft, multi-engine, turbine engine-powered—20 hours; or

4. Airplane, turbojet-powered—25 hours.

The hours of operating experience may be reduced to not less than 50% of the hours required above by the substitution of one additional takeoff and landing for each hour of flight. (PLT407) — 14 CFR §135.244

ATS
8110. A pilot's experience includes 8 hours in a particular make and basic model multiengine, turboprop airplane while acting as pilot-in-command. Which additional pilot-in-command experience meets the requirements for designation as pilot in command of that airplane when operated by a commuter air carrier in passenger-carrying service?

A— Twelve takeoffs and landings.
B— Five takeoffs and landings, and 2 hours.
C— Ten takeoffs and landings, and 2 hours.

No certificate holder may use any person, nor may any person serve, as a pilot-in-command of an aircraft operated by "commuter operations" in passenger-carrying operations, unless that person has completed, on that make and basic model aircraft and in that crewmember position the following operating experience:

1. Aircraft, single engine—10 hours;

2. Aircraft, multi-engine, reciprocating engine-powered—15 hours;

3. Aircraft, multi-engine, turbine engine-powered—20 hours; or

4. Airplane, turbojet-powered—25 hours.

The hours of operating experience may be reduced to not less than 50% of the hours required above by the substitution of one additional takeoff and landing for each hour of flight. (PLT407) — 14 CFR §135.244

ATS
8111. A person is acting as pilot in command of a single-engine airplane operated in passenger-carrying service by a commuter air carrier. If six takeoffs and landings have been accomplished in that make and basic model, which additional pilot-in-command experience meets the requirement for designation as pilot in command?

A— 4 hours
B— 5 hours
C— 6 hours

No certificate holder may use any person, nor may any person serve, as a pilot-in-command of an aircraft operated by "commuter operations" in passenger-carrying operations, unless that person has completed, on that make and basic model aircraft and in that crewmember position the following operating experience:

1. Aircraft, single engine—10 hours;

2. Aircraft, multi-engine, reciprocating engine-powered—15 hours;

3. Aircraft, multi-engine, turbine engine-powered—20 hours; or

4. Airplane, turbojet-powered—25 hours.

The hours of operating experience may be reduced to not less than 50% of the hours required above by the substitution of one additional takeoff and landing for each hour of flight. (PLT407) — 14 CFR §135.244

Answers

| 8109 | [B] | 8110 | [C] | 8111 | [B] |

ATS

9618. (Refer to Figures 168 and 301.) The PIC (single pilot 135 with A/P) of PTZ 70 has less than 100 hours of PIC time in the BE 1900. Due to BUF weather being 100 feet, 1/4 mile in blowing snow, which is below landing minimums, the PIC requested and received clearance to SYR, the filed alternate. Under Part 135, what are the PIC's minimums at SYR for the ILS RWY 10?

A— 800/2.
B— 719/42.
C— 619/50.

The MDA or DA/DH and visibility landing minimums prescribed in 14 CFR Part 97 or in the operator's operations specifications are increased by 100 feet and 1/2 mile respectively, but not to exceed the ceiling and visibility minimums for that airport when used as an alternate airport, for each pilot-in-command of a turbine-powered airplane who has not served at least 100 hours as pilot-in-command in that type of airplane. Since the pilot is operating with an autopilot, as noted in the question with "(single pilot 135 with A/P)," the chart notes indicate that an RVR of 1800 is authorized. Adding a 1/2 mile (or 2400 RVR) to that would make the visibility requirement 4200 RVR. (PLT407) — 14 CFR §135.225

ATS

9632. (Refer to Figure 182A.) The PIC on EAB 90 has not flown 100 hours as PIC in the BE 1900 (CAT B aircraft). What are the minimums for the PIC when flying the ILS RWY 09R, at PHL?

A— 321/42.
B— 221/18.
C— 321/36.

If the PIC of a turbine-powered airplane does not have 100 hours of PIC time in type, he/she must raise the approach minimums by 100-1/2 above the published minimums. The pilot does not have to raise the approach minimums above the published alternate minimums. Note: 2,400 RVR is equal to 1/2 mile visibility. (PLT407) — 14 CFR §135.225

ATS

9633. (Refer to Figure 182A.) The PIC of EAB 90 has 89 hours and 29 landings as PIC in the BE 1900, while operating under Part 135. The PIC has 1,234 hours and 579 landings as PIC in the DC-3 while operating under Part 135. What are the minimums for the ILS RWY 9R approach at PHL, for this PIC?

A— 221/18.
B— 321/24.
C— 321/42.

If the PIC of a turbine-powered airplane does not have 100 hours of PIC time in type, he/she must raise the approach minimums by 100-1/2 above the published minimums. The pilot does not have to raise the approach minimums above the published alternate minimums. Note: 2,400 RVR is equal to 1/2 mile visibility. (PLT443) — 14 CFR §135.225

ATS

9634. (Refer to Figures 183 and 183A.) When the weather at PHL goes below the PICs minimums, the flight diverts to ACY. Upon arrival at ACY, EAB 90 is cleared for the ILS RWY 13 approach. The PIC has 89 hours of PIC time in the BE 1900. What are the PICs minimums?

A— 700-2.
B— 276/18.
C— 376/42.

If the PIC of a turbine-powered airplane does not have 100 hours of PIC time in type, he/she must raise the approach minimums by 100-1/2 above the published minimums. The pilot does not have to raise the approach minimums above the published alternate minimums. Note: 2,400 RVR is equal to 1/2 mile visibility. (PLT443) — 14 CFR §135.225

Answers

9618   [B]   9632   [A]   9633   [C]   9634   [C]

ATS, RTC

8018. Which person, other than the second in command, may the pilot in command permit to manipulate the flight controls?

A— A member of the National Transportation Safety Board who holds a pilot certificate appropriate for the aircraft.

B— An authorized FAA safety representative who is qualified in the aircraft, and is checking flight operations.

C— A pilot employed by an engineering firm who is authorized by the certificate holder to conduct flight tests.

No pilot-in-command may allow any person to manipulate the controls of an aircraft during flight unless that person is:

1. A pilot employed by the certificate holder and qualified in the aircraft; or

2. An authorized safety representative of the Administrator who has permission of the pilot-in-command, is qualified in the aircraft, and is checking flight operations.

(PLT444) — 14 CFR §135.115

ATS, RTC

8026. A flight attendant crewmember is required on aircraft having a passenger seating configuration, excluding any pilot seat, of

A— 15 or more.
B— 19 or more.
C— 20 or more

No certificate holder may operate an aircraft that has a passenger seating configuration, excluding any pilot seat, of more than 19 unless there is a flight attendant crewmember on board the aircraft. (PLT440) — 14 CFR §135.107

ATS, RTC

8027. Before each takeoff, the pilot in command of an aircraft carrying passengers shall ensure that all passengers have been orally briefed on the

A— location of normal and emergency exits, oxygen masks, and life preservers.

B— use of safety belts, location and operation of fire extinguishers, and smoking.

C— use of seatbelts, smoking, and location and use of survival equipment.

Before each takeoff the pilot-in-command shall ensure that all passengers have been orally briefed on:

1. Smoking;

2. Use of seatbelts;

3. The placement of seat backs in an upright position before takeoff and landing;

4. Location and means of opening the passenger entry door and emergency exits;

5. Location of survival equipment;

6. If the flight involves extended overwater operation, ditching procedures and the use of required flotation equipment;

7. If the flight involves operations above 12,000 feet MSL, the normal and emergency use of oxygen; and

8. Location and operation of fire extinguishers.

(PLT384) — 14 CFR §135.117

ATS, RTC

8028. Before takeoff, the pilot in command of an aircraft carrying passengers shall ensure that all passengers have been orally briefed on the normal and emergency use of oxygen

A— if the flight involves operations above 12,000 feet MSL.

B— regardless of the altitude at which the flight will operate.

C— if the flight involves operations at or above 12,000 feet MSL for more than 30 minutes.

Before each takeoff the pilot-in-command shall ensure that all passengers have been orally briefed on the normal and emergency use of oxygen if the flight involves operations above 12,000 feet MSL. (PLT438) — 14 CFR §135.117

ATS, RTC

8029. The oral before flight briefing required on passenger-carrying aircraft shall be

A— supplemented by an actual demonstration of emergency exit door operation by a crewmember.

B— presented by the pilot in command or another flight crewmember, as a crewmember demonstrates the operation of the emergency equipment.

C— conducted by a crewmember or the pilot in command and supplemented by printed cards for the use of each passenger.

The required oral briefing must be given by the pilot-in-command or other crewmember. It must be supplemented by printed cards which must be carried in the aircraft in locations convenient for the use of each passenger. (PLT384) — 14 CFR §135.117

ATS, RTC

8034. A commuter air carrier certificate holder plans to assign a pilot as pilot in command of an aircraft having eight passenger seats to be used in passenger-carrying operations. Which experience requirement must that pilot meet if the aircraft is to be flown with an operative approved autopilot and no second in command?

A— 100 hours as pilot in command in the category, class, and type.

B— 50 hours and 10 landings as pilot in command in the make and model.

C— 100 hours as pilot in command in the make and model.

When using an autopilot in lieu of a second-in-command in commuter airline passenger-carrying operations, the pilot-in-command must have at least 100 hours of PIC time in the make and model of aircraft to be flown. (PLT407) — 14 CFR §135.105

ATS, RTC

8035. Which is a condition that must be met by a commuter air carrier certificate holder to have an aircraft approved for operation with an autopilot system and no second in command?

A— The passenger seating configuration is 10 or more, including any pilot seat.

B— The autopilot system is capable of operating the controls to maintain flight and to maneuver the aircraft about the three axes.

C— The operation is restricted to VFR or VFR over-the-top.

The autopilot used in lieu of a second-in-command must be capable of operating the aircraft controls to maintain flight and maneuver it about the three axes. (PLT443) — 14 CFR §135.105

ATS, RTC

8036. An autopilot may not be used in place of a second in command in any aircraft

A— being operated in commuter air carrier service.

B— having a passenger seating configuration, excluding any pilot's seat, of 10 seats or more.

C— having a total seating capacity of 10 or more seats and being operated in commuter air service.

Unless two pilots are required by 14 CFR for operations under VFR, a person may operate an aircraft without a second-in-command, if it is equipped with an operative approved autopilot system and the use of that system is authorized by appropriate operations specifications. No certificate holder may operate an aircraft without a second-in-command if that aircraft has a passenger seating configuration, excluding any pilot seat, of 10 seats or more. (PLT443) — 14 CFR §135.99 and §135.105

ATS, RTC

8044. What is the minimum passenger seating configuration that requires a second in command?

A— 15 seats.

B— 12 seats.

C— 10 seats.

No certificate holder may operate an aircraft without a second-in-command if that aircraft has a passenger seating configuration, excluding any pilot seat, of 10 seats or more. (PLT443) — 14 CFR §135.99

Answers

8029 [C]   8034 [C]   8035 [B]   8036 [B]   8044 [C]

ATS, RTC
8076. When is a pilot not required to keep the shoulder harness fastened during takeoff and landing while at a pilot station?

A— When operating an aircraft having a passenger seating configuration, excluding any pilot seat, of 10 seats or less.
B— When the pilot cannot perform the required duties with the shoulder harness fastened.
C— When serving as pilot in command or second in command of an aircraft having a total seating capacity of eight seats or less.

Each flight crewmember occupying a station equipped with a shoulder harness must fasten the shoulder harness during takeoff and landing, except that the shoulder harness may be unfastened if the crewmember is unable to perform required duties with the shoulder harness fastened. (PLT464) — 14 CFR §135.171

ATS, RTC
8095. To serve as pilot in command in an IFR operation, a person must have passed a line check

A— consisting of a flight over the route to be flown, with at least three instrument approaches at representative airports, within the past 12 calendar months, in one type of aircraft which that pilot is to fly.
B— within the past 12 months, which include a portion of a civil airway and one instrument approach at one representative airport, in one of the types of aircraft which that pilot is to fly.
C— since the beginning of the 12th month before that service, which included at least one flight over a civil airway, or approved off-airway route, or any portion of either, in one type of aircraft which that pilot is to fly.

No certificate holder may use a pilot, nor may any person serve, as a pilot-in-command of a flight unless, since the beginning of the 12th calendar month before that service, that pilot has passed a flight check (line check) in one of the types of aircraft that pilot is to fly. The flight check shall:

1. Be given by an approved check pilot or by the FAA;

2. Consist of at least one flight over one route segment; and

3. Include takeoffs and landings at one or more representative airports;

4. For a pilot authorized for IFR operations, at least one flight shall be flown over a civil airway, an approved off-airway route, or a portion of either of them.

(PLT442) — 14 CFR §135.299

ATS, RTC
8096. What are the minimum requirements for the line check required of each pilot in command authorized for IFR air taxi operations? The line check shall be given over

A— one route segment in each type of airplane the pilot is to fly and includes takeoffs and landings at one or more representative airports.
B— a civil airway or an approved off-airway route, or a portion of either of them, in one type of airplane the pilot is to fly and includes takeoffs and landings at one or more representative airports.
C— a civil airway or an approved off-airway route in each make and model airplane the pilot is to fly and includes takeoffs and landings at one or more representative airports.

No certificate holder may use a pilot, nor may any person serve, as a pilot-in-command of a flight unless, since the beginning of the 12th calendar month before that service, that pilot has passed a flight check (line check) in one of the types of aircraft that pilot is to fly. The flight check shall:

1. Be given by an approved check pilot or by the FAA;

2. Consist of at least one flight over one route segment; and

3. Include takeoffs and landings at one or more representative airports;

4. For a pilot authorized for IFR operations, at least one flight shall be flown over a civil airway, an approved off-airway route, or a portion of either of them.

(PLT442) — 14 CFR §135.299

ATS, RTC
8097. No certificate holder may use a person as pilot in command unless that person has passed a line check

A— since the beginning of the 12th month before serving as pilot in command.
B— since the beginning of the 6th month before serving as pilot in command.
C— within the past 6 months.

No certificate holder may use a pilot, nor may any person serve, as a pilot-in-command of a flight unless, since the beginning of the 12th calendar month before that service, that pilot has passed a flight check (line check) in one of the types of aircraft that pilot is to fly. (PLT442) — 14 CFR §135.299

ATS, RTC

8098. A person may act as pilot in command of both type A and type B aircraft under IFR, if an instrument proficiency check has been passed in

A— either type A or B since the beginning of the 12th month before time to serve.
B— type A since the beginning of the 12th month, and in type B since the beginning of the 6th month before time to serve.
C— type A since the beginning of the 12th month, and in type B since the beginning of the 24th month before time to serve.

No certificate holder may use a pilot, nor may any person serve, as a pilot-in-command of an aircraft under IFR unless, since the beginning of the 6th calendar month before that service, that pilot has passed an instrument proficiency check given by the FAA or authorized check pilot. If the pilot-in-command is assigned to pilot more than one type of aircraft, that pilot must take the instrument proficiency check for each type of aircraft to which that pilot is assigned in rotation, but not more than one flight check in each period. (PLT442) — 14 CFR §135.297

ATS, RTC

8099. A pilot in command is authorized to use an autopilot system in place of a second in command. During the instrument proficiency check, that person is required to demonstrate (without a second in command) the ability to

A— comply with complex ATC instructions with, but not without, the autopilot.
B— properly conduct air-ground communications with, but not without, the autopilot.
C— properly conduct instrument operations competently both with, and without, the autopilot.

If the pilot-in-command is authorized to use an autopilot system in place of a second-in-command, that pilot must show during the required instrument proficiency check, that the pilot is able both with and without using the autopilot to:

1. Conduct instrument operations competently; and

2. Properly conduct air-ground communications and comply with complex air traffic control instructions. (PLT442) — 14 CFR §135.297

ATS, RTC

8101. A person may not serve as pilot in command in an IFR operation unless that person has passed an

A— aircraft competency, an instrument proficiency, and autopilot check within the previous 6 calendar months prior to the date to serve.
B— instrument proficiency check in the airplane in which to serve, or in an approved aircraft simulator, within the previous 12 calendar months.
C— instrument proficiency check under actual or simulated IFR conditions, since the beginning of the 6th calendar month prior to the date to serve.

No certificate holder may use a pilot, nor may any person serve as a pilot-in-command of an aircraft under IFR unless, since the beginning of the 6th calendar month before that service, that pilot has passed an instrument proficiency check given by the FAA or authorized check pilot. If the pilot-in-command is assigned to both single-engine aircraft and multi-engine aircraft, that pilot must initially take the instrument proficiency check in a multi-engine aircraft and each succeeding check alternately in single-engine and multi-engine aircraft. (PLT442) — 14 CFR §135.297

ATS, RTC

8102. A pilot in command who is authorized to use an autopilot system, in place of a second in command, may take the autopilot check

A— concurrently with the instrument proficiency check, but at 12 month intervals.
B— in any aircraft appropriately equipped, providing the check is taken at 6 month intervals.
C— concurrently with the competency check, providing the check is taken at 12 month intervals.

If the pilot-in-command is authorized to use an autopilot system in place of a second-in-command, that pilot must show during the required instrument proficiency check, that the pilot is able both with and without using the autopilot to:

1. Conduct instrument operations competently; and

2. Properly conduct air-ground communications and comply with complex air traffic control instructions.

(PLT424) — 14 CFR §135.297

Answers

| 8098 | [B] | 8099 | [C] | 8101 | [C] | 8102 | [A] |

ATS, RTC
8104. Pilot flight time limitations under 14 CFR Part 135 are based

A— on the flight time accumulated in any commercial flying.
B— solely on flight time accumulated in air taxi operations.
C— solely on flight time accumulated during commercial flying, in the last 30 day and/or 12 month period.

Pilot flight time limitations are based on the flight time accumulated under 14 CFR Part 135 and any other commercial flying time. (PLT409) — 14 CFR §135.265

ATS, RTC
8105. No person may serve, as second in command of an aircraft (under part 135), unless they hold a commercial pilot certificate with the appropriate category, class rating and an instrument rating. For flight under IFR, that person must have accomplished within the last 6 months, the recent instrument requirements of

A— using the navigation systems for interception and tracking of courses, 6 instrument low approaches and holding.
B— using the navigation systems to intercept and track 3 inbound/3 outbound courses, 6 holding patterns and 6 instrument approaches.
C— holding procedures, using the navigation systems for intercepting and tracking courses, and 6 instrument approaches.

To act as second-in-command under IFR, a person must meet the recent instrument experience requirements of 14 CFR Part 61. These requirements are: in the last 6 months, the pilot must have logged 6 instrument approaches, performed holding procedures, and intercepted and tracked courses through the use of navigation systems. (PLT442) — 14 CFR §135.245

ATS, RTC
8106. With regard to flight crewmember duties, which operations are considered to be in the "critical phase of flight"?

A— All ground operations involving taxi, takeoff, landing, and all other operations conducted below 10,000 feet MSL, including cruise flight.
B— Descent, approach, landing, and taxi operations, irrespective of altitudes MSL.
C— All ground operations involving taxi, takeoff, landing, and all other operations conducted below 10,000 feet, excluding cruise flight.

For the purpose of this section, critical phases of flight include all ground operations involving taxi, takeoff and landing, and all other flight operations conducted below 10,000 feet, except cruise flight. (PLT029) — 14 CFR §135.100

ATS, RTC
8113. Other than in cruise flight, below what altitude are non-safety related cockpit activities by flight crewmembers prohibited?

A— 12,000 feet.
B— 10,000 feet.
C— 8,000 feet.

No certificate holder shall require, nor may any flight crewmember perform, any duties during a critical phase of flight except those duties required for the safe operation of the aircraft. For purposes of this section, critical phases of flight include all ground operations involving taxi, takeoff and landing, and all other flight operations conducted below 10,000 feet, except cruise flight. (PLT440) — 14 CFR §135.100

Answers

8104 [A]   8105 [C]   8106 [C]   8113 [B]

Flight Crew Duty Time Limits

Familiarize yourself with 14 CFR Part 117 to understand flight crew duty time limits. The limitations of Part 117 apply to all flying by flightcrew members on behalf of any certificate holder or 91K program manager during the applicable periods. Each flightcrew member must report for any flight duty period rested and prepared to perform his or her assigned duties. Each certificate holder must develop and implement education and awareness training program that is approved by the Administrator. This program must provide the training to all employees of the certificate holder who are responsible for administering the provisions of Part 117, including flightcrew members, dispatchers, individuals directly involved in the scheduling of flightcrew members or in operational control, and any employee providing direct management oversight of these areas.

A person cannot be assigned to any ground or flight duties during required rest periods. The term "**deadhead**" is used to describe the transportation of crewmembers by the air carrier to or from their flight assignments when that transportation is not local in character. Time spent in deadhead air transportation cannot be considered as part of a required rest period.

Other new terms and definitions associated with Part 117 to be aware of are as follows:

Airport/standby reserve means a defined duty period during which a flightcrew member is required by a certificate holder to be at an airport for a possible assignment. For airport/standby reserve, all time spent in a reserve status is part of the flightcrew member's flight duty period.

Augmented, or unaugmented operations. An unaugmented flight contains the minimum number of flightcrew members necessary to safely pilot an aircraft. An augmented flight contains additional flightcrew members and at least one onboard rest facility, which allows flightcrew members to work in shifts and sleep during the flight.

Calendar day means a 24-hour period from 0000 through 2359 using Coordinated Universal Time or local time.

Fatigue means a physiological state of reduced mental or physical performance capability resulting from lack of sleep or increased physical activity, which can reduce a flightcrew member's alertness and ability to safely operate an aircraft or perform safety-related duties.

Physiological night's rest means 10 hours of rest that encompasses the hours of 0100 and 0700 at the flightcrew member's home base, unless the individual has acclimated to a different theater. If the flightcrew member has acclimated to a different theater, the rest must encompass the hours of 0100 and 0700 at the acclimated location.

Rest period means a continuous period determined prospectively during which the flightcrew member is free from all restraint by the certificate holder, including freedom from present responsibility for work should the occasion arise.

Short-call reserve means a period of time in which a flightcrew member is assigned to a reserve availability period. For short-call reserve, the reserve availability period may not exceed 14 hours.

Theater means a geographical area in which the distance between the flightcrew member's flight duty period departure point and arrival point differs by no more than 60 degrees longitude. The applicable flight duty period is based on the local time at the theater in which the flightcrew member was last acclimated.

Unforeseen operational circumstance means an unplanned event of insufficient duration to allow for adjustments to schedules, including unforecast weather, equipment malfunction, or air traffic delay that is not reasonably expected. For augmented and unaugmented operations, if unforeseen operational

Continued

circumstances arise **prior** to takeoff, the pilot-in-command and the certificate holder may extend the maximum flight duty period permitted up to 2 hours. For augmented and unaugmented operations, if unforeseen operational circumstances arise **after** takeoff, the pilot-in-command and the certificate holder may extend maximum flight duty periods to the extent necessary to safely land the aircraft at the next destination airport or alternate airport, as appropriate.

Window of circadian low means a period of maximum sleepiness that occurs between 0200 and 0559 during a physiological night's rest. No certificate holder may schedule and no flightcrew member may accept more than three consecutive flight duty periods that infringe upon the window of circadian low.

Flight Duty Periods

No certificate holder may schedule, and no flightcrew member may accept an assignment if the flight-crew member's total flight duty period (FDP) will exceed 60 flight duty hours in any 168 consecutive hours. Before beginning any reserve or flight duty period, a flightcrew member must be given at least 30 consecutive hours free from all duty within the past 168 consecutive-hour period.

No certificate holder may schedule, and no flightcrew member may accept an assignment if the flightcrew member's total flight duty period will exceed 190 FDP hours in any 672 consecutive hours.

No certificate holder may schedule, and no flightcrew member may accept an assignment for any reserve or flight duty period unless the flightcrew member is given a rest period of at least 10 consecutive hours immediately before beginning the reserve or flight duty period measured from the time the flightcrew member is released from duty. The 10-hour rest period must provide the flightcrew member with a minimum of 8 uninterrupted hours of sleep opportunity. If a flightcrew member determines that this rest period will not provide eight uninterrupted hours of sleep opportunity, he or she must notify the certificate holder. The flightcrew member cannot report for the assigned flight duty period until he or she receives this specified rest period.

For an unaugmented operation only, if a flightcrew member is provided with a rest opportunity (an opportunity to sleep) in a suitable accommodation during his or her flight duty period, the time that the flightcrew member spends there is not part of his/her flight duty period if the time spent in that accommodation is at least 3 hours, measured from the time that the flightcrew member arrives there.

A Part 117 excerpt will be available for your reference during the FAA test. You will not be required to memorize the tables; however, you will need to know which table to use—that is, which one is applicable to the question being asked.

The maximum flight time for unaugmented operations is as follows (14 CFR Part 117.11 Table A):

Time of report (acclimated)	Maximum flight time (hours)
0000-0459	8
0500-1959	9
2000-2359	8

The maximum flight duty period (hours) for lineholders is based on the number of flight segments and the scheduled time of start (14 CFR 117.13 Table B):

Scheduled time of start (acclimated time)	Maximum flight duty period (hours) for lineholders based on number of flight segments						
	1	2	3	4	5	6	7+
0000-0359	9	9	9	9	9	9	9
0400-0459	10	10	10	10	9	9	9
0500-0559	12	12	12	12	11.5	11	10.5
0600-0659	13	13	12	12	11.5	11	10.5
0700-1159	14	14	13	13	12.5	12	11.5
1200-1259	13	13	13	13	12.5	12	11.5
1300-1659	12	12	12	12	11.5	11	10.5
1700-2159	12	12	11	11	10	9	9
2200-2259	11	11	10	10	9	9	9
2300-2359	10	10	10	9	9	9	9

If the flightcrew member is not acclimated, the maximum flight duty period in Table C of Part 117 is reduced by 30 minutes (14 CFR Part 117 Table C):

Scheduled time of start (acclimated time)	Maximum flight duty period (hours) based on rest facility and number of pilots					
	Class 1 rest facility		Class 2 rest facility		Class 3 rest facility	
	3 pilots	4 pilots	3 pilots	4 pilots	3 pilots	4 pilots
0000-0559	15	17	14	15.5	13	13.5
0600-0659	16	18.5	15	16.5	14	14.5
0700-1259	17	19	16.5	18	15	15.5
1300-1659	16	18.5	15	16.5	14	14.5
1700-2359	15	17	14	15.5	13	13.5

ALL

8706. Fatigue can be evident in others if they

A— talk more than usual.
B— yawn excessively.
C— are overly helpful.

Physical signs of fatigue include yawning repeatedly, heavy eyelids or microsleeps, eye-rubbing, nodding off or head dropping, headaches, nausea, upset stomach, slowed reaction time, lack of energy, weakness, and light headedness. (PLT409) — FAA-H-8083-2

ALL

8707. You did not get a good night's rest and have been on duty for several hours. A sign you may be fatigued is

A— improved dexterity.
B— decreased short term memory.
C— mental acuteness.

Short term memory loss is a sign of mental fatigue. Additional signs of mental fatigue include: difficulty concentrating on tasks, lapse in attention, failure to communicate important information, failure to antici-pate events or actions, making mistakes even on well-practiced tasks, forgetfulness, difficulty thinking clearly, and poor decision making. (PLT409) — FAA-H-8083-2

ATM, DSP

8708. Under 14 CFR 121, a required flightcrew member of an unaugmented two-pilot flag operation may not exceed how many hours duty in a seven consecutive day period?

A— 48.
B— 52.
C— 32.

No pilot may fly more than 32 hours during any seven consecutive days, and each pilot must be relieved from all duty for at least 24 consecutive hours at least once during any seven consecutive days. (PLT409) — 14 CFR §121.481

ATM, DSP

8709. Under 14 CFR 121, a required flightcrew member of an unaugmented two-pilot flag operation may not exceed how many hours duty in a one calendar month period?

A— 120.
B— 100.
C— 80.

No pilot may fly as a member of a crew more than 100 hours during any one calendar month. (PLT409) — 14 CFR §121.481

ATM, DSP

8227. How does deadhead transportation, going to or from a duty assignment, affect the computation of flight time limits for air carrier flight crewmembers? It is

A— considered part of the rest period if the flightcrew includes more than two pilots.
B— considered part of the rest period for flight engineers and navigators.
C— not considered to be part of a rest period.

Time spent in deadhead transportation to or from duty assignment is not considered part of a rest period. (PLT409) — 14 CFR §§121.471, 121.491, and 121.519

Answer (A) is incorrect because deadhead transportation does not count for part of the required rest period. Answer (B) is incorrect because flight engineers and navigators are defined as flight crew-members. The same rest period requirements apply to them as to pilot and copilot.

ATM, DSP

8228. Flight duty period hours for flightcrew members are limited to

A— 190 hours in any 672 consecutive hours.
B— 180 hours in any 672 consecutive hours.
C— 170 hours in any 672 consecutive hours.

No certificate holder may schedule and no flightcrew member may accept an assignment if the flightcrew member's total Flight Duty Period will exceed 190 flight duty period hours in any 672 consecutive hours. (PLT409) — 14 CFR §117.23

ATM, DSP

8220. Flight duty period hours for flightcrew members are limited to

A— 180 hours in any 28 consecutive days.
B— 190 hours in any 672 consecutive hours.
C— 170 hours in any 672 consecutive hours.

Answers

8706 [B]	8707 [B]	8708 [C]	8709 [B]	8227 [C]	8228 [A]
8220 [B]					

No certificate holder may schedule and no flightcrew member may accept an assignment if the flightcrew member's total Flight Duty Period will exceed 190 flight duty period hours in any 672 consecutive hours. (PLT409) — 14 CFR §117.23

ATM, DSP

8221. "Window of circadian low" means a period of maximum sleepiness that occurs between

A— 0100 – 0500.
B— 1200 – 0459.
C— 0200 – 0559.

Window of circadian low means a period of maximum sleepiness that occurs between 0200 and 0559 during a physiological night's rest. (PLT409) — 14 CFR §117.3

ATM, DSP

8219. For a short-call reserve, the reserve availability period may not exceed

A— 12 hours.
B— 14 hours.
C— 16 hours.

Short-call reserve means a period of time in which a flightcrew member is assigned to a reserve availability period. For short-call reserve, the reserve availability period may not exceed 14 hours. (PLT409) — 14 CFR §117.21

ATM, DSP

8222. If the crew van breaks down en route to the rest facility and delays arrival for nearly 2 hours, does the flightcrew member need to notify the certificate holder?

A— No, as long as the crew member has the opportunity for 9 hours of uninterrupted rest.
B— No, as long as the crew member has the opportunity for 8 hours rest.
C— Yes, if the flightcrew member does not have the opportunity for 10 hours of uninterrupted hours free from duty.

No certificate holder may schedule and no flightcrew member may accept an assignment for any reserve or flight duty period unless the flightcrew member is given a rest period of at least 10 consecutive hours immediately before beginning the reserve or flight duty period measured from the time the flightcrew member is released from duty. The 10 hour rest period must provide the flightcrew member with a minimum of 8 uninterrupted hours of sleep opportunity. If a flightcrew

member determines that this rest period will not provide eight uninterrupted hours of sleep opportunity, the flightcrew member must notify the certificate holder. The flightcrew member cannot report for the assigned flight duty period until he or she receives this specified rest period. (PLT409) — 14 CFR §117.25

ATM, DSP

8223. "Airport standby reserve" means

A— a specified 15-hour period of reserve in close proximity of assignment being available for flight duty assignments in less than 2 hours.
B— being within 90 minutes of the airport and available for immediate flight duty assignments of 8 hours duration.
C— a defined duty period during which a flight crewmember is required by the certificate holder to be available for possible assignment.

Airport/standby reserve means a defined duty period during which a flightcrew member is required by a certificate holder to be at an airport for a possible assignment. (PLT409) — 14 CFR §117.3

ATM, DSP

9714. Each flightcrew member must report

A— in uniform and properly prepared to accomplish all assignments.
B— to the airport on time and fully prepared to accomplish assigned duty.
C— for any flight duty period rested and prepared to perform his duty.

Each flightcrew member must report for any flight duty period rested and prepared to perform his or her assigned duties. (PLT409) — 14 CFR §117.5

ATM, DSP

8211. You are on the last day of a four day trip and haven't slept well. What is a warning sign that you are fatigued?

A— Improved dexterity.
B— Head bobbing.
C— Mental acuteness.

Common physical signs of fatigue include yawning repeatedly, heavy eyelids, microsleeps, eye rubbing, nodding off or head dropping, headaches, nausea, or upset stomach, slowed reaction time, lack of energy, weakness, or light headedness. (PLT409) — FAA-H-8083-2, 14 CFR §117.3

Answers

| 8221 [C] | 8219 [B] | 8222 [B] | 8223 [C] | 9714 [C] | 8211 [B] |

ATM, DSP

8224. No flightcrew member may accept an assignment for any reserve or flight duty period unless the flight crew member is given

A— 10 consecutive hours of rest immediately before beginning a flight duty period or a reserve period.

B— 12 consecutive hours of rest immediately before beginning a flight duty period or a reserve period.

C— 8 consecutive hours of rest immediately before beginning a flight duty period or a reserve period.

No certificate holder may schedule and no flightcrew member may accept an assignment for any reserve or flight duty period unless the flightcrew member is given a rest period of at least 10 consecutive hours immediately before beginning the reserve or flight duty period measured from the time the flightcrew member is released from duty. The 10-hour rest period must provide the flightcrew member with a minimum of 8 uninterrupted hours of sleep opportunity. (PLT409) — 14 CFR §117.25

ATM, DSP

8229. You are a pilot operating under 14 CFR Part 121 and are in a required rest period. When can you be contacted about your next day duty assignment?

A— At any time during your required rest period.

B— At the end of your required rest period.

C— No earlier than 1 hour before the end of your required rest period.

No certificate holder may assign and no flightcrew member may accept assignment to any reserve or duty with the certificate holder during any required rest period. (PLT409) — 14 CFR §117.25

ATM, DSP

8231. "Rest period" means

A— an 8-hour continuous period determined prospectively during which the flightcrew member is free from all restraint by the certificate holder.

B— a continuous period determined prospectively during which the flightcrew member is free from all restraint by the certificate holder.

C— a 12-hour continuous period determined prospectively during which the flightcrew member is free from all restraint by the certificate holder.

Rest period *means a continuous period determined prospectively during which the flightcrew member is free from all restraint by the certificate holder, including freedom from present responsibility for work should the occasion arise. (PLT409) — 14 CFR §117.3*

ATM, DSP

8238. "Theater" means

A— a geographical area in which the distance between the flightcrew member flight duty period departure point and arrival point differs by no more than 90 degrees longitude.

B— a geographical area in which the distance between the flightcrew member flight duty period departure point and arrival point differs by no more than 75 degrees longitude.

C— a geographical area in which the distance between the flightcrew member flight duty period departure point and arrival point differs by no more than 60 degrees longitude.

Theater *means a geographical area in which the distance between the flightcrew member's flight duty period departure point and arrival point differs by no more than 60 degrees longitude. The applicable flight duty period is based on the local time at the theater in which the flightcrew member was last acclimated. (PLT409) — 14 CFR §117.3 and §117.13*

ATM, DSP

9837. "Physiological night's rest" means

A— 9 hours of rest that encompasses the hours of 0100 and 0700 at the crewmember's home base.

B— 10 hours of rest that encompasses the hours of 0100 and 0700 at the crewmember's home base.

C— 12 hours of rest that encompasses any continuous 8 hour period for uninterrupted or disturbed rest.

Physiological night's rest *means 10 hours of rest that encompasses the hours of 0100 and 0700 at the flightcrew member's home base, unless the individual has acclimated to a different theater. If the flightcrew member has acclimated to a different theater, the rest must encompass the hours of 0100 and 0700 at the acclimated location. (PLT395) — 14 CFR §117.3*

ATM, DSP

9838. In order to be assigned for duty, each flightcrew member must report

A— on time, in uniform, and properly prepared to accomplish all assigned duties.

B— to the airport on time, after the designated rest period and fully prepared to accomplish assigned duties.

C— for any flight duty period rested and prepared to perform his/her assigned duties.

Answers

| 8224 | [A] | 8229 | [B] | 8231 | [B] | 8238 | [C] | 9837 | [B] | 9838 | [C] |

Each flightcrew member must report for any flight duty period rested and prepared to perform his or her assigned duties. (PLT409) — 14 CFR §117.5

ATM, DSP

9839. Flightcrew members must receive fatigue education and awareness training

A— with all required air carrier dispatcher and every flightcrew member training activity.
B— annually for flightcrew members and every 24 months for dispatchers, flightcrew member schedulers, and operational control individuals.
C— annually for flightcrew member schedulers, operational control individuals and flightcrew members and dispatchers.

Each certificate holder must develop and implement an education and awareness training program that is approved by the Administrator. This program must provide the training to all employees of the certificate holder responsible for administering the provisions of Part 117, including flightcrew members, dispatchers, individuals directly involved in the scheduling of flightcrew members or in operational control, and any employee providing direct management oversight of these areas. (PLT409) — 14 CFR §117.9

ATM, DSP

9840. In an airplane assigned with a minimum flight crew of two, your flight time may not exceed

A— 9 hours if assigned to report at 0330.
B— 9 hours if assigned to report at 0500.
C— 9 hours if assigned to report at 2030.

The maximum flight time for unaugmented operations is as follows:

Time of report (acclimated)	Maximum flight time (hours)
0000-0459	8
0500-1959	9
2000-2359	8

A Part 117 excerpt will be available for your reference during the FAA test. You will not be required to memorize the tables; however, you will need to know which table to use as applicable to the question being asked. (PLT409) — 14 CFR §117.11 and Table A

ATM, DSP

9841. For unaugmented flightcrew operations, your maximum flight duty period limit is

A— 13 hours if assigned to report at 0700 for 4 flight segments.
B— 13 hours if assigned to report at 2030 for 3 flight segments.
C— 10.5 hours if assigned to report at 1730 for 6 flight segments.

The maximum flight duty period (hours) for lineholders is based on the number of flight segments and the scheduled time of start.

Scheduled time of start (acclimated time)	Maximum flight duty period (hours) for lineholders base on number of flight segments						
	1	2	3	4	5	6	7+
0000-0359	9	9	9	9	9	9	9
0400-0459	10	10	10	10	9	9	9
0500-0559	12	12	12	12	11.5	11	10.5
0600-0659	13	13	12	12	11.5	11	10.5
0700-1159	14	14	13	13	12.5	12	11.5
1200-1259	13	13	13	13	12.5	12	11.5
1300-1659	12	12	12	12	11.5	11	10.5
1700-2159	12	12	11	11	10	9	9
2200-2259	11	11	10	10	9	9	9
2300-2359	10	10	10	9	9	9	9

A Part 117 excerpt will be available for your reference during the FAA test. You will not be required to memorize the tables; however, you will need to know which table to use as applicable to the question being asked. (PLT409) — 14 CFR §117.13 and Table B

Answers

9839 [C]	9840 [B]	9841 [A]

ATM, DSP

9842. In an airplane with an augmented crew of three flightcrew members assigned, the maximum flight duty period is

A— 17 hours if assigned to report at 1200 with a Class 3 rest facility available.
B— 16 hours if assigned to report at 0630 with a Class 1 rest facility available
C— 15 hours if assigned to report at 1730 with a Class 2 rest facility available.

Scheduled time of start (acclimated time)	Maximum flight duty period (hours) for lineholders base on number of flight segments					
	Class 1 rest facility		Class 2 rest facility		Class 3 rest facility	
	3 pilots	4 pilots	3 pilots	4 pilots	3 pilots	4 pilots
0000-0559	15	17	14	15.5	13	13.5
0600-0659	16	18.5	15	16.5	14	14.5
0700-1259	17	19	16.5	18	15	15.5
1300-1659	16	18.5	15	16.5	14	14.5
1700-2359	15	17	14	15.5	13	13.5

A Part 117 excerpt will be available for your reference during the FAA test. You will not be required to memorize the tables; however, you will need to know which table to use as applicable to the question being asked. (PLT409) — 14 CFR §117.17 and Table C

ATM, DSP

9843. The time spent resting during unaugmented operations will not be counted towards the flight duty period limitation if the rest period is at least

A— 3 hours long after reaching suitable accommodations.
B— 4 hours long after reaching suitable accommodations.
C— 4 hours long which can include transportation to suitable accommodations.

For an unaugmented operation only, if a flightcrew member is provided with a rest opportunity (an opportunity to sleep) in a suitable accommodation during his or her flight duty period, the time that the flightcrew member spends in the suitable accommodation is not part of that flightcrew member's flight duty period if the time spent in that accommodation is at least 3 hours, measured from the time that the flightcrew member reaches the accommodation. (PLT409) — 14 CFR §117.15

ATM, DSP

9844. Notification of the rest opportunity period during unaugmented operations, must be

A— given before the next to last flight segment.
B— given before the beginning of the flight duty period.
C— provided no later than after the first flight segment offered after the first flight segment is completed.

For an unaugmented operation only, if a flightcrew member is provided with a rest opportunity (an opportunity to sleep) in a suitable accommodation during his or her flight duty period, the time that the flightcrew member spends in that accommodation is not part of that flightcrew member's flight duty period if the rest opportunity is scheduled before the beginning of the flight duty period in which that rest is taken. (PLT409) — 14 CFR §117.15

ATM, DSP

9845. If the augmented flightcrew member is not acclimated, the

A— maximum flight duty period given in 14 CFR part 117, Table C (not included herein) is reduced by 30 minutes.
B— flight duty period assignment must be reduced 15 minutes by each 15 degrees of longitude difference from the previous rest location.
C— minimum rest period must be extended by 3 hours.

If the flightcrew member is not acclimated the maximum flight duty period in Table C of Part 117 is reduced by 30 minutes. (PLT409) — 14 CFR §117.17

ATM, DSP

9846. The flight duty period may be extended due to unforeseen circumstances before takeoff by as much as

A— 2 hours.
B— 1 hour.
C— 30 minutes.

For augmented and unaugmented operations, if unforeseen operational circumstances arise prior to takeoff, the pilot-in-command and the certificate holder may extend the maximum flight duty period permitted up to 2 hours. (PLT409) — 14 CFR §117.19

Answers

9842   [B]   9843   [A]   9844   [B]   9845   [A]   9846   [A]

ATM, DSP

9847. After takeoff, unforeseen circumstances arise. In this case, the flight duty period may be extended by as much as

A— 2 hours.
B— necessary to reach the closest suitable alternate crew base airport.
C— necessary to land at the next destination airport or alternate airport.

For augmented and unaugmented operations, if unforeseen operational circumstances arise after takeoff, the pilot-in-command and the certificate holder may extend maximum flight duty periods to the extent necessary to safely land the aircraft at the next destination airport or alternate airport, as appropriate. (PLT409) — 14 CFR §117.19

ATM, DSP

9847-1. "Unforeseen operational circumstance" means an

A— unplanned event of insufficient duration to allow for adjustments to schedules.
B— unforecast weather and expected ATC delays.
C— event of sufficient duration to create increased flight times for the certificate holder's operation.

***Unforeseen operational circumstance** means an unplanned event of insufficient duration to allow for adjustments to schedules, including unforecast weather, equipment malfunction, or air traffic delay that is not reasonably expected. (PLT407) — 14 CFR §117.3*

ATM, DSP

9848. For airport/standby reserve, all time spent in airport/standby reserve time is

A— not part of the flightcrew member's flight duty period.
B— part of the flightcrew member's flight duty period.
C— part of the flightcrew member's flight duty period after being alerted for flight assignment.

For airport/standby reserve, all time spent in a reserve status is part of the flightcrew member's flight duty period (PLT409) — 14 CFR §117.21

ATM, DSP

9849. Limiting flight time for all flightcrew members will include

A— instruction flight hours, commercial flying, and flying for any certificate holder.
B— any flying by flightcrew members for any certificate holder or 91K program manager.
C— flying by flightcrew members for any certificate holder or 91K program manager and any other commercial flight time.

The limitations of Part 117 include all flying by flightcrew members on behalf of any certificate holder or 91K program manager during the applicable periods. (PLT409) — 14 CFR §117.23

ATM, DSP

9850. Flightcrew member's flight duty periods are limited to

A— 60 hours in any 168 consecutive hours.
B— 70 hours in any 168 consecutive hours.
C— 60 hours in any 7 days.

No certificate holder may schedule and no flightcrew member may accept an assignment if the flightcrew member's total flight duty period will exceed 60 flight duty hours in any 168 consecutive hours. (PLT409) — 14 CFR §117.23

ATM, DSP

9851. A flightcrew member must be given a rest period before beginning any reserve or flight duty period of

A— 24 consecutive hours free from any duty in the past 7 consecutive calendar days.
B— 36 consecutive hours in the past 168 consecutive hours.
C— 30 consecutive hours in the past 168 consecutive hours.

Before beginning any reserve or flight duty period, a flightcrew member must be given at least 30 consecutive hours free from all duty within the past 168 consecutive-hour period. (PLT409) — 14 CFR §117.25

Answers

| 9847 [C] | 9847-1 [A] | 9848 [B] | 9849 [B] | 9850 [A] | 9851 [C] |

ATM, DSP

9852. No flightcrew member may accept an assignment without scheduled rest opportunities for

A— more than 3 consecutive nighttime flights that infringe on the window of circadian low.

B— more than 4 consecutive nighttime flights that infringe on the window of circadian low in a 168 hour period.

C— consecutive nighttime flights beginning after 0001 hours local home base time.

No certificate holder may schedule and no flightcrew member may accept more than three consecutive flight duty periods that infringe on the window of circadian low. (PLT409) — 14 CFR §117.27

DSP

8194. Normally, a dispatcher for domestic or flag operations should be scheduled for no more than

A— 10 hours of duty in any 24 consecutive hours.

B— 8 hours of service in any 24 consecutive hours.

C— 10 consecutive hours of duty.

Except in cases where circumstances or emergency conditions beyond the control of the certificate holder, no certificate holder conducting domestic or flag operations may schedule a dispatcher for more than 10 consecutive hours of duty. (PLT450) — 14 CFR §121.465

ATM, DSP

8724. What is the minimum rest period required before a flight or reserve duty period?

A— 8 consecutive hours rest.

B— 10 consecutive hours rest.

C— 12 consecutive hours rest.

No certificate holder may schedule and no flightcrew member may accept an assignment for any reserve or flight duty period unless the flightcrew member is given a rest period of at least 10 consecutive hours immediately before beginning the reserve or flight duty period measured from the time the flightcrew member is released from duty. The 10 hour rest period must provide the flightcrew member with a minimum of 8 uninterrupted hours of sleep opportunity. (PLT409) — 14 CFR §117.25

Dispatching and Flight Release

Operational control with respect to a flight, means the exercise of authority over initiating, conducting or terminating a flight.

The air carrier or commercial operator is responsible for operational control. The pilot-in-command and the director of operations are jointly responsible for the initiation, continuation, diversion, and termination of flight in compliance with regulations and the company's operations specifications. The pilot-in-command is responsible for the preflight planning and the operation of the flight.

Each flag and domestic flight must have a **dispatch release** on board. The dispatch release can be in any form but must contain the following information.

- The identification number of the aircraft
- The trip number
- The departure, destination, intermediate and alternate airports
- The type of operation (IFR or VFR)
- The minimum fuel supply
- The latest weather reports and forecasts for the complete flight (may be attached to the release rather than be part of it)

The aircraft dispatcher must provide the pilot-in-command with all available current reports or information on airport conditions and irregularities of navigation facilities that may affect the safety of flight. The aircraft dispatcher must provide the pilot-in-command with all available weather reports and forecasts of weather phenomena that may affect the safety of flight including adverse weather. The aircraft dispatcher must update this information during a flight.

Answers

9852   [A]   8194   [C]   8724   [B]

When a domestic flight lands at an intermediate airport named in its original dispatch release and departs again within 1 hour, it does not need a new dispatch release. If it remains on the ground for more than 1 hour, a redispatch release must be issued.

When a flag flight lands at an intermediate airport named in its original dispatch release and departs again within 6 hours, it does not need a new dispatch release. If it remains on the ground for more than 6 hours, a redispatch is required.

The pilot-in-command of a flight shall carry in the airplane to its destination:

• A copy of the completed load manifest
• A copy of the dispatch release
• A copy of the flight plan.

The air carrier must keep copies of these documents for at least 3 months.

Each supplemental carrier or commercial operator flight must have a **flight release** on board. The flight release can be in any form but must contain the following information:

• The company or organization name
• Make, model and registration number of the aircraft used
• The flight or trip number and the date of the flight
• The name of each flight crewmember, flight attendant and the pilot designated as pilot-in-command
• The departure, destination, intermediate and alternate airports and route
• The type of operation (e.g., IFR or VFR)
• The minimum fuel supply
• The latest weather reports and forecasts for the complete flight (may be attached to the release rather than be part of it)

Before beginning a flight, the pilot-in-command must obtain all available current reports or information on airport conditions and irregularities of navigation facilities that may affect the safety of the flight. During a flight, the pilot-in-command must obtain any additional available information of meteorological conditions and irregularities of facilities and services that may affect the safety of the flight.

A provisional airport is defined as an airport approved by the Administrator for use by a certificate holder for the purpose of providing service to a community when the regular airport used by the certificate holder is not available. A person who is not authorized to conduct direct air carrier operations, but who is authorized by the Administrator to conduct operations as a U.S. commercial operator, will be issued an Operating Certificate. Each certificate holder conducting domestic, flag, or commuter operations must obtain operations specifications containing, among many other provisions, the kinds of operations authorized.

Extended-range twin-engine operational performance standards (ETOPS) is a rating accompanied by a time limit (such as 180-minute ETOPS) that allows twin-engine civil transport aircraft to fly over oceans and deserts provided that the aircraft is never more than 180 minutes away from a suitable airfield. An ETOPS "entry point" is the first point on an ETOPS route at which the airplane is farther than a distance of 60 minutes flying time, with one engine inoperative, from an emergency or diversion airport that is adequate for an airplane with two engines.

When filing an alternate using the 180-minute ETOPS rule, the alternate airport must have rescue and fire fighting services (RFFS) that meet ICAO Category 4 standard or higher. If filing an alternate using the beyond-180-minute ETOPS rule, the alternate must have RFFS that meet the ICAO Category 4 standard or higher, and the aircraft must remain within the ETOPS authorized diversion time from an adequate airport that has RFFS equal to ICAO Category 7 or higher.

ALL

9326. "Operational control" of a flight refer to

A— the specific duties of any required crewmember.
B— exercising authority over initiating, conducting, or terminating a flight.
C— exercising the privileges of pilot-in-command of an aircraft.

"Operational Control," with respect to flight, means the exercise of authority over initiating, conducting or terminating a flight. (PLT432) — 14 CFR §1.1

Answer (A) is incorrect because "crewmember" refers to any person assigned to perform duty in an aircraft during flight time, which includes cabin crew as well as cockpit crew. Answer (C) is incorrect because "pilot-in-command" refers to the pilot responsible for the operation and safety of an aircraft during flight time, which does not include the initiation of a flight.

ALL

8003. Which document specifically authorizes a person to operate an aircraft in a particular geographic area?

A— Operations Specifications.
B— Operating Certificate.
C— Dispatch Release.

Each certificate holder conducting domestic, flag, or commuter operations must obtain operations specifications containing authorization and limitations for routes and areas of operations. (PLT389) — 14 CFR §119.49

ALL

9745. No person may operate a U.S. registered civil aircraft

A— for which an AFM or RFM is required by part 21 section 21.5 unless there is a current, approved operator's manual available.
B— for which an AFM or RFM is required by part 21 section 21.5 unless there is a current, approved AFM or RFM available.
C— for which an AFM or RFM is required by part 21 section 21.5 unless there is a current, approved AFM or RFM available or the manual specified in part 135 section 135.19(b).

No person may operate a U.S.-registered civil aircraft for which an Airplane or Rotorcraft Flight Manual is required by §21.5 unless there is available in the aircraft a current, approved Airplane or Rotorcraft Flight Manual or the manual provided for in §121.141(b). (PLT373) — 14 CFR §91.9

ALL

8429. An airport approved by the Administrator for use by an air carrier certificate holder for the purpose of providing service to a community when the regular airport is not available is a/an:

A— destination airport.
B— provisional airport.
C— alternate airport.

A provisional airport is defined as an airport approved by the Administrator for use by a certificate holder for the purpose of providing service to a community when the regular airport used by the certificate holder is not available. (PLT395) — 14 CFR §119.3

Answer (A) is incorrect because the destination airport is the term used to describe the primary airport of intended landing. Answer (C) is incorrect because the alternate airport is generally defined as an airport at which an aircraft may land if a landing at the intended airport becomes inadvisable.

ALL

8430. A provisional airport is an airport approved by the Administrator for use by an air carrier certificate holder for the purpose of

A— obtaining provisions and fuel when unable, due to winds, to proceed direct to the regular airport.
B— having the aircraft catered (foods, beverages, or supplies).
C— providing service to a community when the regular airport is unavailable.

A provisional airport is defined as an airport approved by the Administrator for use by a certificate holder for the purpose of providing service to a community when the regular airport used by the certificate holder is not available. (PLT389) — 14 CFR §119.3

ALL

8767. A person who is not authorized to conduct direct air carrier operations, but who is authorized by the Administrator to conduct operations as a U.S. commercial operator, will be issued

A— an Air Carrier Certificate.
B— a Supplemental Air Carrier Certificate.
C— an Operating Certificate.

A person who is not authorized to conduct direct air carrier operations, but who is authorized by the Administrator to conduct operations as a U.S. commercial operator, will be issued an Operating Certificate. (PLT389) — 14 CFR §119.5

Answers

9326	[B]		8003	[A]		9745	[B]	8429	[B]	8430	[C]	8767	[C]

Answer (A) is incorrect because a person authorized by the Administrator to conduct operations as a direct air carrier is issued an Air Carrier Certificate. Answer (B) is incorrect because wherever in the Federal Aviation Regulations the term "supplemental air carrier operating certificate" appears, it shall be deemed to mean an "Air Carrier Operating Certificate."

ALL

8768. The kinds of operation that a certificate holder is authorized to conduct are specified in the

A— certificate holder's operations specifications.
B— application submitted for an Air Carrier or Operating Certificate, by the applicant.
C— Air Carrier Certificate or Operating Certificate.

Each certificate holder conducting domestic, flag, or commuter operations must obtain operations specifications containing, among many other provisions, the kinds of operations authorized. (PLT389) — 14 CFR §119.49

Answers (B) and (C) are incorrect because the operations specifications are continually updated and amended relative to the operator's needs and not contained in the original application or on the certificate itself.

ALL

9782. All 14 CFR Part 139 airports must report

A— accident and incident data annually.
B— noise complaint statistics for each departure procedure or runway.
C— declared distances for each runway.

All 14 CFR Part 139 airports report declared runway distance for each runway. (PLT078) — AIM ¶4-3-6

Answers (A) and (B) are incorrect because this information is only furnished upon request by the administrator per 14 CFR §139.301.

ATM, DSP

8243. The persons jointly responsible for the initiation, continuation, diversion, and termination of a supplemental air carrier or commercial operator flight are the

A— pilot in command and chief pilot.
B— pilot in command and director of operations.
C— pilot in command and the flight follower.

For operations of supplemental air carriers or commercial operators, the pilot-in-command and the director of operations are jointly responsible for the initiation, continuation, diversion, and termination of a flight. (PLT444) — 14 CFR §121.537

ATM, DSP

8290. Which information must be contained in, or attached to, the dispatch release for a flag air carrier flight?

A— Type of operation (e.g., IFR, VFR), trip number.
B— Total fuel supply and minimum fuel required on board the airplane.
C— Passenger manifest, company or organization name, and cargo weight.

The dispatch release of a flag or domestic air carrier may be in any form but must contain at least the following information concerning the flight:

1. *Identification number of the aircraft;*
2. *Trip number;*
3. *Departure airport, intermediate stops, destination airports, and alternate airports;*
4. *A statement of the type of operation (IFR, VFR);*
5. *Minimum fuel supply.*

(PLT455) — 14 CFR §121.687

Answers (B) and (C) are incorrect because fuel on board, a passenger list, and cargo weights are found in the load manifest. Although separate items, both the dispatch release and the load manifest are required to be carried on the flight.

ATM, DSP

8292. What information must be contained in, or attached to, the dispatch release for a domestic air carrier flight?

A— Departure airport, intermediate stops, destinations, alternate airports, and trip number.
B— Names of all passengers on board and minimum fuel supply.
C— Cargo load, weight and balance data, and identification number of the aircraft.

The dispatch release of a flag or domestic air carrier may be in any form but must contain at least the following information concerning the flight:

1. *Identification number of the aircraft;*
2. *Trip number;*
3. *Departure airport, intermediate stops, destination airports, and alternate airports;*
4. *A statement of the type of operation (IFR, VFR);*
5. *Minimum fuel supply.*

(PLT400) — 14 CFR §121.687

Answers (B) and (C) are incorrect because the passenger names, cargo load, and weight and balance data are part of the required load manifest. A copy of the load manifest must also be carried on the flight. The load manifest is not part of the dispatch release.

Answers

8768 [A]	9782 [C]	8243 [B]	8290 [A]	8292 [A]

ATM, DSP

8293. What information must be included on a domestic air carrier dispatch release?

A— Evidence that the airplane is loaded according to schedule, and a statement of the type of operation.
B— Minimum fuel supply and trip number.
C— Company or organization name and identification number of the aircraft.

The dispatch release of a flag or domestic air carrier may be in any form but must contain at least the following information concerning the flight:

1. Identification number of the aircraft;

2. Trip number;

3. Departure airport, intermediate stops, destination airports, and alternate airports;

4. A statement of the type of operation (IFR, VFR);

5. Minimum fuel supply.

(PLT412) — 14 CFR §121.687

Answer (A) is incorrect because the proper loading of the airplane is documented in the load manifest. Answer (C) is incorrect because the company or organization name is not required on the dispatch release.

ATM, DSP

8294. A dispatch release for a flag or domestic air carrier must contain or have attached to it

A— minimum fuel supply and weather information for the complete flight.
B— trip number and weight and balance data.
C— weather information for the complete flight and a crew list.

The dispatch release must contain, or have attached to it, weather reports, available weather forecasts, or a combination thereof, for the destination airport, intermediate stops, and alternate airports, that are the latest available at the time the release is signed by the pilot-in-command and dispatcher. It may include any additional available weather reports or forecasts that the pilot-in-command or the aircraft dispatcher considers necessary or desirable. (PLT412) — 14 CFR §121.687

ATM, DSP

8280. By regulation, who shall provide the pilot in command of a domestic or flag air carrier airplane information concerning weather, and irregularities of facilities and services?

A— The aircraft dispatcher.
B— Air route traffic control center.
C— Director of operations.

The aircraft dispatcher for a flag or domestic flight shall provide the pilot-in-command all available reports or information on airport conditions and irregularities of navigation facilities that may affect safety of the flight. (PLT398) — 14 CFR §121.601

Answer (B) is incorrect because air route traffic control center may have information concerning irregularities of facilities and service, but it is not the proper source of that information. That information should be provided by the aircraft dispatcher. Answer (C) is incorrect because the director of operations (who may also be the general manager) is an administrative person, responsible for the day-to-day operations and not usually involved in specific flight operations.

ATM, DSP

8283. Where can the pilot of a flag air carrier airplane find the latest FDC NOTAMs?

A— Any company dispatch facility.
B— Notices To Airmen publication.
C— Chart Supplements U.S.

The Aircraft Dispatcher for a flag or domestic flight shall provide the pilot-in-command all available reports or information on airport conditions and irregularities of navigation facilities that may affect safety of the flight. Since FDC NOTAMs are regulatory in nature and apply to instrument approach procedures and enroute charts, they would have to be available. (PLT323) — 14 CFR §121.601

ATM, DSP

8284. Who is responsible, by regulation, for briefing a domestic or flag air carrier pilot in command on all available weather information?

A— Company meteorologist.
B— Aircraft dispatcher.
C— Director of operations.

Before the beginning of a flag or domestic flight, the aircraft dispatcher shall provide the pilot-in-command with all available weather reports and forecasts of weather phenomena that may affect the safety of flight. (PLT398) — 14 CFR §121.601

Answers

| 8293 | [B] | 8294 | [A] | 8280 | [A] | 8283 | [A] | 8284 | [B] |

ATM, DSP

8232. A domestic air carrier flight has a delay while on the ground, at an intermediate airport. How long before a redispatch release is required?

A— Not more than 1 hour.
B— Not more than 2 hours.
C— More than 6 hours.

Except when a domestic air carrier airplane lands at an intermediate airport specified in the original dispatch release and remains there for not more than 1 hour, no person may start a flight unless an aircraft dispatcher specifically authorizes that flight. (PLT452) — 14 CFR §121.593

Answer (B) is incorrect because domestic air carriers may remain at an intermediate stop for 1 hour before a redispatch release is required. Answer (C) is incorrect because flag, supplemental, and commercial operators may remain at an intermediate stop up to 6 hours before a redispatch release is required.

ATM, DSP

8260. A domestic air carrier airplane lands at an intermediate airport at 1815Z. The latest time it may depart without a specific authorization from an aircraft dispatcher is

A— 1945Z.
B— 1915Z.
C— 1845Z.

Except when a domestic air carrier airplane lands at an intermediate airport specified in the original dispatch release and remains there for not more than 1 hour, no person may start a flight unless an aircraft dispatcher specifically authorizes that flight. (PLT398) — 14 CFR §121.593

ATM, DSP

8259. A flag air carrier flight lands at an intermediate airport at 1805Z. The latest time that it may depart without being redispatched is

A— 2005Z.
B— 1905Z.
C— 0005Z.

No person may continue a flag air carrier flight from an intermediate airport without redispatch if the airplane has been on the ground more than 6 hours. (PLT398) — 14 CFR §121.595

ATM, DSP

8266. When a flag air carrier airplane lands at an intermediate airport at 1822Z, what is the latest time it may continue a flight without receiving a redispatch authorization?

A— 1922Z.
B— 1952Z.
C— 0022Z.

No person may continue a flag air carrier flight from an intermediate airport without redispatch if the airplane has been on the ground more than 6 hours. (PLT398) — 14 CFR §121.595

ATM, DSP

8267. If a flag air carrier flight lands at an intermediate airport at 1845Z, and experiences a delay, what is the latest time it may depart for the next airport without a redispatch release?

A— 1945Z.
B— 2015Z.
C— 0045Z.

No person may continue a flag air carrier flight from an intermediate airport without redispatch if the airplane has been on the ground more than 6 hours. (PLT398) — 14 CFR §121.595

ATM, DSP

8226. What information must the pilot in command of a supplemental air carrier flight or commercial operator carry to the destination airport?

A— Cargo and passenger distribution information.
B— Copy of the flight plan.
C— Names of all crewmembers and designated pilot in command.

The pilot-in-command shall carry in the airplane to its destination: load manifest, flight release, airworthiness release, pilot route certification, and flight plan. (PLT400) — 14 CFR §121.687

Answer (A) is incorrect because this information is only part of the load manifest. Answer (C) is incorrect because this is only one element of the flight release which is required on board.

Answers

8232 [A]	8260 [B]	8259 [C]	8266 [C]	8267 [C]	8226 [B]

ATM, DSP

8286. Which documents are required to be carried aboard each domestic air carrier flight?

A— Load manifest (or information from it) and flight release.

B— Dispatch release and weight and balance release.

C— Dispatch release, load manifest (or information from it), and flight plan.

The pilot-in-command of a domestic or flag air carrier flight shall carry in the airplane to its destination:

1. A copy of the completed load manifest;

2. A copy of the dispatch release; and

3. A copy of the flight plan.

(PLT400) — 14 CFR §121.695

ATM, DSP

8288. A domestic or flag air carrier shall keep copies of the flight plans, dispatch releases, and load manifests for at least

A— 3 months.

B— 6 months.

C— 30 days.

The air carrier shall keep copies of the flight plans, dispatch releases, and load manifests for at least 3 months. (PLT453) — 14 CFR §121.695

ATM, DSP

8296. Which documents are required to be carried aboard each flag air carrier flight?

A— Dispatch release, flight plan, and weight and balance release.

B— Load manifest, flight plan, and flight release.

C— Dispatch release, load manifest, and flight plan.

The pilot-in-command of a domestic or flag air carrier flight shall carry in the airplane to its destination:

1. A copy of the completed load manifest;

2. A copy of the dispatch release; and

3. A copy of the flight plan.

(PLT400) — 14 CFR §121.695

Answer (A) is incorrect because a dispatch release is required but there is no required document called a weight and balance release. Answer (B) is incorrect because a flight release is used by supplemental air carriers and commercial operators.

ATM, DSP

8287. How long shall a supplemental air carrier or commercial operator retain a record of the load manifest, airworthiness release, pilot route certification, flight release, and flight plan?

A— 1 month.

B— 3 months.

C— 12 months.

A supplemental air carrier must retain a copy of each load manifest, flight release and flight plan at its principal operations base for at least 3 months. (PLT453) — 14 CFR §121.697

ATM, DSP

8291. The certificated air carrier and operators who must attach to, or include on, the flight release form the name of each flight crewmember, flight attendant, and designated pilot in command are

A— supplemental and commercial.

B— supplemental and domestic.

C— flag and commercial.

Supplemental air carrier and commercial operators must attach to, or include on, the flight release form, containing at least the following information concerning each flight:

1. Company or organization name;

2. Make, model and registration number of the aircraft being used;

3. Flight or trip number and the date of the flight;

4. Name of each flight crewmember, flight attendant, and pilot designated as pilot-in-command;

5. Departure airport, destination airports, alternate airports, and route;

6. Minimum fuel supply; and

7. A statement of the type of operation (IFR, VFR).

(PLT455) — 14 CFR §121.689

Answers (B) and (C) are incorrect because domestic and flag carriers, unlike supplemental and commercial operators, utilize a dispatch release. Commercial operators and supplemental carriers utilize a flight release. A flight release contains the crew names, but a dispatch release does not.

Answers

8286 [C]	8288 [A]	8296 [C]	8287 [B]	8291 [A]

ATM, DSP

8295. The information required in the flight release for supplemental air carriers and commercial operators that is not required in the dispatch release for flag and domestic air carriers is the

A— weather reports and forecasts.
B— names of all crewmembers.
C— minimum fuel supply.

The flight release of a supplemental air carrier or commercial operator may be in any form but must contain at least the following information concerning each flight:

1. *Company or organization name;*

2. *Make, model and registration number of the aircraft being used;*

3. *Flight or trip number and the date of the flight;*

4. *Name of each flight crewmember, flight attendant, and pilot designated as pilot-in-command;*

5. *Departure airport, destination airports, alternate airports, and route;*

6. *Minimum fuel supply; and*

7. *A statement of the type of operation (IFR, VFR).*

The dispatch release of a flag or domestic air carrier may be in any form but must contain at least the following information concerning the flight:

1. *Identification number of the aircraft;*

2. *Trip number;*

3. *Departure airport, intermediate stops, destination airports, and alternate airports;*

4. *A statement of the type of operation (IFR, VFR);*

5. *Minimum fuel supply.*

(PLT412) — 14 CFR §121.689

Answers (A) and (C) are incorrect because weather reports and forecasts and minimum fuel supply information are required in the flight release for supplemental and commercial operators and in the dispatch release for flag and domestic air carriers.

ATM, DSP

9746. Before an ETOPS flight may commence, an ETOPS

A— preflight check must be conducted by a certified A&P and signed off in the logbook.
B— pre-departure service check must be certified by a PDSC Signatory Person.
C— pre-departure check must be signed off by an A&P or the PIC for the flight.

An appropriately-trained, ETOPS-qualified maintenance person must accomplish and certify by signature ETOPS specific tasks. Before an ETOPS flight may commence, an ETOPS pre-departure service check (PDSC) Signatory Person, who has been authorized by the certificate holder, must certify by signature, that the ETOPS PDSC has been completed. (PLT425) — 14 CFR §121.374

ATM, DSP

9746-1. An ETOPS entry point means

A— the first entry point on the route of flight of an ETOPS flight using one-engine-inoperative cruise speed that is more than 60 minutes from an adequate airport for airplanes having two engines.
B— the first entry point on the route of flight of an ETOPS flight using one-engine-inoperative cruise speed that is more than 200 minutes from an adequate airport for airplanes having more than two engines.
C— the first entry point on the route of flight of an ETOPS flight using one-engine-inoperative cruise speed that is more than 90 minutes from an adequate airport for airplanes having two engines.

"ETOPS entry point" means the first point on the route of an ETOPS flight that is (1) more than 60 minutes from an adequate airport for airplanes with two engines, and (2) more than 180 minutes from an adequate airport for passenger-carrying airplanes with more than two engines. This is determined using a one-engine-inoperative cruise speed under standard conditions in still air. (PLT425) — 14 CFR §121.7

Answers

8295   [B]   9746   [B]   9746-1   [A]

ATM, DSP

9746-2. For flight planning, a Designated ETOPS Alternate Airport

A— for ETOPS up to 180 minutes, must have RFFS equivalent to that specified by ICAO category 4, unless the airport's RFFS can be augmented by local fire fighting assets within 30 minutes.

B— for ETOPS up to 180 minutes, must have RFFS equivalent to that specified by ICAO category 3, unless the airport's RFFS can be augmented by local fire fighting assets within 45 minutes.

C— for ETOPS up to 180 minutes, must have RFFS equivalent to that specified by ICAO category 4, unless the airport's RFFS can be augmented by local fire fighting assets within 45 minutes.

For ETOPS up to 180 minutes, each designated ETOPS alternate airport must have RFFS equivalent to that specified by ICAO as Category 4 or higher. If the equipment and personnel required are not immediately available at an airport, the certificate holder may still list the airport on the dispatch or flight release if the airport's RFFS can be augmented from local fire fighting assets. A 30-minute response time for augmentation is adequate if the local assets can be notified while the diverting airplane is en route. (PLT398) — 14 CFR §121.106

ALL

9761. What is considered "north polar"?

A— north of 60° N latitude.
B— north of 68° N latitude.
C— north of 78° N latitude.

As an example, operations in the "North Polar Area" and "South Polar Area" require a specific passenger recovery plan for each diversion airport. North Polar Area means the entire area north of 78° N latitude. (PLT425) — 14 CFR §121.7

ALL

9762. What is considered "south polar"?

A— south of 60° S latitude.
B— south of 68° S latitude.
C— south of 78° S latitude.

As an example, operations in the "North Polar Area" and "South Polar Area" require a specific passenger recovery plan for each diversion airport. South Polar Area means the entire area south of 60° S latitude. (PLT425) — 14 CFR §121.7

ATM, DSP

8281. Who is responsible for obtaining information on all current airport conditions, weather, and irregularities of navigation facilities for a supplemental air carrier flight?

A— Aircraft dispatcher.
B— Director of operations or flight follower.
C— Pilot in command.

Before beginning a flight, each pilot-in-command of a supplemental air carrier or commercial operator flight shall obtain all available current reports or information on airport conditions and irregularities or navigation facilities that may affect the safety of the flight. (PLT444) — 14 CFR §121.603

Answer (A) is incorrect because an aircraft dispatcher is responsible for briefing a flag or domestic (not supplemental) air carrier pilot. Answer (B) is incorrect because the director of operations (who may also be the general manager) is an administrative person, responsible for the day-to-day operations and not usually involved in specific flight operations.

ATM, DSP

8282. During a supplemental air carrier flight, who is responsible for obtaining information on meteorological conditions?

A— Aircraft dispatcher.
B— Pilot in command.
C— Director of operations or flight follower.

During a flight, the pilot-in-command of a supplemental air carrier or commercial operator flight shall obtain any additional available information of meteorological conditions and irregularities of facilities and services that may affect the safety of the flight. (PLT444) — 14 CFR §121.603

Answer (A) is incorrect because an aircraft dispatcher is responsible for obtaining weather information for a flag or domestic air carrier flight. Answer (C) is incorrect because the director of operations (who may also be the general manager) or flight follower is an administrative person, responsible for day-to-day operations and not usually involved in specific flight operations.

Answers

9746-2 [A]	9761 [C]	9762 [A]	8281 [C]	8282 [B]

Fuel Requirements

All **domestic flights** must have enough fuel to:

1. Fly to the airport to which the flight was dispatched;

2. Thereafter, fly to and land at the most distant alternate airport (if an alternate is required) and

3. Thereafter, fly for 45 minutes at normal cruising fuel consumption.

(The fuel required for a **flag flight** landing in the 48 contiguous states or the District of Columbia is the same as for domestic flights.)

(The fuel requirements for **reciprocating-powered supplemental or commercial operations** landing in the contiguous 48 states is the same as for domestic operations.)

If an **alternate is not required** or the flight is being made to a remote airport where **no alternate is available**, the fuel requirements are:

1. Enough fuel to fly to the destination, and then;

2. Fly for two hours at normal cruising fuel consumption.

A **turbojet supplemental flight** (with an alternate available) landing outside the 48 contiguous states must have fuel to:

1. Fly to the destination, then

2. Fly 10% of the total time required to fly to the destination, then

3. Fly to the alternate, then

4. Fly for 30 minutes at holding speed at 1,500 feet above the alternate.

Propeller driven flag flights must have enough fuel to:

1. Fly to the airport to which the flight was dispatched;

2. Thereafter, fly to and land at the most distant alternate; and

3. Thereafter, fly for 30 minutes plus 15% of the total flying time to the destination and the alternate at normal cruising fuel consumption; or fly for 90 minutes, whichever is less.

If an **alternate is not required** or the flight is being made to a remote airport where **no alternate is available**, the fuel requirements for **reciprocating engine powered flights** are:

1. Enough fuel to fly to the destination, and then;

2. Fly for 3 hours at normal cruising fuel consumption.

ATM, DSP

8268. The reserve fuel supply for a domestic air carrier flight is

A— 30 minutes plus 15 percent at normal fuel consumption in addition to the fuel required to the alternate airport.

B— 45 minutes at normal fuel consumption in addition to the fuel required to fly to and land at the most distant alternate airport.

C— 45 minutes at normal fuel consumption in addition to the fuel required to the alternate airport.

For domestic operations, no person may dispatch or takeoff an airplane unless it has enough fuel to:

1. *Fly to the airport to which it was dispatched;*

2. *Thereafter, to fly to and land at the most distant alternate airport (if an alternate is required); and*

3. *Thereafter, to fly for 45 minutes at normal cruising fuel consumption.*

(PLT413) — 14 CFR §121.639

ATM, DSP

8269. The minimum amount (planned) of fuel to be aboard a flag air carrier turbojet airplane on a flight within the 48 contiguous United States, after reaching the most distant alternate airport, should be

A— 45 minutes at normal cruising fuel consumption.

B— 2 hours at normal cruising fuel consumption.

C— enough fuel to return to the destination airport or to fly for 90 minutes at normal cruising fuel consumption, whichever is less.

A turbine-engined flag air carrier operation within the 48 contiguous United States and the District of Columbia may use the fuel requirements of a domestic air carrier. For domestic operations, no person may dispatch or takeoff in an airplane unless it has enough fuel to:

1. *Fly to the airport to which it was dispatched;*

2. *Thereafter, to fly to and land at the most distant alternate airport (if an alternate is required); and*

3. *Thereafter, to fly for 45 minutes at normal cruising fuel consumption.*

(PLT413) — 14 CFR §121.639

Answer (B) is incorrect because 2 hours normal cruising fuel is required at the destination airport when an alternate is not specified and the flight is conducted outside the 48 contiguous United States. Answer (C) is incorrect because there is no provision for return to the destination airport in calculating fuel requirements.

ATM, DSP

8271. For a flag air carrier flight to be released to an island airport for which an alternate airport is not available, a turbojet-powered airplane must have enough fuel to fly to that airport and thereafter to fly

A— at least 2 hours at normal cruising fuel consumption.

B— for 3 hours at normal cruising fuel consumption.

C— back to the departure airport.

No person may dispatch a turbojet-powered airplane to an airport for which no alternate is available unless it has enough fuel, considering wind and other weather conditions, to fly to that airport and thereafter to fly for at least 2 hours at normal cruising fuel consumption. (PLT413) — 14 CFR §121.645

ATM, DSP

8272. An alternate airport is not required for a supplemental or commercial air carrier, turbojet-powered airplane on an IFR flight outside the 48 contiguous United States, if enough fuel

A— is aboard to fly to the destination at normal cruise speed and thereafter at least 2 hours at normal holding speed.

B— is aboard the airplane to fly to the destination and then to fly for at least 2 more hours at normal cruising fuel consumption.

C— to fly over the destination for 30 minutes at holding airspeed at 1,500 feet AGL is carried aboard the airplane.

No person may dispatch a turbojet-powered airplane to an airport for which no alternate is available unless it has enough fuel, considering wind and other weather conditions, to fly to that airport and thereafter to fly for at least 2 hours at normal cruising fuel consumption. (PLT413) — 14 CFR §121.645

Answers

| 8268 | [B] | 8269 | [A] | 8271 | [A] | 8272 | [B] |

ATM, DSP

8276. A turbine-engine-powered flag air carrier airplane is released to an airport which has no available alternate. What is the required fuel reserve?

A— 2 hours at normal cruise speed in a no wind condition fuel consumption.
B— 2 hours at normal cruise fuel consumption.
C— 30 minutes, plus 10 percent of the total flight time.

No person may dispatch a turbojet-powered airplane to an airport for which no alternate is available unless it has enough fuel, considering wind and other weather conditions, to fly to that airport and thereafter to fly for at least 2 hours at normal cruising fuel consumption. (PLT413) — 14 CFR §121.645

ATM, DSP

8273. The fuel reserve required for a turbine-engine-powered (other than turbopropeller) supplemental air carrier airplane upon arrival over the most distant alternate airport outside the 48 contiguous United States is

A— 30 minutes at holding speed, at 1,500 feet over the airport.
B— 30 minutes, over the airport, at 1,500 feet, at cruising speed.
C— 2 hours at the normal cruising fuel consumption rate.

For any flag air carrier, supplemental air carrier, or commercial operator operation outside the 48 contiguous United States or District of Columbia, no person may release for flight or takeoff a turbine engine-powered airplane (other than a turbopropeller-powered airplane) unless, considering wind and other weather conditions expected, it has enough fuel:

1. *To fly to and land at the airport to which it was released;*

2. *After that, to fly for a period of 10% of the total time required to fly from the airport of departure to and land at, the airport to which it was released;*

3. *After that, to fly to and land at the most distant alternate airport specified in the flight release, if an alternate is required; and*

4. *After that, to fly for 30 minutes at holding speed at 1,500 feet above the alternate airport (or destination airport if no alternate is required) under standard temperature conditions.*

(PLT413) — 14 CFR §121.645

ATM, DSP

8270. What is the fuel reserve requirement for a commercially operated reciprocating-engine-powered airplane flying within the 48 contiguous United States upon arrival at the most distant alternate airport specified in the flight release? Enough fuel to fly

A— 30 minutes plus 15 percent of total time required to fly at normal cruising consumption to the alternate.
B— to fly for 90 minutes at normal cruising fuel consumption.
C— 45 minutes at normal cruising fuel consumption.

No person may release for flight or takeoff a nonturbine or turbopropeller-powered airplane unless, considering the wind and other weather conditions expected, it has enough fuel to:

1. *Fly to the airport to which it was released;*

2. *Thereafter, to fly to and land at the most distant alternate airport specified in the flight release; and*

3. *Thereafter, to fly for 45 minutes at normal cruising fuel consumption.*

(PLT413) — 14 CFR §121.643

ATM, DSP

8277. The fuel reserve required for a reciprocating-engine-powered supplemental air carrier airplane upon arrival at the most distant alternate airport during a flight in the 48 contiguous United States is

A— 45 minutes at normal cruising fuel consumption.
B— the fuel required to fly to the alternate, plus 10 percent.
C— 3 hours at normal cruising fuel consumption.

No person may release for flight or takeoff a nonturbine or turbopropeller-powered airplane unless, considering the wind and other weather conditions expected, it has enough fuel to:

1. *Fly to the airport to which it was released;*

2. *Thereafter, to fly to and land at the most distant alternate airport specified in the flight release; and*

3. *Thereafter, to fly for 45 minutes at normal cruising fuel consumption.*

(PLT413) — 14 CFR §121.643

Answers

8276 [B]   8273 [A]   8270 [C]   8277 [A]

ATM, DSP

8274. Upon arriving at the most distant airport, what is the fuel reserve requirement for a turbopropeller flag air carrier airplane?

A— 90 minutes at holding altitude and speed fuel consumption or 30 minutes plus 15 percent of cruise fuel consumption, whichever is less.

B— 45 minutes at holding altitude.

C— 30 minutes plus 15 percent of the total time required, or 90 minutes at normal cruise, whichever is less.

No person may dispatch or takeoff in a flag air carrier nonturbine or turbopropeller-powered airplane unless, considering the wind and other weather conditions expected, it has enough fuel:

1. *To fly to and land at the airport to which it is dispatched;*

2. *Thereafter, to fly to and land at the most distant alternate airport specified in the dispatch release; and*

3. *Thereafter to fly for 30 minutes plus 15% of numbers 1 and 2 above, or to fly for 90 minutes at normal cruising fuel consumption, whichever is less.*

(PLT413) — 14 CFR §121.641

ATM, DSP

8275. The fuel reserve required, for a turbopropeller supplemental air carrier airplane upon the arrival at a destination airport for which an alternate airport is not specified, is

A— 3 hours at normal consumption, no wind condition.

B— 3 hours at normal cruising fuel consumption.

C— 2 hours at normal cruising fuel consumption.

No supplemental air carrier or commercial operator may release a nonturbine or turbopropeller-powered airplane to an airport for which no alternate is specified unless it has enough fuel, considering wind and weather conditions expected, to fly to that airport and thereafter to fly for 3 hours at normal cruising fuel consumption. (PLT413) — 14 CFR §121.643

Answers

8274   [C]   8275   [B]

Carriage of Passengers and Cargo

Before takeoff all the passengers must be briefed on:

- Smoking,

- the location of emergency exits,

- the use of seatbelts,

- the location and use of any required means of emergency flotation.

After the seatbelt sign has been turned off in flight, the passengers must be briefed to keep their seatbelts fastened while seated. In addition to the required briefings, passengers must be provided with printed cards that contain diagrams of and methods of operating the emergency exits and the use of other emergency equipment. Before flight is conducted above FL250, a crewmember must instruct the passengers on the necessity of using oxygen in the event of cabin depressurization, and must point out to them the location and demonstrate the use of the oxygen dispensing equipment.

Each passenger two years old and older must have their own seat or berth and approved seatbelt. During takeoff and landing, all passengers must be in their seat with their seatbelts fastened. A child under two may be held by an adult. During the enroute portion of a flight, two passengers may share a seatbelt while seated in a multiple lounge or divan seat.

There are certain persons who have to be admitted to the flight deck in flight (such as crewmembers, FAA inspectors, etc.) and certain others who may be admitted (e.g., deadheading crew), but the pilot-in-command has emergency authority to exclude any person from the flight deck in the interest of safety. In what is commonly known as the "sterile cockpit rule," crewmembers are required to refrain from nonessential activities during critical phases of flight. As defined in the regulation, critical phases of flight are all ground operations involving taxi, takeoff, and landing, and all other flight operations below 10,000 feet except cruise flight. Nonessential activities include such activities as eating, reading a newspaper, or chatting.

Law enforcement officers may carry firearms on board an air carrier flight if their duties so require. Except in an emergency, the carrier should be given at least one hour prior notice that a person carrying a deadly weapon is going to be on the flight. If a passenger is carrying a firearm in their checked baggage, the weapon must be unloaded and the bag locked. The passenger must retain the key to the bag. The bag must be stowed in a portion of the aircraft that is inaccessible to both the passenger and to crewmembers in flight.

Prisoners are sometimes carried on air carrier flights. The prisoners are always escorted and no more than one prisoner who is classified as "maximum risk" can be allowed on the aircraft. Certain rules apply to the carriage of prisoners. These include:

- The prisoner and escort must be boarded before all other passengers and must stay on board until all other passengers have deplaned.

- The prisoner and escort must sit in the most rearward passenger seats and the escort must sit between the prisoner and the aisle.

- The carrier may serve the prisoner and the escort food and beverages, but neither of them may be served alcohol.

Continued

If a person who appears to be intoxicated creates a disturbance on a flight, a report of the incident must be made to the Administrator (the FAA) within 5 days.

Certain passengers may be carried on an all-cargo flight without the carrier having to comply with all the passenger-carrying rules. Passengers carried on an all-cargo flight must have a seat with an approved seatbelt in the cargo compartment. They must have access to the pilot compartment or to an exit. The pilot-in-command must be able to notify them when they must have their seatbelt fastened and when smoking is prohibited. They must receive an emergency briefing from a crewmember prior to takeoff. The pilot-in-command may authorize the passenger to be admitted to the flight crew compartment.

Cargo (including carry-on baggage) may be carried in the passenger compartment of an aircraft if certain conditions are met. If the cargo is carried in an approved cargo bin, it can be located anywhere in the passenger compartment. The bin:

- Must withstand the load factor required of passenger seats multiplied by 1.15

- May not be installed in a position that restricts access to or use of any required emergency exit, or of the aisle in the passenger cabin

- Must be completely enclosed and made of material that is at least flame resistant

If the cargo is not placed in an approved cargo bin it must be located aft of a bulkhead or divider (i.e., not aft of a passenger) and it must meet certain other requirements. These include:

- It must be properly secured by a safety belt or other tie down.

- It must be packaged or covered in a manner so as to avoid injury to occupants of the passenger cabin.

- It must not impose an excessive load on the floor or seat structures of the aircraft.

- Its location must not restrict access to or use of the aisle, any regular exit or any required emergency exit.

- Its location must not obscure any passenger's view of the "seatbelt," "no smoking" or required "exit" signs unless an auxiliary sign is installed.

Each person who has duties concerning the handling or carriage of dangerous articles or magnetized materials must have completed a training course within the preceding 12 calendar months.

ALL
8131. A certificate holder is notified that a person specifically authorized to carry a deadly weapon is to be aboard an aircraft. Except in an emergency, how long before loading that flight should the air carrier be notified?

A— Notification is not required, if the certificate holder has a security coordinator.
B— A minimum of 1 hour.
C— A minimum of 2 hours.

The certificate holder, except in an emergency, must be given at least 1 hour notice when an authorized person intends to have a weapon accessible in flight. (PLT498) — 49 CFR §1544.219

ALL
8137. When a passenger notifies the certificate holder prior to checking baggage that an unloaded weapon is in the baggage, what action is required by regulation regarding this baggage?

A— The baggage may be carried in the flightcrew compartment, provided the baggage remains locked, and the key is given to the pilot in command.
B— The baggage must remain locked and carried in an area that is inaccessible to the passenger, and only the passenger retains the key.
C— The baggage must remain locked and stored where it would be inaccessible, and custody of the key shall remain with a designated crewmember.

Answers
8131   [B]   8137   [B]

No certificate holder may knowingly permit any person to transport any unloaded firearm in checked baggage unless the baggage in which it is carried is locked and only the passenger checking the baggage retains the key or combination. The baggage containing the fire-arm must be carried in an area, other than the flight crew compartment, that is inaccessible to passengers. (PLT498) — 49 CFR §1544.203(f)

Answers (A) and (C) are incorrect because the baggage containing the unloaded firearm will be carried in the baggage area, and only the passenger checking the baggage retains the key.

ALL

9763. What is meant by "sterile cockpit"?

A— All preflight checks are complete and the aircraft is ready for engine starting.

B— Crewmembers refrain from nonessential activities during critical phases of flight.

C— Crewmembers are seated and buckled at their required stations.

Commonly known as the "sterile cockpit rule," 14 CFR §121.542 requires flight crewmembers to refrain from nonessential activities during critical phases of flight. As defined in the regulation, critical phases of flight are all ground operations involving taxi, takeoff, and land-ing, and all other flight operations below 10,000 feet except cruise flight. Nonessential activities include such activities as eating, reading a newspaper, or chatting. (PLT498) — 14 CFR §121.542

ALL

8132. When a person in the custody of law enforcement personnel is scheduled on a flight, what procedures are required regarding boarding of this person and the escort?

A— They shall be boarded before all other passengers board, and deplaned after all the other passengers have left the aircraft.

B— They shall be boarded after all other passengers board, and deplaned before all the other passengers leave the aircraft.

C— They shall board and depart before the other passengers.

When a person in custody of law enforcement is to be carried on a flight, the prisoner and escort must be boarded before any other passengers and deplaned after all other passengers have deplaned. (PLT325) — 49 CFR §1544.221(f)(1)

ALL

8136. Which applies to the carriage of a person in the custody of law enforcement personnel?

A— The air carrier is not allowed to serve beverages to the person in custody or the law enforcement escort.

B— No more than one person considered to be in the maximum risk category may be carried on a flight, and that person must have at least two armed law enforcement escorts.

C— The person in custody must be seated between the escort and the aisle.

No more than one passenger, of whom the certificate holder has been notified as being in a maximum risk category, can be carried on an airplane. (PLT325) — 49 CFR §1544.221(c)(2), (d)(3)

ATM, DSP

8225. Which announcement must be made if the seat belt sign will be turned off during flight?

A— Clearly explain the location of the fire extinguishers and emergency exits.

B— Passenger should keep their seat belts fastened while seated.

C— Passengers are free to leave their seats once the seat belt sign is turned off.

After each takeoff, immediately before or immediately after turning the seat belt sign off, an announcement shall be made that passengers should keep their seat belts fastened, while seated, even when the seat belt sign is off. (PLT384) — 14 CFR §121.571

ATM, DSP

8181. A passenger briefing by a crewmember shall be given, instructing passengers on the necessity of using oxygen in the event of cabin depressurization, prior to flights conducted above

A— FL 200.

B— FL 240.

C— FL 250.

Before flight is conducted above FL250, a crewmember shall instruct the passengers on the necessity of using oxygen in the event of cabin depressurization, and shall point out to them the location and demonstrate the use of the oxygen dispensing equipment. (PLT438) — 14 CFR §121.333

Answers

9763 [B]	8132 [A]	8136 [B]	8225 [B]	8181 [C]

ATM, DSP

8153. When may two persons share one approved safety belt in a lounge seat?

A— When one is an adult and one is a child under 3 years of age.
B— Only during the en route flight.
C— During all operations except the takeoff and landing portion of a flight.

No person may operate an airplane unless there are available during the takeoff, enroute flight, and landing an approved seatbelt for separate use by each person on board the airplane who has reached his/her second birthday, except that two persons occupying a berth may share one approved seatbelt and two persons occupying a multiple lounge or divan seat may share one approved seatbelt during en route flight only. (PLT465) — 14 CFR §121.311

Answer (A) is incorrect because the regulations do not specify an age of persons sharing a seatbelt on a lounge seat. Sharing a seatbelt in a lounge seat can only be done during the enroute portion of the flight. Answer (C) is incorrect because two persons may share one seatbelt in a lounge seat only during the enroute portion of the flight, which excludes taxi and takeoff as well as landing.

ATM, DSP

8244. The pilot in command has emergency authority to exclude any and all persons from admittance to the flight deck

A— except a FAA inspector doing enroute checks.
B— in the interest of safety.
C— except persons who have authorization from the certificate holder and the FAA or NTSB.

The pilot-in-command has the emergency authority to exclude anyone from the flight deck in the interest of safety. (PLT444) — 14 CFR §121.547

Answers (A) and (C) are incorrect because persons who have specific authorization of the certificate holder and FAA inspectors may be admitted to the flight deck except when excluded in an emergency.

ATM, DSP

8233. If an intoxicated person creates a disturbance aboard an air carrier aircraft, the certificate holder must submit a report, concerning the incident, to the Administrator within

A— 7 days.
B— 5 days.
C— 48 hours.

If an intoxicated person causes an incident on the aircraft the certificate holder shall, within 5 days, report that incident to the Administrator. (PLT366) — 14 CFR §121.575

ATM, DSP

8234. When carrying a passenger aboard an all-cargo aircraft, which of the following applies?

A— The passenger must have access to a seat in the pilot compartment.
B— The pilot in command may authorize the passenger to be admitted to the crew compartment.
C— Crew-type oxygen must be provided for the passenger.

When a passenger is allowed on an all-cargo flight, the pilot-in-command may authorize admittance to the flight deck. (PLT444) — 14 CFR §121.583

Answer (A) is incorrect because the seat does not have to be on the flight deck, but there must be an approved seat with an approved seatbelt for each person. Answer (C) is incorrect because crew-type oxygen is not required for passengers. It is only required that the person be briefed on the use of oxygen and emergency oxygen equipment.

ATM, DSP

8139. What requirement must be met regarding cargo that is carried anywhere in the passenger compartment of an air carrier airplane?

A— The bin in which the cargo is carried may not be installed in a position that restricts access to, or use of, any exit.
B— The bin in which the cargo is carried may not be installed in a position that restricts access to, or use of, any aisle in the passenger compartment.
C— The container or bin in which the cargo is carried must be made of material which is at least flash resistant.

Cargo may be carried anywhere in the passenger compartment if it is carried in an approved cargo bin. The bin must meet the following requirements:

1. *The bin must be able to withstand the load factors and emergency landing conditions applicable to the passenger seats of the airplane in which it is installed, multiplied by a factor of 1.15;*

2. *The cargo bin may not be installed in a position that restricts access to or use of any required emergency exit, or of the aisle in the passenger compartment;*

3. *The bin must be fully enclosed and made of material that is at least flame resistant.*

(PLT385) — 14 CFR §121.285

Answer (A) is incorrect because the bin may not be installed in a position that restricts access to or use of any required emergency exit. Answer (C) is incorrect because the bin must be fully enclosed and made of material that is at least flame resistant.

Answers

| 8153 | [B] | 8244 | [B] | 8233 | [B] | 8234 | [B] | 8139 | [B] |

ATM, DSP

8175. Which restriction applies to a cargo bin in a passenger compartment? The bin

A— may have an open top if it is placed in front of the passengers and the cargo is secured by a cargo net.

B— must withstand the load factor required of passenger seats, multiplied by 1.15, using the combined weight of the bin and the maximum weight of the cargo that may be carried in the bin.

C— must be constructed of flame retardant material and fully enclosed.

Cargo may be carried anywhere in the passenger compartment if it is carried in an approved cargo bin. The bin must meet the following requirements:

1. *The bin must be able to withstand the load factors and emergency landing conditions applicable to the passenger seats of the airplane in which it is installed, multiplied by a factor of 1.15;*

2. *The cargo bin may not be installed in a position that restricts access to or use of any required emergency exit, or of the aisle in the passenger compartment;*

3. *The bin must be fully enclosed and made of material that is at least flame resistant.*

(PLT385) — 14 CFR §121.285

Answers (A) and (C) are incorrect because the cargo bin must be fully enclosed, and be constructed of materials that are at least flame resistant.

ATM, DSP

8138. What restrictions must be observed regarding the carrying of cargo in the passenger compartment of an airplane operated under 14 CFR Part 121?

A— All cargo must be separated from the passengers by a partition capable of withstanding certain load stresses.

B— All cargo must be carried in a suitable flame resistant bin and the bin must be secured to the floor structure of the airplane.

C— Cargo may be carried aft of a divider if properly secured by a safety belt or other tiedown having enough strength to eliminate the possibility of shifting.

Cargo may be carried aft of a bulkhead or divider in any passenger compartment provided the cargo is restrained to required load factors, and it is properly secured by a safety belt or other tiedown having enough strength to eliminate the possibility of shifting under all normally anticipated flight and ground conditions. (PLT385) — 14 CFR §121.285

Answers (A) and (B) are incorrect because cargo may be carried in the passenger compartment if it is properly covered and secured so as not to be a hazard.

Part 135 Carriage of Passengers and Cargo Requirements

ATS, RTC

8007. Where must a certificate holder keep copies of completed load manifests and for what period of time?

A— 1 month at its principal operations base, or at a location approved by the Administrator.
B— 30 days at its principal operations base, or another location used by it and approved by the Administrator.
C— 30 days, at the flight's destination.

The certificate holder shall keep copies of completed load manifests for at least 30 days at its principal operations base, or at another location used by it and approved by the Administrator. (PLT400) — 14 CFR §135.63

ATS, RTC

8008. Which is NOT a required item on the load manifest?

A— List of passenger names and the weight of each.
B— Aircraft registration number or flight number.
C— Identification of crewmembers and their crew position.

The load manifest must be prepared before each takeoff and must include:

1. The number of passengers;

2. The total weight of the loaded aircraft;

3. The maximum allowable takeoff weight for that flight;

4. The center of gravity limits;

5. The center of gravity of the loaded aircraft;

6. The registration number of the aircraft or flight number;

7. The origin and destination; and

8. Identification of crewmembers and their crew position assignments.

(PLT440) — 14 CFR §135.63

ATS, RTC

8009. Who is responsible for the preparation of a required load manifest?

A— PIC or the Dispatcher.
B— Company official designated by the Administrator.
C— The certificate holder.

For multi-engine aircraft, each certificate holder is responsible for the preparation and accuracy of a load manifest. (PLT440) — 14 CFR §135.63

ATS, RTC

8032. Which restriction must be observed regarding the carrying of cargo in the passenger compartment?

A— It is packaged or covered to avoid possible injury to occupants.
B— All cargo must be carried in a suitable bin and secured to a passenger seat or the floor structure of the aircraft.
C— Cargo carried in passenger seats must be forward of all passengers.

No person may carry cargo, including carry-on baggage, in or on any aircraft unless one of the three following criteria is met:

1. It is carried in an approved cargo rack, bin or compartment;

2. It is secured by approved means; or

3. If number 1 or 2 is not met, then all of the following are met:

a. For cargo, it is properly secured by a safety belt or other tie-down having enough strength to eliminate the possibility of shifting under all normally anticipated flight and ground conditions, or for carry-on baggage, it is restrained so as to prevent its movement during air turbulence;

b. It is packaged or covered to avoid possible injury to occupants;

c. It does not impose any load on seats or on the floor structure that exceeds the load limitation for those components;

d. It is not located in a position that obstructs the access to, or use of, any required emergency or regular exit, or the use of the aisle between the crew and passenger compartment, or located in a position that obscures any passenger's view of the "seatbelt" sign, "no smoking" sign or any required exit sign;

e. It is not carried directly above seated occupants.

(PLT385) — 14 CFR §135.87

Answers

8007   [B]   8008   [A]   8009   [C]   8032   [A]

ATS, RTC

9720. A person whose duties include the handling or carriage of dangerous articles and/or magnetized materials must have satisfactorily completed an approved training program established by the certificate holder within the previous

A— 6 calendar months.
B— 12 calendar months.
C— 24 calendar months.

No certificate holder may use any person or perform, and no person may perform, any assigned duties and responsibilities for the handling or carriage of hazardous materials unless within the preceding 12 calendar months that person has satisfactorily completed initial or recurrent training in an appropriate training program established by the certificate holder. (PLT407) — 14 CFR, SFAR 99

ATS, RTC

8039. In a cargo-only operation, cargo must be loaded

A— so that it does not obstruct the aisle between the crew and cargo compartments.
B— in such a manner that at least one emergency or regular exit is available to all occupants.
C— in such a manner that at least one emergency or regular exit is available to all crewmembers, if an emergency occurs.

For cargo-only operations, the cargo must be loaded so at least one emergency or regular exit is available to provide all occupants of the aircraft a means of unobstructed exit from the aircraft if an emergency occurs. (PLT385) — 14 CFR §135.87

ATS, RTC

8040. Which is a requirement governing the carriage of cargo, on a scheduled passenger flight?

A— Cargo must be carried in an approved rack, bin, or compartment.
B— Cargo not stowed in an approved bin must be secured by a safety belt or approved tiedown device.
C— All cargo carried in the passenger compartment must be packaged and stowed ahead of the foremost seated passenger.

No person may carry cargo, including carry-on baggage, in or on any aircraft unless one of the three following criteria is met:

1. *It is carried in an approved cargo rack, bin or compartment;*

2. *It is secured by approved means; or*

3. *If number 1 or 2 is not met, then all of the following are met:*

   a. *For cargo, it is properly secured by a safety belt or other tie-down having enough strength to eliminate the possibility of shifting under all normally anticipated flight and ground conditions, or for carry-on baggage, it is restrained so as to prevent its movement during air turbulence;*

   b. *It is packaged or covered to avoid possible injury to occupants;*

   c. *It does not impose any load on seats or on the floor structure that exceeds the load limitation for those components;*

   d. *It is not located in a position that obstructs the access to, or use of, any required emergency or regular exit, or the use of the aisle between the crew and passenger compartment, or located in a position that obscures any passenger's view of the "seatbelt" sign, "no smoking" sign or any required exit sign;*

   e. *It is not carried directly above seated occupants.*

(PLT385) — 14 CFR §135.87

Answers

9720 [B]   8039 [B]   8040 [B]

ATS, RTC
8041. Which is a requirement governing the carriage of carry-on baggage?

A— All carry-on baggage must be restrained so that its movement is prevented during air turbulence.
B— Carry-on baggage must be stowed under the seat in front of the owner.
C— Pieces of carry-on baggage weighing more than 10 pounds must be carried in an approved rack or bin.

No person may carry cargo, including carry-on baggage, in or on any aircraft unless one of the three following criteria is met:

1. It is carried in an approved cargo rack, bin or compartment;

2. It is secured by approved means; or

3. If number 1 or 2 is not met, then all of the following are met:

> *a. For cargo, it is properly secured by a safety belt or other tie-down having enough strength to eliminate the possibility of shifting under all normally anticipated flight and ground conditions, or for carry-on baggage, it is restrained so as to prevent its movement during air turbulence;*

> *b. It is packaged or covered to avoid possible injury to occupants;*

> *c. It does not impose any load on seats or on the floor structure that exceeds the load limitation for those components;*

> *d. It is not located in a position that obstructs the access to, or use of, any required emergency or regular exit, or the use of the aisle between the crew and passenger compartment, or located in a position that obscures any passenger's view of the "seatbelt" sign, "no smoking" sign or any required exit sign;*

> *e. It is not carried directly above seated occupants.*

(PLT385) — 14 CFR §135.87

ATS, RTC
8042. If carry-on baggage or cargo is carried in the passenger compartment, it must be

A— stowed ahead of the foremost seated passengers and secured by approved means.
B— placed in an approved rack, bin, or compartment installed in the aircraft.
C— so located that it does not obstruct the access to, or the use of, any required emergency or regular exit.

No person may carry cargo, including carry-on baggage, in or on any aircraft unless one of the three following criteria is met:

1. It is carried in an approved cargo rack, bin or compartment;

2. It is secured by approved means; or

3. If number 1 or 2 is not met, then all of the following are met:

> *a. For cargo, it is properly secured by a safety belt or other tie-down having enough strength to eliminate the possibility of shifting under all normally anticipated flight and ground conditions, or for carry-on baggage, it is restrained so as to prevent its movement during air turbulence;*

> *b. It is packaged or covered to avoid possible injury to occupants;*

> *c. It does not impose any load on seats or on the floor structure that exceeds the load limitation for those components;*

> *d. It is not located in a position that obstructs the access to, or use of, any required emergency or regular exit, or the use of the aisle between the crew and passenger compartment, or located in a position that obscures any passenger's view of the "seatbelt" sign, "no smoking" sign or any required exit sign;*

> *e. It is not carried directly above seated occupants.*

(PLT385) — 14 CFR §135.87

ATS, RTC
8043. The load manifest must be prepared prior to each takeoff for

A— any aircraft with a passenger seating capacity of 10 seats or more.
B— any aircraft with more than one engine.
C— all helicopters and large aircraft operated by a commuter air carrier.

For multi-engine aircraft, each certificate holder is responsible for the preparation and accuracy of a load manifest. (PLT440) — 14 CFR §135.63

Answers

8041 **[A]**   8042 **[C]**   8043 **[B]**

Emergency Equipment and Operations

Certain emergency equipment must be carried on every air carrier airplane. This equipment includes fire extinguishers, megaphones, first aid kits and a crash ax. All this equipment must:

- Be inspected regularly.
- Be readily accessible to the crew and, for items carried in the passenger cabin, to the passengers.
- Be clearly identified and marked with its method of operation (this applies to any containers in which the equipment is carried).

Only one crash ax is required on the airplane and must be carried on the flight deck. At least one hand fire extinguisher must be carried on the flight deck. The number of extinguishers carried in the cabin is determined by the number of installed passenger seats. The following table applies.

Minimum Number of Hand Fire Extinguishers in the Passenger Cabin:

Passenger Seating Capacity	Extinguishers Required
6 through 30	1
31 through 60	2
61 through 200	3
201 through 300	4
301 through 400	5
401 through 500	6
501 through 600	7
601 or more	8

The number of megaphones carried on the airplane is determined by the number of installed passenger seats. On airplanes with a seating capacity of 60 through 99 passengers, one megaphone must be carried in the most rearward location in the passenger cabin that is readily accessible to a normal flight attendant seat. On airplanes with a seating capacity of 100 or more seats, one megaphone must be carried at the rear of the cabin and another megaphone must be carried at the front of the cabin.

Passenger carrying airplanes must have an emergency exit light system. This system must be operable manually from both the flight crew station and from a point in the passenger compartment readily accessible to a flight attendant. When the system is armed it must come on automatically with the interruption of the airplane's normal electrical power. The exit lights must be armed or turned on during taxiing, takeoff and landing. Every emergency exit (other than an over wing exit) that is more than 6 feet from the ground must have a means of assisting occupants to the ground in the event of an emergency evacuation. The most common means of complying with this requirement is an inflatable slide that deploys automatically when the door is opened. If such an automatic escape slide is installed, it must be armed during taxi, takeoff and landing. If any required emergency exit for passengers is located in other than the passenger compartment (such as the flight deck), the door separating the compartments must be latched open during takeoff and landing.

A public address system and a separate crewmember interphone system must be installed on all airplanes with a seating capacity of more than 19 seats.

Each crewmember on a flight must have a flashlight in good working order readily available.

Continued

When operating at flight altitudes above 10,000 feet there must be enough oxygen for all crewmembers for the entire flight at those altitudes, and in no event less than a 2-hour supply.

When operating at flight altitudes above FL250 each flight crewmember on flight deck duty must have an oxygen mask, within immediate reach, so designed that it can be rapidly placed on his/her face. This is commonly referred to as a "**quick-donning**" oxygen mask. To meet the requirements, regulations require that the mask be designed so that it can be put on the user's face within 5 seconds. If, while operating above FL250, one pilot leaves his/her station, the other pilot must put on his/her oxygen mask.

Above FL410 one pilot must wear his/her mask at all times. Notice that the rule applies only to the pilots. Above FL250 the flight engineer need only have a quick-donning mask readily available. *Note:* For Part 135 operations one pilot must wear the oxygen mask above FL350.

The oxygen requirements for passengers vary with the type of aircraft, but oxygen must be provided to all passengers for the entire time the cabin altitude is above 15,000 feet.

Passengers on turbine powered airplanes must be supplied oxygen according to the following schedule.

- For flights at cabin pressure altitudes above 10,000 feet, up to and including 14,000 feet, there must be enough oxygen to supply 10% of the passengers for any time at those altitudes in excess of 30 minutes.

- For flights at cabin pressure altitudes above 14,000 feet, up to and including 15,000 feet, there must be enough oxygen for 30% of the passengers for the entire time at those altitudes.

- For flights at cabin pressure altitudes above 15,000 feet there must be enough oxygen for all the passengers for the entire time of flight at those altitudes.

The amount of oxygen carried for passengers in the event of loss of pressurization varies depending on the ability of the airplane to make an emergency descent. If the aircraft can make a descent to 14,000 feet within 4 minutes it may carry less oxygen than would otherwise be required.

A certain amount of **first aid oxygen** must be carried for passengers on flights that operate above FL250. The amount of oxygen is determined by the actual number of passengers but in no case may there be less than 2 oxygen dispensing units.

On extended over-water flights (more than 50 nautical miles from the shoreline) the airplane must have a life preserver for each occupant of the aircraft, and enough life rafts to accommodate all the occupants. This equipment must be easily accessible in the event of a ditching.

- Each life raft and each life vest must be equipped with a survivor locator light.

- A survival kit, appropriate for the route flown, must be attached to each life raft.

- There must be at least one portable emergency radio transmitter carried on the airplane.

When flag or supplemental carriers or commercial operators fly over uninhabited terrain, the following survival equipment must be carried on the airplane:

- Suitable pyrotechnic signaling devices.

- A survival-type emergency locator transmitter.

- Enough survival kits, appropriate for the route flown, for all the occupants of the airplane.

In an emergency situation that requires immediate decision and action, the pilot-in-command may take any action that he/she considers necessary under the circumstances. In such a case the PIC may deviate from prescribed procedures and methods, weather minimums and regulations to the extent required in the interest of safety. In an emergency situation arising during flight that requires immediate decision and action by an aircraft dispatcher, the dispatcher must advise the pilot-in-command of the emergency, shall ascertain the decision of the pilot-in-command and shall have that decision recorded. If the dispatcher cannot communicate with the pilot, he/she shall declare an emergency and take any action he/she considers necessary under the circumstances.

Each certificate holder (airline) must, for each type and model of airplane, assign to each category of crewmember, as appropriate, the necessary functions to be performed in an emergency or in a situation requiring emergency evacuation. The certificate holder must describe those duties in its manual.

Crewmembers must receive emergency training annually on several subjects. Besides the training they must perform emergency drills in:

- The operation of emergency exits;

- Hand fire extinguishers;

- The emergency oxygen system and protective breathing equipment;

- Donning, inflation and use of individual flotation equipment; and

- Ditching.

Crewmembers who serve above 25,000 feet must receive instruction in hypoxia, respiration and decompression. Crewmembers must actually operate certain emergency equipment in their recurrent training at least once every 24 months.

The pilot-in-command must make a report to the appropriate ground radio station of the stoppage of an engine's rotation in flight (due either to failure or intentional shutdown) as soon as practicable and must keep that station informed of the progress of the flight. As a general rule, when an engine fails or is shutdown, the pilot-in-command must land the aircraft at the nearest suitable airport, time-wise, at which a safe landing can be made. There is an exception to the rule for airplanes with 3 or more engines. If only 1 engine has failed, the pilot-in-command may elect to continue to a more distant airport (possibly the original destination) if this is considered as safe as landing at the nearest suitable airport.

The certificate holder must provide a **cockpit check procedure** (checklist) for each type of aircraft it operates. The procedures must include each item necessary for flight crewmembers to check for safety before starting engines, taking-off or landing, and in engine and systems emergencies. The procedures must be designed so that a flight crewmember will not need to rely on memory for items to be checked. The flight crew must use the approved check procedure.

Whenever a pilot-in-command or dispatcher exercises emergency authority, he/she shall keep the appropriate ATC facility and dispatch centers fully informed of the progress of the flight. The person declaring the emergency shall send a written report of any deviation through the air carrier's operations manager to the Administrator (FAA). A dispatcher must send this report within 10 days after the date of the emergency. A pilot-in-command must send the report within 10 days after returning to his/her home base.

When ATC gives priority to an aircraft in an emergency, the chief of the ATC facility involved may ask the pilot-in-command to submit a report. If asked, the pilot-in-command must submit a detailed written report to the ATC facility manager within 48 hours. This is required whether or not there was a deviation from regulations.

ALL

9625. (Refer to Legend 15 and Figure 177.) Lewiston – Nez Perce Co. is a 14 CFR Part 139 airport. What is the minimum number of aircraft rescue and fire fighting vehicles, and the type and amount of fire fighting agents that the airport should have?

A— Two vehicles and 600 pounds dry chemical (DC) or Halon 1211 or 500 pounds of DC plus 100 gallons of water.
B— One vehicle and 500 pounds of dry chemical (DC) or Halon 1211 or 450 pounds DC plus 100 gallons of water.
C— One vehicle and 500 pounds of dry chemical (DC) or Halon 1211 or 350 pounds DC and 1,000 gallons of water.

Using FAA Figure 177, the second line of the Lewiston entry indicates it is an ARFF (Aircraft Rescue and Fire Fighting) Index A airport. FAA Legend 15 indicates that an index A airport must have at least one vehicle with either 500 pounds of dry chemical or Halon 1211, or 450 pounds of dry chemical plus 100 gallons of water. (PLT078) — Chart Supplements U.S.

ALL

9636. (Refer to Legend 15.) Newport News/Williamsburg Intl is a 14 CFR Part 139 airport. The Chart Supplements U.S. (previously A/FD) contains the following entry: ARFF Index A. What is the minimum number of aircraft rescue and fire fighting vehicles, and the type and amount of fire fighting agents that the airport should have?

A— Two vehicles and 600 pounds dry chemical (DC) or Halon 1211 or 500 pounds of DC plus 100 gallons of water.
B— One vehicle and 500 pounds of dry chemical (DC) or Halon 1211 or 450 pounds DC plus 100 gallons of water.
C— One vehicle and 500 pounds of dry chemical (DC) or Halon 1211 or 350 pounds DC and 1,000 gallons of water.

FAA Legend 15 indicates that an index A airport must have at least one vehicle with either 500 pounds of dry chemical or Halon 1211, or 450 pounds of dry chemical plus 100 gallons of water. (PLT143) — Chart Supplements U.S.

ALL

9668. (Refer to Legend 15 and Figure 185A.) McCarran Intl (LAS) is a 14 CFR Part 139 airport. What is the minimum number of aircraft rescue and fire fighting vehicles and the type and amount of fire fighting agents that the airport should have?

A— Three vehicles and 500 pounds of dry chemical (DC) or Halon 1211 or 450 pounds DC and 4,000 gallons of water.
B— Two vehicles and 600 pounds dry chemical (DC) or Halon 1211 or 500 pounds of DC plus 4,000 gallons of water.
C— Three vehicles and 500 pounds of dry chemical (DC) or Halon 1211 or 450 pounds DC plus 3,000 gallons of water.

The second line of the Chart Supplements U.S. (previously A/FD) for McCarran indicates that it is an index D airport. FAA Legend 15 indicates that an index D airport must have at least three vehicles with either 500 pounds of dry chemical or Halon 1211, or 450 pounds of dry chemical plus 4,000 gallons of water. (PLT143) — Chart Supplements U.S.

ALL

9669. (Refer to Legend 15 and Figure 205.) San Francisco Intl (SFO) is a 14 CFR Part 139 airport. What is the minimum number of aircraft rescue and fire fighting vehicles, and the type and amount of fire fighting agents that the airport should have?

A— Three vehicles and 500 pounds of dry chemical (DC) or Halon 1211 or 450 pounds DC and 4,000 gallons of water.
B— Three vehicles and 500 pounds of dry chemical (DC) or Halon 1211 or 500 pounds of DC plus 5,000 gallons of water.
C— Three vehicles and 500 pounds of dry chemical (DC) or Halon 1211 or 450 pounds DC plus 6,000 gallons of water.

The second line of the Chart Supplements U.S. for San Francisco indicates that it is an index E airport. FAA Legend 15 indicates that an index E airport must have at least three vehicles with either 500 pounds of dry chemical or Halon 1211, or 450 pounds of dry chemical plus 6,000 gallons of water. (PLT143) — Chart Supplements U.S.

Answers

9625 [B]   9636 [B]   9668 [A]   9669 [C]

ALL

9690. (Refer to Legend 15 and Figure 215.) Windsor Locks/Bradley Intl, is an 14 CFR Part 139 airport. What minimum number of aircraft rescue and fire-fighting vehicles, and what type and amount of fire-fighting agents are the airport required to have?

A— Two vehicles and 600 pounds dry chemical (DC), or Halon 1211 or 500 pounds of DC plus 4,000 gallons of water.

B— Three vehicles and 500 pounds of dry chemical (DC), or Halon 1211 or 450 pounds DC plus 3,000 gallons of water.

C— Three vehicles and 500 pounds of dry chemical (DC), or Halon 1211 or 450 pounds DC and 4,000 gallons of water.

The Chart Supplements U.S. indicates the Windsor Locks/Bradley Intl is an index D airport. FAA Legend 15 indicates that an index D airport must have at least three vehicles with either 500 pounds of dry chemical or Halon 1211, or 450 pounds of dry chemical plus 4,000 gallons of water. (PLT143) — Chart Supplements U.S.

ALL

9379. During an emergency, a pilot-in-command does not deviate from a 14 CFR rule but is given priority by ATC. To whom or under what condition is the pilot required to submit a written report?

A— To the manager of the General Aviation District Office within 10 days.

B— To the manager of the facility in control within 10 days.

C— Upon request by ATC, submit a written report within 48 hours to the ATC manager.

Each pilot-in-command who (though not deviating from a rule) is given priority by ATC in an emergency, shall, if requested by ATC, submit a detailed report of that emergency within 48 hours to the chief of that ATC facility. (PLT383) — 14 CFR §91.123

ALL

9388. When may ATC request a detailed report on an emergency even though a rule has not been violated?

A— When priority has been given.

B— Anytime an emergency occurs.

C— When the emergency occurs in controlled airspace.

Each pilot-in-command who (though not deviating from a rule) is given priority by ATC in an emergency, shall, if requested by ATC, submit a detailed report of that emergency within 48 hours to the chief of that ATC facility. (PLT044) — 14 CFR §91.123

Answer (B) is incorrect because a pilot may deviate from a regulation in order to meet an emergency, as long as ATC is notified immediately. A detailed report is usually not required if ATC priority was not given. Answer (C) is incorrect because, regardless of the type of airspace in which it occurs, only when priority has been given may a detailed report be requested by ATC.

ATM, DSP

8177. Which requirement applies to emergency equipment (fire extinguishers, megaphones, first-aid kits, and crash ax) installed in an air carrier airplane?

A— All emergency equipment, must be readily accessible to the passengers.

B— Emergency equipment cannot be located in a compartment or area where it is not immediately visible to a flight attendant in the passenger compartment.

C— Emergency equipment must be clearly identified and clearly marked to indicate its method of operation.

Each item of required emergency equipment must be clearly identified and clearly marked to indicate its method of operation. (PLT404) — 14 CFR §121.309

Answers (A) and (B) are incorrect because the requirement is that the emergency equipment be "readily accessible" to the crew.

ATM, DSP

8176. Which factor determines the minimum number of hand fire extinguishers required for flight under 14 CFR Part 121?

A— Number of passengers and crewmembers aboard.

B— Number of passenger cabin occupants.

C— Airplane passenger seating accommodations.

The minimum number of hand fire extinguishers carried on an air carrier flight is determined by the seating capacity of the airplane. (PLT408) — 14 CFR §121.309

Answers (A) and (B) are incorrect because passenger capacity, not actual passenger count, determines the number of extinguishers required.

Answers

9690 [C]	9379 [C]	9388 [A]	8177 [C]	8176 [C]

ATM, DSP

8160. Where should the portable battery-powered megaphone be located if only one is required on a passenger-carrying airplane?

A— The most forward location in the passenger cabin.

B— In the cabin near the over-the-wing emergency exit.

C— The most rearward location in the passenger cabin.

One megaphone must be installed on each airplane with a seating capacity of more than 60 and less than 100 passengers, at the most rearward location in the passenger cabin where it would be readily accessible to a normal flight attendant seat. (PLT462) — 14 CFR §121.309

ATM, DSP

8161. How many portable battery-powered megaphones are required on an air carrier airplane with a seating capacity of 100 passengers on a trip segment when 45 passengers are carried?

A— Two; one at the forward end, and the other at the most rearward location in the passenger cabin.

B— Two; one at the most rearward and one in the center of the passenger cabin.

C— Two; one located near or accessible to the flightcrew, and one located near the center of the passenger cabin.

Two megaphones are required in the passenger cabin of each airplane with a seating capacity of more than 99 passengers, one installed at the forward end and the other at the rearward location where it would be readily accessible to a normal flight attendant seat. (PLT462) — 14 CFR §121.309

ATM, DSP

8162. How many portable battery-powered megaphones are required on an air carrier airplane with a seating capacity of 150 passengers on a trip segment when 75 passengers are carried?

A— Two; one located near or accessible to the flightcrew, and one located near the center of the passenger cabin.

B— Two; one at the most rearward and one in the center of the passenger cabin.

C— Two; one at the forward end, and the other at the most rearward location of the passenger cabin.

Two megaphones are required in the passenger cabin of each airplane with a seating capacity of more than 99 passengers, one installed at the forward end and the other at the rearward location where it would be readily accessible to a normal flight attendant seat. (PLT462) — 14 CFR §121.309

ATM, DSP

8144. The emergency lights on a passenger-carrying airplane must be armed or turned on during

A— taxiing, takeoff, cruise, and landing.

B— taxiing, takeoff, and landing.

C— takeoff, cruise, and landing.

Each emergency exit light must be armed or turned on during taxiing, takeoff, and landing. (PLT404) — 14 CFR §121.310

Answers (A) and (C) are incorrect because the emergency lights are not required to be armed or turned on during cruise.

ATM, DSP

8159. Federal Aviation Regulations require that interior emergency lights must

A— operate automatically when subjected to a negative G load.

B— be operable manually from the flightcrew station and a point in the passenger compartment.

C— be armed or turned on during taxiing and all flight operations.

The emergency exit light system must be operable from both the flight crew station and from a point in the passenger compartment that is readily accessible to a normal flight attendant seat. Each emergency exit light

must be armed or turned on during taxiing, takeoff, and landing. (PLT404) — 14 CFR §121.310

Answer (A) is incorrect because interior emergency lights must operate automatically with the interruption of the airplane's normal electrical power. Answer (C) is incorrect because the interior emergency light system must only be armed during taxi, takeoff, and landing portions of the flight.

ATM, DSP

8157. If a passenger-carrying landplane is required to have an automatic deploying escape slide system, when must this system be armed?

A— For taxi, takeoff, and landing.
B— Only for takeoff and landing.
C— During taxi, takeoff, landing, and after ditching.

Each passenger-carrying landplane with an emergency exit (other than over-the-wing) that is more than 6 feet from the ground must have an approved means to assist the occupants in descending to the ground. An assisting means that deploys automatically must be armed during taxi, takeoffs, and landings. (PLT404) — 14 CFR §121.310

ATM, DSP

8158. If there is a required emergency exit located in the flightcrew compartment, the door which separates the compartment from the passenger cabin must be

A— unlocked during takeoff and landing.
B— locked at all times, except during any emergency declared by the pilot in command.
C— latched open during takeoff and landing.

If it is necessary to pass through a doorway separating the passenger cabin from other areas to reach a required emergency exit from any passenger seat, the door must have means to latch it open, and the door must be latched open during each takeoff and landing. (PLT459) — 14 CFR §121.310

Answers (A) and (B) are incorrect because the door must always be latched open during takeoff and landing.

ATM, DSP

8178. A crewmember interphone system is required on which airplane?

A— A large airplane.
B— A turbojet airplane.
C— An airplane with more than 19 passenger seats.

No person may operate an airplane with a seating capacity of more than 19 passengers unless the airplane is equipped with a crewmember interphone system. (PLT462) — 14 CFR §121.319

Answers (A) and (B) are incorrect because the crewmember interphone system requirement is based upon the number of seats.

ATM, DSP

8179. An air carrier airplane must have an operating public address system if it

A— has a seating capacity of 19 passengers.
B— has a seating capacity for more than 19 passengers.
C— weighs more than 12,500 pounds.

No person may operate an airplane with a seating capacity of more than 19 passengers unless the airplane is equipped with an operating public address system. (PLT462) — 14 CFR §121.318

ATM, DSP

8235. Each crewmember shall have readily available for individual use on each flight a

A— key to the flight deck door.
B— certificate holder's manual.
C— flashlight in good working order.

Each crewmember shall, on each flight, have readily available for use a flashlight that is in good working order. (PLT405) — 14 CFR §121.549

ATM, DSP

8173. How much supplemental oxygen for emergency descent must a pressurized turbine-powered air transport airplane carry for each flight crewmember on flight deck duty when operating at flight altitudes above 10,000 feet?

A— A minimum of 2-hours' supply.
B— Sufficient for the duration of the flight above 8,000 feet cabin pressure altitude.
C— Sufficient for the duration of the flight at 10,000 feet flight altitude, not to exceed 1 hour and 50 minutes.

When operating at flight altitudes above 10,000 feet, the certificate holder shall supply enough oxygen for each crewmember for the entire flight at those altitudes and not less than a 2-hour supply for each flight crewmember on flight deck duty. (PLT438) — 14 CFR §121.331 and §121.333

Answers

| 8157 | [A] | 8158 | [C] | 8178 | [C] | 8179 | [B] | 8235 | [C] | 8173 | [A] |

ATM, DSP

8183. Each air carrier flight deck crewmember on flight deck duty must be provided with an oxygen mask that can be rapidly placed on his face when operating at flight altitudes

A— of FL 260.
B— of FL 250.
C— above FL 250.

When operating at flight altitudes above flight level 250, each flight crewmember on flight deck duty must be provided with an oxygen mask so designed that it can be rapidly placed on his/her face from its ready position, properly secured, sealed, and supplying oxygen within 5 seconds; and so designed that after being placed on the face it does not prevent immediate communication between the flight crewmember and other crewmembers over the airplane intercom system. When not being used at flight altitudes above flight level 250, the mask must be kept ready for use and within immediate reach. (PLT438) — 14 CFR §121.333

ATM, DSP

8184. A flight crewmember must be able to don and use a quick-donning oxygen mask within

A— 5 seconds.
B— 10 seconds.
C— 15 seconds.

When operating at flight altitudes above flight level 250, each flight crewmember on flight deck duty must be provided with an oxygen mask so designed that it can be rapidly placed on his/her face from its ready position, properly secured, sealed, and supplying oxygen within 5 seconds; and so designed that after being placed on the face it does not prevent immediate communication between the flight crewmember and other crewmembers over the airplane intercom system. When not being used at flight altitudes above flight level 250, the mask must be kept ready for use and within immediate reach. (PLT438) — 14 CFR §121.333

ATM, DSP

8155. If either pilot of an air carrier airplane leaves the duty station while flying at FL 410, the other pilot

A— and the flight engineer shall put on their oxygen masks and breathe oxygen.
B— shall put on the oxygen mask and breathe oxygen.
C— must have a quick-donning type oxygen mask available.

If for any reason at any time it is necessary for one pilot to leave the station at the controls of the airplane when operating at flight altitudes above flight level 250, the remaining pilot at the controls shall put on and use his/her oxygen mask until the other pilot has returned to the duty station. (PLT440) — 14 CFR §121.333

Answer (A) is incorrect because only the remaining pilot is required to put on and use an oxygen mask. Answer (C) is incorrect because the remaining pilot must put on an oxygen mask, not just have a quick-donning type available.

ATM, DSP

8156. If a turbine-engine-powered, pressurized airplane is not equipped with quick-donning oxygen masks, what is the maximum flight altitude authorized without one pilot wearing and using an oxygen mask?

A— FL 200.
B— FL 300.
C— FL 250.

When operating at flight altitudes above flight level 250, one pilot at the controls of the airplane shall at all times wear and use an oxygen mask secured, sealed, and supplying oxygen, except that the one pilot need not wear and use an oxygen mask while at or below flight level 410 if each flight crewmember on flight deck duty has a quick-donning type oxygen mask. (PLT438) — 14 CFR §121.333

ATM, DSP

8187. What is the highest flight level that operations may be conducted without the pilot at the controls wearing and using an oxygen mask, while the other pilot is away from the duty station?

A— FL 240.
B— FL 250.
C— Above FL 250.

If for any reason at any time it is necessary for one pilot to leave the station at the controls of the airplane when operating at flight altitudes above flight level 250, the remaining pilot at the controls shall put on and use his/her oxygen mask until the other pilot has returned to the duty station. (PLT438) — 14 CFR §121.333

Answers

8183   [C]   8184   [A]   8155   [B]   8156   [C]   8187   [B]

ATM, DSP

8174. What is the passenger oxygen supply requirement for a flight, in a turbine-powered aircraft, with a cabin pressure altitude in excess of 15,000 feet? Enough oxygen for

A— each passengers for the entire flight above 15,000 feet cabin altitude.
B— 30 percent of the passengers.
C— 10 percent of the passengers for 30 minutes.

For flights at cabin pressure altitudes above 15,000 feet, the certificate holder must provide enough oxygen for each passenger carried during the entire flight at those altitudes. (PLT438) — 14 CFR §§121.327, 121.329

ATM, DSP

8186. For flights above which cabin altitude must oxygen be provided for all passengers during the entire flight at those altitudes?

A— 15,000 feet.
B— 16,000 feet.
C— 14,000 feet.

For flights at cabin pressure altitudes above 15,000 feet, the certificate holder must provide enough oxygen for each passenger carried during the entire flight at those altitudes. (PLT438) — 14 CFR §§121.327, 121.329

ATM, DSP

8185. For a 2-hour flight in a reciprocating engine-powered airplane at a cabin pressure altitude of 12,000 feet, how much supplemental oxygen for sustenance must be provided? Enough oxygen for

A— 30 minutes for 10 percent of the passengers.
B— 10 percent of the passengers for 1.5 hours.
C— each passenger for 30 minutes.

For flight in reciprocating-engine-powered airplanes, at cabin pressure altitudes above 8,000 feet, up to and including 14,000 feet, each certificate holder shall provide enough oxygen for 30 minutes for 10 percent of the passengers. (PLT438) — 14 CFR §121.327

ATM, DSP

8182. The supplemental oxygen requirements for passengers when a flight is operated at FL 250 is dependent upon the airplane's ability to make an emergency descent to a flight altitude of

A— 10,000 feet within 4 minutes.
B— 14,000 feet within 4 minutes.
C— 12,000 feet within 4 minutes or at a minimum rate of 2,500 ft/min, whichever is quicker.

The supplemental oxygen requirements for passengers on pressurized aircraft is dependent upon the ability of the aircraft to descend to 14,000 feet within 4 minutes in the event of a loss of pressurization. (PLT438) — 14 CFR §121.333

ATM, DSP

8180. What is the minimum number of acceptable oxygen-dispensing units for first-aid treatment of occupants who might require undiluted oxygen for physiological reasons?

A— Two.
B— Four.
C— Three.

There must be an appropriate number of oxygen dispensing units for first aid treatment of passengers, but in no case less than 2. (PLT438) — 14 CFR §121.333

Answers

| 8174 | [A] | 8186 | [A] | 8185 | [A] | 8182 | [B] | 8180 | [A] |

ATM, DSP

8164. Which emergency equipment is required for a flag air carrier flight between John F. Kennedy International Airport and London, England?

A— A life preserver equipped with an approved survivor locator light or other flotation device for the full seating capacity of the airplane.

B— An appropriately equipped survival kit attached to each required liferaft.

C— A self-buoyant, water resistant, portable survival-type emergency locator transmitter for each required liferaft.

No person may operate an airplane in extended over-water operations without having on the airplane the following equipment:

1. *A life preserver equipped with an approved survivor locator light for each occupant of the airplane;*

2. *Enough life rafts (each equipped with an approved survivor locator light) to accommodate the occupants of the airplane;*

3. *At least one pyrotechnic signaling device for each life raft;*

4. *One survival-type emergency locator transmitter;*

5. *A survival kit, appropriately equipped for the route to be flown, must be attached to each life raft.*

(PLT404) — 14 CFR §121.339

Answer (A) is incorrect because a life preserver or other flotation device for each occupant is required. The requirement is not based upon seating capacity. Answer (C) is incorrect because only one survival type emergency locator transmitter is required to be carried in the aircraft, not one for each life raft.

ATM, DSP

8166. Each large aircraft operating over water must have a life preserver for each

A— aircraft occupant.

B— seat on the aircraft.

C— passenger seat, plus 10 percent.

No person may operate an airplane in extended over-water operations without having on the airplane the following equipment:

1. *A life preserver equipped with an approved survivor locator light for each occupant of the airplane;*

2. *Enough life rafts (each equipped with an approved survivor locator light) to accommodate the occupants of the airplane;*

3. *At least one pyrotechnic signaling device for each life raft;*

4. *One survival-type emergency locator transmitter;*

5. *A survival kit, appropriately equipped for the route to be flown, must be attached to each life raft.*

(PLT417) — 14 CFR §121.339

Answers (B) and (C) are incorrect because unlike some regulations that are based upon the number of seats in the aircraft, the number of life preservers required is based on the number of occupants for a particular flight.

ATM, DSP

8169. Life preservers required for overwater operations are stored

A— within easy reach of each passenger.

B— under each occupant seat.

C— within easy reach of each seated occupant.

The required life rafts, life preservers, and survival-type emergency locator transmitter must be easily accessible in the event of a ditching without appreciable time for preparatory procedures. (PLT417) — 14 CFR §121.339

ATM, DSP

8167. For a flight over uninhabited terrain, an airplane operated by a flag or supplemental air carrier must carry enough appropriately equipped survival kits for

A— all of the passengers, plus 10 percent.

B— all aircraft occupants.

C— all passenger seats.

Unless it has the following equipment, no flag or supplemental carrier or commercial operator may conduct an operation over an uninhabited area:

1. *Suitable pyrotechnic signaling devices;*

2. *A survival-type emergency locator transmitter; and*

3. *Enough survival kits, appropriately equipped for the route to be flown, for the number of occupants of the airplane.*

(PLT404) — 14 CFR §121.353

ATM, DSP

8168. When a supplemental air carrier is operating over an uninhabited area, how many appropriately equipped survival kits are required aboard the aircraft?

A— One for each passenger seat.

B— One for each passenger, plus 10 percent.

C— One for each occupant of the aircraft.

Answers

8164 [B]   8166   [A]   8169   [C]   8167   [B]   8168   [C]

Unless it has the following equipment, no flag or supplemental carrier or commercial operator may conduct an operation over an uninhabited area:

1. *Suitable pyrotechnic signaling devices;*

2. *A survival-type emergency locator transmitter; and*

3. *Enough survival kits, appropriately equipped for the route to be flown, for the number of occupants of the airplane.*

(PLT404) — 14 CFR §121.353

ATM, DSP

8170. An airplane operated by a supplemental air carrier flying over uninhabited terrain must carry which emergency equipment?

A— Survival kit for each passenger.
B— Suitable pyrotechnic signaling devices.
C— Colored smoke flares and a signal mirror.

Unless it has the following equipment, no flag or supplemental carrier or commercial operator may conduct an operation over an uninhabited area:

1. *Suitable pyrotechnic signaling devices;*

2. *A survival-type emergency locator transmitter; and*

3. *Enough survival kits, appropriately equipped for the route to be flown, for the number of occupants of the airplane.*

(PLT404) — 14 CFR §121.353

ATM, DSP

8171. An airplane operated by a commercial operator flying over uninhabited terrain must carry which emergency equipment?

A— A signal mirror and colored smoke flares.
B— Survival kit for each passenger.
C— An approved survival-type emergency locator transmitter.

Unless it has the following equipment, no flag or supplemental carrier or commercial operator may conduct an operation over an uninhabited area:

1. *Suitable pyrotechnic signaling devices;*

2. *A survival-type emergency locator transmitter; and*

3. *Enough survival kits, appropriately equipped for the route to be flown, for the number of occupants of the airplane.*

(PLT402) — 14 CFR §121.353

ATM, DSP

8172. An airplane operated by a flag air carrier operator flying over uninhabited terrain must carry which emergency equipment?

A— Suitable pyrotechnic signaling devices.
B— Colored smoke flares and a signal mirror.
C— Survival kit for each passenger.

Unless it has the following equipment, no flag or supplemental carrier or commercial operator may conduct an operation over an uninhabited area:

1. *Suitable pyrotechnic signaling devices;*

2. *A survival-type emergency locator transmitter; and*

3. *Enough survival kits, appropriately equipped for the route to be flown, for the number of occupants of the airplane.*

(PLT404) — 14 CFR §121.353

ATM, DSP

8245. If an aircraft dispatcher cannot communicate with the pilot of an air carrier flight during an emergency, the aircraft dispatcher should

A— take any action considered necessary under the circumstances.
B— comply with the company's lost aircraft plan.
C— phone the ARTCC where the flight is located and ask for a phone patch with the flight.

If the aircraft dispatcher cannot communicate with the pilot, he/she shall declare an emergency and take any action considered necessary under the circumstances. (PLT403) — 14 CFR §121.557

ATM, DSP

8198. Which document includes descriptions of the required crewmember functions to be performed in the event of an emergency?

A— Airplane Flight Manual.
B— Certificate holder's manual.
C— Pilot's Emergency Procedures Handbook.

Each certificate holder shall, for each type and model of airplane, assign to each category of required crewmember, as appropriate, the necessary functions to be performed in an emergency or a situation requiring emergency evacuation. The certificate holder shall describe in its manual the functions of each category of required crewmember. (PLT436) — 14 CFR §121.397

Answer (A) is incorrect because the Airplane Flight Manual may contain emergency procedures as a convenience, but they are not required by 14 CFR §121.141. Answer (C) is incorrect because an "Emergency Procedures Handbook" does not exist.

Answers

8170 [B]	8171 [C]	8172 [A]	8245 [A]	8198 [B]

ATM, DSP

8200. The required crewmember functions that are to be performed in the event of an emergency shall be assigned by the

A— pilot in command.
B— air carrier's chief pilot.
C— certificate holder.

Each certificate holder shall, for each type and model of airplane, assign to each category of required crewmember, as appropriate, the necessary functions to be performed in an emergency or a situation requiring emergency evacuation. The certificate holder shall describe in its manual the functions of each category of required crewmember. (PLT374) — 14 CFR §121.397

Answer (A) is incorrect because, although the pilot-in-command may assign duties as necessary during an emergency, the required crewmember functions shall be assigned and described in the certificate holder's manual. Answer (B) is incorrect because the chief pilot does not have the authority to assign crewmember functions that are to be performed in the event of an emergency. Those functions shall be described in the certificate holder's manual.

ATM, DSP

8204. The air carrier must give instruction on such subjects as respiration, hypoxia, and decompression to crewmembers serving on pressurized airplanes operated above

A— FL 180.
B— FL 200.
C— FL 250.

Crewmembers who serve in operations above 25,000 feet must receive instruction in respiration, hypoxia, and decompression. (PLT460) — 14 CFR §121.417

ATM, DSP

8218. How often must a crewmember actually operate the airplane emergency equipment, after initial training? Once every

A— 6 calendar months.
B— 12 calendar months.
C— 24 calendar months.

Emergency drill requirements must be accomplished during initial training and once each 24 calendar months during recurrent training. (PLT407) — 14 CFR §121.417

ATM, DSP

8236. If an engine's rotation is stopped in flight, the pilot in command must report it, as soon as practicable, to the

A— appropriate ground radio station.
B— nearest FAA district office.
C— operations manager (or director of operations).

The pilot-in-command shall report each stoppage of engine rotation in flight to the appropriate ground radio station as soon as practicable and shall keep that station fully informed of the progress of the flight. (PLT366) — 14 CFR §121.565

ATM, DSP

8237. If it becomes necessary to shut down one engine on a domestic air carrier three-engine turbojet airplane, the pilot in command

A— must land at the nearest suitable airport, in point of time, at which a safe landing can be made.
B— may continue to the planned destination if approved by the company aircraft dispatcher.
C— may continue to the planned destination if this is considered as safe as landing at the nearest suitable airport.

If not more than one engine of an airplane that has three or more engines fails or its rotation is stopped, the pilot-in-command may proceed to an airport that he/she selects if, after considering the following, he/she decides that proceeding to that airport is as safe as landing at the nearest suitable airport. (PLT406) — 14 CFR §121.565

ATM, DSP

8241. What action shall the pilot in command take if it becomes necessary to shut down one of the two engines on an air carrier airplane?

A— Land at the airport which the pilot considers to be as safe as the nearest suitable airport in point of time.
B— Land at the nearest suitable airport in point of time at which a safe landing can be made.
C— Land at the nearest airport, including military, that has a crash and rescue unit.

Whenever an engine of an airplane fails or whenever the rotation of an engine is stopped to prevent possible damage, the pilot-in-command shall land the airplane at the nearest suitable airport, time-wise, at which a safe landing can be made. Note: There are no exceptions to this rule for two-engine airplanes. (PLT223) — 14 CFR §121.565

Answers

| 8200 | [C] | 8204 | [C] | 8218 | [C] | 8236 | [A] | 8237 | [C] | 8241 | [B] |

ATM, DSP

8163. In the event of an engine emergency, the use of a cockpit check procedure by the flightcrew is

A— encouraged; it helps to ensure that all items on the procedure are accomplished.
B— required by regulations to prevent reliance upon memorized procedures.
C— required by the FAA as a doublecheck after the memorized procedure has been accomplished.

Each certificate holder shall provide an approved cockpit check procedure for each type of aircraft. The approved procedures must include each item necessary for flight crewmembers to check for safety before starting engines, taking off, or landing, and in engine and systems emergencies. The procedures must be designed so that a flight crewmember will not need to rely upon memory for items to be checked. (PLT404) — 14 CFR §121.315

ATM, DSP

8240. When the pilot in command is responsible for a deviation during an emergency, the pilot should submit a written report within

A— 10 days after the deviation.
B— 10 days after returning home.
C— 10 days after returning to home base.

A pilot-in-command declaring an emergency shall send a written report of any deviation, through the air carrier's director of operations, to the Administrator within 10 days after returning to the home base. (PLT403) — 14 CFR §121.557

ATM, DSP

8246. Who is required to submit a written report on a deviation that occurs during an emergency?

A— Pilot in command.
B— Dispatcher.
C— Person who declares the emergency.

The person declaring the emergency shall send a written report of any deviation, through the air carrier's director of operations, to the Administrator within 10 days. (PLT366) — 14 CFR §121.557

DSP

8239. An aircraft dispatcher declares an emergency for a flight and a deviation results. A written report shall be sent through the air carrier's operations manager by the

A— dispatcher to the FAA Administrator within 10 days of the event.
B— certificate holder to the FAA Administrator within 10 days of the event.
C— pilot in command to the FAA Administrator within 10 days of the event.

An aircraft dispatcher declaring an emergency shall send a written report of any deviation, through the air carrier's director of operations, to the Administrator within 10 days after the date of the emergency. (PLT394) — 14 CFR §121.557

ATM, ATS

8725. Bird strikes in flight will be reported to the

A— nearest state or federal wildlife office on company letterhead.
B— FAA on an FAA form 5200-7.
C— nearest FSS via telephone.

Pilots are urged to report any bird or other wildlife strike using FAA Form 5200–7, Bird/Other Wildlife Strike Report (Appendix 1). (PLT366) — AIM ¶7-4-3

Answers

8163 [B]	8240 [C]	8246 [C]	8239 [A]	8725 [B]

Part 135 Oxygen Requirements

ATS
8020. Which is a requirement for flightcrew use of oxygen masks in a pressurized cabin airplane?

A— Both pilots at the controls shall use oxygen masks above FL 350.

B— At altitudes above 25,000 feet MSL, if one pilot leaves the pilot duty station, the remaining pilot at the controls shall use an oxygen mask.

C— At altitudes above FL 250, one of the two pilots at the controls shall use an oxygen mask continuously.

One pilot of a pressurized aircraft must wear an oxygen mask any time the aircraft is flown above 35,000 feet MSL. In addition, one pilot must wear an oxygen mask above a flight altitude of 25,000 feet MSL if the other pilot leaves the duty station. (PLT438) — 14 CFR §135.89

ATS
8022. Which is a requirement for pilot use of oxygen in a pressurized airplane?

A— The pilot at the controls shall use oxygen continuously any time the cabin pressure altitude is more than 12,000 feet MSL.

B— At FL 250 and above, each pilot shall have an approved quick-donning oxygen mask.

C— At FL 250 and above, the pilot at the controls must have an approved oxygen mask any time the other pilot is away from the duty station.

Each pilot of an unpressurized aircraft shall use oxygen continuously when flying:

1. At altitudes above 10,000 feet through 12,000 feet MSL for that part of the flight at those altitudes that is more than 30 minutes duration; and

2. Above 12,000 feet MSL.

Whenever a pressurized aircraft is operated with the cabin pressure altitude more than 10,000 feet MSL, each pilot shall comply with the rules for unpressurized aircraft.

Whenever a pressurized airplane is operated above 25,000 feet MSL flight altitude both pilots must have a "quick-donning"-type oxygen mask.

One pilot of a pressurized aircraft must wear an oxygen mask any time the aircraft is flown above 35,000 feet MSL. In addition, one pilot must wear an oxygen mask above a flight altitude of 25,000 feet MSL if the other pilot leaves the duty station. (PLT438) — 14 CFR §135.89

Answer (B) is incorrect because the regulation states "above 25,000 feet MSL." Answer (C) is incorrect because above 25,000 feet MSL, the pilot at the controls must wear an approved oxygen mask any time the other pilot is away from the duty station.

ATS
8055. The two pilot stations of a pressurized aircraft are equipped with approved quick-donning oxygen masks. What is the maximum altitude authorized if one pilot is not wearing an oxygen mask and breathing oxygen?

A— 41,000 feet MSL.

B— 35,000 feet MSL.

C— 25,000 feet MSL.

One pilot of a pressurized aircraft must wear an oxygen mask any time the aircraft is flown above 35,000 feet MSL. (PLT438) — 14 CFR §135.89

ATS
8056. At altitudes above 10,000 feet through 12,000 feet MSL, each pilot of an unpressurized airplane must use supplemental oxygen for that part of the flight that is of a duration of more than

A— 20 minutes.

B— 30 minutes.

C— 45 minutes.

Each pilot of an unpressurized aircraft shall use oxygen continuously when flying:

1. At altitudes above 10,000 feet through 12,000 feet MSL for the part of the flight, at those altitudes, that is more than 30 minutes duration; and

2. Above 12,000 feet MSL.

(PLT438) — 14 CFR §135.89

ATS
8072. A pressurized airplane being operated at FL 330 can descend safely to 15,000 feet MSL in 3.5 minutes. What oxygen supply must be carried for all occupants other than the pilots?

A— 60 minutes.

B— 45 minutes.

C— 30 minutes.

No person may operate a pressurized aircraft above 15,000 feet MSL unless it is equipped to supply oxygen to each occupant, other than the pilots, for 1 hour. This is reduced to a 30-minute supply if the aircraft, at all times during flight above 15,000 feet MSL, can safely descend to 15,000 feet within 4 minutes. (PLT438) — 14 CFR §135.157

ATS

8073. At what altitude, in an unpressurized airplane, must all passengers be supplied oxygen?

A— Above 12,000 feet MSL.
B— Above 14,000 feet MSL.
C— Above 15,000 feet MSL.

In unpressurized aircraft, at altitudes above 10,000 feet MSL through 15,000 feet MSL, oxygen must be available for 10% of the occupants, other than the pilots, for the part of the flight, at those altitudes, in excess of 30-minute duration. Above 15,000 feet MSL, oxygen must be available to all occupants, other than the pilots. (PLT438) — 14 CFR §135.157

ATS

8074. Between what altitudes must oxygen be available to at least 10 percent of the occupants, in an unpressurized airplane, other than the pilots?

A— Above 12,000 feet through 16,000 feet MSL, for any time period.
B— Above 10,000 feet through 15,000 feet MSL, if flight at those altitudes is of more than a 30-minute duration.
C— 10,000 feet to 15,000 feet MSL, if flight at those altitudes is of more than a 30-minute duration.

In unpressurized aircraft, at altitudes above 10,000 feet MSL through 15,000 feet MSL, oxygen must be available for 10% of the occupants, other than the pilots, for that part of the flight at those altitudes in excess of 30-minute duration. Above 15,000 feet MSL, oxygen must be available to all occupants. (PLT438) — 14 CFR §135.157

ATS

8080. The oxygen requirements for occupants of a pressurized airplane operated at altitudes above FL 250 is dependent upon the airplane's ability to descend safely to an altitude of

A— 10,000 feet MSL in 4 minutes.
B— 12,000 feet MSL at a minimum rate of 2,500 ft/min.
C— 15,000 feet MSL in 4 minutes.

No person may operate a pressurized aircraft above 15,000 feet MSL unless it is equipped to supply oxygen to each occupant, other than the pilots, for 1 hour. This is reduced to a 30-minute supply if the aircraft, at all times during flight above 15,000 feet MSL, can safely descend to 15,000 feet within 4 minutes. (PLT438) — 14 CFR §135.157

ATS, RTC

8021. Above which altitude/flight level must at least one of the two pilots, at the controls of a pressurized aircraft (with quick-donning masks) wear a secured and sealed oxygen mask?

A— FL 300.
B— FL 350.
C— FL 250.

One pilot of a pressurized aircraft must wear an oxygen mask any time the aircraft is flown above 35,000 feet MSL. (PLT438) — 14 CFR §135.89

ATS, RTC

8023. Which is a pilot requirement for oxygen?

A— Each pilot of a pressurized aircraft operating at FL 180 and above shall have an approved quick-donning type oxygen mask.
B— On pressurized aircraft requiring a flightcrew of two pilots, both shall continuously wear oxygen masks whenever the cabin pressure altitude exceeds 12,000 feet MSL.
C— On unpressurized aircraft, flying above 12,000 feet MSL, pilots shall use oxygen continuously.

Each pilot of an unpressurized aircraft shall use oxygen continuously when flying:

1. At altitudes above 10,000 feet through 12,000 feet MSL for that part of the flight at those altitudes that is more than 30 minutes duration; and

2. Above 12,000 feet MSL.

(PLT438) — 14 CFR §135.89

Answer (A) is incorrect because quick-donning type oxygen masks are required above 25,000 feet MSL. Answer (B) is incorrect because both pilots should continuously use oxygen masks when the cabin pressure altitude is more than 10,000 feet MSL.

Answers

8073   [C]   8074   [B]   8080   [C]   8021   [B]   8023   [C]

ATS, RTC

8024. Which requirement applies when oxygen is stored in liquid form?

A— Smoking is not permitted within 50 feet of stored liquid oxygen.

B— Liquefied oxygen is a hazardous material and must be kept in an isolated storage facility.

C— The equipment used to store liquid oxygen must be covered in the certificate holder's approved maintenance program.

When the oxygen is stored in the form of a liquid, the equipment must have been under the certificate holder's approved maintenance program since its purchase new, or since the storage container was last purged. (PLT438) — 14 CFR §135.91

ATS, RTC

8025. Which is a condition that must be met when a person is administered medical oxygen in flight?

A— The distance between a person using medical oxygen and any electrical unit must not be less than 5 feet.

B— A person using oxygen equipment must be seated to avoid restricting access to, or use of, any required exit.

C— A person being administered oxygen must be monitored by equipment that displays and records pulse and respiration.

Oxygen equipment must be stowed, and each person using the equipment must be seated, so as not to restrict access to or use of any required emergency or regular exit, or of the aisle in the passenger compartment. (PLT438) — 14 CFR §135.91

ATS, RTC

8030. Which is a requirement regarding the carriage and operation of oxygen equipment for medical use by passengers?

A— No person may smoke within 10 feet of oxygen storage and dispensing equipment.

B— When oxygen equipment is used for the medical treatment of a patient, the rules pertaining to emergency exit access are waived.

C— No person may connect oxygen bottles or any other ancillary equipment until all passengers are aboard the aircraft and seated.

No person may smoke within 10 feet of oxygen-dispensing equipment. (PLT438) — 14 CFR §135.91

ATS, RTC

8031. If a certificate holder deviates from the provisions of regulations which pertain to medical use of oxygen by passengers, a complete report of the incident shall be sent to the FAA within

A— 7 working days.

B— 10 working days.

C— 10 days of the deviation.

Each certificate holder who deviates from the provisions of the regulations pertaining to use of medical oxygen by passengers, must send a report of the deviation to the FAA Flight Standards District Office within 10 days excluding Saturdays, Sundays, and federal holidays. (PLT438) — 14 CFR §135.91

ATS, RTC

8081. An unpressurized aircraft with 20 occupants other than the pilots will be cruising at 14,000 feet MSL for 25 minutes. For how many, if any, of these occupants must there be an oxygen supply?

A— Five.

B— Two.

C— None.

In unpressurized aircraft, at altitudes above 10,000 feet MSL through 15,000 feet MSL, oxygen must be available for 10% of the occupants, other than the pilots, for the part of the flight, at those altitudes, in excess of 30-minutes duration. Above 15,000 feet MSL, oxygen must be available to all occupants, other than the pilots. (PLT438) — 14 CFR §135.157

RTC

9576. (Refer to Figures 113 and 114.) When must the pilots use oxygen, under 14 CFR Part 135, on this flight from 0O2 to LAX?

A— Starting 30 minutes after climbing through 10,000 feet until descending below 10,000 feet.

B— 30 minutes after level off until descending below 10,000 feet.

C— All the time they are above 10,000 feet MSL.

Each pilot of an unpressurized aircraft shall use oxygen continuously when flying—

1. At altitudes above 10,000 feet through 12,000 feet MSL for the part of the flight at those altitudes that is more than 30 minutes duration; and

2. Above 12,000 feet MSL.

(PLT438) — 14 CFR §135.89

Answers

| 8024 [C] | 8025 [B] | 8030 [A] | 8031 [B] | 8081 [C] | 9576 [A] |

ATS, RTC

9819. What are the oxygen requirements for passengers if operating at 14,000 feet?

A— 30 minutes for each passenger.
B— available for 10% of the occupants.
C— available for 10% of the occupants other than the pilots.

In unpressurized aircraft at altitudes above 10,000 feet MSL through 15,000 feet MSL, oxygen must be available for 10% of the occupants, other than the pilots, for the part of the flight at those altitudes in excess of 30-minutes duration. Above 15,000 feet MSL, oxygen must be available to all occupants, other than the pilots. (PLT438) — 14 CFR §135.157

RTC

9577. (Refer to Figures 113 and 114.) What are the passenger oxygen requirements, under 14 CFR Part 135, on this flight from 0O2 to LAX?

A— Starting 30 minutes after level off, 10 percent of the aircraft occupants must be supplied oxygen until descending below 10,000 feet.
B— When above 10,000 through 15,000 feet, oxygen must be supplied to at least 10 percent of the aircraft occupants.
C— Starting 30 minutes after climbing through 10,000 feet, 10 percent of the aircraft occupants, except the pilots, must be supplied oxygen until descending below 10,000 feet.

No person may operate an unpressurized aircraft at altitudes prescribed in this section unless it is equipped with enough oxygen dispensers and oxygen to supply the pilots under §135.89(a) and to supply when flying—

1. At altitudes above 10,000 feet through 15,000 MSL, oxygen to at least 10% of the occupants of the aircraft, other than pilots, for the part of the flight at those altitudes that is more than 30 minutes duration; and

2. Above 15,000 feet MSL, oxygen to each occupant of the aircraft other than the pilots.

(PLT438) — 14 CFR §135.157

RTC

9605. (Refer to Figures 162, 163, 164, 165, and 167.) When are the pilots required to use oxygen on this flight from RYN to AEG?

A— Upon climbing through 12,000 feet on ascent, until passing through 12,000 feet on descent.
B— Starting 30 minutes after level off until descending below 10,000 feet.
C— Starting 30 minutes after climbing through 10,000 feet until descending below 10,000 feet.

Each pilot of an unpressurized aircraft shall use oxygen continuously when flying—

1. At altitudes above 10,000 feet through 12,000 feet MSL for the part of the flight at those altitudes that is more than 30 minutes duration; and

2. Above 12,000 feet MSL.

(PLT438) — 14 CFR §135.89

RTC

9606. (Refer to Figures 162, 163, 164, 165, and 167.) What are the passenger oxygen requirements on this flight, from Tucson/Ryan to Albuquerque/Double Eagle II?

A— Starting 30 minutes after climbing through 10,000 feet, 10 percent of the aircraft occupants must be supplied oxygen until descending below 10,000 feet.
B— Starting 30 minutes after climbing through 10,000 feet, 10 percent of the aircraft occupants, except pilots, must be supplied oxygen until descending below 10,000 feet.
C— When above 10,000 feet through 15,000 feet, oxygen must be supplied to at least 10 percent of the aircraft occupants, including the pilots.

No person may operate an unpressurized aircraft at altitudes prescribed in this section unless it is equipped with enough oxygen dispensers and oxygen to supply the pilots under §135.89(a) and to supply when flying—

1. At altitudes above 10,000 feet through 15,000 MSL, oxygen to at least 10% of the occupants of the aircraft, other than pilots, for the part of the flight at those altitudes that is more than 30 minutes duration; and

2. Above 15,000 feet MSL, oxygen to each occupant of the aircraft other than the pilots.

(PLT438) — 14 CFR §135.157

Answers

9819 [C]　　　　9577 [C]　　　　9605 [C]　　　　9606 [B]

RTC
9637. (Refer to Figures 184, 186, 187, 188, and 188A.) When are the pilots required to use oxygen on this 14 CFR Part 135 flight from LAS to PVU?

A— Starting 30 minutes after climbing through 10,000 feet until descending below 10,000 feet.
B— Upon climbing through 12,000 feet on ascent, until passing through 12,000 feet on descent.
C— Starting 30 minutes after takeoff until descending below 10,000 feet.

Each pilot of an unpressurized aircraft shall use oxygen continuously when flying—

1. At altitudes above 10,000 feet through 12,000 feet MSL for the part of the flight at those altitudes that is more than 30 minutes duration; and

2. Above 12,000 feet MSL.

(PLT078) — 14 CFR §135.89

RTC
9638. (Refer to Figures 184, 186, 187, 188, and 188A.) What are the passenger oxygen requirements on this 14 CFR Part 135 flight from Las Vegas to Provo?

A— When above 10,000 feet through 15,000 feet, oxygen must be supplied to at least 10 percent of the aircraft occupants, including the pilots.
B— Starting 30 minutes after climbing through 10,000 feet, 10 percent of the aircraft occupants until reaching cruise at 15,000 feet then all occupants must be supplied oxygen until descending below 15,000 feet, then 10 percent down to 10,000 feet.
C— Starting 30 minutes after climbing through 10,000 feet, 10 percent of the aircraft occupants, except pilots, must be supplied oxygen until descending below 10,000 feet.

No person may operate an unpressurized aircraft at altitudes prescribed in this section unless it is equipped with enough oxygen dispensers and oxygen to supply the pilots under §135.89(a) and to supply when flying—

1. At altitudes above 10,000 feet through 15,000 MSL, oxygen to at least 10% of the occupants of the aircraft, other than pilots, for the part of the flight at those altitudes that is more than 30 minutes duration; and

2. Above 15,000 feet MSL, oxygen to each occupant of the aircraft other than the pilots.

(PLT438) — 14 CFR §135.157

RTC
9650. (Refer to Figures 197 and 199.) When are the pilots required to use oxygen on this flight from EGE to SLC?

A— Starting 30 minutes after level off until descending below 10,000 feet.
B— Starting 30 minutes after climbing through 10,000 feet until descending below 10,000 feet.
C— Upon climbing through 12,000 feet on ascent.

Each pilot of an unpressurized aircraft shall use oxygen continuously when flying—

1. At altitudes above 10,000 feet through 12,000 feet MSL for the part of the flight at those altitudes that is more than 30 minutes duration; and

2. Above 12,000 feet MSL.

(PLT438) — 14 CFR §135.89

RTC
9651. (Refer to Figures 197 and 199.) What are the passenger oxygen requirements on this flight from Eagle County Regional (EGE) to Salt Lake City Intl?

A— Starting 30 minutes after climbing through 10,000 feet, 10 percent of the aircraft occupants must be supplied oxygen until descending below 10,000 feet.
B— Starting 30 minutes after climbing through 10,000 feet, 10 percent of the aircraft occupants, except pilots, must be supplied oxygen until descending below 10,000 feet.
C— When above 10,000 feet through 15,000 feet, oxygen must be supplied to at least 10 percent of the aircraft occupants, including the pilots.

No person may operate an unpressurized aircraft at altitudes prescribed in this section unless it is equipped with enough oxygen dispensers and oxygen to supply the pilots under §135.89(a) and to supply when flying—

1. At altitudes above 10,000 feet through 15,000 MSL, oxygen to at least 10% of the occupants of the aircraft, other than pilots, for the part of the flight at those altitudes that is more than 30 minutes duration; and

2. Above 15,000 feet MSL, oxygen to each occupant of the aircraft other than the pilots.

(PLT438) — 14 CFR §135.157

Answers

9637 [A]   9638 [C]   9650 [C]   9651 [B]

National Transportation Safety Board (NTSB)

Aircraft accident means an occurrence associated with the operation of an aircraft that takes place between the time any person boards the aircraft with the intention of flight, and the time all such persons have disembarked, and in which any person suffers death or serious injury, or in which the aircraft receives substantial damage.

Serious injury means any injury that:

- Requires hospitalization for more than 48 hours commencing within 7 days from the date the injury was received.

- Results in fracture of any bone (except simple fractures of fingers, toes or nose).

- Causes severe hemorrhages, nerve, muscle or tendon damage.

- Involves any internal organ.

- Involves second or third degree burns or any burns affecting more than 5% of the body surface.

Substantial damage means damage or failure that adversely affects the structural strength, performance or flight characteristics of the aircraft and that would normally require major repair or replacement of the affected component. Damage not considered substantial for accident reporting purposes are as follows: engine failure or damage limited to an engine if only one engine fails or is damaged, bent fairings or cowling, dented skin, small punctured holes in the skin or fabric, ground damage to rotor or propeller blades, and damage to the landing gear, wheels, tires, flaps, engine accessories, brakes or wing tips.

The operator of an aircraft must immediately notify the nearest National Transportation Safety Board field office if any of the following occur:

- Flight control system malfunction

- An aircraft accident

- Inability of any required flight crewmember to perform his normal flight duties as the result of injury or illness

- Failure of structural components of a turbine engine excluding compressor and turbine blades and vanes

- Inflight fire

- Aircraft collide in flight

- Damage to property, other than the aircraft, estimate to exceed $25,000 for repair or fair market value in the event of total loss whichever is less

- Certain incidents on large, multi-engine airplanes

- An aircraft is overdue and is believed to have been involved in an accident

The operator of an aircraft must submit a written report of an aircraft accident within 10 days of the accident. The operator of an overdue aircraft must submit a written report within 7 days if the aircraft is still missing. The operator of an aircraft that was involved in an incident requiring immediate notification of the NTSB must submit a written report of the incident only if requested to do so by the NTSB.

ALL

8317. What period of time must a person be hospitalized before an injury may be defined by the NTSB as a "serious injury"?

A— 72 hours; commencing within 10 days after date of injury.

B— 48 hours; commencing within 7 days after date of the injury.

C— 10 days, with no other extenuating circumstances.

"Serious injury" means any injury which requires hospitalization for more than 48 hours, commencing within 7 days from the date the injury was received. (PLT366) — NTSB §830.2

ALL

8319. Which of the following constitutes "substantial damage" according to NTSB Part 830?

A— Ground damage to landing gear, wheels, or tires.

B— Damage to wingtips (or rotor blades, in the case of a helicopter).

C— Failure of a component which would adversely affect the performance, and which would require replacement.

"Substantial damage" is defined as damage or failure which would adversely affect the structural strength, performance, or flight characteristics of the aircraft which would normally require major repair or replacement of the damaged component. (PLT395) — NTSB §830.2

Answer (A) is incorrect because ground damage to landing gear, wheels, or tires is not considered "substantial damage" for the purpose of NTSB Part 830. Answer (B) is incorrect because damage to wing tips (or rotorblades, in the case of a helicopter) is not considered "substantial damage" for the purpose of NTSB Part 830.

ALL

8320. Which of the following meets the requirements of a "serious injury" as defined by the NTSB?

A— A simple fracture of the nose or other extremity.

B— An injury which caused severe tendon damage.

C— First-degree burns over 5 percent of the body.

"Serious injury" includes severe tendon damage and second or third degree burns covering more than five percent of the body. (PLT395) — NTSB §830.2

Answer (A) is incorrect because simple fractures, such as of the finger, toe, or nose, are not considered a serious injury. Answer (C) is incorrect because only second and third degree burns or first degree burns over more than 5% of the body are defined as a serious injury. (First degree burns are less serious than second and third degree burns.)

ALL

8318. Within what time period should the nearest NTSB field office be notified when an aircraft is involved in an accident which results in substantial damage?

A— Immediately.

B— 7 calendar days.

C— 10 days.

The operator of an aircraft shall immediately, and by the most expeditious means available, notify the nearest NTSB field office when an aircraft accident occurs. (PLT366) — NTSB §830.5

ALL

8321. Which incident requires an immediate notification to NTSB?

A— Aircraft colliding on the ground.

B— Flight control system malfunction.

C— Damage to property, other than the aircraft, estimated to exceed $10,000.

The NTSB lists a flight control malfunction or failure as an incident requiring immediate notification to the field office. (PLT416) — NTSB §830.5

ALL

8322. Within how many days must the operator of an aircraft involved in an accident file a report to the NTSB?

A— 3 days.

B— 7 days.

C— 10 days.

The NTSB requires a report to be filed within 10 days of the accident. (PLT366) — NTSB §830.15

ALL

8323. When is an operator of an aircraft, which has been involved in an incident, required to submit a report to the nearest field office of the NTSB?

A— Within 7 days.

B— Within 10 days.

C— Only if requested to do so by the NTSB.

An aircraft involved in an incident is required to file a report only on request from the NTSB. (PLT366) — NTSB §830.15

Answers

8317	[B]	8319	[C]	8320	[B]	8318	[A]	8321	[B]	8322	[C]
8323	[C]						

ALL

9836. Pilots and/or flightcrew members involved in near midair collision (NMAC) occurrences are urged to report each incident immediately

A— by cell phone to the nearest Flight Standards District Office, as this is an emergency.
B— to local law enforcement.
C— by radio or telephone to the nearest FAA ATC facility or FSS.

The primary purpose of the Near Midair Collision (NMAC) Reporting Program is to provide information for use in enhancing the safety and efficiency of the National Airspace System. Pilots and/or flightcrew members involved in NMAC occurrences are urged to report each incident immediately by radio or telephone to the nearest FAA ATC facility or FSS. (PLT526) — AIM ¶7-6-3

Part 135 Regulations

ATS

8053. What aircraft operating under 14 CFR Part 135 are required to have a third gyroscopic bank-and-pitch indicator installed?

A— All airplanes that are turbojet powered.
B— All multiengine airplanes that require a two pilot flightcrew.
C— All turbine powered aircraft having a passenger seating capacity of 30 seats or more.

A third gyroscopic pitch-and-bank indicator is required on all turbojet-powered airplanes. (PLT405) — 14 CFR §135.149

ATS

8054. In airplanes where a third gyroscopic bank-and-pitch indicator is required, that instrument must

A— continue reliable operation for at least 30 minutes after the output of the airplane's electrical generating system falls below an optimum level.
B— be operable by a selector switch which may be actuated from either pilot station.
C— continue reliable operation for a minimum of 30 minutes after total failure of the electrical generating system.

A third gyroscopic pitch-and-bank indicator is required on all turbojet-powered airplanes. This indicator must be able to continue reliable operation for at least 30 minutes after the failure of the aircraft's electrical generating system. (PLT405) — 14 CFR §135.149

ATS

8069. In which airplanes is a Class A TAWS required?

A— All airplanes having a passenger seating configuration, excluding any pilot seat, of 10 seats or more.
B— Turbine-powered airplanes having a passenger seating configuration, excluding any pilot seat, of 10 seats or more.
C— Turbine-powered aircraft having a passenger seating configuration, including any pilot seat, of 10 seats or more.

No person may operate a turbine-powered airplane having a passenger seating configuration, excluding any pilot seat, of 10 seats or more unless it is equipped with a terrain awareness system (TAWS). (PLT139) — 14 CFR §135.153

ATS

8075. Which airplanes must have a shoulder harness installed at each flight crewmember station?

A— All airplanes used in commuter air service, having a passenger seating configuration of 9, excluding any pilot seat.
B— All airplanes operating under 14 CFR Part 135, having a seating configuration for 10 persons.
C— All turbojet-powered airplanes.

No person may operate a turbojet aircraft or an aircraft having a passenger seating configuration, excluding any pilot seat, of 10 seats or more unless it is equipped with an approved shoulder harness installed for each flight crewmember station. (PLT464) — 14 CFR §135.171

Answers

9836 [C]   8053 [A]   8054 [C]   8069 [B]   8075 [C]

ATS

8165. What emergency equipment is required for extended overwater operations?

A— A portable survival emergency locator transmitter for each liferaft.

B— A pyrotechnic signaling device for each life preserver.

C— A life preserver equipped with a survivor locator light, for each person on the airplane.

No person may operate an aircraft in extended overwater operations unless it carries an approved life preserver (easily accessible to each seated occupant) equipped with an approved survivor locator light for each occupant of the aircraft, and enough approved life rafts of a rated capacity and buoyancy to accommodate the occupants of the aircraft. An approved survival-type emergency locator transmitter must be attached to one of the life rafts. (PLT404) — 14 CFR §135.167

Answer (A) is incorrect because only one survival emergency locator transmitter is required to be carried on the airplane. Answer (B) is incorrect because one pyrotechnic signaling device is required for each life raft.

ATS

8088. If the weather forecasts do not require the listing of an alternate airport on an IFR flight, the airplane must carry sufficient fuel to fly to the destination airport and

A— make one missed approach and thereafter have a 45-minute reserve at normal cruising speed.

B— fly thereafter for 45 minutes at normal cruising speed.

C— fly for 45 minutes thereafter at normal cruise climb speed.

No person may operate an aircraft in IFR conditions unless it carries enough fuel (considering weather reports and forecasts) to:

1. Complete the flight to the first airport of intended landing;

2. Fly from that airport to the alternate airport (if one is required); and

3. Fly after that for 45 minutes at normal cruising speed.

(PLT413) — 14 CFR §135.223

ATS

8089. If the weather forecasts require the listing of an alternate airport on an IFR flight, the airplane must carry enough fuel to fly to the first airport of intended landing, then to the alternate, and fly thereafter for a minimum of

A— 45 minutes at normal holding speed.

B— 45 minutes at normal cruise speed and then complete an approach and landing.

C— 45 minutes at normal cruise speed.

No person may operate an aircraft in IFR conditions unless it carries enough fuel (considering weather reports and forecasts) to:

1. Complete the flight to the first airport of intended landing;

2. Fly from that airport to the alternate airport (if one is required); and

3. Fly after that for 45 minutes at normal cruising speed.

(PLT413) — 14 CFR §135.223

ATS

8115. When computing the takeoff data for reciprocating powered airplanes, what is the percentage of the reported headwind component that may be applied to the "still air" data?

A— Not more than 150 percent.

B— Not more than 100 percent.

C— Not more than 50 percent.

When computing takeoff data not more than 50% of the reported headwind component may be taken into account. (PLT011) — 14 CFR §135.389

ATS

8116. When computing takeoff data, what is the percentage of the effective tailwind component which may be applied to the "still air" data?

A— Not less than 150 percent.

B— Not less than 100 percent.

C— Not more than 50 percent.

When computing takeoff data not less than 150% of the reported tailwind component may be taken into account. (PLT011) — 14 CFR §135.389

Answers

8165 [C]	8088 [B]	8089 [C]	8115 [C]	8116 [A]

ATS

8050. Which performance requirement applies to passenger-carrying land airplanes being operated over water?

A— Multiengine airplanes must be able to climb, with the critical engine inoperative, at least 50 ft/min at 1,500 feet above the surface.

B— Single-engine airplanes must be operated at an altitude that will allow them to reach land in case of engine failure.

C— Multiengine airplanes must be able to climb, with the critical engine inoperative, at least 100 ft/min at 1,000 feet above the surface.

No person may operate a land aircraft carrying passengers over water unless it is operated at an altitude that allows it to reach land in the case of engine failure. (PLT437) — 14 CFR §135.183

ATS

8051. What performance is required of a multiengine airplane with the critical engine inoperative, while carrying passengers for hire in IFR weather conditions?

A— Climb at least 100 ft/min at the highest MEA of the route to be flown or 5,000 feet MSL, whichever is higher.

B— Climb at least 50 ft/min at the MEA's of the route to be flown or 5,000 feet AGL, whichever is higher.

C— Climb at least 50 ft/min at the MEA's of the route to be flown or 5,000 feet MSL, whichever is higher.

No person may operate a multi-engine airplane carrying passengers Over-The-Top or in IFR conditions at a weight that will not allow it to climb, with the critical engine inoperative, at least 50 feet a minute when operating at the MEAs of the route to be flown or 5,000 feet MSL, whichever is higher. (PLT223) — 14 CFR §135.181

ATS

8792. The crewmember interphone system on a large turbojet-powered airplane provides a means of two-way communications between ground personnel and at least one of two flight crewmembers in the pilot compartment, when the aircraft is on the ground. The interphone station for use by ground personnel must be located so that those using the system from that station

A— are always visible, from within the airplane.

B— are able to avoid the intake areas of the engines.

C— may avoid visible detection from within the airplane.

The interphone system station for use by ground personnel must be so located that personnel using the system may avoid visible detection from within the airplane. (PLT462) — 14 CFR §135.150

ATS

8831. For which of these aircraft may part of the "clearway" distance, for a particular runway, be considered in computing the takeoff distance?

A— Passenger-carrying transport aircraft.

B— Turbine-engine-powered transport airplanes, certificated after September 30, 1958.

C— U.S. certified transport airplane, certificated before August 26, 1957.

"Clearway" may be used in computing the takeoff distance of turbine-engine-powered airplanes certificated after September 30, 1958. (PLT456) — 14 CFR §1.1

ATS

8832. What requirement must be met regarding cargo that is carried anywhere in the passenger compartment of a commuter air carrier airplane?

A— Cargo may not be carried anywhere in the rear of the passenger compartment.

B— The bin in which the cargo is carried may not be installed in a position that restricts access to, or use of the aisle between the crew and the passenger compartment.

C— The container or bin in which the cargo is carried must be made of material which is at least flash resistant.

No person may carry cargo, including carry-on baggage in an aircraft unless it is in an approved cargo rack, bin, or compartment, and it does not obstruct access to, or use of, the aisle between the passenger and crew compartment. (PLT385) — 14 CFR §135.87

Answers

8050 [B]　　　8051 [C]　　　8792 [C]　　　8831 [B]　　　8832 [B]

ATS

8833. Information recorded during normal operation of a cockpit voice recorder in a multiengine turbine powered airplane

A— may all be erased or otherwise obliterated except for the last 30 minutes.

B— may all be erased or otherwise obliterated except for the last 30 minutes prior to landing.

C— may all be erased, prior to each flight, unless the NTSB has requested that it be kept for 60 days.

Information recorded more than 30 minutes earlier may be erased or obliterated. (PLT388) — 14 CFR §135.151

ATS

8842. An airplane, operated by a commuter air carrier, flying in extended overwater operations must carry enough approved liferafts of a rated capacity and buoyancy to accommodate the occupants of the aircraft. Each liferaft must be equipped with

A— one approved pyrotechnic signaling device.

B— colored smoke flares and a signal mirror.

C— one fishing kit for each person the raft is rated to carry.

Every aircraft flown in extended overwater operations must carry enough appropriately equipped life rafts to accommodate the occupants of the aircraft. Each raft must have an approved pyrotechnic signaling device (either smoke or flare type flare). (PLT082) — 14 CFR §135.167

Answer (B) is incorrect because the survival kit is not required to have colored smoke flares. Answer (C) is incorrect because the survival kit is only required to have one fishing kit per liferaft, not one per person.

ATS, RTC

8001. A certificate holder must have "exclusive use" of

A— at least one aircraft that meets the requirements of each kind of operation authorized in the Operations Specifications.

B— at least one aircraft that meets the requirements of at least one kind of operation authorized in the certificate holder's Operations Specifications.

C— at least one aircraft that meets the requirements of the specific operations authorized in the certificate holder's Operations Specifications.

Each certificate holder must have the exclusive use of at least one aircraft that meets the requirements for at least one kind of operation authorized in the certificate holder's operations specifications. (PLT454) — 14 CFR §135.25

ATS, RTC

8005. Where is the certificate holder required to list the name and title of each person authorized to exercise operational control for a particular flight?

A— Operations Specifications.

B— Attached to the load manifest.

C— Certificate holder's manual.

Each certificate holder is responsible for operational control and shall list in the manual the name and title of each person authorized to exercise operational control. (PLT282) — 14 CFR §135.77

ATS, RTC

8010. An aircraft being operated outside of the United States, over a foreign country, by a 14 CFR part 135 operator must comply with

A— the International Civil Aviation Organization (ICAO), Annex 3, Rules of the Air.

B— regulations of the foreign country.

C— rules of the U.S. State Department and the foreign country.

Each person operating an aircraft under Part 135 while operating outside the United States, shall comply with Annex 2, Rules of the Air, to the Convention of International Civil Aviation or the regulations of any foreign country, whichever applies. (PLT392) — 14 CFR §135.3

ATS, RTC

8011. Who is responsible for keeping copies of the certificate holder's manual up to date with approved changes or additions?

A— Each of the certificate holder's employees who are furnished a manual.

B— An employee designated by the certificate holder.

C— A representative of the certificate holder approved by the Administrator.

Each employee of the certificate holder to whom a manual (or appropriate portions of it) is furnished shall keep it up to date with changes and additions furnished to them. (PLT282) — 14 CFR §135.21

Answers

| 8833 | [A] | 8842 | [A] | 8001 | [B] | 8005 | [C] | 8010 | [B] | 8011 | [A] |

ATS, RTC

9807. No person may operate a U.S. registered civil aircraft

A— for which an AFM or RFM is required by part 21 section 21.5 unless there is a current, approved operator's manual available.

B— for which an AFM or RFM is required by part 21 section 21.5 unless there is a current, approved AFM or RFM available.

C— for which an AFM or RFM is required by part 21 section 21.5 unless there is a current, approved AFM or RFM available or the manual specified in part 135 section 135.19(b).

Per 14 CFR §21.5, with each airplane or rotorcraft not type certificated with an Airplane or Rotorcraft Flight Manual and having no flight time before March 1, 1979, the holder of a type certificate (including amended or supplemental type certificates) or the licensee of a type certificate must make available to the owner at the time of delivery of the aircraft a current approved Airplane or Rotorcraft Flight Manual. (PLT373) — 14 CFR §21.5

ATS, RTC

8013. What is the lowest altitude above the terrain that an autopilot may be used during en route operations, if the Airplane Flight Manual specifies a malfunction under cruise conditions?

A— 1,000 feet.
B— 500 feet.
C— 100 feet.

Except for approaches, no person may use an autopilot at an altitude above the terrain which is less than 500 feet or less than twice the maximum altitude loss specified in the approved Aircraft Flight Manual or equivalent for a malfunction of the autopilot, whichever is higher. (PLT424) — 14 CFR §135.93

ATS, RTC

8033. Who may be allowed to carry a deadly weapon on board an aircraft operated under 14 CFR Part 135?

A— Official bodyguards attached to foreign legations.
B— Crewmembers and/or others authorized by the certificate holder.
C— Employees of a municipality or a state, or of the United States.

No person may carry a deadly weapon on a Part 135 flight except for:

1. *Officials or employees of a municipality or a state or of the United States, who are authorized to carry arms; or*

2. *Crewmembers and other persons authorized by the certificate holder to carry arms.*

(PLT440) — 14 CFR §135.119

ATS, RTC

8038. Which person may be carried aboard an aircraft without complying with the passenger-carrying requirements of 14 CFR Part 135?

A— An individual who is necessary for the safe handling of hazardous material on the aircraft.
B— A representative of the Administrator, traveling to attend a meeting.
C— A member of the United States diplomatic corps on an official courier mission.

The following persons may be carried on an aircraft without complying with the passenger-carrying rules of Part 135:

1. *A crewmember or other employee of the certificate holder;*

2. *A person necessary for the safe handling of animals on the aircraft;*

3. *A person necessary for the safe handling of hazardous materials;*

4. *A person performing duty as a security or honor guard accompanying a shipment made by or under the authority of the U.S. Government;*

5. *A military courier or a military route supervisor carried by a military cargo contract air carrier or commercial operator;*

6. *An authorized representative of the Administrator conducting an enroute inspection; or*

7. *A person, authorized by the Administrator, who is performing a duty connected with a cargo operation of the certificate holder.*

(PLT385) — 14 CFR §135.85

Answers

9807 **[B]**   8013 **[B]**   8033 **[B]**   8038 **[A]**

ATS, RTC

8004. If previous arrangements have not been made by the operator, where can the procedures for servicing the aircraft be found?

A— Certificate holder's maintenance manual.
B— Certificate holder's manual.
C— Pilot's Handbook.

The certificate holder's manual must contain procedures to be followed by the pilot-in-command to obtain maintenance, preventative maintenance, and servicing of the aircraft at a place where previous arrangements have not been made by the operator, when the pilot is authorized to so act for the operator. (PLT282) — 14 CFR §135.23

ATS, RTC

8006. Who is directly responsible for determining the status of each mechanical irregularity previously entered in the aircraft maintenance log?

A— Aircraft dispatcher.
B— Line maintenance supervisor.
C— The next pilot in command.

Before each flight, the pilot-in-command shall determine, if the pilot does not already know, the status of each irregularity entered in the maintenance log at the end of the preceding flight. (PLT374) — 14 CFR §135.65

ATS, RTC

8012. What document contains procedures that explain how the required return-to-service conditions have been met?

A— Maintenance manual.
B— Pilot's Handbook.
C— Certificate holder's manual.

The certificate holder's manual must include procedures for ensuring that the pilot-in-command knows that required airworthiness inspections have been made and that the aircraft has been returned to service in compliance with applicable maintenance requirements. (PLT375) — 14 CFR §135.23

ATS, RTC

8019. Procedures for keeping copies of the aircraft maintenance log in the aircraft and available to appropriate personnel shall be set forth in

A— the certificate holder's manual.
B— the maintenance procedures handbook.
C— the Operations Specifications.

Each certificate holder shall establish a procedure for keeping copies of the aircraft maintenance log in the aircraft for access by appropriate personnel and shall include that procedure in the manual. (PLT282) — 14 CFR §135.65

ATS, RTC

8093. If a certificate holder makes arrangements for another person to perform aircraft maintenance, that maintenance shall be performed in accordance with the

A— certificate holder's manual and 14 CFR Parts 43, 91, and 135.
B— provisions of a contract prepared by a certificate holder and approved by the supervising FAA district office.
C— provisions and standards as outlined in the certificate holder's manual.

The certificate holder shall ensure that any maintenance, preventative maintenance, or alteration that is performed by another person is performed under the certificate holder's manual and regulations. (PLT282) — 14 CFR §135.413

ATS, RTC

8112. Who is responsible for submitting a Mechanical Reliability Report?

A— Each certificate holder.
B— Director of maintenance at the facility that discovers the reportable condition.
C— Chief inspector at the facility where the condition is found.

The certificate holder is responsible for submitting required mechanical reliability reports. (PLT443) — 14 CFR §135.415

Answers

8004 [B]	8006 [C]	8012 [C]	8019 [A]	8093 [A]	8112 [A]

ATS, RTC

8014. The maximum altitude loss specified for malfunction of a certain autopilot under cruise conditions is 50 feet. What is the lowest altitude this autopilot may be used en route?

A— 500 feet AGL.
B— 550 feet AGL.
C— 600 feet AGL.

Except for approaches, no person may use an autopilot at an altitude above the terrain which is less than 500 feet or less than twice the maximum altitude loss specified in the approved Aircraft Flight Manual or equivalent for a malfunction of the autopilot, whichever is higher. (PLT424) — 14 CFR §135.93

ATS, RTC

8015. The maximum altitude loss for a particular malfunctioning autopilot under approach conditions is 55 feet. If the TDZE is 571 feet and the MDA is 1,100 feet, to which minimum altitude may you use this autopilot?

A— 626 feet MSL.
B— 990 feet MSL.
C— 1,050 feet MSL.

When using an instrument approach facility other than ILS, no person may use an autopilot at an altitude above the terrain that is less than 50 feet below the approved minimum descent altitude for that procedure, or less than twice the maximum loss specified in the approved Airplane Flight Manual or equivalent for malfunction of the autopilot under approach conditions, whichever is higher. (PLT424) — 14 CFR §135.93

ATS, RTC

8016. The maximum altitude loss for a malfunctioning autopilot with an approach coupler is 40 feet. To which minimum altitude may the autopilot be used during an ILS approach in less than basic VFR conditions?

A— 40 feet AGL.
B— 50 feet AGL.
C— 80 feet AGL.

For ILS approaches, when reported weather is less than VFR, no person may use an autopilot with an approach coupler at an altitude that is less than 50 feet above the terrain, or the maximum altitude loss specified in the approved Airplane Flight Manual or equivalent, for the malfunction of the autopilot with an approach coupler, whichever is higher. (PLT424) — 14 CFR §135.93

ATS, RTC

8017. The maximum altitude loss for a malfunctioning autopilot without an approach coupler is 45 feet. If the MDA is 1,620 feet MSL and the TDZE is 1,294 feet, to which minimum altitude may you use the autopilot?

A— 1,510 feet MSL.
B— 1,339 feet MSL.
C— 1,570 feet MSL.

When using an instrument approach facility other than ILS, no person may use an autopilot at an altitude above the terrain that is less than 50 feet below the approved minimum descent altitude for that procedure, or less than twice the maximum loss specified in the approved Airplane Flight Manual or equivalent for malfunction of the autopilot under approach conditions, whichever is higher. (PLT424) — 14 CFR §135.93

ATS, RTC

8037. The altitude loss for a particular malfunctioning autopilot with an approach coupler is 60 feet. If the reported weather is below basic VFR minimums and an ILS approach using the approach coupler is to be used, what minimum altitude may be used?

A— 50 feet AGL.
B— 55 feet AGL.
C— 60 feet AGL.

For ILS approaches, when reported weather is less than VFR, no person may use an autopilot with an approach coupler at an altitude that is less than 50 feet above the terrain, or the maximum altitude loss specified in the approved Airplane Flight Manual or equivalent, for the malfunction of the autopilot with an approach coupler, whichever is higher. (PLT424) — 14 CFR §135.93

ATS, RTC

8045. During which time period must a required voice recorder of a passenger-carrying airplane be continuously operated?

A— From the beginning of taxi to the end of the landing roll.
B— From engine start at departure airport to engine shutdown at landing airport.
C— From the use of the checklist before the flight to completion of the final check at the end of the flight.

Continued

Answers

8014 [A]   8015 [C]   8016 [B]   8017 [C]   8037 [C]   8045 [C]

No person may operate a multi-engine, turbine-powered airplane or rotorcraft having a passenger seating configuration of 20 or more seats unless it is equipped with an approved cockpit voice recorder that:

1. *Is installed in compliance with Part 23, 25, 27 or 29 as applicable to Part 135; and*

2. *Is operated continuously from the use of the checklist before the flight to completion of the final check at the end of the flight.*

(PLT405) — 14 CFR §135.151

ATS, RTC

8046. An approved cockpit voice recorder is required equipment in

A— large turbine-powered airplanes having a maximum passenger capacity of 20 or more seats.

B— multiengine, turbine-powered airplanes having a passenger seating configuration of 20 or more seats.

C— all aircraft operated in commuter air carrier service having a passenger seating configuration of 20 seats or more.

No person may operate a multi-engine, turbine-powered airplane or rotorcraft having a passenger seating configuration of 20 or more seats unless it is equipped with an approved cockpit voice recorder. (PLT405) — 14 CFR §135.151

ATS, RTC

8047. Information recorded during normal operations by a required cockpit voice recorder

A— must be erased or obliterated, except for the last 30 minutes.

B— may be erased or obliterated, only once each flight.

C— may be erased or obliterated, except the last 30 minutes.

No person may operate a multi-engine, turbine-powered airplane or rotorcraft having a passenger seating configuration of 20 or more seats unless it is equipped with an approved cockpit voice recorder that:

1. *Is installed in compliance with Part 23, 25, 27 or 29 as applicable to Part 135; and*

2. *Is operated continuously from the use of the checklist before the flight to completion of the final check at the end of the flight.*

In complying with this section, information recorded more than 30 minutes earlier may be erased or otherwise obliterated. (PLT388) — 14 CFR §135.151

ATS, RTC

8048. Which aircraft must be equipped with an approved public address and crewmember interphone system?

A— All turbine-engine-powered aircraft having a seating configuration of more than 19 seats.

B— Aircraft having a passenger seating configuration, excluding any pilot seat, of more than 19 seats.

C— Multiengine aircraft having a passenger seating configuration of 10 seats or more.

No person may operate an aircraft having a passenger seating configuration, excluding any pilot seat, of more than 19 unless an approved public address and crew interphone system is installed. (PLT462) — 14 CFR §135.150

ATS, RTC

8052. To operate an aircraft with certain equipment inoperative under the provisions of a minimum equipment list, what document authorizing it must be issued to the certificate holder?

A— Letter of Authorization from the Regional Airworthiness Office authorizing such an operation.

B— Operations specifications issued by the FAA district office having certification responsibility.

C— Letter of Authorization issued by the FAA district office having certification responsibility.

No person may takeoff with inoperable instruments or equipment installed unless the following conditions are met:

1. *An approved Minimum Equipment List exists for that aircraft.*

2. *The certificate-holding district office has issued the certificate holder operations specifications authorizing operations in accordance with an approved Minimum Equipment List. The flight crew shall have direct access at all times prior to flight to all of the information contained in the approved Minimum Equipment List through printed or other means approved by the Administrator in the certificate holders operations specifications. An approved Minimum Equipment List, as authorized by the operations specifications, constitutes an approved change to the type design without requiring recertification*

(PLT428) — 14 CFR §135.179

Answers

8046 [B]   8047 [C]   8048 [B]   8052 [B]

ATS, RTC

8058. When a crash ax is required equipment on an aircraft, where should it be located?

A— In the flight crew compartment.
B— At a location inaccessible to the passengers during normal operations.
C— At a location accessible to both the crew and passengers during normal operations.

No person may operate an aircraft having a passenger seating configuration, excluding any pilot seat, of more than 19 seats unless it is equipped with a crash ax carried that is accessible to the crew but inaccessible to passengers during normal operations. (PLT404) — 14 CFR §135.177

ATS, RTC

8059. How many, if any, approved first aid kits are required on an aircraft having a passenger seating configuration of 20 seats and a passenger load of 14?

A— None.
B— One.
C— Two.

No person may operate an aircraft having a passenger seating configuration, excluding any pilot seat, of more than 19 seats unless it is equipped with one approved first aid kit for the treatment of injuries likely to occur in flight or in a minor accident. (PLT404) — 14 CFR §135.177

ATS, RTC

8060. An aircraft has a passenger seating configuration of 19 seats, excluding any pilot seats. How many, if any, approved first aid kits are required?

A— One.
B— Two.
C— None.

No person may operate an aircraft having a passenger seating configuration, excluding any pilot seat, of more than 19 seats unless it is equipped with one approved first aid kit for the treatment of injuries likely to occur in flight or in a minor accident. (PLT404) — 14 CFR §135.177

ATS, RTC

8061. Airborne weather radar equipment must be installed in large transport category aircraft, in the conterminous 48 United States,

A— that are engaged in passenger-carrying operations.
B— that are engaged in either cargo or passenger-carrying operations.
C— and be fully operational, although weather forecasts indicate no hazardous conditions.

No person may operate a large, transport category aircraft in passenger-carrying operations unless approved airborne weather radar equipment is installed in the aircraft. (PLT367) — 14 CFR §135.175

ATS, RTC

8062. In which aircraft, or under what conditions, is airborne thunderstorm detection equipment required?

A— Large multiengine turbine-powered aircraft having a passenger seating configuration of 19 seats or more being operated by a commuter air carrier.
B— Any aircraft having a passenger seating configuration of 19 seats or more that is engaged in passenger-carrying operations under IFR or at night.
C— Small aircraft having a passenger seating configuration of 10 seats or more, excluding any pilot seat, that are engaged in passenger-carrying operations.

No person may operate an aircraft that has a passenger seating configuration, excluding any pilot seat, of 10 seats or more in passenger-carrying operations unless the aircraft is equipped with either approved thunderstorm detection equipment or approved airborne weather radar equipment. (PLT367) — 14 CFR §135.173

Answers

8058 [B]	8059 [B]	8060 [C]	8061 [A]	8062 [C]

ATS, RTC

8070. When a ground proximity warning system is required under 14 CFR Part 135, it must

A— convey warnings of any deviation below glide slope and of excessive closure rate with the terrain.

B— convey warnings for excessive closure rates with the terrain but not for deviation from an ILS glide slope.

C— alert the pilot by an audible and visual warning signals when deviation above or below glide slope occurs.

An approved ground proximity warning system must convey warnings of excessive closure rates with the terrain and any deviations below glide slope by visual and audible means. (PLT139) — 14 CFR §135.153

ATS, RTC

8071. When a ground proximity warning system is required, it must

A— apply corrective control pressure when deviation below glide slope occurs.

B— incorporate a means of alerting the pilot when a system malfunction occurs.

C— incorporate a backup feature that activates automatically upon total failure of the aircraft's electrical generating system.

An approved ground proximity warning system must convey warnings of excessive closure rates with the terrain and any deviations below glide slope by visual and audible means. It must also incorporate a means of alerting the pilot when a malfunction occurs. (PLT139) — 14 CFR §135.153

ATS, RTC

8077. Which group of aircraft must have a shoulder harness installed at each flight crewmember station?

A— Aircraft having a passenger seating configuration, excluding any pilot seat, of 10 seats or more.

B— All passenger-carrying aircraft operating under 14 CFR Part 135, having a seating configuration for 10 persons.

C— Large aircraft being operated in commuter air service, having a passenger seating configuration of 9, excluding any pilot seat.

No person may operate a turbojet aircraft or an aircraft having a passenger seating configuration, excluding any pilot seat, of 10 seats or more unless it is equipped with an approved shoulder harness installed for each flight crewmember station. (PLT464) — 14 CFR §135.171

ATS, RTC

8078. Which is a requirement for life preservers during extended overwater operations? Each life preserver must be equipped with

A— a dye marker.

B— an approved survivor locator light.

C— one flashlight having at least two size "D" cells or equivalent.

No person may operate an aircraft in extended over-water operations unless it carries an approved life preserver equipped with an approved survivor locator light for each occupant of the aircraft. (PLT437) — 14 CFR §135.167

ATS, RTC

8079. In addition to fully-equipped liferafts and life preservers, what emergency equipment must be provided during extended overwater operations?

A— One water resistant, self-buoyant, portable survival-type emergency radio transmitter for each liferaft.

B— Each aircraft must have at least one liferaft, equipped with a survival-type emergency locator transmitter.

C— One pyrotechnic signaling device for each aircraft.

No person may operate an aircraft in extended over-water operations unless there is attached to one of the required life rafts, a survival-type emergency locator transmitter. (PLT437) — 14 CFR §135.167

ATS, RTC

8057. A pilot may make an IFR departure from an airport that does not have an approved standard instrument approach procedure if

A— there is a departure alternate within 60 minutes and the weather there is above landing minimums.

B— the Administrator has issued Operations Specifications to the certificate holder approving the procedure.

C— the departure airport is within 30 minutes flying time of another airport that has an approved standard instrument approach procedure.

The Administrator may issue operations specifications to the certificate holder to allow it to depart at an airport that does not have an approved standard instrument approach procedure when the Administrator determines that it is necessary to make an IFR departure from that airport and that the proposed operations can be conducted safely. (PLT459) — 14 CFR §135.215

Answers

8070 [A]   8071 [B]   8077 [A]   8078 [B]   8079 [B]   8057 [B]

ATS, RTC

8063. Assuming the required ceiling exists, an alternate for the destination airport is not required under 14 CFR 135 if, for at least 1 hour before and after the ETA, the forecast visibility is at least

A— 5 miles, or 3 miles more than the lowest applicable visibility minimums for the instrument approach procedure to be used, whichever is greater.
B— 3 miles, or 2 miles more than the lowest applicable visibility minimums for the instrument approach procedure to be used, whichever is greater.
C— 3 nautical miles, or 2 nautical miles more than the lowest applicable visibility minimums for the approach procedure to be used, which ever is greater.

An alternate airport need not be designated if the ceiling criteria is met and the visibility is forecast to be at least 3 miles or 2 miles more than the lowest applicable visibility minimums, whichever is the greater, for the instrument approach procedure to be used at the destination airport. (PLT379) — 14 CFR §135.223

ATS, RTC

8064. A pilot may not designate an airport as an alternate unless the weather reports, or forecasts, or any combination of them indicate that it will be at or above alternate airport landing minimum at the

A— time of departure.
B— estimated time of arrival, plus or minus 1 hour.
C— estimated time of arrival.

No person may designate an alternate airport unless the weather reports or forecasts, or any combination of them, indicate that the weather conditions will be at or above authorized alternate airport landing minimums for that airport at the estimated time of arrival. (E04) — 14 CFR §135.221

ATS, RTC

8065. A takeoff may not be made from an airport that is below the authorized IFR landing minimums unless

A— there is an alternate airport with the required IFR landing minimums within 60 minutes flying time, at normal cruising speed in still air.
B— the departure airport is forecast to have the required IFR landing minimums within 1 hour.
C— there is an alternate airport with the required IFR landing minimums within 60 minutes flying time, at normal cruising speed in still air with one engine inoperative.

No person may takeoff an aircraft under IFR from an airport where weather conditions are at or above takeoff minimums, but are below landing minimums, unless there is an alternate airport within one hour's flying time (at normal cruising speed in still air) of the airport of departure. (PLT459) — 14 CFR §135.217

ATS, RTC

8066. A pilot may not begin an IFR operation unless the next airport of intended landing is forecast to be at or above authorized IFR landing minimums at

A— the estimated time of arrival, ±1 hour.
B— the estimated time of arrival.
C— the estimated time of arrival, ±30 minutes.

No person may takeoff an aircraft under IFR or begin an IFR or over-the-top operation unless the latest weather reports or forecasts, or any combination of them, indicate that weather conditions at the estimated time of arrival at the next airport of intended landing will be at or above authorized IFR landing minimums. (PLT459) — 14 CFR §135.219

ATS, RTC

8068. Which condition must be met to conduct IFR operations from an airport that is not at the location where weather observations are made?

A— An "Authorization Letter" permitting the procedure must be issued by the FAA district office charged with the overall inspection of the certificate holder.
B— A "Letter of Waiver" authorizing the procedure must be issued by the Administrator, after an investigation by the U.S. National Weather Service and the FSDO which find the standard of safety to be satisfactory.
C— The Administrator must issue Operations Specifications that permit the procedure.

The Administrator may issue operations specifications to the certificate holder to allow it to depart at an airport that does not have an approved standard instrument approach procedure when the Administrator determines that it is necessary to make an IFR departure from that airport and that the proposed operations can be conducted safely. (PLT282) — 14 CFR §135.215

Answers

8063 [B]   8064 [C]   8065 [A]   8066 [B]   8068 [C]

ATS, RTC

8084. Which is an operational requirement concerning ice, snow, or frost on structural surfaces?

A— A takeoff may be made with ice, snow, or frost adhering to the wings or stabilizing or control surfaces, but polished smooth, if the anti-icing and deicing equipment is operating.

B— If snow, ice, or frost is adhering to the airplane's lift or control surfaces, but polished smooth, a takeoff may be made.

C— A takeoff may not be made if ice or snow is adhering to the wings or stabilizing or control surfaces.

No pilot may takeoff in an aircraft that has snow or ice adhering to the wings, stabilizing, or control surfaces. (PLT493) — 14 CFR §135.227

ATS, RTC

8085. Which is one required condition for a pilot to take off under IFR with less-than-standard takeoff minimums at an airport where a straight-in instrument approach procedure is authorized and there is an approved weather reporting source?

A— The pilot must have at least 100 hours as pilot in command in the type airplane to be flown.

B— The certificate holder has been approved for such operation and the visibility at the time of takeoff must be at least RVR 16.

C— Wind direction and velocity must be such that a straight-in approach can be made to the runway served by the procedure.

At airports where straight-in instrument approach procedures are authorized, a pilot may takeoff in an aircraft under IFR when the weather conditions are equal to or better than the lowest straight-in landing minimums if:

1. The wind direction and velocity at the time of takeoff are such that a straight-in instrument approach can be made to the runway served by instrument approach;

2. The associated ground facilities upon which the landing minimums are predicated and the related airborne equipment are in normal operation; and

3. The certificate holder has been approved for such operations.

(PLT459) — 14 CFR §135.225

ATS, RTC

8086. After passing the final approach fix on a VOR approach, a weather report is received indicating the visibility is below prescribed minimums. In this situation, the pilot

A— may continue the approach and land, if at the MDA, the actual weather conditions are at least equal to the minimums prescribed for the procedure.

B— may continue the approach and land regardless of the visibility observed at the MDA, if prior to beginning the approach, the visibility was reported at or above minimums.

C— should leveloff and continue to fly the approach to the MAP, and execute the missed approach.

If a pilot has begun the final approach segment of a VOR, NDB or comparable approach procedure and has passed the final approach fix when he/she receives a weather report indicating below minimum conditions, he/she may continue the approach and, if upon reaching the MDA finds the weather at least equal to the prescribed minimums, may land. (PLT379) — 14 CFR §135.225

ATS, RTC

8087. An alternate for a destination airport (circling not authorized) is not required if, for at least 1 hour before and after the ETA, the required visibility exists, and the forecast ceiling is at least

A— 1,500 feet above the lowest published minimum, or 2,000 feet above the airport elevation, whichever is higher.

B— 1,500 feet above the lowest MDA or 2,000 feet above the runway touchdown zone elevation, whichever is higher.

C— 1,000 feet above the lowest published minimum, or 1,500 feet above the airport elevation, whichever is higher.

An alternate airport need not be designated if the required visibility criteria exists and the ceiling is forecast to be at least 1,500 feet above the lowest circling approach MDA. If no circling approach is authorized the ceiling must be forecast to be 1,500 feet above the lowest published minimum, or 2,000 feet above the airport elevation, whichever is higher. (PLT380) — 14 CFR §135.223

Answers

8084 [C]	8085 [C]	8086 [A]	8087 [A]

ATS, RTC

8090. At a military airport, a pilot may not take off under IFR unless the reported weather conditions indicate that the

A— visibility is at least 1 mile.
B— ceiling is at least 500 feet and the visibility is 1 mile or more.
C— airport has landing minimums.

Each pilot making an IFR takeoff or approach and landing at a military or foreign airport shall comply with applicable instrument approach procedures and weather minimums prescribed by the authority having jurisdiction over that airport. In addition, no pilot may takeoff at that airport when the visibility is less than one mile. (PLT459) — 14 CFR §135.225

ATS, RTC

8091. A pilot may not take off under IFR at a foreign airport unless the visibility is

A— 1/2 mile or more above landing minimums.
B— 1 mile or more and the ceiling is 500 feet or more.
C— at least 1 mile.

Each pilot making an IFR takeoff or approach and landing at a military or foreign airport shall comply with applicable instrument approach procedures and weather minimums prescribed by the authority having jurisdiction over that airport. In addition, no pilot may takeoff at that airport when the visibility is less than one mile. (PLT459) — 14 CFR §135.225

ATS, RTC

8092. An instrument approach procedure to an airport may not be initiated unless the latest weather report issued by an authorized weather reporting facility indicates that weather conditions

A— are at or above the circling minimums for the runway the pilot intends to use.
B— are at or above the authorized IFR landing minimums for that procedure.
C— exceed the straight-in minimums for all nonprecision approaches.

No pilot may begin an instrument approach procedure to an airport unless the latest weather report issued by that weather reporting facility indicates that weather conditions are at or above the authorized IFR landing minimums for that airport. (PLT420) — 14 CFR §135.225

ATS, RTC

8114. What is the minimum ceiling and visibility for an airplane to operate under VFR in Class G airspace?

A— 2,000-foot ceiling; 1-mile visibility.
B— 2,000-foot ceiling; 1-mile flight visibility.
C— 1,000-foot ceiling; 2-miles flight visibility.

No person may operate an airplane under VFR in uncontrolled airspace when the ceiling is less than 1,000 feet unless flight visibility is at least 2 miles. (PLT163) — 14 CFR §135.205

ATS, RTC

8807. Which document would constitute an approved change to the type design without requiring a recertification?

A— An approved Minimum Equipment List.
B— The Operations Specifications as approved by the Administrator.
C— A special flight permit.

An approved Minimum Equipment List, as authorized by the operations specifications, constitutes an approved change to the type design without requiring recertification. (PLT428) — 14 CFR §135.179

ATS, RTC

8808. No person may operate an aircraft under 14 CFR Part 135, carrying passengers under VFR at night, unless

A— each flight crewmember has a flashlight having at least two size "D" batteries or the equivalent.
B— it is equipped with a flashlight having at least two size "D" cell or the equivalent.
C— each crewmember has a flashlight having at least two size "D" cells and a spare bulb.

No person may operate an aircraft carrying passengers under VFR at night unless it is equipped with a flashlight having at least two size "D" cells or equivalent. (PLT405) — 14 CFR §135.159

Answers

8090 [A]   8091 [C]   8092 [B]   8114 [C]   8807 [A]   8808 [B]

ATS, RTC

8809. For operations during the period beginning 1 hour after sunset and ending 1 hour before sunrise (as published in the Air Almanac), no certificate holder may use any person, nor may any person serve, as pilot in command of an aircraft carrying passengers unless that person has made three takeoffs and three landings, within the preceding 90 days,

A— as the sole manipulator of the flight controls in an aircraft of the same category and class and, if a type rating is required, of the same type in which that person is to serve.
B— as pilot in command of an aircraft of the same category and class and, if a type rating is required, of the same type in which that person is to serve.
C— as the sole manipulator of the flight controls in an aircraft of the same type in which that person is to serve.

No person may serve as pilot-in-command of an aircraft carrying passengers unless, within the preceding 90 days, that person has, for operation during the period beginning 1 hour after sunset and ending 1 hour before sunrise (as published in the air almanac), made 3 take-offs and 3 landings as the sole manipulator of the flight controls in an aircraft of the same category and class and, if a type rating is required, of the same type in which the person is to serve. (PLT442) — 14 CFR §135.247

ATS, RTC

8813. An employee who performs safety-sensitive functions, for a certificate holder, who has actual knowledge of an accident involving an aircraft for which he or she performed a safety-sensitive function at or near the time of the accident shall not use alcohol

A— until 4 hours after the accident.
B— within 8 hours of the accident.
C— until given a release by the NTSB or FAA.

No covered employee who has actual knowledge of an accident involving an aircraft for which he or she has performed a safety-sensitive function at or near the time of the accident shall use alcohol for 8 hours following the accident. (PLT463) — 14 CFR §135.253

ATS, RTC

8814. What is the maximum number of hours that a pilot may fly in 7 consecutive days as a pilot in commercial flying and as a pilot for a commuter air carrier?

A— 32 hours.
B— 34 hours.
C— 35 hours.

No certificate holder may schedule any flight crewmember for flight in scheduled operations if that crewmember's total time in commercial flying will exceed:

1. 1,200 hours in any calendar year.

2. 120 hours in any calendar month.

3. 34 hours in any seven consecutive days.

(PLT409) — 14 CFR §135.265

ATS, RTC

8815. What is the maximum number of hours that a commuter air carrier may schedule a flight crewmember to fly in scheduled operations and other commercial flying in any calendar month?

A— 100.
B— 110.
C— 120.

No certificate holder may schedule any flight crewmember for flight in scheduled operations if that crewmember's total time in commercial flying will exceed:

1. 1,200 hours in any calendar year.

2. 120 hours in any calendar month.

3. 34 hours in any seven consecutive days.

(PLT409) — 14 CFR §135.265

ATS, RTC

8819. The pilot in command may deviate from 14 CFR Part 135 during an emergency involving the safety of persons or property only

A— after ATC is notified of the emergency and the extent of deviation required.
B— to the extent required to meet that emergency.
C— if required to, by the emergency cockpit checklist.

In an emergency involving the safety of persons or property, the pilot-in-command may deviate from the rules of 14 CFR Part 135 to the extent required to meet that emergency. (PLT444) — 14 CFR §135.19

Answers

8809 [A]	8813 [B]	8814 [B]	8815 [C]	8819 [B]

ATS, RTC

8820. The training required for flight crewmembers who have not qualified and served in the same capacity on an aircraft is

A— upgrade training.
B— transition training.
C— initial training.

Initial training is the term used for the training required for crewmembers who have not qualified and served in the same capacity on an aircraft. (PLT407) — 14 CFR §135.321

ATS, RTC

8821. A crewmember who has served as second in command on a particular aircraft type (e.g., BE-1900), may serve as pilot in command upon completing which training program?

A— Upgrade training.
B— Transition training.
C— Initial training.

Upgrade training is the training required of crewmembers who have qualified and served as second-in-command on a particular aircraft before they serve as pilot-in-command of that aircraft. (PLT407) — 14 CFR §135.321

ATS, RTC

8827. The training required for crewmembers who have been qualified and served in the same capacity on another aircraft is

A— difference training.
B— transition training.
C— upgrade training.

Transition training is the training required of crewmembers who have qualified and served in the same capacity on another aircraft. (PLT407) — 14 CFR §135.321

ATS, RTC

8828. The certificate holder must give instruction on such subjects as respiration, hypoxia, gas expansion, and decompression to crewmembers who serve in operations above

A— FL 180.
B— FL 200.
C— FL 250.

Crewmembers who serve in operations above 25,000 feet must receive instruction in respiration, hypoxia, duration of consciousness without supplemental oxygen at altitude, gas expansion, gas bubble formation and physical phenomena and incidents of decompression. (PLT460) — 14 CFR §135.331

ATS, RTC

8829. The air carrier must give instruction on such subjects as gas bubble formation, hypoxia, decompression, and length of consciousness without supplemental oxygen at altitude to crewmembers serving on aircraft operated above

A— FL 250.
B— FL 200.
C— FL 180.

Crewmembers who serve in operations above 25,000 feet must receive instruction in respiration, hypoxia, duration of consciousness without supplemental oxygen at altitude, gas expansion, gas bubble formation and physical phenomena and incidents of decompression. (PLT407) — 14 CFR §135.331

ATS, RTC

8830. What is one of the requirements that must be met by a pilot in command to re-establish recency of experience?

A— At least one full stop landing must be made from a circling approach.
B— Three takeoffs and landings must be made as the sole manipulator of the controls, in the type, if a type rating is required, if not in the same category and class aircraft that the person is to serve.
C— At least one nonprecision approach must be made to the lowest minimums authorized for the certificate holder.

No person may serve as pilot-in-command of an aircraft carrying passengers unless, within the preceding 90 days, that person has made 3 takeoffs and 3 landings as the sole manipulator of the flight controls in an aircraft of the same category and class and, if a type rating is required, of the same type in which the person is to serve. (PLT442) — 14 CFR §135.247

Answers

8820 [C]   8821 [A]   8827 [B]   8828 [C]   8829 [A]   8830 [B]

ATS, RTC
8834. Federal Aviation Regulations require that interior emergency lights, on aircraft having a passenger seating configuration of 20 to

A— operate automatically when subjected to a negative G load.
B— be operable manually from the flight crew station and a point in the passenger compartment.
C— be armed or turned on during taxiing and all flight operations.

Emergency exit lights must be operable manually from the flight crew station and from a station in the passenger compartment that is readily accessible to a normal flight attendant seat. (PLT404) — 14 CFR §135.178

Answer (A) is incorrect because the lights must operate automatically either with loss of normal electrical power or when an emergency assist means is activated, depending on the aircraft certification. Answer (C) is incorrect because the lights must be armed or turned on during taxi, takeoff and landing but not necessarily during all other flight operations.

ATS, RTC
8838. What emergency equipment is required for extended overwater operations?

A— A portable survival emergency locator transmitter for each life raft.
B— A pyrotechnic signaling device for each life preserver.
C— A life preserver equipped with a survivor locator light, for each person on the airplane.

Every aircraft flown in extended overwater operations must carry an approved life preserver for every occupant of the aircraft. This life preserver must be equipped with an approved survivor locator light. A life preserver must be readily accessible to each seated occupant. In addition, there must be enough appropriately equipped life rafts to accommodate all the occupants of the aircraft. One of the life rafts must have a survival type emergency locator transmitter. (PLT437) — 14 CFR §135.167

ATS, RTC
8840. Each aircraft being operated in extended overwater operations, must have a life preserver for each

A— aircraft occupant.
B— seat on the aircraft.
C— passenger seat, plus 10 percent.

Every aircraft flown in extended overwater operations must carry an approved life preserver for every occupant of the aircraft. (PLT437) — 14 CFR §135.167

ATS, RTC
8841. Life preservers required for extended overwater operations are stored

A— within easy reach of each passenger.
B— under each occupant seat.
C— within easy access of each seated occupant.

Every aircraft flown in extended overwater operations must carry an approved life preserver for every occupant of the aircraft. A life preserver must be readily accessible to each seated occupant. (PLT437) — 14 CFR §135.167

ATS, RTC
8843. No person may takeoff an aircraft under IFR from an airport that has takeoff weather minimums but that is below landing minimums unless there is an alternate airport within

A— 1 hour at normal indicated airspeed of the departure airport.
B— 1 hour at normal cruise speed in still air of the departure airport.
C— 1 hour at normal cruise speed in still air with one engine operating.

No person may takeoff an aircraft under IFR from an airport where weather conditions are at or above takeoff minimums, but are below authorized IFR landing minimums unless there is an alternate airport within 1 hour's flying time (in still air) of the airport of departure. (PLT459) — 14 CFR §135.217

Answers

8834 [B]   8838 [C]   8840 [A]   8841 [C]   8843 [B]

Helicopter Regulations

RTC

8002. What minimum rest period must be provided for a pilot assigned to Helicopter Hospital Emergency Medical Evacuation Service (HEMES) who has been on duty for a 47 hour period?

A— 16 consecutive hours.
B— 14 consecutive hours.
C— 12 consecutive hours.

Each pilot must be given a rest period upon completion of the HEMES assignment and prior to being assigned any further duty with the certificate holder of at least 12 consecutive hours for an assignment of less than 48 hours, and at least 16 consecutive hours for an assignment of more than 48 hours. (PLT409) — 14 CFR §135.271

RTC

9043. What is a helicopter pilot's responsibility when cleared to "air taxi" on the airport?

A— Taxi direct to destination as quickly as possible.
B— Taxi at hover altitude using taxiways.
C— Taxi below 100 feet AGL avoiding other aircraft and personnel.

Air taxi is the preferred method for helicopter ground movements on airports. Unless otherwise requested or instructed, pilots are expected to remain below 100 feet AGL. Helicopters should avoid overflight of other aircraft, vehicles, and personnel during air taxi operations. (PLT112) — AIM ¶4-3-17

RTC

9336. What minimum instrument experience in the past 6 calendar months meets the second-in-command requirement to maintain IFR currency in a helicopter?

A— 6 hours in actual IFR conditions or 3 hours actual and 3 hours simulated IFR in a helicopter plus six instrument approaches.
B— Holding procedures, intercepting and tracking courses using the navigation equipment, six instrument approaches logged in actual or simulated IFR in a helicopter, simulator or a flight training device.
C— 6 hours of actual or simulated time in a helicopter of the same type, plus six instrument approaches.

For flight under IFR, the second-in-command must meet the recent instrument requirements of Part 61: No pilot may act as pilot-in-command under IFR unless the pilot has performed and logged, within the past 6 calendar months, at least 6 instrument approaches, holding procedures, and intercepting and tracking courses through the use of navigation systems in the appropriate category of aircraft for the instrument privileges sought. (PLT442) — 14 CFR §135.245 and §61.57

RTC

9337. What minimum conditions are necessary for the instrument approaches required for second-in-command IFR currency in a helicopter?

A— Six must be performed and logged under actual or simulated instrument conditions in a rotorcraft.
B— Six must be performed and logged under actual or simulated instrument conditions; three must be in a rotorcraft, three may be in an airplane or an approved flight simulator.
C— All must be made in a rotorcraft category of aircraft, or approved simulator, or flight training device and logged while under actual or simulated IFR conditions.

For flight under IFR, the second-in-command must meet the recent instrument requirements of Part 61: No pilot may act as pilot-in-command under IFR unless the pilot has performed and logged, within the past 6 calendar months, at least 6 instrument approaches, holding procedures, and intercepting and tracking courses through the use of navigation systems in the appropriate category of aircraft for the instrument privileges sought. (PLT442) — 14 CFR §135.245 and §61.57

Answers

8002　[C]　　　9043　[C]　　　9336　[B]　　　9337　[C]

RTC

9338. Within the past 6 months, a pilot has accomplished:

Two approaches in a helicopter.
Two approaches in an airplane.
Two approaches in a glider.

What additional instrument experience must the pilot obtain prior to acting as second in command (under 14 CFR part 135) on an IFR flight?

A— Four approaches in an aircraft, approved training device, flight simulator (that is representative of the aircraft category), holding, intercepting and tracking courses using the navigation systems.
B— Passes an instrument proficiency check in any category aircraft, approved simulator or training device.
C— Holding, intercepting and tracking courses (using the navigation systems) in an aircraft, approved simulator or approved flight training device.

For flight under IFR, the second-in-command must meet the recent instrument requirements of Part 61: No pilot may act as pilot-in-command under IFR unless the pilot has performed and logged, within the past 6 calendar months, at least 6 instrument approaches, holding procedures, and intercepting and tracking courses through the use of navigation systems in the appropriate category of aircraft for the instrument privileges sought. (PLT442) — 14 CFR §135.245 and §61.57

RTC

9341. Within the past 6 months, a pilot has accomplished:

Two approaches and intercepting, tracking courses using the navigation systems in a helicopter.
Two approaches, missed approaches and holding in an approved airplane flight simulator.
Two approaches and holding in an approved rotorcraft flight training device.

What additional instrument experience, if any, must the pilot perform to act as second in command (under 14 CFR part 135) on an IFR helicopter flight?

A— None.
B— Two approaches in a rotorcraft category aircraft.
C— Two approaches in either a helicopter or an airplane.

For flight under IFR, the second-in-command must meet the recent instrument requirements of Part 61: No pilot may act as pilot-in-command under IFR unless the pilot has performed and logged, within the past 6 calendar months, at least 6 instrument approaches, holding procedures, and intercepting and tracking courses through the use of navigation systems in the appropriate category of aircraft for the instrument privileges sought. (PLT442) — 14 CFR §135.245, §61.57

RTC

9366. Unless otherwise prescribed, what is the rule regarding altitude and course to be maintained by a helicopter during an off-airways IFR flight over non-mountainous terrain?

A— 1,000 feet above the highest obstacle within 4 nautical miles of course.
B— 2,000 feet above the highest obstacle within 5 statute miles of course.
C— 1,500 feet above the highest obstacle within a horizontal distance of 3 statute miles of course.

In the case of operations over areas that are not designated as mountainous areas; no person may operate an aircraft under IFR below an altitude of 1,000 feet above the highest obstacle within a horizontal distance of 4 nautical miles from the course to be flown. (PLT430) — 14 CFR §91.177

RTC

9367. Unless otherwise prescribed, what is the rule regarding altitude and course to be maintained by a helicopter during an IFR off-airways flight over mountainous terrain?

A— 1,000 feet above the highest obstacle within a horizontal distance of 5 statute miles of course.
B— 2,500 feet above the highest obstacle within a horizontal distance of 3 nautical miles of course.
C— 2,000 feet above the highest obstacle within 5 statute miles of course.

In the case of operations over areas designated as mountainous; no person may operate an aircraft under IFR below an altitude of 2,000 feet above the highest obstacle within a horizontal distance of 5 statute miles from the course to be flown. (PLT430) — 14 CFR §91.177

Answers

9338   [A]   9341   [B]   9366   [A]   9367   [C]

RTC
9371. According to 14 CFR Part 91, when takeoff minimums are not prescribed for a civil airport, what are the takeoff minimums under IFR for a multiengine helicopter?

A— 1 SM visibility.
B— 1/2 SM visibility.
C— 1200 RVR.

If takeoff minimums are not prescribed under Part 97, the takeoff minimums under IFR for helicopters are 1/2 statute mile visibility. (PLT459) — 14 CFR §91.175

RTC
9372. According to 14 CFR Part 91, when takeoff minimums are not prescribed for a civil airport, what are the takeoff minimums under IFR for a single-engine helicopter?

A— 1/2 SM visibility.
B— 1 SM visibility.
C— 1200 RVR.

If takeoff minimums are not prescribed under Part 97, the takeoff minimums under IFR for helicopters are 1/2 statute mile visibility. (PLT459) — 14 CFR §91.175

RTC
9373. What minimum altitude should a helicopter maintain while en route?

A— Over congested areas such as towns, no lower than 1,000 feet over the highest obstacle within a horizontal radius of 2,000 feet of the helicopter.
B— That specifically prescribed by the air carrier for the operation.
C— That prescribed by the Administrator.

Each person operating a helicopter shall comply with routes or altitudes specifically prescribed for helicopters by the Administrator. (PLT430) — 14 CFR §91.119

RTC
9414. In addition to a two-way radio capable of communicating with ATC on appropriate frequencies, which equipment is the helicopter required to have to operate within Class B airspace? (Letter of agreement not applicable.)

A— A VOR or TACAN receiver.
B— DME, a VOR or TACAN receiver, and an appropriate transponder beacon.
C— An appropriate ATC transponder.

An operable ATC transponder is required to operate all aircraft in Class B airspace except for helicopters operated at or below 1,000 feet AGL under the terms of a letter of agreement. (PLT405) — 14 CFR §91.131 and §91.215

RTC
9415. Which of the following is a transponder requirement for helicopter operations?

A— Helicopters with a certified gross weight of more than 12,500 pounds that are engaged in commercial operations are required to be equipped with operable ATC transponders.
B— Helicopters may not be operated at or below 1,000 feet AGL within Class B airspace without an operable ATC transponder.
C— Operable ATC transponders are required when operating helicopters within Class D airspace at night under special VFR.

An operable ATC transponder is required to operate all aircraft in Class B airspace except as authorized by ATC. (PLT405) — 14 CFR §91.215

RTC
8975. Which of the following are required for a helicopter ILS approach with a decision height lower than 200 feet HAT?

A— Special aircrew training and aircraft certification.
B— Both a marker beacon and a radio altimeter.
C— ATP helicopter certificate and CAT II certification.

Approaches with a HAT below 200 feet are annotated with the note: "Special Aircraft & Aircraft Certification Required" since the FAA must approve the helicopter and its avionics, and the flight crew must have the required experience, training, and checking. (PLT356) — FAA-H-8083-16

Answers

9371 [B]	9372 [A]	9373 [C]	9414 [C]	9415 [B]	8975 [A]

Chapter 2
Equipment, Navigation and Facilities

Inoperative Equipment

A certificate holder's manual must contain enroute flight, navigation and communication procedures, including procedures for the dispatch, release or continuance of a flight if a required piece of equipment becomes inoperative.

When any required instrument or equipment in an aircraft is inoperative, the airplane cannot be flown unless that aircraft's **Minimum Equipment List (MEL)** allows such a flight.

The pilot-in-command of an aircraft operating IFR in controlled airspace shall report to ATC immediately any malfunction of navigational, approach or communications equipment that occurs in flight. The report must include:

- Aircraft identification;

- Equipment affected;

- Degree to which the capability of the aircraft to operate IFR in the ATC system is impaired; and

- Nature and extent of assistance desired from ATC.

ALL

9407. An approved minimum equipment list or FAA Letter of Authorization allows certain instruments or equipment

A— to be inoperative prior to beginning a flight in an aircraft if prescribed procedures are followed.
B— to be inoperative anytime with no other documentation required or procedures to be followed.
C— to be inoperative for a one-time ferry flight of a large airplane to a maintenance base without further documentation from the operator or FAA with passengers on board.

The Minimum Equipment List and the letter of authorization constitute a supplemental type certificate for the aircraft. The approved Minimum Equipment List must provide for the operation of the aircraft with the instruments and equipment in an inoperable condition (PLT405) — 14 CFR §91.213

ALL

9380. What action is necessary when a partial loss of ILS receiver capability occurs while operating in controlled airspace under IFR?

A— Continue as cleared and file a written report to the Administrator if requested.
B— If the aircraft is equipped with other radios suitable for executing an instrument approach, no further action is necessary.
C— Report the malfunction immediately to ATC.

The pilot-in-command of an aircraft operating IFR in controlled airspace shall report to ATC as soon as practical any malfunction of navigational, approach or communication equipment that occurs in flight. (PLT356) — 14 CFR §91.187

Answer (A) is incorrect because any malfunction of approach equipment must be reported in flight, not by a written report. Answer (B) is incorrect because, although another type of instrument approach may be executed if permission is granted by ATC, any malfunction of approach equipment should be reported.

ALL

9381. What action should be taken if one of the two VHF radios fail while IFR in controlled airspace?

A— Notify ATC immediately.
B— Squawk 7600.
C— Monitor the VOR receiver.

The pilot-in-command of an aircraft operating IFR in controlled airspace shall report to ATC as soon as practical any malfunction of navigational, approach or communication equipment that occurs in flight. (PLT162) — 14 CFR §91.187

Answer (B) is incorrect because, although you have experienced a communications failure, it is only a partial one. You still have one operational VHF radio and all other radios are working normally, so a squawk of 7600 is not needed. Answer (C) is incorrect because you still have an operable VHF radio for communication, so monitoring of a NAVAID is not needed. The only pilot action required is notification to ATC of the problem.

Answers

9407 [A] 9380 [C] 9381 [A]

ALL

9386. While flying IFR in controlled airspace, if one of the two VOR receivers fails, which course of action should the pilot-in-command follow?

A— No call is required if one of the two VOR receivers is operating properly.
B— Advise ATC immediately.
C— Notify the dispatcher via company frequency.

The pilot-in-command of an aircraft operating IFR in controlled airspace shall report to ATC as soon as practical any malfunction of navigational, approach or communication equipment that occurs in flight. (PLT406) — 14 CFR §91.187

Answer (A) is incorrect because any malfunction of a navigational radio should be reported, no matter how slightly it may affect the conduct of the flight. Answer (C) is incorrect because, although this may be a common practice among the air carriers, the regulations require notification to ATC of the malfunction.

ALL

9387. While flying in controlled airspace under IFR, the ADF fails. What action is required?

A— Descend below Class A airspace.
B— Advise dispatch via company frequency.
C— Notify ATC immediately.

The pilot-in-command of an aircraft operating IFR in controlled airspace shall report to ATC as soon as practical any malfunction of navigational, approach or communication equipment that occurs in flight. (PLT406) — 14 CFR §91.187

Answer (A) is incorrect because controlled airspace exists far below positive control airspace (base of 18,000 feet MSL), and any loss of a navigational aid should be reported to ATC. Answer (B) is incorrect because, although this may be a common practice among the air carriers, the regulations require notification to ATC of the malfunction.

ATM, DSP

8278. If a required instrument on a multiengine airplane becomes inoperative, which document dictates whether the flight may continue en route?

A— A Master Minimum Equipment List for the airplane.
B— Original dispatch release.
C— Certificate holder's manual.

Each certificate holder's manual must contain enroute flight, navigation, and communication procedures for the dispatch, release or continuance of flight if any item of equipment required for the particular type of operation becomes inoperative or unserviceable en route. (PLT436) — 14 CFR §121.135

Pitot-Static Instruments

Modern jet transports usually have three pitot-static systems. There are separate systems for the captain's and co-pilot's instruments plus an auxiliary system that provides a backup for either of the two primary systems. The instruments that require static pressure input are **airspeed, Mach, altitude** and **vertical speed indicators**. In addition, the airspeed and Mach indicators need a source of pitot pressure. Besides the flight instruments, static pressure input is required for the Mach warning, autopilot, flight director, flight recorder and cabin differential pressure. Pitot input is required for all those systems except for cabin differential pressure. The usual source for these non-flight instruments is the auxiliary pitot-static system. *See* Figure 2-1.

Altimeters compare the sea level pressure setting in their window with the outside air pressure sensed through the static system. The difference is displayed as the altitude above sea level. Part of the preflight check is to verify the accuracy of the altimeters. An altimeter should be considered questionable if the indicated altitude varies by more the 75 feet from a known field elevation.

The altimeter setting used by pilots is always the station pressure of the reporting station corrected to sea level. **Station pressure** is the actual pressure at field elevation.

True altitude is the actual height of the aircraft above sea level. This is the same as indicated altitude when standard temperatures exist. When the temperature is warmer than standard, true altitude is higher than indicated altitude. When the temperature is colder than standard day conditions, just the opposite is true. Corrected altitude (approximately true altitude) can be calculated but it is neither practical

Answers

9386   [B]   9387   [C]   8278   [C]

nor useful to do so in most situations. When setting an altimeter, a pilot should just use the appropriate altimeter setting and disregard the effects of nonstandard atmospheric pressures and temperatures.

Pressure altitude is the altitude indicated when the altimeter is set to standard sea level pressure of 29.92" Hg. Density altitude is used in aircraft performance computations. It is pressure altitude corrected for nonstandard temperatures. If the temperature is warmer than standard, density altitude will be higher than pressure altitude.

The local altimeter setting is used when flying below FL180 and the altimeter is 31.00" Hg or less. Special procedures apply when the local pressure is more than 31.00" Hg because most altimeters cannot be set higher than that. In the United States, all altimeters are set to 29.92" Hg when climbing through FL180. Caution: outside the United States the transition altitude is often something other than FL180.

A common reason for altimeter errors is incorrect setting of the altimeter. If the setting in the altimeter is higher than the actual sea level pressure, the altimeter will read higher than the actual altitude. If the setting is too low, the altimeter will read lower than it really is. As a rough rule of thumb, the magnitude of the error is about 1,000 feet for each 1" Hg that the altimeter is off. For example, if the altimeter is set to 29.92" Hg, but the real sea level pressure is 30.57" Hg, the altimeter will read about 650 feet lower than the actual airplane's altitude (30.57 − 29.92 = .65" Hg = 650 feet). In this example, the airplane would be 650 feet higher than the indicated altitude.

Continued

Figure 2-1. Typical pitot-static system

The airspeed indicators compare pitot pressure with static pressure and display the difference as **indicated airspeed**. This indicated airspeed equals the aircraft's actual speed through the air (True Airspeed) only under standard day conditions at sea level. Under almost all flight conditions, true airspeed will be higher than indicated airspeed because of the lower ambient pressures at altitude.

The Machmeter displays aircraft speed as a percentage of the speed of sound. For example, an aircraft cruising at a Mach number of .82 is flying at 82% of the speed of sound. The Machmeter works in a manner similar to the airspeed indicator in that it compares pitot and static pressure, but these inputs are corrected by an altimeter mechanism.

If a pitot tube becomes blocked, the airspeed and Mach indicators will read inaccurately. If pressure is trapped in the pitot line, the airspeed will read inaccurately high as the aircraft climbs, low as it descends, and will be unresponsive to changes in airspeed. The airspeed indicator acts as an altimeter because only the static pressure changes. This situation occurs in icing conditions if both the ram air inlet and the drain hole of the pitot tube become completely blocked by ice.

If the pitot tube is blocked but the static port and the pitot drain hole remain open, the indicated airspeed will drop to zero. The drain pitot tube drain hole allows the pressure in the pitot line to drop to atmospheric and therefore there is no differential between the static and pitot pressures.

Pitot tubes and static ports are electrically heated to prevent ice formations that could interfere with proper operation of the systems. They are required to have "power on" indicator lights to show proper operation. In addition, many aircraft have an ammeter that shows the actual current flow to the pitot and static ports.

Since the magnetic compass is the only direction-seeking instrument in most airplanes, the pilot must be able to turn the airplane to a magnetic compass heading and maintain this heading. It is influenced by magnetic dip which causes northerly turning error and acceleration/deceleration error. When northerly turning error occurs, the compass will lag behind the actual aircraft heading while turning through headings in the northern half of the compass rose, and lead the aircraft's actual heading in the southern half. The error is most pronounced when turning through north or south, and is approximately equal in degrees to the latitude.

The acceleration/deceleration error is most pronounced on headings of east and west. When accelerating, the compass indicates a turn toward the north, and when decelerating it indicates a turn toward the south. The acronym **ANDS** is a good memory aid:

A accelerate

N north

D decelerate

S south

No errors are apparent while on east or west headings, when turning either north or south.

ALL

9174. Which pressure is defined as station pressure?

A— Altimeter setting.
B— Actual pressure at field elevation.
C— Station barometric pressure reduced to sea level.

The pressure measured at a station or airport is "station pressure" or the actual pressure at field elevation. (PLT166) — AC 00-6

Answer (A) is incorrect because altimeter setting is the value to which the scale of a pressure altimeter is adjusted to read field elevation. Answer (C) is incorrect because station barometric pressure reduced to sea level is a method to readily compare station pressures between stations at different altitudes.

ALL

9164. What is corrected altitude (approximate true altitude)?

A— Pressure altitude corrected for instrument error.
B— Indicated altitude corrected for temperature variation from standard.
C— Density altitude corrected for temperature variation from standard.

True altitude is indicated altitude corrected for the fact that nonstandard temperatures will result in nonstandard pressure lapse rates. (PLT023) — AC 00-6

Answer (A) is incorrect because pressure altitude corrected for instrument error is a nonexistent concept. Answer (C) is incorrect because density altitude is pressure altitude corrected for temperature variation from standard. Density altitude is a final figure and not subject to additional adjustments.

ALL

9099. When setting the altimeter, pilots should disregard

A— effects of nonstandard atmospheric temperatures and pressures.
B— corrections for static pressure systems.
C— corrections for instrument error.

Pilots should disregard the effect of nonstandard atmospheric temperatures and pressures except that low temperatures and pressures need to be considered for terrain clearance purposes. (PLT166) — AIM ¶7-2-2

Answers (B) and (C) are incorrect because altimeters are subject to instrument errors and to errors in the static pressure system. A pilot should set the current reported altimeter setting on the altimeter setting scale. The altimeter should read within 75 feet of field elevation. If not, it is questionable and should be evaluated by a repair station.

ALL

9173. If the ambient temperature is colder than standard at FL310, what is the relationship between true altitude and pressure altitude?

A— They are both the same, 31,000 feet.
B— True altitude is lower than 31,000 feet.
C— Pressure altitude is lower than true altitude.

True altitude is indicated altitude corrected for the fact that nonstandard temperatures will result in nonstandard pressure lapse rates. In warm air, you fly at a true altitude higher than indicated. In cold air, you fly at a true altitude lower than indicated. Pressure altitude is the altitude indicated when the altimeter is set to the standard sea level pressure (29.92" Hg). In the United States, altimeters are always set to 29.92" Hg at and above 18,000 feet. This question assumes the difference between the pressure altitude and the indicated altitude (local altimeter setting) is not significant enough to reverse the effects of the temperature. (PLT023) — AC 00-6

Answer (A) is incorrect because both true and pressure altitude would be the same at FL310 if the ambient air temperature was standard. Answer (C) is incorrect because pressure altitude would be lower than true altitude in warmer than standard air temperature.

ALL

9173-1. When the temperature is -20°C at 15,000 feet indicated, you know that

A— altimeters automatically compensate for temperature variations.
B— the altimeter is indicating higher than true altitude.
C— the altimeter is indicating lower than true altitude.

The ISA for 15,000 feet is -15°C. When the temperature is colder than standard, the altimeter will indicate higher than true altitude. (PLT023) — AC 00-6

Answers

9174 [B]	9164 [B]	9099 [A]	9173 [B]	9173-1 [B]

ALL
9172. If the ambient temperature is warmer than standard at FL350, what is the density altitude compared to pressure altitude?

A— Lower than pressure altitude.
B— Higher than pressure altitude.
C— Impossible to determine without information on possible inversion layers at lower altitudes.

Pressure altitude is the altitude indicated when the altimeter is set to the standard sea level pressure (29.92" Hg). Density altitude is pressure altitude corrected for nonstandard temperature. A warmer than standard temperature will result in a density altitude higher than the pressure altitude. (PLT023) — AC 00-6

Answer (A) is incorrect because density altitude is higher when air temperature is warmer than standard. Answer (C) is incorrect because density altitude is pressure altitude corrected for nonstandard temperatures. Pressure altitude is based on a standard pressure atmosphere at a particular altitude, and inversion layers at lower levels have no effect on pressure altitude.

ALL
9813. Given

Pressure altitude... 1,000 ft
True air temperature... 10°C

From the conditions given, the approximate density altitude is

A— 1,000 feet MSL
B— 650 feet MSL
C— 450 feet MSL

1. *Using an E6B flight computer, refer to the right-hand "Density Altitude" window. Note that the scale above the window is labeled air temperature (°C). The scale inside the window itself is labeled pressure altitude (in thousands of feet). Rotate the disc and place the pressure altitude of 1,000 feet opposite an air temperature of 10°C.*

2. *The density altitude shown in the window is 650 feet.*

You can also answer this using an electronic flight computer, such as the CX-3. Select Altitude from the CX-3 FLT menu. (PLT005) — AC 00-6

ALL
9163. En route at FL270, the altimeter is set correctly. On descent, a pilot fails to set the local altimeter setting of 30.57. If the field elevation is 650 feet, and the altimeter is functioning properly, what will it indicate upon landing?

A— 585 feet.
B— 1,300 feet.
C— Sea level.

One inch of Hg pressure is equal to about 1,000 feet of altitude. In the United States, altimeters are always set to 29.92" Hg at and above 18,000 feet. If the altimeter is not reset when descending into an area with a local altimeter setting of 30.57" Hg, an error of 650 feet will result (30.57 – 29.92 = .65 = 650 feet). If the altimeter is set lower than the actual setting, it will read lower than the actual altitude. (PLT166) — AC 00-6

Answer (A) is incorrect because 585 feet is the result of subtracting 65 feet rather than subtracting 650 feet. Answer (B) is incorrect because 1,300 feet is the result of adding 650 feet rather than subtracting 650 feet.

ALL
9080. During an en route descent in a fixed-thrust and fixed-pitch attitude configuration, both the ram air input and drain hole of the pitot system become completely blocked by ice. What airspeed indication can be expected?

A— Increase in indicated airspeed.
B— Decrease in indicated airspeed.
C— Indicated airspeed remains at the value prior to icing.

If both the ram air input and the drain hole are blocked, the pressure trapped in the pitot line cannot change and the airspeed indicator may react as an altimeter. The airspeed will not change in level flight even when actual airspeed is varied by large power changes. During a climb the airspeed indication will increase. During a descent the airspeed indication will decrease. (PLT128) — AC 91-43

Answer (A) is incorrect because indicated airspeed will decrease in a descent. Answer (C) is incorrect because indicated airspeed will remain at the same value during level flight.

Answers

9172   [B]   9813   [B]   9163   [C]   9080   [B]

ALL

9081. What can a pilot expect if the pitot system ram air input and drain hole are blocked by ice?

A— The airspeed indicator may act as an altimeter.
B— The airspeed indicator will show a decrease with an increase in altitude.
C— No airspeed indicator change will occur during climbs or descents.

If both the ram air input and the drain hole are blocked, the pressure trapped in the pitot line cannot change and the airspeed indicator may react as an altimeter. The airspeed will not change in level flight even when actual airspeed is varied by large power changes. During a climb the airspeed indication will increase. During a descent the airspeed indication will decrease. (PLT337) — AC 91-43

Answer (B) is incorrect because the airspeed indicator will show an increase (not decrease) with an increase in altitude. Answer (C) is incorrect because differential pressure between the pitot tube and static air source changes, and so does indicated airspeed.

ALL

9082. If both the ram air input and drain hole of the pitot system are blocked by ice, what airspeed indication can be expected?

A— No variation of indicated airspeed in level flight if large power changes are made.
B— Decrease of indicated airspeed during a climb.
C— Constant indicated airspeed during a descent.

If both the ram air input and the drain hole are blocked, the pressure trapped in the pitot line cannot change and the airspeed indicator may react as an altimeter. The airspeed will not change in level flight even when actual airspeed is varied by large power changes. During a climb the airspeed indication will increase. During a descent the airspeed indication will decrease. (PLT337) — AC 91-43

Answer (B) is incorrect because, during a climb, it will indicate an increase due to the stronger differential pressure in the blocked pitot tube relative to the static vents. Answer (C) is incorrect because indicated airspeed would change with changes in altitude.

ALL

9222. How will the airspeed indicator react if the ram air input to the pitot head is blocked by ice, but the drain hole and static port are not?

A— Indication will drop to zero.
B— Indication will rise to the top of the scale.
C— Indication will remain constant but will increase in a climb.

If the pitot tube becomes blocked but pressure is not trapped in the pitot lines, the indicated airspeed will drop to zero since the pitot pressure will be approximately equal to the static pressure. (PLT337) — AC 00-6

Answer (B) is incorrect because the airspeed indication will drop if only the ram air input is blocked. Answer (C) is incorrect because the pressure in the airspeed line will vent out through the hole and the indication will drop to zero.

Answers

9081 [A]   9082 [A]   9222 [A]

Electronic Flight Instruments

Electronic flight instrument systems integrate many individual instruments into a single presentation called a primary flight display (PFD). Flight instrument presentations on a PFD differ from conventional instrumentation not only in format, but sometimes in location as well. For example, the attitude indicator on the PFD is often larger than conventional round-dial presentations of an artificial horizon. Airspeed and altitude indications are presented on vertical tape displays that appear on the left and right sides of the primary flight display. The vertical speed indicator is depicted using conventional analog presentation. Turn coordination is shown using a segmented triangle near the top of the attitude indicator. The rate-of-turn indicator appears as a curved line display at the top of the heading/navigation instrument in the lower half of the PFD.

Figure 2-2. A typical primary flight display (PFD)

ALL

8206. (*See* Figure shown below.) You see the indication in the figure on your PFD, but your standby indicator reads 120 knots and the power is set for 120-knot cruise in level flight. You decide the

A— pitot tube may be plugged with ice or a bug.
B— standby indicator is defective because there is no red 'X' on the speed tape display.
C— airspeed means attitude is incorrect.

The airspeed indicator on the PFD is indicating a TAS of 64 knots. If this instrument had failed, the numbers would be replaced with a large red X. The stand-by airspeed indicator reading 120 knots suggests this instrument is working fine. The line coming out of the pitot tube splits to feed multiple instruments. The most likely culprit is a bug or ice blockage occurring past the split, in the line that feeds the Air Data Computer (ADC) for the PFD. This would allow the stand-by gauge to work properly, but cause the ASI on the PFD to give a false indication. True Airspeed is calculated in the ADC by correcting CAS with OAT probe data, so this explains why

Question 8206

the TAS is correspondingly low. The pitot lines need to be cleared; applying pitot heat may or may not help at this point. (PLT524) — FAA-H-8083-6

Answer (B) is incorrect because you cannot assume the standby is failed if you have cruise power and level attitude; the red Xs appear on the speed tape when the ADC fails or when one of the pressure transducers fail. Answer (C) is incorrect because an attitude instrument savvy pilot would discern attitude correctness by cross referencing other instruments and hearing the pitch of the engine would decide that power and a level attitude must be an indicator problem and have nothing to do with attitude correctness.

ALL

9769. Automated flight decks or cockpits

A— enhance basic pilot flight skills.
B— decrease the workload in terminal areas.
C— often create much larger pilot errors than traditional cockpits.

Advanced avionics were designed to increase safety as well as the utility of the aircraft, particularly during increased workload phases, such as in the terminal areas. (PLT524) — FAA-H-8083-6

Answer (A) is incorrect because automation has been shown to erode some flying skills when they are not kept proficient. Answer (C) is incorrect because while automation can make some errors more evident and hide others, it does not result in larger pilot errors than traditional cockpits.

Answers

8206   [A]   9769   [B]

ALL

9769-1. Automated flight decks or cockpits

A— improve basic flight skills.
B— decrease the workload in terminal areas.
C— sometimes hide errors.

Automation can make some errors more evident and hide others. (PLT524) — FAA-H-8083-6

ALL

9769-2. When flying an aircraft with electronic flight displays (EFDs), risk increases

A— if the pilot expects the electronics to enhance flight safety and remove pilot error.
B— when the pilot expects the equipment to malfunction on occasion.
C— if the pilot believes the EFD will compensate for lack of skill and knowledge.

Automation has been shown to erode some flying skills when they are not kept proficient. (PLT524) — FAA-H-8083-6

ALL

9830. Automation has been found to

A— create higher workloads in terminal areas.
B— improve crew situational awareness skills.
C— substitute for a lack of aviation experience.

Advanced avionics were designed to increase safety as well as the utility of the aircraft. Safety is enhanced by enabling better situational awareness. (PLT104) — FAA-H-8083-6

ALL

9853. When a pilot believes advanced avionics enable operations closer to personal or environmental limits,

A— greater utilization of the aircraft is achieved.
B— risk is increased.
C— risk is decreased.

Advanced avionics can sometimes have a negative effect on pilot risk-taking behavior, where more information results in pilots taking more risk than they might be willing to accept without the information. Advanced avionics should be used to increase safety, not risk. (PLT104) — FAA-H-8083-6

ALL

9854. Automation in aircraft has proven

A— to present new hazards in its limitations.
B— that automation is basically flawless.
C— effective in preventing accidents.

Advanced avionics were designed to increase safety as well as the utility of the aircraft. However, the systems are not infallible. While automation does help prevent many existing types of errors, it has also created new kinds of errors. (PLT104) — FAA-H-8083-6

ALL

9855. The lighter workloads associated with glass (digital) flight instrumentation

A— are useful in decreasing flightcrew fatigue.
B— have proven to increase safety in operations.
C— may lead to complacency by the flightcrew.

Risk management is the last of the three flight management skills needed for mastery of the advanced avionics aircraft. The enhanced situational awareness and automation capabilities offered by a glass flight deck vastly expand its safety and utility, especially for personal transportation use. At the same time, there is some risk that lighter workloads could lead to complacency. (PLT104) — FAA-H-8083-2

ALL

9857. Humans are characteristically

A— disposed to appreciate the workload imposed by automation.
B— disposed to expect automation to fail often.
C— poor monitors of automated systems.

Humans are characteristically poor monitors of automated systems. When passively monitoring an automated system for faults, abnormalities, or other infrequent events, humans perform poorly. The more reliable the system is, the worse the human performance becomes. For example, the pilot monitors only a backup alert system, rather than the situation that the alert system is designed to safeguard. It is a paradox of automation that technically advanced avionics can both increase and decrease pilot awareness. (PLT104) — FAA-H-8083-2

Answers

9769-1 [C]	9769-2 [C]	9830 [B]	9853 [B]	9854 [A]	9855 [C]
9857 [C]					

ALL
8711. Reliance on automation can translate to

A— decreased cockpit workload.
B— increased error awareness.
C— lack of manual handling skills.

A reliance on automation translates into a lack of basic flying skills that may affect the pilot's ability to cope with an in-flight emergency, such as a sudden mechanical failure. (PLT104) — FAA-8083-25

Safety of Flight Equipment

Airborne weather radar is used to detect and avoid areas of heavy precipitation such as thunderstorms. With few exceptions, all air carrier aircraft must be equipped with an approved airborne weather radar unit. The radar must be in satisfactory operating condition prior to dispatch on an IFR or night VFR flight if thunderstorms (or other hazardous weather) that could be detected by the radar are forecast along the intended route of flight. An aircraft may be dispatched with an inoperative radar unit if one of two conditions is met:

• The flight will be able to remain in day VFR flight conditions, or

• Hazardous weather is not forecast.

An air carrier's operations manual must contain procedures for the flight crew to follow if the weather radar fails in flight.

A ground proximity warning system (GPWS) must be installed on all large turbine powered airplanes. The GPWS gives aural and visual warnings when an aircraft too close to the terrain is in an improper configuration for landing, or when it deviates below glide slope on an ILS approach.

TCAS I (Traffic Alert and Collision Avoidance System) provides proximity warning only, to assist the pilot in the visual acquisition of intruder aircraft. No recommended avoidance maneuvers are provided nor authorized as a result of a TCAS I warning. TCAS II provides traffic advisories (TAs) and resolution advisories (RAs). Resolution advisories provide recommended maneuvers in a vertical direction to avoid conflicting traffic. TCAS does not alter or diminish the pilot's basic authority and responsibility to ensure safe flight. After the conflict, return to the ATC clearance in effect. If a deviation occurs, contact ATC as soon as practical.

Cockpit voice recorders are required on large turbine engine powered airplanes and large four engine reciprocating powered airplanes. The recorder must operate from before the start of the before starting checklist to the completion of the secure cockpit checklist. Although the recorder runs for the entire flight, only the most recent 30 minutes of information need be retained on the recorder tape.

An approved flight recorder must be installed on all airplanes certified for operations above 25,000 feet and on all turbine powered airplanes. What the flight recorder must record varies from airplane to airplane, but at a minimum it must record:

• Time

• Altitude

• Airspeed

• Vertical acceleration

• Heading

• Time of each radio transmission to or from ATC.

Answers

8711   [C]

An air carrier must keep the flight recorder data until an aircraft has been operated at least 25 hours after the data was removed. However, 1 hour of the oldest recorded data may be erased to test the flight recorder.

The cockpit voice and flight recorder data can be used to identify malfunctions and irregularities with the aircraft and in carrying out investigations under NTSB Part 830. It cannot be used by the FAA for enforcement purposes. If an incident occurs which would require the immediate notification of the NTSB, the data must be kept by the operator for at least 60 days.

ALL

9410. Information obtained from flight data and cockpit voice recorders shall be used only for determining

A— who was responsible for any accident or incident.
B— evidence for use in civil penalty or certificate action.
C— possible causes of accidents or incidents.

Information obtained from flight data and cockpit voice recorders is used to assist in determining the cause of accidents or occurrences in connection with investigation under NTSB Part 830. The Administrator does not use the cockpit voice recorder record in any civil penalty or certificate action. (PLT388) — 14 CFR §91.609

Answer (A) is incorrect because flight data or cockpit voice recorders are only used to determine possible causes of accidents or incidents. Answer (B) is incorrect because flight data or cockpit voice recorders may not be used for any civil penalty or certificate action.

ALL

9356. For what purpose may cockpit voice recorders and flight data recorders NOT be used?

A— Determining causes of accidents and occurrences under investigation by the NTSB.
B— Determining any certificate action, or civil penalty, arising out of an accident or occurrence.
C— Identifying procedures that may have been conducive to any accident, or occurrence resulting in investigation under NTSB Part 830.

Information obtained from flight data and cockpit voice recorders is used to assist in determining the cause of accidents or occurrences in connection with investigation under NTSB Part 830. The Administrator does not use the cockpit voice recorder record in any civil penalty or certificate action. (PLT388) — 14 CFR §91.609

Answer (A) is incorrect because cockpit voice recorders and flight data recorders are used to determine causes of accidents and occurrences. Answer (C) is incorrect because flight data recorders and cockpit voice recorders are used to identify any procedures, malfunction, or failure that may have contributed to an accident or occurrence.

ALL

9357. How long is cockpit voice recorder and flight recorder data kept, in the event of an accident or occurrence resulting in terminating the flight?

A— 60 days.
B— 90 days.
C— 30 days.

In the event of an accident or occurrence requiring immediate notification to NTSB Part 830, and that results in the termination of a flight, any operator who has installed approved flight recorders and approved cockpit voice recorders shall keep the recorded information for at least 60 days. (PLT388) — 14 CFR §91.609

ATM, ATS

9428. Each pilot who deviates from an ATC clearance in response to a TCAS II, resolution advisory (RA) is expected to

A— maintain the course and altitude resulting from the deviation, as ATC has radar contact.
B— request ATC clearance for the deviation.
C— notify ATC of the deviation as soon as practicable.

Each pilot who deviates from an ATC clearance in response to a TCAS II RA shall notify ATC of that deviation as soon as practicable and expeditiously return to the current ATC clearance when the traffic conflict is resolved. (PLT195) — AIM ¶4-4-16

Answers

9410 [C]	9356 [B]	9357 [A]	9428 [C]

ATM, ATS, RTC

9425. TCAS I provides

A— traffic and resolution advisories.
B— proximity warning.
C— recommended maneuvers to avoid conflicting traffic.

TCAS I provides proximity warning only, to assist the pilot in the visual acquisition of intruder aircraft. No recommended avoidance maneuvers are provided nor authorized as a result of a TCAS I warning. (PLT195) — AIM ¶4-4-16

Answer (A) is incorrect because traffic and resolution advisories are provided by TCAS II. Answer (C) is incorrect because no recommended avoidance maneuvers are provided nor authorized as a result of a TCAS I warning.

ATM, ATS, RTC

9426. TCAS II provides

A— traffic and resolution advisories.
B— proximity warning.
C— maneuvers in all directions to avoid the conflicting traffic.

TCAS II provides traffic advisories (TAs) and resolution advisories (RAs). (PLT195) — AIM ¶4-4-16

Answer (B) is incorrect because TCAS I provides proximity warning only. Answer (C) is incorrect because resolution advisories provide recommended maneuvers in a vertical direction only to avoid conflicting traffic.

ATM, ATS, RTC

9750. With no traffic identified by TCAS, you

A— can rest assured that no other aircraft are in the area.
B— must continually scan for other traffic in visual conditions.
C— must scan only for hot air balloons.

Traffic data systems are designed to enhance "see and avoid" capabilities. Do not use traffic data systems as a substitute for visual scanning and acquisition of surrounding traffic. (PLT524) – FAA-H-8083-6

Answer (A) is incorrect because TCAS can fail or be affected by power spikes, weather and other onboard aircraft disturbances. Answer (C) is incorrect because TCAS data is supplemental to your traffic awareness for all aircraft.

ATM, ATS, RTC

9427. Each pilot who deviates from an ATC clearance in response to a TCAS advisory is expected to notify ATC and

A— maintain the course and altitude resulting from the deviation, as ATC has radar contact.
B— request a new ATC clearance.
C— expeditiously return to the ATC clearance in effect prior to the advisory, after the conflict is resolved.

Each pilot who deviates from an ATC clearance in response to a TCAS II RA shall notify ATC of that deviation as soon as practicable and expeditiously return to the current ATC clearance when the traffic conflict is resolved. (PLT195) — AIM ¶4-4-16

ALL

9427-1. With no traffic identified by TCAS when in 10 miles of visibility, you

A— can rest assured that no other aircraft is near.
B— must continually scan for other traffic.
C— must scan only for hot air balloons and gliders.

TCAS does not alter or diminish the pilot's basic authority and responsibility to ensure safe flight. Since TCAS does not respond to aircraft that are not transponder-equipped or aircraft with a transponder failure, TCAS alone does not ensure safe separation in every case. (PLT195) — AIM ¶4-4-16

ATM, DSP

8150. If an air carrier airplane's airborne radar is inoperative and thunderstorms are forecast along the proposed route of flight, an airplane may be dispatched only

A— when able to climb and descend VFR and maintain VFR/OT en route.
B— in VFR conditions.
C— in day VFR conditions.

No person may dispatch an airplane under IFR or night VFR conditions when current weather reports indicate that thunderstorms, or other potentially hazardous weather conditions that can be detected with airborne weather radar, may reasonably be expected along the route to be flown, unless the weather radar is in satisfactory operating condition. (PLT469) — 14 CFR §121.357

Answers

9425 [B]   9426 [A]   9750 [B]   9427 [C]   9427-1 [B]   8150 [C]

ATM, DSP

8151. An air carrier airplane's airborne radar must be in satisfactory operating condition prior to dispatch, if the flight will be

A— conducted under VFR conditions at night with scattered thunderstorms reported en route.
B— carrying passengers, but not if it is "all cargo."
C— conducted IFR, and ATC is able to radar vector the flight around areas of weather.

No person may dispatch an airplane under IFR or night VFR conditions when current weather reports indicate that thunderstorms, or other potentially hazardous weather conditions that can be detected with airborne weather radar, may reasonably be expected along the route to be flown, unless the weather radar is in satisfactory operating condition. (PLT469) — 14 CFR §121.357

Answer (B) is incorrect because there is no difference between "all cargo" and "passenger" air carrier operations. The airborne radar must be operational prior to dispatch into an area of expected thunderstorms. Answer (C) is incorrect because airborne radar needs to be in operating condition for IFR or night VFR conditions, regardless of ATC's ability to vector the flight around the areas of weather.

ATM, DSP

8148. What action should be taken by the pilot in command of a transport category airplane if the airborne weather radar becomes inoperative en route on an IFR flight for which weather reports indicate possible thunderstorms?

A— Request radar vectors from ATC to the nearest suitable airport and land.
B— Proceed in accordance with the approved instructions and procedures specified in the operations manual for such an event.
C— Return to the departure airport if the thunderstorms have not been encountered, and there is enough fuel remaining.

No person may dispatch an airplane under IFR or night VFR conditions when current weather reports indicate that thunderstorms, or other potentially hazardous weather conditions that can be detected with airborne weather radar, may reasonably be expected along the route to be flown, unless the weather radar is in satisfactory operating condition. If the airborne radar becomes inoperative en route, the airplane must be operated in accordance with the approved instructions and procedures specified in the operations manual for such an event. (PLT469) — 14 CFR §121.357

Answer (A) is incorrect because radar vectors to land at the nearest suitable airport are not required when airborne weather detection radar malfunctions. Radar vectors to avoid weather would be a wise request. Answer (C) is incorrect because return to the departure airport upon malfunction of airborne weather detection radar would be the correct action if it were the procedure specified in the air carrier's operations manual. However, it is not required by regulation.

ATM, DSP

8154. Which airplanes are required to be equipped with a ground proximity warning glide slope deviation alerting system?

A— All turbine powered airplanes.
B— Passenger-carrying turbine-powered airplanes only.
C— Large turbine-powered airplanes only.

No person may operate a turbine-powered airplane unless it is equipped with a ground proximity warning/ glide slope deviation alerting system. (PLT139) — 14 CFR §121.360

ATM, DSP

8140. Information recorded during normal operation of a cockpit voice recorder in a large pressurized airplane with four reciprocating engines

A— may all be erased or otherwise obliterated except for the last 30 minutes.
B— may be erased or otherwise obliterated except for the last 30 minutes prior to landing.
C— may all be erased, as the voice recorder is not required on an aircraft with reciprocating engines.

When a cockpit voice recorder is required on an airplane, it must be operated continuously from the start of the use of the checklist (before starting engines for the purpose of flight), to completion of the final checklist at the termination of flight. Information recorded more than 30 minutes earlier may be erased or otherwise obliterated. (PLT405) — 14 CFR §121.359

Answer (B) is incorrect because there is no requirement for information to be retained for 30 minutes after landing. However, under some circumstances involving an accident or occurrence, the certificate holder may be required to retain the information up to 60 days. Answer (C) is incorrect because a cockpit voice recorder is required in large pressurized airplanes with four reciprocating engines.

Answers

8151 **[A]**   8148 **[B]**   8154 **[A]**   8140 **[A]**

ATM, DSP

8141. Which rule applies to the use of the cockpit voice recorder erasure feature?

A— All recorded information may be erased, except for the last 30 minutes prior to landing.
B— Any information more than 30 minutes old may be erased.
C— All recorded information may be erased, unless the NTSB needs to be notified of an occurrence.

When a cockpit voice recorder is required on an airplane, it must be operated continuously from the start of the use of the checklist (before starting engines for the purpose of flight), to completion of the final checklist at the termination of flight. Information recorded more than 30 minutes earlier may be erased or otherwise obliterated. (PLT388) — 14 CFR §121.359

Answer (A) is incorrect because the requirement is that any information more than 30 minutes old may be erased. Answer (C) is incorrect because the requirement is to retain any information that was recorded within the last 30 minutes.

ATM, DSP

8143. A cockpit voice recorder must be operated

A— from the start of the before starting engine checklist to completion of final checklist upon termination of flight.
B— from the start of the before starting engine checklist to completion of checklist prior to engine shutdown.
C— when starting to taxi for takeoff to the engine shutdown checklist after termination of the flight.

When a cockpit voice recorder is required on an airplane, it must be operated continuously from the start of the use of the checklist (before starting engines for the purpose of flight), to completion of the final checklist at the termination of flight. Information recorded more than 30 minutes earlier may be erased or otherwise obliterated. (PLT388) — 14 CFR §121.359

ATM, DSP

8142. For the purpose of testing the flight recorder system,

A— a minimum of 1 hour of the oldest recorded data must be erased to get a valid test.
B— a total of 1 hour of the oldest recorded data accumulated at the time of testing may be erased.
C— a total of no more than 1 hour of recorded data may be erased.

A total of 1 hour of recorded data may be erased for the purpose of testing a flight recorder or flight recorder system. Any erasure must be of the oldest recorded data accumulated at the time of testing. (PLT388) — 14 CFR §121.343

Answer (A) is incorrect because a maximum of 1 hour of data may be erased for testing. Answer (C) is incorrect because a total of no more than 1 hour of flight recorder data may be erased, but it must be 1 hour of the oldest recorded data.

Answers

8141 [B]   8143 [A]   8142 [B]

Communications

Each flag and domestic operator must have a two-way radio system that, under normal conditions, allows reliable and rapid communications between its aircraft and the appropriate dispatch office. For operations within the 48 contiguous states, this system must be independent of any operated by the U.S. government.

ALL

9258. ATC asks you to follow the B737 3 NM ahead of you on the approach path. ATC is responsible to ensure

A— wake turbulence avoidance.
B— traffic separation only.
C— wind shear avoidance.

A pilot's acceptance of instructions to follow another aircraft or provide visual separation from it is an acknowledgment that the pilot will maneuver the aircraft as necessary to avoid the other aircraft or to maintain in-trail separation. In operations conducted behind heavy jet aircraft, it is also an acknowledgment that the pilot accepts the responsibility for wake turbulence separation. (PLT149) — AIM ¶4-4-14

ATM, DSP

8135. Who must the crew of a domestic or flag air carrier airplane be able to communicate with, under normal conditions, along the entire route (in either direction) of flight?

A— ARINC.
B— Any FSS.
C— Appropriate dispatch office.

Each domestic and flag air carrier must show that a two-way air/ground radio communications system is available at points that will ensure reliable and rapid communications, under normal operating conditions over the entire route (either direct or via approved point to point circuits) between each airplane and the appropriate dispatch office, and between each airplane and the appropriate air traffic control unit. (PLT390) — 14 CFR §121.99

Answer (A) is incorrect because the aircraft must be able to communicate directly with the air carrier dispatch office, not just ARINC. ARINC is a commercial message company which subscribers may use to relay messages, telephone calls, etc. Answer (B) is incorrect because regulations require that the company communications system be independent of any system operated by the FAA or any other third party.

ALL

9783. When should transponders be operated on the ground while taxiing?

A— Only when ATC specifically requests that the transponder to be activated.
B— Any time the airport is operating under IFR.
C— All the time when at an airport with ASDE-X.

If operating at an airport with Airport Surface Detection Equipment - Model X (ASDE-X), transponders should be transmitting "on" with altitude reporting continuously while moving on the airport surface if so equipped. (PLT149) — AIM ¶4-1-20

ALL

9783-1. If you notice ATC is unusually quiet and one of your VHF transmit lights is illuminated, then you should suspect

A— your VHF receiver is inoperative.
B— your VHF transmitter is keyed and you probably have a stuck microphone.
C— the radio is performing a self-test function.

If radio communications are unusually quiet, suspect radio problems or a stuck microphone, and then contact ATC and look for light gun signals. (PLT362) — AIM

ALL

9784. When taxiing on an airport with ASDE-X, you should

A— operate the transponder only when the airport is under IFR or at night during your taxi.
B— operate the transponder with altitude reporting all of the time during taxiing.
C— be ready to activate the transponder upon ATC request while taxing.

If operating at an airport with Airport Surface Detection Equipment - Model X (ASDE-X), transponders should be transmitting "on" with altitude reporting continuously while moving on the airport surface if so equipped. (PLT149) — AIM ¶4-1-20

Answers

| 9258 | [B] | 8135 | [C] | 9783 | [C] | 9783-1 | [B] | 9784 | [B] |

Navigation Equipment

When an aircraft is flown IFR or VFR Over-the-Top it must have a dual installation of the navigation radios required to fly that route. This means that an aircraft flying Victor airways or jet routes must have two operable VOR systems. Only one ILS system and one marker beacon system is required under Part 121.

When an aircraft is navigating over routes using low frequency, ADF or Radio Range, it only needs one receiver for those NAVAIDs, if it is also equipped with two VOR receivers. If that is the case, the VOR stations must be located such that the aircraft could complete the flight to a suitable airport and make an instrument approach if the low frequency system fails. The airplane must also be fueled to allow for such a failure.

Whenever a different VOR station is tuned, the pilot must listen to the Morse code identification. This will ensure that the correct frequency has been tuned and that a usable signal is available. Occasionally, when a VOR station is undergoing routine maintenance, it will broadcast a signal that is not reliable enough to use for navigation. This condition is indicated in one of two ways. Either the coded ident will be turned off or the ident will be changed to the letters T - E - S - T. Other than the identifier, the station may appear to be broadcasting a normal signal.

To be flown IFR, an aircraft must have had its VORs checked within the past 30 days. The pilots may check the accuracy of the VORs in one of several ways.

The VORs may be checked using a VOT facility on an airport. The VOT broadcasts the 360° radial and so the CDI needle should center either on a setting of 360° with a FROM indication or on 180° with a TO indication. A deviation of ±4° is acceptable for a VOT check.

If a VOT is not available, a VOR checkpoint may be used instead. The aircraft must be moved to the checkpoint and the designated radial set in the CDI course. The acceptable variation for a ground check is ±4°. For an airborne check the allowable variation is ±6°.

If no VOT or VOR check point is available, the VORs may be checked against each other. This is called a "dual VOR check." Tune the VORs to the same station and check the difference in indicated bearing. If they are within 4° of each other, the check is satisfactory. This check can be performed on the ground or in the air.

The person making a VOR check must make an entry in the aircraft log or other record. A proper entry includes the date, place and bearing error. The checker must sign the entry. Besides the VOR check, the altimeter system and the transponder must have been checked within the last 24 calendar months (14 CFR §91.411 and §91.413).

Whenever VOR receivers are required on board an aircraft operating within the United States, it must also have at least one DME receiver on board as well. *Note:* 14 CFR §91.205 requires a DME only if the aircraft is operated above FL240. 14 CFR §121.349 makes the DME required equipment for all air carrier aircraft operating in the U.S. If the DME fails in flight, the pilot must inform ATC as soon as possible.

DME indicates the actual distance from the station to the receiving aircraft in nautical miles. That is different from the horizontal distance because the aircraft is always higher than the DME ground station and altitude is included in the slant range. As a practical matter, the difference between the horizontal distance and the "slant range" is insignificant at distances of more than 10 miles from the station. There is a considerable error close to the station when the aircraft is at high altitudes. In such a situation, almost all of the slant range distance is vertical. When an aircraft passes over a DME station, the distance indicated at station passage is the altitude of the aircraft above the station in nautical miles. For example, if an airplane flew over a VORTAC site 12,000 feet above the station, the DME would indicate 2.0 NM.

A multi-function display (MFD) presents information drawn from a variety of aircraft information systems. The moving map function uses the MFD to provide a pictorial view of the present position of the aircraft, the route programmed into the flight management system, the surrounding airspace, and geographical features. The MFD and moving map can help you maintain the "big picture" and awareness of potential landing sites.

ALL

9019. What would be the identification when a VORTAC is undergoing routine maintenance and is considered unreliable?

A— A test signal, "TESTING," is sent every 30 seconds.
B— Identifier is preceded by "M" and an intermittent "OFF" flag would appear.
C— The identifier would be removed.

During periods of routine or emergency maintenance, coded identification (or code and voice, where applicable) is removed from certain FAA NAVAIDs. During periods of maintenance, VHF ranges may radiate a T-E-S-T code. (PLT300) — AIM ¶1-1-3

Answer (A) is incorrect because a facility may send a T-E-S-T code (not "TESTING") during periods of maintenance. Answer (B) is incorrect because an identifier preceded by "M" designates an identification group for the Microwave Landing System (MLS), a system no longer in operation.

ALL

9020. Which indication may be received when a VOR is undergoing maintenance and is considered unreliable?

A— Coded identification T-E-S-T.
B— Identifier is preceded by "M" and an intermittent "OFF" flag might appear.
C— An automatic voice recording stating the VOR is out-of-service for maintenance.

During periods of routine or emergency maintenance, coded identification (or code and voice, where applicable) is removed from certain FAA NAVAIDs. During periods of maintenance, VHF ranges may radiate a T-E-S-T code. (PLT300) — AIM ¶1-1-3

Answer (B) is incorrect because an identifier preceded by "M" designates an identification group for the Microwave Landing System (MLS), a system no longer in operation. Answer (C) is incorrect because this is used to identify a station and it is removed when the VOR is undergoing maintenance and is considered unreliable.

ALL

9375. What is the maximum permissible variation between the two bearing indicators on a dual VOR system when checking one VOR against the other?

A— 4° on the ground and in flight.
B— 6° on the ground and in flight.
C— 6° in flight and 4° on the ground.

If a dual system VOR (units independent of each other except for the antenna) is installed in the aircraft, the person checking the equipment may check one system against the other. The maximum permissible variation between the two indicated bearings is 4°. (PLT508) — 14 CFR §91.171

Answer (B) is incorrect because 6° is the maximum permissible bearing error when checking a single VOR system against a published radial while in the air, not when checking a dual VOR system. Answer (C) is incorrect because 6° is the maximum permissible bearing error when checking a single VOR system while in the air. Regardless of whether you are on the ground or airborne, the maximum permissible bearing error is only 4° when using a cross-check between dual VORs.

ALL

9405. During a VOT check of the VOR equipment, the course deviation indicator centers on 356° with the TO/FROM reading FROM. This VOR equipment may

A— be used if 4° is entered on a correction card and subtracted from all VOR courses.
B— be used during IFR flights, since the error is within limits.
C— not be used during IFR flights, since the TO/FROM should read TO.

With the course deviation indicator (CDI) centered, the omni-bearing selector should read 0° (±4°) with the TO/FROM indicator showing FROM or 180° (±4°) with the TO/FROM indicator showing TO. (PLT508) — 14 CFR §91.171

Answer (A) is incorrect because 4° is the maximum permissible bearing error for a VOT check, and no correction card exists for VORs. VORs are either within or not within acceptable limits. Answer (C) is incorrect because a "TO" reading would be indicated if the omni-bearing selector were selected to 180°, not 0°.

Answers

9019 [C]   9020 [A]   9375 [A]   9405 [B]

ALL

9406. If an airborne checkpoint is used to check the VOR system for IFR operations, the maximum bearing error permissible is

A— plus or minus 6°.
B— plus 6° or minus 4°.
C— plus or minus 4°.

If neither a VOT nor a designated ground checkpoint is available, a pilot may use a designated airborne checkpoint for the VOR check. The maximum permissible bearing error is ±6°. (PLT508) — 14 CFR §91.171

Answer (B) is incorrect because the maximum bearing error is ±6. Answer (C) is incorrect because ±4° is the maximum permissible bearing error when using a VOT check or a radio repair facility.

ALL

9376. Which entry shall be recorded by the person performing a VOR operational check?

A— Frequency, radial and facility used, and bearing error.
B— Flight hours and number of days since last check, and bearing error.
C— Date, place, bearing error, and signature.

Each person making the VOR operational check required by regulations shall enter the date, place, bearing error and sign the aircraft log or other record. (PLT508) — 14 CFR §91.171

Answer (A) is incorrect because the frequency and radial used are not required entry items. Answer (B) is incorrect because flight hours and number of days since last check are not required entry items.

ALL

9404. What record shall be made by the pilot performing a VOR operational check?

A— The date, frequency of VOR or VOT, number of hours flown since last check, and signature in the aircraft log.
B— The date, place, bearing error, and signature in the aircraft log or other record.
C— The date, approval or disapproval, tach reading, and signature in the aircraft log or other permanent record.

Each person making the VOR operational check required by regulations shall enter the date, place, bearing error and sign the aircraft log or other record. (PLT508) — 14 CFR §91.171

Answer (A) is incorrect because neither the frequency nor number of hours flown since the last check need to be entered in the log or record. Answer (C) is incorrect because neither the tach reading nor approval or disapproval need to be entered in the record of a VOR operational check.

ALL

9377. Which checks and inspections of flight instruments or instrument systems must be accomplished before an aircraft can be flown under IFR?

A— VOR within 30 days and altimeter systems and transponder within 24 calendar months.
B— ELT test within 30 days, altimeter systems within 12 calendar months, and transponder within 24 calendar months.
C— Airspeed indicator within 24 calendar months, altimeter system within 24 calendar months, and transponder within 12 calendar months.

No person may operate an aircraft under IFR using the VOR system of radio navigation unless the VOR equipment of that aircraft has been operationally checked within the preceding 30 days. No person may operate an airplane in controlled airspace under IFR unless, within the preceding 24 calendar months, each static pressure system, each altimeter instrument, and each automatic pressure altitude reporting system has been tested and inspected. No person may use an ATC transponder required by regulations unless, within the preceding 24 calendar months, it has been tested and inspected. (PLT508) — 14 CFR §§91.171, 91.411, 91.413

Answer (B) is incorrect because ELTs do not have to be tested every 30 days, and the altimeter must be checked along with transponder every 24 calendar months (not 12 months). Answer (C) is incorrect because the airspeed indicator is part of the pitot-static system which must be inspected every 24 calendar months and the transponder which must be inspected every 24 calendar months.

ALL

9408. When is DME or suitable RNAV required for an instrument flight?

A— At or above 24,000 feet MSL if VOR navigational equipment is required.
B— In terminal radar service areas.
C— Above 12,500 feet MSL.

If VOR navigational equipment is required, no person may operate a U.S.-registered civil aircraft within the 50 states and District of Columbia, at or above 24,000 feet MSL, unless that aircraft is equipped with approved distance measuring equipment (DME) or a suitable RNAV system. (PLT429) — 14 CFR §91.205

Answers

| 9406 | [A] | 9376 | [C] | 9404 | [B] | 9377 | [A] | 9408 | [A] |

ALL

9023. What DME indications should a pilot observe when directly over a VORTAC site at 12,000 feet?

A— 0 DME miles.
B— 2 DME miles.
C— 2.3 DME miles.

Distance information displayed on DME equipment is slant range from the station in nautical miles. 12,000 feet directly over a VORTAC is almost exactly 2 NM. (PLT202) — FAA-H-8083-15

Answer (A) is incorrect because the DME would indicate 0 DME miles if the DME were sitting on top of the VORTAC site. Answer (C) is incorrect because 2.3 DME miles would be indicated if the airplane were at 13,800 feet (6,000 x 2.3) above the VORTAC site.

ALL

9024. Where does the DME indicator have the greatest error between the ground distance and displayed distance to the VORTAC?

A— High altitudes close to the VORTAC.
B— Low altitudes close to the VORTAC.
C— Low altitudes far from the VORTAC.

Distance information displayed on DME equipment is slant range from the station in nautical miles. The greatest difference between displayed distance and ground distance will occur at high altitudes close to the VORTAC. (PLT202) — FAA-H-8083-15

Answer (B) is incorrect because at low altitudes close to the VORTAC, the slant-range error is less than at high altitudes close to the VORTAC. Answer (C) is incorrect because the slant-range error is at its smallest at low altitudes far from the VORTAC.

ALL

9570. (Refer to Figure 112.) While arcing left on the IAH 10 DME Arc, the pilot experiences a left crosswind component. Where should the bearing pointer be referenced relative to the 90° (wingtip) position to maintain the 10 DME range?

A— On the left wingtip reference.
B— Behind the left wingtip reference.
C— Ahead of the left wingtip reference.

If an aircraft was flying a perfect 10 DME arc to the left in no wind conditions, the RMI bearing would remain on the left wing-tip reference mark indicating that the VOR was exactly 90° to the left of the aircraft's heading. With a left crosswind, the pilot would have to turn the aircraft toward the wind to compensate for the drift to the right. That would place the bearing to the VOR less than 90°, and the bearing pointer would be ahead of the wing-tip reference. (PLT202) — Fly the Wing

ATM, DSP

8145. When an air carrier flight is operated under IFR or over-the-top on "victor airways," which navigation equipment is required to be installed in duplicate?

A— VOR.
B— ADF.
C— VOR and DME.

No person may operate IFR or Over-the-Top unless the airplane is equipped with the radio equipment necessary for the route, and is able to satisfactorily receive radio navigational signals from all primary en route and approach navigational facilities intended for use, by either of two independent systems. (PLT322) — 14 CFR §121.349

ATM, DSP

8195. An air carrier operates a flight in VFR over-the-top conditions. What radio navigation equipment is required to be a dual installation?

A— VOR.
B— VOR and ILS.
C— VOR and DME.

No person may operate IFR or Over-the-Top unless the airplane is equipped with the radio equipment necessary for the route and is able to satisfactorily receive radio navigational signals from all primary en route and approach navigational facilities intended for use, by either of two independent systems. (PLT429) — 14 CFR §121.349

ATM, DSP

8195-1. An air carrier operates a flight in VFR over-the-top conditions where pilotage is not used. What radio navigation equipment is required?

A— single VOR and DME installed.
B— dual approved independent navigation systems.
C— dual VOR, ILS's, and DME.

No person may operate IFR or over-the-top unless the airplane is equipped with the radio equipment necessary for the route and is able to satisfactorily receive radio navigational signals from all primary en route and approach navigational facilities intended for use, by either of two independent systems. (PLT429) — 14 CFR §121.349

Answers

9023 [B]　　9024 [A]　　9570 [C]　　8145 [A]　　8195 [A]　　8195-1 [B]

ATM, DSP

8149. If an air carrier airplane is flying IFR using a single ADF navigation receiver and the ADF equipment fails, the flight must be able to

A— proceed safely to a suitable airport using VOR aids and complete an instrument approach by use of the remaining airplane radio system.

B— continue to the destination airport by means of dead reckoning navigation.

C— proceed to a suitable airport using VOR aids, complete an instrument approach and land.

In the case of IFR operation over routes in which navigation is based on low-frequency radio range or automatic direction finding, only one low-frequency radio range or ADF receiver need be installed if the airplane is equipped with two VOR receivers, and VOR navigational aids are so located and the airplane is fueled so that, in the case of failure of the low-frequency radio range or ADF receiver, the flight may proceed safely to a suitable airport by means of VOR aids and complete an instrument approach by use of the remaining airplane radio system. (PLT429) — 14 CFR §121.349

ATM, DSP

8147. When a pilot plans a flight using NDB NAVAIDs, which rule applies?

A— The airplane must have sufficient fuel to proceed, by means of one other independent navigation system, to a suitable airport and complete an instrument approach by use of the remaining airplane radio system.

B— The pilot must be able to return to the departure airport using other navigation radios anywhere along the route with 150% of the forecast headwinds.

C— The airplane must have sufficient fuel to proceed, by means of VOR NAVAIDS, to a suitable airport and land anywhere along the route with 150% of the forecast headwinds.

In the case of IFR operation over routes in which navigation is based on low-frequency radio range or automatic direction finding, only one low-frequency radio range or ADF receiver need be installed if the airplane is equipped with two VOR receivers, and VOR navigational aids are so located and the airplane is fueled so that, in the case of failure of the low-frequency radio range or ADF receiver, the flight may proceed safely to a suitable airport by means of VOR aids and complete an instrument approach by use of the remaining airplane radio system. (PLT322) — 14 CFR §121.349

ATM, DSP

8146. When must an air carrier airplane be DME/suitable RNAV system equipped?

A— In Class E airspace for all IFR or VFR on Top operations.

B— Whenever VOR navigation equipment is required.

C— For flights at or above FL 180.

Whenever VOR navigational receivers are required by regulation, at least one approved distance measuring equipment (DME) unit or suitable RNAV system capable of receiving and indicating distance information from VORTAC facilities must be installed on each airplane when operated in the 50 states and the District of Columbia. (PLT405) — 14 CFR §121.349

Answer (A) is incorrect because DME is only required if VOR equipment is required and not only in Class E airspace. Answer (C) is incorrect because DME is only required if VOR receivers are required.

ATM, DSP

8152. While on an IFR flight in controlled airspace, the failure of which unit will precipitate an immediate report to ATC?

A— One engine, on a multiengine aircraft.

B— Airborne radar.

C— DME.

If the distance measuring equipment (DME) becomes inoperative enroute, the pilot shall notify ATC of that failure as soon as it occurs. (PLT429) — 14 CFR §121.349

Answers

8149	[A]	8147	[A]	8146	[B]	8152	[C]

ALL

9751. (*See* Figure shown at right.) The moving map below reflects a loss of

A— position information.
B— the AHRS.
C— the ADC.

Failure indications on the moving map can be quite subtle. The MFD in Figure 242 reflects a loss of position information, indicated by the removal of the aircraft symbol, compass labels, and other subtle differences. (PLT524) — FAA-H-8083-6

Answers (B) and (C) are incorrect because an AHRS or ADC failure would be depicted by red X's on the PFD.

Question 9751

Horizontal Situation Indicator (HSI)

The **Horizontal Situation Indicator (HSI)** is a combination of two instruments: the heading indicator and the VOR. *See* Figure 2-3.

The aircraft heading displayed on the rotating azimuth card under the upper lubber line in Figure 2-2 is 330°. The course-indicating arrowhead that is shown is set to 300°. The tail of the course-indicating arrow indicates the reciprocal, or 120°.

The course deviation bar operates with a VOR/LOC navigation receiver to indicate either left or right deviations from the course that is selected with the course-indicating arrow. It moves left or right to indicate deviation from the centerline in the same manner that the angular movement of a conventional VOR/LOC needle indicates deviation from course.

The desired course is selected by rotating the course-indicating arrow in relation to the azimuth card by means of the course set knob. This gives the pilot a pictorial presentation. The fixed aircraft symbol and the course deviation bar display the aircraft relative to the selected course as though the pilot was above the aircraft looking down.

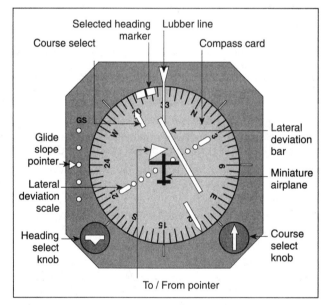

Figure 2-3. Horizontal Situation Indicator (HSI)

The TO/FROM indicator is a triangular-shaped pointer. When this indicator points to the head of the course arrow, it indicates that the course selected, and if properly intercepted and flown, will take the aircraft TO the selected facility, and vice versa.

The glide slope deviation pointer indicates the relationship of the aircraft to the glide slope. When the pointer is below the center position, the aircraft is above the glide slope and an increased rate of descent is required.

Continued

Answers

9751   [A]

To orient where the aircraft is in relation to the facility, first determine which radial is selected (look at the arrowhead). Next, determine whether the aircraft is flying to or away from the station (look at the TO/FROM indicator) to find which hemisphere the aircraft is in. Next, determine how far from the selected course the aircraft is (look at the deviation bar) to find which quadrant the aircraft is in. Last, consider the aircraft heading (under the lubber line) to determine the aircraft's position within the quadrant.

Aircraft displacement from course is approximately 200 feet per dot per nautical mile. For example, at 30 NM from the station, 1-dot deflection indicates approximately 1 NM displacement of the aircraft from the course centerline. Therefore, a 2.5-dot deflection at 60 NM would mean the aircraft is approximately 5 NM from the course centerline.

ALL

8999. (Refer to Figures 142 and 143.) To which aircraft position does HSI presentation "D" correspond?

A— 4.
B— 15.
C— 17.

HSI Indicator "D" has a course selection of 180°, and the TO/FROM indicator is pointing to the tail of the course arrow. So the aircraft is flying away FROM the station, and is south of R-270 and R-090. The CDI bar is deflected left, which means the aircraft is west of R-180. The aircraft heading is 180°, which describes position 17. (PLT355) — FAA-H-8083-15

Answer (A) is incorrect because position 4 is to the north of the 270/090 radials, which would require a TO indication. Answer (B) is incorrect because the course deflection bar on position 15 would have a centered deflection bar and a heading of 360°.

ALL

9000. (Refer to Figures 142 and 143.) To which aircraft position does HSI presentation "E" correspond?

A— 5.
B— 6.
C— 15.

HSI Indicator "E" has a course selection of 360°, and the TO/FROM indicator is pointing to the tail of the course arrow. So the aircraft is flying away FROM the station, and is north of R-270 and R-090. The CDI bar is deflected left, which means the aircraft is east of R-180. The aircraft heading is 360°, which describes position 6. (PLT355) — FAA-H-8083-15

Answer (A) is incorrect because position 5 would have a centered deflection bar and a heading of 180°. Answer (C) is incorrect because position 15 is to the south of the R-270 and R-090, which would require a TO indication, and the deflection bar would be centered.

ALL

9001. (Refer to Figures 142 and 143.) To which aircraft position does HSI presentation "F" correspond?

A— 10.
B— 14.
C— 16.

HSI Indicator "F" has a course selection of 180°, and the TO/FROM indicator is pointing to the tail of the course arrow. So the aircraft is flying away FROM the station, and is south of R-270 and R-090. The CDI bar is centered, which means the aircraft is on R-180. The aircraft heading is 045°, which describes position 16. (PLT355) — FAA-H-8083-15

Answer (A) is incorrect because position 10 is north of R-270 and R-090 and east of R-360 and R-180, which would require a TO indication and a right course deflection. Answer (B) is incorrect because position 14 is to the east of R-180, which would require a right course deflection.

ALL

9002. (Refer to Figures 142 and 143.) To which aircraft position does HSI presentation "A" correspond?

A— 1.
B— 8.
C— 11.

HSI Indicator "A" has a course selection of 090°, and the TO/FROM indicator is pointing to the head of the course arrow. So the aircraft is flying TO the station, and is west of R-180 and R-000. The CDI bar is deflected right, which means the aircraft is north of R-270. The aircraft heading is 205°, which describes position 1. (PLT355) — FAA-H-8083-15

Answer (B) is incorrect because position 8 is to the right of R-360 and R-180, which would require a FROM indication. Answer (C) is incorrect because airplane 11 is to the right of R-360 and R-180 and is south of R-270 and R-090, which would require a FROM indication and a left deviation indication.

Answers

| 8999 | [C] | 9000 | [B] | 9001 | [C] | 9002 | [A] |

ALL
9003. (Refer to Figures 142 and 143.) To which aircraft position does HSI presentation "B" correspond?

A— 9.
B— 13.
C— 19.

HSI Indicator "B" has a course selection of 270°, and the TO/FROM indicator is pointing to the tail of the course arrow. So the aircraft is flying away FROM the station, and is west of R-180 and R-000. The CDI bar is deflected right, which means the aircraft is south of R-270. The aircraft heading is 135°, which describes position 19. (PLT355) — FAA-H-8083-15

Answer (A) is incorrect because position 9 would require a left course deflection bar indication and a TO indication. Answer (B) is incorrect because position 13 is to the right of R-360 and R-180 and would require a TO indication.

ALL
9004. (Refer to Figures 142 and 143.) To which aircraft position does HSI presentation "C" correspond?

A— 6.
B— 7.
C— 12.

HSI Indicator "C" has a course selection of 360°, and the TO/FROM indicator is pointing to the head of the course arrow. So the aircraft is flying TO the station, and is south of R-270 and R-090. The CDI bar is deflected left, which means the aircraft is east of R-180. The aircraft heading is 310°, which describes position 12. (PLT355) — FAA-H-8083-15

Answer (A) is incorrect because position 6 has a heading of 360° and is north of R-270 and R-090, which would require a FROM indication. Answer (B) is incorrect because position 7 is north of R-270 and R-090 radials, which would require a FROM indication.

ALL
8984. (Refer to Figure 139.) What is the lateral displacement of the aircraft in nautical miles from the radial selected on the No. 1 NAV?

A— 5.0 NM.
B— 7.5 NM.
C— 10.0 NM.

Aircraft displacement from course is approximately 200 feet per dot per nautical mile. For example, at 30 NM from the station, 1-dot deflection indicates approximately 1 NM displacement of the aircraft from the course centerline. Therefore, a 2.5-dot deflection at 60 NM would mean the aircraft is approximately 5 NM from the course centerline. (PLT276) — FAA-H-8083-15

Answer (B) is incorrect because 7.5 NM would be indicated by a displacement of almost 4 dots. Answer (C) is incorrect because 10.0 NM would be indicated by a full deflection.

ALL
8985. (Refer to Figure 139.) On which radial is the aircraft as indicated by the No. 1 NAV?

A— R-175.
B— R-165.
C— R-345.

The No. 1 Nav has a course selection of 350°, and the TO/FROM indicator is pointing to the tail of the course arrow. So the aircraft is flying away FROM the station, and is in the north hemisphere. The CDI bar is deflected right, which means the aircraft is in the northwestern quadrant. The aircraft heading is 140°. The only answer choice in the northwest is R-345. (PLT276) — FAA-H-8083-15

Answer (A) is incorrect because R-175 would require a TO indicator. Answer (B) is incorrect because R-165 would require a TO indicator and a left deflection.

ALL
8986. (Refer to Figure 139.) Which OBS selection on the No. 1 NAV would center the CDI and change the ambiguity indication to a TO?

A— 175.
B— 165.
C— 345.

The No. 1 Nav has a course selection of 350°, and the TO/FROM indicator is pointing to the tail of the course arrow. So the aircraft is flying away FROM the station, and is in the north hemisphere. The CDI bar is deflected 2.5° right and the aircraft heading is 140°, which would put the aircraft on R-345. To center the CDI and change the ambiguity indication to a TO, rotate the OBS to 165° (the reciprocal of R-345). (PLT276) — FAA-H-8083-15

Answers (A) and (C) are incorrect because the aircraft is currently on R-345.

Answers

9003 [C]	9004 [C]	8984 [A]	8985 [C]	8986 [B]

ALL

8987. (Refer to Figure 139.) What is the lateral displacement in degrees from the desired radial on the No. 2 NAV?

A— 1°.
B— 2°.
C— 4°.

Full scale deflection is 10°, so each dot represents 2°. The CDI is displaced two dots. Therefore, the lateral displacement is: 2 dots × 2°/dot = 4°. (PLT276) — FAA-H-8083-15

Answer (A) is incorrect because a 1° lateral displacement would be indicated by a 1/2-dot displacement of the CDI. Answer (B) is incorrect because a 2° lateral displacement would be indicated by a 1-dot displacement of the CDI.

ALL

8988. (Refer to Figure 139.) Which OBS selection on the No. 2 NAV would center the CDI?

A— 174.
B— 166.
C— 335.

Full scale deflection is 10°, so each dot represents 2°. The CDI is displaced two dots (4°). The OBS is set at 170° with a FROM indication, and the aircraft is 4° to the right of course (or on R-174). Simply rotating the OBS to 174° would center the CDI. (PLT276) — FAA-H-8083-15

Answer (B) is incorrect because a right deflection would indicate R-166. Answer (C) is incorrect because the TO-FROM indicator is on FROM, not TO.

ALL

8989. (Refer to Figure 139.) Which OBS selection on the No. 2 NAV would center the CDI and change the ambiguity indication to a TO?

A— 166.
B— 346.
C— 354.

Rotating the OBS to the reciprocal of 170° (350°) under the course arrow will cause the ambiguity indication to change to a TO. The CDI indicates that the aircraft is 4° to the left of course. Rotating the OBS to 354° will center the CDI. (PLT276) — FAA-H-8083-15

Answer (A) is incorrect because a right deflection would currently mean the airplane is on R-166. To change the ambiguity indicator to a TO, 180° must be added to the current radial. Answer (B) is incorrect because a right deflection would mean the airplane is currently on R-166.

ALL

8990. (Refer to Figures 140 and 141.) To which aircraft position(s) does HSI presentation "A" correspond?

A— 9 and 6.
B— 9 only.
C— 6 only.

HSI Indicator "A" is set up with the head of the arrow pointing to 270° (normal sensing). The Course Deviation Indicator is centered; therefore, the aircraft is on the extended centerline of runway #9 and #27. With a heading of 360, Indicator "A" represents an aircraft at position #6 or #9. See the figure below. (PLT355) — FAA-H-8083-15

Answers (B) and (C) are incorrect because the indication will be the same on both the front course and the back course.

Question 8990

ALL

8991. (Refer to Figures 140 and 141.) To which aircraft position(s) does HSI presentation "B" correspond?

A— 11.
B— 5 and 13.
C— 7 and 11.

HSI Indicator "B" is set up with the head of the arrow pointing to 090° (reverse sensing). The CDI indication is deflected right, which means the aircraft is actually to the south of the extended centerline. Indicator "B" then, with the aircraft flying on a heading of 090°, could be at position #13 and #5. Remember that the local receiver does not know where you are in relationship to the antenna site. See the figure below. (PLT355) — FAA-H-8083-15

Answer (A) is incorrect because position 11 has a 270° heading. Answer (C) is incorrect because positions 7 and 11 have 270° headings.

Question 8991

Answers

8987 [C]   8988 [A]   8989 [C]   8990 [A]   8991 [B]

ALL
8992. (Refer to Figures 140 and 141.) To which aircraft position does HSI presentation "C" correspond?

A— 9.
B— 4.
C— 12.

HSI Indicator "C" is set up with the head of the arrow pointing to 090° (reverse sensing). With the CDI centered, the aircraft is on the extended centerline. With a heading of 090°, position #12 is the only one which would have that indication. See the figure below. (PLT355) — FAA-H-8083-15

Answer (A) is incorrect because position 9 has a 360° heading. Answer (B) is incorrect because position 4 has a 270° heading.

Question 8992

ALL
8993. (Refer to Figures 140 and 141.) To which aircraft position does HSI presentation "D" correspond?

A— 1.
B— 10.
C— 2.

HSI Indicator "D" is set up with the head of the arrow pointing to 090° (reverse sensing). The CDI is deflected right, which means the aircraft is to the south of course. On a heading of 310°, position #2 is the only choice. See the figure below. (PLT355) — FAA-H-8083-15

Answer (A) is incorrect because position 1 is on a 225° heading and is north of the localizer. Answer (B) is incorrect because position 10 has a 135° heading, and is north of the localizer.

Question 8993

ALL
8994. (Refer to Figures 140 and 141.) To which aircraft position(s) does HSI presentation "E" correspond?

A— 8 only.
B— 8 and 3.
C— 3 only.

HSI Indicator "E" is set up with the head of the arrow pointing to 090° (reverse sensing). With the CDI deflected right, the aircraft is to the south of the extended centerline. On a heading of 045°, position #8 or #3 are the only answers. See the figure below. (PLT355) — FAA-H-8083-15

Answers (A) and (C) are incorrect because both positions 8 and 3 have a 045° heading and are south of the localizer.

Question 8994

ALL
8995. (Refer to Figures 140 and 141.) To which aircraft position does HSI presentation "F" correspond?

A— 4.
B— 11.
C— 5.

HSI Indicator "F" is set up with the head of the arrow pointing to 270° (normal sensing). The CDI is centered; therefore, the aircraft is on the extended centerline of runway #9 and #27. With a heading of 270°, Indicator "F" represents an aircraft at position #4. See the figure below. (PLT355) — FAA-H-8083-15

Answer (B) is incorrect because position 11 has a left CDI deflection. Answer (C) is incorrect because position 5 has a 090° heading. It also should have a right deflection because it is south of the localizer.

Question 8995

Answers

8992 [C]   8993 [C]   8994 [B]   8995 [A]

ALL

8996. (Refer to Figures 140 and 141.) To which aircraft position(s) does HSI presentation "G" correspond?

A— 7 only.
B— 7 and 11.
C— 5 and 13.

HSI Indicator "G" is set up with the head of the arrow pointing to 270° (normal sensing). The CDI is deflected left; therefore, the aircraft is right of the extended centerline of runway #9 and #27. With a heading of 270°, Indicator "G" represents an aircraft at positions #7 or #11. See the figure below. (PLT355) — FAA-H-8083-15

Answer (A) is incorrect because position 11 is also north of the localizer with a 270° heading. Answer (C) is incorrect because positions 5 and 13 have a 190° heading and are south of the localizer.

Question 8996

ALL

8997. (Refer to Figures 140 and 141.) To which aircraft position does HSI presentation "H" correspond?

A— 8.
B— 1.
C— 2.

HSI Indicator "H" is set up with the head of the arrow pointing to 270° (normal sensing). The CDI is deflected left; therefore, the aircraft is right of the extended centerline of runway #9 and #27. With a heading of 215°, Indicator "H" represents an aircraft at position #1. See the figure below. (PLT355) — FAA-H-8083-15

Answer (A) is incorrect because position 8 has a heading of 045° and is located south of the localizer. Answer (C) is incorrect because position 2 has a heading of 315° and is located south of the localizer.

Question 8997

ALL

8998. (Refer to Figures 140 and 141.) To which aircraft position does HSI presentation "I" correspond?

A— 4.
B— 12.
C— 11.

HSI Indicator "I" is set up with the head of the arrow pointing to 090° (reverse sensing). The CDI is deflected left; therefore, the aircraft is north of the extended centerline of runway #9 and #27. With a heading of 270°, Indicator "I" represents an aircraft at positions #7 or #11. See the figure below. (PLT355) — FAA-H-8083-15

Answer (A) is incorrect because position 4 is on the localizer, and has a centered CDI. Answer (B) is incorrect because position 12 is heading 090° and is on the localizer.

Question 8998

Answers

8996　[B]　　　　8997　[B]　　　　8998　[C]

Global Navigation

When an air carrier operates on routes outside of the 48 contiguous states where the aircraft's position cannot be reliably fixed for more than one hour, special rules apply. The aircraft must either be equipped with a "specialized means of navigation" (INS or Doppler Radar), or one of the flight crewmembers must have a current flight navigator certificate. The FAA may also require either a navigator or the specialized navigation on routes which meet the one hour rule if they feel it's necessary. All routes that require either the navigator or specialized means of navigation must be listed in the air carrier's operations specifications.

Certain routes over the North Atlantic Ocean between North America and Europe require better than normal standards of navigation. Appendix C of 14 CFR Part 91 defines these routes and the required navigation standards. The Administrator (the FAA) has the authority to grant a deviation from the navigation standards of Appendix C if an operator requests one.

ALL
9352. Which publication includes information on operations in the North Atlantic High Level Airspace (NAT HLA)?

A— 14 CFR Part 121.
B— ICAO Annex 1, Chapter 2.
C— 14 CFR Part 91.

Appendix C of 14 CFR Part 91 establishes performance standards for navigation in the North Atlantic (NAT) airspace. (PLT393) — 14 CFR §91.705

Answer (A) is incorrect because 14 CFR Part 121 provides rules in the United States regarding certification and operations: domestic, flag, and supplemental air carriers and commercial operators of large aircraft. Answer (B) is incorrect because ICAO Annex 1, Chapter 2 concerns licenses and ratings for pilots.

ALL
9353. How may an aircraft operate in North Atlantic (NAT) Minimum Navigation Performance Specifications Airspace with less than the minimum navigation capability required by 14 CFR Part 91, Appendix C?

A— By operating under VFR conditions only.
B— By requesting a deviation from the Administrator.
C— By operating only between 2400Z and 0600Z.

Appendix C of 14 CFR Part 91 establishes performance standards for navigation in the North Atlantic (NAT) airspace. The Administrator authorizes deviations from the requirements of Appendix C. (PLT393) — 14 CFR §91.703

Answer (A) is incorrect because NAT flights, with or without MNPS, may be conducted in IFR weather conditions as well as VFR. Answer (C) is incorrect because NAT flights, with or without MNPS, do not have time restrictions.

ATM, DSP
8196. Routes that require a flight navigator are listed in the

A— Airplane Flight Manual.
B— International Flight Information Manual.
C— Air Carrier's Operations Specifications.

Operations where a flight navigator, special navigation equipment, or both are required, are specified in the operations specifications of the air carrier or commercial operator. (PLT389) — 14 CFR §121.389

ATM, DSP
8197. Where is a list maintained for routes that require special navigation equipment?

A— Air Carrier's Operations Specifications.
B— International Flight Information Manual.
C— Airplane Flight Manual.

Operations where a flight navigator, special navigation equipment, or both are required, are specified in the operations specifications of the air carrier or commercial operator. (PLT389) — 14 CFR §121.389

Answers (B) and (C) are incorrect because while the International Notices to Airmen and the International Aeronautical Information Manual may contain information on the location and operation of the flight navigation equipment, the air carrier's operations specifications determine the routes in which a flight navigator is required.

Answers

| 9352 | [C] | 9353 | [B] | 8196 | [C] | 8197 | [A] |

DSP

9811. What document(s) must be in a person's possession for that person to act as a flight navigator?

A— Third-Class Medical Certificate and current Flight Navigator Certificate.

B— Current Flight Navigator Certificate and a current Second-Class (or higher) Medical Certificate.

C— Current Flight Navigator Certificate and a valid passport.

No person may act as a flight navigator of a civil aircraft of U.S. registry unless he has in his personal possession a current flight navigator certificate issued to him under this part and a second-class (or higher) medical certificate issued to him under Part 67 within the preceding 12 months. (PLT427) — 14 CFR §63.3

ATM, DSP

8199. A flight navigator or a specialized means of navigation is required aboard an air carrier airplane operated outside the 48 contiguous United States and District of Columbia when

A— operations are conducted IFR or VFR on Top.

B— operations are conducted over water more than 50 miles from shore.

C— the airplane's position cannot be reliably fixed for a period of more than 1 hour.

No certificate holder may operate an airplane outside the 48 contiguous states and the District of Columbia, when its position cannot be reliably fixed for a period of more than one hour, without a flight crewmember who holds a current flight navigator certificate, or unless the aircraft is equipped with an approved specialized means of navigation. (PLT374) — 14 CFR §121.389

Answer (A) is incorrect because whether IFR or VFR-On-Top, the requirement applies if the airplane's position cannot be reliably fixed for more than 1 hour. Answer (B) is incorrect because the requirement applies over water or land if the airplane's position cannot be reliably fixed for more than 1 hour.

Approach Systems

The primary instrument approach system in the United States is the **Instrument Landing System (ILS)**. The system can be divided operationally into three parts: guidance, range and visual information. If any of the elements is unusable, the approach minimums may be raised or the approach may not be authorized at all.

The guidance information consists of the localizer for horizontal guidance and the glide slope for vertical guidance. The localizer operates on one of 40 frequencies from 108.10 MHz to 111.95 MHz. The glide slope operates on one of 40 paired UHF frequencies. The Morse code identifier of the localizer is the letter "I" (· ·) followed by three other letters unique to that facility. The portion of the localizer used for the ILS approach is called the front course. The portion of the localizer extending from the far end of the runway is called the back course. The back course may be used for missed approach procedures or for a back course approach if one is published.

Range information is usually provided by 75 MHz marker beacons or, occasionally, by DME. There are four types of marker beacons associated with ILS approaches — the outer marker, the middle marker, the inner marker and the back course marker. Flying over any marker beacon will result in both visual and aural indications. The outer marker is identified by a blue light and continuous dashes in Morse code at a rate of 2 per second. The middle marker is indicated by a flashing amber light and alternating dots and dashes at a rate of 2 per second. The inner marker flashes the white light and sounds continuous dots at 6 per second. The back course marker will also flash the white light and sound a series of 2-dot combinations. *See* Figure 2-4 on the next page.

Often, an ADF facility (called a compass locator) is associated with an ILS approach. Usually it is located at the outer marker, but occasionally it is co-located with the middle marker. An outer compass locator is identified with the first 2 letters of the localizer identification group. A middle compass locator is identified by the last 2 letters of the localizer.

Answers

9811   [B]   8199   [C]

VHF Localizer
Provides horizontal guidance
108.10 to 111.95 MHz. Radiates about 100 watts. Horizontal polarization. Modulation frequencies 90 and 150 Hz. Modulation depth on course 20% for each frequency. Code identification (1020 Hz, 5%) and voice communication (modulated 50%) provided on same channel.

ILS approach charts should be consulted to obtain variations of individual systems.

1,000' typical. Localizer transmitter building is offset 250' minimum from center of antenna array and within 90° ±30° from approach end. Antenna is on centerline and normally is under 50/1 clearance plane.

Flag indicates if facility not on the air or receiver malfunctioning

Runway length 7,000' (typical)

250' to 600' from centerline of runway

Sited to provide 55' (±5') runway threshold crossing height

Point of intersection runway and glide slope extended.

Middle Marker
Indicates approximate decision height point
Modulation 1,300 Hz, 95%

Keying: 95 alternate dot & dash combinations/minute

Amber Light

Outer Marker
Provides final approach fix for non-precision approach
Modulation 400 Hz, 95%

Keying: Two dashes/second

Blue Light

UHF Glide Slope Transmitter
Provides vertical guidance
329.3 to 335.0 MHz. Radiates about 5 watts. Horizontal polarization, modulation on path 40% for 90 Hz and 150 Hz. The standard glide slope angle is 3.0 degrees. It may be higher depending on local terrain.

3,000' to 6,000' from threshold

*200'

Localizer modulation frequency
90 Hz   150 Hz

90 Hz   150 Hz
Glide slope modulation frequency

Approximately 1.4° width (full scale limits.)

0.7° (approx.)

3° above horizontal (optimum)

Outer marker located 4 to 7 miles from end of runway, where glide slope intersects the procedure turn (minimum holding) altitude, ±50' vertically.

All marker transmitters approximately 2 watts of 75 MHz modulated about 95%.

Course width varies between 3° to 6° tailored to provide 700' at threshold (full scale limits)

Rate of Descent Chart (feet per minute)

Speed (Knots)	Angle		
	2.5°	2.75°	3°
90	400	440	475
110	485	535	585
130	575	630	690
150	665	730	795
160	707	778	849

Compass locators, rated at 25 watts output 190 to 535 KHz, are installed at many outer and some middle markers. A 400 Hz or a 1020 Hz tone, modulating the carrier about 95%, is keyed with the first two letters of the ILS identification on the outer locator and the last two letters on the middle locator. At some locations, simultaneous voice transmissions from the control tower are provided, with appropriate reduction in identification percentage.

*Figures marked with asterisk are typical. Actual figures vary with deviations in distances to markers, glide angles and localizer widths.

Figure 2-4. Instrument Landing System (ILS)

If a middle marker is out of service, the middle compass locator or PAR radar can be substituted. The middle marker being inoperative does not affect minimums during a Category I ILS approach.

The visual information portion of the ILS consists of approach lights, touchdown and centerline lights and runway lights.

The localizer is very narrow. In fact a full scale deflection (CDI moving from the center to full scale left or right) is only about 700 feet at the runway threshold.

Continued

Different aircraft will require different rates of descent to stay on glide slope. A good rule of thumb is that the vertical speed in feet per minute will be equal to about five times the ground speed in knots. For example, an aircraft with an approach speed of 140 knots will require a descent rate of about 700 feet per minute (140 x 5 = 700).

The lowest approach minimums that can be used for a normal (Category I) ILS approach are a DH of 200 feet and 1,800 feet RVR. A Category II ILS approach will have minimums as low as a DH of 100 feet and a visibility requirement of 1,200 feet RVR. The approach has to be approved for Category II minimums. In addition to suitable localizer, glide slope and marker beacons, the approach must have certain additional equipment working on the landing runway. This equipment includes an approach light system, High Intensity Runway Lights (HIRL), Touchdown Zone Lights (TDZL), Runway Centerline Lights (CL) and Runway Visual Range (RVR). Radar, VASI and Runway End Identifier Lights (REIL) are not required components of a Category II approach system. To descend below the DH from a Category II approach the pilot must be able to see one of the following:

- The runway threshold;
- The threshold markings;
- The threshold lights;
- The touchdown zone or the touchdown zone markings;
- The touchdown zone lights; or
- The approach light system, except that a pilot may not descend below 100 feet above the touchdown zone unless the red terminating bars or the red side row bars are distinctly visible and identifiable.

The Simplified Directional Facility (SDF) and the Localizer-type Directional Air (LDA) are approach systems that give a localizer-type indication to the pilot, but with some significant differences. The LDA is essentially a localizer, but it is not aligned within 3° of the runway as a localizer must be. The localizer can be any width from 3° to 6° wide. If the LDA is within 30°, straight-in minimums will be published for it; if not, only circling minimums will be published. The SDF may or may not be aligned with the runway. The main difference between it and a localizer is that its width is fixed at either 6° or 12°.

ALL

8961. Within what frequency range does the localizer transmitter of the ILS operate?

A— 108.10 to 118.10 MHz.
B— 108.10 to 111.95 MHz.
C— 108.10 to 117.95 MHz.

The localizer transmitter operates on one of 40 ILS channels within the frequency range of 108.10 to 111.95 MHz. (PLT358) — AIM ¶1-1-9

Answer (A) is incorrect because communications frequencies are above 117.95 MHz. Answer (C) is incorrect because 108.10 to 117.95 MHz is the frequency band in which VORs operate.

ALL

8966. What functions are provided by ILS?

A— Azimuth, distance, and vertical angle.
B— Azimuth, range, and vertical angle.
C— Guidance, range, and visual information.

The ILS system may be divided into three functional parts:

1. *Guidance information — localizer, glide slope;*

2. *Range information — marker beacon, DME; and*

3. *Visual information — approach lights, touchdown and centerline lights, runway lights.*

(PLT356) — AIM ¶1-1-9

Answer (A) is incorrect because azimuth and distance information are provided by a TACAN. Answer (B) is incorrect because a localizer/DME approach provides azimuth and range information.

Answers

8961 [B]   8966 [C]

ALL

8958. What aural and visual indications should be observed over an ILS inner marker?

A— Continuous dots at the rate of six per second.

B— Continuous dashes at the rate of two per second.

C— Alternate dots and dashes at the rate of two per second.

The code and light identifications of marker beacons are as follows:

Marker	Code	Light
OM	_ _ _	BLUE
MM	• — • —	AMBER
IM	• • • •	WHITE
BC	• • • •	WHITE

(PLT356) — AIM ¶1-1-9

Answer (B) is incorrect because continuous dashes at the rate of two per second indicate the ILS outer marker. Answer (C) is incorrect because alternate dots and dashes at the rate of two per second indicate the ILS middle marker.

ALL

8959. What aural and visual indications should be observed over an ILS middle marker?

A— Continuous dots at the rate of six per second, identified as a high pitch tone.

B— Continuous dashes at the rate of two per second, identified as a low-pitched tone.

C— Alternate dots and dashes identified as a low-pitched tone.

The code and light identifications of marker beacons are as follows:

Marker	Code	Light
OM	_ _ _	BLUE
MM	• — • —	AMBER
IM	• • • •	WHITE
BC	• • • •	WHITE

(PLT277) — AIM ¶1-1-9

Answer (A) is incorrect because continuous dots at the rate of six per second indicate an ILS inner marker. Answer (B) is incorrect because continuous dashes at the rate of two per second indicate an ILS outer marker.

ALL

8960. What aural and visual indications should be observed over an ILS outer marker?

A— Continuous dots at the rate of six per second.

B— Continuous dashes at the rate of two per second.

C— Alternate dots and dashes at the rate of two per second.

The code and light identifications of marker beacons are as follows:

Marker	Code	Light
OM	— — —	BLUE
MM	• — • —	AMBER
IM	• • • •	WHITE
BC	• • • •	WHITE

(PLT277) — AIM ¶1-1-9

Answer (A) is incorrect because continuous dots at the rate of six per second indicate an ILS inner marker. Answer (C) is incorrect because alternating dots and dashes at the rate of two per second indicate an ILS middle marker.

ALL

8962. If installed, what aural and visual indications should be observed over the ILS back course marker?

A— A series of two dot combinations, and a white marker beacon light.

B— Continuous dashes at the rate of one per second, and a white marker beacon light.

C— A series of two dash combinations, and a white marker beacon light.

The code and light identifications of marker beacons are as follows:

Marker	Code	Light
OM	— — —	BLUE
MM	• — • —	AMBER
IM	• • • •	WHITE
BC	• • • •	WHITE

(PLT277) — AIM ¶1-1-9

Answer (B) is incorrect because this is not a marker indication of any kind, but it most closely resembles an ILS outer marker. Answer (C) is incorrect because this is not marker indication of any kind, but it most closely resembles an ILS middle marker.

Answers

8958	[A]	8959	[C]	8960	[B]	8962	[A]

ALL

8956. Which component associated with the ILS is identified by the last two letters of the localizer group?

A— Inner marker.
B— Middle compass locator.
C— Outer compass locator.

Compass locators transmit two-letter identification groups. The outer locator transmits the first two letters of the localizer identification group, and the middle locator transmits the last two letters of the localizer identification group. (PLT356) — AIM ¶1-1-9

Answer (A) is incorrect because a simple marker beacon is not identified by letters; only compass locators are so identified. Answer (C) is incorrect because an outer compass locator is identified by the first two letters of the localizer identification group.

ALL

8957. Which component associated with the ILS is identified by the first two letters of the localizer identification group?

A— Inner marker.
B— Middle compass locator.
C— Outer compass locator.

Compass locators transmit two-letter identification groups. The outer locator transmits the first two letters of the localizer identification group, and the middle locator transmits the last two letters of the localizer identification group. (PLT356) — AIM ¶1-1-9

Answer (A) is incorrect because marker beacons are not identified by letters; only compass locators. Answer (B) is incorrect because a middle compass locator is identified by the last two letters of the localizer identification group.

ALL

9403. Which facility may be substituted for the middle marker during a Category I ILS approach?

A— VOR/DME FIX.
B— Surveillance radar.
C— Compass locator.

A compass locator or precision radar may be substituted for the outer or middle marker. (PLT356)—14 CFR §91.175

Answer (A) is incorrect because VOR/DME may be substituted for the outer marker only. Answer (B) is incorrect because surveillance radar may be substituted for the outer marker only.

ALL

8970. If the middle marker for a Category I ILS approach is inoperative,

A— the RVR required to begin the approach in increased by 20%.
B— the DA/DH is increased by 50 feet.
C— the inoperative middle marker has no effect on straight-in minimums.

The middle marker being inoperative does not affect minimums. (PLT277) — 14 CFR §91.175

ALL

8968. When is the course deviation indicator (CDI) considered to have a full-scale deflection?

A— When the CDI deflects from full-scale left to full-scale right, or vice versa.
B— When the CDI deflects from the center of the scale to full-scale left or right.
C— When the CDI deflects from half-scale left to half-scale right, or vice versa.

Full-scale deflection is 5 dots to either side of center. (PLT276) — FAA-H-8083-15

Answers (A) and (C) are incorrect because when the CDI deflects full-scale left to full-scale right (or vice versa), this represents 2 full-scale deflections.

ALL

8969. Which "rule-of-thumb" may be used to approximate the rate of descent required for a 3° glidepath?

A— 5 times groundspeed in knots.
B— 8 times groundspeed in knots.
C— 10 times groundspeed in knots.

The descent rate in feet per minute required to maintain a 3° glide slope is roughly five times your ground speed in knots. (PLT170) — FAA-P-8740-48

Answer (B) is incorrect because 8 times the ground speed in knots would result in a 5% glide slope. Answer (C) is incorrect because 10 times the ground speed in knots would result in a 6% glide slope.

ALL

9749. The rate of descent for a 3.5° angle of descent glidescope is

A— 740 ft/min at 105 knots groundspeed.
B— 740 ft/min at 120 knots airspeed.
C— 740 ft/min at 120 knots groundspeed.

Reference Legend 9. Follow 3.5° to right to 740 ft/min and go up to find the ground speed of 120. (PLT045) — AIM ¶1-1-20

Answers

ALL

8971. (Refer to Figures 135 and 138.) Which displacement from the localizer and glide slope at the 1.9 NM point is indicated?

A— 710 feet to the left of the localizer centerline and 140 feet below the glide slope.
B— 710 feet to the right of the localizer centerline and 140 feet above the glide slope.
C— 430 feet to the right of the localizer centerline and 28 feet above the glide slope.

With the CDI two dots to the left, we are to the right of course, and according to FAA Figure 138, at the 1.9 NM location 710 feet to the right of course. The glide slope indication is two dots above the glide slope and at the 1.9 NM mark on FAA Figure 138, that would put you 140 feet above the glide slope. (PLT141) — FAA-H-8083-15

Answer (A) is incorrect because the aircraft is to the right of the localizer and above the glide slope. Answer (C) is incorrect because the 430 feet and 28 feet deviations are at 1,300 feet.

ALL

8972. (Refer to Figures 136 and 138.) Which displacement from the localizer centerline and glide slope at the 1,300-foot point from the runway is indicated?

A— 21 feet below the glide slope and approximately 320 feet to the right of the runway centerline.
B— 28 feet above the glide slope and approximately 250 feet to the left of the runway centerline.
C— 21 feet above the glide slope and approximately 320 feet to the left of the runway centerline.

FAA Figure 136 shows the aircraft is displaced a dot and a half left of course and a dot and a half above the glide slope, eliminating Answer A. Interpolating at the 1,300-foot point, the aircraft is 21 feet above the glide slope and 322 feet left of course. (PLT049) — FAA-H-8083-15

Answer (A) is incorrect because the airplane is above the glide slope, and to the left of the localizer. Answer (B) is incorrect because 28 feet is 2 dots, and 250 feet is less than 1-1/4 dots.

ALL

8973. (Refer to Figures 137 and 138.) Which displacement from the localizer and glide slope at the outer marker is indicated?

A— 1,550 feet to the left of the localizer centerline and 210 feet below the glide slope.
B— 1,550 feet to the right of the localizer centerline and 210 feet above the glide slope.
C— 775 feet to the left of the localizer centerline and 420 feet below the glide slope.

FAA Figure 137 shows the aircraft to be 1 dot below the glide slope and 2 dots left of the localizer, eliminating answer choice B. FAA Figure 138 shows the displacement from the glide slope to be 210 feet and from localizer, 1,550 feet at the outer marker (OM). (PLT276) — FAA-H-8083-15

Answer (B) is incorrect because the airplane is to the left of the localizer, and below the glide slope. Answer (C) is incorrect because at the OM 775 feet is one dot on the localizer, not the glide slope, and 420 feet is two dots on the glide slope.

ALL

8963. The lowest ILS Category II minimums are

A— DH 50 feet and RVR 1,200 feet.
B— DH 100 feet and RVR 1,000 feet.
C— DH 150 feet and RVR 1,500 feet.

The lowest authorized ILS minimums with all required ground and airborne systems components operative, are:

Category I—Decision Height (DH) 200 feet and Runway Visual Range (RVR) 2,400 feet (with touchdown zone and runway centerline lighting, RVR 1,800 Category A, B, C; RVR 2,000 Category D),

Category II—DH 100 feet and RVR 1,000 feet, and

Category IIIA—RVR 700 feet.

(PLT356) — AIM ¶1-1-9

Answer (A) is incorrect because a DH of 50 feet is for Category III operations. Answer (C) is incorrect because a DH of 150 feet is for a pilot's initial Category II authorization (for the initial 6-month period) only and is not the lowest DH for Category II operations.

ALL

9411. Which ground components are required to be operative for a Category II approach in addition to LOC, glide slope, marker beacons, and approach lights?

A— Radar, VOR, ADF, taxiway lead-off lights and RVR.
B— RCLS and REIL.
C— All of the required ground components.

No person may operate a civil aircraft in a Category II or Category III operation unless each ground component required for that operation and the related airborne equipment is installed and operating. (PLT420) — 14 CFR §91.189

Answer (A) is incorrect because radar is not a required Category II ILS ground component. Answer (B) is incorrect because runway end identifier lights (REIL) are used to provide rapid identification of the approach component for Category II ILS.

Answers

| 8971 | [B] | 8972 | [C] | 8973 | [A] | 8963 | [B] | 9411 | [C] |

ALL

9412. When may a pilot descend below 100 feet above the touchdown zone elevation during a Category II ILS instrument approach when only the approach lights are visible?

A— After passing the visual descent point (VDP).
B— When the RVR is 1,600 feet or more.
C— When the red terminal bar of the approach light systems are in sight.

A pilot may descend below the DH on a Category II approach using the approach light system as the sole visual reference. However, the pilot may not descend below 100 feet above touchdown zone elevation (TDZE) using the approach lights as a reference unless the red terminating bars or the red side row bars are also distinctly visible and identifiable. (PLT356) — 14 CFR §91.189

Answer (A) is incorrect because a VDP is not used in conjunction with Category II ILS instrument approaches. Answer (B) is incorrect because, although 1,600 feet may be the required inflight visibility, in order to descend below 100 feet above the touchdown zone elevation based on the approach lights also requires sighting of the red terminating bars.

ALL

9413. In addition to the localizer, glide slope, marker beacons, approach lighting, and HIRL, which ground components are required to be operative for a Category II instrument approach to a DH below 150 feet AGL?

A— RCLS and REIL.
B— Radar, VOR, ADF, runway exit lights, and RVR.
C— Each required ground component.

In addition to localizer, glide slope, marker beacons, and approach light system a Category II ILS must have high-intensity runway lights (HIRL), runway centerline lights (RCLS), touchdown zone lights (TDZL), and runway visual range (RVR). (PLT420) — 14 CFR §91.189

Answer (A) is incorrect because runway end identifier lights (REIL) are used to provide rapid identification of the approach end of a runway. Answer (B) is incorrect because radar is not a required ground component for Category II ILS operations.

ALL

8967. How does the LDA differ from an ILS LOC?

A— LDA. 6° or 12° wide, ILS – 3° to 6°.
B— LDA. offset from runway plus 3°, ILS – aligned with runway.
C— LDA. 15° usable off course indications, ILS – 35°.

The LDA is not aligned with the runway. (PLT356) — AIM ¶1-1-9

Answer (A) is incorrect because an SDF (not LDA) is fixed at either 6° or 12° wide. Answer (C) is incorrect because the usable off-course indications are limited to 35° for both types of approaches within 10 NM.

ALL

8965. How does the SDF differ from an ILS LOC?

A— SDF – 6° or 12° wide, ILS – 3° to 6°.
B— SDF – offset from runway plus 4°, ILS – aligned with runway.
C— SDF – 15° usable off course indications, ILS – 35°.

The SDF signal is fixed at either 6° or 12° as necessary to provide maximum flyability and optimum course quality. (PLT361) — AIM ¶1-1-10

Answer (B) is incorrect because an SDF may or may not be aligned with the centerline of the runway. Answer (C) is incorrect because the usable off course indications are limited to 35° for both types of approaches.

ALL

9794. (Refer to Figure 251). You are cleared to HNL and plan to use the RNAV (RNP) RWY 26L approach. Assuming you have received the training, you

A— should be prepared to program the FMS/GPS with the radio frequency to fly this approach.
B— can use the GPS and radio frequency communications to fly this approach to minimums.
C— must know ahead of time whether or not your FMS/GPS has GPS and radius-to-fix capability.

Some RNP approaches have a curved path, also called a radius-to-fix (RF) leg. Since not all aircraft have the capability to fly these arcs, pilots are responsible for knowing ahead of time whether or not they can conduct an RNP approach with an arc. (PLT354) — AIM ¶5-4-18

Answers

9412　[C]　　　　9413　[C]　　　　8967　[B]　　　　8965　[A]　　　　9794　[C]

RTC

9795. (Refer to Figure 253.) You are cleared to LXV in your helicopter and expect to be given the GPS RWY 16 approach. Your helicopter is equipped with an IFR certified WAAS GPS. Your approach minimums will be

A— 11,360' MDA and 3/4 mi.
B— 11,360' MDA and 1-1/4 mi.
C— 11,360' MDA and 6,600 RVR, or 1-1/2 mi.

Helicopters flying conventional (non-copter) SIAP's may reduce the visibility minima to not less than one half the published Category A landing visibility minima, or 1/4 statute mile visibility/1200 RVR, whichever is greater unless the procedure is annotated with "Visibility Reduction by Helicopters NA." (PLT354) — AIM ¶10-1-2

ALL

9796. (Refer to Figure 250.) You arrive at DUMBB for the RNAV (GPS) at CHA. The preflight briefer issued an unreliable advisory before takeoff. Your avionics are good and you have full GPS service. You

A— can descend to the LNAV MDA of 1,200 feet and 2,400 RVR due to the FSS advisory.
B— descend to the LPV minima of 882 feet and 2,400 RVR in your CAT B aircraft.
C— can descend to the LNAV MDA of 518 feet due to the FSS advisory.

Upon commencing an approach at locations with a "WAAS UNRELIABLE" NOTAM, if the WAAS avionics indicate LNAV/VNAV or LPV service is available, then vertical guidance may be used to complete the approach using the displayed level of service. (PLT354) — AIM ¶1-1-20

ALL

9796-1. (Refer to Figure 249.) You arrive at PILOC. The preflight briefer issued you an "unreliable" advisory on the approach before you took off. Your avionics indicates good signal. You

A— know you can only fly the approach down to LNAV DA minimum of 459 ft. because of the FSS advisory.
B— can use the LPV minimum of 368'DA and 2400 RVR in your CAT B airplane.
C— can only fly the approach down to the LNAV MDA of 560'.

Upon commencing an approach at locations with a "WAAS UNRELIABLE" NOTAM, if the WAAS avionics indicate LNAV/VNAV or LPV service is available, then vertical guidance may be used to complete the approach using the displayed level of service. (PLT354) — AIM ¶1-1-20

ALL

8703. (Refer to Figure 251.) In the RNAV (RNP) RWL 26L at HNL profile, what does the shaded triangle below the DA indicate?

A— The visual segment below the DA is not clear of obstacles.
B— The approach does not have a visual glide slope landing aid.
C— The visual segment is clear.

The shaded fan (or triangle) indicates visual segment below DA is clear of obstacles on a 34:1 slope. (PLT354) — Instrument Approach Procedures

GPS

The Global Positioning System (GPS) is a satellite-based radio navigational, positioning, and time transfer system. The GPS receiver verifies the integrity (usability) of the signals received from the GPS satellites through receiver autonomous integrity monitoring (RAIM) to determine if a satellite is providing corrupted information. Without RAIM capability, the pilot has no assurance of the accuracy of the GPS position. If RAIM is not available, another type of navigation and approach system must be used, another destination selected, or the trip delayed until RAIM is predicted to be available on arrival. The authorization to use GPS to fly instrument approaches is limited to U.S. airspace. The use of GPS in any other airspace must be expressly authorized by the appropriate sovereign authority.

If a visual descent point (VDP) is published, it will not be included in the sequence of waypoints. Pilots are expected to use normal piloting techniques for beginning the visual descent. The database may not contain all of the transitions or departures from all runways and some GPS receivers do not

Continued

Answers

9795   [A]   9796   [B]   9796-1   [B]   8703   [C]

contain DPs in the database. The GPS receiver must be set to terminal (±1 NM) course deviation indicator (CDI) sensitivity and the navigation routes contained in the database in order to fly published IFR charted departures and DPs. Terminal RAIM should be automatically provided by the receiver. Terminal RAIM for departure may not be available unless the waypoints are part of the active flight plan rather than proceeding direct to the first destination. Overriding an automatically selected sensitivity during an approach will cancel the approach mode annunciation. The RAIM and CDI sensitivity will not ramp down, and the pilot should not descend to MDA, but fly to the MAWP and execute a missed approach.

It is necessary that helicopter procedures be flown at 70 knots or less since helicopter departure procedures and missed approaches use a 20:1 obstacle clearance surface (OCS), which is double the fixed-wing OCS, and turning areas are based on this speed as well.

The pilot must be thoroughly familiar with the activation procedure for the particular GPS receiver installed in the aircraft and must initiate appropriate action after the missed approach waypoint (MAWP). Activating the missed approach prior to the MAWP will cause CDI sensitivity to immediately change to terminal (±1 NM) sensitivity and the receiver will continue to navigate to the MAWP. The receiver will not sequence past the MAWP. Turns should not begin prior to the MAWP. A GPS missed approach requires pilot action to sequence the receiver past the MAWP to the missed approach portion of the procedure. If the missed approach is not activated, the GPS receiver will display an extension of the inbound final approach course and the ATD will increase from the MAWP until it is manually sequenced after crossing the MAWP.

Any required alternate airport must have an approved instrument approach procedure other than GPS, which is anticipated to be operational and available at the estimated time of arrival and which the aircraft is equipped to fly. Missed approach routings in which the first track is via a course rather than direct to the next waypoint require additional action by the pilot to set the course. Being familiar with all of the inputs required is especially critical during this phase of flight.

ALL

9429. If Receiver Autonomous Integrity Monitoring (RAIM) is not available when setting up for GPS approach, the pilot should

A— continue to the MAP and hold until the satellites are recaptured.
B— proceed as cleared to the IAF and hold until satellite reception is satisfactory.
C— select another type of approach using another type of navigation aid.

If RAIM is not available, another type of navigation and approach system must be used, another destination selected, or the trip delayed until RAIM is predicted to be available on arrival. (PLT354) — AIM ¶1-1-19

ALL

9430. Without Receiver Autonomous Integrity Monitoring (RAIM) capability, the accuracy of the GPS derived

A— altitude information should not be relied upon to determine aircraft altitude.
B— position is not affected.
C— velocity information should be relied upon to determine aircraft groundspeed.

The GPS receiver verifies the integrity (usability) of the signals received from the GPS constellation through RAIM, to determine if a satellite is providing corrupted information. Without RAIM capability, the pilot has no assurance of the accuracy of the GPS position. (PLT354) — AIM ¶1-1-19

Answers

9429 [C]   9430 [A]

ALL

9431. Overriding an automatically selected sensitivity during a GPS approach will

A— cancel the approach mode annunciation.
B— require flying point-to-point on the approach to comply with the published approach procedure.
C— have no affect if the approach is flown manually.

Overriding an automatically selected sensitivity during an approach will cancel the approach mode annunciation. The RAIM and CDI sensitivity will not ramp down, and the pilot should not descend to MDA, but fly to the MAWP and execute a missed approach. (PLT354) — AIM ¶1-1-19

ALL

9432. If a visual descent point (VDP) is published on a GPS approach, it

A— will be coded in the waypoint sequence and identified using ATD.
B— will not be included in the sequence of waypoints.
C— must be included in the normal waypoints.

If a visual descent point (VDP) is published, it will not be included in the sequence of waypoints. Pilots are expected to use normal piloting techniques for beginning the visual descent. (PLT354) — AIM ¶1-1-19

ALL

9722. GPS instrument approach operations, outside the United States, must be authorized by

A— the FAA-approved aircraft flight manual (AFM) or flight manual supplement.
B— a sovereign country or governmental unit.
C— the FAA Administrator only.

The authorization to use GPS to fly instrument approaches is provided by a sovereign country or governmental unit. (PLT354) — AIM ¶1-1-19

ALL

9723. Authorization to conduct any GPS operation under IFR requires that

A— the equipment be approved in accordance with TSO C-115a.
B— the pilot review appropriate weather, aircraft flight manual (AFM), and operation of the particular GPS receiver.
C— air carrier and commercial operators must meet the appropriate provisions of their approved operations specifications.

The GPS operation must be conducted in accordance with the FAA-approved aircraft flight manual (AFM) or flight manual supplement. Flight crewmembers must be thoroughly familiar with the particular GPS equipment installed in the aircraft, the receiver operation manual, and the AFM or flight manual supplement. Air carrier and commercial operators must meet the appropriate provisions of their approved operations specifications. (PLT354) — AIM ¶1-1-19

Answer (A) is incorrect because the equipment must be approved in accordance with TSO C-129, not TSO C-115a. Answer (B) is incorrect because while the pilot is responsible for reviewing the weather before any flight, this requirement is not specific to GPS operations.

ALL

9812. What does the absence of the shaded arrowhead after the VDP on a GPS approach indicate?

A— Obstacle obstructions between the VDP and the runway.
B— A 20:1 glideslope.
C— A 60:1 glideslope.

Absence of the shaded area indicates that the 34:1 visual surface area is not clear of obstructions. (PLT354) — AIM ¶5-4-5

ALL

9812-1. (Refer to Figure 252.) In reviewing the RNAV/GPS procedure RWY 4 LEW, the lack of shaded fan from the 1.6 NM point to the runway indicates

A— the visual segment below the MDA/DA is not clear of obstacles on a 34-to-1 slope.
B— it does not have VASI.
C— you can descend on a 20-to-1 slope and remain clear of all obstacles.

This question is referring to the area near the black triangle symbol in the IAP profile view that is pointing to the 1.6 NM to RW04 location. For RNAV approaches only, the presence of a gray-shaded line (or "fan," or arrowhead-shaped symbol) from the MDA to the runway symbol in the profile view, is an indication that the visual segment below the MDA is clear of obstructions on the 34:1 slope. Absence of this gray-shaded area indicates that the 34:1 visual surface area is not free of obstructions. (PLT354) — AIM ¶5-4-5, FAA-H-8083-16

Answers

9431 [A]	9432 [B]	9722 [B]	9723 [C]	9812 [A]	9812-1 [A]

ALL
9742. A pilot employed by an air carrier and/or commercial operator may conduct GPS/WAAS instrument approaches

A— if they are not prohibited by the FAA-approved aircraft flight manual and the flight manual supplement.
B— only if approved in their air carrier/commercial operator operations specifications.
C— only if the pilot was evaluated on GPS/WAAS approach procedures during their most recent proficiency check.

Air carrier and commercial operators must meet the appropriate provisions of their approved operations specifications. (PLT420) — AIM ¶1-1-20

ALL
9724. Authorization to conduct any GPS operation under IFR requires that

A— the pilot review appropriate weather, aircraft flight manual (AFM), and operation of the particular GPS receiver.
B— air carrier and commercial operators must meet the appropriate provisions of their approved operations specifications.
C— the equipment be approved in accordance with TSO C-115a.

Properly certified GPS equipment may be used as a supplemental means of IFR navigation for domestic enroute, terminal operations, and certain instrument approach procedures (IAPs). This approval permits the use of GPS in a manner that is consistent with current navigation requirements as well as approved air carrier operations specifications. (PLT389) — AIM ¶1-1-19

Answer (A) is incorrect because while the pilot is responsible for reviewing the weather before any flight, this requirement is not specific to GPS operation. Answer (C) is incorrect because the equipment must be approved in accordance with TSO C-129, not TSO C-115a.

ALL
9725. When using GPS for navigation and instrument approaches, a required alternate airport must have

A— an approved instrument approach procedure, besides GPS, that is expected to be operational and available at the ETA.
B— a GPS approach that is expected to be operational and available at the ETA.
C— authorization to fly approaches under IFR using GPS avionics.

Use of a GPS for IFR requires that the avionics necessary to receive all of the ground based facilities appropriate for the route to the destination airport and any required alternate airport must be installed and operational. (PLT354) — AIM ¶1-1-19

Answer (B) is incorrect because the operational nature of GPS is not facility dependent. Answer (C) is incorrect because the GPS equipment, not the pilot-in-command, is authorized for use under IFR.

ALL
9727. A GPS missed approach requires that the pilot take action to sequence the receiver

A— over the MAWP.
B— after the MAWP.
C— just prior to the MAWP.

The pilot must be thoroughly familiar with the activation procedure for the particular GPS receiver installed in the aircraft and must initiate appropriate action after the MAWP. Activating the missed approach prior to the MAWP will cause CDI sensitivity to immediately change to terminal (±1 NM) sensitivity and the receiver will continue to navigate to the MAWP. The receiver will not sequence past the MAWP. Turns should not begin prior to the MAWP. (PLT354) — AIM ¶1-1-19

ALL
9728. If the missed approach is not activated, the GPS receiver will display

A— an extension of the outbound final approach course, and the ATD will increase from the MAWP.
B— an extension of the outbound final approach course.
C— an extension of the inbound final approach course.

A GPS missed approach requires pilot action to sequence the receiver past the MAWP to the missed approach portion of the procedure. If the missed approach is not activated, the GPS receiver will display an extension of the inbound final approach course and the ATD will increase from the MAWP until it is manually sequenced after crossing the MAWP. (PLT354) — AIM ¶1-1-19

Answers

9742 **[B]**	9724 **[B]**	9725 **[A]**	9727 **[B]**	9728 **[C]**

ALL

9739. "Unreliable," as indicated in the following GPS NOTAMS: SFO 12/051 SFO WAAS LNAV/VNAV AND LPV MNM UNRELBL WEF0512182025-0512182049 means

A— within the time parameters of the NOTAM, the predicted level of service will not support LPV approaches.
B— satellite signals are currently unavailable to support LPV and LNAV/VNAV approaches.
C— within the time parameters of the NOTAM, the predicted level of service will not support RNAV and MLS approaches.

The term "unreliable" is used in conjunction with GPS NOTAMs; the term is an advisory to pilots indicating the expected level of service may not be available. GPS operation may be NOTAMed UNRELIABLE due to testing or anomalies. (PLT354) — AIM ¶1-1-19

ALL

9743. What does "UNREL" indicate in the following GPS and WAAS NOTAM: BOS WAAS LPV AND LNAV/VNAV MNM UNREL WEF 0305231700 -0305231815?

A— Satellite signals are currently unavailable to support LPV and LNAV/VNAV approaches to the Boston airport.
B— The predicted level of service, within the time parameters of the NOTAM, may not support LPV approaches.
C— The predicted level of service, within the time parameters of the NOTAM, will not support LNAV/VNAV and MLS approaches.

The term UNRELIABLE is used in conjunction with GPS and WAAS NOTAMs for flight planning purposes. The term UNRELIABLE is an advisory to pilots indicating the expected level of WAAS service (LNAV/VNAV, LPV) may not be available. (PLT354) — AIM ¶1-1-20

Answer (A) is incorrect because UNREL indicates the expected level of WAAS service merely **might not** be available, and this states that it is **definitely** unavailable. Answer (C) is incorrect because MLS approaches are not included in the UNREL advisory.

ALL

9917. It is important for a pilot to ask for site-specific WAAS UNRELIABLE NOTAMS for your destination airport before a flight because

A— Air Traffic Control will not advise pilots of site-specific WAAS UNRELIABLE NOTAMS.
B— Air Traffic Control will confirm that you have site-specific information from a pre-flight briefing.
C— this provides for a second level of safety in the National Airspace System.

Site-specific WAAS MAY NOT BE AVBL NOTAMs indicate an expected level of service; for example, LNAV/VNAV, LP, or LPV may not be available. Pilots must request site-specific WAAS NOTAMs during flight planning. In flight, Air Traffic Control will not advise pilots of WAAS MAY NOT BE AVBL NOTAMs. (PLT354) — AIM ¶1-1-18

ALL

9729. If flying a published GPS departure,

A— the data base will contain all of the transition or departures from all runways.
B— and if RAIM is available, manual intervention by the pilot should not be required.
C— the GPS receiver must be set to terminal course deviation indicator sensitivity.

The GPS receiver must be set to terminal (±1 NM) course deviation indicator (CDI) sensitivity and the navigation routes contained in the data base in order to fly published IFR charted departures and SIDs. Terminal RAIM should be automatically provided by the receiver. Terminal RAIM for departure may not be available unless the waypoints are part of the active flight plan rather than proceeding direct to the first destination. (PLT354) — AIM ¶1-1-19

Answer (A) is incorrect because the data base may **not** contain all of the transitions or departures from all runways and some GPS receivers do not contain SIDs in the data base. Answer (B) is incorrect because certain segments of a SID may require some manual intervention by the pilot, especially when radar vectored to a course or required to intercept a specific course to a waypoint.

Answers

9739	[A]	9743	[B]	9917	[A]	9729	[C]

ALL

9729-1. To use a substitute means of guidance on departure procedures, pilots of aircraft with RNAV systems using DME/DME/IRU without GPS input must

A— ensure their aircraft navigation system position is confirmed within 1,000 feet at the start point of takeoff roll.

B— ensure their aircraft navigation system position is confirmed within 2,000 feet of the initialization point.

C— ensure their aircraft navigation system position is confirmed within 1,000 feet of pushback.

For RNAV 1 DPs and STARs, pilots of aircraft without GPS using DME/DME/IRU, must ensure the aircraft navigation system position is confirmed within 1,000 feet at the start point of take-off roll. (PLT354) — AIM ¶5-5-16

ALL

9730. Missed approach routing in which the first track is via a course rather than direct to the next waypoint requires

A— that the GPS receiver be sequenced to the missed approach portion of the procedure.

B— manual intervention by the pilot, but will not be required, if RAIM is available.

C— additional action by the operator to set the course.

Missed approach routings in which the first track is via a course rather than direct to the next waypoint require additional action by the pilot to set the course. Being familiar with all of the inputs required is especially critical during this phase of flight. (PLT354) — AIM ¶1-1-19

Answer (A) is incorrect because a GPS missed approach requires pilot action to sequence the receiver, and routing in which the first track is via a course requires additional action by the operator. Answer (B) is incorrect because manual intervention for GPS missed approach routing is not dependent upon RAIM availability.

RTC

9721. Obstacles in most areas where "Copter GPS" instrument approaches are needed, require the approach speed must be limited to

A— 80 knots on initial and final segments.

B— 60 knots on all segments except the missed approach.

C— 70 knots on final and missed approach segments.

As long as the obstacle environment permits, helicopter approaches can be flown at a speed of 70 knots from the initial approach waypoint until reaching the missed approach holding waypoint. It is necessary that helicopter procedures be flown at 70 knots or less since helicopter departure procedures and missed approaches use a 20:1 obstacle clearance surface. (PLT382) — AIM ¶1-1-19

RTC

9726. The maximum speed and obstacle clearance surface (OCS) that a "Copter GPS" standard instrument departure (SID) or departure procedure (DP) is based upon is

A— 70 knots and 20:1 OCS.

B— 70 knots and 10:1 OCS.

C— 60 knots and 20:1 OCS.

As long as the obstacle environment permits, helicopter approaches can be flown at a speed of 70 knots from the initial approach waypoint until reaching the missed approach holding waypoint. It is necessary that helicopter procedures be flown at 70 knots or less since helicopter departure procedures and missed approaches use a 20:1 obstacle clearance surface. (PLT354) — AIM ¶1-1-19

Airport Lighting and Marking

A rotating beacon not only aids in locating an airport at night or in low visibility, it can also help to identify which airport is seen. Civilian airports have a beacon that alternately flashes green and white. A military airport has the same green and white beacon but the white beam is split to give a dual flash of white. A lighted heliport has a green, yellow and white beacon.

FAA Figure 129 shows the basic marking and lighting for a runway with a nonprecision approach. The threshold is marked with 4 stripes on either side of the centerline. 1,000 feet from the threshold, a broad "fixed distance" marker is painted on either side of the centerline (A). The runway lights are white for the entire length of the runway (as are the centerline lights if installed). The threshold is lit with red lights.

Answers

9729-1 [A]	9730 [C]	9721 [C]	9726 [A]

FAA Figure 130 shows the somewhat more elaborate ICAO markings for a nonprecision runway. In addition to the fixed distance marker, there are stripes painted on the runway every 500 feet to a distance of 3,000 feet from the threshold. This runway has either High Intensity Runway Lights (HIRL) or Medium Intensity Runway Lights (MIRL) installed. These lights are amber rather than white in the areas within 2,000 feet of the threshold. This gives the pilot a "caution zone" on landing rollout.

FAA Figure 131 shows the lighting and marking for a precision instrument runway. The runway striping has been modified to make it easier to tell exactly how much runway remains. The stripes are still at 500 foot intervals for the 3,000 feet from the threshold. The HIRL or MIRL turns amber for the 2,000 feet closest to the threshold. The centerline lighting has alternating red and white lights from 3,000 feet to 1,000 feet to go, and has all red lights in the 1,000 feet closest to the threshold.

In addition to the markings discussed above, some runways have distance remaining markers. These are simply signs showing the remaining runway in thousands of feet.

Taxi leadoff lights associated with runway centerline lights are green and yellow alternating lights, curving from the centerline of the runway to a point on the exit.

Some runways have Runway End Identifier Lights (REIL) installed at the threshold. These are synchronized flashing lights (usually strobes) placed laterally at either side of the runway threshold. Their purpose is to facilitate identification of a runway surrounded by numerous other lighting systems.

LAHSO is an acronym for "Land And Hold Short Operations." These operations include landing and holding short of an intersecting runway, an intersecting taxiway, or some other designated point on a runway other than an intersecting runway or taxiway. At controlled airports, ATC may clear a pilot to land and hold short. The pilot-in-command has the final authority to accept or decline any land and hold short clearance. The safety and operation of the aircraft remain the responsibility of the pilot. To conduct LAHSO, pilots should become familiar with all available information concerning LAHSO at their destination airport. Pilots should have, readily available, the published Available Landing Distance (ALD) and runway slope information for all LAHSO runway combinations at each airport of intended landing. Additionally, knowledge about landing performance data permits the pilot to readily determine that the ALD for the assigned runway is sufficient for safe LAHSO. If, for any reason, such as difficulty in discerning the location of a LAHSO intersection, wind conditions, aircraft condition, etc., the pilot elects to request to land on the full length of the runway, to land on another runway, or to decline LAHSO, a pilot is expected to promptly inform ATC, ideally even before the clearance is issued. A LAHSO clearance, once accepted, must be adhered to, just as any other ATC clearance, unless an amended clearance is obtained or an emergency occurs. However, a LAHSO clearance does not preclude a rejected landing. The airport markings, signage, and lighting associated with LAHSO consist of a three-part system of yellow hold-short markings, red and white signage and, in certain cases, in-pavement lighting.

ALL
8905. How can a pilot identify a military airport at night?

A— Green, yellow, and white beacon light.
B— White and red beacon light with dual flash of the white.
C— Green and white beacon light with dual flash of the white.

Military airport beacons flash alternately white and green, but are differentiated from civil beacons by a dual peaked (two quick) white flashes between the green flashes. (PLT141) — AIM ¶2-1-9

Answer (A) is incorrect because a sequential green, yellow, and white beacon light identifies a lighted civilian heliport. Answer (B) is incorrect because no type of airfield is marked by a beacon with a red and white light with dual flash of the white.

Answers

8905   [C]

ALL

8906. How can a pilot identify a lighted heliport at night?

A— Green, yellow, and white beacon light.
B— White and red beacon light with dual flash of the white.
C— Green and white beacon light with dual flash of the white.

A rotating beacon flashing green, yellow and white identifies a lighted heliport. (PLT141) — AIM ¶2-1-9

Answer (B) is incorrect because no type of airfield is marked by a white and red beacon with a dual flash of white. Answer (C) is incorrect because a green and white beacon light with a dual flash of the white identifies a military airfield.

ALL

9421. Holding position signs have

A— white inscriptions on a red background.
B— red inscriptions on a white background.
C— yellow inscriptions on a red background.

Holding position signs are mandatory instruction signs, and mandatory instruction signs have a red background with a white inscription. (PLT141) — AIM ¶2-3-8

ALL

9421-1. The most important markings on an airport are

A— ILS critical area.
B— hold markings.
C— taxiway identification markings.

The hold markings depict where the aircraft is supposed to stop and are a critical component to safe airport operations. (PLT141) — AIM ¶2-3-5

ALL

9421-2. In the United States, there is an average of

A— 2 runway incursions every week.
B— 3 runway incursions every day.
C— 4 runway incursions every month.

Runway safety is a significant challenge and a top priority for everyone in aviation. In the United States, an average of three runway incursions occur daily. (PLT141) — FAA-H-8083-25

ALL

9421-3. Detailed investigations of runway incursions have identified

A— 2 major areas of contributing factors.
B— 3 major areas of contributing factors.
C— 4 major areas of contributing factors.

Detailed investigations of runway incursions have identified 3 major areas contributing to these events: (1) failure to comply with ATC instructions; (2) lack of airport familiarity; (3) nonconformance with standard operating procedures. (PLT149) — FAA-H-8083-25

ALL

9422. Airport information signs, used to provide destination or information, have

A— yellow inscriptions on a black background.
B— white inscriptions on a black background.
C— black inscriptions on a yellow background.

Information signs have a yellow background with a black inscription. They are used to provide the pilot with information on such things as areas that cannot be seen from the control tower, applicable radio frequencies, and noise abatement procedures. (PLT141) — AIM ¶2-3-12

ALL

9735. (Refer to Figure 223.) The "runway hold position" sign denotes

A— an area protected for an aircraft approaching a runway.
B— an entrance to runway from a taxiway.
C— intersecting runways.

Runway holding position signs are located at the holding position on taxiways that intersect a runway or on runways that intersect other runways. (PLT141) — AIM ¶2-3-8

ALL

9735-1. (Refer to Figure 228.) What is the purpose of the runway/runway hold position sign?

A— Denotes entrance to runway from a taxiway.
B— Denotes area protected for an aircraft approaching or departing a runway.
C— Denotes intersecting runways.

Answers

8906	[A]		9421	[A]		9421-1	[B]		9421-2	[B]
9735	[C]		9735-1	[C]						

And continuing: 9421-3 [B], 9422 [C]

Mandatory instruction signs are used to denote an entrance to a runway or critical area and areas where an aircraft is prohibited from entering. The runway holding position sign is located at the holding position on taxiways that intersect a runway or on runways that intersect other runways. (PLT141) — AIM ¶2-3-8

ALL
9735-2. (Refer to Figure 225.) What is the purpose of No Entry sign?

A— Identifies paved area where aircraft are prohibited from entering.
B— Identifies area that does not continue beyond intersection.
C— Identifies the exit boundary for the runway protected area.

The no entry sign prohibits an aircraft from entering an area. Typically, this sign would be located on a taxiway intended to be used in only one direction or at the intersection of vehicle roadways with runways, taxiways or aprons where the roadway may be mistaken as a taxiway or other aircraft movement surface. (PLT141) — AIM ¶2-3-8

Answer (B) is incorrect because this is the purpose of a hold position sign. Answer (C) is incorrect because this is the purpose of the runway boundary sign.

ALL
9735-3. (Refer to Figure 226.) What does the outbound destination sign identify?

A— Identifies entrance to the runway from a taxiway.
B— Identifies runway on which an aircraft is located.
C— Identifies direction to take-off runways.

Outbound destination signs define directions to takeoff runways. (PLT141) — AIM ¶2-3-11

Answer (A) is incorrect because this is a runway marking. Answer (B) is incorrect because this is a runway location sign.

ALL
8901. What is the advantage of HIRL or MIRL on an IFR runway as compared to a VFR runway?

A— Lights are closer together and easily distinguished from surrounding lights.
B— Amber lights replace white on the last 2,000 feet of runway for a caution zone.
C— Alternate red and white lights replace the white on the last 3,000 feet of runway for a caution zone.

Runway edge lights (HIRL or MIRL) are white, except on instrument runways, amber replaces white on the last 2,000 feet or half the runway length, whichever is less, to form a caution zone for landing. (PLT148) — AIM ¶2-1-4

Answer (A) is incorrect because MIRL and HIRL are runway edge light systems, and are not spaced closer together on instrument runways. Answer (C) is incorrect because alternate red and white runway centerline lights are on the last 3,000 feet of a runway to the last 1,000 feet of runway (the last 1,000 feet of runway centerline lights are marked by red lights).

ALL
8902. Identify touchdown zone lighting (TDZL).

A— Two rows of transverse light bars disposed symmetrically about the runway centerline.
B— Flush centerline lights spaced at 50-foot intervals extending through the touchdown zone.
C— Alternate white and green centerline lights extending from 75 feet from the threshold through the touchdown zone.

Touchdown Zone Lighting (TDZL) consists of two rows of transverse light bars disposed symmetrically about the runway centerline in the runway touchdown zone. (PLT148) — AIM ¶2-1-5

Answer (B) is incorrect because flush centerline lights spaced at 50-foot intervals extending the length of the runway, including the touchdown zone, are runway centerline lighting. Answer (C) is incorrect because runway centerline lights extend from 75 feet from the threshold through the touchdown zone and are white, not alternating white and green.

ALL
8722. When approaching a holding position sign for a runway approach area you must

A— obtain ATC clearance prior to crossing.
B— hold only when specifically instructed by ATC.
C— hold only when the weather is below 800 feet and 2 miles visibility.

At some airports, it is necessary to hold an aircraft on a taxiway located in the approach or departure area for a runway so that the aircraft does not interfere with operations on that runway. In these situations, a sign with the designation of the approach end of the runway followed by a "dash" (-) and letters "APCH" will be located at the holding position on the taxiway. (PLT141) — AIM ¶2-3-8

Answers

9735-2	[A]	9735-3	[C]	8901	[B]	8902	[A]	8722	[A]

ALL

8903. Identify runway remaining lighting on centerline lighting systems.

A— Amber lights from 3,000 feet to 1,000 feet, then alternate red and white lights to the end.

B— Alternate red and white lights from 3,000 feet to 1,000 feet, then red lights to the end.

C— Alternate red and white lights from 3,000 feet to the end of the runway.

Centerline lighting systems consist of alternating red and white lights from 3,000 feet remaining to the 1,000-foot point, and all red lights for the last 1,000 feet of the runway. (PLT141) — AIM ¶2-1-5

Answer (A) is incorrect because alternate red and white lights are from 3,000 feet to 1,000 feet, then red lights to the end. Answer (C) is incorrect because runway remaining lighting alternates red and white lights from 3,000 feet to 1,000 feet, and red lights from 1,000 feet to the end of the runway.

ALL

8904. Identify taxi leadoff lights associated with the centerline lighting system.

A— Alternate green and yellow lights curving from the centerline of the runway to the centerline of the taxiway.

B— Alternate green and yellow lights curving from the centerline of the runway to the edge of the taxiway.

C— Alternate green and yellow lights curving from the centerline of the runway to a point on the exit.

Taxiway leadoff lights extend from the runway centerline to a point on an exit taxiway to expedite movement of aircraft from the runway. These lights alternate green and yellow from the runway centerline to the runway holding position or the ILS critical area, as appropriate. (PLT141) — AIM ¶2-1-5

ALL

8907. Identify the runway distance remaining markers.

A— Signs with increments of 1,000 feet distance remaining.

B— Red markers laterally placed across the runway at 3,000 feet from the end.

C— Yellow marker laterally placed across the runway with signs on the side denoting distance to end.

Runway distance remaining markers are signs located along the sides of a runway to indicate the remaining runway distance in increments of 1,000 feet. (PLT141) — AIM ¶2-3-3

Answers (B) and (C) are incorrect because distance remaining markers are along the side of the runway and are black and white.

ALL

8922. (Refer to Figure 129.) What is the runway distance remaining at "A" for a daytime takeoff on runway 9?

A— 1,000 feet.

B— 1,500 feet.

C— 2,000 feet.

The fixed distance marker is located 1,000 feet from the threshold (in this case the end of the runway). (PLT141) — AIM ¶2-3-3

Answer (B) is incorrect because the 1,500 feet distance of runway remaining is not marked on an FAA nonprecision runway. Answer (C) is incorrect because 2,000 feet is the distance remaining on an ICAO (not FAA) nonprecision instrument runway where the runway edge lights are amber.

ALL

8923. (Refer to Figure 130.) What is the runway distance remaining at "A" for a nighttime takeoff on runway 9?

A— 1,000 feet.

B— 2,000 feet.

C— 2,500 feet.

According to the key, a half-shaded circle indicates yellow lights. Each fixed-distance marker marks off 500 feet. Four markers from the departure end to the first yellow light measures 2,000 feet remaining. (PLT141) — AIM ¶2-3-3

Answers (A) and (C) are incorrect because the beginning of yellow runway edge lights on an ICAO nonprecision instrument runway indicates 2,000 feet of runway remaining.

ALL

8924. (Refer to Figure 130.) What is the runway distance remaining at "B" for a daytime takeoff on runway 9?

A— 2,000 feet.

B— 2,500 feet.

C— 3,000 feet.

Each fixed-distance marker measures 500 feet. From the departure end, it is 3,000 feet. (PLT141) — AIM ¶2-3-3

Answer (A) is incorrect because 2,000 feet would be the third distance marker encountered. At night, 2,000 feet is identified by the beginning of amber runway edge lights. Answer (B) is incorrect because 2,500 feet would be the second distance marker encountered.

Answers

| 8903 | [B] | 8904 | [C] | 8907 | [A] | 8922 | [A] | 8923 | [B] | 8924 | [C] |

ALL
8925. (Refer to Figure 130.) What is the runway distance remaining at "C" for a daytime takeoff on runway 9?

A— 2,500 feet.
B— 2,000 feet.
C— 1,500 feet.

Since each fixed-distance marker in this problem represents 500 feet, the distance to "C" from the departure end is 2,000 feet. (PLT141) — AIM ¶2-3-3

Answer (A) is incorrect because 2,500 feet would be the second distance marker encountered. Answer (C) is incorrect because 1,500 feet would be the fourth distance marker encountered.

ALL
8926. (Refer to Figure 130.) What is the runway distance remaining at "D" for a daytime takeoff on runway 9?

A— 500 feet.
B— 1,000 feet.
C— 1,500 feet.

The fixed-distance marker at "D" corresponds to 1,000 feet remaining. (PLT141) — AIM ¶2-3-3

Answer (A) is incorrect because 500 feet would be the sixth distance marker encountered. Answer (C) is incorrect because 1,500 feet would be the fourth distance marker encountered.

ALL
8927. (Refer to Figure 131.) What is the runway distance remaining at "E" for a daytime takeoff on runway 9?

A— 1,500 feet.
B— 2,000 feet.
C— 2,500 feet.

Each fixed-distance marker marks off 500 feet. "E" is 2,000 feet from the departure end. (PLT141) — AIM ¶2-3-3

Answer (A) is incorrect because 1,500 feet would be the second pair of double markers encountered on either side of the centerline. Answer (C) is incorrect because 2,500 feet would be the second pair of single markers encountered on either side of the centerline.

ALL
8928. (Refer to Figure 131.) What is the runway distance remaining at "A" for a nighttime takeoff on runway 9?

A— 2,000 feet.
B— 3,000 feet.
C— 3,500 feet.

This question and figure reference remaining runway lighting/centerline lighting systems in the final 2,000 feet as viewed from the takeoff or approach position. Alternate

red and white lights are seen from the 3,000-foot points to the 1,000-foot points, and all red lights are seen for the last 1,000 feet of the runway. (PLT141) — AIM ¶2-1-5

Answer (A) is incorrect because 2,000 feet is marked by the beginning of amber runway edge lights. Answer (C) is incorrect because the runway remaining lights begin alternating between red and white at 3,000 feet of remaining runway.

ALL
8929. (Refer to Figure 131.) What is the runway distance remaining at "D" for a daytime takeoff on runway 9?

A— 3,000 feet.
B— 2,500 feet.
C— 1,500 feet.

Each fixed-distance marker marks off 500 feet. "D" corresponds to 3,000 feet. (PLT141) — AIM ¶2-3-3

Answer (B) is incorrect because 2,500 feet would be the second pair of single markers encountered on either side of the centerline. Answer (C) is incorrect because 1,500 feet would be the second pair of double markers encountered on either side of the centerline.

ALL
8930. (Refer to Figure 131.) What is the runway distance remaining at "B" for a nighttime takeoff on runway 9?

A— 1,000 feet.
B— 2,000 feet.
C— 2,500 feet.

The runway edge lights are white, except on instrument runways. There, amber replaces white on the last 2,000 feet or half the runway length, whichever is less, to form a caution zone for landings. (PLT141) — AIM ¶2-1-4

Answer (A) is incorrect because 1,000 feet would be indicated by the start of red centerline lighting. Answer (C) is incorrect because the beginning of yellow runway edge lights on an instrument runway indicates 2,000 feet of remaining runway.

ALL
8931. (Refer to Figure 131.) What is the runway distance remaining at "F" for a daytime takeoff on runway 9?

A— 2,000 feet.
B— 1,500 feet.
C— 1,000 feet.

Each fixed-distance marker marks off 500 feet. "F" corresponds to the 1,000-foot fixed-distance marker. (PLT141) — AIM ¶2-3-3

Answer (A) is incorrect because 2,000 feet would be the first pair of double markers encountered on either side of the centerline. At night it is marked by the beginning of amber runway edge lights. Answer (B) is incorrect because 1,500 feet would be the second pair of double markers encountered on either side of the centerline.

Answers

8925 [B]	8926 [B]	8927 [B]	8928 [B]	8929 [A]	8930 [B]
8931 [C]					

ALL
8932. (Refer to Figure 131.) What is the runway distance remaining at "C" for a nighttime takeoff on runway 9?

A— 1,000 feet.
B— 1,500 feet.
C— 1,800 feet.

All red lights along the runway centerline correspond to the last 1,000 feet of runway. (PLT141) — AIM ¶2-1-5

Answer (B) is incorrect because the start of red lights on centerline lighting indicates 1,000 feet of remaining runway. Answer (C) is incorrect because the start of red lights on centerline lighting indicates 1,000 feet of remaining runway.

ALL
8914. What is the purpose of REIL?

A— Identification of a runway surrounded by a preponderance of other lighting.
B— Identification of the touchdown zone to prevent landing short.
C— Establish visual descent guidance information during an approach.

Runway End Identifier Lights (REIL) are effective for:

1. *Identification of a runway surrounded by numerous other lighting systems,*

2. *Identification of a runway which lacks contrast with surrounding terrain, or*

3. *Identification of a runway during reduced visibility.*

(PLT145) — AIM ¶2-1-3

Answer (B) is incorrect because the touchdown zone is identified by in-runway lighting of two rows of transverse light bars on either side of the runway centerline from 100 feet to 3,000 feet from the landing threshold. Answer (C) is incorrect because a VASI (not REIL) assists in providing visual descent guidance information during an approach.

ALL
8915. Identify REIL.

A— Amber lights for the first 2,000 feet of runway.
B— Green lights at the threshold and red lights at far end of runway.
C— Synchronized flashing lights laterally at each side of the runway threshold.

The REIL system consists of a pair of synchronized flashing lights located laterally on each side of the runway threshold. (PLT145) — AIM ¶2-1-3

Answer (A) is incorrect because amber lights are used on the last 2,000 feet of runway edge lights to form a caution zone on instrument runways. Answer (B) is incorrect because green lights at the threshold mark the runway edge for landing aircraft and red lights at the far end mark the runway edge to a departing or landing aircraft.

ALL
9731. Land and Hold Short Operations (LAHSO) include landing and holding short:

A— of an intersecting taxiway only.
B— of some designated point on the runway.
C— only of an intersecting runway or taxiway.

Land And Hold Short Operations (LAHSO) include landing and holding short of an intersecting runway, an intersecting taxiway, or some other designated point on a runway other than an intersecting runway or taxiway. (PLT140) — AIM ¶4-3-11

ALL
9732. A Land and Hold Short Operations (LAHSO) clearance, that the pilot accepts:

A— must result in a landing.
B— does not preclude a rejected landing.
C— precludes a rejected landing.

A LAHSO clearance, once accepted, must be adhered to unless an amended clearance is obtained or an emergency occurs. However, a LAHSO clearance does not preclude a rejected landing. (PLT140) — AIM ¶4-3-11

ALL
9733. In conducting Land and Hold Short Operations (LAHSO), the pilot should have readily available:

A— the published Available Landing Distance (ALD), landing performance of the aircraft, and slope of all LAHSO combinations at the destination airport.
B— the published runway length and slope for all LAHSO combinations at the airport of intended landing.
C— the landing performance of the aircraft, published Available Landing Distance (ALD) for all LAHSO combinations at the airport of intended landing, plus the forecast winds.

To conduct LAHSO, pilots should become familiar with all available information concerning LAHSO at their destination airport. Pilots should have, readily available, the published Available Landing Distance (ALD) and runway slope information for all LAHSO runway combinations at each airport of intended landing. Additionally, knowledge about landing performance data permits the pilot to readily determine that the ALD for the assigned runway is sufficient for safe LAHSO. (PLT140) — AIM ¶4-3-11

Answers

8932 [A]   8914 [A]   8915 [C]   9731 [B]   9732 [B]   9733 [A]

ALL

9734. The airport markings, signage and lighting associated with Land and Hold Short (LAHSO) consists of:

A— yellow hold-short markings, red and white signage, and in-pavement lights.
B— red and white signage, yellow hold-short markings, and at some airports, in-pavement lights.
C— red and black signage, in-pavement lights, and yellow hold-short markings.

The airport markings, signage, and lighting associated with LAHSO consist of a three-part system of yellow hold-short markings, red and white signage and, in certain cases, in-pavement lighting. (PLT140) — AIM ¶4-3-11

ALL

9416-1. (Refer to Figure 224.) The ILS critical area markings denote

A— where you are clear of the runway.
B— where you must be to start your ILS procedure.
C— where you are clear of the ILS critical area.

The ILS critical area sign is located adjacent to the ILS holding position marking on the pavement and can be seen by pilots leaving the critical area. The sign is intended to provide pilots with another visual cue which they can use as a guide in deciding when they are clear of the ILS critical area. (PLT141) — AIM ¶2-3-9

ALL

9416-2. The ILS critical area sign indicates

A— where aircraft are prohibited.
B— the edge of the ILS critical area.
C— the exit boundary.

The ILS critical area sign is located adjacent to the ILS holding position marking on the pavement and can be seen by pilots leaving the critical area. The sign is intended to provide pilots with another visual cue to use as a guide in deciding when they are clear of the ILS critical area. (PLT141) — AIM ¶2-3-9

ALL

9423-1. (Refer to Figure 227.) The "taxiway ending" marker

A— identifies area where aircraft are prohibited.
B— indicates taxiway does not continue.
C— provides general taxiing direction to named taxiway.

Taxiway ending marker is an airport sign indicating the taxiway does not continue. (PLT141) — AIM ¶2-3-11

Answer (A) is incorrect because this is the purpose of a no entry sign. Answer (C) is incorrect because this is the purpose of direction signs.

ATM, ATS, RTC

9423. Hold line markings at the intersection of taxiways and runways consist of four lines (two solid and two dashed) that extend across the width of the taxiway. These lines are

A— white in color and the dashed lines are nearest the runway.
B— yellow in color and the dashed lines are nearest the runway.
C— yellow in color and the solid lines are nearest the runway.

Holding position markings for taxiway/runway intersections consist of four yellow lines—two solid and two dashed. The solid lines are always on the same side where the aircraft is to hold. (PLT141) — AIM ¶2-3-5

ALL

8203. All runway hold markings consist of

A— 2 dashed and 1 solid yellow line.
B— 2 dashed and 2 solid yellow lines.
C— 1 dashed and 1 solid yellow line.

Holding position markings for taxiway/runway intersections consist of four yellow lines—two solid and two dashed. The solid lines are always on the same side where the aircraft is to hold. (PLT149) — AIM ¶2-3-5

Answers

9734 [B]	9416-1 [C]	9416-2 [B]	9423-1 [B]	9423 [B]	8203 [B]

ATM, ATS, RTC

9436. (Refer to Figure 156.) This sign, which is visible to the pilot on the runway, indicates

A— a point at which the pilot should contact ground control without being instructed by the tower.
B— a point at which the aircraft will be clear of the runway.
C— the point at which the emergency arresting gear is stretched across the runway.

The runway boundary sign has a yellow background with a black inscription with a graphic depicting the pavement holding position. This sign, which faces the runway and is visible to the pilot exiting the runway, is located adjacent to the holding position marking on the pavement. The sign is intended to provide pilots with another visual cue which they can use as a guide in deciding when they are "clear of the runway." (PLT141) — AIM ¶2-3-9

ATM, ATS, RTC

9417. You have just landed at JFK and the tower tells you to call ground control when clear of the runway. You are considered clear of the runway when

A— the aft end of the aircraft is even with the taxiway location sign.
B— the flight deck area of the aircraft is even with the hold line.
C— all parts of the aircraft have crossed the hold line.

An aircraft is not "clear of the runway" until all parts have crossed the applicable holding position marking. (PLT141) — AIM ¶2-3-5

ALL

9764. Taxiway Centerline Lead-Off Lights are color coded to warn pilots that

A— they are within the runway environment or run-up danger critical area.
B— they are within the runway environment or ILS critical area.
C— they are within the taxiway end environment or ILS critical area.

Taxiway centerline lead-off lights provide visual guidance to persons exiting the runway. They are color-coded to warn pilots and vehicle drivers that they are within the runway environment or ILS critical area, whichever is more restrictive. Alternate green and yellow lights are installed, beginning with green, from the runway centerline to one centerline light position beyond the runway holding position or ILS critical area holding position. (PLT141) — AIM ¶2-1-5

ALL

9785. THL is the acronym for

A— Takeoff hold lights.
B— Taxi holding lights.
C— Terminal holding lights.

The Takeoff Hold Lights (THL) system is composed of in-pavement, unidirectional fixtures in a double longitudinal row aligned either side of the runway centerline lighting. Fixtures are focused toward the arrival end of the runway at the "position and hold" point, and they extend for 1,500 feet in front of the holding aircraft. Illuminated red lights provide a signal, to an aircraft in position for takeoff or rolling, indicating that it is unsafe to takeoff because the runway is occupied or about to be occupied by another aircraft or ground vehicle. Two aircraft, or a surface vehicle and an aircraft, are required for the lights to illuminate. The departing aircraft must be in position for takeoff or beginning takeoff roll. Another aircraft or a surface vehicle must be on or about to cross the runway. (PLT141) — AIM ¶2-1-6

ALL

9785-1. Takeoff hold lights (THL) are a part of the

A— automatic runway status light system.
B— tower operated runway stop light system.
C— ground controller operated ramp status holding light system.

Runway Status Light (RWSL) System is a fully automated system that provides runway status information to pilots and surface vehicle operators to clearly indicate when it is unsafe to enter, cross, takeoff from, or land on a runway. The RWSL system processes information from surveillance systems and activates Runway Entrance Lights (REL), Takeoff Hold Lights (THL), Runway Intersection Lights (RIL), and Final Approach Runway Occupancy Signal (FAROS) in accordance with the position and velocity of the detected surface traffic and approach traffic. REL, THL, and RIL are in-pavement light fixtures that are directly visible to pilots and surface vehicle operators. (PLT141) — AIM ¶2-1-6

ALL

9786. REL is the acronym for

A— Runway exit lights.
B— Runway entrance lights.
C— Ramp entry lights.

Answers

9436   [B]   9417   [C]   9764   [B]   9785   [A]   9785-1   [A]   9786   [B]

The Runway Entrance Lights (REL) system is composed of flush mounted, in-pavement, unidirectional fixtures that are parallel to and focused along the taxiway centerline and directed toward the pilot at the hold line. A specific array of REL lights include the first light at the hold line followed by a series of evenly spaced lights to the runway edge; and one additional light at the runway centerline in line with the last two lights before the runway edge. When activated, these red lights indicate that there is high-speed traffic on the runway or there is an aircraft on final approach within the activation area. (PLT141) — AIM ¶2-1-6

ALL

9786-1. Runway Status Lights (REL) are

A— an independent light system.
B— automatically activated.
C— ATC tower controlled.

The runway status light (RWSL) system, which includes runway entrance lights (REL), is a fully automated system that provides runway status information to pilots and surface vehicle operators to clearly indicate when it is unsafe to enter, cross, takeoff from, or land on a runway. RWSL is an independent safety enhancement that does not substitute for or convey an ATC clearance. (PLT141) — AIM ¶2-1-6

ALL

9787. (Refer to Figure 241). Hot Spots are depicted on airport diagrams as

A— squares or rectangles around "HS" and a number.
B— circles or polygons around "HS" and a number.
C— triangles or blocks filled with "HS" and a number.

Runway hotspots (some FAA Regions refer to them as high alert areas) are locations on particular airports that historically have hazardous intersections. Hotspots are depicted on some airport charts as circled areas. (PLT149) — FAA-H-8083-16

ATM, ATS, RTC

9437. (Refer to Figure 157.) This is an example of

A— an ILS Critical Area Holding Position Sign.
B— a Runway Boundary Sign.
C— an ILS Critical Area Boundary Sign.

This sign has a yellow background with a black inscription with a graphic depicting the ILS pavement holding position marking. This is located adjacent to the ILS holding position marking on the pavement and can be seen by the pilots leaving the critical area. (PLT141) — AIM ¶2-3-9

ATM, ATS, RTC

9416. When instructed by ATC to "Hold short of a runway (ILS critical area, etc.)," the pilot should stop

A— with the nose gear on the hold line.
B— so that no part of the aircraft extends beyond the hold line.
C— so the flight deck area of the aircraft is even with the hold line.

When the ILS critical area is being protected the pilot should stop so no part of the aircraft extends beyond the holding position marking. (PLT141) — AIM ¶2-3-5

ALL

9798. When you see this pavement marking from the cockpit, you

A— can taxi past this point at your own risk.
B— must hold short until "cleared" to taxi onto or past the runway.
C— may not cross the line until ATC allows you to "enter" or "cross" by instruction.

This question will likely include an onscreen image depicting runway hold position markings. These markings indicate where an aircraft is supposed to stop when approaching a runway. ATC will not use the word "cleared" in conjunction with authorization for aircraft to taxi. (PLT141) — AIM ¶2-3-5, 4-3-18

ALL

9799. The sign shown is an example of

A— a mandatory instruction sign.
B— runway heading notification signage.
C— an airport directional sign.

This question will likely include an onscreen image depicting a runway hold position sign. This is a mandatory instruction sign, used to hold an aircraft on a taxiway located in the approach or departure area for a runway so the aircraft does not interfere with operations on that runway. (PLT141) — AIM ¶2-3-8

Answers

9786-1 [A]	9787 [B]	9437 [C]	9416 [B]	9798 [C]	9799 [A]

ALL

8701. Airport "hot spots" are

A— reserved for contaminated aircraft.

B— parking spots for military aircraft.

C— known hazardous runway intersections.

A hot spot is defined as a location on an airport movement area with a history of potential risk of collision or runway incursion, and where heightened attention by pilots and drivers is necessary. (PLT149) — FAA-H-8083-16

Approach Lighting

An airplane approaching to land on a runway served by a **Visual Approach Slope Indicator (VASI)** must remain on or above the glide slope (except for normal bracketing) until a lower altitude is necessary for a safe landing.

A VASI gives the pilot a visual glide slope to follow when landing on certain runways. A VASI glide slope is normally about 3° (the same as an ILS) and the aim point is about 1,000 feet down the runway from the threshold. The angle and aim point of the VASI can be adjusted as necessary to accommodate the runway conditions. If a pilot of a high performance airplane is flying a VASI with a glide slope steeper than 3.5°, he/she should be aware that a longer than normal roll-out may result from the flare maneuver required by the steep angle.

Many runways used by air carrier aircraft have a three-bar VASI system to accommodate aircraft with a high cockpit such as Boeing 747 or DC-10. These aircraft need a glide slope that has an aim point further down the runway to ensure adequate clearance for the landing gear at the runway threshold. The pilot of such an airplane must use the two upwind lights (middle and far bars) for glide slope information.

The **Precision Approach Path Indicator (PAPI)** approach light system consists of a row of four lights perpendicular to the runway. Each light can be either red or white depending on the aircraft's position relative to the glide slope. The glide slope indications of a PAPI are as follows:

- High — 4 white lights
- Slightly high — 1 red, 3 white lights
- On glidepath — 2 red, 2 white lights
- Slightly low — 1 white, 3 red lights
- Low — 4 red lights

Pulsating visual approach slope indicators normally consist of a single light unit projecting a two-color visual approach path. The below glidepath indication is normally pulsating red and the above glidepath indication is normally pulsating white. The "on glide slope" indication for one type of system is a steady white light, while for another type it is an alternating red and white.

ALL

9378. A pilot approaching to land a turbine-powered aircraft on a runway served by a VASI shall

A— not use the VASI unless a clearance for a VASI approach is received.

B— use the VASI only when weather conditions are below basic VFR.

C— maintain an altitude at or above the glide slope until a lower altitude is necessary for a safe landing.

An airplane approaching to land on a runway served by a visual approach slope indicator (VASI), shall maintain an altitude at or above the glide slope until a lower altitude is necessary for a safe landing. (PLT147) — 14 CFR §91.129

Answer (A) is incorrect because a VASI should be used at all times when available, and is not considered an instrument approach. Answer (B) is incorrect because a VASI should be used at all times in both VFR and when transitioning out of IFR weather.

Answers

8701   [C]   9378   [C]

ALL
8912. A pilot of a high-performance airplane should be aware that flying a steeper-than-normal VASI glide slope angle may result in

A— a hard landing.
B— increased landing rollout.
C— landing short of the runway threshold.

Although normal VASI glidepath angles are 3°, angles at some locations may be as high as 4.5° to give proper obstacle clearance. Pilots of high performance aircraft are cautioned that use of VASI angles in excess of 3.5° may cause an increase in runway length required for landing and rollout. (PLT147) — AIM ¶2-1-2

Answer (A) is incorrect because flying a steeper-than-normal VASI may result in an increased landing rollout in a high-performance airplane. Answer (C) is incorrect because a landing short of the runway threshold would be a result of flying a lower-than-normal VASI glide slope angle.

ALL
8911. What is the advantage of a three-bar VASI?

A— Pilots have a choice of glide angles.
B— A normal glide angle is afforded both high and low cockpit aircraft.
C— The three-bar VASI is much more visible and can be used at a greater height.

Three-bar VASI installations provide two visual glidepaths. The lower glidepath is provided by the near and middle bars and is normally set at 3° while the upper glidepath, provided by the middle and far bars is normally 1/4° higher. This higher glidepath is intended for use only by high cockpit aircraft to provide a sufficient threshold crossing height. (PLT147) — AIM ¶2-1-2

Answer (A) is incorrect because the three-bar VASI provides a glide slope for high cockpit aircraft, not a choice of glide angles for pilots. Answer (C) is incorrect because both the two- and three-bar VASI are visible from 3-5 miles during the day and up to 20 miles or more at night, and the three-bar VASI does not provide use at a greater height.

ALL
8913. The higher glide slope of the three-bar VASI is intended for use by

A— high performance aircraft.
B— helicopters.
C— high cockpit aircraft.

Three-bar VASI installations provide two visual glidepaths. The lower glidepath is provided by the near and middle bars and is normally set at 3° while the upper glidepath, provided by the middle and far bars is normally 1/4° higher. This higher glidepath is intended for use only by high cockpit aircraft to provide a sufficient threshold crossing height. (PLT147) — AIM ¶2-1-2

Answer (A) is incorrect because the higher glide slope of a three-bar VASI is for use only by high cockpit aircraft, which may or may not be high performance aircraft. Answer (B) is incorrect because the higher glide slope of a three-bar VASI is for use only by high cockpit aircraft, not specifically for use by helicopters.

ALL
8921. What does the Precision Approach Path Indicator (PAPI) consist of?

A— Row of four lights parallel to the runway; red, white, and green.
B— Row of four lights perpendicular to the runway; red and white.
C— One light projector with two colors; red and white.

The Precision Approach Path Indicator (PAPI) uses light units similar to the VASI but are installed in a single row of either two- or four-light units. (PLT147) — AIM ¶2-1-2

Answer (A) is incorrect because PAPI has a row of four lights perpendicular to the runway, and projects red and white light. Answer (C) is incorrect because PAPI consists of a row of four light projectors emitting red or white light.

ALL
8908. What are the indications of Precision Approach Path Indicator (PAPI)?

A— High – white, on glidepath – red and white; low – red.
B— High – white, on glidepath – green; low – red.
C— High – white and green, on glidepath – green; low – red.

The Precision Approach Path Indicator (PAPI) uses light units similar to the VASI but are installed in a single row of either two or four light units:

High	4 white lights
Slightly high	1 red, 3 white lights
On glide path	2 red, 2 white lights
Slightly low	1 white, 3 red lights
Low	4 red lights

(PLT147) — AIM ¶2-1-2

Answer (B) is incorrect because the on glidepath indication of PAPI is both red and white lights. Answer (C) is incorrect because above the glidepath indication of PAPI is all white, on glidepath is two red and two white, and below glidepath is all red.

Answers

8912 [B]	8911 [B]	8913 [C]	8921 [B]	8908 [A]

ALL

8909. What does the pulsating VASI consist of?

A— Three-light system, two pulsing and one steady.
B— Two-light projectors, one pulsing and one steady.
C— One-light projector, pulsing white when above glide slope or red when more than slightly below glide slope, steady white when on glide slope, steady red for slightly below glide path.

Pulsating visual approach slope indicators normally consist of a single light unit projecting a two-color visual approach path into the final approach area of the runway upon which the indicator is installed. The below glidepath indication is normally pulsating red, and the above glidepath indication is normally pulsating white. The on glidepath indication for one type of system is a steady white light, while for another type system, the on glidepath indication consists of an alternating red and white. (PLT147) — AIM ¶2-1-2

Answer (A) is incorrect because the pulsating VASI is a two-light system, in which below glidepath is pulsating red, above glidepath is pulsating white, and on glidepath is a steady white light. Answer (B) is incorrect because the pulsating VASI is a single light projecting unit emitting a two-color visual approach path into the final approach area of the runway.

ALL

8910. What are the indications of the pulsating VASI?

A— High – pulsing white, on glidepath – green, low – pulsing red.
B— High – pulsing white, on glidepath – steady white, slightly below glide slope steady red, low – pulsing red.
C— High – pulsing white, on course and on glidepath – steady white, off course but on glidepath – pulsing white and red; low – pulsing red.

Pulsating visual approach slope indicators normally consist of a single light unit projecting a two-color visual approach path into the final approach area of the runway upon which the indicator is installed. The below glidepath indication is normally pulsating red, and the above glidepath indication is normally pulsating white. The on glidepath indication for one type of system is a steady white light, while for another type system the on glidepath indication consists of an alternating red and white. (PLT147) — AIM ¶2-1-2

Answer (A) is incorrect because the on glidepath indication of a pulsating VASI is either a pulsing red and white or steady white, not green. Answer (C) is incorrect because the pulsating VASI only provides glidepath indications, not lateral, or course, indications. Above glidepath is pulsing white, on glidepath is pulsing red and white or steady white, and below glidepath is pulsing red.

ALL

8705. Lights which indicate the runway is occupied are

A— strobe lights located next to the PAPIs.
B— flashing PAPIs.
C— yellow flashing lights located below the PAPIs.

The standalone final approach runway occupancy signal (FAROS) is a fully automated system that provides runway occupancy status to pilots on final approach to indicate whether it may be unsafe to land. When an aircraft or vehicle is detected on the runway, the precision approach path indicator (PAPI) light fixtures flash as a signal to indicate the runway is occupied and that it may be unsafe to land. (PLT147) — AIM ¶2-1-7

Answers

8909 [C]   8910 [B]   8705 [B]

Chapter 3
Aerodynamics

Lift and Drag

The four forces acting on an aircraft in flight are **lift, weight, thrust** and **drag**. Weight always acts vertically toward the center of the earth. Lift acts perpendicular to the relative wind (not always vertically). Thrust and drag act opposite each other and parallel to the relative wind.

Lift is produced by air flowing over the curved wing surfaces. The air flowing over the upper surface of the wing is deflected further than that flowing across the lower surface and therefore is accelerated. **Bernoulli's Principle** states that when a gas is accelerated, its pressure decreases. Thus the pressure on the upper wing surface is lower than that on the lower surface and lift is produced.

Angle of attack is the angle between the relative wind and chord line of wing. At zero angle of attack, the pressure on the upper surface of the wing is still less than atmospheric, but the wing is producing minimum lift. As the angle of attack is increased, the lift developed by the wing increases proportionately. This is true until the angle of attack exceeds a critical value, when the air flowing over the top of the wing breaks up into a turbulent flow and the wing stalls.

Angle of attack and indicated airspeed determine the total lift. An increase in either indicated airspeed or angle of attack increases total lift (up to the stalling angle of attack) and a decrease in either decreases total lift. To maintain the same total lift (i.e., maintain level flight), a pilot has to change the angle of attack anytime indicated airspeed is changed. For example, as indicated airspeed is decreased, the angle of attack must be increased to compensate for the loss of lift. The relationship between indicated airspeed and lift for a given angle of attack involves the law of squares. If the angle of attack does not change, total lift varies with the square of the indicated airspeed. For example, if the airspeed doubles, the lift will increase by four times.

Indicated airspeed can be thought of as having two elements — the actual speed of the airplane through the air (true airspeed) and the density of the air. As altitude increases, air density decreases. To maintain the same indicated airspeed at altitude an aircraft must fly at a higher true airspeed. To produce the same amount of lift at altitude, a higher true airspeed is required for a given angle of attack.

A wing will always stall at the same angle of attack. The load factor, weight and density altitude will cause the stalling true airspeed to vary, but the stall angle of attack will always be the same.

A curve comparing total drag to parasite and induced drag reveals an airspeed at which drag is at a minimum value. At higher airspeeds, total drag increases because of increasing parasite drag. At lower airspeeds, induced drag increases which increases the total drag. Since the lift stays constant (equal to weight), the low point on the curve is the airspeed that produces the best lift to drag (L/D) ratio. This point is referred to as **L/D$_{MAX}$**. *See* Figure 3-1.

A change in weight changes the L/D curve. The amount of parasite drag is mainly a function of indicated airspeed. The amount of induced drag is a function of angle of attack. When an aircraft's weight is increased, any indicated airspeed will require a higher angle of attack to produce the required lift. This means that induced drag will increase with increases in weight while there will be little change in parasite drag.

When an airplane is within about one wingspan of the ground, the flow of air around the wingtips is inhibited by the close proximity of the ground. This **ground effect** reduces induced drag (and therefore total drag) and increases lift. As an airplane flies out of ground effect on takeoff, the increased induced drag will require a higher angle of attack.

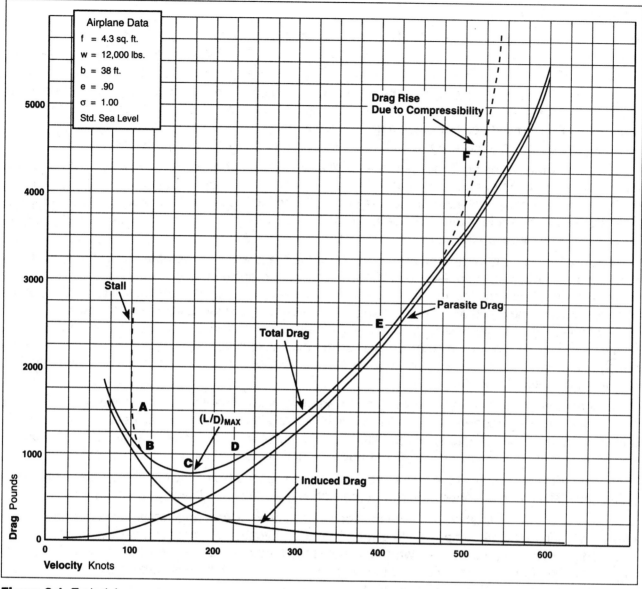

Figure 3-1. Typical drag curves

ALL

8377. What will be the ratio between airspeed and lift if the angle of attack and other factors remain constant and airspeed is doubled? Lift will be

A— the same.
B— two times greater.
C— four times greater.

Lift is proportional to the square of the airplane's velocity. For example, an airplane traveling at 200 knots has four times the lift as the same airplane traveling at 100 knots if the angle of attack and other factors remain constant. (PLT242) — FAA-H-8083-25

Answer (A) is incorrect because lift is proportional to the square of the airplane's velocity, it is not constant. Answer (B) is incorrect because, as airspeed is doubled, the lift will be four times greater.

ALL

8378. What true airspeed and angle of attack should be used to generate the same amount of lift as altitude is increased?

A— The same true airspeed and angle of attack.
B— A higher true airspeed for any given angle of attack.
C— A lower true airspeed and higher angle of attack.

If the density factor is decreased and the total lift must equal the total weight to remain in flight, it follows that one of the other factors must be increased. The factors usually increased are the airspeed or the angle of attack, because these can be controlled by the pilot. (PLT168) — FAA-H-8083-25

Answer (A) is incorrect because true airspeed must be increased (not remain the same) as altitude increases. Answer (C) is incorrect because true airspeed must increase (not decrease) for any given angle of attack.

ALL

8348. What affects indicated stall speed?

A— Weight, load factor, and power.
B— Load factor, angle of attack, and power.
C— Angle of attack, weight, and air density.

An airplane will always stall at the same angle of attack. The indicated airspeed at which the stalling angle of attack is reached will vary with weight, load factor, and (to an extent) power setting. (PLT477) — FAA-H-8083-25

Answers (B) and (C) are incorrect because indicated stall speed is not affected by the angle of attack or air density.

ALL

9808. The stall speed of an airplane

A— is constant regardless of weight or airfoil configuration.
B— is affected by weight, and bank angle.
C— is not affected by dynamic pressures and lift co-efficient.

Airplanes stall at the same angle of attack regardless of weight, dynamic pressure, bank angle, etc. The stall speed of the aircraft will be affected by weight, bank angle, and other factors since the product of dynamic pressure, wing area, and lift coefficient must produce the required lift. (PLT477) — ANA

ALL

8346. What is the effect on total drag of an aircraft if the airspeed decreases in level flight below that speed for maximum L/D?

A— Drag increases because of increased induced drag.
B— Drag increases because of increased parasite drag.
C— Drag decreases because of lower induced drag.

Note in the following figure that the airspeed at which minimum drag occurs is the same airspeed at which the maximum lift/drag ratio (L/D) takes place. At speeds below maximum L/D, any decrease in airspeed will result in an increase in total drag due to the increase in induced drag. (PLT303) — FAA-H-8083-25

Answer (B) is incorrect because parasite drag varies directly (not inversely) with airspeed. Answer (C) is incorrect because drag increases (not decreases) from any speed other than that for maximum L/D.

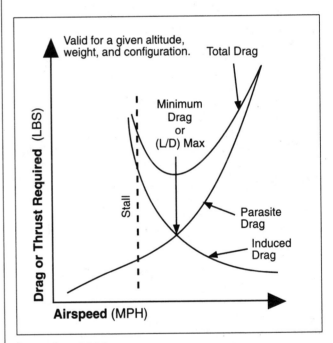

Question 8346

ALL

8397. What is the relationship between induced and parasite drag when the gross weight is increased?

A— Parasite drag increases more than induced drag.
B— Induced drag increases more than parasite drag.
C— Both parasite and induced drag are equally increased.

Lift is required to counteract the aircraft's weight. If weight is increased, lift must be also. To increase lift, angle of attack must be increased, so induced drag also increases. Parasite drag is due to form and friction drag, so there would be little or no change in parasite drag. (PLT015) — ANA

Answer (A) is incorrect because parasite drag increases less (not more) than induced drag as airplane weight increases. Answer (C) is incorrect because induced drag increases more than parasite drag with increases in airplane gross weight.

ALL

9767. How does V_S (KTAS) speed vary with altitude?

A— Remains the same at all altitudes.
B— Varies directly with altitude.
C— Varies inversely with altitude.

True airspeed (KTAS) is based on the density of the air, which is affected by pressure, temperature, and humidity—together, these determine air density. While flying at a constant indicated airspeed, an increase in density altitude will indicate that the air has become less dense, and the true airspeed as well as ground speed will increase. (PLT124) — FAA-H-8083-25

ALL

8368. What is the reason for variations in geometric pitch along a propeller or rotor blade?

A— It permits a relatively constant angle of attack along its length when in cruising flight.
B— It prevents the portion of the blade near the hub or root from stalling during cruising flight.
C— It permits a relatively constant angle of incidence along its length when in cruising flight.

"Twisting," or variations in the geometric pitch of the blades permits the propeller to operate with a relatively constant angle of attack along its length when in cruising flight. (PLT214) — FAA-H-8083-25

ALL

8375. What flight condition should be expected when an aircraft leaves ground effect?

A— An increase in induced drag requiring a higher angle of attack.
B— A decrease in parasite drag permitting a lower angle of attack.
C— An increase in dynamic stability.

An airplane leaving ground effect will require an increase in angle of attack to maintain the same lift coefficient, experience an increase in induced drag and thrust required, experience a decrease in stability with a nose-up change in pitch, and produce a reduction in static source pressure and increase in indicated airspeed. (PLT131) — FAA-H-8083-25

Answer (B) is incorrect because, at slow airspeeds when taking off, induced (not parasite) drag predominates. Answer (C) is incorrect because, when leaving ground effect, expect a decrease in stability and a nose-up change in moment.

ATM, ATS, DSP

8382. By changing the angle of attack of a wing, the pilot can control the airplane's

A— lift, gross weight, and drag.
B— lift, airspeed, and drag.
C— lift and airspeed, but not drag.

By changing the angle of attack, the pilot can control lift, airspeed, and drag. Even the total load supported in flight by the wing may be modified by variations in angle of attack. (PLT004) — FAA-H-8083-3

Answer (A) is incorrect because angle of attack cannot control the airplane's gross weight. Answer (C) is incorrect because the pilot can control the amount of induced drag by changing the angle of attack.

ATM, ATS, DSP

8399. At which speed will increasing the pitch attitude cause an airplane to climb?

A— Low speed.
B— High speed.
C— Any speed.

When operating at speeds below L/D$_{MAX}$, an increase in pitch or decrease in speed causes total drag to increase, thus causing a descent with a fixed power setting. When operating at speeds above L/D$_{MAX}$ and pitch is increased (or airspeed is decreased), total drag will decrease, thus causing a climb with a fixed power setting. (PLT303) — ANA

Answers (A) and (C) are incorrect because below L/D$_{MAX}$, performance decreases with increases in pitch.

Answers

8397 [B]	9767 [B]	8368 [A]	8375 [A]	8382 [B]	8399 [B]

ATM, ATS, DSP

8379. How can an airplane produce the same lift in ground effect as when out of ground effect?

A— The same angle of attack.
B— A lower angle of attack.
C— A higher angle of attack.

The reduction of the wing-tip vortices due to ground effect alters the spanwise lift distribution and reduces the induced angle of attack and induced drag. Therefore, the wing will require a lower angle of attack in ground effect to produce the same lift coefficient. (PLT131) — FAA-H-8083-3

Answer (A) is incorrect because, if the same angle of attack is maintained, an increase in lift coefficient will result. Answer (C) is incorrect because a lower angle of attack is required to produce the same lift in ground effect.

Critical Engine and V_{MC}

Because of "P-Factor" on most propeller-driven airplanes, the loss of one particular engine at high angles of attack would be more detrimental to performance than the loss of the other. One of the engines has its thrust line closer to the aircraft centerline (*see* Figure 3-2). The loss of this engine would more adversely affect the performance and handling of the aircraft; therefore this is the "critical engine."

For unsupercharged engines, V_{MC} decreases as altitude is increased. Stalls should never be practiced with one engine inoperative because of the potential for loss of control. Engine out approaches and landings should be made the same as normal approaches and landings.

Banking at least 5° into the good engine ensures the airplane will be controllable at any speed above the certificated V_{MC}, that the airplane will be in a minimum drag configuration for best climb performance, and that the stall characteristics will not be degraded. Engine out flight with the ball centered is never correct.

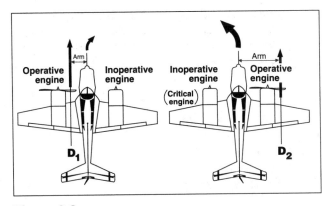

Figure 3-2

ATM

8357. In a light, twin-engine airplane with one engine inoperative, when is it acceptable to allow the ball of a slip-skid indicator to be deflected outside the reference lines?

A— While maneuvering at minimum controllable airspeed or less to avoid overbanking.
B— When operating at any airspeed of V_{MC} or greater with only enough deflection to zero the side slip.
C— When practicing imminent stalls in a banked attitude of over 60°.

Banking at least 5° into the good engine ensures that the airplane will be controllable at any speed above the certificated V_{MC}, that the airplane will be in a minimum drag configuration for best climb performance, and that the stall characteristics will not be degraded. Engine out flight with the ball centered is never correct. (PLT223) — FAA-H-8083-3

ATM

8358. What is the safest and most efficient takeoff and initial climb procedure in a light, twin-engine airplane? Accelerate to

A— best engine-out, rate-of-climb airspeed while on the ground, then lift off and climb at that speed.
B— V_{MC}, then lift off at that speed and climb at maximum angle-of-climb airspeed.
C— an airspeed slightly above V_{MC}, then lift off and climb at the best rate-of-climb airspeed.

Lift-off should be made at no less than V_{MC} + 5. After lift-off, the airplane should be allowed to accelerate to the all-engine best-rate-of-climb speed V_Y, and then the climb maintained at this speed with takeoff power until a safe maneuvering altitude is attained. (PLT459) — FAA-H-8083-3

Answers

8379   [B]   8357   [B]   8358   [C]

ATM

8360. What performance should a pilot of a light, twin-engine airplane be able to maintain at V_{MC}?

A— Heading.
B— Heading and altitude.
C— Heading, altitude, and ability to climb 50 ft/min.

V_{MC} can be defined as the minimum airspeed at which the airplane is controllable when the critical engine is suddenly made inoperative, and the remaining engine is producing takeoff power. This does not mean that the airplane must be able to climb or even hold altitude. It only means that a heading can be maintained. (PLT208) — FAA-H-8083-3

ATM

8364. What does the blue radial line on the airspeed indicator of a light, twin-engine airplane represent?

A— Maximum single-engine rate of climb.
B— Maximum single-engine angle of climb.
C— Minimum controllable airspeed for single-engine operation.

The airspeed indicator in a twin-engine airplane is marked with a red radial line at the minimum controllable airspeed with the critical engine inoperative (V_{MC}), and a blue radial line at the best rate of climb airspeed with one engine inoperative (V_{YSE}). (PLT132) — FAA-H-8083-3

ATM, DSP

8359. What procedure is recommended for an engine-out approach and landing?

A— The flightpath and procedures should be almost identical to a normal approach and landing.
B— The altitude and airspeed should be considerably higher than normal throughout the approach.
C— A normal approach, except do not extend the landing gear or flaps until over the runway threshold.

Essentially, an engine-out approach and landing is the same as a normal approach and landing. (PLT223) — FAA-H-8083-3

ATM, DSP

8361. Which engine is the "critical" engine of a twin-engine airplane?

A— The one with the center of thrust closest to the centerline of the fuselage.
B— The one designated by the manufacturer which develops most usable thrust.
C— The one with the center of thrust farthest from the centerline of the fuselage.

The critical engine is defined as the engine whose failure would most adversely affect performance or handling. Because of "P-factor," most propeller-driven airplanes do not develop symmetrical thrust at high angles of attack. If the engine with the thrust line closest to the airplane centerline fails, the resulting yawing moment will be greater than if the other engine had failed. (PLT347) — FAA-H-8083-3

ATM, DSP

8362. What effect, if any, does altitude have on V_{MC} for an airplane with unsupercharged engines?

A— None.
B— Increases with altitude.
C— Decreases with altitude.

For an airplane without supercharged engines, V_{MC} decreases as altitude is increased. Consequently, directional control can be maintained at a lower airspeed than at sea level. (PLT314) — FAA-H-8083-3

ATM, DSP

8363. Under what condition should stalls never be practiced in a twin-engine airplane?

A— With one engine inoperative.
B— With climb power on.
C— With full flaps and gear extended.

With full power applied to the operative engine, as the airspeed drops below V_{MC}, the airplane tends to roll as well as yaw into the inoperative engine. This tendency becomes greater as the airspeed is further reduced. Since this tendency must be counteracted by aileron control, the yaw condition is aggravated by aileron roll (the "down" aileron creates more drag than the "up" aileron). If a stall occurs in this condition, a violent roll into the dead engine may be experienced. (PLT459) — FAA-H-8083-3

Answers

8360 [A]	8364 [A]	8359 [A]	8361 [A]	8362 [C]	8363 [A]

Maneuvering Flight

In a **turn**, centrifugal force is counterbalanced by a portion of the lift of the wing. The horizontal component of lift turns the airplane and the vertical component of lift opposes gravity. When the pilot rolls the airplane into a turn he must increase the total lift of the wing so that the vertical component is equal to the airplane's weight. This is done by increasing the angle of attack. If no compensation is made for the loss of vertical component of lift in a turn, the aircraft will develop a sink rate.

Load factor is the ratio of the weight supported by the wings to the actual weight of the aircraft. For example, if an aircraft with a gross weight of 2,000 pounds were subjected to a total load of 6,000 pounds in flight, the load factor would be 3 Gs. On the ground or in unaccelerated flight the load factor is one. Conditions which can increase the load factor are vertical gusts (turbulence) and level turns. In a **level turn**, the load factor is dependent only on the angle of bank. Airspeed, turn rate or aircraft weight have no effect on load factor.

Rate of turn is the number of degrees per second at which the aircraft turns. The rate of turn is dependent on both the aircraft's airspeed and its angle of bank. To increase the rate of turn, the pilot must increase the angle of bank or decrease the airspeed or both. The rate of turn will decrease if the bank angle is decreased or if the airspeed is increased. The **radius of turn** is also dependent on both the bank angle and the airspeed. If angle of bank is increased or airspeed is decreased, the radius of turn will decrease. If bank angle is shallowed or if airspeed is increased, the radius of turn will increase.

ALL
8349. If no corrective action is taken by the pilot as angle of bank is increased, how is the vertical component of lift and sink rate affected?

A— Lift increases and the sink rate increases.
B— Lift decreases and the sink rate decreases.
C— Lift decreases and the sink rate increases.

When an airplane is banked, its lift can be broken into two vectors, a vertical component of lift and a horizontal component. If the airplane is to maintain altitude in the turn, the vertical component of lift must be equal to the aircraft's weight. This means that total lift must be increased. Lift can be increased either by increasing airspeed or by increasing angle of attack. If the vertical component of lift is less than the aircraft's weight, the airplane will descend. (PLT348) — FAA-H-8083-3

Answer (A) is incorrect because lift will decrease, not increase. Answer (B) is incorrect because the sink rate increases as the lift decreases.

ALL
8350. Why must the angle of attack be increased during a turn to maintain altitude?

A— Compensate for loss of vertical component of lift.
B— Increase the horizontal component of lift equal to the vertical component.
C— Compensate for increase in drag.

When an airplane is banked, its lift can be broken into two vectors, a vertical component of lift and a horizontal component. If the airplane is to maintain altitude in the turn, the vertical component of lift must be equal to the aircraft's weight. This means that total lift must be increased. Lift can be increased either by increasing airspeed or by increasing angle of attack. If the vertical component of lift is less than the aircraft's weight, the airplane will descend. (PLT348) — FAA-H-8083-3

Answer (B) is incorrect because angle of attack is increased in order to increase the vertical component of lift to equal weight. Answer (C) is incorrect because additional thrust (power) is used to compensate for increase in drag.

ALL
8347. What is load factor?

A— Lift multiplied by the total weight.
B— Lift subtracted from the total weight.
C— Lift divided by the total weight.

Load factor is the ratio of the total load supported by the airplane's wings to the actual weight of the airplane and its contents, or the actual load supported by the wings' lift divided by the total weight of the airplane. (PLT310) — FAA-H-8083-25

Answers

8349   [C]   8350   [A]   8347   [C]

ALL

9823. During a turn with constant power

A—the aircraft nose will pitch down.
B—the aircraft will decelerate.
C—the rate of descent will increase.

While in a turn, part of the vertical component of lift has been diverted to horizontal lift. If total lift is not increased (increase in angle of attack) the aircraft nose will pitch down. (PLT348) — FAA-H-8083-3

ALL

9740. During a skidding turn to the right, what is the relationship between the component of lift and centrifugal force?

A—Centrifugal force is less than the horizontal lift component and the load factor is increased.
B—Centrifugal force is greater than the horizontal lift component.
C—Centrifugal force and the horizontal lift component are equal, and the load factor is decreased.

A skidding turn results from excess centrifugal force over the horizontal lift component, pulling the aircraft toward the outside of the turn. As centrifugal force increases, the load factor also increases. (PLT234) — FAA-H-8083-15

Answer (A) is incorrect because a slipping turn will occur if centrifugal force is less than horizontal lift. Answer (C) is incorrect because centrifugal force and horizontal lift are equal in a coordinated turn and load factor will increase.

ALL

8354. If an aircraft with a gross weight of 2,000 pounds were subjected to a total load of 6,000 pounds in flight, the load factor would be

A—2 Gs.
B—3 Gs.
C—9 Gs.

Load factor is the ratio of the total load supported by the airplane's wings to the actual weight of the airplane and its contents, or the actual load supported by the wings divided by the total weight of the airplane:

6,000 pounds ÷ 2,000 pounds = 3 Gs

(PLT018) — FAA-H-8083-25

ALL

8353. Upon which factor does wing loading during a level coordinated turn in smooth air depend?

A—Rate of turn.
B—Angle of bank.
C—True airspeed.

Load factor is independent of airspeed and dependent on angle of bank; therefore, with a constant bank angle, load factor is not affected. There is no change in centrifugal force for any given bank — the load factor remains the same. (PLT248) — FAA-H-8083-25

Answer (A) is incorrect because in a coordinated turn, the rate of turn does not have any impact on the load factor — it is determined wholly by the angle of bank. Answer (C) is incorrect because true airspeed has no impact on the load factor.

ALL

8396. For a given angle of bank, the load factor imposed on both the aircraft and pilot in a coordinated constant-altitude turn

A—is directly related to the airplane's gross weight.
B—varies with the rate of turn.
C—is constant.

For any given angle of bank, the load factor remains constant. (PLT309) — FAA-H-8083-25

ALL

8351. How can the pilot increase the rate of turn and decrease the radius at the same time?

A—Steepen the bank and increase airspeed.
B—Steepen the bank and decrease airspeed.
C—Shallow the bank and increase airspeed.

Any increase in the angle of bank will increase the rate of turn and decrease the radius of turn. Turn radius will decrease with decreasing airspeed. (PLT348) — FAA-H-8083-3

Answers

9823 [A]	9740 [B]	8354 [B]	8353 [B]	8396 [C]	8351 [B]

ALL

8352. What is the relationship of the rate of turn with the radius of turn with a constant angle of bank but increasing airspeed?

A— Rate will decrease and radius will increase.
B— Rate will increase and radius will decrease.
C— Rate and radius will increase.

For any given angle of bank, the rate of turn varies with the airspeed. If the angle of bank is held constant and the airspeed is increased, the rate of turn will decrease. The radius of turn will vary with airspeed. As airspeed is increased the radius will also increase. (PLT248) — FAA-H-8083-3

Answer (B) is incorrect because to maintain a constant angle of bank while increasing airspeed, the radius of turn will increase. Answer (C) is incorrect because to maintain a constant angle of bank while increasing airspeed, the rate of turn will decrease.

ALL

8345. What effect does an increase in airspeed have on a coordinated turn while maintaining a constant angle of bank and altitude?

A— The rate of turn will decrease resulting in a decreased load factor.
B— The rate of turn will increase resulting in an increased load factor.
C— The rate of turn will decrease resulting in no changes in load factor.

For any given angle of bank, the rate of turn varies with the airspeed. A constant bank angle does not change the load factor. If the angle of bank is held constant and the airspeed is increased, the rate of turn will decrease. The radius of turn will vary with airspeed. As airspeed is increased the radius will also increase. (PLT248) — FAA-H-8083-25

Answer (A) is incorrect because, at a constant bank angle, the higher airspeed will decrease the rate of turn to compensate for added centrifugal force, allowing the load factor to remain the same. Answer (B) is incorrect because, for any bank angle, the rate of turn varies with the airspeed; the higher the speed, the slower the rate of turn.

ATM, ATS, DSP

8345-1. Generally, the turning performance of an airplane is defined by

A— structural and power limits at high altitude.
B— aerodynamic and structural limits at low altitude.
C— control and structural limits at high altitude.

Each of the three limiting factors (aerodynamic, structural, and power) may combine to define the turning performance of an airplane. Generally, aerodynamic and structural limits predominate at low altitude while aerodynamic and power limits predominate at high altitude. The knowledge of this turning performance is particularly necessary for effective operation of fighter and interceptor types of airplanes. (PLT237) — ANA

ATM, ATS, DSP

8345-2. A bank angle of 15° will increase induced drag by about

A— 3%.
B— 7%.
C— 15%.

Due to the increased load factor in a coordinated turn, there will be an increase in stall speed and—of greater importance to engine-out performance—an increase in induced drag. A bank angle of 15 degrees will increase induced drag by about 7%. (PLT237) — ANA

Answers

8352   [A]   8345   [C]   8345-1   [B]   8345-2   [B]

Stability

Static stability describes the initial reaction of an aircraft after it has been disturbed from equilibrium in one or more of its axes of rotation. If the aircraft has an initial tendency to return to its original attitude of equilibrium, it has **positive static stability**. When it continues to diverge, it exhibits **negative static** stability. If an aircraft tends to remain in its new, disturbed state, it has **neutral static stability**. Most airplanes have positive static stability in pitch and yaw, and are close to neutrally stable in roll.

When an aircraft exhibits positive static stability in one of its axes, the term "dynamic stability" describes the long term tendency of the aircraft. When an aircraft is disturbed from equilibrium and then tries to return, it will invariably overshoot the original attitude and then pitch back. This results in a series of oscillations. If the oscillations become smaller with time, the aircraft has positive dynamic stability. If the aircraft diverges further away from its original attitude with each oscillation, it has negative dynamic stability.

The entire design of an aircraft contributes to its **stability** (or lack of it) in each of its axes of rotation. However, the vertical tail is the primary source of direction stability (yaw), and the horizontal tail is the primary source of pitch stability. The **center of gravity (CG)** location also affects stability. If the CG is toward its rearward limit, the aircraft will be less stable in both roll and pitch. As the CG is moved forward, the stability improves. Even though an airplane will be less stable with a rearward CG, it will have some desirable aerodynamic characteristics due to reduced aerodynamic loading of horizontal tail surface. This type of an airplane will have a slightly lower stall speed and will cruise faster for a given power setting.

ALL

8365. Identify the type stability if the aircraft attitude remains in the new position after the controls have been neutralized.

A— Negative longitudinal static stability.
B— Neutral longitudinal dynamic stability.
C— Neutral longitudinal static stability.

Neutral static stability is the initial tendency of an airplane to remain in a new position after its equilibrium has been disturbed. (PLT236) — FAA-H-8083-25

Answer (A) is incorrect because a negative longitudinal static stability means the airplane would tend to move even further from the original position. Answer (B) is incorrect because, with neutral longitudinal dynamic stability, the airplane would continue to oscillate without a tendency to increase or decrease.

ALL

8372. Identify the type stability if the aircraft attitude tends to move farther from its original position after the controls have been neutralized.

A— Negative static stability.
B— Positive static stability.
C— Negative dynamic stability.

Negative static stability is the initial tendency of the airplane to continue away from the original state of equilibrium after being disturbed. (PLT213) — FAA-H-8083-25

ALL

8373. Identify the type stability if the aircraft attitude tends to return to its original position after the controls have been neutralized.

A— Positive dynamic stability.
B— Positive static stability.
C— Neutral dynamic stability.

Positive static stability is the initial tendency of the airplane to return to the original state of equilibrium after being disturbed. (PLT236) — FAA-H-8083-25

Answer (A) is incorrect because positive dynamic stability refers to oscillations being dampened or decreasing. Answer (C) is incorrect because neutral dynamic stability refers to oscillations continuing without a tendency to increase or decrease.

ALL

8366. What is a characteristic of longitudinal instability?

A— Pitch oscillations becoming progressively greater.
B— Bank oscillations becoming progressively greater.
C— Aircraft constantly tries to pitch down.

A longitudinally unstable airplane has a tendency to dive or climb progressively into a very steep dive or climb, or even a stall. (PLT213) — FAA-H-8083-25

Answer (B) is incorrect because longitudinal stability refers to pitch (not bank) oscillations. Answer (C) is incorrect because this is not considered a stability problem. Stability is the reaction of the airplane when its equilibrium is disturbed.

Answers

8365 [C]   8372 [A]   8373 [B]   8366 [A]

ALL

8367. Describe dynamic longitudinal stability.

A— Motion about the longitudinal axis.
B— Motion about the lateral axis.
C— Motion about the vertical axis.

Longitudinal stability is the quality which makes an airplane stable about its lateral axis. (PLT236) — FAA-H-8083-25

Answer (A) is incorrect because motion about the airplane's longitudinal axis is lateral (not longitudinal) stability. Answer (C) is incorrect because motion about the vertical axis is directional stability.

ALL

8376. What characteristic should exist if an airplane is loaded to the rear of its CG range?

A— Sluggish in aileron control.
B— Sluggish in rudder control.
C— Unstable about the lateral axis.

If an airplane is loaded too far rearward it may not dampen out a vertical displacement of the nose. Instead, when the nose is momentarily pulled up, it may alternately climb and dive becoming steeper with each oscillation. (PLT236) — FAA-H-8083-25

Answer (A) is incorrect because an aft location of the CG has a greater effect on the longitudinal stability, not the lateral (aileron) controllability. Answer (B) is incorrect because an aft CG has a greater effect on the longitudinal stability, not vertical (rudder) controllability.

ATM, ATS, DSP

8380. What are some characteristics of an airplane loaded with the CG at the aft limit?

A— Lowest stall speed, highest cruise speed, and least stability.
B— Highest stall speed, highest cruise speed, and least stability.
C— Lowest stall speed, lowest cruise speed, and highest stability.

An airplane loaded with the CG at its aft limit will have a lower stall speed, higher cruise speed, but be less stable. (PLT240) — FAA-H-8083-3

Answer (B) is incorrect because an aft CG would cause the airplane to have the lowest stall speed. Answer (C) is incorrect because an aft CG would cause an airplane to have the highest cruise speed and the least stability.

High Speed Flight

Mach number is the ratio of the true airspeed to the speed of sound (TAS ÷ Speed of Sound). For example, an aircraft cruising at Mach .80 is flying at 80% of the speed of sound. The speed of sound is Mach 1.0.

A large increase in drag occurs when the air flow around the aircraft exceeds the speed of sound (Mach 1.0). Because lift is generated by accelerating air across the upper surface of the wing, local air flow velocities will reach sonic speeds while the aircraft Mach number is still considerably below the speed of sound. With respect to **Mach cruise control**, flight speeds can be divided into three regimes — subsonic, transonic and supersonic. The **subsonic regime** can be considered to occur at aircraft Mach numbers where all the local air flow is less than the speed of sound. The **transonic range** is where some but not all the local air flow velocities are Mach 1.0 or above. In **supersonic** flight, all the air flow around the aircraft exceeds Mach 1.0. The exact Mach numbers will vary with each aircraft type but as a very rough rule of thumb the subsonic regime occurs below Mach .75, the transonic regime between Mach .75 and Mach 1.20, and the supersonic regime over Mach 1.20.

Continued

Answers

8367   [B]   8376   [C]   8380   [A]

A limiting speed for a subsonic transport aircraft is its critical Mach number (M_{CRIT}). That is the speed at which airflow over the wing first reaches, but does not exceed, the speed of sound. At M_{CRIT} there may be sonic but no supersonic flow.

When an airplane exceeds its critical Mach number, a shock wave forms on the wing surface that can cause a phenomenon known as shock stall. If this shock stall occurs symmetrically at the wing roots, the loss of lift and loss of downwash on the tail will cause the aircraft to pitch down or "tuck under." This tendency is further aggravated in sweptwing aircraft because the center of pressure moves aft as the wing roots shock stall. If the wing tips of a sweptwing airplane shock stall first, the wing's center of pressure would move inward and forward causing a pitch up motion. *See* Figure 3-3.

The less airflow is accelerated across the wing, the higher the critical Mach number (i.e., the maximum flow velocity is closer to the aircraft's Mach number). Two ways of increasing M_{CRIT} in jet transport designs are to give the wing a lower camber and increase wing sweep. A thin airfoil section (lower camber) causes less airflow acceleration. The sweptwing design has the effect of creating a thin airfoil section by inducing a spanwise flow, thus increasing the effective chord length. *See* Figure 3-4.

Although a sweptwing design gives an airplane a higher critical Mach number (and therefore a higher maximum cruise speed), it results in some undesirable flight characteristics. One of these is a reduced maximum coefficient of lift. This requires that sweptwing airplanes extensively employ high lift devices, such as slats and slotted flaps, to get acceptably low takeoff and landing speeds. The purpose of high lift devices such as flaps, slats and slots is to increase lift at low airspeeds and to delay stall to a higher angle of attack.

Another disadvantage of the sweptwing design is the tendency, at low airspeeds, for the wing tips to stall first. This results in loss of aileron control early in the stall, and in very little aerodynamic buffet on the tail surfaces.

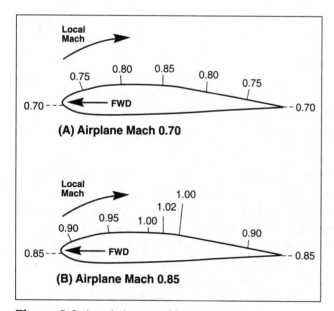

Figure 3-3. Local airstream Mach numbers

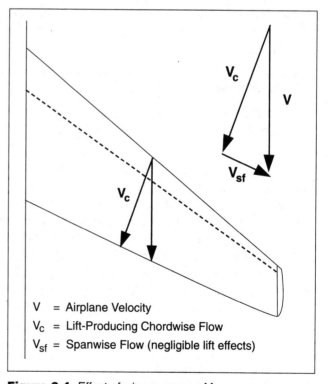

Figure 3-4. Effect of wing sweep on M_{CRIT}

ATM, ATS, DSP

8387. Within what Mach range does transonic flight regimes usually occur?

A— .50 to .75 Mach.
B— .75 to 1.20 Mach.
C— 1.20 to 2.50 Mach.

Flight regimes are defined as follows:

Subsonic – Mach numbers below 0.75
Transonic – Mach numbers from 0.75 to 1.20
Supersonic – Mach numbers from 1.20 to 5.00
Hypersonic – Mach numbers above 5.00.

(PLT032) — ANA

Answer (A) is incorrect because .50 to .75 Mach would be subsonic flight. Answer (C) is incorrect because 1.20 to 2.50 Mach would be supersonic flight.

ATM, ATS, DSP

8390. At what Mach range does the subsonic flight range normally occur?

A— Below .75 Mach.
B— From .75 to 1.20 Mach.
C— From 1.20 to 2.50 Mach.

Flight regimes are defined as follows:

Subsonic – Mach numbers below 0.75
Transonic – Mach numbers from 0.75 to 1.20
Supersonic – Mach numbers from 1.20 to 5.00
Hypersonic – Mach numbers above 5.00.

(PLT214) — ANA

Answer (B) is incorrect because .75 to 1.20 Mach would be transonic flight. Answer (C) is incorrect because 1.20 to 2.50 Mach would be supersonic flight.

ATM, ATS, DSP

8388. What is the highest speed possible without supersonic flow over the wing?

A— Initial buffet speed.
B— Critical Mach number.
C— Transonic index.

The highest speed possible without supersonic flow is called the Critical Mach Number. (PLT214) — ANA

ATM, ATS, DSP

8389. What is the free stream Mach number which produces first evidence of local sonic flow?

A— Supersonic Mach number.
B— Transonic Mach number.
C— Critical Mach number.

The highest speed possible without supersonic flow is called the Critical Mach Number. (PLT214) — ANA

ATM, ATS, DSP

8392. What is the result of a shock-induced separation of airflow occurring symmetrically near the wing root of a sweptwing aircraft?

A— A high-speed stall and sudden pitchup.
B— A severe moment or "Mach tuck."
C— Severe porpoising.

If the shock-induced separation occurs symmetrically near the wing root, there is an accompanying loss of lift. A decrease in downwash on the horizontal tail will create a diving moment and the aircraft will "tuck under." (PLT214) — ANA

Answer (A) is incorrect because there is a sudden pitch down when a shock-induced separation of airflow occurs symmetrically near the wing root of a sweptwing aircraft. Answer (C) is incorrect because there is a diving moment when a shock-induced separation of airflow occurs symmetrically near the wing root of a sweptwing aircraft.

ATM, ATS, DSP

8395. What is the movement of the center of pressure when the wingtips of a sweptwing airplane are shock-stalled first?

A— Inward and aft.
B— Inward and forward.
C— Outward and forward.

Shock formation at the wing tip first moves the center of pressure forward and inboard and the resulting climbing moment and tail downwash can contribute to "pitch up." (PLT214) — ANA

Answer (A) is incorrect because when the wing tips are shock-stalled first, the center of pressure moves forward. Answer (C) is incorrect because when the wing tips are shock-stalled first, the center of pressure moves inward.

Answers

8387 [B]	8390 [A]	8388 [B]	8389 [C]	8392 [B]	8395 [B]

ATM, ATS, DSP

8391. What is the principal advantage of a sweepback design wing over a straightwing design?

A— The critical Mach number will increase significantly.
B— Sweepback will increase changes in the magnitude of force coefficients due to compressibility.
C— Sweepback will accelerate the onset of compressibility effect.

One of the most important advantages of sweep is an increase in critical Mach number, force divergence Mach number, and the Mach number at which the drag rise will peak. In other words, the sweep will delay the onset of compressibility effects. (PLT214) — ANA

ATM, ATS, DSP

8391-1. Swept wings

A— improve specific fuel consumption.
B— increase the critical Mach number.
C— increase the speed of sound quotient.

One of the advantages of sweep in wing design is the increase in the critical Mach number it creates. The increase in critical Mach number, force divergence Mach number, and the Mach number at which the drag-rise peaks will delay the onset of compressibility effects. (PLT094) — ANA

ATM, ATS, DSP

8391-2. For significant benefit, wing sweep must be at least

A— 30 to 35°.
B— 45 to 50°.
C— 55°or more to substantially delay compressibility effects.

If sweepback is to be used at all, at least 30 to 35 degrees must be used to produce any significant benefit. (PLT094) — ANA

ATM, ATS, DSP

8393. What is one disadvantage of a sweptwing design?

A— The wing root stalls prior to the wingtip section.
B— The wingtip section stalls prior to the wing root.
C— Severe pitchdown moment when the center of pressure shifts forward.

When sweepback is combined with taper there is an extremely powerful tendency for the wing tip to stall first. (PLT214) — ANA

ATM, ATS, DSP

9803. Swept wings causes a significant

A— increase in effectiveness of flaps.
B— reduction in effectiveness of flaps.
C— flap actuation reliability issue.

Thin airfoil sections with sweepback impose distinct limitations on the effectiveness of flaps. (PLT266) — ANA

ATM, ATS, DSP

8394-2. A turbojet airplane has an increase in specific range with altitude, which can be attributed to three factors. One of those factors is

A— an increase in altitude in the troposphere results in higher energy air flow.
B— an increase in proportion of velocity versus thrust required.
C— decreased engine turbine speeds.

One of the three factors that leads to the increase in specific range with altitude in a turbojet airplane is that higher altitude increases the proportion of V/Tr (velocity versus required thrust), which in turn provides a greater true airspeed for the same amount of thrust.

The other two factors involved are that, (1) an increase in tropospheric altitude produces a lower inlet air temperature, which then reduces the specific fuel consumption, and (2) an increase in altitude requires increased engine RPM for cruise thrust, and then the specific fuel consumption is reduced as the engine approaches the normal-rated RPM. (PLT094) — ANA

Answers

8391 [A]	8391-1 [B]	8391-2 [A]	8393 [B]	9803 [B]	8394-2 [B]

Primary Flight Controls

Because of the high air loads, it is very difficult to move the flight control surfaces of jet aircraft with just mechanical and aerodynamic forces. So flight controls are usually moved by hydraulic actuators. Flight controls are divided into **primary flight controls** and **secondary** or **auxiliary flight controls**. The primary flight controls are those that maneuver the aircraft in roll, pitch and yaw. These include the ailerons, elevator and rudder. Secondary (or auxiliary) flight controls include tabs, trailing-edge flaps, leading-edge flaps, spoilers and slats. *See* Figure 3-5.

Roll control of most jet aircraft is accomplished by ailerons and flight spoilers. The exact mix of controls is determined by the aircraft's flight regime. In low speed flight all control surfaces operate to provide the desired roll control. As the aircraft moves into higher speed operations, control surface movement is reduced to provide approximately the same roll response to a given input through a wide range of speeds.

Many aircraft have two sets of ailerons — inboard and outboard. The inboard ailerons operate in all flight regimes. The outboard ailerons work only when the wing flaps are extended and are automatically locked out when flaps are retracted. This allows good roll response in low speed flight with the flaps extended and prevents excessive roll and wing bending at high speeds when the flaps are retracted.

Spoilers increase drag and reduce lift on the wing. If raised on only one wing, they aid roll control by causing that wing to drop. If the spoilers raise symmetrically in flight, the aircraft can either be slowed in level flight or can descend rapidly without an increase in airspeed. When the spoilers rise on the ground at high speeds, they destroy the wing's lift which puts more of the aircraft's weight on its wheels which in turn makes the brakes more effective.

Often aircraft have both flight and ground spoilers. The flight spoilers are available both in flight and on the ground. However, the ground spoilers can only be raised when the weight of the aircraft is on the landing gear. When the spoilers deploy on the ground, they decrease lift and make the brakes more effective. In flight, a ground-sensing switch on the landing gear prevents deployment of the ground spoilers.

Vortex generators are small (an inch or so high) aerodynamic surfaces located in different places on different airplanes. They prevent undesirable airflow separation from the surface by mixing the boundary airflow with the high energy airflow just above the surface. When located on the upper surface of a wing, the vortex generators prevent shock-induced separation from the wing as the aircraft approaches its critical Mach number. This increases aileron effectiveness at high speeds.

Figure 3-5. Typical transport aircraft flight controls

ATM, ATS, DSP

8326. Which of the following is considered a primary flight control?

A— Slats.
B— Elevator.
C— Dorsal fin.

The primary group of flight control surfaces consists of ailerons, elevators, and rudders. (PLT346) — FAA-H-8083-25

Answer (A) is incorrect because slats are high-lift devices, not a flight control device. Answer (C) is incorrect because a dorsal fin is not a primary flight control, but is used to provide directional stability.

ATM, ATS, DSP

8327. Which of the following is considered an auxiliary flight control?

A— Ruddervator.
B— Upper rudder.
C— Leading-edge flaps.

Auxiliary wing flight surfaces include trailing edge flaps, leading edge flaps, speed brakes, spoilers, and leading edge slats. (PLT473) — FAA-H-8083-25

Answer (A) is incorrect because a ruddervator is a primary flight control surface that incorporates both a rudder and elevator into one surface. Answer (B) is incorrect because upper rudders (found on the B-727) are stand-by rudders, which are used in the event of a hydraulic system failure.

Answers

8326   [B]   8327   [C]

ATM, ATS, DSP

8343. Precise roll control using a rudder on a transport category airplane

A— can be effective when turbulence is encountered.
B— is difficult and therefore not recommended.
C— should be considered to assist the yaw damper.

The lateral control of an airplane is accomplished by producing differential lift on the wings. The differential lift for control in roll is usually obtained by some type of ailerons or spoilers. Rudders are not recommended as the primary method to achieve precise roll control as they can contribute to dihedral effect. Excessive dihedral effect can lead to many problems including Dutch rolls. (PLT346) — ANA

ATM, ATS, DSP

8324. When are inboard ailerons normally used?

A— Low-speed flight only.
B— High-speed flight only.
C— Low-speed and high-speed flight.

During low-speed flight, all lateral control surfaces operate to provide maximum stability. This includes all four ailerons, flaps, and spoilers. (PLT346) — FAA-H-8083-25

Answers (A) and (B) are incorrect because the inboard ailerons are used during both high- and low-speed flight.

ATM, ATS, DSP

8325. When are outboard ailerons normally used?

A— Low-speed flight only.
B— High-speed flight only.
C— Low-speed and high-speed flight.

At high speeds, flaps are retracted and the outboard ailerons are locked out of the aileron control system. (PLT346) — FAA-H-8083-25

Answers (B) and (C) are incorrect because the outboard ailerons are locked when airspeed is increased and flaps are raised.

ATM, ATS, DSP

8342. Why do some airplanes equipped with inboard/outboard ailerons use the outboards for slow flight only?

A— Increased surface area provides greater controllability with flap extension.
B— Aerodynamic loads on the outboard ailerons tend to twist the wingtips at high speeds.
C— Locking out the outboard ailerons in high-speed flight provides variable flight control feel.

Aerodynamic loads on the outboard ailerons tend to twist the wing tips at high speeds. This results in deformation great enough to nullify the effect of aileron deflection and create rolling moments opposite to the direction commanded. Because of this, outboard ailerons are used for slow flight only. (PLT346) — FAA-H-8083-25

ATM, ATS, DSP

8332. What is a purpose of flight spoilers?

A— Increase the camber of the wing.
B— Reduce lift without decreasing airspeed.
C— Direct airflow over the top of the wing at high angles of attack.

The purpose of the spoilers is to disturb the smooth airflow across the top of the wing thereby creating an increased amount of drag and a reduced amount of lift. (PLT473) — FAA-H-8083-25

Answer (A) is incorrect because flaps (not spoilers) increase the camber of the wing. Answer (C) is incorrect because slots and slats direct airflow over the top of the wing at high angles of attack.

ATM, ATS, DSP

8333. For which purpose may flight spoilers be used?

A— Reduce the wings' lift upon landing.
B— Increase the rate of descent without increasing aerodynamic drag.
C— Aid in longitudinal balance when rolling an airplane into a turn.

An additional purpose or use for flight spoilers is to reduce lift when the aircraft lands. (PLT473) — FAA-H-8083-25

Answer (B) is incorrect because spoilers will increase the aerodynamic drag. Answer (C) is incorrect because trim devices (not spoilers) aid in balancing forces on an aircraft about the three axes.

ATM, ATS, DSP

8336. Which is a purpose of ground spoilers?

A— Reduce the wings' lift upon landing.
B— Aid in rolling an airplane into a turn.
C— Increase the rate of descent without gaining airspeed.

Ground spoilers are speed brakes extended on the ground or landing roll to kill lift and keep the aircraft from flying again after touchdown. (PLT473) — FAA-H-8083-25

Answer (B) is incorrect because an aid in rolling an airplane into a turn is a flight spoiler. Answer (C) is incorrect because increasing the rate of descent without gaining airspeed is the purpose of a flight spoiler.

Answers

8343 [B]	8324 [C]	8325 [A]	8342 [B]	8332 [B]	8333 [A]
8336 [A]					

ATM, ATS, DSP

9793. Upon landing, spoilers

A— decrease directional stability on the landing rollout.
B— function by increasing tire to ground friction.
C— should be extended after the thrust reversers have been deployed.

Spoilers should be deployed immediately after touch-down because they are most effective at high speed. The spoilers increase wheel loading by as much as 200 percent in the landing flap configuration. This increases the tire ground friction force making the maximum tire braking and cornering forces available. (PLT170) — FAA-H-8083-3A

ATM, ATS, DSP

9793-1. Aerodynamic braking is only effective up to approximately

A— 30% of touchdown speed.
B— 40 to 50% of touchdown speed.
C— 60 to 70% of touchdown speed.

The aerodynamic drag of the airplane must be considered during the landing roll. Because of the reduced induced drag when in ground effect, aerodynamic braking will be of greatest significance only when partial stalling of the wing can be accomplished. The reduced drag when in ground effect accounts for the fact that the brakes are the most effective source of deceleration for the majority of airplane configurations. At speeds less than 60 to 70 percent of the touchdown speed, aerodynamic drag is so slight as to be of little use, and therefore aerodynamic braking must be utilized to produce continued deceleration of the airplane. (PLT247) — ANA

ATM, ATS, DSP

8341. Which is a purpose of wing-mounted vortex generators?

A— Delays the onset of drag divergence at high speeds and aids in maintaining aileron effectiveness at high speeds.
B— Increase the onset of drag divergence and aid in aileron effectiveness at low speeds.
C— Breaks the airflow over the wing so the stall will progress from the root out to the tip of the wing.

"Vortex generators" are used to delay or prevent shock wave-induced boundary layer separation encountered in transonic flight. Vortex generators create a vortex which mixes the boundary airflow with the high energy airflow just above the surface. This produces higher surface velocities and increases the energy of the boundary layer. Thus, a stronger shock wave will be necessary to produce airflow separation. (PLT266) — FAA-H-8083-25

Answer (B) is incorrect because vortex generators are most effective at high speeds and the increased drag that they produce is not their primary function. Answer (C) is incorrect because a stall strip breaks the airflow over the wing so the stall will progress from the root out to the tip of the wing.

ATM, ATS, DSP

8356. Airflow separation over the wing can be delayed by using vortex generators

A— directing high pressure air over the top of the wing or flap through slots and making the wing surface smooth.
B— directing a suction over the top of the wing or flap through slots and making the wing surface smooth.
C— making the wing surface rough and/or directing high pressure air over the top of the wing or flap through slots.

Vortex generators prevent undesirable airflow separation from the surface by mixing the boundary airflow with the high energy airflow just above the surface. The vortex generators mix the turbulent outer layers of the boundary layers with the slow moving laminar lower layers thus reenergizing them. (PLT266) — FAA-H-8083-25

ALL

9759. If the boundary layer separates

A— drag is decreased.
B— the wing is about to stall and stop producing lift.
C— ice will sublimate and not freeze.

The boundary layer gives any object an "effective" shape that is usually slightly different from the physical shape. The boundary layer may also separate from the body, thus creating an effective shape much different from the physical shape of the object. This change in the physical shape of the boundary layer causes a dramatic decrease in lift and an increase in drag. When this happens, the airfoil has stalled. (PLT266) — FAA-H-8083-25

Answers

9793 [B]	9793-1 [C]	8341 [A]	8356 [C]	9759 [B]

Tabs

Flight control surfaces are sometimes equipped with **servo tabs**. These tabs are on the trailing edge of the control surface and are mechanically linked to move opposite the direction of the surface. If the tab moves up, the surface moves down. This "servo" movement moves the control surface. *See* Figure 3-6.

One method of modifying the downward tail load through changes in airspeed and configuration is by using **trim tabs**. Trim tabs are moved by a separate trim control from the cockpit. Movement of the trim tab (like the servo tab) is opposite that of the primary control surface.

Anti-servo tabs move in the same direction as the primary control surface. This means that as the control surface deflects, the aerodynamic load is increased by movement of the anti-servo tab. This helps to prevent the control surface from moving to a full deflection. It also makes a hydraulically-boosted flight control more aerodynamically effective than it would otherwise be.

Some jet aircraft have **control tabs** for use in the event of loss of all hydraulic pressure. Movement of the control wheel moves the control tab which causes the aerodynamic movement of the control surface. The control tab is used only during manual reversion; that is, with the loss of hydraulic pressure. They work the same as a servo tab but only in the manual mode.

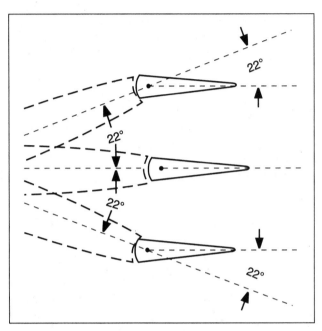

Figure 3-6

ATM, ATS, DSP
8330. What is the purpose of a servo tab?

A— Move the flight controls in the event of manual reversion.
B— Reduce control forces by deflecting in the proper direction to move a primary flight control.
C— Prevent a control surface from moving to a full-deflection position due to aerodynamic forces.

The servo tab moves in response to the cockpit control. The force of the airflow on the servo tab then moves the primary control surface. (PLT473) — FAA-H-8083-25

Answer (A) is incorrect because, in the event of "manual reversion" on some transport category aircraft, the control tabs would move the flight controls. Answer (C) is incorrect because the purpose of the anti-servo tab is to preclude full deflection of control surfaces.

ATM, ATS, DSP
8338. Which direction from the primary control surface does a servo tab move?

A— Same direction.
B— Opposite direction.
C— Remains fixed for all positions.

The servo tab attached to the flight control moves in the opposite direction, to assist in moving and holding the flight control by way of the airflow against it. (PLT473) — FAA-H-8083-25

Answer (A) is incorrect because an anti-servo tab, as found on the trailing edge of stabilators, moves in the same direction as the stabilator to provide a feel to the pilot control pressures. Answer (C) is incorrect because servo tabs move in response to the pilot's control movements.

Answers

8330 [B]   8338 [B]

ATM, ATS, DSP

8339. Which direction from the primary control surface does an elevator adjustable trim tab move when the control surface is moved?

A— Same direction.
B— Opposite direction.
C— Remains fixed for all positions.

Trim tabs remain fixed for all positions of primary control surface movement until mechanically adjusted from the cockpit. A trim tab is hinged to its parent primary control surface but is operated by an independent control. (PLT473) — FAA-H-8083-25

Answer (A) is incorrect because once adjusted, trim tabs remain fixed to the primary control surface as the primary control surface is moved. Answer (B) is incorrect because a tab having a linkage designed to move in the opposite direction from the main control surface is called a balance tab.

ATM, ATS, DSP

8340. What is the purpose of an elevator trim tab?

A— Provide horizontal balance as airspeed is increased to allow hands-off flight.
B— Adjust the speed tail load for different airspeeds in flight allowing neutral control forces.
C— Modify the downward tail load for various airspeeds in flight eliminating flight-control pressures.

The air flowing downward behind the trailing edge of the wing strikes the upper surface of the horizontal stabilizer, creating a downward tail force. The use of the trim tab will allow the pilot to reduce the hinge moment to zero and trim the control forces to zero for a given flight condition. (PLT473) — FAA-H-8083-25

Answer (A) is incorrect because the elevator trim tab permits "hands-off" flight at any airspeed, not only when the airspeed is increasing, and provides longitudinal balance. Answer (B) is incorrect because the elevator trim tab adjusts the downward tail load for various airspeeds in flight allowing neutral control forces.

ATM, ATS, DSP

8329. What is the purpose of an anti-servo tab?

A— Move the flight controls in the event of manual reversion.
B— Reduce control forces by deflecting in the proper direction to move a primary flight control.
C— Prevent a control surface from moving to a full-deflection position due to aerodynamic forces.

Anti-servo tabs add resistance and increase control forces required as the surface moves toward its limit to avoid overcontrolling and offset deflection caused by aerodynamic forces rather than control input. (PLT473) — FAA-H-8083-25

Answer (A) is incorrect because in the event of "manual reversion" the control tabs (not servo or anti-servo tabs) would move the flight controls. Answer (B) is incorrect because the anti-servo usually will increase the pressure required to deflect the control surfaces (the anti-servo tab moves in the same direction as the control surface).

ATM, ATS, DSP

8337. Which direction from the primary control surface does an anti-servo tab move?

A— Same direction.
B— Opposite direction.
C— Remains fixed for all positions.

Anti-servo tabs move in the same direction as the primary control surface. (PLT346) — FAA-H-8083-25

Answer (B) is incorrect because a servo tab moves in the opposite direction from the primary control surface. Answer (C) is incorrect because trim tabs remain fixed during control inputs.

ATM, ATS, DSP

8328. What is the purpose of a control tab?

A— Move the flight controls in the event of manual reversion.
B— Reduce control forces by deflecting in the proper direction to move a primary flight control.
C— Prevent a control surface from moving to a full-deflection position due to aerodynamic forces.

The flight controls of large jet airplanes are usually hydraulically powered. They are equipped with control tabs in the event of a total hydraulic failure. When this happens, the control tab can still be moved with control wheel input and the tab displacement creates an aerodynamic force which moves the control surface. (PLT473) — FAA-H-8083-25

Answer (B) is incorrect because servo tabs reduce control forces by deflecting primary flight controls in the proper direction. Answer (C) is incorrect because this is the purpose and function of an anti-servo tab.

Answers

8339 [C]   8340 [C]   8329 [C]   8337 [A]   8328 [A]

High-Lift Devices

Sweptwing jet aircraft are equipped with a number of high-lift devices. These include leading edge flaps, slots or slats, and trailing edge flaps. The primary purpose of high-lift devices (flaps, slots, slats, etc.) is to increase the **maximum coefficient of lift** (CL_{MAX}) of the airplane and reduce the stall speed. The takeoff and landing speeds are consequently reduced.

The two most common types of **leading-edge devices** are **slats** and **Krueger flaps**. The Krueger flap extends from the leading edge of the wing, increasing its camber. The slat also extends from the wing's leading edge but it creates a gap or slot. This slot allows high energy from under the wing to flow over the top of the wing that delays stall to a higher angle of attack than would otherwise occur. It is common to find Krueger flaps and slats on the same wing.

ATM, ATS, DSP

8384. The primary purpose of high-lift devices is to increase the

A— L/D$_{MAX}$.
B— lift at low speeds.
C— drag and reduce airspeed.

The primary purpose of high-lift devices (flaps, slots, slats, etc.) is to increase the CL_{MAX} of the airplane and to reduce the stall speed. The takeoff and landing speeds are consequently reduced. (PLT266) — ANA

Answer (A) is incorrect because increasing the lift component is an objective of high-lift devices which increase the ratio of L/D. The primary purpose of high-lift devices is to increase lift at low speeds. Answer (C) is incorrect because increasing the drag to reduce airspeed is the function of spoilers, not high-lift devices.

ATM, ATS, DSP

8331. Which is a purpose of leading-edge flaps?

A— Increase the camber of the wing.
B— Reduce lift without increasing airspeed.
C— Direct airflow over the top of the wing at high angles of attack.

The leading-edge flap extends in a downward direction to increase the camber or total curve of the wing's shape. (PLT473) — ANA

Answer (B) is incorrect because leading-edge flaps increase the maximum lift coefficient at higher angles of attack. Answer (C) is incorrect because a slot will direct airflow over the top of the wing at high angles of attack.

ATM, ATS, DSP

8385. What is the primary function of the leading edge flaps in landing configuration during the flare before touchdown?

A— Prevent flow separation.
B— Decrease rate of sink.
C— Increase profile drag.

The primary purpose of high-lift devices (flaps, slots, slats, etc.) is to increase the CL_{MAX} of the airplane and to reduce the stall speed. The takeoff and landing speeds are consequently reduced. (PLT266) — ANA

Answer (B) is incorrect because, to decrease the rate of sink, the coefficient of lift (CL) must increase. This is done by using leading-edge lift devices, slats, flaps, and other devices with the correct power setting. Answer (C) is incorrect because spoilers increase profile drag and are usually deployed after touchdown to reduce lift.

ATM, ATS, DSP

8334. Which is a purpose of leading-edge slats on high-performance wings?

A— Increase lift at relative slow speeds.
B— Improve aileron control during low angles of attack.
C— Direct air from the low-pressure area under the leading edge along the top of the wing.

The primary purpose of high-lift devices (flaps, slots, slats, etc.) is to increase the CL_{MAX} of the airplane and reduce the stall speed. The takeoff and landing speeds are consequently reduced. (PLT473) — ANA

Answer (B) is incorrect because the leading-edge slats are used during high angle-of-attack situations such as takeoffs and landings. Answer (C) is incorrect because the area under the leading edge is high pressure.

Answers

8384 [B]	8331 [A]	8385 [A]	8334 [A]

ATM, ATS, DSP

8386. What effect does the leading edge slot in the wing have on performance?

A— Decreases profile drag.
B— Changes the stalling angle of attack to a higher angle.
C— Decelerates the upper surface boundary layer air.

The slot delays stall to a higher angle of attack. (PLT266) — ANA

Answer (A) is incorrect because, at low angles of attack, there is little or no profile drag increase. At high angles of attack, the slot delays the stall characteristics of the wing. Answer (C) is incorrect because the leading-edge slot actually increases airflow on the upper wing surface to allow higher angles of attack.

ATM, ATS, DSP

9765. What is a difference between the fowler flap system and split flap system?

A— Fowler flaps produce the greatest change in pitching moment.
B— Fowler flaps produce more drag.
C— Split flaps cause the greatest change in twisting loads.

Fowler flaps slide out and downward from the trailing edge of the wing. When lowered, they increase the wing area as well as the wing camber. The Fowler flap is characterized by the largest increase in CL_{MAX} with the least changes in drag. The Fowler flap also creates the greatest change in pitching moment. Split flaps consist of a hinged plate that deflects downward from the lower surface of the wing and produce the least change in the pitching moments of a wing when it is lowered. The deflection of a flap causes large nose-down moments which create significant twisting loads on the structure and pitching moments that must be controlled with the horizontal tail. Unfortunately, the flap types producing the greatest increases in CL_{MAX} usually cause the greatest twisting moments. The Fowler flap causes the greatest change in twisting moment while the split flap causes the least. (PLT266) — ANA

ATM, ATS, DSP

9766. On which type of wing are flaps most effective?

A— Thin wing.
B— Thick wing.
C— Sweptback wing.

The effectiveness of flaps on a wing configuration depends on many different factors, of which an important one is the amount of the wing area affected by the flaps. Since a certain amount of the span is reserved for ailerons, the actual wing maximum lift properties will be less than that resulting from the flapped two-dimensional section. If the basic wing has a low thickness, any type of flap will be less effective than on a wing of greater thickness. Sweepback of the wing can also cause a significant reduction in the effectiveness of flaps. (PLT266) — ANA

ATM, ATS, DSP

9771. When compared to plain flaps, split flaps

A— produce more lift with less drag.
B— produce only slightly more lift, but much more drag.
C— enhance takeoff performance in high density conditions.

The split flap produces a slightly greater change in CL_{MAX} than the plain flap. However, a much larger change in drag results from the substantial and turbulent wake produced by this type of flap; although greater drag may be advantageous, for example, when steeper landing approaches over obstacles are required. (PLT266) – ANA

Answers

8386 [B]   9765 [A]   9766 [B]   9771 [B]

Helicopter Aerodynamics

RTC

8355. What is the ratio between the total load supported by the rotor disc and the gross weight of a helicopter in flight?

A— Power loading.
B— Load factor.
C— Aspect ratio.

The load factor is the actual load on the rotor blades at any time, divided by the gross weight (or apparent gross weight; i.e., when the helicopter is in a bank, the apparent gross weight increases). (PLT310) — FAA-H-8083-21

RTC

8402. How should the pilot execute a pinnacle-type approach to a rooftop heliport in conditions of high wind and turbulence?

A— Steeper-than-normal approach, maintaining the desired angle of descent with collective.
B— Normal approach, maintaining a slower-than-normal rate of descent with cyclic.
C— Shallow approach, maintaining a constant line of descent with cyclic.

High winds can cause severe turbulence and downdrafts on the leeward side of rooftop helipads. Under these conditions, a steeper-than-normal approach to avoid downdrafts is desired. Angle of descent is maintained with collective and rate of closure (airspeed) is controlled with cyclic. (PLT170) — FAA-H-8083-21

RTC

8403. How should a quick stop be initiated?

A— Raise collective pitch.
B— Apply aft cyclic.
C— Decrease RPM while raising collective pitch.

The deceleration (or slowing) is initiated by applying aft cyclic to reduce forward speed and simultaneously lowering the collective to counteract any ballooning or climbing tendency. (PLT170) — FAA-H-8083-21

RTC

8404. How does V_{NE} speed vary with altitude?

A— Remains the same at all altitudes.
B— Increases with an increase in altitude.
C— Decreases with altitude an increase in altitude.

V_{NE} will decrease with an increase in altitude. Several factors contribute to V_{NE} including temperature, weight, altitude, and design limitations. (PLT124) — FAA-H-8083-21

RTC

8405. What limits the high airspeed potential of a helicopter?

A— Harmonic resonance.
B— Retreating blade stall.
C— Rotor RPM limitations.

The airflow over the retreating blade decreases and the airflow over the advancing blade increases in forward flight. To correct for the resulting dissymmetry of lift, the retreating blade must operate at increasingly higher angles of attack as the forward speed increases, until the retreating blade will stall at some high forward airspeed. (PLT124) — FAA-H-8083-21

RTC

8406. What corrective action can a pilot take to recover from settling with power?

A— Increase forward speed and raise collective pitch.
B— Decrease forward speed and partially raise collective pitch.
C— Increase forward speed and partially lower collective pitch.

By increasing forward speed and/or (if possible) partially lowering collective pitch, the conditions necessary for settling with power are reduced or eliminated. (PLT208) — FAA-H-8083-21

Answers

8355 [B]	8402 [A]	8403 [B]	8404 [C]	8405 [B]	8406 [C]

RTC
8408. The lift differential that exists between the advancing main rotor blade and the retreating main rotor blade is known as

A— Coriolis effect.
B— dissymmetry of lift.
C— translating tendency.

Dissymmetry of lift is created by horizontal flight or by wind during hovering flight, and is the difference in lift that exists between the advancing blade of the rotor disc and the retreating blade of the rotor disc. (PLT470) — FAA-H-8083-21

RTC
8409. During a hover, a helicopter tends to drift in the direction of tail rotor thrust. What is this movement called?

A— Translating tendency.
B— Transverse flow effect.
C— Gyroscopic precession.

The entire helicopter has a tendency to move in the direction of tail rotor thrust when hovering, which is often referred to as "drift or translating tendency." (PLT268) — FAA-H-8083-21

RTC
8410. What is the purpose of the lead-lag (drag) hinge in a three-bladed, fully articulated helicopter rotor system?

A— Offset lateral instability during autorotation.
B— Compensate for Coriolis effect.
C— Provide geometric balance.

When a rotor blade of a three-bladed rotor system flaps upward, the center mass of that blade moves closer to the axis of rotation and blade acceleration takes place. When the blade flaps downward, its center of mass moves further from the axis of rotation and blade deceleration (or slowing) occurs. This increase and decrease of blade velocity in the plane of rotation due to mass movement is known as Coriolis effect. The acceleration and deceleration actions (leading and lagging) are absorbed by dampers or the blade structure itself (hinges) in a three-bladed system. (PLT470) — FAA-H-8083-21

RTC
8411. During an autorotation (collective pitch full down), what is an increase in rotor RPM associated with?

A— An increase in airflow through the rotor system.
B— A decrease in airflow through the rotor system.
C— A decrease in airspeed.

During an autorotation, the flow of air is upward through the rotor. The portion of the blade that produces the forces causing the rotor to turn in autorotation (approximately 25 to 70% of the radius outward from the center) is the driving region. An increase in the aerodynamic forces along the driving region (increase in the airflow through the rotor) tends to speed up the blade rotation. (PLT470) — FAA-H-8083-21

RTC
8412. What corrective action can a pilot take to prevent a retreating blade stall at its onset?

A— Reduce collective pitch and increase rotor RPM.
B— Increase collective pitch and increase rotor RPM.
C— Reduce collective pitch and decrease rotor RPM.

At the onset of blade stall vibration, the pilot should reduce collective pitch, increase rotor RPM, reduce forward airspeed and minimize maneuvering. (PLT470) — FAA-H-8083-21

RTC
8413. Which is a major warning of approaching retreating blade stall?

A— High frequency vibration.
B— Tendency to roll opposite the stalled side of the rotor.
C— Pitchup of the nose.

The major warnings of approaching retreating blade stall are: low-frequency vibration equal to the number of blades per revolution of the main rotor system, pitchup of the nose and tendency for the helicopter to roll towards the stalled (retreating blade) side of the rotor system. (PLT470) — FAA-H-8083-21

Answers

| 8408 | [B] | 8409 | [A] | 8410 | [B] | 8411 | [A] | 8412 | [A] | 8413 | [C] |

RTC

8417. How does high density altitude affect helicopter performance?

A— Engine and rotor efficiency are increased.
B— Engine and rotor efficiency are reduced.
C— Engine efficiency is reduced, but rotor efficiency is increased.

High elevations, high temperatures, and high moisture content (relative humidity) all contribute to high density altitude, which lessens helicopter performance. The thinner air at high density altitudes reduces the amount of lift of the rotor blades, and unsupercharged engines produce less power. (PLT124) — FAA-H-8083-21

RTC

8418. How is helicopter climb performance most adversely affected?

A— Higher-than-standard temperature and high relative humidity.
B— Lower-than-standard temperature and high relative humidity.
C— Higher-than-standard temperature and low relative humidity.

High elevations, high temperatures, and high moisture content (relative humidity) all contribute to high density altitude, which lessens helicopter performance. The thinner air at high density altitudes reduces the amount of lift of the rotor blades, and unsupercharged engines produce less power. (PLT124) — FAA-H-8083-21

RTC

8420. What causes Coriolis effect?

A— Differential thrust of rotor blades.
B— Changing angle of attack of blades during rotation.
C— Shift in center of mass of flapping blade.

When a rotor blade of a three-bladed rotor system flaps upward, the center mass of that blade moves closer to the axis of rotation and blade acceleration takes place. When the blade flaps downward, its center of mass moves further from the axis of rotation and blade deceleration (or slowing) occurs. This increase and decrease of blade velocity in the plane of rotation due to mass movement is known as Coriolis effect. (PLT197) — FAA-H-8083-21

RTC

8421. Why are the rotor blades more efficient when operating in ground effect?

A— Induced drag is reduced.
B— Induced angle of attack is increased.
C— Downwash velocity is accelerated.

When a helicopter is operated near the surface, the downwash velocity of the rotor blades cannot be fully developed. The reduction in downwash velocity causes the induced angle of attack of each rotor blade to be reduced, which causes the induced drag to be less. (PLT237) — FAA-H-8083-21

RTC

8422. What result does a level turn have on the total lift required and load factor with a constant airspeed?

A— Lift required remains constant and the load factor increases.
B— Lift required increases and the load factor decreases.
C— Both total lift force and load factor increase.

When a helicopter is placed in a bank, the resultant lifting force acts more horizontally and less vertically. To maintain a level turn, the resultant lifting force (total lift force) must be increased. When a helicopter assumes a curved flight path, centrifugal force causes additional stresses (load factor) to be imposed. (PLT248) — FAA-H-8083-21

RTC

8423. What causes a helicopter to turn?

A— Centrifugal force.
B— Horizontal component of lift.
C— Greater angle of attack of rotor blades on upward side of the rotor disc.

When a helicopter is placed in a bank, the rotor disc is tilted sideward causing the horizontal component of lift to be increased. The increased horizontal lift component pulls the helicopter from its straight course. (PLT248) — FAA-H-8083-21

Answers

8417 [B]   8418 [A]   8420 [C]   8421 [A]   8422 [C]   8423 [B]

RTC

8424. What is the primary purpose of the tail rotor system?

A— Maintain heading during forward flight.
B— Act as a rudder to assist in coordinated turns.
C— Counteract the torque effect of the main rotor.

As the main rotor of a helicopter turns in one direction, the fuselage tends to rotate in the opposite direction (Newton's Third Law of Motion: For every action there is an equal and opposite reaction). This tendency to rotate is called torque. The tail rotor is used to produce thrust to counteract the torque effect of the main rotor. (PLT470) — FAA-H-8083-21

RTC

8425. Under what condition would it be necessary to cause the tail rotor to direct thrust to the left on an American-made helicopter?

A— To maintain heading with a left crosswind.
B— To counteract the drag of the transmission during autorotation.
C— To execute hovering turns to the right.

The capability for tail rotors to produce thrust to the left (negative pitch angle) is necessary because during autorotation, the drag of the transmission (with no torque effect present) tends to yaw the nose to the left, in the same direction that the main rotor is turning. (PLT470) — FAA-H-8083-21

RTC

9318. Which statement describes the term "V$_{TOSS}$"?

A— The takeoff safety speed in a turbine-engine powered transport category airplane.
B— The takeoff safety speed in a Category A helicopter.
C— The takeoff stall speed in the takeoff configuration in a turbopropeller powered airplane.

V$_{TOSS}$ means takeoff safety speed for Category A helicopters. (PLT466) — 14 CFR §1.2

RTC

9831. A level attitude in flight in a helicopter indicates

A— acceleration.
B— descent.
C— stable flight.

In straight-and-level, unaccelerated forward flight, lift equals weight and thrust equals drag (straight-and-level flight is flight with a constant heading and at a constant altitude). If lift exceeds weight, the helicopter climbs; if lift is less than weight, the helicopter descends. If thrust exceeds drag, the helicopter speeds up; if thrust is less than drag, it slows down. (PLT219) — FAA-H-8083-21

Answers

8424 [C]	8425 [B]	9318 [B]	9381 [C]

Chapter 4
Performance

Continued

Engine Performance

Note applicable to Chapters 4 and 5: The ATP Single-engine exam (ATS) focuses on the Cessna 208 and the ATP Multi-engine exam (ATM) focuses on the Bombardier CRJ200 and Q400.

There are four types of engines in use on modern airplanes: **reciprocating engine, turboprop engine, turbofan engine** and **turbojet engine**. The type of engine selected for a particular airplane design depends primarily on the speed range of the aircraft. The reciprocating engine is most efficient for aircraft with cruising speeds below 250 MPH, the turboprop works best in the 250 MPH to 450 MPH range and the turbofan and turbojet engines are most efficient above 450 MPH.

Manifold pressure (MAP) is a measurement of the power output of a reciprocating engine. It is basically the pressure in the engine's air inlet system. In a normally-aspirated (unsupercharged) engine, the MAP will drop as the aircraft climbs to altitude. This severely limits a piston-powered airplane's altitude capability.

Most piston-powered airplanes flown by air carriers are turbocharged. On this type of engine, exhaust gas from the engine is used as a power source for a compressor that in turn raises the MAP at any given altitude. The flow of exhaust gas to the turbocharger is controlled by a device called a **waste gate**.

Turbocharging allows an aircraft to fly at much higher altitudes than it would be able to with normally-aspirated engines. The term **critical altitude** is used to describe the effect of turbocharging on the aircraft's performance. The critical altitude of a turbocharged reciprocating engine is the highest altitude at which a desired manifold pressure can be maintained.

The pilots of reciprocating-engine-powered aircraft must be very careful to observe the published limits on manifold pressure and engine RPM. In particular, high RPM and low MAP can produce severe wear, fatigue and damage.

Turboprops, turbofans and turbojet engines are types of **gas turbine engines**. Turbine engines are classified by the type of compressors they use — centrifugal flow, axial flow, and centrifugal-axial flow. All gas turbine engines consist of an air inlet section, a compressor section, the combustion section, the turbine section and the exhaust. Air enters the inlet at roughly ambient temperature and pressure. As it passes through the compressor the pressure increases and so does the temperature due to the heat of compression. **Bleed air** is tapped off the compressor for such accessories as air conditioning and thermal anti-icing.

The section connecting the compressor and the combustion sections is called the diffuser. In the diffuser, the cross sectional area of the engine increases. This allows the air stream from the compressor to slow and its pressure to increase. In fact, the highest pressure in the engine is attained at this point.

Next, the air enters the combustion section where it is mixed with fuel and the mixture is ignited. Note that after the initial start of the engine there is no need for an ignition system that operates continuously (such as the spark plugs in a piston engine) because the uninterrupted flow of fuel and air will sustain combustion after the initial "light off." The combustion of the fuel-air mixture causes a great increase in volume and because there is higher pressure at the diffuser, the gas exits through the turbine section. The temperature of the gas rises rapidly as it passes from the front to the rear of the combustion section. It reaches its highest point in the engine at the turbine inlet. The maximum turbine inlet temperature is a major limitation on turbojet performance, and without cooling, it could easily reach up to 4,000°F, far beyond the limits of the materials used in the turbine section. To keep the temperature down to an acceptable 1,100° to 1,500°F, surplus cooling air from the compressor is mixed aft of the burners.

The purpose of the turbine(s) is to drive the compressor(s) and they are connected by a drive shaft. Since the turbines take energy from the gas, both the temperature and pressure drop.

Continued

The gases exit the turbine section at very high velocity into the tailpipe. The tailpipe is shaped so that the gas is accelerated even more, reaching maximum velocity as it exits into the atmosphere. *See* Figure 4-1.

Combinations of slow airspeed and high engine RPM can cause a phenomenon in turbine engines called **compressor stall**. This occurs when the angle of attack of the engine's compressor blades becomes excessive and they stall. If a transient stall condition exists, the pilot will hear an intermittent "bang" as backfires and flow reversals in the compressor take place. If the transient condition develops into a steady state stall, the pilot will hear a loud roar and experience severe engine vibrations. The steady state compressor stall has the most potential for severe engine damage, which can occur literally within seconds of the onset of the stall.

If a compressor stall occurs in flight, the pilot should reduce fuel flow, reduce the aircraft's angle of attack and increase airspeed.

The turboprop is a turbine engine that drives a conventional propeller. It can develop much more power per pound than can a piston engine and is more fuel efficient than the turbojet engine. Compared to a turbojet engine, it is limited to slower speeds and lower altitudes (25,000 feet to the tropopause). The term **equivalent shaft horsepower (ESHP)** is used to describe the total engine output. This term combines its output in shaft horsepower (used to drive the propeller) and the jet thrust it develops.

As the density altitude is increased, engine performance will decrease. When the air becomes less dense, there is not as much oxygen available for combustion and the potential thrust output is decreased accordingly. Density altitude is increased by increasing the pressure altitude or by increasing the ambient temperature. Relative humidity will also affect engine performance. Reciprocating engines in particular will experience a significant loss of BHP (Brake Horsepower). Turbine engines are not affected as much by high humidity and will experience very little loss of thrust.

Figure 4-1. Turbojet engine

ALL
9072. Where is the critical altitude of a supercharged-reciprocating engine?

A— The highest altitude at which a desired manifold pressure can be obtained.
B— Highest altitude where the mixture can be leaned to best power ratio.
C— The altitude at which maximum allowable BMEP can be obtained.

The critical altitude of a supercharged reciprocating engine is the highest altitude at which a desired MAP can be maintained. (PLT343) — FAA-H-8083-25

Answer (B) is incorrect because critical altitude is the highest altitude at which a manifold pressure can be obtained. Answer (C) is incorrect because BMEP is pressure representing the mean gas load on the piston during the power stroke.

ALL
9073. What is controlled by the waste gate of a turbocharged-reciprocating engine?

A— Supercharger gear ratio.
B— Exhaust gas discharge.
C— Throttle opening.

A turbocharger drives exhaust gas from the engine. The waste gate controls the flow of the exhaust gas through the turbocharger's turbine. (PLT343) — FAA-H-8083-25

Answer (A) is incorrect because supercharger gear ratio is not controlled by the waste gate. Answer (C) is incorrect because the throttle opening sets the desired manifold pressure.

ALL
9068. Under normal operating conditions, which combination of MAP and RPM produce the most severe wear, fatigue, and damage to high performance reciprocating engines?

A— High RPM and low MAP.
B— Low RPM and high MAP.
C— High RPM and high MAP.

The most severe rate of wear and fatigue damage occurs at high RPM and low MAP. (PLT365) — FAA-H-8083-25

Answer (B) is incorrect because while low RPM and high MAP produce severe wear to high performance reciprocating engines, the most damage is done by high RPM and low manifold pressure. Answer (C) is incorrect because a high RPM and a low MAP produce the most severe wear to high performance reciprocating engines.

ALL
9068-1. How are turbine engines classified?

A— The type of compressor or combination of compressors they use.
B— The method in which the air/fuel mixture is ignited.
C— The flow of air through the engine and how power is produced.

Turbine engines are classified by the type of compressors they use—centrifugal flow, axial flow, and centrifugal-axial flow. (PLT365) — FAA-H-8083-25

ALL
9058. Which place in the turbojet engine is subjected to the highest temperature?

A— Compressor discharge.
B— Fuel spray nozzles.
C— Turbine inlet.

The highest temperatures in any turbine engine will occur at the turbine inlet. This TIT (Turbine Inlet Temperature) is usually the limiting factor in the engine operation. (PLT499) — FAA-H-8083-25

ALL
8394. A hot start in a turbine engine is caused by

A— failed ignition.
B— the engine's failure to accelerate.
C— too much fuel in the combustion chamber.

A hot start occurs when the exhaust gas temperature exceeds the safe limit of an aircraft. Caused by either too much fuel entering the combustion chamber or insufficient turbine RPM, this condition is also known as a hung start. (PLT499) — FAA-H-8083-25

Answers

9072 [A]	9073 [B]	9068 [A]	9068-1 [A]	9058 [C]	8394 [C]

ALL
9060. The most important restriction to the operation of turbojet or turboprop engines is

A— limiting compressor speed.
B— limiting exhaust gas temperature.
C— limiting torque.

The highest temperatures in any turbine engine will occur at the turbine inlet. This TIT (Turbine Inlet Temperature) is usually the limiting factor in the engine operation. In many engines, TIT is measured indirectly as EGT (Exhaust Gas Temperature). (PLT499) — FAA-H-8083-25

Answer (A) is incorrect because the turbine section is the most critical element of the turbojet engine. Temperature control is more restrictive than compressor speed, which may operate above 10,000 RPM continuously. Answer (C) is incorrect because torque is a performance measure used on turbopropeller airplanes, but not generally applicable to turbojet engines. The most important restriction is temperature, even though in cooler weather a torque limitation may be reached before the temperature limitation in a turbopropeller airplane.

ALL
9064. What characterizes a transient compressor stall?

A— Loud, steady roar accompanied by heavy shuddering.
B— Sudden loss of thrust accompanied by a loud whine.
C— Intermittent "bang," as backfires and flow reversals take place.

If a compressor stall is transient and intermittent, the indication will be an intermittent "bang" as backfire and flow reversal take place. If the stall develops and becomes steady, strong vibration and a loud roar develop from the continuous flow reversal. The possibility of damage is immediate from a steady stall. Recovery must be accomplished quickly by reducing throttle setting, lowering the airplane angle of attack, and increasing airspeed. (PLT343) — FAA-H-8083-25

Answer (A) is incorrect because this describes a developed and steady stall. Answer (B) is incorrect because a transient stall is characterized by an intermittent "bang."

ALL
9768. What prevents turbine engines from developing compressor stalls?

A— Deice valves-fuel heat.
B— TKS system.
C— Compressor bleed valves.

At a low RPM, sudden full power application will tend to overfuel the engine resulting in possible compressor surge, excessive turbine temperatures, compressor stall, and/or flameout. To prevent this, various limiters such as compressor bleed valves are contained in the system and serve to restrict the engine until it is at an RPM at which it can respond to a rapid acceleration demand without distress. (PLT499) — FAA-H-8083-3

ALL
9065. What indicates that a compressor stall has developed and become steady?

A— Strong vibrations and loud roar.
B— Occasional loud "bang" and flow reversal.
C— Complete loss of power with severe reduction in airspeed.

If a compressor stall is transient and intermittent, the indication will be an intermittent "bang" as backfire and flow reversal take place. If the stall develops and becomes steady, strong vibration and a loud roar develop from the continuous flow reversal. The possibility of damage is immediate from a steady stall. Recovery must be accomplished quickly by reducing throttle setting, lowering the airplane angle of attack, and increasing airspeed. (PLT343) — FAA-H-8083-25

Answer (B) is incorrect because this describes an indication of a transient stall. Answer (C) is incorrect because a compressor stall will not cause a complete loss of power.

ALL
9066. Which type of compressor stall has the greatest potential for severe engine damage?

A— Intermittent "backfire" stall.
B— Transient "backfire" stall.
C— Steady, continuous flow reversal stall.

If a compressor stall is transient and intermittent, the indication will be an intermittent "bang" as backfire and flow reversal take place. If the stall develops and becomes steady, strong vibration and a loud roar develop from the continuous flow reversal. The possibility of damage is immediate from a steady stall. Recovery must be accomplished quickly by reducing throttle setting, lowering the airplane angle of attack, and increasing airspeed. (PLT343) — FAA-H-8083-25

Answers

9060 [B]	9064 [C]	9768 [C]	9065 [A]	9066 [C]

ALL
8974. Which part(s) in the turbojet engine is subjected to the high temperatures and severe centrifugal forces?

A— Turbine wheel(s).
B— Turbine vanes.
C— Compressor rotor(s) or impeller(s).

The turbine wheels are found at the back of the turbine section, in the area of very high temperatures and high centrifugal forces. Very hot, high pressure gases enter the turbine section from the combustor. The function of the gas generator's turbine wheels is to transfer the energy from the hot, high pressure gases to drive the shaft which is connected to the compressor wheel at the front of the engine. This in turn compresses air into the combustor where fuel is added and ignited. During normal operations, the turbine wheel rotates at many thousands of RPM. (PLT499) — FAA-H-8083-25

Answer (B) is incorrect because although turbine vanes (inlet guide vanes) are exposed to higher temperatures, they are stationary and thus are not subject to centrifugal forces. Answer (C) is incorrect because turbine wheels, or disks, with their attached blades, are the most highly stressed components on a turbojet engine.

ALL
9067. What recovery would be appropriate in the event of compressor stall?

A— Reduce the throttle and then rapidly advance the throttle to decrease the angle of attack on the compressor blades, creating more airflow.
B— Reduce the throttle and then slowly advance the throttle again and decrease the aircraft's angle of attack.
C— Advance the throttle slowly to increase airflow and decrease the angle of attack on one or more compressor blades.

If a compressor stall is transient and intermittent, the indication will be an intermittent "bang" as backfire and flow reversal take place. If the stall develops and becomes steady, strong vibration and a loud roar develop from the continuous flow reversal. The possibility of damage is immediate from a steady stall. Recovery must be accomplished quickly by reducing throttle setting, lowering the airplane angle of attack, and increasing airspeed. (PLT343) — FAA-H-8083-25

ALL
9070. Equivalent shaft horsepower (ESHP) of a turbo-prop engine is a measure of

A— turbine inlet temperature.
B— shaft horsepower and jet thrust.
C— propeller thrust only.

Turboprop engines get 15 to 25% of their total thrust output from jet exhaust. ESHP (Equivalent Shaft Horse-power) is the term used to describe the shaft horsepower applied to the propeller plus this jet thrust. (PLT500) — FAA-H-8083-25

ALL
9071. Minimum specific fuel consumption of the turboprop engine is normally available in which altitude range?

A— 10,000 feet to 25,000 feet.
B— 25,000 feet to the tropopause.
C— The tropopause to 45,000 feet.

Minimum specific fuel consumption of a turboprop engine will be obtained in an altitude range of 25,000 to 35,000 feet. The tropopause will be in the neighborhood of 35,000 feet depending on the season and latitude. (PLT130) — FAA-H-8083-25

ALL
9059. What effect would a change in ambient temperature or air density have on gas-turbine-engine performance?

A— As air density decreases, thrust increases.
B— As temperature increases, thrust increases.
C— As temperature increases, thrust decreases.

Turbine engine thrust varies directly with air density. As air density decreases, so does thrust. An increase in temperature will decrease air density. (PLT127) — FAA-H-8083-25

ALL
9061. As outside air pressure decreases, thrust output will

A— increase due to greater efficiency of jet aircraft in thin air.
B— remain the same since compression of inlet air will compensate for any decrease in air pressure.
C— decrease due to higher density altitude.

Thrust output decreases with increasing density altitude. Decreasing air pressure increases density altitude. (PLT127) — FAA-H-8083-25

Answers

8974 [A]	9067 [B]	9070 [B]	9071 [B]	9059 [C]	9061 [C]

9061-1. Low pressure air decreases aircraft performance because

A— the air is denser than higher pressure air.
B— the air is less dense than high pressure air.
C— air expands in the engine during the combustion process.

Thrust output decreases with increasing density altitude. Decreasing air pressure increases density altitude. (PLT127) — FAA-H-8083-25

9062. What effect will an increase in altitude have upon the available equivalent shaft horsepower (ESHP) of a turboprop engine?

A— Lower air density and engine mass flow will cause a decrease in power.
B— Higher propeller efficiency will cause an increase in usable power (ESHP) and thrust.
C— Power will remain the same but propeller efficiency will decrease.

As altitude is increased, the ESHP of a turboprop engine will decrease due to lower engine mass flow and decreased propeller efficiency. (PLT127) — FAA-H-8083-25

9063. What effect, if any, does high ambient temperature have upon the thrust output of a turbine engine?

A— Thrust will be reduced due to the decrease in air density.
B— Thrust will remain the same, but turbine temperature will be higher.
C— Thrust will be higher because more heat energy is extracted from the hotter air.

Turbine engine thrust varies directly with air density. As air density decreases, so does thrust. An increase in temperature will decrease air density. (PLT127) — FAA-H-8083-25

9069. What effect does high relative humidity have upon the maximum power output of modern aircraft engines?

A— Neither turbojet nor reciprocating engines are affected.
B— Reciprocating engines will experience a significant loss of BHP.
C— Turbojet engines will experience a significant loss of thrust.

While turbojet engines are almost unaffected by high relative humidity, reciprocating engines will experience a significant loss of BHP (Brake Horsepower). (PLT365) — FAA-H-8083-25

Answer (A) is incorrect because both reciprocating and turbojet engines are affected by high relative humidity to some degree. Answer (C) is incorrect because turbojet engines will have a negligible loss of thrust.

Answers

| 9061-1 | [B] | 9062 | [A] | 9063 | [A] | 9069 | [B] |

Helicopter Systems

RTC
8407. Which type rotor system is more susceptible to ground resonance?

A— Fully articulated rotor system.
B— Semi-rigid rotor system.
C— Rigid rotor system.

Due to the lead/lag of the blades in a fully articulated rotor system, a shock from a landing gear striking the surface can be transmitted through the fuselage to the rotor, forcing the blades straddling the contact point closer together and unbalancing the rotor system. This can cause a pendulum-like oscillation which will increase rapidly unless immediate corrective action is taken. (PLT470) — FAA-H-8083-21

RTC
9781. Ground resonance occurs when

A— a fully articulated rotor system is unbalanced.
B— a semi-rigid rotor system is out of balance.
C— a pilot lands with over inflated tires.

Ground resonance is an aerodynamic phenomenon associated with fully articulated rotor systems. It develops when the rotor blades move out of phase with each other and cause the rotor disc to become unbalanced. (PLT470) — FAA-H-8083-21

RTC
8414. What type frequency vibration is associated with a defective transmission?

A— Low frequency only.
B— Medium or low frequency.
C— High or medium frequency.

High-frequency vibrations (2,000 cycles per minute or higher) are associated with the engine in most helicopters. Any bearings in the transmission that go bad will result in vibrations with frequencies directly related to the speed of the engine. (PLT472) — FAA-H-8083-21

RTC
8415. What type frequency vibration is associated with the main rotor system?

A— Low frequency.
B— Medium frequency.
C— High frequency.

Abnormal vibrations in the low-frequency range (100 to 400 cycles per minute) are always associated with the main rotor system, and will be somewhat related to the rotor RPM and the number of blades of the main rotor. (PLT472) — FAA-H-8083-21

RTC
9800. A medium or higher frequency vibration mainly present in the anti-torque pedals is

A— usually traceable to engine cooling fan assembly.
B— probably caused by the tail rotor.
C— to be expected and accepted as normal.

Medium-frequency vibrations are a result of trouble with the tail rotor in most helicopters. Improper rigging, imbalance, defective blades, or bad bearings in the tail rotor are all sources of these vibrations. If the vibration occurs only during turns, the trouble may be caused by insufficient tail rotor flapping action. (PLT472) — FAA-H-8083-21

RTC
8416. What type frequency vibration is indicative of a defective tail rotor system?

A— Low and medium frequency.
B— Medium and high frequency.
C— Low and high frequency.

Medium frequency vibrations (1,000–2,000 cycles per minute) and high frequency vibrations (2,000 cycles per minute or higher) are normally associated with out-of-balance components that rotate at a high RPM, such as the tail rotor, engine, cooling fans, and components of the drive train, including transmissions, drive shafts, bearings, pulleys, and belts. (PLT472) — FAA-H-8083-21

Answers
8407 [A]   9781 [A]   8414 [C]   8415 [A]   9800 [B]   8416 [B]

RTC

8426. What is the primary purpose of the free-wheeling unit?

A— To provide speed reduction between the engine, main rotor system, and tail rotor system.
B— To provide disengagement of the engine from the rotor system for autorotation purposes.
C— To transmit engine power to the main rotor, tail rotor, generator/alternator, and other accessories.

The freewheeling coupling provides for autorotative capabilities by disconnecting the rotor system from the engine when the engine stops or slows below the RPM of the rotor system. This allows the transmission to be driven by the main rotor. The tail rotor will continue to be turned by the transmission. (PLT470) — FAA-H-8083-21

RTC

8427. The main rotor blades of a fully articulated rotor system can

A— flap, drag, and feather collectively.
B— flap, drag, and feather independently of each other.
C— flap and drag individually, but can only feather collectively.

Fully articulated rotor systems usually have three or more rotor blades, each of which is attached to the rotor hub by a horizontal hinge (flapping), a vertical hinge (drag), and can be feathered (rotated about their spanwise axis) independently of the other blades. (PLT470) — FAA-H-8083-21

RTC

8428. The main rotor blades of a semi-rigid system can

A— flap and feather as a unit.
B— flap, drag, and feather independently.
C— flap and drag individually, but can only feather collectively.

In a semirigid (two-bladed) rotor system, the blades are rigidly interconnected to the hub and flap as a unit (when one blade flaps up, the other blade flaps down an equal amount). The swash plate changes the pitch angle in each blade (feathers) an equal amount. (PLT470) — FAA-H-8083-21

Takeoff Performance Terminology

Clearway — a plane beyond the end of a runway which does not contain obstructions and can be considered when calculating takeoff performance of turbine-powered transport category airplanes. The first segment of the takeoff of a turbine-powered airplane is considered complete when it reaches a height of 35 feet above the runway and has achieved V_2 speed. Clearway may be used for the climb to 35 feet.

Stopway — an area designated for use in decelerating an aborted takeoff. It cannot be used as a part of the takeoff distance but can be considered as part of the accelerate-stop distance. *See* Figure 4-2.

Regulation requires that a transport category airplane's takeoff weight be such that, if at any time during the takeoff run the critical engine fails, the airplane can either be stopped on the runway and stopway remaining, or that it can safely continue the takeoff. This means that a **maximum takeoff weight** must be computed for each takeoff. Factors which determine the maximum takeoff weight for an airplane include runway length, wind, flap position, runway braking action, pressure altitude and temperature.

In addition to the runway-limited takeoff weight, each takeoff requires a computation of a climb-limited takeoff weight that will guarantee acceptable climb performance after takeoff with an engine inoperative. The climb-limited takeoff weight is determined by flap position, pressure altitude and temperature.

When the runway-limited and climb-limited takeoff weights are determined, they are compared to the maximum structural takeoff weight. The lowest of the three weights is the limit that must be observed for that takeoff. If the airplane's actual weight is at or below the lowest of the three limits, adequate takeoff performance is ensured. If the actual weight is above any of the limits a takeoff cannot be made until the weight is reduced or one or more limiting factors (runway, flap setting, etc.) is changed to raise the limiting weight.

Answers

8426 [B]	8427 [B]	8428 [A]

After the maximum takeoff weight is computed and it is determined that the airplane's actual weight is within limits, then V_1, V_R and V_2 are computed. These takeoff speed limits are contained in performance charts and tables of the airplane flight manual, and are observed on the captain's airspeed indicator. By definition they are indicated airspeeds. *See* Figure 4-3.

V_1 **(Takeoff Decision Speed)** is the speed during the takeoff at which the airplane can experience a failure of the critical engine and the pilot can abort the takeoff and come to a full safe stop on the runway and stopway remaining, or the pilot can continue the takeoff safely. If an engine fails at a speed less than V_1, the pilot must abort; if the failure occurs at a speed above V_1 he/she must continue the takeoff.

V_R **(Rotation Speed)** is the IAS at which the aircraft is rotated to its takeoff attitude with or without an engine failure. V_R is at or just above V_1.

V_2 **(Takeoff Safety Speed)** ensures that the airplane can maintain an acceptable climb gradient with the critical engine inoperative.

V_{MU} **(Minimum Unstick Speed)** is the minimum speed at which the airplane may be flown off the runway without a tail strike. This speed is determined by manufacturer's tests and establishes minimum V_1 and V_R speeds. The flight crew does not normally compute the V_{MU} speed separately.

V_1 is computed using the actual airplane gross weight, flap setting, pressure altitude and temperature. Raising the pressure altitude, temperature or gross weight will all increase the computed V_1 speed. Lowering any of those variables will lower the V_1 speed.

A wind will change the takeoff distance. A headwind will decrease it and a tailwind will increase it. While a headwind or tailwind component does affect the runway limited takeoff weight, it usually has no direct effect on the computed V_1 speed. The performance tables for a few airplanes include a small correction to V_1 for very strong winds. For those airplanes, a headwind will increase V_1 and a tailwind will decrease it.

A runway slope has the same effect on takeoff performance as a wind. A runway which slopes uphill will increase the takeoff distance for an airplane and a downslope will decrease it. A significant slope may require an adjustment in the V_1 speed. An upslope will require an increase in V_1 and a downslope will require a decrease.

If there is slush on the runway or if the antiskid system is inoperative, the stopping performance of the airplane is degraded. This requires that any aborted takeoff be started at a lower speed and with more runway and stopway remaining. This means that both the runway-limited takeoff weight and the V_1 used for takeoff be lower than normal.

Figure 4-2. Takeoff runway definitions

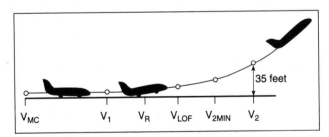

Figure 4-3. Takeoff speeds

ATM, ATS, DSP

9324. What is the name of an area beyond the end of a runway which does not contain obstructions and can be considered when calculating takeoff performance of turbine-powered aircraft?

A— Clearway.
B— Stopway.
C— Obstruction clearance plane.

"Clearway" means, for turbine-powered airplanes, an area beyond the end of the runway, centrally located about the extended centerline and under the control of the airport authorities. Clearway distance may be used in the calculation of takeoff distance. (PLT395) — 14 CFR §1.1

Answer (B) is incorrect because a stopway is an area beyond the takeoff runway, not any less wide than the runway, centered upon the extended centerline of the runway, and able to support the airplane during an aborted takeoff. Answer (C) is incorrect because an obstruction clearance plane is not defined in 14 CFR Part 1.

ATM, ATS, DSP

9327. What is an area identified by the term "stopway"?

A— An area, at least the same width as the runway, capable of supporting an airplane during a normal takeoff.
B— An area designated for use in decelerating an aborted takeoff.
C— An area, not as wide as the runway, capable of supporting an airplane during a normal takeoff.

"Stopway" means an area beyond the takeoff runway, able to support the airplane, for use in decelerating the airplane during an aborted takeoff. (PLT395) — 14 CFR §1.1

Answer (A) is incorrect because it describes the nonlanding portion of a runway behind a displaced threshold, which may be suitable for taxiing, landing rollout, and takeoff of aircraft. Answer (C) is incorrect because it would describe an area that exists before a displaced threshold.

ATM, ATS, DSP

8134. For which of these aircraft is the "clearway" for a particular runway considered in computing takeoff weight limitations?

A— Those passenger-carrying transport aircraft certified between August 26, 1957 and August 30, 1959.
B— Turbine-engine-powered transport airplanes certificated after September 30, 1958.
C— U.S. certified air carrier airplanes certificated after August 29, 1959.

"Clearway" may be considered when determining the takeoff distance of turbine-engine-powered transport category airplane certificated after August 29, 1959. (PLT034) — 14 CFR §121.189 and §1.1

Answers (A) and (C) are incorrect because the passenger-carrying transport aircraft and air carrier airplane would have to be turbine-engine-powered in order to include the clearway in determining runway length for takeoff purposes.

ATM, ATS, DSP

9317. Which is a definition of V_2 speed?

A— Takeoff decision speed.
B— Takeoff safety speed.
C— Minimum takeoff speed.

V_2 means takeoff safety speed. (PLT466) — 14 CFR §1.2

Answer (A) is incorrect because V_1 is takeoff decision speed. Answer (C) is incorrect because minimum takeoff speed doesn't describe a defined speed.

ATM, ATS, DSP

9319. What is the correct symbol for minimum unstick speed?

A— V_{MU}.
B— V_{MD}.
C— V_{FC}.

V_{MU} means minimum unstick speed. (PLT466) — 14 CFR §1.2

Answer (B) is incorrect because V_{MD} is not a concept that is defined in 14 CFR §1.2. Answer (C) is incorrect because V_{FC}/M_{FC} is maximum speed for stability characteristics.

ATM, ATS, DSP

8774. The maximum speed during takeoff that the pilot may abort the takeoff and stop the airplane within the accelerate-stop distance is

A— V_2.
B— V_{EF}.
C— V_1.

The takeoff decision speed, V_1, is the calibrated airspeed on the ground at which, as a result of engine failure or other reasons, the pilot is assumed to have made a decision to continue or discontinue the takeoff. (PLT506) — 14 CFR §1.2

Answer (A) is incorrect because V_2 is the takeoff safety speed. Answer (B) is incorrect because V_{EF} is the calibrated airspeed at which the critical engine is assumed to fail.

Answers

| 9324 [A] | 9327 [B] | 8134 [B] | 9317 [B] | 9319 [A] | 8774 [C] |

ATM, ATS, DSP

8775. The minimum speed during takeoff, following a failure of the critical engine at V_{EF}, at which the pilot may continue the takeoff and achieve the required height above the takeoff surface within the takeoff distance is indicated by symbol

A— V_{2min}.
B— V_1.
C— V_{LOF}.

The takeoff decision speed, V_1, is the calibrated airspeed on the ground at which, as a result of engine failure or other reasons, the pilot is assumed to have made a decision to continue or discontinue the takeoff. V_1 is also the speed at which the airplane can be rotated for takeoff and shown to be adequate to safely continue the takeoff, using normal piloting skill, when the critical engine is suddenly made inoperative. (PLT466) — 14 CFR §1.2

Answer (A) is incorrect because V_{2min} is the minimum takeoff safety speed. Answer (C) is incorrect because V_{LOF} is the liftoff speed.

ATM, ATS, DSP

8780. The symbol for the speed at which the critical engine is assumed to fail during takeoff is

A— V_2.
B— V_1.
C— V_{EF}.

V_{EF} is the calibrated airspeed at which the critical engine is assumed to fail. V_{EF} must be selected by the applicant but must not be less than 1.05 V_{MC} or, at the option of the applicant, not less than V_{MCG}. (PLT466) — 14 CFR §23.51

Answer (A) is incorrect because V_2 is the takeoff safety speed. Answer (B) is incorrect because V_1 is takeoff decision speed.

ATM, ATS, DSP

9076. Which performance factor decreases as airplane gross weight increases, for a given runway?

A— Critical engine failure speed.
B— Rotation speed.
C— Accelerate-stop distance.

Critical Engine Failure Speed (also called V_1) increases with an increase in weight, resulting in a decrease in performance. (PLT011) — ANA

ATM, ATS, DSP

9085. Which condition has the effect of reducing critical engine failure speed?

A— Slush on the runway or inoperative antiskid.
B— Low gross weight.
C— High density altitude.

Critical Engine Failure Speed is an obsolete term for V_1 which is now called Takeoff Decision Speed. Lowering the airplane's weight will always have the effect of decreasing V_1, while increasing the density altitude will have the effect of increasing V_1. However, inoperative antiskid or slush on the runway will cause a reduction in the maximum allowable takeoff weight which has the effect of lowering V_1. (PLT347) — ANA

ATM, ATS, DSP

9083. What effect does an uphill runway slope have upon takeoff performance?

A— Increases takeoff distance.
B— Decreases takeoff speed.
C— Decreases takeoff distance.

An uphill runway will have the effect of decreasing an airplane's rate of acceleration during the takeoff roll thus causing it to reach its takeoff speeds (V_1 and V_R) further down the runway than would otherwise be the case. An uphill runway will also necessitate an increased V_1 speed in some airplanes. (PLT129) — ANA

ATM, ATS, DSP

9075. Which condition reduces the required runway for takeoff?

A— Higher-than-recommended airspeed before rotation.
B— Lower-than-standard air density.
C— Increased headwind component.

A headwind, in effect, gives an airplane part of its airspeed prior to starting the takeoff roll. This allows the airplane to reach its takeoff speed after a shorter takeoff roll than in no wind conditions. High rotation speeds and lower air density (high density altitude) both have the effect of increasing takeoff distance. (PLT134) — ANA

Answers (A) and (B) are incorrect because higher-than-recommended airspeed before rotation and lower-than-standard air density would increase the required runway for takeoff.

Answers

8775 [B]	8780 [C]	9076 [A]	9085 [A]	9083 [A]	9075 [C]

ATM, ATS, DSP

9797. You are rolling out after touchdown and decide you really need to abort your landing, and takeoff. Your airplane is at 116 knots and your engines have spooled down to 71% idle. You need a V_2 of 142 to safely lift off and climb. The airplane will require 6 seconds to accelerate after the engines spool up to takeoff thrust, which requires 4 seconds. How much runway will you require for a safe landing abort from your decision point? (Use an average of 129 knots ground speed.)

A— 1,738 feet.
B— 2,178 feet.
C— 3,601 feet.

At a ground speed of 129 knots, the question assumes it takes 10 seconds to takeoff. The distance required to fly to the decision point would be calculated using 129 knots ground speed. 1 knot = 1.69 feet per second = 218 ft/seconds. 218 x 10 sec = 2,180 feet. (PLT011) — FAA-H-8083-25

ATM, ATS, DSP

9797-1. You touchdown long with a speed of 145 knots on a 9,001 foot runway and the braking is not working, so you decide to takeoff and climb out. The engines require 5 seconds to spool up and then the airplane requires 10 seconds of acceleration time to lift off again. The 5,000 foot marker flashes by. Do you have enough runway to lift off? (Use 132 knots for the average groundspeed.)

A— Yes, there will be a margin of 850 feet and almost 3 seconds of decision time.
B— Yes, there will be a margin of 2,001 feet and almost 5 seconds of decision time.
C— No, the runway is 1,340 feet too short and my decision is about 6 seconds too late.

1. *Calculate distance traveled per second (1 knot = 1.69 feet per second) at 132 knots x 1.69 feet per second for 223.08 feet per second.*

2. *Calculate Liftoff Distance—Total of 15 seconds (5 for spool up and 10 for liftoff) multiplied by distance traveled per second 223.08 = 3,346.2 feet of liftoff distance needed.*

3. *Calculate Distance remaining (at 5000 marker) 5,000 - 3,346.2 (liftoff distance) = 1,653.8 feet remaining.*

4. *Calculate time for decision by dividing 1,653.8 by 223.08 (distance traveled per second) = 7.41 seconds available to make a decision.*

(PLT011) — FAA-H-8083-25

ATM, ATS, DSP

9797-2. You touchdown long with a speed of 145 knots on a 8,501 foot runway and the braking is not working, so you decide to takeoff and climbout. The engines require 5 seconds to spool up and then the airplane requires 10 seconds of acceleration to lift off again. The 4,000 foot marker flashed by 2 seconds ago. Do you have enough runway to lift off? (Use 143 knots for average ground speed due to the tailwind.)

A— Yes, there will be a margin of about 850 feet which is almost 3 seconds of decision time.
B— Yes, there will be a margin of almost 101 feet which is about 1.5 seconds of decision time.
C— No, the runway is 99 feet too short and my decision was about 0.4 seconds too late.

1. *Calculate distance traveled per second (1 knot = 1.69 feet per second) at 143 knots x 1.69 feet per second for 241.67 feet per second.*

2. *Calculate distance past 4,000 marker by 241.67 (distance traveled per second) x 2 (time past marker) = 483.34 feet.*

3. *Subtract distance past marker from the marker passed (4,000 - 483.34 = 3,516.66) to find remaining runway.*

4. *Calculate Liftoff Distance—Total of 15 seconds (5 for spool up and 10 for liftoff) multiplied by distance traveled per second 241.67 = 3,625.05 feet of liftoff distance needed.*

5. *Calculate if any excess runway is present—3,516.66 feet remaining - 3,625.05 required for liftoff = -108.39 feet available*

This calculation indicates an extra 108.39 feet would be needed to make this takeoff.

6. *Calculate time needed to make a decision 108.39 feet required / 241.67 feet per second =.448 seconds*

This calculation indicates the decision would have needed to be made .448 seconds ago. (PLT011) — FAA-H-8083-25

Answers

9797 [B]   9797-1 [B]   9797-2 [C]

ATM, ATS, DSP

9801. One typical takeoff error is

A— delayed rotation, which may extend the climb distance.
B— premature rotation, which may increase takeoff distance.
C— extended rotation, which may degrade acceleration.

In training it is common for the pilot to overshoot V_R and then overshoot V_2 because the pilot not flying will call for rotation at, or just past V_R. The reaction of the pilot flying is to visually verify V_R and then rotate. The airplane then leaves the ground at or above V_2. The excess airspeed may be of little concern on a normal takeoff, but a delayed rotation can be critical when runway length or obstacle clearance is limited. (PLT134) — FAA-H-8083-3

ATM, ATS, DSP

9802. Excessive takeoff speeds may result in approximately a

A— 4% takeoff distance increase for each 1% of additional takeoff speed.
B— 1% takeoff distance increase for each 2% of additional takeoff speed.
C— 2% takeoff distance increase for each 1% of additional takeoff speed.

An excessive airspeed at takeoff may improve the initial rate of climb and "feel" of the airplane but will produce an undesirable increase in takeoff distance. Assuming that the acceleration is essentially unaffected, the takeoff distance varies as the square of the takeoff velocity. Thus, a 10% increase excess airspeed would increase the takeoff distance 21%. (PLT134) — ANA

Calculating V-Speeds

The table in FAA Figure 82 is used in several problems to determine the pressure altitude from the indicated altitude and the local altimeter setting. The table uses the local altimeter setting to indicate the proper correction to field elevation. For example, assume the local altimeter setting is 29.36" Hg. Enter the table in the left-hand column labeled "QNH IN. HG." and then find the range of altimeter settings that contains 29.36" Hg. Read the correction to elevation in the center column. In this case, add 500 feet to the field elevation to determine the pressure altitude. If the altimeter setting is given in millibars, enter the table in the right-hand column.

CRJ200 V-Speeds

V_1, V_R, and V_2 are calculated by using the charts in FAA Figures 450, 452, and 454. In order to use these charts, you must first find a "Reference A" speed in FAA Figure 451. Once you have the Reference A speed, enter the chart in either Figure 452 or 454 at that speed and then move across directly right to determine the minimum V_{1MCA}.

From there, continuing to the right, intersect the aircraft weight line and proceed directly down, correcting for runway slope (if present), to note the V_R speed. If V_R is greater than $1.05 \times V_{1MCA}$, proceed to the right until entering the Chart B region; otherwise, use Chart A. Once intersecting the aircraft weight line in Chart A or B, move directly down and read the V_2 speed.

Q400 V-Speeds

V_1, V_R and V_2 for the Q400 are calculated from the charts contained in FAA Figures 470, 471, and 472. Using operating conditions given either through airport diagrams or as part of the question, you must be able to calculate these important speeds.

Figure 470 is the chart used to determine V_1 and V_R. Start on this chart at the lower left with the OAT and move up to the field elevation. Move across to the right until intersecting the reference line. Then proceed diagonally until intersecting the aircraft weight line. From there, move across to the right and

Continued

Answers

9801   [A]   9802   [C]

note the V_R speed. Continue to the right and intersect the reference line, then move down and to the left in parallel with the diagonal lines until intersecting the correct V_1/V_R ratio. Move directly right and find your V_1 speed. Note that V_1 cannot be less than V_R.

B-737 V-Speeds

Using Operating Conditions R-1 (FAA Figure 53), follow the steps for determining the V-speeds (*See* FAA Figure 55). Enter the table at the top left in the row appropriate for the pressure altitude and go across until in a column containing a temperature range which includes the given value. In this case, enter in the row labeled -1 to 1 (pressure altitude = 500 feet, refer to FAA Figure 54) and go to the first column which contains the temperature of +50°F (be sure to use the Fahrenheit or Celsius ranges as appropriate). Go down the first column until in the row appropriate for a flap setting of 15° and a gross weight of 90,000 pounds. The V_1 speed is 120 knots, the V_R speed is 121 knots and the V_2 speed is 128 knots. There are two possible adjustments to make to the V_1 speed only. They are noted at the bottom of the table.

DC-9 V-Speeds

The first step for calculating V_1 and V_R is to find the basic speeds in the table at the top of FAA Figure 47. Using the conditions from Operating Conditions A-1 from FAA Figure 45, the V-speeds for a weight of 75,000 pounds are: V_1 = 120.5, and V_R = 123.5 knots. Next, a series of corrections must be applied for pressure altitude, ambient temperature, runway slope, wind component, and engine and wing ice protection. There are table values for all these corrections at the bottom of FAA Figure 47 except for pressure altitude and ambient temperature.

The first step in the altitude correction is to use the table in FAA Figure 46 to determine the pressure altitude. Using the altimeter setting from Operating Conditions A-1 (29.40" Hg), the table shows a correction of +500 feet. The pressure altitude then is 3,000 feet (2,500 + 500).

Next, enter the graphs as shown in FAA Figure 47. Draw two vertical lines representing the pressure altitude of 3,000 feet. Next, draw a horizontal line through the ambient temperature (+10°F) to intersect each of the vertical lines. In this case, the lines meet in the "zero" correction area for both V_1 and V_R. Notice that the correction is marked by bands. For example, if the lines crossed anywhere in the highest shaded band, the correction would be +1 knot.

Next, set up a table similar to the one below to apply any necessary corrections:

	V_1	V_R
Table Value	120.5	123.5
Pressure Alt & Temp	0	0
Slope (+1%)	+ 1.5	+ .9
10 HW	+ .3	0
Ice Protection	+ .8	+ .8
Corrected Speeds	123.1	125.2

ATM, DSP

8717. (Refer to Figures 340, 451, and 452.) With a reported temperature of 20°C, flaps set at 8, engine bleeds closed, and a takeoff weight of 79,500 pounds, the takeoff safety speed is

A— 154 knots.
B— 160 knots.
C— 162 knots.

1. On Figure 340, find an airport elevation of 23 feet.

2. Use Figure 451 to find Reference A. Locate the portion of the chart marked Engine Bleeds Closed. Enter the chart at 20°C and work your way up to a Pressure Altitude of 23 feet. Move right to find a Reference A of 15.

3. On Figure 452, enter the chart from the left at Reference A of 15. Move right to the chart B area—the notes indicate this is the correct area because V_{MCA} is 114 knots and V_R is 146 knots (V_R is greater than 1.05 x V_{MCA} of 114). Intersect your takeoff weight of 79,500 pounds, then read the takeoff speed below of 154 knots.

(PLT011) — FAA-H-8083-25

ATM, DSP

8718. (Refer to Figures 336, 451, and 452). With a reported temperature of 5°C, flaps set at 8, engine bleeds closed, and a takeoff weight off 82,000 pounds, the V_R is

A— 150 knots.
B— 147 knots.
C— 158 knots.

1. On Figure 336, find a field elevation of 9 feet.

2. Use Figure 451 to find a Reference A. Locate the portion of the graph with column marked Engine Bleeds Closed. Enter the chart at 5°C moving up to intersect an altitude of 9 feet. Move straight across to the right to find a Reference A of 15.4.

3. On Figure 452, enter the chart from the left at Reference A of 15.4. Move right to intersect your takeoff weight of 82,000 pounds. Moving straight down, locate the V_R of 147 knots.

(PLT011) — FAA-H-8083-25

ATM, DSP

8719. (Refer to Figures 340 and 450.) With a reported temperature of 35°C, flaps set at 8, and 5 knots of headwind at a takeoff weight of 82,300 pounds, the V_{1MBE} is

A— 174 knots.
B— 169 knots.
C— 154 knots.

1. On Figure 340, the field elevation is 23 feet. Note that there is no runway slope indicated for runway 10.

2. On Figure 450, start with the ambient temperature of 35°C, and move right to intersect an airport pressure altitude of 23 feet. Then move straight down all the way to the REF. LINE in the wind section. From this reference line, move up and right in parallel with the diagonal lines until you reach the 5 knot wind mark. From here, proceed straight down to the REF. LINE in the runway slope section. Because there is no slope, move straight down and determine the V_{1MBE} speed of 171 knots.

3. Reference Note 2 in the upper right side of chart and see that for each 2,200 pounds under 84,500 pounds, add 3 knots. Since 84,500 – 82,300 = 2,200, add 3 knots, with the result of an V_{1MBE} speed of 174 knots.

(PLT089) — FAA-H-8083-25

ATM, DSP

8720. (Refer to Figures 342 and 450.) With a reported temperature of 40°C, flaps set at 20, and a 3 knot tailwind at a takeoff weight of 84,500, the V_{1MBE} is

A— 160 knots.
B— 143 knots.
C— 166 knots.

In Figure 450, enter the chart on the left at 40°C. Move right to locate an airport altitude of 10 feet. Move straight down to intersect the tailwind portion of the chart following the line parallel and to the right to -3 knots. Read a V_{1MBE} of 165 on the bottom portion of the chart. Note 1 states with flaps set at 20 degrees increase V_{1MBE} value by 1 knot.

165 + 1 = 166 knots

(PLT012) — FAA-H-8083-25

Answers

| 8717 [A] | 8718 [B] | 8719 [A] | 8720 [C] |

ATM, DSP

8721. (Refer to Figures 342, 451, and 452.) With a reported temperature of -10°C, flaps set at 8, cowl anti-ice on, and at a takeoff weight off 77,000 lbs, the V_R and V_2 speeds are

A— 143 and 153 knots.
B— 153 and 143 knots.
C— 123 and 133 knots.

1. Start with Figure 342 to determine an airport elevation of 10 feet.

2. Enter Figure 451 at -10°C in the first column labeled Cowl and Anti-Ice On, and proceed up to a pressure altitude of approximately 10 feet. Move straight across to the right to determine a Reference A of 13.9.

3. On Figure 452, enter the chart at your Reference A of 13.9. Move across to intersect the take-off weight of 77,000 lbs. Proceed straight down to note a V_R speed of 143.

4. To find V_2 speed, once again enter the chart at 13.9 moving straight across to intersect the weight of 77,000 lbs on Chart B. Proceed straight down to note a V_2 speed of 153 knots.

(PLT012) — FAA-H-8083-25

ATM, DSP

8583. (Refer to Figures 321 and 471.) With a reported temperature of -5°C and gross weight of 49,000 pounds, the chart V_2 value is

A— 118 knots.
B— 120 knots.
C— 122 knots.

1. From Figure 321, determine the field elevation of 6,535 feet.

2. On Figure 471, with a gross weight of 49,000 pounds, start on the lower right side of the chart at aircraft weight. Proceed directly up from 49,000 pounds until you intersect the diagonal reference line. Then proceed straight to the right to note a V_2 speed of 117 knots.

(PLT123) — FAA-H-8083-25

ATM, DSP

8584. (Refer to Figure 465.) At a weight of 60,000 pounds with 35 flaps, the Reference Stall Speed is

A— 96 knots.
B— 93 knots.
C— 89 knots.

Start at the bottom of Figure 465 at the weight of 60,000 pounds. Move straight up until you intersect the 35° flap angle reference line. Move straight left and note a stall speed of 96 knots. (PLT123) — FAA-H-8083-25

ATM, DSP

8585. (Refer to Figure 466.) At a weight of 60,500 pounds with 5 flaps, the 1.3 V_{SR} speed is

A— 146 knots.
B— 149 knots.
C— 152 knots.

Start at the bottom of the Flap 5° chart on Figure 466. Find 60,500 pounds and move straight up until intersecting the 1.3 V_{SR} reference line. Move straight left and note a speed of 149 knots. (PLT123) — FAA-H-8083-25

ATM, DSP

8586. (Refer to Figure 470.) What are the V_1 and V_R speeds at 25°C at sea level for an aircraft weighing 54,500 lbs. and a maximum V_1/V_R ratio of .93?

A— 110 and 114 knots.
B— 102 and 109 knots.
C— 97 and 102 knots.

1. Start at the bottom left on Figure 470 and find 25°C. Move straight up until intersecting the sea level line. Move straight to the right until intersecting the reference line. Move diagonally up and to the right staying parallel with the lines until you intersect the 54,500 lbs line. Move directly to the right and note a V_R speed of 109 knots.

2. Continue to the right until intersecting the reference line. Move diagonally down and to the left in parallel with the lines until intersecting the .93 V_1/V_R ratio line. Move directly to the right and note a V_1 of 102 knots.

(PLT123) — FAA-H-8083-25

Answers

8721 [A]	8583 [A]	8584 [A]	8585 [B]	8586 [B]

ATM, DSP

8587. (Refer to Figure 470.) What are the V_1 and V_R speeds at ISA+30°C and a field elevation of 4,500 feet for an aircraft weighing 64,000 lbs. and a maximum V_1/V_R ratio of .98?

A— 100 and 104 knots.
B— 112 and 115 knots.
C— 119 and 121 knots.

Pressure altitude = 1,500 feet

1. *Start at the ISA+30°C point in the middle left portion of Figure 470. Move down and to the right until intersecting the 4,500 foot line. Move straight to the right until intersecting the reference line. Move diagonally up and to the right staying parallel with the lines until you intersect the 64,000 lbs line. Move directly to the right and note a V_R speed of 121 knots.*

2. *Continue to the right until intersecting the reference line. Move diagonally down and to the left in parallel with the lines until intersecting the .98 V_1/V_R ratio line. Move directly to the right and note a V_1 of 119 knots.*

(PLT123) — FAA-H-8083-25

DSP

8618. (Refer to Figures 53, 54, and 55.) What is the takeoff safety speed for Operating Conditions R-1?

A— 128 knots.
B— 121 knots.
C— 133 knots.

Pressure altitude = 500 feet
$V_1 = 120 + 1$ *(slope)* $= 121$
$V_R = 121$
$V_2 = 128$

Note: V_2 is defined as Takeoff Safety Speed.

(PLT011) — FAA-H-8083-25

Answer (B) is incorrect because 121 knots is the rotation (V_R) speed. Answer (C) is incorrect because 133 knots is the V_2 speed using 5 flaps.

DSP

8619. (Refer to Figures 53, 54, and 55.) What is the rotation speed for Operating Conditions R-2?

A— 147 knots.
B— 152 knots.
C— 146 knots.

Pressure altitude = 3,500 feet
$V_1 = 144 - 1$ *(Wind)* $- 1$ *(Slope)* $= 142$
$V_R = 146$
$V_2 = 150$

Note: V_R is defined as Rotation Speed.

(PLT011) — FAA-H-8083-25

DSP

8620. (Refer to Figures 53, 54, and 55.) What are V_1, V_R, and V_2 speeds for Operating Conditions R-3?

A— 143, 143, and 147 knots.
B— 138, 138, and 142 knots.
C— 136, 138, and 143 knots.

Pressure altitude = 1,450 feet
$V_1 = 136 + 1$ *(Wind)* $+ 1$ *(Slope)* $= 138$
$V_R = 138$
$V_2 = 142$

(PLT011) — FAA-H-8083-25

DSP

8621. (Refer to Figures 53, 54, and 55.) What are critical engine failure and takeoff safety speeds for Operating Conditions R-4?

A— 131 and 133 knots.
B— 123 and 134 knots.
C— 122 and 130 knots.

Pressure altitude = 1,900 feet
$V_1 = 127 - 2$ *(Wind)* $- 2$ *(Slope)* $= 123$
$V_R = 129$
$V_2 = 134$

Note: Critical Engine Failure Speed is an obsolete term for V_1. V_2 is Takeoff Safety Speed.

(PLT012) — FAA-H-8083-25

DSP

8622. (Refer to Figures 53, 54, and 55.) What are rotation and V_2 bug speeds for Operating Conditions R-5?

A— 138 and 143 knots.
B— 136 and 138 knots.
C— 134 and 141 knots.

Pressure altitude = -150 feet
$V_R = 138$
$V_2 = 143$

(PLT012) — FAA-H-8083-25

Answers

8587 [C]	8618 [A]	8619 [C]	8620 [B]	8621 [B]	8622 [A]

DSP
9864. (Refer to Figures 45, 46, and 47.) What are V₁ and V_R speeds for Operating Conditions A-1?

A— V₁ 123.1 knots; V_R 125.2 knots.
B— V₁ 120.5 knots; V_R 123.5 knots.
C— V₁ 122.3 knots; V_R 124.1 knots.

Pressure altitude = 3,000 feet

	V₁	**V_R**
Table value	120.5	123.5
Pressure alt & temp	0	0
Slope (+1%)	+ 1.5	+ .9
10 HW	+ .3	0
Ice protection	+ .8	+ .8
Corrected speeds	123.1	125.2

(PLT011) — FAA-H-8083-25

DSP
9865. (Refer to Figures 45, 46, and 47.) What are V₁ and V_R speeds for Operating Conditions A-2?

A— V₁ 129.7 knots; V_R 134.0 knots.
B— V₁ 127.2 knots; V_R 133.2 knots.
C— V₁ 127.4 knots; V_R 133.6 knots.

Pressure altitude = 100 feet

	V₁	**V_R**
Table value	129.50	134.00
Pressure alt & temp	+ 1.00	+ 1.00
Slope (-1.5%)	− 2.25	− 1.35
10 TW	− .80	0
Ice protection	—	—
Corrected speeds	127.45	133.65

(PLT011) — FAA-H-8083-25

Answer (A) is incorrect because 134.0 knots is V_R unadjusted. Answer (B) is incorrect because V₁ and V_R are more than 127.2 and 133.2, respectively.

DSP
9866. (Refer to Figures 45, 46, and 47.) What are V₁ and V_R speeds for Operating Conditions A-3?

A— V₁ 136.8 knots; V_R 141.8 knots.
B— V₁ 134.8 knots; V_R 139.0 knots.
C— V₁ 133.5 knots; V_R 141.0 knots.

Pressure altitude = 4,000 feet

	V₁	**V_R**
Table value	133.50	139.00
Pressure alt & temp	+ 2.00	+ 2.00
Slope (+0%)	—	—
15 HW	+ .45	—
Ice protection	+ .80	+ .80
Corrected speeds	136.75	141.80

(PLT011) — FAA-H-8083-25

DSP
9867. (Refer to Figures 45, 46, and 47.) What are V₁ and V_R speeds for Operating Conditions A-4?

A— V₁ 128.0 knots; V_R 130.5 knots.
B— V₁ 129.9 knots; V_R 133.4 knots.
C— V₁ 128.6 knots; V_R 131.1 knots.

Pressure altitude = 5,600 feet

	V₁	**V_R**
Table value	125.00	129.00
Pressure alt & temp	+ 3.00	+ 3.00
Slope (+1.5%)	+ 2.25	+ 1.35
5 TW	− .40	0
Ice protection	—	—
Corrected speeds	129.85	133.35

Note: No correction is required if engine ice protection only is used. See remarks on table at the top of FAA Figure 47.

(PLT011) — FAA-H-8083-25

DSP
9868. (Refer to Figures 45, 46, and 47.) What are V₁ and V_R speeds for Operating Conditions A-5?

A— V₁ 110.4 knots; V_R 110.9 knots.
B— V₁ 109.6 knots; V_R 112.7 knots.
C— V₁ 106.4 knots; V_R 106.4 knots.

Pressure altitude = 1,500 feet

	V₁	**V_R**
Table value	110.0	112.5
Pressure alt & temp	+ 2.0	+ 2.0
Slope (-2%)	− 3.0	− 1.8
20 HW	+ .6	0
Ice protection	—	—
Corrected speeds	109.6	112.7

(PLT011) — FAA-H-8083-25

Answers

9864 [A] 9865 [C] 9866 [A] 9867 [B] 9868 [B]

DSP
8642-4. (Refer to Figures 237 and 238.) Given the following conditions, what are the takeoff V speeds?

Weight .... 170,000 lb
Flaps ....10°
Temperature (OAT) .... 25°C
Field pressure altitude .... 427 ft.
Runway slope 0%
Wind (kts) headwind ....8 kts
Runway condition .... wet runway

For V_R more than or equal to .1 V_R, round up V_R to the next value (example: 140 + .1 = 141)

A— V_1 133 kts, V_R 140 kts, V_2 145 kts.
B— V_1 140 kts, V_R 140 kts, V_2 145 kts.
C— V_1 138 kts, V_R 141 kts, V_2 145 kts.

1. *Start on FAA Figure 238 since a wet runway is specified.*
2. *Enter the Takeoff speeds chart at 170 (1,000 pounds) and proceed to the Flaps 10 column for V_1 – 133, V_R – 139, V_2 – 145.*
3. *Enter the adjustments table at 27°C and interpolate in each column for pressure altitude of 500 feet.*
4. *Enter the V_1 Slope and Wind adjustments table at the given weight of 170 (1,000 lbs). Since there is no runway slope, continue right to the wind column of 10 knots (rounding up from the given 8-knot headwind). Note a minimal -1 knot decrease adjustment for V_1.*
5. *For V_1, round down to 133 knots, for V_R round up to 140 knots, for V_2 the adjustment is 0 so it remains 145.*

(PLT011) — FAA-H-8083-25

Calculating Takeoff Power

CRJ200 Takeoff Thrust Settings

Calculating the appropriate thrust settings for the CRJ200 is accomplished by using FAA Figures 428 through 431. Pay special attention to the "Notes" at the bottom of each of these figures, as this tells how to determine the correct chart to use. For example, Figure 428 depicts thrust settings based on all engines operating with the bleed valves closed, which is a typical takeoff for the CRJ200. Enter the chart at the left at the correct temperature and move to the right until intersecting the correct pressure altitude. This will yield the correct N_1 power thrust setting to be used during takeoff.

Q400 Takeoff Power

The Q400 takeoff power settings are determined by the charts in FAA Figures 467 and 468. Figure 467 depicts the appropriate power settings while on the ground and Figure 468 is used in flight (during the climb). To determine the correct takeoff torque setting, use Figure 467. Start at the bottom of the chart at the OAT, then move directly up until intersecting the airport elevation. Move directly to the right to find the torque setting.

B-737 Takeoff EPR

The Takeoff EPR table at the top of FAA Figure 55 is similar to the B-727 takeoff EPR. In the table of FAA Figure 55, two EPR values are found: one for temperature and one for altitude (be sure to use the table in FAA Figure 54 to determine the pressure altitude). The lower of the two is the takeoff EPR. For example if the temperature is 50°F at a pressure altitude of 500 feet, the temperature-limited EPR is 2.04 and the altitude-limited EPR is 2.035. (The altitude-limited EPR is 2.01 from sea level up to 1,000 feet.) The only possible correction would be for if the air conditioning bleeds are off.

Answers

8642-4   [A]

ATM, DSP

8712. (Refer to Figures 363 and 429.) At a reported temperature of 10°C with cowl anti-ice on and packs on, the takeoff thrust setting is

A— 90.0%.
B— 89.1%.
C— 87.4%.

Using Figure 363, determine an airport elevation of 3,877 feet. On Figure 429, find the row marked 10°C and column marked 4,000. Determine an approximate takeoff thrust setting of 90.0%. (PLT011) — FAA-H-8083-25

ATM, DSP

8713. (Refer to Figures 330 and 428.) At a reported temperature of 30°C with engine bleeds closed, the takeoff thrust setting is

A— 91.9%.
B— 87.4%.
C— 90.9%.

Using Figure 330, determine an airport elevation of 13 feet. On Figure 428, find the row marked 30°C and column marked zero. Determine an approximate takeoff thrust setting of 91.9%. (PLT011) — FAA-H-8083-25

ATM, DSP

8714. (Refer to Figures 329 and 428.) At a reported temperature of 20°C with engine bleeds closed, the takeoff thrust setting is

A— 92.1%.
B— 92.3%.
C— 88.4%.

Using Figure 329, determine an airport elevation of 4,473 feet. On Figure 428, find the row marked 30°C and column marked 4,000. Interpolate to find an approximate takeoff thrust setting of 92.3%. (PLT011) — FAA-H-8083-25

ATM, DSP

8715. (Refer to Figures 329 and 429.) At a reported temperature of -10°C with cowl anti-ice on and packs on, the takeoff thrust setting is

A— 87.0%.
B— 87.2%.
C— 87.7%.

Using Figure 329, determine an airport elevation of 4,473 feet. On Figure 429 find the row marked -10°C and column marked 4,000. Interpolate to find an approximate takeoff thrust setting of 87.2%. (PLT011) — FAA-H-8083-25

ATM, DSP

8716. (Refer to Figures 332 and 428.) At a reported temperature of 5°C with engine bleeds off, the takeoff thrust setting is

A— 87.0%.
B— 87.2%.
C— 88.2%.

Using Figure 332, determine an airport elevation of 13 feet. On Figure 428, find the row marked 5°C and column marked zero. Interpolate to find an approximate takeoff thrust setting of 88.2%. (PLT011) — FAA-H-8083-25

ATM, ATS, DSP

8613. (Refer to Figure 393.) (Note: Applicants may request a printed copy of the chart(s) or graph(s) for use while computing the answer. All printed pages must be returned to test proctor.) With an OAT of 10°C, inertial separator in bypass and cabin heater, you calculate maximum torque for climb to be

A— 1,795 ft-lbs.
B— 1,695 ft-lbs.
C— 1,615 ft-lbs.

On Figure 393, find the OAT of 10°C at the bottom of the chart and move straight up. No pressure altitude is given, therefore you can move to the maximum torque limit of 1,865 foot-pounds. Because the inertial separator is on, the torque is reduced by 100. Furthermore, assuming the question is asking for cabin heat on, the torque is reduced by another 80 pounds. This yields a torque of 1,685 foot-pounds. (PLT011) — FAA-H-8083-25

DSP

9874. (Refer to Figures 53, 54, and 55.) What is the takeoff EPR for Operating Conditions R-1?

A— 2.04.
B— 2.01.
C— 2.035.

Pressure altitude = 500 feet
Altitude-limited EPR = 2.035
Temperature-limited EPR = 2.04

(PLT007) — FAA-H-8083-25

Answers

| 8712 | [A] | 8713 | [A] | 8714 | [B] | 8715 | [B] | 8716 | [C] | 8613 | [B] |
| 9874 | [C] | | | | | | | | | | |

DSP
8614. (Refer to Figures 53, 54, and 55.) What is the takeoff EPR for Operating Conditions R-2?

A— 2.19.
B— 2.18.
C— 2.16.

Pressure altitude = 3,500 feet
Altitude-limited EPR = 2.19
Temperature-limited EPR = 2.19

(PLT011) — FAA-H-8083-25

DSP
8615. (Refer to Figures 53, 54, and 55.) What is the takeoff EPR for Operating Conditions R-3?

A— 2.01.
B— 2.083.
C— 2.04.

Pressure altitude = 1,450 feet
Altitude-limited EPR = 2.083
Temperature-limited EPR = 2.01

Add .03 for air conditioning off.

(PLT007) — FAA-H-8083-25

DSP
8616. (Refer to Figures 53, 54, and 55.) What is the takeoff EPR for Operating Conditions R-4?

A— 2.06.
B— 2.105.
C— 2.11.

Pressure altitude = 1,900 feet
Altitude-limited EPR = 2.105
Temperature-limited EPR = 2.11

(PLT007) — FAA-H-8083-25

DSP
8617. (Refer to Figures 53, 54, and 55.) What is the takeoff EPR for Operating Conditions R-5?

A— 1.98.
B— 1.95.
C— 1.96.

Pressure altitude = -150 feet
Altitude-limited EPR = 2.003
Temperature-limited EPR = 1.95

Add .03 for air conditioning off.

(PLT007) — FAA-H-8083-25

Climb Performance

The **best rate-of-climb speed** for any airplane is the speed at which there is the greatest difference between the power required for level flight and the power available from the engines. The L/D_{MAX} speed for any airplane is the one that requires the least power for level flight since it is the lowest drag speed. Because the power output of prop-driven airplanes is relatively constant at all speeds, L/D_{MAX} is the best rate-of-climb speed for them.

Turbojet engines produce more power as the aircraft speed increases. Even though drag increases at speeds above L/D_{MAX}, the engine's power output increases even more so that the maximum difference between power required and power available is achieved at a higher airspeed. For a turbojet, the best rate-of-climb speed is faster than L/D_{MAX}.

CRJ200 Performance Tables

FAA Figures 432 through 454 contain the information needed to correctly calculate takeoff performance data, including V-speeds, takeoff weights, and climb performance. It is very important to note that these tables are divided into two categories based upon flap setting used on takeoff. Note the boxed "Flaps 8" or "Flaps 20" usually found in the lower right-hand side of the figure in order to choose the correct chart.

Q400 Performance Tables

FAA Figures 475 and 476 contain the data needed to calculate first- and second-segment climb performance. This is done with one engine operating and is part of the performance pre-planning conducted

Continued

Answers

8614 [A]   8615 [C]   8616 [B]   8617 [A]

prior to each flight. Note that you will start with the OAT on the bottom of the chart and move up. Most of the time you do not need to worry about the ISA lines — simply intersect the appropriate pressure altitude. Move right to the "Reference Line," follow the diagonal lines to the aircraft weight, and then move across to the right to find your climb gradient.

Q400 Climb and Cruise Power Tables

The Q400 figures include FAA Figures 481 (radius of turn), and Figure 482 (maximum-climb ceiling chart). The radius of turn depicts the radius in feet that will be flown given a 15-degree steady-state turn. This can be helpful when calculating distance needed to maneuver during single-engine operations. The enroute climb ceiling chart (Figure 482) uses two parameters — aircraft weight and temperature — to determine the maximum ceiling during single-engine operations.

B-737 Climb Performance Tables

The tables in FAA Figures 57 and 58 allow you to determine the time and fuel required for a climb to cruising altitude after takeoff. The table in FAA Figure 57 is for ISA temperatures, and the table in FAA Figure 58 is for ISA +10°C. Each intersection of Brake Release Weight and Cruise Altitude has a box with four numbers. These are the time, the fuel, the distance and the TAS required to climb from a sea level airport to cruise altitude in calm wind conditions. For example, with a brake release weight of 110,000 pounds, a climb to 33,000 feet in ISA +10°C conditions will require 26 minutes, 4,100 pounds of fuel and cover a distance of 154 NM.

A headwind or tailwind component in the climb will change the distance flown. Assume that there is an average 20-knot headwind in the climb described above. The first step is to compute the average "no wind" GS. A distance of 154 NM flown in 26 minutes works out to a GS of 355.4 knots. A headwind component of 20 knots will reduce this GS to 335.4 knots. The distance flown in 26 minutes at 335.4 knots is 145.3 NM.

Note: Using a CX-3 computer, select "Ground Speed" from the FLT menu and enter Duration and GS. Do not use the TAS from the table as that will result in an inaccurate answer.

Departure from an airport that is significantly above sea level will reduce the fuel required for the climb. Notice that departure from a 2,000-foot airport will reduce the climb fuel by 100 pounds, however the effect on time and distance flown is negligible.

B-737 Climb and Cruise Power Tables

The Max Climb & Max Continuous EPR Table at the top of FAA Figure 60 is similar to the one discussed in Takeoff EPR. In this table two EPR values are found — one for temperature and one for altitude. The lower of the two is the maximum climb/continuous EPR. For example, if the temperature is +10°C at a pressure altitude of 10,000 feet, the temperature-limited EPR is 2.04 and the altitude-limited EPR is 2.30. (The altitude-limited EPR is 2.30 from 5,660 feet and up.) The max EPR is 2.04.

The Max Cruise EPR Table supplies one EPR value for a given TAT (Total Air Temperature) in one of two altitude ranges. The correction tables are similar to ones used previously and apply to both tables.

ATM, ATS, DSP

8400. At what speed, with reference to L/D$_{MAX}$, does maximum rate-of-climb for a jet airplane occur?

A— A speed greater than that for L/D$_{MAX}$.
B— A speed equal to that for L/D$_{MAX}$.
C— A speed less than that for L/D$_{MAX}$.

An airplane's best rate-of-climb is achieved at the airspeed where there is the maximum difference between the power available from the engines and the power required for level flight. The L/D$_{MAX}$ airspeed will require the minimum power for level flight since drag is at its minimum. However, turbojet engines produce more power at high speed than at lower speeds and so the speed with the greatest difference between power required and power available is higher than L/D$_{MAX}$. (PLT303) — ANA

Answer (B) is incorrect because a speed equal to that of L/D$_{MAX}$ is the maximum rate-of-climb for a propeller airplane. Answer (C) is incorrect because the maximum rate-of-climb is at a speed greater than L/D$_{MAX}$.

ATM, DSP

8593. (Refer to Figures 273 and 475.) With a reported temperature of 32°C, and a weight of 58,000 pounds, the second segment takeoff gross climb gradient is

A— 0.059%.
B— 0.062%.
C— 0.065%.

1. From Figure 273, find the field elevation of 1,135 feet.

2. On Figure 475, start at the bottom left and find 32°C. Move straight up until you intersect the 1,135 foot line. Move straight to the right until you intersect the reference line. Move down and to the right following the diagonal lines in parallel until you intersect the 58,000 pound line. Move directly to the right and note a second segment climb gradient of .059%.

(PLT004) — FAA-H-8083-25

ATM, DSP

8594. (Refer to Figures 273 and 474.) With a reported temperature of 45°C, and a weight of 52,000 pounds, the first segment takeoff gross climb gradient is

A— 0.048%.
B— 0.044%.
C— 0.0419%.

1. From Figure 273, find the field elevation of 1,135 feet.

2. On Figure 474, start at the bottom left side of chart and note the temperature of 45°C. Move straight up until you intersect the 1,135 foot line. Move straight to the right until intersecting the reference line. Move down and to the right following the diagonal lines in parallel until you intersect the 52,000 pound line. Move directly to the right and note a first segment climb gradient of .045%.

(PLT004) — FAA-H-8083-25

ATM, DSP

8595. (Refer to Figure 472.) With a gross weight of 54,500 pounds, the final takeoff climb speed is

A— 142 knots.
B— 145 knots.
C— 148 knots.

On Figure 472, find 54,500 pounds at the bottom of the chart. Move straight up until you intersect the reference line. Move directly to the left and note a final takeoff climb speed of 145 knots. (PLT004) — FAA-H-8083-25

ATM, DSP

8628. (Refer to Figures 56, 57, and 58.) What is the ground distance covered during en route climb for Operating Conditions V-1?

A— 145 NM.
B— 137 NM.
C— 134 NM.

No wind time = 26 minutes
No wind distance = 154 NM
No wind GS = 355.4 knots
Wind adjusted GS = 335.4 knots
Wind adjusted distance = 145.3 NM

(PLT004) — FAA-H-8083-25

Answers

8400 [A]	8593 [A]	8594 [B]	8595 [B]	8628 [A]

ATM, DSP

8629. (Refer to Figures 56, 57, and 58.) What is the ground distance covered during en route climb for Operating Conditions V-2?

A— 84 NM.
B— 65 NM.
C— 69 NM.

No wind time = 13 minutes
No wind distance = 65 NM
No wind GS = 300 knots
Wind adjusted GS = 320 knots
Wind adjusted distance = 69.3 NM

(PLT004) — FAA-H-8083-25

ATM, DSP

8630. (Refer to Figures 56, 57, and 58.) What is the ground distance covered during en route climb for Operating Conditions V-3?

A— 95 NM.
B— 79 NM.
C— 57 NM.

No wind time = 16 minutes
No wind distance = 87 NM
No wind GS = 326.3 knots
Wind adjusted GS = 296.3 knots
Wind adjusted distance = 79 NM

(PLT004) — FAA-H-8083-25

ATM, DSP

8631. (Refer to Figures 56, 57, and 58.) What is the ground distance covered during en route climb for Operating Conditions V-4?

A— 63 NM.
B— 53 NM.
C— 65 NM.

No wind time = 13 minutes
No wind distance = 61 NM
No wind GS = 281.5 knots
Wind adjusted GS = 291.5 knots
Wind adjusted distance = 63.2 NM

(PLT004) — FAA-H-8083-25

ATM, DSP

8632. (Refer to Figures 56, 57, and 58.) What is the ground distance covered during en route climb for Operating Conditions V-5?

A— 70 NM.
B— 52 NM.
C— 61 NM.

No wind time = 13 minutes
No wind distance = 70 NM
No wind GS = 323.1 knots
Wind adjusted GS = 283.1 knots
Wind adjusted distance = 61.3 NM

(PLT004) — FAA-H-8083-25

ATM, DSP

8633. (Refer to Figures 56, 57, and 58.) How much fuel is burned during en route climb for Operating Conditions V-1?

A— 4,100 pounds.
B— 3,600 pounds.
C— 4,000 pounds.

Fuel to climb from sea level = 4,100 lbs
Correction factor = -100 lbs

(PLT012) — FAA-H-8083-25

ATM, DSP

8634. (Refer to Figures 56, 57, and 58.) How much fuel is burned during en route climb for Operating Conditions V-2?

A— 2,250 pounds.
B— 2,600 pounds.
C— 2,400 pounds.

Fuel to climb from sea level = 2,400 lbs
Correction factor = -150 lbs

(PLT012) — FAA-H-8083-25

ATM, DSP

8635. (Refer to Figures 56, 57, and 58.) What is the aircraft weight at the top of climb for Operating Conditions V-3?

A— 82,100 pounds.
B— 82,500 pounds.
C— 82,200 pounds.

Fuel to climb from sea level = 2,600 lbs
Correction factor = -100 lbs
Final weight = 85,000 – 2,500 = 82,500 lbs

(PLT004) — FAA-H-8083-25

Answers

8629 [C] 8630 [B] 8631 [A] 8632 [C] 8633 [C] 8634 [A]
8635 [B]

ATM, DSP

8636. (Refer to Figures 56, 57, and 58.) What is the aircraft weight at the top of climb for Operating Conditions V-4?

A— 102,900 pounds.
B— 102,600 pounds.
C— 103,100 pounds.

Fuel to climb from sea level = 2,400 lbs
Correction factor = -300 lbs
Final weight = 105,000 – 2,100 = 102,900 lbs

(PLT004) — FAA-H-8083-25

ATM, DSP

8637. (Refer to Figures 56, 57, and 58.) What is the aircraft weight at the top of climb for Operating Conditions V-5?

A— 73,000 pounds.
B— 72,900 pounds.
C— 72,800 pounds.

Fuel to climb from sea level = 2,100 lbs
Correction factor = -100 lbs
Final weight = 75,000 – 2,000 = 73,000 lbs

(PLT004) — FAA-H-8083-25

ATM, DSP

8638. (Refer to Figures 59 and 60.) What is the max climb EPR for Operating Conditions T-1?

A— 1.82.
B— 1.96.
C— 2.04.

Altitude-limited EPR = 2.30
TAT-limited EPR = 1.90
Correction for engine anti-ice = -.08
Max climb EPR setting = 1.82

(PLT007) — FAA-H-8083-25

*Answer (B) is incorrect because 1.96 is the max continuous EPR.
Answer (C) is incorrect because 2.04 is the max continuous EPR
without the bleed air correction for the engine anti-ice ON.*

ATM, DSP

8639. (Refer to Figures 59 and 60.) What is the max continuous EPR for Operating Conditions T-2?

A— 2.10.
B— 1.99.
C— 2.02.

Altitude-limited EPR = 2.20
TAT-limited EPR = 2.10
Engine and wing anti-ice correction = -.12
Air conditioning off correction = +.04
Max continuous EPR setting = 2.02

(PLT007) — FAA-H-8083-25

ATM, DSP

8640. (Refer to Figures 59 and 60.) What is the max cruise EPR for Operating Conditions T-3?

A— 2.11.
B— 2.02.
C— 1.90.

Max cruise EPR = 2.02
Engine and wing anti-ice correction = -.12
Max cruise EPR setting = 1.90

(PLT007) — FAA-H-8083-25

ATM, DSP

8641. (Refer to Figures 59 and 60.) What is the max climb EPR for Operating Conditions T-4?

A— 2.20.
B— 2.07.
C— 2.06.

Altitude-limited EPR = 2.30
TAT-limited EPR = 2.20
Engine and wing anti-ice correction = -.14
Max climb EPR setting = 2.06

(PLT007) — FAA-H-8083-25

ATM, DSP

8642-1. (Refer to Figures 59 and 60.) What is the max continuous EPR for Operating Conditions T-5?

A— 2.00.
B— 2.04.
C— 1.96.

Altitude-limited EPR = 2.30
TAT-limited EPR = 2.00
Air conditioning off correction = +.04
Max continuous EPR setting = 2.04

(PLT007) — FAA-H-8083-25

Answers

8636	[A]	8637	[A]	8638	[A]	8639	[C]	8640	[C]	8641	[C]
8642-1	[B]										

ATM, DSP

8642-2. (Refer to Figure 231.) Given the following conditions, what is the takeoff climb limit?

Airport OAT .... 38°C
Airport Pressure Altitude .... 14 ft.
Flaps .... 15°
Engine Bleed for packs .... On
Anti-ice .... Off

A— 136,000 lb.
B— 137,500 lb.
C— 139,000 lb.

1. *Enter FAA Figure 231 at 38° OAT and proceed up to the 0 ft pressure altitude (this is closest to 14 feet).*

2. *From the point of intersection on the pressure altitude line, draw a line horizontally to the Climb Limit Brake Release Weight of 136,000 pounds.*

(PLT085) — FAA-H-8083-25

ATM, DSP

8642-3. (Refer to Figures 235 and 236.) Given the following conditions, what is the maximum Slush/Standing Water takeoff weight?

Dry field/obstacle limit weight .... 180,000 lb.
Slush/standing water depth .... 25 inches
Temperature (OAT) .... 30°C
Field pressure altitude .... 5431 ft
Field length available .... 9000 ft
No reverse thrust

A— 130,850 lb.
B— 147,550 lb.
C— 139,850 lb.

1. *Enter FAA Figure 235 which is the no reverse thrust chart with an Obstacle Limit Weight of 180 (1,000 pounds).*

2. *Proceed across to the .25 inches water depth column and interpolate to find an adjustment of -40.03 (between 5,000 and 10,000).*

3. *Subtract 40,030 from 180,000 to get 139,970 pounds.*

4. *Determine ISA temperature in order to calculate field length in next step.*
ISA (°C) = 15 – ((FL/1000) x 2)
15 – (5.431 x 2) = 4.138°C

5. *Go down to the V_1 (MCG) chart and figure out the adjusted field length based on Note 2 and 30°C:*
Note 2: Adjust field length available by -150 feet for every 5°C above
30°C – 4.138°C = 25.862°C
25.862°C / 5°C = 5.2
5.2 x (-150) = -780
9,000 – 780 = 8,220 feet.

6. *Enter the Limit Weight table at 8,200 feet and proceed across to the .25 inches column. Interpolating between 5,000 and 10,000 gives you 138.445.*

7. *Enter the Limit Weight table again at 8,600 feet to find the interpolated adjustment to use between 5,000 and 10,000 feet: 159.91.*

8. *Interpolate between the 8,200 feet adjustment (138.445) and the 8,600 adjustment (159.91) for a field length of 8,220 feet (from step 4):*
159.91 – 138.445 = 21.465
21.465/400 = 0.053662
0.053662 x 20 = 1.07325
138.445 + 1.07325= 139.5182
139.5182 x 1000 = 139,518

9. *Compare 139,970 pounds to 139,518 pounds as per note 4 and the lesser of the weights is 139,518 pounds.*

(PLT069) — FAA-H-8083-25

DSP

9875. (Refer to Figures 48, 49, and 50.) What is the ground distance covered during en route climb for Operating Conditions W-1?

A— 104.0 NM.
B— 99.2 NM.
C— 109.7 NM.

Long range climb:

No wind time = 17.1 minutes
No wind distance = 109.7 NM
No wind GS = 384.9 knots
Wind adjusted GS = 364.9 knots
Wind adjusted distance = 104 NM

(PLT004) — FAA-H-8083-25

Answers

8642-2   [A]   8642-3   [C]   9875   [A]

DSP

9876. (Refer to Figures 48, 49, and 50.) What is the ground distance covered during en route climb for Operating Conditions W-2?

A— 85.8 NM.
B— 87.8 NM.
C— 79.4 NM.

High speed climb:

No wind time = 12.8 minutes
No wind distance = 85.8 NM
No wind GS = 402.2 knots
Wind adjusted GS = 372.2 knots
Wind adjusted distance = 79.4 NM

(PLT004) — FAA-H-8083-25

DSP

9877. (Refer to Figures 48, 49, and 50.) What is the ground distance covered during en route climb for Operating Conditions W-3?

A— 86.4 NM.
B— 84.2 NM.
C— 85.1 NM.

Long range climb:

No wind time = 13.3 minutes
No wind distance = 84.2 NM
No wind GS = 379.8 knots
Wind adjusted GS = 389.8 knots
Wind adjusted distance = 86.4 NM

(PLT004) — FAA-H-8083-25

DSP

8596. (Refer to Figures 48, 49, and 50.) What is the ground distance covered during en route climb for Operating Conditions W-4?

A— 58.4 NM.
B— 61.4 NM.
C— 60.3 NM.

High speed climb:

No wind time = 9.1 minutes
No wind distance = 58.4 NM
No wind GS = 385.1 knots
Wind adjusted GS = 405.1 knots
Wind adjusted distance = 61.4 NM

(PLT004) — FAA-H-8083-25

DSP

8597. (Refer to Figures 48, 49, and 50.) What is the ground distance covered during en route climb for Operating Conditions W-5?

A— 68.0 NM.
B— 73.9 NM.
C— 66.4 NM.

High speed climb:

No wind time = 11.3 minutes
No wind distance = 73.9 NM
No wind GS = 392.4 knots
Wind adjusted GS = 352.4 knots
Wind adjusted distance = 66.4 NM

(PLT004) — FAA-H-8083-25

DSP

8598. (Refer to Figures 48, 49, and 50.) What is the aircraft weight at the top of climb for Operating Conditions W-1?

A— 81,600 pounds.
B— 81,400 pounds.
C— 81,550 pounds.

Long range climb:

Initial weight	*84,000*
Burn	*– 2,570*
TOC weight	*81,430*

(PLT004) — FAA-H-8083-25

DSP

8599. (Refer to Figures 48, 49, and 50.) What is the aircraft weight at the top of climb for Operating Conditions W-2?

A— 82,775 pounds.
B— 83,650 pounds.
C— 83,775 pounds.

High speed climb:

Initial weight	*86,000*
Burn	*– 2,225*
TOC weight	*83,775*

(PLT004) — FAA-H-8083-25

Answers

9876 [C]	9877 [A]	8596 [B]	8597 [C]	8598 [B]	8599 [C]

DSP
8600. (Refer to Figures 48, 49, and 50.) What is the aircraft weight at the top of climb for Operating Conditions W-3?

A— 75,750 pounds.
B— 75,900 pounds.
C— 76,100 pounds.

Long range climb:

Initial weight	*78,000*
Burn	*– 2,102*
TOC weight	*75,898*

(PLT004) — FAA-H-8083-25

DSP
8601. (Refer to Figures 48, 49, and 50.) What is the aircraft weight at the top of climb for Operating Conditions W-4?

A— 86,150 pounds.
B— 86,260 pounds.
C— 86,450 pounds.

High speed climb:

Initial weight	*88,000*
Burn	*– 1,738*
TOC weight	*86,262*

(PLT004) — FAA-H-8083-25

DSP
8602. (Refer to Figures 48, 49, and 50.) What is the aircraft weight at the top of climb for Operating Conditions W-5?

A— 89,900 pounds.
B— 90,000 pounds.
C— 90,100 pounds.

Long-range climb:

Initial weight	*92,000*
Burn	*– 2,079*
TOC weight	*89,921*

(PLT004) — FAA-H-8083-25

Cruise Performance

The maximum range speed for an aircraft is determined by its L/D curve. Propeller-driven airplanes will achieve best range performance if they are flown at the speed that yields L/D_{MAX}. In turbojet aircraft, a somewhat more complex relationship between lift and drag determines best range. Turbojets always have a best range speed higher than L/D_{MAX}.

A headwind or tailwind will affect the miles per unit of fuel burned. If an airplane is operating at its best-range airspeed and encounters a headwind, it should speed up to minimize the time in the adverse wind. By the same token, an airplane with a tailwind can slow down and let the wind maintain its ground speed with a lower fuel flow. The exact amount of airspeed change that is useful varies with airplane type.

Turbojet engines have a strong preference for operations at high altitudes and airspeeds. Both lower temperatures and higher altitudes increase engine efficiency by requiring a lower fuel flow for a given thrust. Besides increased engine efficiency, lift and drag both decrease at higher altitudes, so less thrust is required.

Turbine engines are much more efficient when operated at the upper end of their RPM range. Generally, the optimum cruise altitude for a turbojet airplane is the highest at which it is possible to maintain the optimum aerodynamic conditions (best angle of attack) at maximum continuous power. The optimum altitude is determined mainly by the aircraft's gross weight at the beginning of cruise.

As an aircraft burns fuel and becomes lighter, the optimum cruise altitude slowly increases and the speed that yields the optimum cruise performance slowly decreases. Since it is seldom practical to change speed and altitude constantly, it is common procedure to maintain a constant Mach cruise at a flight level close to optimum. As fuel is burned, thrust is reduced to maintain the constant Mach number.

Answers

8600   [B]   8601   [B]   8602   [A]

ATM, ATS, DSP

8383. What performance is characteristic of flight at maximum L/D in a propeller-driven airplane?

A— Maximum range and distance glide.
B— Best angle of climb.
C— Maximum endurance.

Maximum range and glide distance is achieved at L/D_{MAX}*. (PLT242) — FAA-H-8083-3*

Answer (B) is incorrect because best angle of climb is at a high angle of attack with both high lift and high drag coefficients, which would not result in a maximum L/D ratio. Answer (C) is incorrect because maximum endurance would be obtained at the point of minimum power required, since this would require the lowest fuel flow to keep the airplane in steady, level flight. This is not at maximum L/D.

ATM, ATS, DSP

8401. At what speed, with reference to L/D_{MAX}, does maximum range for a jet airplane occur?

A— A speed less than that for L/D_{MAX}.
B— A speed equal to that for L/D_{MAX}.
C— A speed greater than that for L/D_{MAX}.

Maximum range is obtained at the aerodynamic condition which produces a maximum proportion between the square root of the lift coefficient and the drag coefficient. It occurs where the proportion between velocity and thrust required is greatest. This point is located by a straight line from the origin tangent to the curve, and is consequently at a higher airspeed than L/D_{MAX}. (PLT303) — ANA

Answer (A) is incorrect because a speed greater than L/D_{MAX} will obtain maximum range for a jet airplane. Answer (B) is incorrect because a speed equal to that of L/D_{MAX} is a jet airplane's maximum endurance, not range.

ATM, ATS, DSP

8398. What should a pilot do to maintain "best range" airplane performance when a tailwind is encountered?

A— Increase speed.
B— Maintain speed.
C— Decrease speed.

While it is only necessary to consider wind velocity effect on cruise speed at wind velocities that exceed 25 percent of the zero wind cruise speed, generally you should increase cruise speed with a headwind and decrease cruise speed with a tailwind. (PLT303) — FAA-H-8083-25

ATM, ATS, DSP

9078. Which procedure produces the minimum fuel consumption for a given leg of the cruise flight?

A— Increase speed for a headwind.
B— Increase speed for a tailwind.
C— Increase altitude for a headwind, decrease altitude for a tailwind.

When flying into a headwind the airspeed should be increased above that used for maximum range in calm winds. Airspeed should be decreased for a tailwind. (PLT015) — ANA

ATM, ATS, DSP

8381. Which maximum range factor decreases as weight decreases?

A— Angle of attack.
B— Altitude.
C— Airspeed.

As fuel is consumed and the airplane's weight decreases, the optimum airspeed and power setting may decrease, or the optimum altitude may increase. The optimum angle of attack does not change with changes in weight. (PLT006) — FAA-H-8083-3

Answer (A) is incorrect because the factors of maximum range are weight, altitude, and aerodynamic configuration of the airplane, not angle of attack. Answer (B) is incorrect because maximum range altitude may increase with a decrease in weight.

ATM, ATS, DSP

9077. Maximum range performance of a turbojet aircraft is obtained by which procedure as aircraft weight reduces?

A— Increasing speed or altitude.
B— Increasing altitude or decreasing speed.
C— Increasing speed or decreasing altitude.

As a turbojet-powered airplane burns fuel, its maximum range of profile can be maintained by increasing the cruise altitude to improve the specific fuel consumption of the engines and by decreasing airspeed to maintain the optimum L/D ratio. (PLT015) — ANA

Answer (A) is incorrect because, as weight decreases, the optimum speed decreases, or altitude increases. Answer (C) is incorrect because, as weight decreases, speed decreases, or altitude increases.

Answers

8383 [A]	8401 [C]	8398 [C]	9078 [A]	8381 [C]	9077 [B]

Landing Considerations

V_S — stalling speed or the minimum steady flight speed at which the airplane is controllable.

V_{S0} — stalling speed or the minimum steady flight speed in the landing configuration.

V_{REF} — reference speed. It is normally 1.3 x V_{S0}.

Even with all the aircraft's high lift devices extended, a typical air carrier airplane has a high approach speed and a long landing roll. An airplane is normally flown at 1.3 times the V_{S0} speed for the aircraft's weight. Of course, 1.3 times V_{S0} is an indicated airspeed and the ground speed will vary depending on wind, altitude and temperature. A high temperature or high altitude approach will increase an aircraft's ground speed for any given approach speed.

Once an airplane has touched down on a runway there are 3 ways of slowing it to a stop: aerodynamic braking, use of the wheel brakes, and reverse thrust.

The typical technique for stopping an aircraft on a normal landing is to apply reverse thrust (or prop reverse) once the nosewheel is on the ground. This takes maximum advantage of reverse thrust when it is most effective and it saves wear on the wheel brakes, which heat up very rapidly at high ground speeds. Shortly after touchdown, the spoilers are deployed. This reduces lift and increases drag. As the aircraft slows, the main wheel brakes are applied to bring it down to taxiing speed. The brakes are most effective when lift has been reduced (by spoilers and low airspeed) and more of the aircraft's weight is carried by the landing gear.

Water on a runway will increase the landing rollout because the reduced coefficient of friction makes the wheel brakes less effective. This is particularly true at high ground speeds.

A very dangerous possibility when landing on a wet runway is **hydroplaning**. When hydroplaning occurs, the wheel brakes are almost totally ineffective. This not only greatly increases the landing rollout, but also introduces the possibility of losing directional control on sliding off the side of the runway. There are three types of hydroplaning.

Dynamic hydroplaning occurs when a tire rolls through standing water, forms a bow wave, and then rolls up on top of the wave, losing all contact with the runway. The minimum speed at which dynamic hydroplaning can start is related to tire pressure. As a rule of thumb, dynamic hydroplaning will start at speeds of greater than nine times the square root of the tire pressure in pounds per square inch. The practical application is that your nose wheel can hydroplane at a lower speed than the mains because of its lower pressure. Once dynamic hydroplaning has started, it can continue to much lower speeds.

Viscous hydroplaning occurs when there is a thin film of water covering a smooth surface such as a painted or rubber-coated portion of the runway. Viscous hydroplaning can occur at much lower speeds than dynamic hydroplaning.

Reverted rubber hydroplaning occurs during a locked wheel skid. Water trapped between the tire and the runway is heated by friction, and the tire rides along a pocket of steam.

When landing on a water-covered runway, fly the approach as close to "on speed" as possible. Landing at a higher than recommended speed will greatly increase the potential for hydroplaning. After touchdown, use aerodynamic braking and reverse thrust to maximum possible extent, saving the use of wheel brakes until the speed is low enough to minimize the possibility of hydroplaning.

Regulations (14 CFR §121.195) require that when a turbojet aircraft is dispatched to an airport where the runways are forecast to be wet or slippery, the effective length of the landing runway must be 115% of what is required under dry conditions. Since runways cannot be lengthened, the effect of this rule is to lower the maximum allowable landing weight of aircraft on wet runways for dispatch purposes.

ATM, ATS, DSP

9323. Which is the correct symbol for the stalling speed or the minimum steady flight speed at which the airplane is controllable?

A— V_{S0}.
B— V_S.
C— V_{S1}.

V_S means the stalling speed or the minimum steady flight speed at which the airplane is controllable. (PLT466) — 14 CFR §1.2

Answer (A) is incorrect because V_{S0} is the stalling speed or the minimum steady flight speed in the landing configuration. Answer (C) is incorrect because V_{S1} is the stalling speed or the minimum steady flight speed in a specific configuration.

ATM, ATS, DSP

9322. Which is the correct symbol for the minimum steady-flight speed or stalling speed in the landing configuration?

A— V_S.
B— V_{S1}.
C— V_{S0}.

V_{S0} means the stalling speed or the minimum steady flight speed in the landing configuration. (PLT466) — 14 CFR §1.2

Answer (A) is incorrect because V_S is the stalling speed or the minimum steady flight speed at which the airplane is controllable. Answer (B) is incorrect because V_{S1} is the stalling speed or the minimum steady flight speed in a specific configuration.

ATM, ATS, DSP

8374. What effect does landing at high elevation airports have on groundspeed with comparable conditions relative to temperature, wind, and airplane weight?

A— Higher than at low elevation.
B— Lower than at low elevation.
C— The same as at low elevation.

An airplane at altitude will land at the same indicated airspeed as at sea level but, because of the reduced air density, the true airspeed will be greater. Given the same wind conditions, this will also make the ground speed higher than at sea level. (PLT124) — FAA-H-8083-25

Answer (B) is incorrect because at high elevation there is reduced air density, and thus TAS will increase. As TAS increases, ground speed will increase. Answer (C) is incorrect because, under comparable conditions, TAS will increase and cause the ground speed to be higher, at higher elevation.

ATM, ATS, DSP

9074. How should thrust reversers be applied to reduce landing distance for turbojet aircraft?

A— Immediately after ground contact.
B— Immediately prior to touchdown.
C— After applying maximum wheel braking.

Thrust reversers are most effective at high speeds and should be deployed immediately after touchdown. (PLT170) — FAA-H-8083-3

ATM, ATS, DSP

9074-1. Upon landing, thrust reversers

A— are required to obtain the calculated stopping distances.
B— should be deployed as soon as the nose wheel is in firm contact with the runway.
C— should be deployed immediately upon landing when airspeeds are highest.

If operating an aircraft such as the MD-80, thrust reversers should be deployed as soon as the nose wheel is in firm contact with the runway. (PLT170) — FAA-H-8083-3

ATM, ATS, DSP

9079. How should reverse thrust propellers be used during landing for maximum effectiveness in stopping?

A— Gradually increase reverse power to maximum as rollout speed decreases.
B— Use maximum reverse power as soon as possible after touchdown.
C— Select reverse-pitch after landing and use idle power setting of the engines.

Reverse thrust is most effective at high airspeeds. It should be used as soon as possible after touchdown. (PLT244) — FAA-H-8083-25

Answers

9323 [B]	9322 [C]	8374 [A]	9074 [A]	9074-1 [B]	9079 [B]

ATM, ATS, DSP

9084. Under which condition during the landing roll are the main wheel brakes at maximum effectiveness?

A— When wing lift has been reduced.
B— At high groundspeeds.
C— When the wheels are locked and skidding.

Wheel brakes are at maximum effectiveness when the weight of the airplane is used to hold the tires in contact with the runway and the rate of wheel deceleration (or slowing) is just below that which would induce a skid. To place the maximum weight on the tires it is necessary to reduce lift as soon as possible after touchdown by lowering the nose wheel to the runway and deploying wing spoilers. Wheel brakes become more effective as an airplane decelerates (or slows down) because of loss of residual lift as the airspeed decreases. (PLT170) — FAA-H-8083-25

Answer (B) is incorrect because, at high ground speeds, the lift is greater and the normal force on the wheels is small, thus the braking friction force is small. Answer (C) is incorrect because, when the wheels are locked and skidding, the braking friction force is small.

ATM, ATS, DSP

8935. At what minimum speed (rounded off) could dynamic hydroplaning occur on main tires having a pressure of 121 PSI?

A— 90 knots.
B— 96 knots.
C— 110 knots.

Dynamic hydroplaning occurs when there is standing water on the runway surface. Water about 1/10th of an inch deep acts to lift the tire off the runway. The minimum speed at which dynamic hydroplaning occurs has been determined to be about 9 times the square root of the tire pressure in pounds per square inch:

Square root of 121 = 11
11 x 9 = 99

(PLT144) — FAA-H-8083-3

ATM, ATS, DSP

8936. At what minimum speed will dynamic hydroplaning begin if a tire has an air pressure of 70 PSI?

A— 85 knots.
B— 80 knots.
C— 75 knots.

Dynamic hydroplaning occurs when there is standing water on the runway surface. Water about 1/10th of an inch deep acts to lift the tire off the runway. The minimum speed at which dynamic hydroplaning occurs has been determined to be about 9 times the square root of the tire pressure in pounds per square inch:

Square root of 70 = 8.37
8.37 x 9 = 75.3

(PLT144) — FAA-H-8083-3

Answer (A) is incorrect because hydroplaning would occur at 85 knots with a tire pressure of 95 PSI. Answer (B) is incorrect because hydroplaning would occur at 80 knots with a tire pressure of 84 PSI.

ATM, ATS, DSP

8933. A definition of the term "viscous hydroplaning" is where

A— the airplane rides on standing water.
B— a film of moisture covers the painted or rubber-coated portion of the runway.
C— the tires of the airplane are actually riding on a mixture of steam and melted rubber.

Either the moisture or the originally slick surface could cause problems, and the combination is especially dangerous. (PLT144) — FAA-H-8083-3

Answer (A) is incorrect because dynamic hydroplaning occurs when the airplane tires ride on standing water. Answer (C) is incorrect because reverted rubber hydroplaning occurs when the tires of the airplane are actually riding on a mixture of steam and melted rubber.

ATM, ATS, DSP

8938. Compared to dynamic hydroplaning, at what speed does viscous hydroplaning occur when landing on a smooth, wet runway?

A— At approximately 2.0 times the speed that dynamic hydroplaning occurs.
B— At a lower speed than dynamic hydroplaning.
C— At the same speed as dynamic hydroplaning.

Viscous hydroplaning occurs due to the viscous properties of water. In this type, a thin film of fluid (not more than 1/1,000 of an inch in depth) cannot be penetrated by the tire and the tire rolls on top of the film. This can occur at a much lower speed than dynamic hydroplaning but requires a smooth acting surface. (PLT144) — FAA-H-8083-3

Answers

9084	[A]	8935	[B]	8936	[C]	8933	[B]	8938	[B]

ATM, ATS, DSP

8934. Which term describes the hydroplaning which occurs when an airplane's tire is effectively held off a smooth runway surface by steam generated by friction?

A— Reverted rubber hydroplaning.
B— Dynamic hydroplaning.
C— Viscous hydroplaning.

This would typically occur if excessive braking kept a wheel from rotating. (PLT144) — FAA-H-8083-3

Answer (B) is incorrect because dynamic hydroplaning occurs when there is standing water or slush on the runway which forms a wedge that lifts the tire away from contact with the runway surface. Answer (C) is incorrect because viscous hydroplaning occurs on a thin film of water on a smooth (e.g., painted or rubber-coated) runway surface.

ATM, ATS, DSP

8937. What is the best method of speed reduction if hydroplaning is experienced on landing?

A— Apply full main wheel braking only.
B— Apply nosewheel and main wheel braking alternately and abruptly.
C— Apply aerodynamic braking to the fullest advantage.

Since occurrence of dynamic hydroplaning is related to speed, it is prudent to slow the aircraft with spoilers, reverse thrust, etc., as much as possible prior to applying the brakes. (PLT144) — FAA-H-8083-3

Answer (A) is incorrect because applying full main wheel braking may increase or compound the problems associated with hydroplaning. If any brakes are used, a pumping or modulating motion like an antiskid system can be used. Aerodynamic braking is recommended. Answer (B) is incorrect because abrupt use of either the nose wheel or main wheel brakes will lock the wheels and compound the problem.

ATM, ATS, DSP

8939. What effect, if any, will landing at a higher-than-recommended touchdown speed have on hydroplaning?

A— No effect on hydroplaning, but increases landing roll.
B— Reduces hydroplaning potential if heavy braking is applied.
C— Increases hydroplaning potential regardless of braking.

Hydroplaning is most likely to occur during conditions of standing water or slush on a runway with a smooth textured surface. The higher the aircraft speed, the more likely it is to hydroplane. (PLT144) — FAA-H-8083-3

ATM, DSP

8133. What effective runway length is required for a turbojet-powered airplane at the destination airport if the runways are forecast to be wet or slippery at the ETA?

A— 70 percent of the actual runway available, from a height of 50 feet over the threshold.
B— 115 percent of the runway length required for a dry runway.
C— 115 percent of the runway length required for a wet runway.

No person may takeoff in a turbojet-powered airplane when the appropriate weather reports and forecasts, or combination thereof, indicate that the runways at the destination airport may be wet or slippery at the estimated time of arrival unless the effective runway length at the destination airport is at least 115% of the runway length required for a landing on a dry runway. (PLT144) — 14 CFR §121.195

Answer (A) is incorrect because 70% is the requirement for the turbopropeller aircraft. Answer (C) is incorrect because the effective runway length is based on a dry runway.

Landing Performance Tables and Graphs

FAA Figures 457 and 458 are examples of landing performance charts. These are used to calculate both the appropriate landing reference speeds and landing distances. As in most performance charts, OAT, pressure altitude, wind and runway slope are the determining factors for calculating speeds and distances used. As a general rule, always move to the next reference line on the chart, before making any adjustments.

Answers

8934 [A]   8937 [C]   8939 [C]   8133 [B]

ALL

9791. Approaching the runway 1° below glidepath can add how many feet to the landing distance?

A— 250 feet.
B— 500 feet.
C— 1,000 feet.

On final approach, at a constant airspeed, the glidepath angle and rate of descent is controlled with pitch attitude and elevator. The optimum glidepath angle is 2.5° to 3° whether or not an electronic glidepath reference is being used. On visual approaches, pilots may have a tendency to make flat approaches. A flat approach, however, will increase landing distance and should be avoided. For example, an approach angle of 2° instead of a recommended 3° will add 500 feet to landing distance. (PLT170) — FAA-H-8083-3A

ALL

9792. Arriving over the runway 10 knots over V$_{REF}$ would add approximately how many feet to the dry landing distance?

A— 800 feet.
B— 1,700 feet.
C— 2,800 feet.

Excess approach speed carried through the threshold window and onto the runway will increase the minimum stopping distance required by 20–30 feet per knot of excess speed for a dry runway. Worse yet, the excess speed will increase the chances of an extended flare, which will increase the distance to touchdown by approximately 250 feet for each excess knot in speed. (PLT170) — FAA-H-8083-3A

ATM, DSP

8742. (Refer to Figures 327 and 457.) With a weight of 69,000 pounds, flaps 45, calm winds, the V$_{REF}$ is

A— 136 knots.
B— 133 knots.
C— 129 knots.

1. *On Figure 327, note the field elevation of 7,680 feet.*

2. *On Figure 457, start at 69,000 pounds on lower left of chart. Move straight up until you intersect the 10,000 foot line. Move directly to the right and note a V$_{REF}$ speed of 136 knots.*

(PLT008) — FAA-H-8083-25

ATM, DSP

8743. (Refer to Figure 460.) At a weight of 77,500 pounds, and a landing elevation below 5,000 feet, the V$_{REF}$ is

A— 139 knots.
B— 141 knots.
C— 143 knots.

On Figure 460, start on the right side of chart and locate 77,500 pounds. Move left until intersecting the reference line for 5,000 feet and below. Move straight down and note the V$_{REF}$ speed of 143 knots. (PLT008) — FAA-H-8083-25

ATM, DSP

8744. (Refer to Figures 331 and 461.) At a weight of 73,500 pounds, the expected landing field length is

A— 6,700 feet.
B— 5,650 feet.
C— 6,450 feet.

1. *On Figure 331, note the field elevation of 13 feet.*

2. *On Figure 461, start on the right side of the page at 73,500 pounds. Move directly to the left until you intersect the S.L. line. Move straight down and note the 5,650 feet landing field length.*

(PLT008) — FAA-H-8083-25

ATM, DSP

8745. (Refer to Figures 331 and 461.) What is the maximum landing weight which will permit stopping 2,000 feet short of the end of a 7,500-foot dry runway?

A— 32,200 pounds.
B— 71,000 pounds.
C— 72,500 pounds.

A landing weight of about 71,000 pounds will require a distance of about 5,500 feet. (PLT008) — FAA-H-8083-25

Answer (A) is incorrect because 32,000 is shown on the chart in kg. Answer (C) is incorrect because a landing weight of 72,500 pounds would require a landing distance greater than 5,500 feet.

Answers

| 9791 [B] | 9792 [C] | 8742 [A] | 8743 [C] | 8744 [B] | 8745 [B] |

ATM, DSP
8746. (Refer to Figures 321 and 458.) With a reported temperature of 15°C, a 0.8% upslope, and calm winds, the maximum permissible quick turn-around landing weight is

A— 81,000 pounds.
B— 81,600 pounds.
C— 82,000 pounds.

1. On Figure 321, note the field elevation of 6,535 feet.

2. On Figure 458, start at the temperature of 15°C and move directly right. Intersect the airport pressure altitude of 6,535 feet. Move down until intersecting the wind reference line. Winds are calm, so you can move down to the runway slope reference line. Move diagonally up and to the right in parallel with the diagonal lines until intersecting the .8% upslope line. Move directly down and note the 81,000 pound maximum permissible landing weight.

(PLT121) — FAA-H-8083-25

ATM, DSP
8750. (Refer to Figure 461.) What is the maximum landing weight which will permit stopping 700 feet short of the end of a 5,600 foot runway at sea level?

A— 61,000 pounds.
B— 59,000 pounds.
C— 63,000 pounds.

A landing weight of 61,000 pounds will cause the aircraft to stop approximately 700 feet short of the end of the runway. (PLT008) — FAA-8083-25

Answer (B) is incorrect because the aircraft will stop 950 feet short. Answer (C) is incorrect because the aircraft will stop more than 700 feet short of the end of the runway.

ATM, DSP
8753. (Refer to Figures 273 and 457). What is the landing field length on a wet runway with a headwind of 7 knots and an aircraft weight of 83,000 pounds?

A— 6,600 feet.
B— 7,200 feet.
C— 5,900 feet.

1. On Figure 273, note the field elevation of 1,135 feet.

2. On Figure 457, start in the left section at the bottom of the graph, at 83,000 pounds. Move up until you intersect the 1,135 foot pressure altitude line. Move directly to the right until you intersect the reference

line. Move diagonally down and to the right in parallel with the diagonal lines until you intersect the 7 knot line. Move right until you intersect the REF line. Move up and to the right in parallel with the diagonal line until intersecting the WET reference line. Move directly to the right and note a landing field length of 6,600 feet.

(PLT008) — FAA-H-8083-25

ATM, DSP
8756. (Refer to Figures 331 and 457.) What approach speed and landing distance will be needed when landing at a weight of 75,000 pounds on a dry runway with calm winds?

A— 131 knots and 5,600 feet.
B— 141 knots and 4,600 feet.
C— 141 knots and 5,600 feet.

Figure 331 shows an approximate airport elevation of 13 feet. At 75,000 pounds, the vertical line indicates a V_{REF} speed of 141 knots and a landing distance of 5,600 feet in calm dry conditions. (PLT008) — FAA-H-8083-25

ATM, DSP
8692. (Refer to Figures 73, 74, and 75.) What is V_{REF} for Operating Conditions L-1?

A— 143 knots.
B— 144 knots.
C— 145 knots.

Table value	135 knots
Wind correction	+ 7 knots
V_{REF}	142 knots

(PLT008) — FAA-H-8083-25

ATM, DSP
8693. (Refer to Figures 73, 74, and 75.) What is the reference speed for Operating Conditions L-2?

A— 140 knots.
B— 145 knots.
C— 148 knots.

Table value	140 knots
Wind correction	+ 5 knots
V_{REF}	145 knots

(PLT012) — FAA-H-8083-25

Answers

8746 [A]	8750 [A]	8753 [A]	8756 [C]	8692 [A]	8693 [B]

ATM, DSP

8694. (Refer to Figures 73, 74, and 75.) What is V$_{REF}$ +20 for Operating Conditions L-3?

A— 151 knots.
B— 169 knots.
C— 149 knots.

Table value	141	knots
Wind correction	+ 8	knots
V$_{REF}$	149	knots
	+ 20	
	169	knots

(PLT012) — FAA-H-8083-25

ATM, DSP

8695. (Refer to Figures 73, 74, and 75.) What is V$_{REF}$ +10 for Operating Conditions L-4?

A— 152 knots.
B— 138 knots.
C— 148 knots.

Table value	134	knots
Wind correction	+ 3	knots
V$_{REF}$	137	knots
	+ 10	
	147	knots

(PLT012) — FAA-H-8083-25

ATM, DSP

8696. (Refer to Figures 73, 74, and 75.) What is the maneuvering speed for Operating Conditions L-5?

A— 124 knots.
B— 137 knots.
C— 130 knots.

Table value	124	knots
Wind correction	+ 6	knots
V$_{REF}$	130	knots

(PLT002) — FAA-H-8083-25

ATM, DSP

8687. (Refer to Figures 73 and 75.) What is the go-around EPR for Operating Conditions L-1?

A— 2.01 EPR.
B— 2.03 EPR.
C— 2.04 EPR.

Temperature scale = TAT
Temperature-limited EPR = 2.00
Altitude-limited EPR = 2.04, 1.98 (need to interpolate to find 2.01)
Air conditioning correction = +.03

(PLT007) — FAA-H-8083-25

ATM, DSP

8688. (Refer to Figures 73 and 75.) What is the go-around EPR for Operating Conditions L-2?

A— 2.115 EPR.
B— 2.10 EPR.
C— 2.06 EPR.

Temperature scale = OAT°F
Temperature-limited EPR = 2.10
Altitude-limited EPR = 2.15
Anti-ice correction = -.04

(PLT007) — FAA-H-8083-25

ATM, DSP

8689. (Refer to Figures 73 and 75.) What is the go-around EPR for Operating Conditions L-3?

A— 2.06 EPR.
B— 2.07 EPR.
C— 2.09 EPR.

Temperature scale = OAT°C
Temperature-limited EPR = 2.13
Altitude-limited EPR = 2.09, 2.15 (need to interpolate, finding 2.12)
Anti-ice correction = -.06

(PLT007) — FAA-H-8083-25

ATM, DSP

8690. (Refer to Figures 73 and 75.) What is the go-around EPR for Operating Conditions L-4?

A— 2.056 EPR.
B— 2.12 EPR.
C— 2.096 EPR.

Temperature scale = TAT
Temperature-limited EPR = 2.16
Altitude-limited EPR = 2.09, 2.15 (need to interpolate to find 2.096)
Anti-ice correction = -.04

(PLT007) — FAA-H-8083-25

Answers

8694   [B]   8695   [C]   8696   [C]   8687   [B]   8688   [C]   8689   [A]
8690   [A]

ATM, DSP

8691. (Refer to Figures 73 and 75.) What is the go-around EPR for Operating Conditions L-5?

A— 2.00 EPR.
B— 2.04 EPR.
C— 2.05 EPR.

Temperature scale = OAT°F
Temperature-limited EPR = 2.00
Altitude-limited EPR = 2.04

(PLT007) — FAA-H-8083-25

Miscellaneous Performance

V_C — design cruising speed.

V_{MO}/M_{MO} — maximum operating limit speed.

An encounter with strong turbulence can result in structural damage to an aircraft, or inadvertent stall. The sudden changes in wind direction and speed can result in very rapid changes in an aircraft's angle of attack. A sudden increase in angle of attack will cause the airplane to accelerate upward, increasing both the load factor and the stalling speed.

For any combination of weight and altitude there will be a recommended "rough air" speed that provides the best protection from stalls and from the possibility of overstressing the aircraft. When clear air turbulence has been reported in the area, a pilot should slow to the rough air speed upon encountering the first ripple of turbulence.

In severe turbulence, it may be impossible to maintain a constant airspeed or altitude. If this happens, the pilot should set the power to that which would maintain the desired airspeed and maintain a level flight attitude, accepting large variations in airspeed and altitude.

ALL

9321. Which is the correct symbol for design cruising speed?

A— V_C.
B— V_S.
C— V_A.

V_C—design cruising speed.

(PLT132) — 14 CFR §1.2

Answer (B) is incorrect because V_S is the stalling speed or minimum steady flight speed at which the airplane is controllable. Answer (C) is incorrect because V_A is maneuvering speed.

ALL

8344. How can turbulent air cause an increase in stalling speed of an airfoil?

A— An abrupt change in relative wind.
B— A decrease in angle of attack.
C— Sudden decrease in load factor.

When an airplane flying at a high speed with a low angle of attack suddenly encounters a vertical current of air moving upward, the relative wind changes in an upward direction as it meets the airfoil. This increases the angle of attack. A downward gust would have the effect of decreasing the angle of attack. (PLT245) — FAA-H-8083-25

Answer (B) is incorrect because a decrease in angle of attack would decrease the possibility of a stall. Answer (C) is incorrect because a sudden decrease in load factor would decrease the stalling speed.

Answers

8691 [A]   9321 [A]   8344 [A]

ALL

9129. If severe turbulence is encountered, which procedure is recommended?

A— Maintain a constant altitude.
B— Maintain a constant attitude.
C— Maintain constant airspeed and altitude.

In severe turbulence, the airspeed indicator is inaccurate; therefore the pilot should set power for the recommended rough air speed and then maintain a level flight attitude, accepting variations in indicated airspeed and altitude. (PLT501) — AC 00-30

Answers (A) and (C) are incorrect because severe turbulence causes large variations in both indicated airspeed and altitude. Any attempt to maintain constant airspeed and altitude may overstress the aircraft.

ATM, ATS, DSP

9320. Which speed symbol indicates the maximum operating limit speed for an airplane?

A— V_{LE}.
B— V_{MO}/M_{MO}.
C— V_{LO}/M_{LO}.

V_{MO}/M_{MO}—maximum operating limit speed.

(PLT466) — 14 CFR §1.2

Answer (A) is incorrect because V_{LE} is maximum landing gear extended speed. Answer (C) is incorrect because V_{LO}/M_{LO} is the maximum speed for operating the landing gear.

ATM, DSP

8668. (Refer to Figures 68 and 69.) What are the recommended IAS and EPR settings for holding under Operating Conditions O-1?

A— 219 knots and 1.83 EPR.
B— 223 knots and 2.01 EPR.
C— 217 knots and 1.81 EPR.

Interpolation is required for FL310 and 102,000 pounds. At FL350, the EPR value for 102,000 is 1.97. At FL300, the EPR value for 102,000 is 1.77. Interpolation for FL310 results in an EPR value of 1.81. At FL350 the IAS for 102,000 is 219 knots. At FL300 the IAS for 102,000 is 217 knots. Interpolating for FL310 results in an IAS value of 217 knots. (PLT007) — FAA-H-8083-25

ATM, DSP

8669. (Refer to Figures 68 and 69.) What are the recommended IAS and EPR settings for holding under Operating Conditions O-2?

A— 210 knots and 1.57 EPR.
B— 210 knots and 1.51 EPR.
C— 210 knots and 1.45 EPR.

Interpolation is required for FL230 and 93,000 pounds. At FL250, the EPR value for 93,000 is 1.56. At FL200, the EPR value for 93,000 is 1.44. Interpolation for FL230 results in an EPR value of 1.51. At FL250, the IAS for 93,000 is 210 knots. At FL200, the IAS for 93,000 is 210 knots. Interpolating for FL230 results in an IAS value of 210 knots. (PLT007) — FAA-H-8083-25

ATM, DSP

8670. (Refer to Figures 68 and 69.) What are the recommended IAS and EPR settings for holding under Operating Conditions O-3?

A— 217 knots and 1.50 EPR.
B— 215 knots and 1.44 EPR.
C— 216 knots and 1.40 EPR.

Interpolation is required for FL170 and 104,000 pounds. At FL200, the EPR value for 104,000 is 1.50. At FL150, the EPR value for 104,000 is 1.40. Interpolation for FL170 results in an EPR value of 1.44. At FL200, the IAS for 104,000 is 216 knots. At FL150, the IAS for 104,000 is 215 knots. Interpolating for FL170 results in an IAS value of 215 knots. (PLT007) — FAA-H-8083-25

ATM, DSP

8671. (Refer to Figures 68 and 69.) What are the recommended IAS and EPR settings for holding under Operating Conditions O-4?

A— 223 knots and 1.33 EPR.
B— 225 knots and 1.33 EPR.
C— 220 knots and 1.28 EPR.

Interpolation is required for FL080 and 113,000 pounds. At FL100, the EPR value for 113,000 is 1.35. At FL050, the EPR value for 113,000 is 1.29. Interpolation for FL080 results in an EPR value of 1.33. At FL100, the IAS for 113,000 is 223 knots. At FL050, the IAS for 113,000 is 222 knots. Interpolating for FL080 results in an IAS value of 223 knots. (PLT007) — FAA-H-8083-25

Answers

| 9129 | [B] | 9320 | [B] | 8668 | [C] | 8669 | [B] | 8670 | [B] | 8671 | [A] |

ATM, DSP
8672. (Refer to Figures 68 and 69.) What are the recommended IAS and EPR settings for holding under Operating Conditions O-5?

A— 219 knots and 1.28 EPR.
B— 214 knots and 1.26 EPR.
C— 218 knots and 1.27 EPR.

Interpolation is required for FL040 and 109,000 pounds. At FL050, the EPR value for 109,000 is 1.28. At FL015, the EPR value for 109,000 is 1.24. Interpolation for FL040 results in an EPR value of 1.27. At FL050, the IAS for 109,000 is 218 knots. At FL015, the IAS for 109,000 is 218 knots. Interpolating for FL040 results in an IAS value of 218 knots. (PLT007) — FAA-H-8083-25

ATM, DSP
8673. (Refer to Figures 68 and 69.) What is the approximate fuel consumed when holding under Operating Conditions O-1?

A— 1,625 pounds.
B— 1,950 pounds.
C— 2,440 pounds.

Compute the fuel flow for the holding time as follows:

*Fuel flow per engine = 2,434 x 2 = 4,868 ÷ 60 x 20
= 1,623*

(PLT012) — FAA-H-8083-25

ATM, DSP
8674. (Refer to Figures 68 and 69.) What is the approximate fuel consumed when holding under Operating Conditions O-2?

A— 2,250 pounds.
B— 2,500 pounds.
C— 3,000 pounds.

Compute the fuel used for the holding time as follows:

*Fuel flow per engine = 2,248 x 2 = 4,496 ÷ 60 x 40
= 2,997*

(PLT012) — FAA-H-8083-25

ATM, DSP
8675. (Refer to Figures 68 and 69.) What is the approximate fuel consumed when holding under Operating Conditions O-3?

A— 2,940 pounds.
B— 2,520 pounds.
C— 3,250 pounds.

Compute the fuel used for the holding time as follows:

*Fuel flow per engine = 2,518 x 2 = 5,036 ÷ 60 x 35
= 2,938*

(PLT012) — FAA-H-8083-25

ATM, DSP
8676. (Refer to Figures 68 and 69.) What is the approximate fuel consumed when holding under Operating Conditions O-4?

A— 2,870 pounds.
B— 2,230 pounds.
C— 1,440 pounds.

Compute the fuel used for the holding time as follows:

*Fuel flow per engine = 2,866 x 2 = 5,732 ÷ 60 x 15
= 1,433*

(PLT012) — FAA-H-8083-25

ATM, DSP
8677. (Refer to Figures 68 and 69.) What is the approximate fuel consumed when holding under Operating Conditions O-5?

A— 2,950 pounds.
B— 2,870 pounds.
C— 2,400 pounds.

Compute the fuel used for the holding time as follows:

*Fuel flow per engine = 2,873 x 2 = 5,746 ÷ 60 x 25
= 2,394*

(PLT012) — FAA-H-8083-25

ATM, DSP
8727. (Refer to Figures 287 and 421.) The winds are reported as 220/15. You compute tailwind component, hoping for a Runway 33 takeoff. You compute the tailwind to be

A— 14 knots.
B— 10 knots.
C— 5 knots.

The angle between the winds and the runway is 110°. On Figure 421, starting on the left side of the chart at zero, move down and to the right along the 110 line until intersecting the 15 knots point. Then move directly to the left and note a tailwind (indicated by the minus sign) of 5 knots. (PLT013) — FAA-H-8083-25

Answers

| 8672 [C] | 8673 [A] | 8674 [C] | 8675 [A] | 8676 [C] | 8677 [C] |
| 8727 [C] | | | | | |

ATM, DSP

8728. (Refer to Figure 422.) At a weight of 68,500 pounds with gear and flaps up, you find the reference stall speed to be

A— 148 knots.
B— 145 knots.
C— 142 knots.

On Figure 422, use the upper chart that indicates FLAP 0/GEAR UP. Find the gross weight of 68,500 pounds at the bottom of the chart and move up until intersecting the reference line. Then move directly to the left and note a reference stall speed of 142 knots. (PLT 018) — FAA-H-8083-25

ATM, DSP

8729. (Refer to Figure 459.) With a payload of 20,000 pounds, the still-air range is

A— 1,350 NM.
B— 1,410 NM.
C— 1,590 NM.

On Figure 459, find the payload of 20,000 pounds on the bottom of the chart. Move directly up until you intersect the MTOW 82500 LB line. Then move directly to the right and note the still-air range of 1,410 NM. (PLT121) — FAA-H-8083-25

ATM, DSP

8730. (Refer to Figure 459.) For a supplemental charter, a still-air range of 2,250 NM is required. The payload for this nonstop trip is

A— 5,100 pounds.
B— 5,600 pounds.
C— 6,100 pounds.

On Figure 459, start at the right side of the chart and find the still-air range of 2,250 NM. Move directly to the left until you intersect the MX FUEL 19450 LB reference line. Then move straight down and note the payload of 5,600 pounds. (PLT121) — FAA-H-8083-25

ATM, DSP

8731. (Refer to Figure 417.) You find one air data computer listed on the MEL as inoperative, leaving one ADC operative during your preflight logbook inspection. This means the flight

A— must fly non-RVSM flight levels above FL330.
B— can only fly between FL290.
C— must remain below FL290 unless dispatch obtains a deviation from ATC.

Figure 417 indicates that two air data computers (ADCs) are required for RVSM operations. Because RVSM airspace starts at FL290, you will not be able to climb above FL 290 unless you receive special permission or a deviation from ATC. (PLT428) — FAA-H-8083-25

ATM, DSP

8732. (Refer to Figure 438.) With an actual runway length of 6,400 feet with 8 flaps, a 1% downslope, a 200 foot clearway, and 4 knots of tailwind, the Reference A is

A— 2.12.
B— 2.02.
C— 1.94.

On Figure 438, start on the left side and find 6,400 feet. Move right until you intersect the REF LINE. Move up and right in parallel with the diagonal lines until you intersect the 200-foot clearway line. Move directly to the right until you intersect the next REF LINE. Move up and left in parallel with the diagonal lines until you intersect the -1 runway slope line. Move directly right until intersecting the Reported Wind REF LINE. Move down and left in parallel with the diagonal lines until you intersect the -4 wind line. Move directly to the right and note the 1.94 Reference A. (PLT428) — FAA-H-8083-25

ATM, DSP

8733. (Refer to Figures 318 and 439.) With a reported temperature of 30°C with packs on and anti-ice off, the Reference B is

A— 28.2.
B— 29.8.
C— 30.7.

1. *On Figure 318 note the field elevation of 4,227 feet.*

2. *On Figure 439, find the section of the chart that indicates ANTI-ICE OFF PACKS ON and start at the bottom of that section at 30°C. Move straight up until you intersect the 4,227 feet line. Move directly to the right and note the Reference B of 29.8.*

(PLT328) — FAA-H-8083-25

ATM, DSP

8734. (Refer to Figure 440, All Engines.) With a Reference A of 3.00 and Reference B of 28.5, the takeoff weight is limited to

A— 78,500 pounds.
B— 76,500 pounds.
C— 75,000 pounds.

Answers

8728 [C]	8729 [B]	8730 [B]	8731 [C]	8732 [C]	8733 [B]
8734 [B]					

On Figure 440, start at the right side of the chart and find the Reference B of 28.5. Move directly right until you intersect the REF LINE. Move up and to the right diagonally until you intersect the Reference A line of 3.00. Move directly to the right and note the aircraft weight of 76,500 pounds. (PLT328) — FAA-H-8083-25

ATM, DSP

9128. What action is appropriate when encountering the first ripple of reported clear air turbulence (CAT)?

A— Extend flaps to decrease wing loading.
B— Extend gear to provide more drag and increase stability.
C— Adjust airspeed to that recommended for rough air.

In an area where significant clear air turbulence has been reported or is forecast, the pilot should adjust the speed to fly at the recommended rough air speed on encountering the first ripple, since the intensity of such turbulence may build up rapidly. (PLT501) — AC 00-30

Answer (A) is incorrect because use of flaps increases the camber of the wing and angle of attack, but does not decrease the amount of wing loading. Answer (B) is incorrect because extending the gear would increase the drag, but would not change the stability of the airplane.

ATM, DSP

8653. (Refer to Figures 63 and 64.) What is the turbulent air penetration N_1 power setting for Operating Conditions Q-1?

A— 82.4 percent.
B— 84.0 percent.
C— 84.8 percent.

TAT = ISA +15°

Table value	82.4%
Temp. correction	+ 2.4%
Corrected N_1	84.8%

(PLT020) — FAA-H-8083-25

ATM, DSP

8654. (Refer to Figures 63 and 64.) What is the turbulent air penetration N_1 power setting for Operating Conditions Q-2?

A— 78.2 percent.
B— 75.2 percent.
C— 76.7 percent.

TAT = ISA -10°

Table value	76.7%
Temp. correction	– 1.5%
Corrected N_1	75.2%

(PLT020) — FAA-H-8083-25

ATM, DSP

8655. (Refer to Figures 63 and 64.) What is the turbulent air penetration N_1 power setting for Operating Conditions Q-3?

A— 77.8 percent.
B— 82.6 percent.
C— 84.2 percent.

TAT = ISA +20°

Table value	81.0%
Temp. correction	+ 3.2%
Corrected N_1	84.2%

(PLT020) — FAA-H-8083-25

ATM, DSP

8656. (Refer to Figures 63 and 64.) What is the turbulent air penetration N_1 power setting for Operating Conditions Q-4?

A— 76.8 percent.
B— 75.4 percent.
C— 74.0 percent.

TAT = ISA +10°

Table value	75.4%
Temp. correction	+ 1.4%
Corrected N_1	76.8%

(PLT020) — FAA-H-8083-25

ATM, DSP

8657. (Refer to Figures 63 and 64.) What is the turbulent air penetration N_1 power setting for Operating Conditions Q-5?

A— 70.9 percent.
B— 72.9 percent.
C— 71.6 percent.

TAT = ISA -15°

Table value	72.90%
Temp. correction	– 1.95%
Corrected N_1	70.95%

(PLT020) — FAA-H-8083-25

Answers

9128 [C]	8653 [C]	8654 [B]	8655 [C]	8656 [A]	8657 [A]

Engine-Out Procedures

V_{MC} — minimum control speed with the critical engine inoperative.

V_{XSE} — best single engine angle-of-climb speed.

V_{YSE} — best single engine rate-of-climb speed.

When an engine fails in flight, the effect on aircraft performance is drastic. For example, the loss of one engine on a two-engine aircraft will result in a loss of climb performance in excess of 50%. Climb performance is determined by the amount of power available in excess of that required for level flight. The one remaining engine must provide all of the power required for level flight. It may be able to develop little or no excess power that would allow for a climb.

When an engine fails in cruise flight, the pilot should slow the aircraft to its best single-engine rate-of-climb speed (V_{YSE}) and apply maximum continuous power on the remaining engine. The airplane may or may not be able to climb. If it cannot climb at the present altitude, at least it will descend at the minimum possible rate of sink and level off at its maximum engine-out altitude. It may be necessary to dump fuel to improve the altitude capability of the aircraft.

A multi-engine airplane should never be flown below its minimum control speed (V_{MC}). If it is below V_{MC} and an engine failure occurs, it may be impossible to maintain directional control with the other engine operating at full power. V_{MC} will vary with the aircraft's center of gravity location. V_{MC} will be highest with the CG at its most rearward-allowed position.

A three- or four-engine turbine-powered airplane, used by an air carrier, may be ferried to a maintenance base with one engine inoperative if certain requirements are met. These requirements include:

- The airplane model must have been test flown to show that such an operation is safe.
- The operator's approved flight manual must contain performance data for such an operation.
- The operating weight of the aircraft must be limited to the minimum required for flight plus any required reserve fuel.
- Takeoffs are usually limited to dry runways.
- The computed takeoff performance must be within acceptable limits (this will vary depending on the type of aircraft).
- The initial climb cannot be over thickly-populated areas.
- Only required flight crewmembers may be on the aircraft.
- Weather conditions at the takeoff and destination airports must be VFR.

ATM, ATS, DSP

8369. If an engine failure occurs at an altitude above single-engine ceiling, what airspeed should be maintained?

A— V_{MC}.
B— V_{YSE}.
C— V_{XSE}.

If an airplane is not capable of maintaining altitude with an engine inoperative under existing circumstances, the airspeed should be maintained within ±5 knots of the engine-out best rate-of-climb speed (V_{YSE}), in order to conserve altitude as long as possible to reach a suitable landing area. (PLT208) — FAA-H-8083-3

Answers

8369 [B]

ATM, ATS, DSP

8370. What is the resulting performance loss when one engine on a twin-engine airplane fails?

A— Reduction of cruise airspeed by 50 percent.
B— Reduction of climb by 80 to 90 percent.
C— Reduction of all performance by 50 percent.

When one engine fails on a light twin, performance is not really halved, but is actually reduced by 80% or more. The performance loss is greater than 50% because an airplane's climb performance is a function of the thrust horsepower, which is in excess of that required for level flight. (PLT223) — FAA-H-8083-3

Answer (A) is incorrect because the power loss affects climb capability much more than it does cruise speed. Answer (C) is incorrect because climb capability is significantly (more than 50%) reduced.

ATM, ATS, DSP

8371. Under what condition is V_{MC} the highest?

A— Gross weight is at the maximum allowable value.
B— CG is at the most rearward allowable position.
C— CG is at the most forward allowable position.

V_{MC} is greater when the center of gravity is at the most rearward-allowed position. (PLT466) — FAA-H-8083-3

Answer (A) is incorrect because the location of the weight (i.e., CG) is more critical than the amount of weight. Answer (C) is incorrect because a forward CG increases rudder effectiveness and reduces V_{MC}.

ATM, ATS, DSP

9355. Which operational requirement must be observed by a commercial operator when ferrying a large, three-engine, turbojet-powered airplane from one facility to another to repair an inoperative engine?

A— The computed takeoff distance to reach V_1 must not exceed 70 percent of the effective runway length.
B— The existing and forecast weather for departure, en route, and approach must be VFR.
C— No passengers may be carried.

A commercial operator of large aircraft may conduct a ferry flight of a four-engine airplane or a turbine-engine-powered, three-engine airplane with one engine inoperative, to a base for the purpose of repairing the engine. Several restrictions apply to such flights. These include:

1. *The Airplane Flight Manual must include procedures and performance data which allow for the safe operation of such a flight.*
2. *The initial climb cannot be over thickly-populated areas.*

3. *Weather conditions at the takeoff and destination airports must be VFR.*
4. *Only required flight crewmembers may be on board the aircraft.*

(PLT367) — 14 CFR §91.611

Answer (A) is incorrect because runway length allowing V_1 in less than 70% of the runway is not required for ferry flights with one engine inoperative. Answer (B) is incorrect because the weather conditions must be VFR only for takeoff and landing.

ATM, ATS, DSP

9355-1. You are assigned to ferry a large, three-engine, turbojet-powered airplane from one facility to another to repair an inoperative engine. You know you are restricted to

A— VFR weather for takeoff, en route, and landing.
B— flight crewmembers only aboard.
C— a computed takeoff distance to reach V_1 that cannot exceed 70 percent of the effective runway length.

A commercial operator of large aircraft may conduct a ferry flight of a four-engine airplane or a turbine-engine-powered, three-engine airplane with one engine inoperative, to a base for the purpose of repairing the engine. Several restrictions apply to such flights. These include:

1. *The Airplane Flight Manual must include procedures and performance data which allow for the safe operation of such a flight.*
2. *The initial climb cannot be over thickly-populated areas.*
3. *Weather conditions at the takeoff and destination airports must be VFR.*
4. *Only required flight crewmembers may be on board the aircraft.*

(PLT367) — 14 CFR §91.611

ATM, ATS, DSP

9358. A commercial operator plans to ferry a large, four-engine, reciprocating-engine-powered airplane from one facility to another to repair an inoperative engine. Which is an operational requirement for the three-engine flight?

A— The gross weight at takeoff may not exceed 75 percent of the maximum certificated gross weight.
B— Weather conditions at the takeoff and destination airports must be VFR.
C— The computed takeoff distance to reach V_1 must not exceed 70 percent of the effective runway length.

Continued

A commercial operator of large aircraft may conduct a ferry flight of a four-engine airplane or a turbine-engine-powered, three-engine airplane with one engine inoperative, to a base for the purpose of repairing the engine. Several restrictions apply to such flights. These include:

1. *The Airplane Flight Manual must include procedures and performance data which allow for the safe operation of such a flight.*

2. *The initial climb cannot be over thickly-populated areas.*

3. *Weather conditions at the takeoff and destination airports must be VFR.*

4. *Only required flight crewmembers may be on board the aircraft.*

(PLT367) — 14 CFR §91.611

ATM, ATS, DSP

9359. Which operational requirement must be observed when ferrying an air carrier airplane when one of its three turbine engines is inoperative?

A— The weather conditions at takeoff and destination must be VFR.

B— The flight cannot be conducted between official sunset and official sunrise.

C— Weather conditions must exceed the basic VFR minimums for the entire route, including takeoff and landing.

A commercial operator of large aircraft may conduct a ferry flight of a four-engine airplane or a turbine-engine-powered, three-engine airplane with one engine inoperative, to a base for the purpose of repairing the engine. Several restrictions apply to such flights. These include:

1. *The Airplane Flight Manual must include procedures and performance data which allow for the safe operation of such a flight.*

2. *The initial climb cannot be over thickly-populated areas.*

3. *Weather conditions at the takeoff and destination airports must be VFR.*

4. *Only required flight crewmembers may be on board the aircraft.*

(PLT367) — 14 CFR §91.611

Answer (B) is incorrect because a ferry flight may be conducted after sunset and before sunrise as long as the takeoff and destination airports are VFR. Answer (C) is incorrect because the weather conditions must be VFR only for takeoff and landing.

ATM, ATS, DSP

9360. Which operational requirement must be observed when ferrying a large, turbine-engine-powered airplane when one of its engines is inoperative?

A— The weather conditions at takeoff and destination must be VFR.

B— Weather conditions must exceed the basic VFR minimums for the entire route, including takeoff and landing.

C— The flight cannot be conducted between official sunset and sunrise.

A commercial operator of large aircraft may conduct a ferry flight of a four-engine airplane or a turbine-engine-powered, three-engine airplane with one engine inoperative, to a base for the purpose of repairing the engine. Several restrictions apply to such flights. These include:

1. *The Airplane Flight Manual must include procedures and performance data which allow for the safe operation of such a flight.*

2. *The initial climb cannot be over thickly-populated areas.*

3. *Weather conditions at the takeoff and destination airports must be VFR.*

4. *Only required flight crewmembers may be on board the aircraft.*

(PLT367) — 14 CFR §91.611

Answer (B) is incorrect because the weather conditions must be VFR only for takeoff and landing. Answer (C) is incorrect because a ferry flight may be conducted after sunset and before sunrise as long as the takeoff and destination airports are VFR.

ATM, ATS, DSP

9361. When a turbine-engine-powered airplane is to be ferried to another base for repair of an inoperative engine, which operational requirement must be observed?

A— Only the required flight crewmembers may be on board the airplane.

B— The existing and forecast weather for departure, en route, and approach must be VFR.

C— No passengers except authorized maintenance personnel may be carried.

A commercial operator of large aircraft may conduct a ferry flight of a four-engine airplane or a turbine-engine-powered, three-engine airplane with one engine inoperative, to a base for the purpose of repairing the engine. Several restrictions apply to such flights. These include:

Answers

9359   [A]   9360   [A]   9361   [A]

1. The Airplane Flight Manual must include procedures and performance data which allow for the safe operation of such a flight.

2. The initial climb cannot be over thickly-populated areas.

3. Weather conditions at the takeoff and destination airports must be VFR.

4. Only required flight crewmembers may be on board the aircraft.

(PLT367) — 14 CFR §91.611

Answer (B) is incorrect because the weather conditions must be VFR only for takeoff and landing. Answer (C) is incorrect because only the required flight crewmembers may be aboard.

ATM, DSP

8678. (Refer to Figure 70.) How many minutes of dump time is required to reach a weight of 144,500 pounds?

Initial weight.. 180,500 lb
Zero fuel weight.. 125,500 lb

A— 13 minutes.
B— 15 minutes.
C— 16 minutes.

1. Initial weight	180,500
Zero fuel wt.	− 125,500
Initial fuel wt.	55,000
2. Ending weight	144,500
Zero fuel wt.	− 125,500
Ending fuel wt.	19,000

3. Dump time = 15.25 minutes

(PLT016) — FAA-H-8083-25

ATM, DSP

8679. (Refer to Figure 70.) How many minutes of dump time is required to reduce fuel load to 25,000 pounds?

Initial weight.. 179,500 lb
Zero fuel weight.. 136,500 lb

A— 10 minutes.
B— 9 minutes.
C— 8 minutes.

1. Initial weight	179,500
Zero fuel wt.	− 136,500
Initial fuel wt.	43,000
2. Ending fuel wt.	25,000

3. Dump time = 7.6 minutes

(PLT016) — FAA-H-8083-25

ATM, DSP

8680. (Refer to Figure 70.) How many minutes of dump time is required to reach a weight of 151,500 pounds?

Initial weight.. 181,500 lb
Zero fuel weight.. 126,000 lb

A— 15 minutes.
B— 14 minutes.
C— 13 minutes.

1. Initial weight	181,500
Zero fuel wt.	− 126,000
Initial fuel wt.	55,500
2. Ending weight	151,500
Zero fuel wt.	− 126,000
Ending fuel wt.	25,500

3. Dump time = 12.875 minutes

(PLT016) — FAA-H-8083-25

ATM, DSP

8681. (Refer to Figure 70.) How many minutes of dump time is required to reduce fuel load to 16,000 pounds (at 2,350 lbs/min)?

Initial weight.. 175,500 lb
Zero fuel weight.. 138,000 lb

A— 9 minutes.
B— 10 minutes.
C— 8 minutes.

1. Initial weight	175,500
Zero fuel wt.	− 138,000
Initial fuel wt.	37,500
2. Ending fuel wt.	16,000

3. Dump time = 8.8125 minutes

(PLT016) — FAA-H-8083-25

ATM, DSP

8682. (Refer to Figures 71 and 72.) What is the approximate level-off pressure altitude after drift-down under Operating Conditions D-1?

A— 19,400 feet.
B— 18,000 feet.
C— 20,200 feet.

Assume the aircraft weighs 100,000 pounds at the time of its engine failure and the engine anti-ice is on. If the temperature is ISA, the level-off altitude is 19,400 feet.
(PLT004) — FAA-H-8083-25

Answers

| 8678 | [B] | | 8679 | [C] | | 8680 | [C] | | 8681 | [A] | | 8682 | [A] |

ATM, DSP

8683. (Refer to Figures 71 and 72.) What is the approximate level-off pressure altitude after drift-down under Operating Conditions D-2?

A— 14,700 feet.
B— 17,500 feet.
C— 18,300 feet.

Assume the aircraft weighs 110,000 pounds at the time of its engine failure. If the temperature is ISA +10°C, the level-off altitude is 17,500 feet. (PLT004) — FAA-H-8083-25

ATM, DSP

8684. (Refer to Figures 71 and 72.) What is the approximate level-off pressure altitude after drift-down under Operating Conditions D-3?

A— 22,200 feet.
B— 19,800 feet.
C— 21,600 feet.

Assume the aircraft weighs 90,000 pounds at the time of its engine failure. If the temperature is ISA -10°C, the level-off altitude is 21,600 feet. (PLT004) — FAA-H-8083-25

ATM, DSP

8685. (Refer to Figures 71 and 72.) What is the approximate level-off pressure altitude after drift-down under Operating Conditions D-4?

A— 27,900 feet.
B— 22,200 feet.
C— 24,400 feet.

Assume the aircraft weighs 80,000 pounds at the time of its engine failure. If the temperature is ISA -10°C, the level-off altitude is 24,400 feet. (PLT004) — FAA-H-8083-25

ATM, DSP

8686. (Refer to Figures 71 and 72.) What is the approximate level-off pressure altitude after drift-down under Operating Conditions D-5?

A— 8,800 feet.
B— 9,600 feet.
C— 13,000 feet.

Assume the aircraft weighs 120,000 pounds at the time of its engine failure. If the temperature is ISA +20°C, the level-off altitude is 8,800 feet. When engine bleed-air for air conditioning is off below 17,000 feet, increase level-off altitude by 800 feet. Therefore, the level-off altitude is 9,600 feet (8,800 + 800). (PLT004) — FAA-H-8083-25

C208 Aircraft Performance

ATS, DSP

8459. (Refer to Figure 392.) Given the following conditions, what is the maximum torque for takeoff?

Pressure altitude...9,000 ft
Temperature (OAT)..+3°C
Cabin Heat...OFF

A— 1,800 foot-pounds.
B— 1,840 foot-pounds.
C— 1,775 foot-pounds.

Enter the graph at +3°C and proceed up to 9,000 feet, then over to the left to read 1,840 foot-pounds of torque. Note that the pressure altitude levels are given in thousand feet increments, therefore 8 is equal to 8,000, 10 is equal to 10,000, etc. (PLT169) — FAA-H-8083-25

ATS, DSP

8460. (Refer to Figure 392.) Given the following conditions, what is the maximum torque for takeoff?

Pressure altitude...4,500 ft
Temperature (OAT)..+35°C
Cabin Heat...OFF

A— 1,760 foot-pounds.
B— 1,840 foot-pounds.
C— 1,675 foot-pounds.

Enter the graph at +35°C and proceed up to 4,500 feet, then over to the left to read 1,760 foot-pounds of torque. Note that the pressure altitude levels are given in thousand feet increments, therefore 8 is equal to 8,000, 10 is equal to 10,000, etc. (PLT169) — FAA-H-8083-25

Answers

| 8683 [B] | 8684 [C] | 8685 [C] | 8686 [B] | 8459 [B] | 8460 [A] |

ATS, DSP

8461. (Refer to Figure 392.) Given the following conditions, what is the maximum torque for takeoff?

Pressure altitude.. 1,000 ft
Temperature (OAT)... +40°C
Cabin Heat.. OFF

A— 1,800 foot-pounds.
B— 1,725 foot-pounds.
C— 1,865 foot-pounds.

Enter the graph at +40°C and proceed up to 1,000 feet, then over to the left to read 1,865 foot-pounds of torque. Note that the pressure altitude levels are given in thousand feet increments, therefore 8 is equal to 8,000, 10 is equal to 10,000, etc. (PLT169) — FAA-H-8083-25

ATS, DSP

8462. (Refer to Figure 392.) Given the following conditions, what is the maximum torque for takeoff?

Pressure altitude.. 6,000 ft
Temperature (OAT)... +25°C
Cabin Heat.. ON

A— 1,800 foot-pounds.
B— 1,735 foot-pounds.
C— 1,865 foot-pounds.

Enter the graph at +25°C and proceed up to 6,000 feet, then over to the left to read 1,800 foot-pounds of torque. Note 4 states that with cabin heat on, decrease torque setting by 65 foot-pounds: 1,800 – 65 = 1,735 foot-pounds. Note that the pressure altitude levels are given in thousand feet increments, therefore 8 is equal to 8,000, 10 is equal to 10,000, etc. (PLT169) — FAA-H-8083-25

ATS, DSP

8463. (Refer to Figure 392.) Given the following conditions, what is the maximum torque for takeoff?

Pressure altitude.. 9,000 ft
Temperature (OAT)... +15°C
Cabin Heat.. ON

A— 1,645 foot-pounds.
B— 1,710 foot-pounds.
C— 1,675 foot-pounds.

Enter the graph at +15°C and proceed up to 9,000 feet, then over to the left to read 1,710 foot-pounds of torque. Note 4 states that with cabin heat on, decrease torque setting by 65 foot-pounds: 1,710 – 65 = 1,645 foot-pounds. Note that the pressure altitude levels are given in thousand feet increments, therefore 8 is equal to 8,000, 10 is equal to 10,000, etc. (PLT169) — FAA-H-8083-25

ATS, DSP

8464. (Refer to Figures 394 and 395.) Given the following conditions, what is the takeoff distance over a 50-foot obstacle?

Pressure Altitude .... Sea Level
Temperature (OAT)....................................... +20°C
Wind .... 11 knots headwind

A— 2,570 feet.
B— 2,313 feet.
C— 2,160 feet.

Find the column marked 20°C and "Total Distance to Clear 50 foot obstacle." Move down to intersect a pressure altitude of sea level, and find 2,570. Note 2 on Figure 394 requires you to reduce the distance by 10% for each 11 knots of headwind.

2,570 x .10 = 257

2,570 – 257 = 2,313 feet

(PLT169) — FAA-H-8083-25

ATS, DSP

8465. (Refer to Figures 394 and 395.) Given the following conditions, what is the takeoff ground roll?

Pressure Altitude .... 4,000 ft
Temperature (OAT)... 0°C
Wind .... 4 knots tailwind

A— 1,655 feet.
B— 1,820 feet.
C— 1,986 feet.

Find the column marked 0°C and "Ground Roll Feet." Move down to intersect a pressure altitude of 4,000 feet and find 1,655 feet. Note 2 requires you to increase ground roll by 10% for each two knots of tailwind, therefore 4 knots total would equal a 20% increase.

1655 x .20 = 331

1655 + 331 = 1,986 feet

(PLT169) — FAA-H-8083-25

Answers

8461 [C]	8462 [B]	8463 [A]	8464 [B]	8465 [C]

ATS, DSP

8466. (Refer to Figures 394 and 395.) Given the following conditions, what is the takeoff distance over a 50-foot obstacle?

Pressure altitude...2,000 ft
Temperature (OAT)..+15°C
Weight ....8750 lbs
Wind ....Calm

A— 2,823 feet.
B— 1,595 feet.
C— 2,905 feet.

At 2,000 feet and 10°C, find 2,740 feet to clear a 50-foot obstacle. At 2,000 and 20°C, find 2,905 feet to clear a 50-foot obstacle. To find the distance to clear a 50-foot obstacle at 15°C, interpolate to find the difference: 2740 + 2905 = 5675 / 2 = 2,823 feet. (PLT011) — FAA-H-8083-25

ATS, DSP

8467. (Refer to Figures 394 and 395.) Given the following conditions, what is the takeoff ground roll?

Pressure altitude...4,000 ft
Temperature (OAT)..+10°C
Weight ....8750 lbs
Wind ....HW 11 knots

A— 1,760 feet.
B— 1,584 feet.
C— 1,936 feet.

At 4,000 feet and 10°C, find a ground roll of 1,760 feet. On Figure 394, Note 2 requires you to decrease distance 10% for each 11 knots of headwind.

1760 x .10 = 176

1760 – 176 = 1,584 feet

(PLT011) — FAA-H-8083-25

ATS, DSP

8468. (Refer to Figures 394 and 395.) Given the following conditions, what is the takeoff distance over a 50-foot obstacle?

Pressure altitude...5,000 ft
Temperature (OAT)..+20°C
Weight ....8,750 lbs
Wind ....Calm

A— 3,530 feet.
B— 3,765 feet.
C— 2,010 feet.

At 4,000 feet and 20°C, find 3,295 feet to clear a 50-foot obstacle. At 6,000 and 20°C, find 3,765 feet to clear a 50-foot obstacle. To find the distance to clear a 50-foot obstacle at 5,000 feet, interpolate between 4,000 feet and 6,000 feet to find 3,530 feet. (PLT011) — FAA-H-8083-25

ATS, DSP

8479. (Refer to Figures 298, 394, and 395.) With an OAT of 30°C, inertial separator set to normal, and a 12-knot headwind, you calculate the short field takeoff distance to clear a 50-foot obstacle to be

A— 3,510 feet.
B— 3,833 feet.
C— 4,370 feet.

1. On Figure 298, find the field elevation of 5,837 feet.

2. On Figure 395, find the OAT of 30°C and note the distances over a 50-foot obstacle to be 3,510 feet at a 4,000-foot pressure altitude and 4,370 feet at a 6,000-foot pressure altitude. Interpolating for 5,837 feet yields a distance of 4,300 feet.

3. Because of the 12-knot headwind, you must reduce the distance by approximately 10.9% (10% for each 11 knots): 4,300 – 469 = 3,831 feet.

(PLT011) — FAA-H-8083-25

ATS, DSP

8480. (Refer Figure 398.) With an OAT of 20°C, inertial separator normal, and gross weight of 8,750 pounds, you calculate the climb gradient at 8,000 feet to be

A— 495 ft/NM.
B— 410 ft/NM.
C— 330 ft/NM.

On Figure 398, locate the gross weight figure of 8,750 in the upper left side of the chart. Proceed to the right at the 8,000 feet pressure altitude level until you intersect the 20°C and note the climb gradient of 330 feet per NM. (PLT004) — FAA-H-8083-25

ATS, DSP

8481. (Refer to Figure 399.) With an OAT of 15°C, inertial separator set in bypass, and a gross weight of 8,750 pounds, you calculate the climb fuel to 12,000 feet to be

A— 105 lbs.
B— 112 lbs.
C— 147 lbs.

Answers

8466 [A]   8467 [B]   8468 [A]   8479 [B]   8480 [C]   8481 [B]

On Figure 399, start at the gross weight of 8,750 pounds and move to the right across the 12,000 feet pressure altitude level until you intersect the "Standard Temperature/Fuel LBS" column. Note the 105 lbs of fuel used in the climb. Note 3 states that for each 2,000 feet of climb, add 1% to this figure. Because of the climb to 12,000 feet, increase the 105 figure by 6% (1% for each 2,000 feet to 12,000). 6% of 105 is 6.3 feet. 105 + 6.3 = 111.3 feet. Note that 15°C is the standard temperature at sea level where the climb begins. (PLT004) — FAA-H-8083-25

ATS
8117. (Refer to Figure 1.) What is the maximum landing distance that may be used by a turbopropeller-powered, small transport category airplane to land on Rwy 24 (dry) at the alternate airport?

A— 5,490 feet.
B— 6,210 feet.
C— 6,405 feet.

The maximum landing percentages for turboprop small transport category airplanes are 60% at destination and 70% at alternate of effective runway length (actual runway minus shaded obstruction clearance portion). Compute for runway 24 as follows:

    10,350
    – 1,200
     9,150 x .7 = 6,405

(PLT008) — 14 CFR §§135.385, 135.387, 135.397

ATS
8118. (Refer to Figure 1.) What is the maximum landing distance that may be used by a reciprocating-engine-powered, small transport category airplane to land on Rwy 24 (dry) at the destination airport?

A— 5,490 feet.
B— 6,210 feet.
C— 6,405 feet.

The maximum landing percentages for reciprocating transport category airplanes are 60% at destination and 70% at alternate of effective runway length (actual runway minus shaded obstruction clearance portion). Compute for runway 24 as follows:

    10,350
    – 1,200
     9,150 x .6 = 5,490

(PLT008) — 14 CFR §§135.375, 135.377, 135.397

ATS
8119. (Refer to Figure 1.) What is the maximum landing distance that may be used by a turbopropeller-powered, small transport category airplane to land on Rwy 6 (dry) at the alternate airport?

A— 5,460 feet.
B— 6,210 feet.
C— 6,370 feet.

The maximum landing percentages for turboprop small transport category airplanes are 60% at destination and 70% at alternate of effective runway length (actual runway minus shaded obstruction clearance portion). Compute for runway 6 as follows:

    10,350
    – 1,250
     9,100 x .7 = 6,370

(PLT008) — 14 CFR §§135.385, 135.387, 135.395

ATS
8120. (Refer to Figure 1.) What is the maximum landing distance that may be used by a reciprocating-engine-powered, small transport category airplane to land on Rwy 6 (dry) at the destination airport?

A— 5,460 feet.
B— 6,210 feet.
C— 6,370 feet.

The maximum landing percentages for reciprocating transport category airplanes are 60% at destination and 70% at alternate of effective runway length (actual runway minus shaded obstruction clearance portion). Compute for runway 6 as follows:

    10,350
    – 1,250
     9,100 x .6 = 5,460

(PLT008) — 14 CFR §§135.375, 135.377, 135.397

Answers

8117   [C]   8118   [A]   8119   [C]   8120   [A]

ATS
8121. (Refer to Figure 1.) What is the maximum landing distance that may be used by a turbine-engine-powered, small transport category airplane to land on Rwy 24 (dry) at the destination airport?

A— 5,460 feet.
B— 5,490 feet.
C— 6,210 feet.

The maximum landing percentages for turbine-engine-powered small transport category airplanes are 60% at destination and 70% at alternate of effective runway length (actual runway minus shaded obstruction clearance portion). Compute for runway 24 as follows:

$$\begin{array}{r} 10,350 \\ -\ 1,200 \\ \hline 9,150 \end{array} \quad x\ .6 = 5,490$$

(PLT008) — 14 CFR §§135.385, 135.387, 135.395

ATS
8122. (Refer to Figure 1.) What is the maximum landing distance that may be used by a turbine-engine-powered, small transport category airplane to land on Rwy 6 (wet) at the destination airport?

A— 5,460 feet.
B— 9,100 feet.
C— 6,279 feet.

The maximum landing percentages for turbine-engine-powered small transport category airplanes are 60% at destination and 70% at alternate of effective runway length (actual runway minus shaded obstruction clearance portion). Compute for runway 6 as follows:

$$\begin{array}{r} 10,350 \\ -\ 1,250 \\ \hline 9,100 \end{array} \quad x\ .6 = 5,460$$

14 CFR §135.385 is misleading here because you must increase actual landing distance by 115% to find the effective runway length wet, but the question asks for maximum landing distance, not effective landing distance. (PLT008) — 14 CFR §§135.385, 135.387, 135.395

ATS
8123. (Refer to Figure 2.) What is the maximum landing distance that may be used by a turbopropeller-powered, small transport category airplane to land on Rwy 19 (dry) at the destination airport?

A— 6,020 feet.
B— 5,820 feet.
C— 5,160 feet.

The maximum landing percentages for turboprop small transport category airplanes are 60% at destination and 70% at alternate of effective runway length (actual runway minus shaded obstruction clearance portion). Compute for runway 19 as follows:

$$\begin{array}{r} 9,700 \\ -\ 1,100 \\ \hline 8,600 \end{array} \quad x\ .6 = 5,160$$

(PLT008) — 14 CFR §§135.377, 135.385, 135.387, 135.397

ATS
8124. (Refer to Figure 2.) What is the maximum landing distance that may be used by a reciprocating-engine-powered, small transport category airplane to land on Rwy 1 (dry) at the destination airport?

A— 5,010 feet.
B— 5,820 feet.
C— 5,845 feet.

The maximum landing percentages for reciprocating transport category airplanes are 60% at destination and 70% at alternate of effective runway length (actual runway minus shaded obstruction clearance portion). Compute for runway 1 as follows:

$$\begin{array}{r} 9,700 \\ -\ 1,350 \\ \hline 8,350 \end{array} \quad x\ .6 = 5,010$$

(PLT008) — 14 CFR §§135.375, 135.377, 135.395

ATS
8125. (Refer to Figure 2.) What is the maximum landing distance that may be used by a turbine-engine-powered, small transport category airplane to land on Rwy 1 (dry) at the destination airport?

A— 5,010 feet.
B— 5,820 feet.
C— 5,845 feet.

The maximum landing percentages for turbine-engine-powered small transport category airplanes are 60% at destination and 70% at alternate of effective runway length (actual runway minus shaded obstruction clearance portion). Compute for runway 1 as follows:

$$\begin{array}{r} 9,700 \\ -\ 1,350 \\ \hline 8,350 \end{array} \quad x\ .6 = 5,010$$

(PLT008) — 14 CFR §§135.385, 135.387, 135.395

Answers

8121 [B]   8122 [A]   8123 [C]   8124 [A]   8125 [A]

ATS
8126. (Refer to Figure 2.) What is the maximum landing distance that may be used by a turbine-engine-powered, small transport category airplane to land on Rwy 19 (dry) at the destination airport?

A— 5,160 feet.
B— 5,820 feet.
C— 6,020 feet.

The maximum landing percentages for turbine-engine-powered small transport category airplanes are 60% at destination and 70% at alternate of effective runway length (actual runway minus shaded obstruction clearance portion). Compute for runway 19 as follows:

$$9,700$$
$$- 1,100$$
$$\overline{8,600} \; x\,.6 = 5,160$$

(PLT008) — 14 CFR §§135.385, 135.387, 135.395

ATS
8127. (Refer to Figure 2.) May a small transport category, turbine-engine-powered airplane that has a computed landing distance of 5,500 feet use one or both of the runways depicted in the illustration at the destination airport?

A— Neither Rwy 1 nor Rwy 19 may be used if dry conditions exist.
B— Only Rwy 19 may be used provided dry conditions exist.
C— Rwy 1 or Rwy 19 may be used whether conditions are wet or dry.

The maximum landing percentages for turbine-engine-powered small transport category airplanes are 60% at destination and 70% at alternate of effective runway length (actual runway minus shaded obstruction clearance portion). Compute as follows:

1. *Runway 1*

$$9,700$$
$$- 1,350$$
$$\overline{8,350} \; x\,.6 = 5,010$$

2. *Runway 19*

$$9,700$$
$$- 1,100$$
$$\overline{8,600} \; x\,.6 = 5,160$$

3. *Computed landing distance is given as 5,500. Since computed landing distance exceeds both runway landing distances even in dry conditions, neither runway 1 nor 19 may be used if dry conditions exist.*

(PLT456) — 14 CFR §135.385

ATS
8128. (Refer to Figure 2.) May a small transport category, turboprop airplane that has a computed landing distance of 6,000 feet use either or both runways depicted in the illustration at the destination airport?

A— Only Rwy 19 may be used if dry conditions exist.
B— Neither Rwy 1 nor Rwy 19 may be used under any conditions.
C— Either Rwy 1 or Rwy 19 may be used whether conditions are wet or dry.

The maximum landing percentages for turboprop small transport category airplanes are 60% at destination and 70% at alternate of effective runway length (actual runway minus shaded obstruction clearance portion). Compute as follows:

1. *Runway 1*

$$9,700$$
$$- 1,350$$
$$\overline{8,350} \; x\,.6 = 5,010$$

2. *Runway 19*

$$9,700$$
$$- 1,100$$
$$\overline{8,600} \; x\,.6 = 5,160$$

3. *Computed landing distance is given as 6,000; therefore neither runway may be used.*

(PLT456) — 14 CFR §§135.385, 135.387, 135.395

ATS
8129. (Refer to Figure 2.) What is the maximum landing distance that may be used for a non-transport category, turbopropeller-driven airplane to land on Rwy 1 (dry) at the alternate airport?

A— 5,010 feet.
B— 5,845 feet.
C— 6,020 feet.

The maximum landing percentages for turboprop small transport category airplanes are 60% at destination and 70% at alternate of effective runway length (actual runway minus shaded obstruction clearance portion). Compute as follows:

$$9,700$$
$$- 1,350$$
$$\overline{8,350} \; x\,.7 = 5,845$$

(PLT008) — 14 CFR §§135.385, 135.387, 135.395

Answers

8126 [A]   8127 [A]   8128 [B]   8129 [B]

ATS
8130. (Refer to Figure 2.) Which condition meets 14 CFR Part 135 operational requirements for a small, transport category, turboprop airplane to land at the destination airport that has the runway environment given in the illustration?

A— The airport may be listed as the destination airport if the landing distance does not exceed 5,160 feet for Rwy 19.

B— The airport may NOT be listed as the destination airport if the landing distance exceeds 5,100 feet for Rwy 19.

C— The airport may be listed as the destination airport if the landing distance does not exceed 5,350 feet for either runway, wet or dry conditions.

The maximum landing percentages for turboprop small transport category airplanes are 60% at destination and 70% at alternate of effective runway length (actual runway minus shaded obstruction clearance portion). Compute as follows:

1. *Runway 1*

$$\begin{array}{r} 9{,}700 \\ -\ 1{,}350 \\ \hline 8{,}350 \end{array} \ \times .6 = 5{,}010$$

2. *Runway 19*

$$\begin{array}{r} 9{,}700 \\ -\ 1{,}100 \\ \hline 8{,}600 \end{array} \ \times .6 = 5{,}160$$

3. *The best answer is to not exceed 5,160 feet.*

(PLT456) — 14 CFR §135.385

Cessna 208 Performance Tables

The Cessna 208 performance tables start with FAA Figure 392 and continue through Figure 403. With Cessna charts, be sure to always read closely the "Notes" associated with a particular chart. A good example of why it's important to read the Notes is shown in the "Engine torque on takeoff" charts in Figures 392 and 393. The inertial separator is set to "Normal" for the chart readings, but when it is placed in bypass, adjustments need to be made. For example, in Figure 392, if you calculate a maximum torque setting of 1,750, you will have to decrease the torque setting by 15 (*see* Note 3).

The takeoff and landing distance charts (FAA Figures 395 and 402) are tabular charts that often require interpolation to obtain accurate results. For example, a landing ground-roll distance is needed (Figure 402) for a sea level airport at 20°C. Examining the chart, this distance is 930 feet. But it gets more complicated if the pressure altitude is 1,000 feet. In this case, the value would be halfway between the sea level value of 930 and the 2,000-foot value of 1,000—or, 965 feet (930 + 1,000 = 1,930 ÷ 2 = 965).

Sometimes the interpolation requires a calculation beyond the simple "halfway-in-between" two published values. There are a few techniques available for solving these problems but the basic idea is to set up a ratio. Let's say the pressure altitude in the above example is a field elevation of 683 feet. We know from the chart that between sea level and 2,000 feet (a difference of 2,000), the ground roll increased 70 feet. That makes a ratio of 70/2000, or, for every 2,000 feet, the ground roll increases by 70 feet. (Note that this relationship only works at *this* altitude, and will change at the higher altitudes.)

In the example, calculate how many feet the ground roll increases when the pressure altitude increases 683 feet. To do this, we cross-multiply: just multiply 683 by 70, and divide by 2,000. This yields 24 feet. Therefore, add 24 to the 930 sea level value, and calculate a ground roll of 954 feet at a pressure altitude of 683 feet. Interpolation can also work between temperature settings.

Again—don't forget to read the Notes in these chart figures; sometimes they can be found on a further page as in FAA Figure 401.

Answers

8130   [A]

ATS, DSP

8505. (Refer to Figures 298, 401, and 402.) With an OAT of 30°C, inertial separator set to Normal, 10 knots of headwind, and a gross weight of 8,500 pounds, you calculate the landing roll to be about

A— 1,080 feet.
B— 1,200 feet.
C— 2,140 feet.

1. *On Figure 298, note the field elevation of 5,837 feet.*

2. *On Figure 402, find the pressure altitude of 4,000 and 6,000 feet at 30°C and note 1,115 feet (at 4,000 feet pressure altitude) and 1,200 feet (at 6,000 feet pressure altitude). Interpolating for 5,837 feet, calculate a ground roll of 1,193 feet.*

3. *Due to the 10-knot headwind, reduce this distance by 9.1% (reduce 10% for each 11 knots of headwind—see Figure 401 for the corresponding note): 1,193 – 109 = 1,084 feet.*

(PLT008) — FAA-H-8083-25

ATS, DSP

8506. (Refer to Figures 299 and 409.) What is your landing distance over a 50-foot obstacle at 10°C and 8,500 pounds?

A— 1,715 feet.
B— 965 feet.
C— 1,747 feet.

1. *On Figure 299, note the field elevation of 647 feet.*

2. *On Figure 409, find the sea level and 2,000-foot pressure altitudes and move across to the right until you find the distances to clear a 50-foot obstacle. Note the 1,715 feet at sea level and the 1,815 feet at 2,000 feet pressure altitude. Interpolating for the field elevation of 647 feet, calculate a distance of 1,747 feet.*

(PLT008) — FAA-H-8083-25

ATS, DSP

8507. (Refer to Figures 295 and 409.) Calculate your landing distance with an OAT of 20°C.

A— 1,000 feet.
B— 1,016 feet.
C— 1,884 feet.

1. *On Figure 295, note the field elevation of 2,417 feet.*

2. *On Figure 409, find the 2,000-foot pressure altitude and the 4,000-foot pressure altitude. Move across to the right until you find the ground roll distances at 20°C. Note the 1,000 feet at 2,000-foot pressure altitude and the 1,075 feet at 4,000-foot pressure altitude. Interpolating for the field elevation of 2,417 feet, calculate a distance of 1,016 feet.*

(PLT008) — FAA-H-8083-25

ATS, DSP

8508. (Refer to Figure 409.) Given the following conditions, what would your distance to clear a 50-foot obstacle be?

Pressure Altitude .... 2,000 feet
OAT .... 40°C
Wind ....calm
Weight .... 8,500 pounds
Runway condition ....Paved, level and dry

A— 1,960 feet.
B— 1,070 feet.
C— 1,742 feet.

On Figure 409, find the 2,000-foot pressure altitude and move across until you intersect the 40°C column. Note the 1,960 feet needed to clear the 50-foot obstacle. (PLT008) — FAA-H-8083-25

ATS, DSP

8509. (Refer to Figure 409.) Given the following conditions, what would your ground roll distance be?

Pressure Altitude .... 4,000 feet
OAT .... 15°C
Wind ....calm
Weight .... 8,500 pounds
Runway condition ....Paved, level and dry

A— 1,040 feet.
B— 1,058 feet.
C— 1,075 feet.

On Figure 409, find the 4,000-foot pressure altitude and move across until you intersect the 10°C and 20°C columns. Note the ground roll distances of 1,040 feet for 10°C and 1,075 feet for 20°C feet. Interpolating for 15°C, find a value of 1,058 feet. (PLT008) — FAA-H-8083-25

Answers

8505 [A]   8506 [C]   8507 [B]   8508 [A]   8509 [B]

ATS, DSP

8510. (Refer to Figure 409.) Given the following conditions, what would your ground roll distance be?

Pressure Altitude .... 1,000 feet
OAT .... -10°C
Wind ....calm
Weight .... 8,500 pounds
Runway condition ....Paved, level and dry

A— 868 feet.
B— 835 feet.
C— 900 feet.

On Figure 409, find the sea level and 2,000-foot pressure altitudes and move across until you intersect the -10°C. Note the ground roll distances of 835 feet at sea level and 900 feet at the 2,000-foot pressure altitude. Interpolating for 1,000 feet pressure altitude, find a value of 868 feet. (PLT008) — FAA-H-8083-25

ATS, DSP

8511. (Refer to Figures 342 and 409.) Calculate your landing distance with an OAT of 5°C.

A— 865 feet.
B— 883 feet.
C— 900 feet.

1. On Figure 342, note the field elevation of 10 feet.

2. On Figure 409, find the sea level pressure altitude. Move across to the right until you find the ground roll distances at 0°C and at 10°C. Note the 0°C distance of 865 feet, and the 10°C distance of 900 feet. Interpolating for the temperature of 5°C, calculate a distance of 883 feet.

(PLT008) — FAA-H-8083-25

ATS, DSP

8512. (Refer to Figures 327 and 409.) Calculate your landing distance over a 50-foot obstacle with an OAT of 10°C.

A— 2,135 feet.
B— 2,030 feet.
C— 2,155 feet.

1. On Figure 327, note the field elevation of 7,680 feet.

2. On Figure 409, find the pressure altitudes of 6,000 and 8,000 feet. Move across to the right until you find the 10°C distances over a 50-foot obstacle at both pressure altitudes. Note the distance of 2,030 feet at the pressure altitude of 6,000 feet, and the distance of 2,155 at the pressure altitude of 8,000 feet. Interpolating for the field elevation of 7,680 feet, calculate a distance of 883 feet.

(PLT008) — FAA-H-8083-25

BE1900 Performance

DSP

9894. (Refer to Figure 12.) Given the following conditions, what is the minimum torque for takeoff?

Pressure altitude... 9,000 ft
Temperature (OAT)..+3°C
Ice vanes .... Extended

A— 3,100 foot-pound.
B— 3,040 foot-pound.
C— 3,180 foot-pound.

The graph on the left of FAA Figure 12 is used if the ice vanes are extended and the graph on the right is used when the ice vanes are retracted. Enter the left-hand graph at +3°C, proceed up to 9,000 feet, then over to the left to read torque of 3,100 foot-pounds. (PLT169) — FAA-H-8083-25

DSP

9895. (Refer to Figure 12.) Given the following conditions, what is the minimum torque for takeoff?

Pressure altitude... 7,500 ft
Temperature (OAT)...+35°C
Ice vanes ....Retracted

A— 2,820 foot-pound.
B— 2,880 foot-pound.
C— 2,780 foot-pound.

The graph on the left of FAA Figure 12 is used if the ice vanes are extended and the graph on the right is used when the ice vanes are retracted. Enter the right-hand graph at +35°C, proceed up to 7,500 feet, then over to the left to read torque of 2,820 foot-pounds. (PLT169) — FAA-H-8083-25

Answers

8510 [A]	8511 [B]	8512 [A]	9894 [A]	9895 [A]

DSP
9896. Refer to Figure 12.) Given the following conditions, what is the minimum torque for takeoff?

Pressure altitude.. 7,500 ft
Temperature (OAT)... +9°C
Ice vanes .... Extended

A— 3,200 foot-pound.
B— 3,160 foot-pound.
C— 3,300 foot-pound.

The graph on the left of FAA Figure 12 is used if the ice vanes are extended and the graph on the right is used when the ice vanes are retracted. Enter the left-hand graph at +9°C, proceed up to 7,500 feet, then over to the left to read torque of 3,160 foot-pounds. (PLT169) — FAA-H-8083-25

DSP
9897. (Refer to Figure 12.) Given the following conditions, what is the minimum torque for takeoff?

Pressure altitude.. 3,500 ft
Temperature (OAT).. +43°C
Ice vanes .... Retracted

A— 3,000 foot-pound.
B— 3,050 foot-pound.
C— 3,110 foot-pound.

The graph on the left of FAA Figure 12 is used if the ice vanes are extended and the graph on the right is used when the ice vanes are retracted. Enter the right-hand graph at +43°C, proceed up to 3,500 feet, then over to the left to read torque of 3,050 foot-pounds. (PLT169) — FAA-H-8083-25

DSP
9898. (Refer to Figure 12.) Given the following conditions, what is the minimum torque for takeoff?

Pressure altitude.. 5,500 ft
Temperature (OAT).. +29°C
Ice vanes .... Retracted

A— 2,950 foot-pound.
B— 3,100 foot-pound.
C— 3,200 foot-pound.

The graph on the left of FAA Figure 12 is used if the ice vanes are extended and the graph on the right is used when the ice vanes are retracted. Enter the right-hand graph at +29°C, proceed up to 5,500 feet, then over to the left to read torque of 3,200 foot-pounds. (PLT169) — FAA-H-8083-25

DSP
9899. (Refer to Figure 13.) Given the following conditions, what is the takeoff distance over a 50-foot obstacle?

Pressure altitude.. Sea Level
Temperature (OAT).. +12°C
Weight .... 16,000 lb
Wind component..16 kts HW
Ice vanes ....Retracted

A— 1,750 feet.
B— 2,800 feet.
C— 2,550 feet.

1. *Enter FAA Figure 13 at the bottom left-hand side at +12°C OAT and proceed upward to the line representing sea level (SL) pressure altitude.*

2. *From the point of intersection on the "pressure altitude" lines, draw a horizontal line to the reference line, then parallel the line which represents an aircraft weight of 16,000 pounds.*

3. *From the point of intersection in the "weight" portion of the graph, draw a horizontal line to the next reference line (wind component), then parallel the line until intersecting with the 16-knot headwind.*

4. *From the point of intersection on the "wind" portion of the graph draw a horizontal line to the next reference line (0-foot obstacle height), then parallel the line required to clear a 50-foot obstacle.*

5. *The distance required is 2,550 feet.*

(PLT011) — FAA-H-8083-25

DSP
9900. (Refer to Figure 13.) Given the following conditions, what is the takeoff ground roll and V_1 speed?

Pressure altitude.. 4,000 ft
Temperature (OAT).. 0°C
Weight .... 15,500 lb
Wind component... 10 kts TW
Ice vanes .... Extended

A— 2,900 feet, 106 knots.
B— 4,250 feet, 102 knots.
C— 2,700 feet, 107 knots.

1. *Enter FAA Figure 13 at the bottom left-hand side at +5°C OAT (adding 5°C to the actual OAT since the ice vanes are extended) and proceed upward to the line representing 4,000 feet pressure altitude.*

2. *From the point of intersection on the "pressure altitude" lines, draw a horizontal line to the reference line, then parallel the line which represents an aircraft weight of 15,500 pounds.*

Continued

Answers

| 9896 | [B] | 9897 | [B] | 9898 | [C] | 9899 | [C] | 9900 | [A] |

3. From the point of intersection in the "weight" portion of the graph, draw a horizontal line to the next reference line (wind component), then parallel the line until intersecting with the 10-knot tailwind.

4. From the point of intersection on the "wind" portion of the graph continue to the edge of the graph to find the ground roll required: 2,900 feet.

5. The V_1 speed is found using the table in the upper right corner of FAA Figure 13. Interpolate between 16,000 and 14,000 to find 106 knots for 15,500 pounds.

(PLT011) — FAA-H-8083-25

DSP
9901. (Refer to Figure 13.) Given the following conditions, what is the takeoff distance over a 50-foot obstacle?

Pressure altitude..2,000 ft
Temperature (OAT)...+15°C
Weight ....16,600 lb
Wind component...Calm
Ice vanes ....Retracted

A— 3,400 feet.
B— 3,700 feet.
C— 4,200 feet.

1. Enter FAA Figure 13 at the bottom left-hand side at +15°C OAT and proceed upward to the line representing 2,000 feet pressure altitude.

2. From the point of intersection on the "pressure altitudes" lines, draw a horizontal line to the reference line, then parallel the line which represents an aircraft weight of 16,600 pounds.

3. Continue past the second reference line to the third reference line (since the wind is calm).

4. From the third reference line (0-foot obstacle height), parallel the line required to clear a 50-foot obstacle.

5. The distance required is 3,700 feet.

(PLT011) — FAA-H-8083-25

DSP
9902. (Refer to Figure 13.) Given the following conditions, what is the takeoff ground roll and V_1 speed?

Pressure altitude...3,000 ft
Temperature (OAT)..-10°C
Weight ....15,000 lb
Wind component...8 kts TW
Ice vanes ....Extended

A— 2,200 feet, 105 knots.
B— 2,000 feet, 113 knots.
C— 1,900 feet, 103 knots.

1. Enter FAA Figure 13 at the bottom left-hand side at -5°C OAT (adding 5°C to the actual OAT since the ice vanes are extended) and proceed upward to the line representing 3,000 feet pressure altitude.

2. From the point of intersection on the "pressure altitude" lines, draw a horizontal line to the reference line, then parallel the line which represents an aircraft weight of 15,000 pounds.

3. From the point of intersection in the "weight" portion of the graph, draw a horizontal line to the next reference line (wind component), then parallel the line until intersecting with the 8-knot tailwind.

4. From the point of intersection on the "wind" portion of the graph continue to the edge of the graph to find the ground roll required: 2,200 feet.

5. The V_1 speed is found using the table in the upper right corner of FAA Figure 13. Interpolate between 16,000 and 14,000 to find 105 knots for 15,000 pounds.

(PLT011) — FAA-H-8083-25

Answers

9901   [B]   9902   [A]

DSP

9903. (Refer to Figure 13.) Given the following conditions, what is the takeoff distance over a 50 foot obstacle?

Pressure altitude.. 6,000 ft
Temperature (OAT).. +35°C
Weight .... 14,500 lb
Wind component.. 10 kts HW
Ice vanes .... Retracted

A— 4,150 feet.
B— 4,550 feet.
C— 2,600 feet.

1. *Enter FAA Figure 13 at the bottom left-hand side at +35°C OAT and proceed upward to the line representing 6,000 feet pressure altitude.*

2. *From the point of intersection on the "pressure altitude" lines, draw a horizontal line to the reference line, then parallel the line which represents an aircraft weight of 14,500 pounds.*

3. *From the point of intersection in the "weight" portion of the graph, draw a horizontal line to the next reference line (wind component), then parallel the line until intersecting with the 10-knot headwind.*

4. *From the point of intersection on the "wind" portion of the graph draw a horizontal line to the next reference line (0-foot obstacle height), then parallel the line required to clear a 50-foot obstacle.*

5. *The distance required is 4,150 feet.*

(PLT011) — FAA-H-8083-25

DSP

8469. (Refer to Figure 14.) Given the following conditions, what is the accelerate-stop field length?

Pressure altitude.. 5,000 ft
Temperature (OAT).. +20°C
Weight .... 15,000 lb
Wind component.. 10 kts HW
Ice vanes .... Retracted

A— 6,300 feet.
B— 4,700 feet.
C— 4,300 feet.

1. *Enter FAA Figure 14 at the bottom left-hand side at +20°C OAT and proceed upward to the line representing 5,000 feet pressure altitude.*

2. *From the point of intersection on the "pressure altitude" lines, draw a horizontal line to the reference line, then parallel the line which represents an aircraft weight of 15,000 pounds.*

3. *From the point of intersection in the "weight" portion of the graph, draw a horizontal line to the next reference line (wind component), then parallel the line until intersecting with the 10-knot headwind.*

4. *Proceed from the wind line to the edge of the chart to read the accelerate/stop distance of 4,300 feet.*

(PLT011) — FAA-H-8083-25

Answers

9903   [A]   8469   [C]

DSP

8470. (Refer to Figure 14.) Given the following conditions, what is the accelerate-stop field length?

Pressure altitude..2,000 ft
Temperature (OAT)...-15°C
Weight .... 16,000 lb
Wind component..5 kts TW
Ice vanes ....Extended

A— 3,750 feet.
B— 4,600 feet.
C— 4,250 feet.

1. *Enter FAA Figure 14 at the bottom left-hand side at -12°C OAT (adding 3°C to the actual OAT for extended ice vanes) and proceed upward to the line representing 2,000 feet pressure altitude.*

2. *From the point of intersection on the "pressure altitude" lines, draw a horizontal line to the reference line, then parallel the line which represents an aircraft weight of 16,000 pounds.*

3. *From the point of intersection in the "weight" portion of the graph, draw a horizontal line to the next reference line (wind component), then parallel the line until intersecting with the 5-knot tailwind.*

4. *Proceed from the wind line to the edge of the chart to read the accelerate/stop distance of 4,250 feet.*

(PLT011) — FAA-H-8083-25

DSP

8471. (Refer to Figure 14.) Given the following conditions, what is the accelerate-stop field length?

Pressure altitude..6,000 ft
Temperature (OAT)...+10°C
Weight .... 16,600 lb
Wind component..15 kts HW
Ice vanes ....Retracted

A— 4,950 feet.
B— 4,800 feet.
C— 5,300 feet.

1. *Enter FAA Figure 14 at the bottom left-hand side at +10°C OAT and proceed upward to the line representing 6,000 feet pressure altitude.*

2. *From the point of intersection on the "pressure altitude" lines, draw a horizontal line to the reference line, then parallel the line which represents an aircraft weight of 16,600 pounds.*

3. *From the point of intersection in the "weight" portion of the graph, draw a horizontal line to the next reference line (wind component), then parallel the line until intersecting with the 15-knot headwind.*

4. *Proceed from the wind line to the edge of the chart to read the accelerate/stop distance of 4,950 feet.*

(PLT011) — FAA-H-8083-25

DSP

8472. (Refer to Figure 14.) Given the following conditions, what is the accelerate-stop field length?

Pressure altitude..8,000 ft
Temperature (OAT)..-5°C
Weight .... 14,000 lb
Wind component..4 kts TW
Ice vanes ....Extended

A— 4,500 feet.
B— 4,800 feet.
C— 5,300 feet.

1. *Enter FAA Figure 14 at the bottom left-hand side at -2°C OAT (adding 3°C to the actual OAT for extended ice vanes) and proceed upward to the line representing 8,000 feet pressure altitude.*

2. *From the point of intersection on the "pressure altitude" lines, draw a horizontal line to the reference line, then parallel the line which represents an aircraft weight of 14,000 pounds.*

3. *From the point of intersection in the "weight" portion of the graph, draw a horizontal line to the next reference line (wind component), then parallel the line until intersecting with the 4-knot tailwind.*

4. *Proceed from the wind line to the edge of the chart to read the accelerate/stop distance of 4,800 feet.*

(PLT011) — FAA-H-8083-25

DSP

8473. (Refer to Figure 14.) Given the following conditions, what is the accelerate-stop field length?

Pressure altitude... Sea Level
Temperature (OAT)...+30°C
Weight .... 13,500 lb
Wind component..14 kts HW
Ice vanes ....Retracted

A— 2,500 feet.
B— 2,850 feet.
C— 3,050 feet.

Answers

8470 [C]   8471 [A]   8472 [B]   8473 [C]

1. *Enter FAA Figure 14 at the bottom left-hand side at +30°C OAT and proceed upward to the line representing sea level (SL) pressure altitude.*

2. *From the point of intersection on the "pressure altitude" lines, draw a horizontal line to the reference line, then parallel the line which represents an aircraft weight of 13,500 pounds.*

3. *From the point of intersection in the "weight" portion of the graph, draw a horizontal line to the next reference line (wind component), then parallel the line until intersecting with the 14-knot headwind.*

4. *Proceed from the wind line to the edge of the chart to read the accelerate/stop distance of 3,050 feet.*

(PLT011) — FAA-H-8083-25

DSP
8474. (Refer to Figures 15, 16, and 17.) What is the two-engine rate of climb after takeoff in climb configuration for Operating Conditions BE-21?

A— 1,350 ft/min.
B— 2,450 ft/min.
C— 2,300 ft/min.

1. *Enter FAA Figure 16 at the bottom left-hand side at +10°C OAT and proceed upward to the line representing 2,000 feet pressure altitude.*

2. *From the point of intersection on the "pressure altitude" lines, draw a horizontal line to the reference line, then parallel the line which represents an aircraft weight of 16,600 pounds.*

3. *From the point of intersection in the "weight" portion of the graph, draw a horizontal line to the edge of the chart to read 2,300 fpm.*

(PLT004) — FAA-H-8083-25

DSP
8475. (Refer to Figures 15, 16, and 17.) What is the single-engine climb gradient after takeoff in climb configuration for Operating Conditions BE-22?

A— 6.8 percent gradient.
B— 7.5 percent gradient.
C— 5.6 percent gradient.

1. *Enter FAA Figure 17 at the bottom left-hand side at 0°C OAT and proceed upward to the line representing 1,000 feet pressure altitude.*

2. *From the point of intersection on the "pressure altitude" lines, draw a horizontal line to the reference line, then parallel the line which represents an aircraft weight of 14,000 pounds.*

3. *From the point of intersection in the "weight" portion of the graph, draw a horizontal line to the edge of the chart to read 870 fpm.*

4. *Adjust the rate of climb for the extended ice vanes, as indicated at the top of the graph. The single-engine rate of climb with ice vanes extended is 755 fpm (870 – 115).*

5. *Find 755 fpm at the right edge of the chart and proceed right to the reference line and determine a climb gradient of 5.6%.*

(PLT004) — FAA-H-8083-25

DSP
8476. (Refer to Figures 15, 16, and 17.) What is the two-engine rate of climb after takeoff in climb configuration for Operating Conditions BE-23?

A— 1,500 ft/min.
B— 2,600 ft/min.
C— 2,490 ft/min.

1. *Enter FAA Figure 16 at the bottom left-hand side at +20°C OAT and proceed upward to the line representing 3,000 feet pressure altitude.*

2. *From the point of intersection on the "pressure altitude" lines, draw a horizontal line to the reference line, then parallel the line which represents an aircraft weight of 15,000 pounds.*

3. *From the point of intersection in the "weight" portion of the graph, draw a horizontal line to the edge of the chart to read 2,600 fpm.*

(PLT004) — FAA-H-8083-25

Answers
8474 [C]   8475 [C]   8476 [B]

DSP
8477. (Refer to Figures 15, 16, and 17.) What is the two-engine rate of climb after takeoff in climb configuration for Operating Conditions BE-24?

A— 2,100 ft/min.
B— 2,400 ft/min.
C— 1,500 ft/min.

1. *Enter FAA Figure 16 at the bottom left-hand side at +25°C OAT and proceed upward to the line representing 4,000 feet pressure altitude.*

2. *From the point of intersection on the "pressure altitude" lines, draw a horizontal line to the reference line, then parallel the line which represents an aircraft weight of 16,000 pounds.*

3. *From the point of intersection in the "weight" portion of the graph, draw a horizontal line to the edge of the chart to read 2,100 fpm.*

(PLT004) — FAA-H-8083-25

DSP
8478. (Refer to Figures 15, 16, and 17.) What is the single-engine rate of climb after takeoff in climb configuration for Operating Conditions BE-25?

A— 385 ft/min.
B— 780 ft/min.
C— 665 ft/min.

1. *Enter FAA Figure 17 at the bottom left-hand side at -10°C OAT and proceed upward to the line representing 5,000 feet pressure altitude.*

2. *From the point of intersection on the "pressure altitude" lines, draw a horizontal line to the reference line, then parallel the line which represents an aircraft weight of 14,000 pounds.*

3. *From the point of intersection in the "weight" portion of the graph, draw a horizontal line to the edge of the chart to read 780 fpm.*

4. *Adjust the rate of climb for the extended ice vanes, as indicated at the top of the graph. The single-engine rate-of-climb with ice vanes extended is 665 fpm (780 – 115).*

(PLT004) — FAA-H-8083-25

DSP
9904. (Refer to Figures 15 and 18.) What are the time, fuel, and distance from the start of climb to cruise altitude for Operating Conditions BE-21?

A— 10.0 minutes; 290 pounds; 35 NM.
B— 10.0 minutes; 165 pounds; 30 NM.
C— 11.5 minutes; 165 pounds; 30 NM.

1. *Enter FAA Figure 18 at the bottom left-hand side at -20°C OAT and proceed upward to the line representing 16,000-foot cruise altitude.*

2. *From the point of intersection on the "pressure altitude" lines, draw a horizontal line to the line which represents an aircraft weight of 16,600 pounds.*

3. *From the point of intersection in the "weight" portion of the graph, draw a line down to the bottom of the chart to read the time to climb of 11.5 minutes.*

4. *Continue down to the fuel to climb line to read 190 pounds fuel burned.*

5. *Continue down to the distance-to-climb line to read 32 NM.*

6. *Repeat steps 1 through 5 using an OAT of +10°C OAT and 2,000 feet pressure altitude, and find the time to climb 1.5 minutes, fuel burn 25 pounds, and distance 2 NM.*

7. *Subtract the results of the airport altitudes from the cruise altitude results. Therefore, from 2,000 feet to 16,000 feet, it will take 10 minutes (11.5 – 1.5), 165 pounds of fuel (190 – 25), and 30 NM (32 – 2).*

(PLT012) — FAA-H-8083-25

DSP
9905. (Refer to Figures 15 and 18.) What are the time, fuel, and distance from the start of climb to cruise altitude for Operating Conditions BE-22?

A— 12.0 minutes; 220 pounds; 40 NM.
B— 11.0 minutes; 185 pounds; 37 NM.
C— 10.5 minutes; 175 pounds; 32 NM.

1. *Enter FAA Figure 18 at the bottom left-hand side at -15°C OAT (accounting for the extended ice vanes) and proceed upward to the line representing 18,000-foot cruise altitude.*

2. *From the point of intersection on the "pressure altitude" lines, draw a horizontal line to the line which represents an aircraft weight of 14,000 pounds.*

3. *From the point of intersection in the "weight" portion of the graph, draw a line down to the bottom of the chart to read the time to climb of 12 minutes.*

Answers

8477 [A]	8478 [C]	9904 [B]	9905 [B]

4. *Continue down to the fuel-to-climb line to read 200 pounds fuel burned.*

5. *Continue down to the distance-to-climb line to read 37.5 NM.*

6. *Repeat steps 1 through 5 using an OAT of +10°C OAT and 1,000 feet pressure altitude, and find the time to climb 1 minute, fuel burn 15 pounds, and distance 0.5 NM.*

7. *Subtract the results of the airport altitudes from the cruise altitude results. Therefore, from 1,000 feet to 18,000 feet, it will take 11 minutes (12 – 1), 185 pounds of fuel (200 – 15), and 37 NM (37.5 – 0.5).*

(PLT012) — FAA-H-8083-25

DSP

9906. (Refer to Figures 15 and 18.) What are the time, fuel, and distance from the start of climb to cruise altitude for Operating Conditions BE-23?

A— 13.0 minutes; 180 pounds; 35 NM.
B— 14.0 minutes; 210 pounds; 40 NM.
C— 15.0 minutes; 240 pounds; 46 NM.

1. *Enter FAA Figure 18 at the bottom left-hand side at ISA and proceed upward to the line representing 20,000-foot cruise altitude.*

2. *From the point of intersection on the "pressure altitude" lines, draw a horizontal line to the line which represents an aircraft weight of 15,000 pounds.*

3. *From the point of intersection in the "weight" portion of the graph, draw a line down to the bottom of the chart to read the time to climb of 15 minutes.*

4. *Continue down to the fuel-to-climb line to read 235 pounds fuel burned.*

5. *Continue down to the distance-to-climb line to read 44 NM.*

6. *Repeat steps 1 through 5 using an OAT of +20°C OAT and 3,000 feet pressure altitude, and find the time to climb 1 minutes, fuel burn 25 pounds, and distance 4 NM.*

7. *Subtract the results of the airport altitudes from the cruise altitude results. Therefore, from 3,000 feet to 20,000 feet, it will take 14 minutes (15 – 1), 210 pounds of fuel (235 – 25), and 40 NM (44 – 4).*

(PLT012) — FAA-H-8083-25

DSP

8482. (Refer to Figures 15 and 18.) What are the time, fuel, and distance from the start of climb to cruise altitude for Operating Conditions BE-24?

A— 12.0 minutes; 220 pounds; 45 NM.
B— 9.0 minutes; 185 pounds; 38 NM.
C— 10.0 minutes; 170 pounds; 30 NM.

1. *Enter FAA Figure 18 at the bottom left-hand side at 0°C OAT and proceed upward to the line representing 14,000-foot cruise altitude.*

2. *From the point of intersection on the "pressure altitude" lines, draw a horizontal line to the line which represents an aircraft weight of 16,000 pounds.*

3. *From the point of intersection in the "weight" portion of the graph, draw a line down to the bottom of the chart to read the time to climb of 13 minutes.*

4. *Continue down to the fuel-to-climb line to read 210 pounds fuel burned.*

5. *Continue down to the distance-to-climb line to read 38 NM.*

6. *Repeat steps 1 through 5 using an OAT of +25°C OAT and 4,000 feet pressure altitude, and find the time to climb 3 minutes, fuel burn 60 pounds, and distance 8 NM.*

7. *Subtract the results of the airport altitudes from the cruise altitude results. Therefore, from 4,000 feet to 14,000 feet, it will take 10 minutes (13 – 3), 150 pounds of fuel (210 – 60), and 30 NM (38 – 8).*

(PLT004) — FAA-H-8083-25

DSP

8483. (Refer to Figures 15 and 18.) What are the time, fuel, and distance from the start of climb to cruise altitude for Operating Conditions BE-25?

A— 11.5 minutes; 170 pounds; 31 NM.
B— 8.0 minutes; 270 pounds; 28 NM.
C— 12.5 minutes; 195 pounds; 38 NM.

1. *Enter FAA Figure 18 at the bottom left-hand side at -30°C OAT (accounting for the extended ice vanes) and proceed upward to the line representing 22,000-foot cruise altitude.*

2. *From the point of intersection on the "pressure altitude" lines, draw a horizontal line to the line which represents an aircraft weight of 14,000 pounds.*

3. *From the point of intersection in the "weight" portion of the graph, draw a line down to the bottom of the chart to read the time to climb of 14.5 minutes.*

Continued

Answers

9906 [B]   8482 [C]   8483 [C]

4. *Continue down to the fuel-to-climb line to read 235 pounds fuel burned.*

5. *Continue down to the distance-to-climb line to read 44 NM.*

6. *Repeat steps 1 through 5 using an OAT of 0°C OAT and 5,000 feet pressure altitude, and find the time to climb 2 minutes, fuel burn 40 pounds, and distance 6 NM.*

7. *Subtract the results of the airport altitudes from the cruise altitude results. Therefore, from 5,000 feet to 22,000 feet, it will take 12.5 minutes (14.5 – 2), 195 pounds of fuel (235 – 40), and 38 NM (44 – 6).*

(PLT012) — FAA-H-8083-25

DSP
8484. (Refer to Figures 19 and 20.) At what altitude is the service ceiling with one engine inoperative for Operating Conditions BE-26?

A— 13,000 feet.
B— 14,200 feet.
C— 13,600 feet.

1. *Enter FAA Figure 20 at the bottom left-hand side (for bleed air on) at -8°C OAT and proceed upward to the line representing 15,500 pounds.*

2. *From the point of intersection in the "weight" portion of the graph, draw a line to the edge of the chart to determine a pressure altitude service ceiling of 13,000 feet with one engine inoperative.*

(PLT065) — FAA-H-8083-25

DSP
8485. (Refer to Figures 19 and 20.) Which statement is true regarding performance with one engine inoperative for Operating Conditions BE-27?

A— Climb rate at the MEA is more than 50 ft/min.
B— Service ceiling is below the MEA.
C— Bleed air OFF improves service ceiling by 3,000 feet.

1. *Enter FAA Figure 20 at the bottom left-hand side (for bleed air on) at +30°C OAT and proceed upward to the line representing 16,600 pounds.*

2. *From the point of intersection in the "weight" portion of the graph, draw a line to the edge of the chart to determine a pressure altitude service ceiling of 5,000 feet with one engine inoperative.*

3. *Therefore, the 5,000-foot service ceiling is below the MEA of 5,500 feet.*

(PLT065) — FAA-H-8083-25

DSP
8486. (Refer to Figures 19 and 20.) At what altitude is the service ceiling with one engine inoperative for Operating Conditions BE-28?

A— 1,500 feet above the MEA.
B— 10,400 feet.
C— 11,800 feet.

1. *Enter FAA Figure 20 at the bottom right-hand side (for bleed air off) at +5°C OAT and proceed upward to the line representing 16,000 pounds.*

2. *From the point of intersection in the "weight" portion of the graph, draw a line to the edge of the chart to determine a pressure altitude service ceiling of 11,800 feet with one engine inoperative.*

3. *11,800 feet is 2,800 feet above the 9,000-foot MEA.*

(PLT065) — FAA-H-8083-25

DSP
8487. (Refer to Figures 19 and 20.) Which statement is true regarding performance with one engine inoperative for Operating Conditions BE-29?

A— Service ceiling is more than 100 feet above the MEA.
B— Bleed air must be OFF to obtain a rate of climb of 50 ft/min at the MEA.
C— Climb is not possible at the MEA.

1. *Enter FAA Figure 20 at the bottom left-hand side (for bleed air on) at +18°C OAT and proceed upward to the line representing 16,300 pounds.*

2. *From the point of intersection in the "weight" portion of the graph, draw a line to the edge of the chart to determine a pressure altitude service ceiling of 7,700 feet with one engine inoperative.*

3. *Therefore, the 7,700-foot service ceiling is above the MEA of 7,000 feet by more than 100 feet.*

(PLT065) — FAA-H-8083-25

DSP
8488. (Refer to Figures 19 and 20.) At what altitude is the service ceiling with one engine inoperative for Operating Conditions BE-30?

A— 9,600 feet.
B— 13,200 feet.
C— 2,100 feet above the MEA.

Answers

8484 [A]	8485 [B]	8486 [C]	8487 [A]	8488 [C]

1. Enter FAA Figure 20 at the bottom right-hand side (for bleed air off) at +22°C OAT and proceed upward to the line representing 14,500 pounds.

2. From the point of intersection in the "weight" portion of the graph, draw a line to the edge of the chart to determine a pressure altitude service ceiling of 11,600 feet with one engine inoperative.

3. Therefore, the 11,600-foot service ceiling is above the MEA of 9,500 feet.

(PLT065) — FAA-H-8083-25

DSP
8489. (Refer to Figures 21, 22, 23, 24, and 25.) What is the en route time of the cruise leg for Operating Conditions BE-31?

A— 1 hour 11 minutes.
B— 1 hour 17 minutes.
C— 1 hour 19 minutes.

Temperature = ISA +10°C
TAS = 228 knots
GS = 216.0 knots
Time = 1 hour 17 minutes 47 seconds

(PLT012) — FAA-H-8083-25

DSP
8490. (Refer to Figures 21, 22, 23, 24, and 25.) What is the en route time of the cruise leg for Operating Conditions BE-32?

A— 1 hour 13 minutes.
B— 1 hour 15 minutes.
C— 1 hour 20 minutes.

Temperature = -19°C
TAS = 252 knots
GS = 261.8 knots
Time = 1 hour 13 minutes 20 seconds

(PLT012) — FAA-H-8083-25

DSP
8491. (Refer to Figures 21, 22, 23, 24, and 25.) What is the en route time of the cruise leg for Operating Conditions BE-33?

A— 1 hour 50 minutes.
B— 1 hour 36 minutes.
C— 1 hour 46 minutes.

Temperature = ISA -10°C
TAS = 256.5 knots
GS = 225.2 knots
Time = 1 hour 46 minutes 33 seconds

(PLT012) — FAA-H-8083-25

DSP
8492. (Refer to Figures 21, 22, 23, 24, and 25.) What is the en route time of the cruise leg for Operating Conditions BE-34?

A— 1 hour 7 minutes.
B— 1 hour 2 minutes.
C— 1 hour 12 minutes.

Temperature = ISA
TAS = 228 knots
GS = 208 knots
Time = 1 hour 06 minutes 15 seconds

(PLT012) — FAA-H-8083-25

DSP
8493. (Refer to Figures 21, 22, 23, 24, and 25.) What is the en route time of the cruise leg for Operating Conditions BE-35?

A— 1 hour 6 minutes.
B— 1 hour 8 minutes.
C— 1 hour 10 minutes.

Temperature = ISA +10°C
TAS = 253 knots
GS = 252.4 knots
Time = 1 hour 11 minutes 19 seconds

(PLT012) — FAA-H-8083-25

DSP
8494. (Refer to Figures 21, 22, 23, 24, and 25.) What is the fuel consumption during the cruise leg for Operating Conditions BE-31?

A— 812 pounds.
B— 749 pounds.
C— 870 pounds.

Temperature = ISA +10°C
Time = 1 hour 17 minutes (see Question 8489)
Fuel flow = 633
Fuel burn = 812.3 pounds

(PLT012) — FAA-H-8083-25

Answers

8489 [B]	8490 [A]	8491 [C]	8492 [A]	8493 [C]	8494 [A]

DSP
8495. (Refer to Figures 21, 22, 23, 24, and 25.) What is the fuel consumption during the cruise leg for Operating Conditions BE-32?

A— 1,028 pounds.
B— 896 pounds.
C— 977 pounds.

Temperature = ISA
Time = 1 hour 13 minutes (see Question 8490)
Fuel flow = 803
Fuel burn = 977.0 pounds

(PLT012) — FAA-H-8083-25

DSP
8496. (Refer to Figures 21, 22, 23, 24, and 25.) What is the fuel consumption during the cruise leg for Operating Conditions BE-33?

A— 1,165 pounds.
B— 1,373 pounds.
C— 976 pounds.

Temperature = ISA -10°C
Time = 1 hour 46 minutes (see Question 8491)
Fuel flow = 777
Fuel burn = 1,372.7 pounds

(PLT012) — FAA-H-8083-25

DSP
8497. (Refer to Figures 21, 22, 23, 24, and 25.) What is the fuel consumption during the cruise leg for Operating Conditions BE-34?

A— 668 pounds.
B— 718 pounds.
C— 737 pounds.

Temperature = ISA
Time = 1 hour 06 minutes (see Question 8492)
Fuel flow = 653
Fuel burn = 718.3 pounds

(PLT012) — FAA-H-8083-25

DSP
8498. (Refer to Figures 21, 23, 24, and 25.) What is the fuel consumption during the cruise leg for Operating Conditions BE-35?

A— 900 pounds.
B— 1,030 pounds.
C— 954 pounds.

Temperature = ISA +10°C
Time = 1 hour 10 minutes (see Question 8493)
Fuel flow = 818
Fuel burn = 954.3 pounds

(PLT012) — FAA-H-8083-25

DSP
8499. (Refer to Figure 26.) What are the time and distance to descend from 18,000 feet to 2,500 feet?

A— 10.3 minutes, 39 NM.
B— 9.8 minutes, 33 NM.
C— 10.0 minutes, 36 NM.

Enter FAA Figure 26 from initial pressure altitude on the left side of the graph. Proceed to heavy reference line, then drop to minutes, pounds and/or distance scales as needed. Repeat this process with the final altitude.

	Time	NM
Descent to SL	12.0	45
Field alt.	− 1.5	− 5
Descent	10.5	40

(PLT012) — FAA-H-8083-25

DSP
8500. (Refer to Figure 26.) What are the distance and fuel consumption to descend from 22,000 feet to 4,500 feet?

A— 44 NAM, 117 pounds.
B— 48 NAM, 112 pounds.
C— 56 NAM, 125 pounds.

Enter FAA Figure 26 from initial pressure altitude on the left side of the graph. Proceed to heavy reference line, then drop to minutes, pounds and/or distance scales as needed. Repeat this process with the final altitude.

	NM	Fuel
Descent to SL	58	142
Field alt.	− 10	− 30
Descent	48	112

(PLT012) — FAA-H-8083-25

Answers

8495 [C] 8496 [B] 8497 [B] 8498 [C] 8499 [A] 8500 [B]

DSP

8501. (Refer to Figure 26.) What are the time and distance to descend from 16,500 feet to 3,500 feet?

A— 9.3 minutes, 37 NAM.
B— 9.1 minutes, 35 NAM.
C— 8.7 minutes, 33 NAM.

Enter FAA Figure 26 from initial pressure altitude on the left side of the graph. Proceed to heavy reference line, then drop to minutes, pounds and/or distance scales as needed. Repeat this process with the final altitude.

	Time	NM
Descent to SL	11.1	41
Field alt.	– 2.4	– 8
Descent	8.7	33

(PLT045) — FAA-H-8083-25

DSP

8502. (Refer to Figure 26.) What are the distance and fuel consumption to descend from 13,500 feet to 1,500 feet?

A— 30 NAM, 87 pounds.
B— 29 NAM, 80 pounds.
C— 38 NAM, 100 pounds.

Enter FAA Figure 26 from initial pressure altitude on the left side of the graph. Proceed to heavy reference line, then drop to minutes, pounds and/or distance scales as needed. Repeat this process with the final altitude.

	NM	Fuel
Descent to SL	32.5	90
Field alt.	– 3.5	– 10
Descent	29	80

(PLT045) — FAA-H-8083-25

DSP

8503. (Refer to Figure 26.) What are the time and distance to descend from 23,000 feet to 600 feet with an average 15-knot headwind?

A— 14.2 minutes, 50 NAM.
B— 14.6 minutes, 56 NAM.
C— 14.9 minutes, 59 NAM.

Enter FAA Figure 26 from initial pressure altitude on the left side of the graph. Proceed to heavy reference line, then drop to minutes, pounds and/or distance scales as needed. Repeat this process with the final altitude.

	Time	NM
Descent to SL	15.4	62
Field alt.	– .5	– 2
Descent	14.9	60

Note: The answers are in NM so no wind correction is necessary.

(PLT045) — FAA-H-8083-25

DSP

8504. (Refer to Figures 27 and 28.) What is the landing distance over a 50-foot obstacle for Operating Conditions B-36?

A— 1,900 feet.
B— 1,625 feet.
C— 950 feet.

1. *Enter FAA Figure 28 at the bottom left-hand side at +30°C OAT and proceed upward to the line representing sea level (SL) pressure altitude.*

2. *From the point of intersection on the "pressure altitude" lines, draw a horizontal line to the reference line, then parallel the line which represents an aircraft weight of 16,000 pounds.*

3. *From the point of intersection in the "weight" portion of the graph, draw a horizontal line to the next reference line (wind component), then parallel the line until intersecting with the 20-knot headwind.*

4. *From the point of intersection on the "wind" portion of the graph draw a horizontal line to the next reference line (0-foot obstacle height), then parallel the line required to clear a 50-foot obstacle.*

5. *The distance required is 1,900 feet.*

(PLT008) — FAA-H-8083-25

Answers

8501	[C]	8502	[B]	8503	[C]	8504	[A]

DSP
9907. (Refer to Figures 27 and 28.) What are the approach speed and ground roll when landing under Operating Conditions B-36?

A— 113 knots and 950 feet.
B— 113 knots and 1,950 feet.
C— 112 knots and 900 feet.

1. *Enter FAA Figure 28 at the bottom left-hand side at +30°C OAT and proceed upward to the line representing sea level (SL) pressure altitude.*

2. *From the point of intersection on the "pressure altitude" lines, draw a horizontal line to the reference line, then parallel the line which represents an aircraft weight of 16,000 pounds.*

3. *From the point of intersection in the "weight" portion of the graph, draw a horizontal line to the next reference line (wind component), then parallel the line until intersecting with the 20-knot headwind.*

4. *From the point of intersection on the "wind" portion of the graph draw a horizontal line to the edge of the chart to find a ground roll of 950 feet.*

5. *The approach speed is found using the table at the top of figure. Interpolate between 16,100 and 14,000 to find the approach speed for 16,000 pounds at 113 knots.*

(PLT008) — FAA-H-8083-25

DSP
9908. (Refer to Figures 27 and 28.) What is the remaining runway length when stopped after landing over a 50-foot obstacle for Operating Conditions B-37?

A— 2,500 feet.
B— 2,000 feet.
C— 2,600 feet.

1. *Enter FAA Figure 28 at the bottom left-hand side at +16°C OAT and proceed upward to the line representing 1,000 feet pressure altitude.*

2. *From the point of intersection on the "pressure altitude" lines, draw a horizontal line to the reference line, then parallel the line which represents an aircraft weight of 14,500 pounds.*

3. *From the point of intersection in the "weight" portion of the graph, draw a horizontal line to the next reference line (wind component), then parallel the line until intersecting with the 10-knot tailwind.*

4. *From the point of intersection on the "wind" portion of the graph draw a horizontal line to the next reference line (0-foot obstacle height), then parallel the line required to clear a 50-foot obstacle.*

5. *The distance required is 2,500 feet.*

6. *The remaining runway length when stopped is the runway distance minus the distance required, which is 2,000 feet (4,500 – 2,500).*

(PLT008) — FAA-H-8083-25

DSP
9909. (Refer to Figures 27 and 28.) What are the approach speed and ground roll when landing under Operating Conditions B-37?

A— 108 knots and 1,400 feet.
B— 109 knots and 900 feet.
C— 107 knots and 1,350 feet.

1. *Enter FAA Figure 28 at the bottom left-hand side at +16°C OAT and proceed upward to the line representing 1,000 feet pressure altitude.*

2. *From the point of intersection on the "pressure altitude" lines, draw a horizontal line to the reference line, then parallel the line which represents an aircraft weight of 14,500 pounds.*

3. *From the point of intersection in the "weight" portion of the graph, draw a horizontal line to the next reference line (wind component), then parallel the line until intersecting with the 10-knot tailwind.*

4. *From the point of intersection on the "wind" portion of the graph draw a horizontal line to the edge of the chart to find a ground roll of 1,400 feet.*

5. *The approach speed is found using the table at the top of figure. Interpolate between 16,100 and 14,000 to find the approach speed for 14,500 pounds at 108 knots.*

(PLT008) — FAA-H-8083-25

Answers

9907 [A]   9908 [B]   9909 [A]

DSP
9910. (Refer to Figures 27 and 28.) What is the landing distance over a 50-foot obstacle for Operating Conditions B-38?

A— 1,850 feet.
B— 1,700 feet.
C— 1,800 feet.

1. *Enter FAA Figure 28 at the bottom left-hand side at 0°C OAT and proceed upward to the line representing 2,000 feet pressure altitude.*

2. *From the point of intersection on the "pressure altitude" lines, draw a horizontal line to the reference line, then parallel the line which represents an aircraft weight of 13,500 pounds.*

3. *From the point of intersection in the "weight" portion of the graph, draw a horizontal line to the next reference line (wind component), then parallel the line until intersecting with the 15-knot headwind.*

4. *From the point of intersection on the "wind" portion of the graph draw a horizontal line to the next reference line (0-foot obstacle height), then parallel the line required to clear a 50-foot obstacle.*

5. *The distance required is 1,700 feet.*

(PLT008) — FAA-H-8083-25

DSP
9911. (Refer to Figures 27 and 28.) What is the total runway used when touchdown is at the 1,000 foot marker for Operating Conditions B-38?

A— 2,000 feet.
B— 1,700 feet.
C— 1,800 feet.

1. *Enter FAA Figure 28 at the bottom left-hand side at 0°C OAT and proceed upward to the line representing 2,000 feet pressure altitude.*

2. *From the point of intersection on the "pressure altitude" lines, draw a horizontal line to the reference line, then parallel the line which represents an aircraft weight of 13,500 pounds.*

3. *From the point of intersection in the "weight" portion of the graph, draw a horizontal line to the next reference line (wind component), then parallel the line until intersecting with the 15-knot headwind.*

4. *From the point of intersection on the "wind" portion of the graph draw a horizontal line to the edge of the chart to find the ground roll distance is 800 feet.*

5. *The total runway used is the distance from the threshold of the runway to the touchdown point, plus the ground roll distance, which is 1,800 feet (1,000 + 800).*

(PLT008) — FAA-H-8083-25

DSP
9912. (Refer to Figures 27 and 28.) What is the remaining runway length when stopped after landing over a 50-foot obstacle for Operating Conditions B-39?

A— 2,300 feet.
B— 2,400 feet.
C— 2,500 feet.

1. *Enter FAA Figure 28 at the bottom left-hand side at +20°C OAT and proceed upward to the line representing 4,000 feet pressure altitude.*

2. *From the point of intersection on the "pressure altitude" lines, draw a horizontal line to the reference line, then parallel the line which represents an aircraft weight of 15,000 pounds.*

3. *From the point of intersection in the "weight" portion of the graph, draw a horizontal line to the next reference line (wind component), then parallel the line until intersecting with the 5-knot tailwind.*

4. *From the point of intersection on the "wind" portion of the graph draw a horizontal line to the next reference line (0-foot obstacle height), then parallel the line required to clear a 50-foot obstacle, which is 2,500 feet.*

5. *The remaining runway length when stopped is the runway length minus the landing distance, which is 2,500 feet (5,000 − 2,500).*

(PLT008) — FAA-H-8083-25

DSP
9913. (Refer to Figures 27 and 28.) What are the approach speed and ground roll when landing under Operating Conditions B-39?

A— 111 knots and 1,550 feet.
B— 110 knots and 1,400 feet.
C— 109 knots and 1,300 feet.

1. *Enter FAA Figure 28 at the bottom left-hand side at +20°C OAT and proceed upward to the line representing 4,000 feet pressure altitude.*

2. *From the point of intersection on the "pressure altitude" lines, draw a horizontal line to the reference line, then parallel the line which represents an aircraft weight of 15,000 pounds.*

Continued

Answers

9910 [B]   9911 [C]   9912 [C]   9913 [B]

3. From the point of intersection in the "weight" portion of the graph, draw a horizontal line to the next reference line (wind component), then parallel the line until intersecting with the 5-knot tailwind.

4. From the point of intersection on the "wind" portion of the graph draw a horizontal line to the edge of the chart to find a ground roll of 1,400 feet.

5. The approach speed is found using the table at the top of figure. Interpolate between 16,100 and 14,000 to find the approach speed for 15,000 pounds at 110 knots.

(PLT008) — FAA-H-8083-25

DSP
9914. (Refer to Figures 27 and 28.) What is the landing distance over a 50-foot obstacle for Operating Conditions B-40?

A— 1,500 feet.
B— 1,750 feet.
C— 1,650 feet.

1. Enter FAA Figure 28 at the ISA line and proceed to the line representing 5,000 feet pressure altitude.

2. From the point of intersection on the "pressure altitude" lines, draw a horizontal line to the reference line, then parallel the line which represents an aircraft weight of 12,500 pounds.

3. From the point of intersection in the "weight" portion of the graph, draw a horizontal line to the next reference line (wind component), then parallel the line until intersecting with the 25-knot headwind.

4. From the point of intersection on the "wind" portion of the graph draw a horizontal line to the next reference line (0-foot obstacle height), then parallel the line required to clear a 50-foot obstacle, which is 1,650 feet.

(PLT008) — FAA-H-8083-25

Helicopter Performance

RTC
8533. (Refer to Figure 36.) Given the following conditions, what is the maximum allowable measured gas temperature (MGT) during the power assurance check?

Engine torque .... 57 percent
Pressure altitude... 2,500 ft
Temperature (OAT)... +5°C

A— 810°C.
B— 815°C.
C— 828°C.

Follow the example in the inset, upper left corner of FAA Figure 36. Begin at 57% torque, draw a line with a straight-edge parallel to the bold line through pressure altitude. From the point where your line intersects with 2,500 feet, draw a second line through the OAT lines. From the intersection of that line and +5°C OAT, draw a perpendicular line to maximum allowable MGT. Read the correct answer of 828°C. (PLT009) — FAA-H-8083-21

RTC
8534. (Refer to Figure 36.) Given the following conditions, what is the maximum allowable measured gas temperature (MGT) during the power assurance check?

Engine torque .... 49 percent
Pressure altitude... 5,500 ft
Temperature (OAT)... +25°C

A— 870°C.
B— 855°C.
C— 880°C.

Follow the example in the inset, upper left corner FAA Figure 36. Begin at 49% torque, draw a line with a straight-edge parallel to the bold line through pressure altitude. From the point where your line intersects with 5,500 feet, draw a second line through the OAT lines. From the intersection of that line and +25°C OAT, draw a perpendicular line to maximum allowable MGT. Read the correct answer of 870°C. (PLT009) — FAA-H-8083-21

Answers

9914   [C]   8533   [C]   8534   [A]

RTC

8535. (Refer to Figure 36.) Given the following conditions, what is the maximum allowable measured gas temperature (MGT) during the power assurance check?

Engine torque .... 54 percent
Pressure altitude... 500 ft
Temperature (OAT)... +25°C

A—840°C.
B—830°C.
C—820°C.

Follow the example in the inset, upper left corner FAA Figure 36. Begin at 54% torque, draw a line with a straight-edge parallel to the bold line through pressure altitude. From the point where your line intersects with 500 feet, draw a second line through the OAT lines. From the intersection of that line and +25°C OAT, draw a perpendicular line to maximum allowable MGT. Read the correct answer of 840°C. (PLT009) — FAA-H-8083-21

RTC

8536. (Refer to Figure 36.) Given the following conditions, what is the maximum allowable measured gas temperature (MGT) during the power assurance check?

Engine torque .... 43 percent
Pressure altitude... 9,000 ft
Temperature (OAT)... -15°C

A—782°C.
B—768°C.
C—750°C.

Follow the example in the inset, upper left corner FAA Figure 36. Begin at 43% torque, draw a line with a straight-edge parallel to the bold line through pressure altitude. From the point where your line intersects with 9,000 feet, draw a second line through the OAT lines. From the intersection of that line and -15°C OAT, draw a perpendicular line to maximum allowable MGT. Read the correct answer of 768°C. (PLT009) — FAA-H-8083-21

RTC

8537. (Refer to Figure 36.) Given the following conditions, what is the maximum allowable measured gas temperature (MGT) during the power assurance check?

Engine torque .... 52 percent
Pressure altitude... 1,500 ft
Temperature (OAT)... +35°C

A—880°C.
B—865°C.
C—872°C.

Follow the example in the inset, upper left corner FAA Figure 36. Begin at 52% torque, draw a line with a straight-edge parallel to the bold line through pressure altitude. From the point where your line intersects with 1,500 feet, draw a second line through the OAT lines. From the intersection of that line and +35°C OAT, draw a perpendicular line to maximum allowable MGT. Read the correct answer of 865°C. (PLT009) — FAA-H-8083-21

RTC

8538. (Refer to Figure 37.) What is the maximum gross weight for hovering in ground effect at 3,000 feet pressure altitude and +25°C?

A— 17,300 pounds.
B— 14,700 pounds.
C— 16,600 pounds.

To determine the maximum gross weight, begin in the lower left corner of FAA Figure 37 at +25°C OAT. With a straight-edge, draw a line vertically to intersect 3,000 feet pressure altitude. Draw a second perpendicular line from that point to the right to intersect +25°C OAT. Draw a third line from this intersection vertically to gross weight. Read the correct answer of 17,300 pounds. (PLT048) — FAA-H-8083-21

RTC

8539. (Refer to Figure 37.) What is the maximum gross weight for hovering in ground effect at 6,000 feet pressure altitude and +15°C?

A— 17,200 pounds.
B— 16,600 pounds.
C— 14,200 pounds.

To determine the maximum gross weight, begin in the lower left corner of FAA Figure 37 at +15°C OAT. With a straight-edge, draw a line vertically to intersect 6,000 feet pressure altitude. Draw a second perpendicular line from that point to the right to intersect +15°C OAT. Draw a third line from this intersection vertically to gross weight. Read the correct answer of 16,600 pounds. (PLT048) — FAA-H-8083-21

Answers

| 8535 [A] | 8536 [B] | 8537 [B] | 8538 [A] | 8539 [B] |

RTC

8540. (Refer to Figure 37.) What is the maximum gross weight for hovering in ground effect at 7,000 feet pressure altitude and +35°C?

A— 13,500 pounds.
B— 14,700 pounds.
C— 12,100 pounds.

To determine the maximum gross weight, begin in the lower left corner of FAA Figure 37 at +35°C OAT. With a straight-edge, draw a line vertically to intersect 7,000 feet pressure altitude. Draw a second perpendicular line from that point to the right to intersect +35°C OAT. Draw a third line from this intersection vertically to gross weight. Read the correct answer of 13,500 pounds. (PLT048) — FAA-H-8083-21

RTC

8541. (Refer to Figure 37.) What is the maximum gross weight for hovering in ground effect at 4,500 feet pressure altitude and +20°C?

A— 14,500 pounds.
B— 16,500 pounds.
C— 17,000 pounds.

To determine the maximum gross weight, begin in the lower left corner of FAA Figure 37 at +20°C OAT. With a straight-edge, draw a line vertically to intersect 4,500 feet pressure altitude. Draw a second perpendicular line from that point to the right to intersect +20°C OAT. Draw a third line from this intersection vertically to gross weight. Read the correct answer of 17,000 pounds. (PLT048) — FAA-H-8083-21

RTC

8542. (Refer to Figure 37.) What is the maximum gross weight for hovering in ground effect at 2,500 feet pressure altitude and +35°C?

A— 16,200 pounds.
B— 16,600 pounds.
C— 14,600 pounds.

To determine the maximum gross weight, begin in the lower left corner of FAA Figure 37 at +35°C OAT. With a straight-edge, draw a line vertically to intersect 2,500 feet pressure altitude. Draw a second perpendicular line from that point to the right to intersect +35°C OAT. Draw a third line from this intersection vertically to gross weight. Read the correct answer of 16,200 pounds. (PLT048) — FAA-H-8083-21

RTC

8543. (Refer to Figure 38.) What is the maximum gross weight for hovering out of ground effect at 3,000 feet pressure altitude and +30°C?

A— 17,500 pounds.
B— 14,300 pounds.
C— 13,400 pounds.

To determine the maximum gross weight, begin in the lower left corner of FAA Figure 38 at +30°C OAT. With a straight-edge, draw a line vertically to intersect 3,000 feet pressure altitude. Draw a second perpendicular line from that point to the right to intersect +30°C OAT. Draw a third line from this intersection vertically to gross weight. Read the correct answer of 14,300 pounds. (PLT048) — FAA-H-8083-21

RTC

8544. (Refer to Figure 38.) What is the maximum gross weight for hovering out of ground effect at 6,000 feet pressure altitude and +15°C?

A— 16,800 pounds.
B— 13,500 pounds.
C— 14,400 pounds.

To determine the maximum gross weight, begin in the lower left corner of FAA Figure 38 at +15°C OAT. With a straight-edge, draw a line vertically to intersect 6,000 feet pressure altitude. Draw a second perpendicular line from that point to the right to intersect +15°C OAT. Draw a third line from this intersection vertically to gross weight. Read the correct answer of 14,400 pounds. (PLT048) — FAA-H-8083-21

RTC

8545. (Refer to Figure 38.) What is the maximum gross weight for hovering out of ground effect at 7,000 feet pressure altitude and +35°C?

A— 14,000 pounds.
B— 11,600 pounds.
C— 12,500 pounds.

To determine the maximum gross weight, begin in the lower left corner of FAA Figure 38 at +35°C OAT. With a straight-edge, draw a line vertically to intersect 7,000 feet pressure altitude. Draw a second perpendicular line from that point to the right to intersect +35°C OAT. Draw a third line from this intersection vertically to gross weight. Read the correct answer of 11,600 pounds. (PLT048) — FAA-H-8083-21

Answers

8540 [A]   8541 [C]   8542 [A]   8543 [B]   8544 [C]   8545 [B]

RTC

8546. (Refer to Figure 38.) What is the maximum gross weight for hovering out of ground effect at 4,500 feet pressure altitude and +20°C?

A— 14,500 pounds.
B— 14,000 pounds.
C— 17,000 pounds.

To determine the maximum gross weight, begin in the lower left corner of FAA Figure 38 at +20°C OAT. With a straight-edge, draw a line vertically to intersect 4,500 feet pressure altitude. Draw a second perpendicular line from that point to the right to intersect +20°C OAT. Draw a third line from this intersection vertically to gross weight. Read the correct answer of 14,500 pounds. (PLT048) — FAA-H-8083-21

RTC

8547. (Refer to Figure 38.) What is the maximum gross weight for hovering out of ground effect at 2,500 feet pressure altitude and +30°C?

A— 17,400 pounds.
B— 15,000 pounds.
C— 14,500 pounds.

To determine the maximum gross weight, begin in the lower left corner of FAA Figure 38 at +30°C OAT. With a straight-edge, draw a line vertically to intersect 2,500 feet pressure altitude. Draw a second perpendicular line from that point to the right to intersect +30°C OAT. Draw a third line from this intersection vertically to gross weight. Read the correct answer of 14,500 pounds. (PLT048) — FAA-H-8083-21

RTC

8548. (Refer to Figure 39.) What is the takeoff distance over a 50-foot obstacle?

Pressure altitude..3,500 ft
Temperature (OAT)..+20°C
Gross weight... 15,000 lb

A— 1,070 feet.
B— 1,020 feet.
C— 1,100 feet.

To determine the takeoff distance, begin at +20°C OAT in the lower left corner of FAA Figure 39. Draw a vertical line upward to intersect 3,500 feet pressure altitude. From that point, draw a perpendicular line to 15,000 pounds gross weight. From this point, draw a vertical line downward to takeoff distance. Read the distance of 1,070 feet. (PLT011) — FAA-H-8083-21

RTC

8549. (Refer to Figure 39.) What is the takeoff distance over a 50-foot obstacle?

Pressure altitude..5,000 ft
Temperature (OAT)...-10°C
Gross weight..11,000 lb

A— 1,000 feet.
B— 920 feet.
C— 870 feet.

To determine the takeoff distance, begin at -10°C OAT in the lower left corner of FAA Figure 39. Draw a vertical line upward to intersect 5,000 feet pressure altitude. From that point, draw a perpendicular line to 11,000 pounds gross weight. From this point, draw a vertical line downward to takeoff distance. Read the distance of 870 feet. (PLT011) — FAA-H-8083-21

RTC

8550. (Refer to Figure 39.) What is the takeoff distance over a 50-foot obstacle?

Pressure altitude..6,500 ft
Temperature (OAT)..0°C
Gross weight... 13,500 lb

A— 1,500 feet.
B— 1,050 feet.
C— 1,100 feet.

To determine the takeoff distance, begin at +0°C OAT in the lower left corner of FAA Figure 39. Draw a vertical line upward to intersect 6,500 feet pressure altitude. From that point, draw a perpendicular line to 13,500 pounds gross weight. From this point, draw a vertical line downward to takeoff distance. Read the distance of 1,050 feet. (PLT011) — FAA-H-8083-21

RTC

8551. (Refer to Figure 39.) What is the takeoff distance over a 50-foot obstacle?

Pressure altitude..9,000 ft
Temperature (OAT)...+20°C
Gross weight... 15,000 lb

A— 1,300 feet.
B— 1,350 feet.
C— 1,250 feet.

To determine the takeoff distance, begin at +20°C OAT in the lower left corner of FAA Figure 39. Draw a verti-cal line upward to intersect 9,000 feet pressure altitude.

Continued

Answers

8546 [A]	8547 [C]	8548 [A]	8549 [C]	8550 [B]	8551 [B]

From that point, draw a perpendicular line to 15,000 pounds gross weight. From this point, draw a vertical line downward to takeoff distance. Read the distance of 1,350 feet. (PLT011) — FAA-H-8083-21

RTC
8552. (Refer to Figure 39.) What is the takeoff distance over a 50-foot obstacle?

Pressure altitude...-1,000 ft
Temperature (OAT)..+25°C
Gross weight.. 14,000 lb

A— 1,000 feet.
B— 900 feet.
C— 950 feet.

To determine the takeoff distance, begin at +25°C OAT in the lower left corner of FAA Figure 39. Draw a vertical line upward to intersect -1,000 feet pressure altitude. From that point, draw a perpendicular line to 14,000 pounds gross weight. From this point, draw a vertical line downward to takeoff distance. Read the distance of 900 feet. (PLT011) — FAA-H-8083-21

RTC
8553. (Refer to Figure 40.) What is the climb performance with both engines operating?

Pressure altitude.. 9,500 ft
Temperature (OAT)..-5°C
Heater..ON

A— 925 ft/min.
B— 600 ft/min.
C— 335 ft/min.

1. *Enter FAA Figure 40 at the left side with 9,500 pressure altitude and draw a horizontal line to the curved line representing -5°C temperature (interpolate between temperatures as necessary).*

2. *From that point of intersection, draw a vertical line to the bottom of the graph and read the rate of climb of 915 fpm.*

3. *With the heater on above 1,800 feet, the rate of climb is 315 fpm less, therefore our rate of climb is 600 fpm.*

(PLT004) — FAA-H-8083-21

RTC
8554. (Refer to Figure 40.) What is the climb performance with both engines operating?

Pressure altitude.. 7,500 ft
Temperature (OAT)..+5°C
Heater..ON

A— 905 ft/min.
B— 765 ft/min.
C— 1,080 ft/min.

1. *Enter FAA Figure 40 at the left side with 7,500 pressure altitude and draw a horizontal line to the curved line representing +5°C temperature (interpolate between temperatures as necessary).*

2. *From that point of intersection, draw a vertical line to the bottom of the graph and read the rate of climb of 1,080 fpm.*

3. *With the heater on above 1,800 feet, the rate of climb is 315 fpm less; therefore, our rate of climb is 765 fpm.*

(PLT004) — FAA-H-8083-21

RTC
8555. (Refer to Figure 40.) What is the climb performance with both engines operating?

Pressure altitude.. 6,500 ft
Temperature (OAT)..+25°C
Heater..OFF

A— 285 ft/min.
B— 600 ft/min.
C— 400 ft/min.

1. *Enter FAA Figure 40 at the left side with 6,500 pressure altitude and draw a horizontal line to the curved line representing +25°C temperature (interpolate between temperatures as necessary).*

2. *From that point of intersection, draw a vertical line to the bottom of the graph and read the rate of climb of 600 fpm.*

(PLT004) — FAA-H-8083-21

Answers

8552 [B]   8553 [B]   8554 [B]   8555 [B]

RTC
8556. (Refer to Figure 40.) What is the climb performance with both engines operating?

Pressure altitude... 11,500 ft
Temperature (OAT)...-15°C
Heater...ON

A— 645 ft/min.
B— 375 ft/min.
C— 330 ft/min.

1. Enter FAA Figure 40 at the left side with 11,500 pressure altitude and draw a horizontal line to the curved line representing -15°C temperature (interpolate between temperatures as necessary).

2. From that point of intersection, draw a vertical line to the bottom of the graph and read the rate of climb of 645 fpm.

3. With the heater on above 1,800 feet, the rate of climb is 315 fpm less; therefore, the rate of climb is 330 fpm.

(PLT004) — FAA-H-8083-21

RTC
8557. (Refer to Figure 40.) What is the climb performance with both engines operating?

Pressure altitude... 3,500 ft
Temperature (OAT)...-10°C
Heater...ON

A— 985 ft/min.
B— 1,300 ft/min.
C— 1,360 ft/min.

1. Enter FAA Figure 40 at the left side with 3,500 pressure altitude and draw a horizontal line to the curved line representing -10°C temperature (interpolate between temperatures as necessary).

2. From that point of intersection, draw a vertical line to the bottom of the graph and read the rate of climb of 1,300 fpm.

3. With the heater on above 1,800 feet, the rate of climb is 315 fpm less; therefore, our rate of climb is 985 fpm.

(PLT004) — FAA-H-8083-21

RTC
8558. (Refer to Figure 41.) What is the single-engine climb or descent performance?

Pressure altitude... 7,500 ft
Temperature (OAT)... 0°C

A— 80 ft/min descent.
B— 10 ft/min climb.
C— 50 ft/min climb.

1. Enter FAA Figure 41 at the left side with 7,500 pressure altitude and draw a horizontal line to the curved line representing 0°C temperature (interpolate between temperatures as necessary).

2. From that point of intersection, draw a vertical line to the bottom of the graph and read the rate of descent of 80 fpm.

(PLT004) — FAA-H-8083-21

RTC
8559. (Refer to Figure 41.) Given the following, what is the single-engine climb or descent performance?

Pressure altitude... 3,000 ft
Temperature (OAT)..+35°C

A— 150 ft/min descent.
B— 350 ft/min climb.
C— 100 ft/min descent.

1. Enter FAA Figure 41 at the left side with 3,000 pressure altitude and draw a horizontal line to the curved line representing +35°C temperature (interpolate between temperatures as necessary).

2. From that point of intersection, draw a vertical line to the bottom of the graph and read the rate of descent of 100 fpm.

(PLT004) — FAA-H-8083-21

RTC
8560. (Refer to Figure 41.) Given the following, what is the single-engine climb or descent performance?

Pressure altitude... 4,700 ft
Temperature (OAT)..+20°C

A— 420 ft/min climb.
B— 60 ft/min climb.
C— 60 ft/min descent.

Continued

1. Enter FAA Figure 41 at the left side with 4,700 pressure altitude and draw a horizontal line to the curved line representing +20°C temperature (interpolate between temperatures as necessary).

2. From that point of intersection, draw a vertical line to the bottom of the graph and read the rate of climb of 60 fpm.

(PLT004) — FAA-H-8083-21

RTC
8561. (Refer to Figure 41.) Given the following, what is the single-engine climb or descent performance?

Pressure altitude.. 9,500 ft
Temperature (OAT)....................................... -10°C

A— 600 ft/min descent.
B— 840 ft/min descent.
C— 280 ft/min descent.

1. Enter FAA Figure 41 at the left side with 9,500 pressure altitude and draw a horizontal line to the curved line representing -10°C temperature (interpolate between temperatures as necessary).

2. From that point of intersection, draw a vertical line to the bottom of the graph and read the rate of descent of 280 fpm.

(PLT004) — FAA-H-8083-21

RTC
8562. (Refer to Figure 41.) Given the following, what is the single-engine climb or descent performance?

Pressure altitude.. 1,500 ft
Temperature (OAT)....................................... +45°C

A— 100 ft/min descent.
B— 360 ft/min climb.
C— 200 ft/min descent.

1. Enter FAA Figure 41 at the left side with 1,500 pressure altitude and draw a horizontal line to the curved line representing +45°C temperature (interpolate between temperatures as necessary).

2. From that point of intersection, draw a vertical line to the bottom of the graph and read the rate of descent of 100 fpm.

(PLT004) — FAA-H-8083-21

RTC
8563. (Refer to Figure 42.) Given the following, what is the airspeed limit (V$_{NE}$)?

Gross weight.. 16,500 lb
Pressure altitude... 5,000 ft
Temperature (OAT)... -15°C

A— 128 KIAS.
B— 133 KIAS.
C— 126 KIAS.

1. Use the right-middle table for an aircraft weighing 16,500 pounds.

2. Start at an OAT of -15°C and interpolate between 6,000 (126) and 4,000 (131) feet to find V$_{NE}$ for 5,000.

3. V$_{NE}$ for 5,000 feet at -15°C is 128.5 knots.

(PLT002) — FAA-H-8083-21

RTC
8564. (Refer to Figure 42.) What is the airspeed limit (V$_{NE}$)?

Gross weight.. 17,500 lb
Pressure altitude... 4,000 ft
Temperature (OAT)... +10°C

A— 114 KIAS.
B— 120 KIAS.
C— 130 KIAS.

1. Use the right-bottom table for an aircraft weighing 17,500 pounds.

2. Interpolate between 0°C and 20°C for 4,000 feet to find V$_{NE}$ for +10°C.

3. V$_{NE}$ for 5,000 feet at +10°C is 120 knots.

(PLT002) — FAA-H-8083-21

RTC
8565. (Refer to Figure 42.) What is the airspeed limit (V$_{NE}$)?

Gross weight.. 15,000 lb
Pressure altitude... 6,000 ft
Temperature (OAT)... 0°C

A— 135 KIAS.
B— 127 KIAS.
C— 143 KIAS.

Answers

8561 [C]   8562 [A]   8563 [A]   8564 [B]   8565 [A]

1. Use the table for 14,500 pounds and 16,500 to interpolate for an aircraft weighing 15,000 pounds.

2. Start at an OAT of 0°C and find 6,000 for both 14,500 pounds (138) and 16,500 pounds (122) feet to find V_{NE} for 15,000 pounds.

3. V_{NE} for 15,000 feet at 0°C is 135 knots.

(PLT002) — FAA-H-8083-21

RTC

8566. (Refer to Figure 42.) What is the airspeed limit (V_{NE})?

Gross weight.. 14,000 lb
Pressure altitude... 8,000 ft
Temperature (OAT)..-15°C

A— 121 KIAS.
B— 123 KIAS.
C— 113 KIAS.

1. Use the table for 13,500 pounds and 14,500 to interpolate for an aircraft weighing 14,000 pounds.

2. Start at an OAT of -15°C and find 8,000 for both 13,500 pounds (121) and 14,500 pounds (121) feet to find V_{NE} for 14,000 pounds.

3. V_{NE} for 14,000 feet at -15°C is 121 knots.

(PLT002) — FAA-H-8083-21

RTC

8567. (Refer to Figure 42.) What is the airspeed limit (V_{NE})?

Gross weight.. 12,500 lb
Pressure altitude.. 14,000 ft
Temperature (OAT)..-20°C

A— 99 KIAS.
B— 108 KIAS.
C— 103 KIAS.

1. Use the table for an aircraft weighing 12,500 pounds.

2. Interpolate between -15°C and -25°C for 14,000 feet to find V_{NE} for -20°C.

3. V_{NE} for 14,000 feet at -20°C is 103 knots.

(PLT002) — FAA-H-8083-21

RTC

8568. (Refer to Figure 43.) What is the single-engine landing distance over a 50-foot obstacle?

Gross weight.. 12,000 lb
Pressure altitude... 3,500 ft
Temperature (OAT)..+30°C

A— 850 feet.
B— 900 feet.
C— 1,000 feet.

1. Enter FAA Figure 43 on the left side at the bottom and draw a vertical line from +30°C OAT to the 3,500 feet pressure altitude (interpolate as necessary).

2. From that point of intersection, draw a horizontal line to the diagonal representing 12,000 pounds, and then a vertical line from there down to the landing distance of 1,000 feet.

(PLT011) — FAA-H-8083-21

RTC

8569. (Refer to Figure 43.) What is the single-engine landing distance over a 50-foot obstacle?

Gross weight.. 16,500 lb
Pressure altitude... 5,500 ft
Temperature (OAT)..-10°C

A— 1,700 feet.
B— 1,550 feet.
C— 1,600 feet.

1. Enter FAA Figure 43 on the left side at the bottom and draw a vertical line from -10°C OAT to the 5,500 feet pressure altitude (interpolate as necessary).

2. From that point of intersection, draw a horizontal line to the diagonal representing 16,500 pounds, and then a vertical line from there down to the landing distance of 1,550 feet.

(PLT011) — FAA-H-8083-21

Answers

8566 [A]	8567 [C]	8568 [C]	8569 [B]

RTC

8570. (Refer to Figure 43.) What is the single-engine landing distance over a 50-foot obstacle?

Gross weight... 15,000 lb
Pressure altitude... 8,000 ft
Temperature (OAT)... +20°C

A— 1,900 feet.
B— 1,800 feet.
C— 2,000 feet.

1. Enter FAA Figure 43 on the left side at the bottom and draw a vertical line from +20°C OAT to the 8,000 feet pressure altitude (interpolate as necessary).

2. From that point of intersection, draw a horizontal line to the diagonal representing 15,000 pounds, and then a vertical line from there down to the landing distance of 1,900 feet.

(PLT011) — FAA-H-8083-21

RTC

8571. (Refer to Figure 43.) What is the single-engine landing distance over a 50-foot obstacle?

Gross weight... 14,000 lb
Pressure altitude... 1,000 ft
Temperature (OAT)... +10°C

A— 650 feet.
B— 920 feet.
C— 800 feet.

1. Enter FAA Figure 43 on the left side at the bottom and draw a vertical line from +10°C OAT to the 1,000 feet pressure altitude (interpolate as necessary).

2. From that point of intersection, draw a horizontal line to the diagonal representing 14,000 pounds, and then a vertical line from there down to the landing distance of 920 feet.

(PLT011) — FAA-H-8083-21

RTC

8572. (Refer to Figure 43.) What is the single-engine landing distance over a 50-foot obstacle?

Gross weight... 17,000 lb
Pressure altitude... 4,000 ft
Temperature (OAT)... +40°C

A— 1,850 feet.
B— 2,200 feet.
C— 2,000 feet.

1. Enter FAA Figure 43 on the left side at the bottom and draw a vertical line from +40°C OAT to the 4,000 feet pressure altitude (interpolate as necessary).

2. From that point of intersection, draw a horizontal line to the diagonal representing 17,000 pounds, and then a vertical line from there down to the landing distance of 2,000 feet.

(PLT011) — FAA-H-8083-21

RTC

8822. (Refer to Figures 113 and 114.) What TAS would be required to arrive at POM VORTAC 52 minutes after passing DAG VORTAC?

A— 114 knots.
B— 117 knots.
C— 120 knots.

Problem may be solved using E6-B or CX-3 Flight Computer:

Distance = 80 NM
GS = 92.3 knots
Wind = 290/36, variation = 15° East
   (found in Figure 113A)
Course = 214°
TAS = 114.2 knots

(PLT012) — FAA-H-8083-15

RTC

8823. (Refer to Figures 113 and 114.) What TAS would be required to arrive at POM VORTAC 1 hour after passing DAG VORTAC?

A— 102 knots.
B— 105 knots.
C— 108 knots.

Problem may be solved using E6-B or CX-3 Flight Computer:

Distance = 80 NM
GS = 80 knots
Wind = 290/36, variation = 15° East
   (found in Figure 113A)
Course = 214°
TAS = 102.4 knots

(PLT012) — FAA-H-8083-15

Answers

| 8570 | [A] | 8571 | [B] | 8572 | [C] | 8822 | [A] | 8823 | [A] |

Flight Planning Graphs and Tables

Aircraft manufacturers publish flight planning graphs or tables that enable flight crews to quickly estimate the time and fuel required to fly certain trips. These tables or graphs allow adjustments for aircraft weight, wind, altitude, cruise speed, and other variables.

FAA Figure 399 represents a performance chart that is often used for performance questions on the Cessna 208: the "time, fuel and distance to climb" chart. This chart is fairly easy to use in that you simply find your weight, and the altitude you are climbing to. Just make sure to subtract your departure elevation altitude. For example, if you were departing from a field elevation of 4,000 feet and climbing to a cruise altitude of 16,000 feet, you would first calculate everything at the 16,000-foot level and then subtract the 4,000-foot field elevation.

In this example, at 8,750 pounds and standard temperature, you would expect to spend 23 minutes in the climb; however, subtract the 4,000-foot time of 5 minutes, which yields a time-to-climb of 18 minutes.

ATM, DSP

8643. (Refer to Figures 61 and 62.) What is the trip time for Operating Conditions X-1?

A— 4 hours 5 minutes.
B— 4 hours 15 minutes.
C— 4 hours.

1. Enter the bottom of FAA Figure 62 at 2,000 and move up to the reference line.

2. From the reference line, follow the diagonal line representing a 50-knot tailwind.

3. Move up to the line representing a pressure altitude of 27,000 feet and move left to the reference line.

4. From the reference line, follow the diagonal line representing ISA +10°C and continue to the edge of the chart.

5. Determine a trip time of 4 hours.

(PLT012) — FAA-H-8083-25

ATM, DSP

8644. (Refer to Figures 61 and 62.) What is the trip time for Operating Conditions X-2?

A— 5 hours 5 minutes.
B— 6 hours 15 minutes.
C— 5 hours 55 minutes.

1. Enter the bottom of FAA Figure 62 at 2,400 and move up to the reference line.

2. From the reference line, follow the diagonal line representing a 50-knot headwind.

3. Move up to the line representing a pressure altitude of 35,000 feet and move left to edge of the chart.

4. Determine a trip time of 6 hours 15 minutes.

(PLT012) — FAA-H-8083-25

ATM, DSP

8645. (Refer to Figures 61 and 62.) What is the trip time for Operating Conditions X-3?

A— 4 hours 15 minutes.
B— 3 hours 40 minutes.
C— 4 hours.

1. Enter the bottom of FAA Figure 62 at 1,800 and move up to the reference line.

2. From the reference line, follow the diagonal line representing a 20-knot headwind.

3. Move up to the line representing a pressure altitude of 20,000 feet and move left to the reference line.

4. From the reference line, follow the diagonal line representing ISA +20°C and continue to the edge of the chart.

5. Determine a trip time of 4 hours.

(PLT012) — FAA-H-8083-25

ATM, DSP

8646. (Refer to Figures 61 and 62.) What is the trip time for Operating Conditions X-4?

A— 6 hours 50 minutes.
B— 5 hours 45 minutes.
C— 5 hours 30 minutes.

1. Enter the bottom of FAA Figure 62 at 2,800 and move up to the reference line.

2. From the reference line, follow the diagonal line representing a 50-knot tailwind.

3. Move up to the line representing a pressure altitude of 29,000 feet and move left to the reference line.

Continued

Answers

8643 [C]	8644 [B]	8645 [C]	8646 [B]

4. *From the reference line, follow the diagonal line representing ISA -10°C and continue to the edge of the chart.*

5. *Determine a trip time of 5 hours 45 minutes.*

(PLT012) — FAA-H-8083-25

ATM, DSP

8647. (Refer to Figures 61 and 62.) What is the trip time for Operating Conditions X-5?

A— 2 hours 55 minutes.
B— 3 hours 10 minutes.
C— 2 hours 59 minutes.

1. *Enter the bottom of FAA Figure 62 at 1,200 and move up to the reference line.*

2. *From the reference line, follow the diagonal line representing a 30-knot headwind.*

3. *Move up to the line representing a pressure altitude of 37,000 feet and move left to the reference line.*

4. *From the reference line, follow the diagonal line representing ISA +10°C and continue to the edge of the chart.*

5. *Determine a trip time of 2 hours 55 minutes.*

(PLT012) — FAA-H-8083-25

ATM, DSP

8648. (Refer to Figures 61 and 62.) What is the trip fuel for Operating Conditions X-1?

A— 25,000 pounds.
B— 26,000 pounds.
C— 24,000 pounds.

1. *Enter the bottom of FAA Figure 62 at 2,000 and move up to the reference line.*

2. *From the reference line, follow the diagonal line representing a 50-knot tailwind.*

3. *Move up to the line representing a pressure altitude of 27,000 feet and move right to the reference line.*

4. *From the reference line, follow the diagonal line representing 70,000 pounds and continue to the edge of the chart.*

5. *Determine a trip fuel of 26,000 pounds.*

(PLT012) — FAA-H-8083-25

ATM, DSP

8649. (Refer to Figures 61 and 62.) What is the trip fuel for Operating Conditions X-2?

A— 33,000 pounds.
B— 28,000 pounds.
C— 35,000 pounds.

1. *Enter the bottom of FAA Figure 62 at 2,400 and move up to the reference line.*

2. *From the reference line, follow the diagonal line representing a 50-knot headwind.*

3. *Move up to the line representing a pressure altitude of 35,000 feet and move right to the reference line.*

4. *From the reference line, follow the diagonal line representing 75,000 pounds and continue to the edge of the chart.*

5. *Determine a trip fuel of 35,000 pounds.*

(PLT012) — FAA-H-8083-25

ATM, DSP

8650. (Refer to Figures 61 and 62.) What is the trip fuel for Operating Conditions X-3?

A— 36,000 pounds.
B— 34,500 pounds.
C— 33,000 pounds.

1. *Enter the bottom of FAA Figure 62 at 1,800 and move up to the reference line.*

2. *From the reference line, follow the diagonal line representing a 20-knot headwind.*

3. *Move up to the line representing a pressure altitude of 20,000 feet and move right to the reference line.*

4. *From the reference line, follow the diagonal line representing 75,000 pounds and continue to the edge of the chart.*

5. *Determine a trip fuel of 34,500 pounds.*

(PLT012) — FAA-H-8083-25

ATM, DSP

8651. (Refer to Figures 61 and 62.) What is the trip fuel for Operating Conditions X-4?

A— 33,000 pounds.
B— 31,500 pounds.
C— 34,000 pounds.

Answers

8647   [A]   8648   [B]   8649   [C]   8650   [B]   8651   [A]

1. Enter the bottom of FAA Figure 62 at 2,800 and move up to the reference line.

2. From the reference line, follow the diagonal line representing a 50-knot tailwind.

3. Move up to the line representing a pressure altitude of 29,000 feet and move right to the reference line.

4. From the reference line, follow the diagonal line representing 65,000 pounds and continue to the edge of the chart.

5. Determine a trip fuel of 33,000 pounds.

(PLT012) — FAA-H-8083-25

ATM, DSP

8652. (Refer to Figures 61 and 62.) What is the trip fuel for Operating Conditions X-5?

A— 15,000 pounds.
B— 20,000 pounds.
C— 19,000 pounds.

1. Enter the bottom of FAA Figure 62 at 1,200 and move up to the reference line.

2. From the reference line, follow the diagonal line representing a 30-knot headwind.

3. Move up to the line representing a pressure altitude of 37,000 feet and move right to the reference line.

4. From the reference line, follow the diagonal line representing 90,000 pounds and continue to the edge of the chart.

5. Determine a trip fuel of 19,000 pounds.

(PLT012) — FAA-H-8083-25

ATM, ATS, DSP

8658. (Refer to Figures 66 and 67.) What is the trip time corrected for wind under Operating Conditions Z-1?

A— 58.1 minutes.
B— 51.9 minutes.
C— 54.7 minutes.

Change in time = Time x Wind Component ÷ TAS
55 x (-25) ÷ 438 = -3.1 minutes

Therefore, the trip time corrected for wind is 51.9 minutes (55 – 3.1).

(PLT012) — FAA-H-8083-25

ATM, ATS, DSP

8659. (Refer to Figures 66 and 67.) What is the trip time corrected for wind under Operating Conditions Z-2?

A— 1 hour 35 minutes.
B— 1 hour 52 minutes.
C— 1 hour 46 minutes.

Table time = 96 minutes
Change in time = 96 minutes x 45 ÷ 433 = +10 minutes
Trip time = 96 min + 10 min = 106 minutes = 1 hour 46 minutes

(PLT012) — FAA-H-8083-25

ATM, ATS, DSP

8660. (Refer to Figures 66 and 67.) What is the trip time corrected for wind under Operating Conditions Z-3?

A— 2 hours 9 minutes.
B— 1 hour 59 minutes.
C— 1 hour 52 minutes.

Table time = 129 minutes
Change in time = 129 min x (-35) ÷ 433 = -10.4 minutes
Trip time = 129 min – 10.4 min = 118.6 minutes = 1 hour 59 minutes

(PLT012) — FAA-H-8083-25

ATM, ATS, DSP

8661. (Refer to Figures 66 and 67.) What is the trip time corrected for wind under Operating Conditions Z-4?

A— 48.3 minutes.
B— 50.7 minutes.
C— 51.3 minutes.

Table time = 48 minutes
Change in time = 48 min x 25 ÷ 443 = 2.7 minutes
Trip time = 48 min + 2.7 min = 50.7 minutes

(PLT012) — FAA-H-8083-25

ATM, ATS, DSP

8662. (Refer to Figures 66 and 67.) What is the trip time corrected for wind under Operating Conditions Z-5?

A— 1 hour 11 minutes.
B— 56 minutes.
C— 62 minutes.

Table time = 62 minutes
Change in time = 62 min x 60 ÷ 433 = 8.6 minutes
Trip time = 62 min + 8.6 min = 70.6 minute = 1 hour 11 minutes

(PLT012) — FAA-H-8083-25

Answers

8652 [C]	8658 [B]	8659 [C]	8660 [B]	8661 [B]	8662 [A]

ATM, ATS, DSP

8663. (Refer to Figures 66 and 67.) What is the estimated fuel consumption for Operating Conditions Z-1?

A— 5,230 pounds.
B— 5,970 pounds.
C— 5,550 pounds.

Table fuel = 5,550 lbs
Change in fuel = 5,500 x (-25) ÷ 438 = -316.8 lbs
Trip fuel = 5,500 lbs – 316.8 lbs = 5,233.2 lbs

(PLT012) — FAA-H-8083-25

ATM, ATS, DSP

8664. (Refer to Figures 66 and 67.) What is the estimated fuel consumption for Operating Conditions Z-2?

A— 10,270 pounds.
B— 9,660 pounds.
C— 10,165 pounds.

Table fuel = 9,300 lbs
Change in fuel = 9,300 x 45 ÷ 433 = 967 lbs
Trip fuel = 9,300 lbs + 967 lbs = 10,267 lbs

(PLT012) — FAA-H-8083-25

ATM, ATS, DSP

8665. (Refer to Figures 66 and 67.) What is the estimated fuel consumption for Operating Conditions Z-3?

A— 12,300 pounds.
B— 11,300 pounds.
C— 13,990 pounds.

Table fuel = 12,300 lbs
Change in fuel = 12,300 x (-35) ÷ 433 = -994 lbs
Trip fuel = 12,300 lbs – 994 lbs = 11,306 lbs

(PLT012) — FAA-H-8083-25

ATM, ATS, DSP

8666. (Refer to Figures 66 and 67.) What is the estimated fuel consumption for Operating Conditions Z-4?

A— 4,950 pounds.
B— 5,380 pounds.
C— 5,230 pounds.

Table fuel = 4,950 lbs
Change in fuel = 4,950 x 25 ÷ 443 = 279 lbs
Trip fuel = 4,950 lbs + 279 lbs = 5,229 lbs

(PLT012) — FAA-H-8083-25

ATM, ATS, DSP

8667. (Refer to Figures 66 and 67.) What is the estimated fuel consumption for Operating Conditions Z-5?

A— 6,250 pounds.
B— 5,380 pounds.
C— 7,120 pounds.

Table fuel = 6,250 lbs
Change in fuel = 6,250 x 60 ÷ 433 = 866 lbs
Trip fuel = 6,250 lbs + 866 lbs = 7,116 lbs

(PLT012) — FAA-H-8083-25

ATM, ATS, DSP

8603. (Refer to Figures 297 and 481.) With a reported temperature of 0°C, at 500 feet AGL after takeoff, and airspeed of 145 knots IAS, the radius of turn is

A— 7,850 feet.
B— 8,150 feet.
C— 8,450 feet.

1. *On Figure 297, note the field elevation of 5,355 feet.*

2. *On Figure 481, start on the lower left side of the chart at 0°C and move straight up until you intersect the altitude of 5,855 feet (field elevation of 5,355 + 500 feet AGL). Move directly to the right until intersecting the REF LINE. Move up and to the right in parallel with the diagonal lines until intersecting the airspeed of 145 knots. Move directly to the right and note the radius of turn of 8,150 feet.*

(PLT011) — FAA-H-8083-25

ATM, DSP

8604. (Refer to Figure 469.) With an OAT of -20°C at 20,000 feet and an IAS of 150, the Maximum Continuous Power Torque Setting is

A— 64%.
B— 66%.
C— 68%.

On Figure 469, start at the bottom of the chart and locate -20°C. Move straight up until intersecting the 20,000 feet line. Move directly to the right and stop at the REF LINE. Because 150 knots intersects with the REF LINE, you continue to the right and note the maximum continuous power torque setting is 66%. (PLT009) — FAA-H-8083-25

Answers

8663 [A]	8664 [A]	8665 [B]	8666 [C]	8667 [C]	8603 [B]
8604 [B]					

DSP
9915. (Refer to Figures 51 and 52.) What is the total time from starting to the alternate through completing the approach for Operating Conditions L-1?

A— 30 minutes.
B— 44 minutes.
C— 29 minutes.

29 minutes	En route
+15 minutes	Holding
44 minutes	Total

Note: Distance is provided as NM so you should disregard the wind component provided in the operating conditions.

(PLT012) — FAA-H-8083-25

DSP
9916. (Refer to Figures 51 and 52.) What is the total time from starting to the alternate through completing the approach for Operating Conditions L-2?

A— 36 minutes.
B— 55 minutes.
C— 40 minutes.

40 minutes	En route
+15 minutes	Holding
55 minutes	Total

(PLT012) — FAA-H-8083-25

DSP
8605. (Refer to Figures 51 and 52.) What is the total time from starting to the alternate through completing the approach for Operating Conditions L-3?

A— 1 hour.
B— 1 hour 15 minutes.
C— 1 hour 24 minutes.

60 minutes	En route
+15 minutes	Holding
75 minutes	Total (1 hour 15 minutes)

(PLT012) — FAA-H-8083-25

DSP
8606. (Refer to Figures 51 and 52.) What is the total time from starting to the alternate through completing the approach for Operating Conditions L-4?

A— 35 minutes.
B— 19 minutes.
C— 20 minutes.

20 minutes	En route
+15 minutes	Holding
35 minutes	Total

(PLT012) — FAA-H-8083-25

DSP
8607. (Refer to Figures 51 and 52.) What is the total time from starting to the alternate through completing the approach for Operating Conditions L-5?

A— 1 hour 3 minutes.
B— 48 minutes.
C— 55 minutes.

48 minutes	En route
+15 minutes	Holding
63 minutes	Total (1 hour 3 minutes)

(PLT012) — FAA-H-8083-25

DSP
8608. (Refer to Figures 51 and 52.) What is the approximate landing weight for Operating Conditions L-1?

A— 78,850 pounds.
B— 80,300 pounds.
C— 81,600 pounds.

85,000 lbs	Weight (start to alt)
– 3,400 lbs	Fuel burn
81,600 lbs	Landing weight

(PLT008) — FAA-H-8083-25

DSP
8609. (Refer to Figures 51 and 52.) What is the approximate landing weight for Operating Conditions L-2?

A— 65,200 pounds.
B— 65,800 pounds.
C— 69,600 pounds.

70,000 lbs	Weight (start to alt)
– 4,200 lbs	Fuel burn
65,800 lbs	Landing weight

(PLT008) — FAA-H-8083-25

Answers

9915 [B]	9916 [B]	8605 [B]	8606 [A]	8607 [A]	8608 [C]
8609 [B]					

DSP
8610. (Refer to Figures 51 and 52.) What is the approximate landing weight for Operating Conditions L-3?

A— 80,300 pounds.
B— 85,400 pounds.
C— 77,700 pounds.

86,000	lbs	Weight (start to alt)
– 5,700	lbs	Fuel burn
80,300	lbs	Landing weight

(PLT008) — FAA-H-8083-25

DSP
8611. (Refer to Figures 51 and 52.) What is the approximate landing weight for Operating Conditions L-4?

A— 73,200 pounds.
B— 74,190 pounds.
C— 73,500 pounds.

76,000	lbs	Weight (start to alt)
– 2,800	lbs	Fuel burn
73,200	lbs	Landing weight

(PLT008) — FAA-H-8083-25

DSP
8612. (Refer to Figures 51 and 52.) What is the approximate landing weight for Operating Conditions L-5?

A— 78,600 pounds.
B— 77,000 pounds.
C— 76,300 pounds.

82,000	lbs	Weight (start to alt)
– 4,700	lbs	Fuel burn
77,300	lbs	Landing weight

(PLT008) — FAA-H-8083-25

Typical Flight Logs

Flight logs are used to accurately plan the time and fuel required for a flight. In the following paragraphs we describe all the steps required to complete a flight log.

1. Determine the magnetic courses for each leg and determine the leg distances.
2. Apply variations to the winds aloft.
3. Determine the temperature in relation to ISA.
4. Determine Mach number and convert to TAS.
5. Compute ground speed.
6. Calculate and record the time for each leg.
7. Compute fuel flow.
8. Compute total fuel.
9. Determine the reserve fuel.
10. Compute fuel burn to alternate.
11. Add the en route, reserve, and alternate fuel to find the total fuel required for the flight.

Computation of Temperature at Cruise Altitude

Temperature is often expressed as a deviation from ISA which is the standard day temperature (i.e., ISA -2°). This temperature can be computed by the following procedure:

1. Compute ISA by multiplying the altitude in thousands of feet times -2° and then adding 15°. For example: ISA at 27,000 feet = 27 x (-2°) +15 = -39°

2. Apply the deviation from ISA. ISA -2° at 27,000 feet = (-39°) + (-2°) = -41°

Answers

8610   [A]   8611   [A]   8612   [B]

Computation of True Airspeed Using Mach Number

True Airspeed (TAS) can be computed from Mach number and Outside Air Temperature (OAT).

Using the CX-3 Flight Computer, select "Airspeed" from the FLT menu, then enter the OAT and the Mach number at the appropriate prompts to get TAS.

Using an E6-B computer, follow these steps:

1. In the small window labeled "Airspeed Correction" or "True Airspeed," align the arrow labeled "Mach Number" with the OAT on the scale adjacent the window.

2. Find the Mach number on the inner of the two main scales and then read the TAS opposite it on the outer scale.

Note: Some "CR"-type mechanical computers have a window in which a Mach Index is aligned with a Mach number inside the window. Don't use this scale. It is designed to use Indicated Temperature and will give an inaccurate TAS when OAT is used.

See the instruction manual of your individual computer for more detailed instructions.

Specific Range

Specific range is the term used to describe the rate of fuel burn per nautical air mile flown. It is calculated by using TAS and fuel flow only. Wind has no effect on specific range. To calculate specific range in nautical air miles per 1,000 pounds, use the formula:

NM/1,000 = TAS x 1,000 ÷ PPH.

TAS should be calculated from the Mach number as in the paragraph above. PPH can be taken directly from the flight log.

ATM, ATS, DSP
8702. A jet airplane is flying at .72 Mach with an OAT of -40°C. What is the true airspeed?

A— 430 knots.
B— 452 knots.
C— 464 knots.

Using your CX-3 Flight Computer select Airspeed from the FLT menu. Enter a MACH of .72 and OAT of -40°C to get a TAS of 428.41 KTS. The closest available answer is 430 knots. (PLT012) — FAA-H-8083-15

ATM, ATS, DSP
9546. (Refer to Figures 94, 95, and 96.) What is the ETE from Chicago Midway Airport to Greater Buffalo Intl?

A— 2 hours 12 minutes.
B— 2 hours 15 minutes.
C— 2 hours 18 minutes.

To answer this question, complete the flight log in FAA Figure 94, using the information given in the problem:

1. *Change the winds aloft of FL190 at GIJ (Gipper) from true to magnetic, using the variation from the flight log (FAA Figure 94). Note: The variation changes with each leg. Winds at GIJ at FL190 are 230° true at 51 knots.*

   230° True
   + 01° West variation
   231° Magnetic

2. *Find the distance flown for the leg. In this case it is 19 nautical miles, since the L/O point is on the GIJ 270° radial at 19 NM. Distances for subsequent legs must be determined by referring to the enroute charts (FAA Figure 96).*

3. *Find the ground speed for the leg from L/O to GIJ using a flight computer:*

   Wind direction 231° (calculated in Step 1).
   Wind speed 51 knots (given on the flight log).
   Course 090° (L/O point is on the GIJ 270° radial).
   TAS 160 knots (given in the flight plan in FAA Figure 94).

   Calculated GS is 196.4 knots.

Continued

Answers

8702   [A]   9546   [A]

4. Compute the time en route for the leg from L/O to GIJ:

> Distance 19 NM (determined in Step 2).
> Ground speed 196.4 (calculated in Step 3).

Calculated leg time is 5 minutes, 48 seconds.

5. Since the next question asks for the fuel required for the flight, calculate the fuel burned on this leg:

> ETE is :5:48 (calculated in Step 4).
> Fuel flow is 610 PPH (in note at the bottom of the flight log).

Fuel burned is 59.0 pounds.

6. Repeat steps for the subsequent legs to fill in the flight log:

FROM	TO	CRS	TAS	GS	NM	ETE	FUEL
MDW	L/O	—	—	—	—	:19:00*	327.0*
L/O	GIJ	090	160	196	19	:05:48	59.0
GIJ	CRL	085	160	200	129	:38:58	392.8
CRL	YXU	065	160	219	118	:32:20	328.7
YXU	T/D	101	160	215	80	:22:18	236.7
T/D	BUF	—	—	—	30	:14:00*	121.5*
						2:12:04	1,455.7

*(given)

(PLT012) — FAA-H-8083-15

ATM, ATS, DSP

9547. (Refer to Figures 94, 95, and 96.) What are the fuel requirements from Chicago Midway Airport to Greater Buffalo Intl?

A— 2,224 pounds.
B— 1,987 pounds.
C— 1,454 pounds.

Fuel from Question 9546:   1,455.7
Fuel for alternate to ROC: 236.0
Fuel for reserve: + 532.5
                2,224.2 pounds

(PLT012) — FAA-H-8083-15

ATM, ATS, DSP

9548. (Refer to Figures 94, 95, and 96.) What TAS should be maintained to arrive over CRL VORTAC 42 minutes after level-off?

A— 166 knots.
B— 168 knots.
C— 171 knots.

1. Determine the required ground speed using a flight calculator:

> Distance flown is 148 NM (distance from L/O to GIJ to CRL).
> Time is 42 minutes (given in the problem).

Calculated GS is 211.4 knots.

2. Determine the required TAS:

> Wind direction is 231° Magnetic (see Steps 1 and 2 in Question 9546).
> Wind speed is 51 knots (given in flight log).
> Course is 087° (average of the two legs).
> GS is 211.4 (calculated in Step 1).

TAS is 172.8.

(PLT012) — FAA-H-8083-15

ATM, ATS, DSP

9556. (Refer to Figures 98, 99, 100, and 102.) What is the ETE from DFW Intl to IAH?

A— 1 hour 2 minutes.
B— 1 hour 4 minutes.
C— 1 hour 6 minutes.

To answer this question, complete the flight log in FAA Figure 98, using the information given in the problem:

1. Change the winds aloft at 15,000 from true to magnetic, using the variation from the Chart Supplements U.S. (previously A/FD). Winds at BILEE are 230° True at 42 knots.

> 230° True
> – 08° East variation
> 222° Magnetic

2. Find the distance flown for the leg. In this case it is 80 NM. The sum of the distances from DFW to BILEE is 107 NM, and 27 NM of that is used by the climb. Distances for subsequent legs must be determined by referring to the enroute charts and the CUGAR Four Arrival (FAA Figures 100 and 102).

3. Find the ground speed for the leg from L/O to BILEE using a flight computer:

> Wind direction 222° (calculated in Step 1).
> Wind speed 42 knots (given on the flight log).
> Course 154° (V369 is on the DFW 154° radial).
> TAS 248 knots (given in the flight plan on FAA Figure 98).

Calculated GS is 229.2 knots.

Answers

9547 [A]   9548 [C]   9556 [B]

4. Compute the time en route for the leg from L/O to BILEE:

> Distance 80 NM (determined in Step 2).
> Ground speed 229.2 (calculated in Step 3).

Calculated leg time is 20 minutes, 57 seconds.

5. Since the next question asks for the fuel required for the flight, calculate the fuel burned on this leg:

> ETE is :20:57 (calculated in Step 4).
> Fuel flow is 850 PPH (in note at the bottom of the flight log).

Fuel burned is 296.7 pounds.

6. Repeat steps for the subsequent legs to fill in the flight log:

FROM	TO	CRS	TAS	GS	NM	ETE	FUEL
DFW	L/O	—	—	—	27	:12:00*	231.0*
L/O	BILEE	154	248	229.2	80	:20:57	296.7
BILEE	CUGAR	125	248	249.6	47	:11:18	160.1
CUGAR	T/D	125	248	249.6	21	:05:03	71.5
T/D	IAH	—	—	—	25	:14:00*	132.0*
						1:03:18	891.3

*(given)

(PLT012) — FAA-H-8083-15

ATM, ATS, DSP
9557. (Refer to Figures 98, 99, 100, and 102.) What is the total fuel required from DFW Intl to IAH?

A— 1,555 pounds.
B— 1,863 pounds.
C— 1,941 pounds.

In this question, the regulation-required fuel must be calculated using the summary box at the bottom of the flight plan.

1. Compute the fuel required to fly the flight:

> Fuel required is 891.3 pounds (see flight plan in Question 9556).

2. Compute the regulation-required reserve fuel (see Question 9556, Step 5):

> Time required is 45 minutes (14 CFR §135.223).
> Fuel flow is 880 PPH (given at bottom of flight plan in FAA Figure 98).

Reserve fuel is 660.0 pounds.

3. Compute ETE to alternate (see Question 9556, Step 4):

> GS is 194 knots (given in flight log).
> Distance 68 NM (given in flight log).

ETE to alternate is 21 minutes, 2 seconds.

4. Compute fuel burn to alternate (see Question 9556, Step 5):

> Time to alternate is :21:02 (computed in previous step).
> Fuel flow is 880 PPH (given in flight log).

Fuel burn to alternate is 308.5 pounds.

5. Add the totals of Steps 1 through 4:

> **FUEL**
> 891.3   En route
> 660.0   Reserve
> + 308.5   Alternate
> 1,859.8   Total

(PLT012) — FAA-H-8083-15, 14 CFR §91.167

ATM, ATS, DSP
9558. (Refer to Figures 98, 99, 100, and 102.) Determine the TAS required to arrive at CUGAR, 31 minutes after level-off.

A— 269 knots.
B— 264 knots.
C— 258 knots.

1. Determine the required ground speed using a flight calculator:

> Distance flown is 127 NM (80 + 47). Time is 31 minutes (stated in the problem).

Calculated GS is 245.8 knots.

2. Determine the required TAS:

> Wind direction is 222° Magnetic (see Step 1 in Question 9556).
> Wind speed is 42 knots (given in flight log).
> Course is 154° (V369).
> GS is 245.8 knots (calculated in Step 1).

TAS is 264.4 knots.

(PLT012) — FAA-H-8083-15

Answers

9557   [B]   9558   [B]

ATM, ATS, DSP
9559. (Refer to Figures 98, 99, 100, and 102.) Determine the TAS required to arrive at CUGAR, 29 minutes after level-off.

A— 285 knots.
B— 290 knots.
C— 295 knots.

1. Determine the required ground speed using a flight calculator:

> Distance flown is 127 NM (80 + 47).
> Time is 29 minutes (stated in the problem).

Calculated GS is 262.8 knots.

2. Determine the required TAS:

> Wind direction is 222° Magnetic (see Step 1 in Question 9556).
> Wind speed is 42 knots (given in flight log).
> Course is 154° (V369).
> GS is 262.8 knots (calculated in Step 1).

TAS is 281.2 knots (the closest answer is 285).

(PLT012) — FAA-H-8083-15

ATM, ATS, DSP
9560. (Refer to Figures 103, 104, 105, and 106.) Estimate the total fuel required to be on the aircraft, prior to taxi at Tucson Intl. (Use 13°E for problem magnetic variation.)

A— 2,223 pounds.
B— 2,327 pounds.
C— 2,447 pounds.

To answer this question, complete the flight log in FAA Figure 103, using the information given in the problem:

1. Change the winds aloft at FL220 from true to magnetic, using the variation given in the question. Winds at GBN are 280° true at 46 knots.

> 280° True
> – 13° East variation
> 267° Magnetic

2. Find the distance flown for the leg. In this case it is 31 NM. The sum of the distances from Tucson to GBN is 104 NM (see the TUCSON 4 Departure), and 73 NM of that is used by the climb. Distances for subsequent legs must be determined by referring to the enroute charts and the DOWNE 3 Arrival (FAA Figures 105 and 106).

3. Find the ground speed for the leg from L/O to GBN using a flight computer:

> Wind direction 267° (calculated in Step 1).
> Wind speed 46 knots (given on the flight log).
> Course 289° (inbound on GBN 109 radial).
> TAS 233 knots (given in the flight plan on FAA Figure 103).

Calculated GS is 189 knots.

4. Compute the time en route for the leg from L/O to GBN:

> Distance 31 NM (determined in Step 2).
> Ground speed 189 (calculated in Step 3).

Calculated leg time is 9 minutes, 49 seconds.

5. Calculate the fuel burned on this leg:

> ETE is :09:49 (calculated in Step 4).
> Fuel flow is 676 PPH (in note at the bottom of the flight log).

Fuel burned is 110.6 pounds.

6. Repeat steps for the subsequent legs to fill in the flight log:

FROM	TO	CRS	TAS	GS	NM	ETE	FUEL
TUS	L/O	—	—	—	73	:25:00*	350.0*
L/O	GBN	289	233	189	31	:09:49	110.6
GBN	Int J104	298	233	192	76	:23:45	267.5
Int J104	PKE	277	233	188	47	:15:01	169.2
PKE	TNP	256	233	187	54	:17:17	194.7
TNP	T/D	250	233	188	81**	:25:49	290.8
T/D	LAX	—	—	—	52	:18:00*	170.0*
						2:14:41	1,552.8

*(given)

**Note: The DOWNE Three arrival is only used when LAX is landing on runways 6 or 7 and the total distance from TNP to LAX on the arrival is 176 NM. However, it is apparent from the answer choices and the approach charts that a straight-in landing on Runway 25L is assumed. This gives a distance of 133 from TNP to LAX. The distance from TNP to T/D was determined by taking the distance from TNP to PIONE Int to LAX (FAA Figure 106) and subtracting the 52 NM used for the descent. In this question, the regulation-required fuel must be calculated using the summary box at the bottom of the flight plan.

7. Compute the fuel required to fly the flight:

> Fuel required is 1,552.8 pounds (see flight plan).

8. Compute the required reserve fuel (see Step 5):

> Time required is 45 minutes (§135.223).
> Fuel flow is 726 PPH (given at bottom of flight plan in FAA Figure 103).

Reserve fuel is 544.2 pounds.

Answers

9559 [A]   9560 [B]

9. Compute fuel burn to alternate (see Step 5):

Time to alternate is :19:00 (given in FAA Figure 103).
Fuel flow is 726 PPH (given in flight log).

Fuel burn to alternate is 229.9 pounds.

10. Add the totals of Steps 7 through 9:

FUEL

1552.8	En route
544.5	Reserve
+ 229.9	Alternate
2,327.2	Total

(PLT012) — FAA-H-8083-15

ATM, ATS, DSP
9561. (Refer to Figures 103, 104, 105, and 106.) Determine the ETE for the flight from Tucson Intl to Los Angeles Intl.

A— 2 hours 10 minutes.
B— 2 hours 15 minutes.
C— 2 hours 19 minutes.

Refer to Question 9560, Steps 1-6.

(PLT012) — FAA-H-8083-15

ATM, ATS, DSP
9578. (Refer to Figures 107, 115, 116, 117, 118, and 118C.) What is the ETE at .78 Mach?

A— 1 hour 08 minutes.
B— 1 hour 02 minutes.
C— 1 hour 05 minutes.

To answer this question, complete the flight log in FAA Figure 115, using the information given in the problem:

1. Change the winds aloft at FL270 from true to magnetic, using the variation from the Chart Supplements U.S. entries for the LAX and PHX VORTACs. Winds at IPL are 300° True at 43 knots.

300°	True
– 15°	East variation
285°	Magnetic

2. Calculate the TAS for Mach .78:

ISA temperature at FL270 is -39°C
((27 x (-2°)) + 15°).
ISA -2° = -41°C

Using a flight calculator, determine that Mach .78 = 463.1 knots.

3. Find the distance flown for the leg. In this case it is 50 NM. The remarks section of the flight plan notes that the L/O point is on the OCN 270° radial at 50 NM. The first leg of the IMPERIAL THREE Departure is from there to OCN. Even though only one line is used for the cruise portion of the IMPERIAL 3 departure, each leg of it should be calculated separately for best accuracy. The same is true of the ARLIN 9 Arrival into PHX.

4. Find the ground speed for the leg from L/O to OCN using a flight computer:

Wind direction 285° (calculated in Step 1).
Wind speed 43 knots (given on the flight log).
Course 090° (L/O point is on the OCN 270° radial).
TAS 463.1 knots (calculated in Step 2).

Calculated GS is 504.5 knots.

5. Compute the time en route for the leg from L/O to OCN:

Distance 50 NM (determined in Step 3).
Ground speed 504.5 (calculated in Step 4).

Calculated leg time is 5 minutes, 57 seconds.

6. Since the next question asks for the fuel required for the flight, calculate the fuel burned on this leg:

ETE is :5:57 (calculated in Step 5).
Fuel flow is 9,600 PPH (in note at the bottom of the flight log).

Fuel burned is 951.4 pounds.

7. Repeat steps for the subsequent legs to fill in the flight log:

FROM	TO	CRS	TAS	GS	NM	ETE	FUEL
LAX	L/O	—	—	—	43	:19:00*	4,510.0*
L/O	OCN	090	463.1	504.5	50	:05:57	951.4
OCN	JLI	083	463.1	502.7	42	:05:01	802.1
JLI	KUMBA	115	463.1	505.4	35	:04:09	664.8
KUMBA	IPL	078	463.1	501.0	27	:03:14	517.4
IPL	BZA	074	463.1	499.4	46	:05:32	885.3
BZA	Mohak Int	075	463.1	499.0	32	:03:51	615.6
Mohak	T/P	067	463.1	494.7	15	:01:49	290.7
T/P	HYDRR	035	463.1	473.9	42	:05:19	850.7
HYDRR	ARLIN	076	463.1	499.0	19	:02:17	365.3
ARLIN	PHX	—	—	—	—	:12:00*	1,140.0*
						1:08:09	11,593.3

*(given)

(PLT012) — FAA-H-8083-15

Answers

9561 [B]   9578 [A]

ATM, ATS, DSP
9579. (Refer to Figures 115, 116, 117, 118, and 118C.)
What is the total fuel required at .78 Mach?

A— 22,140 pounds.
B— 22,556 pounds.
C— 22,972 pounds.

In this question, the regulation-required fuel must be calculated using the summary box at the bottom of the flight plan:

1. *Compute the fuel required to fly the flight:*

   Fuel required is 11,593.3 pounds (see flight plan in Question 9578).

2. *Compute the required reserve fuel (see Question 9578, Step 6):*

   Time required is 45 minutes (§121.639).
   Fuel flow is 9,250 PPH (given at bottom of flight plan in FAA Figure 115).

   Reserve fuel is 6,937.5 pounds.

3. *Determine ETE to alternate:*

   ETE to alternate is 26 minutes (given in the flight log).

4. *Compute fuel burn to alternate (see Question 9578, Step 6):*

   Time to alternate is :26:00 (from Step 3).
   Fuel flow is 9,250 PPH (given in flight log).

   Fuel burn to alternate is 4,008.3 pounds.

5. *Add the totals of Steps 1 through 4:*

   FUEL
11,593.3	En route
6,937.5	Reserve
+ 4,008.3	Alternate
22,539.1	Total

(PLT012) — FAA-H-8083-15

ATM, ATS, DSP
9580. (Refer to Figures 115, 116, 117, 118, and 118C.)
What is the specific range in nautical miles per 1,000 pounds of fuel from level-off to the ARLIN Intersection using .78 Mach?

A— 48.8 NAM/1,000 pounds.
B— 48.2 NAM/1,000 pounds.
C— 47.9 NAM/1,000 pounds.

NM/1,000 is calculated by multiplying TAS times 1,000 and dividing the answer by the fuel flow.

   TAS is 463.1 (calculated in Step 2 of Question 9578).
   Fuel flow is 9,600 PPH (given in the flight log).

NM/1,000 = 48.2

(PLT015) — ANA

ATM, ATS, DSP
9581. (Refer to Figures 107, 115, 116, 117, 118, and 118C.) What is the ETE at .80 Mach?

A— 1 hour 02 minutes.
B— 1 hour 04 minutes.
C— 1 hour 07 minutes.

To answer this question, complete the flight log in FAA Figure 115, using the information given in the problem:

1. *Change the winds aloft at FL270 from true to magnetic, using the variation from the Chart Supplements U.S. entries for the LAX and PHX VORTACs. Winds at IPL are 300° True at 43 knots.*

300°	True
– 15°	East variation
285°	Magnetic

2. *Calculate the TAS for Mach .80:*

   ISA temperature at FL270 is -39°C
   ((27 x (-2°)) + 15°).
   ISA -2°= -41°C

   Using a flight calculator, determine that Mach .80 = 475.0 knots.

3. *Find the distance flown for the leg. In this case it is 50 NM. The remarks section of the flight plan notes that the L/O point is on the OCN 270° radial at 50 NM. The first leg of the IMPERIAL THREE Departure is from there to OCN. Even though only one line is used for the cruise portion of the IMPERIAL 3 departure, each leg of it should be calculated separately for best accuracy. The same is true of the ARLIN 9 Arrival into PHX.*

4. *Find the ground speed for the leg from L/O to OCN using a flight computer:*

   Wind direction 285° (calculated in Step 1).
   Wind speed 43 knots (given on the flight log).
   Course 090° (L/O point is on the OCN 270° radial).
   TAS 475.0 knots (calculated in Step 2).

   Calculated GS is 516.4 knots.

Answers

9579 [B]   9580 [B]   9581 [C]

5. Compute the time en route for the leg from L/O to OCN:

> Distance 50 NM (determined in Step 3).
> Ground speed 516.4 (calculated in Step 4).

Calculated leg time is 5 minutes, 49 seconds.

6. Since the next question asks for the fuel required for the flight, calculate the fuel burned on this leg:

> ETE is :5:49 (calculated in Step 5).
> Fuel flow is 9,600 PPH (in note at the bottom of the flight log).

Fuel burned is 930.7 pounds.

7. Repeat steps for the subsequent legs to fill in the flight log:

FROM	TO	CRS	TAS	GS	NM	ETE	FUEL
LAX	L/O	—	—	—	43	:19:00*	4,510.0*
L/O	OCN	090	475	516.4	50	:05:49	930.7
OCN	JLI	083	475	514.6	42	:04:54	784.0
JLI	KUMBA	115	475	517.3	35	:04:04	650.7
KUMBA	IPL	078	475	512.9	27	:03:10	506.7
IPL	BZA	074	475	510.9	46	:05:24	864.3
BZA	Mohak Int	075	475	510.5	32	:03:46	601.8
Mohak	T/P	067	475	506.6	15	:01:47	285.3
T/P	HYDRR	035	475	485.8	42	:05:11	829.3
HYDRR	ARLIN	076	475	510.9	19	:02:14	357.3
ARLIN	PHX	—	—	—	—	:12:00*	1,140.0*
						1:07:19	11,460.1

*(given)

(PLT012) — FAA-H-8083-15

ATM, ATS, DSP

9582. (Refer to Figures 115, 116, 117, 118, and 118C.) What is the total fuel required at .80 Mach?

A— 22,836 pounds.
B— 22,420 pounds.
C— 22,556 pounds.

In this question, the regulation-required fuel must be calculated using the summary box at the bottom of the flight plan.

1. Compute the fuel required to fly the flight:

> Fuel required is 11,460.1 pounds (see flight plan in Question 9581).

2. Compute the required reserve fuel (see Question 9581, Step 6):

> Time required is 45 minutes (§121.639).
> Fuel flow is 9,250 PPH (given at bottom of flight plan in FAA Figure 115).

Reserve fuel is 6,937.5 pounds.

3. Determine ETE to alternate:

> ETE to alternate is 26 minutes (given in the flight log).

4. Compute fuel burn to alternate (see Question 9581, Step 6):

> Time to alternate is :26:00 (from Step 3).
> Fuel flow is 9,250 PPH (given in flight log).

Fuel burn to alternate is 4,008.3 pounds.

5. Add the totals of Steps 1 through 4:

> **FUEL**
> 11,460.1 En route
> 6,937.5 Reserve
> + 4,008.3 Alternate
> 22,405.9 Total

(PLT012) — FAA-H-8083-15

ATM, ATS, DSP

9583. (Refer to Figures 115, 116, 117, and 118C.) What approximate indicated Mach should be maintained to arrive over the BZA VORTAC 6 minutes after passing IPL VORTAC?

A— .73 Mach.
B— .74 Mach.
C— .715 Mach.

1. Determine the required GS:

> Distance is 46 NM (FAA Figure 117).
> Time is 6 minutes (given in the question).

> GS = 460 knots

2. Determine the required TAS:

> Wind direction is 287° magnetic (300° True from flight log, less 13° east variation).
> Wind speed is 43 knots (given in flight log).
> Course is 074° (FAA Figure 117).
> GS is 460 knots (calculated in Step 1).

> Required TAS = 424.6 knots.

3. Calculate the required Mach number:

> TAS is 424.6 knots (calculated in Step 2).
> Temperature is -41°C (calculated in Question 9581, Step 2).

> Required Mach number is .715.

(PLT012) — FAA-H-8083-15

Answers

9582 [B]   9583 [C]

ATM, ATS, DSP
9584. (Refer to Figures 107, 115, 116, 117, 118, and 118C.) What is the ETE at .82 Mach?

A— 1 hour 05 minutes.
B— 1 hour 07 minutes.
C— 1 hour 03 minutes.

To answer this question, complete the flight log in FAA Figure 115, using the information given in the problem:

1. *Change the winds aloft at FL270 from true to magnetic, using the variation from the Chart Supplements U.S. entries for the LAX and PHX VORTACs. Winds at IPL are 300° true at 43 knots.*

    300° *True*
    − 15° *East variation*
    285° *Magnetic*

2. *Calculate the TAS for Mach .82:*

    *ISA temperature at FL270 is -39°C
    ((27 x (-2°)) + 15°).
    ISA -2° = -41°C*

    Using a flight calculator, determine that Mach .82 = 486.9 knots.

3. *Find the distance flown for the leg. In this case it is 50 NM. The remarks section of the flight plan form notes that the L/O point is on the OCN 270° radial at 50 NM. The first leg of the IMPERIAL 3 Departure is from there to OCN. Even though only one line is used for the cruise portion of the IMPERIAL 3 departure, each leg of it should be calculated separately for best accuracy. The same is true of the ARLIN 9 Arrival into PHX.*

4. *Find the ground speed for the leg from L/O to OCN using a flight computer:*

    *Wind direction 285° (calculated in Step 1).
    Wind speed 43 knots (given in the flight log).
    Course 090° (L/O point is on the OCN
       270° radial).
    TAS 486.9 knots (calculated in Step 2).*

    Calculated GS is 528.3 knots.

5. *Compute the time en route for the leg from L/O to OCN:*

    *Distance 50 NM (determined in Step 3).
    Ground speed 528.3 (calculated in Step 4).*

    Calculated leg time is 5 minutes, 41 seconds.

6. *Since the next question asks for the fuel required for the flight, calculate the fuel burned on this leg:*

    *ETE is :5:41 (calculated in Step 5).
    Fuel flow is 9,600 PPH (in note at the bottom of
       the flight log).*

    Fuel burned is 909.3 pounds.

7. *Repeat steps for the subsequent legs to fill in the flight log:*

FROM	TO	CRS	TAS	GS	NM	ETE	FUEL
LAX	L/O	—	—	—	43	:19:00*	4,510.0*
L/O	OCN	090	486.9	528.3	50	:05:41	909.3
OCN	JLI	083	486.9	526.5	42	:04:47	765.3
JLI	KUMBA	115	486.9	529.2	35	:03:58	634.7
KUMBA	IPL	078	486.9	524.8	27	:03:05	493.3
IPL	BZA	074	486.9	522.4	46	:05:17	845.4
BZA	Mohak Int	075	486.9	522.4	32	:03:41	588.1
Mohak	T/P	067	486.9	518.5	15	:01:44	277.3
T/P	HYDRR	035	486.9	497.7	42	:05:04	810.7
HYDRR	ARLIN	076	486.9	522.8	19	:02:11	349.3
ARLIN	PHX	—	—	—	—	:12:00*	1,140.0*
						1:06:28	11,323.4

*(given)

(PLT012) — FAA-H-8083-15

ATM, ATS, DSP
9585. (Refer to Figures 115, 116, 117, 118, and 118C.) What is the total fuel required at .82 Mach?

A— 22,420 pounds.
B— 22,284 pounds.
C— 22,700 pounds.

In this question, the regulation-required fuel must be calculated using the summary box at the bottom of the flight plan.

1. *Compute the fuel required to fly the flight:*

    *Fuel required is 11,323.4 pounds (see flight
       plan in Question 9584).*

2. *Compute the required reserve fuel (see Question 9584, Step 6):*

    *Time required is 45 minutes (§121.639).
    Fuel flow is 9,250 PPH (given at bottom of flight
       plan in FAA Figure 115).*

    Reserve fuel is 6,937.5 pounds.

3. *Determine ETE to alternate:*

    *ETE to alternate is 26 minutes (given in the
       flight log).*

Answers

9584   [B]   9585   [B]

4. Compute fuel burn to alternate (see Question 9584, Step 6):

> Time to alternate is :26:00 (computed in previous step).
> Fuel flow is 9,250 PPH (given in flight log).

> Fuel burn to alternate is 4,008.3 pounds.

5. Add the totals of Steps 1 through 4:

> **FUEL**
> 11,323.4 En route
> 6,937.5 Reserve
> + 4,008.3 Alternate
> 22,269.2 Total

(PLT012) — FAA-H-8083-15

ATM, ATS, DSP

9591. (Refer to Figures 119, 120, 121, and 122.) What is the ETE from BUF to ORD using .78 Mach?

A— 1 hour 09 minutes.
B— 1 hour 07 minutes.
C— 1 hour 05 minutes.

To answer this question, complete the flight log in FAA Figure 119, using the information given in the problem:

1. Change the winds aloft at FL310 from true to magnetic, using the variation from the remarks section of the flight plan. Winds at BUF are 330° True at 39 knots.

> 330° True
> + 08° West variation
> 338° Magnetic

2. Calculate the TAS for Mach .78:

> ISA temperature at FL310 is -47°C
> ((31 x (-2°)) + 15).
> ISA -6° = -53°C

> Using a flight calculator, determine that Mach .78 = 451.0 knots.

3. Find the distance flown for the leg, in this case 40 NM. FAA Figure 121 shows that it is 110 NM from BUF to YXU via J547. The flight log indicates that 70 NM is needed for the climb.

4. Find the ground speed for the leg from L/O to YXU using a flight computer:

> Wind direction 338° (calculated in Step 1).
> Wind speed 39 knots (given in the flight log).
> Course 282° (L/O point is on the BUF 282° radial).
> TAS 451.0 knots (calculated in Step 2).

> Calculated GS is 428.0 knots.

5. Compute the time en route for the leg from L/O to YXU:

> Distance 40 NM (determined in Step 3).
> Ground speed 428.0 (calculated in Step 4).

> Calculated leg time is 5 minutes, 36 seconds.

6. Since the next question asks for the fuel required for the flight, calculate the fuel burned on this leg:

> ETE is :5:36 (calculated in Step 5).
> Fuel flow is 9,300 PPH (in note at the bottom of the flight log).

> Fuel burned is 869.1 pounds.

7. Repeat steps for the subsequent legs to fill in the flight log:

FROM	TO	CRS	TAS	GS	NM	ETE	FUEL
BUF	L/O	—	—	—	70	:16:00*	4,960.0*
L/O	YXU	282	451	428.0	40	:05:36	869.1
YXU	FNT	270	451	431.9	114	:15:50	2454.5
FNT	T/D	258	451	439.3	94	:12:50	1989.9
T/D	PMM	—	—	—	15	:02:00*	216.7*
PMM	ORD	—	—	—	89	:13:00*	1,408.3*
						1:05:16	11,898.5

*(given)

(PLT012) — FAA-H-8083-15

ATM, ATS, DSP

9592. (Refer to Figures 119, 120, 121, and 122.) What is the total fuel required for the flight from BUF to ORD using .78 Mach?

A— 19,033 pounds.
B— 21,739 pounds.
C— 22,189 pounds.

In this question, the regulation-required fuel must be calculated using the summary box at the bottom of the flight plan.

1. Compute the fuel required to fly the flight:

> Fuel required is 11,898.5 pounds (see flight plan in Question 9591).

2. Compute the required reserve fuel (see Question 9591, Step 6):

> Time required is 45 minutes (§121.639).
> Fuel flow is 9,550 PPH (given at bottom of flight plan in FAA Figure 119).

> Reserve fuel is 7,162.5 pounds.

3. Determine ETE to alternate:

> ETE to alternate is 17 minutes (given in the flight log).

Continued

Answers

9591 [C]   9592 [B]

4. Compute fuel burn to alternate (see Question 9591, Step 6):

> Time to alternate is :17:00 (from Step 3).
> Fuel flow is 9,550 PPH (given in flight log).

> Fuel burn to alternate is 2,705.8 pounds.

5. Add the totals of Steps 1 through 4:

> **FUEL**
> 11,898.5   En route
> 7,162.5   Reserve
> + 2,705.8   Alternate
> 21,766.8   Total

(PLT012) — FAA-H-8083-15

ATM, ATS, DSP

9593. (Refer to Figures 119, 120, 121, and 122.) What is the specific range in nautical air miles per 1,000 pounds of fuel from level-off to start of descent using .78 Mach?

A— 48.9 NAM/1000.
B— 52.5 NAM/1000.
C— 55.9 NAM/1000.

NM/1,000 is calculated by multiplying TAS times 1,000 and dividing the answer by the fuel flow:

> TAS is 451 (calculated in Question 9591, Step 2).
> Fuel flow is 9,300 PPH (given in the flight log).

NM/1,000 = 48.5

(PLT015) — ANA

ATM, ATS, DSP

9594. (Refer to Figures 119, 120, 121, and 122.) What is the ETE from BUF to ORD using .80 Mach?

A— 1 hour 01 minutes.
B— 1 hour 04 minutes.
C— 1 hour 08 minutes.

To answer this question, complete the flight log in FAA Figure 119, using the information given in the problem:

1. Change the winds aloft at FL310 from true to magnetic, using the variation from the remarks section of the flight plan. Winds at BUF are 330° True at 39 knots.

> 330° True
> + 08° West variation
> 338° Magnetic

2. Calculate the TAS for Mach .80:

> ISA temperature at FL310 is -47°C
> ((31 x (-2°)) + 15°).
> ISA -6° = -53°C

Using a flight calculator, determine that Mach .80 = 462.5 knots.

3. Find the distance flown for the leg. In this case it is 40 NM. FAA Figure 121 shows that it is 110 NM from BUF to YXU via J547. The flight log indicates that 70 NM is needed for the climb.

4. Find the ground speed for the leg from L/O to YXU using a flight computer:

> Wind direction 338° (calculated in Step 1).
> Wind speed 39 knots (given in the flight log).
> Course 282° (L/O point is on the BUF 282° radial).
> TAS 462.5 knots (calculated in Step 2).

Calculated GS is 428.0 knots.

5. Compute the time enroute for the leg from L/O to YXU:

> Distance 40 NM (determined in Step 3).
> Ground speed 439.6 (calculated in Step 4).

Calculated leg time is 5 minutes, 28 seconds.

6. Since the next question asks for the fuel required for the flight, calculate the fuel burned on this leg:

> ETE is :5:28 (calculated in Step 5).
> Fuel flow is 9,300 PPH (in note at the bottom of the flight log).

Fuel burned is 846.2 pounds.

7. Repeat steps for the subsequent legs to fill in the flight log:

FROM	TO	CRS	TAS	GS	NM	ETE	FUEL
BUF	L/O	—	—	—	70	:16:00*	4,960.0*
L/O	YXU	282	462.5	439.6	40	:05:28	846.2
YXU	FNT	270	462.5	443.5	114	:15:25	2,390.3
FNT	T/D	258	462.5	450.9	94	:12:30	1938.7
T/D	PMM	—	—	—	15	:02:00*	216.7*
PMM	ORD	—	—	—	89	:13:00*	1,408.3*
						1:04:23	11,760.2

*(given)

(PLT012) — FAA-H-8083-15

ATM, ATS, DSP

9595. (Refer to Figures 119, 120, 121, and 122.) What is the total fuel required for the flight from BUF to ORD using .80 Mach?

A— 19,388 pounds.
B— 22,494 pounds.
C— 21,644 pounds.

In this question, the regulation-required fuel must be calculated using the summary box at the bottom of the flight plan.

1. *Compute the fuel required to fly the flight:*

   Fuel required is 11,760.2 pounds (see flight plan in Question 9594).

2. *Compute the required reserve fuel (see Question 9594, Step 6):*

   Time required is 45 minutes (§121.639).
   Fuel flow is 9,550 PPH (given at bottom of flight plan in FAA Figure 119).

   Reserve fuel is 7,162.5 pounds.

3. *Determine ETE to alternate:*

   ETE to alternate is 17 minutes (given in the flight log).

4. *Compute fuel burn to alternate (see Question 9594, Step 6):*

   Time to alternate is :17:00 (from Step 3).
   Fuel flow is 9,550 PPH (given in flight log).

   Fuel burn to alternate is 2,705.8 pounds.

5. *Add the totals of Steps 1 through 4:*

   FUEL
   11,760.2   *En route*
   7,162.5   *Reserve*
   + 2,705.8   *Alternate*
   ——————
   21,628.5   *Total*

(PLT012) — FAA-H-8083-15

ATM, ATS, DSP

9597. (Refer to Figures 158, 159, 160, 160A, and 161.) The estimated time enroute from STL to LGA for N711JB is

A— 1 hour 46 minutes.
B— 1 hour 50 minutes.
C— 1 hour 54 minutes.

To answer this question, complete the flight log in FAA Figure 158, using the information given in the problem:

1. *Change the winds aloft at FL370 from true to magnetic, using the variation from the remarks section of the flight plan. Notice that the variation changes with each leg. Winds at ROD are 350° True at 96 knots.*

   350° *True*
   + 01° *West variation*
   ——————
   351° *Magnetic*

2. *Find the distance flown for the leg. In this case it is 131 NM. This is the distance from BIB to SHB in FAA Figure 160. Although the flight log provides only one line for the leg from BIB to ROD, the turn at SHB makes it more accurate to compute the ETEs and fuel burns separately.*

3. *Find the ground speed for the leg from BID to SHB using a flight computer:*

   Wind direction 351° (calculated in Step 1).
   Wind speed 96 knots (given in the flight log).
   Course 067° (V394).
   TAS 506 knots (given in the flight plan in FAA Figure 158).

   Calculated GS is 474.1 knots.

4. *Compute the time en route for the leg from BIB to SHB:*

   Distance 131 NM (determined in Step 2).
   Ground speed 474.1 (calculated in Step 3).

   Calculated leg time is 16 minutes, 35 seconds.

5. *Since the next question asks for the fuel required for the flight, calculate the fuel burned on this leg:*

   ETE is :16:35 (calculated in Step 4).
   Fuel flow is 2,389 PPH (in note at the bottom of the flight log).

   Fuel burned is 660.1 pounds.

6. *Repeat steps for the subsequent legs to fill in the flight log:*

FROM	TO	CRS	TAS	GS	NM	ETE	FUEL
STL	BIB	—	—	—	95	:16:00*	987.0*
BIB	SHB	067	506	474.1	131	:16:35	660.1
SHB	ROD	063	506	468.0	91	:11:40	464.5
ROD	DJB	059	506	456.5	107	:14:04	560.0
DJB	PSB	109	506	532.4	191	:21:32	857.1
PSB	MIP	093	506	505.2	61	:07:15	288.4
MIP	SBJ	117	506	540.7	92	:10:13	406.5
SBJ	LGA	—	—	—	52	:16:26*	269.0*
						1:53:45	4,492.6

*(given)

(PLT012) — FAA-H-8083-15

Answers

9595 [C]   9597 [C]

ATM, ATS, DSP
9598. (Refer to Figures 158, 159, 160, 160A, and 161.) The required amount of fuel (in pounds) to be on N711JB at STL, prior to taxi, is

A— 5,933 pounds.
B— 6,408 pounds.
C— 6,641 pounds

In this question, the regulation-required fuel must be calculated using the summary box at the bottom of the flight plan.

1. Compute the fuel required to fly the flight:

   Fuel required is 4,492.6 pounds (see flight plan in Question 9597).

2. Compute the required reserve fuel (see Question 9597, Step 5):

   Time required is 45 minutes (§135.223).
   Fuel flow is 1,898 PPH (given at bottom of flight plan in FAA Figure 158).

   Reserve fuel is 1,423.5 pounds.

3. Determine ETE to alternate:

   ETE to alternate is 15 minutes (given in the flight log).

4. Compute fuel burn to alternate (see Question 9597, Step 5):

   Time to alternate is :15:00 (from Step 3).
   Fuel flow is 1,898 PPH (given in flight log).

   Fuel burn to alternate is 474.5 pounds.

5. Add the totals of Steps 1 through 4:

   FUEL
4,492.6	En route
1,423.5	Reserve
+ 474.5	Alternate
6,390.6	Total

(PLT012) — FAA-H-8083-15

ATM, ATS, DSP
9610. (Refer to Figures 168, 169, 169A, 171, and 172.) What is the ETE for PTZ 70 from Chicago Pal-Waukee Airport to Greater Buffalo Intl Airport?

A— 2 hours 15 minutes.
B— 2 hours 18 minutes.
C— 2 hours 21 minutes.

To answer this question, complete the flight log in FAA Figure 168, using the information given in the problem:

1. Change the winds aloft at FL190 from true to magnetic, using the variation from the remarks section of the flight plan. Notice that the variation changes with each leg. Winds at PMM are 020° True at 61 knots.

020°	True
+ 01°	West variation
021°	Magnetic

2. Find the distance flown for the leg. In this case it is 47 NM. This is noted in the remarks section of the flight plan.

3. Find the ground speed for the leg from L/O to PMM using a flight computer:

   Wind direction 021° (calculated in Step 1).
   Wind speed 61 knots (given in the flight log).
   Course 081° (L/O point is the PMM 261° at 47 NM).
   TAS 247 knots (given in the flight plan in FAA Figure 168).

   Calculated GS is 210.0 knots.

4. Compute the time en route for the leg from L/O to PMM:

   Distance 47 NM (determined in Step 2).
   Ground speed 210.0 (calculated in Step 3).

   Calculated leg time is 13 minutes, 26 seconds.

5. Since the next question asks for the fuel required for the flight, calculate the fuel burned on this leg:

   ETE is :13:26 (calculated in Step 4).
   Fuel flow is 676 PPH (in note at the bottom of the flight log).

   Fuel burned is 151.3 pounds.

6. Repeat steps for the subsequent legs to fill in the flight log:

FROM	TO	CRS	TAS	GS	NM	ETE	FUEL
PWK	L/O	—	—	—	49	:24:00*	410.0*
L/O	PMM	081	247	210.0	47	:13:26	151.3
PMM	FNT	076	247	205.4	109	:31:50	358.7
FNT	YXU	094	247	217.6	114	:31:26	354.1
YXU	T/D	101	247	222.2	70	:18:54	213.0
T/D	BUF	—	—	—	19	:19:00*	163.0*
						2:18:36	1,650.1

*(given)

(PLT012) — FAA-H-8083-15

ATM, ATS, DSP

9611. (Refer to Figures 168, 169, 169A, 171, and 172.) What is the computed fuel usage for PTZ 70 from start of taxi at Chicago Pal-Waukee to landing at Greater Buffalo Intl?

A— 1,642 pounds.
B— 2,005 pounds.
C— 2,550 pounds.

See Steps 1 through 6 in Question 9610. Question 9611 asks only for the fuel burn, so it is not necessary to compute reserve or alternate fuel. (PLT012) — FAA-H-8083-15

ATM, ATS, DSP

9612. (Refer to Figures 168, 171, 172, and 173.) What TAS should PTZ 70 maintain to arrive at FNT 30 minutes after passing PMM?

A— 255 knots.
B— 265 knots.
C— 260 knots.

1. Determine the required GS from PMM to FNT:

   Distance is 109 NM (FAA Figure 171).
   Time is 30 minutes (given in question).

   Required GS is 218.0 knots.

2. Calculate the required TAS:

   Wind direction is 023° magnetic (020 + 3° west
      variation).
   Wind speed is 61 knots (given in flight log).
   Course is 078° (inbound on the FNT
      258° radial).
   GS is 218.0 (calculated in Step 1).

   Required TAS is 257.9.

(PLT012) — FAA-H-8083-15

ATM, ATS, DSP

9627. (Refer to Figures 179, 180, 181, 182, and 182A.) The planned fuel usage from Newport News/Williamsburg Intl to Philadelphia Intl for EAB 90 is

A— 1,132 pounds.
B— 1,107 pounds.
C— 1,084 pounds.

To answer this question, complete the flight log in FAA Figure 179 using the information given in the problem:

1. *Change the winds aloft at FL190 from true to magnetic. Variation is provided in the remarks section of the flight plan (FAA Figure 179). Winds at ORF are 300° True at 70 knots. 300° True + 10° West variation = 310° Magnetic*

2. *Find the distance flown for the leg. In this case it is 42 NM, the distance from ORF to SAWED (FAA Figure 181).*

3. *Find the ground speed for the leg from ORF to SAWED using a flight computer: Wind direction 310° (calculated in Step 1). Wind speed 70 knots (given in the flight log). Course 030° (J121 is the ORF 030° radial). TAS 236 knots (given in the flight plan in FAA Figure 179). Calculated GS is 213.6 knots.*

4. *Compute the time enroute for the leg from ORF to SAWED: Distance 42 NM (determined in Step 2). Ground speed 213.6 (calculated in Step 3). Calculated leg time is 11 minutes, 48 seconds.*

5. *Since the next question asks for the fuel required for the flight, calculate the fuel burned on this leg. ETE is :11:48 (calculated in Step 4). Fuel flow is 689 PPH (in note at the bottom of the flight log). Fuel burned is 133.5 pounds.*

6. *Repeat steps for the subsequent legs to fill in the flight log.*

FROM	TO	CRS	TAS	GS	NM	ETE	FUEL
PHF	ORF	—	—	—	40	:19:00*	312.0*
ORF	SAWED	030	236	213.6	42	:11:48	133.5
SAWED	SLW	039	236	224.2	37	:09:54	113.7
SLW	SIE	035	236	219.4	70	:19:09	219.9
SIE	VCN	354	236	180.6	28	:09:18	106.8
VCN	OOD	301	236	166.6	17	:06:07	70.3
OOD	PHL	—	—	—	30	:16:00*	177.0*
						1:31:16	1,133.2

*(given)

(PLT012) — FAA-H-8083-15

Answers

9611   [A]   9612   [C]   9627   [A]

ATM, ATS, DSP
9628. (Refer to Figures 179, 180, 181, 182, and 183.) The required fuel from Newport News/Williamsburg Intl to Philadelphia Intl for EAB 90 is

A— 1,860 pounds.
B— 1,908 pounds.
C— 2,003 pounds.

In this question, the regulation-required fuel must be calculated using the summary box at the bottom of the flight plan.

1. Compute the fuel required to fly the flight:

> Fuel required is 1,133.2 pounds (see flight plan in Question 9626).

2. Compute the required reserve fuel (see Question 9626, Step 5):

> Time required is 45 minutes (§135.223).
> Fuel flow is 739 PPH (given at bottom of flight plan in FAA Figure 113).

> Reserve fuel is 554.3 pounds.

3. Determine ETE to alternate:

> ETE to alternate is 18 minutes (given in the flight log).

4. Compute fuel burn to alternate (see Question 9626, Step 5):

> Time to alternate is :18:00 (from Step 3).
> Fuel flow is 739 PPH (given in flight log).

> Fuel burn to alternate is 221.7 pounds.

5. Add the totals of Steps 1 through 4:

> **FUEL**
> 1,133.2   En route
> 554.3   Reserve
> + 221.7   Alternate
> 1,909.2   Total

(PLT012) — FAA-H-8083-15

ATM, ATS, DSP
9642. (Refer to Figures 190, 191, 192, 193, 193A, 194, 195, and 195A.) The estimated time enroute from MSP to DEN for PIL 10 is

A— 1 hour 54 minutes.
B— 1 hour 57 minutes.
C— 2 hours 00 minutes.

To answer this question, complete the flight log in FAA Figure 190, using the information given in the problem:

1. Change the winds aloft at FL430 from true to magnetic, using the variation from the remarks section of the flight plan. Winds at FSD are 290° True at 89 knots.

> 290° True
> – 09° East variation
> 281° Magnetic

2. The TAS is 456 knots from the flight plan.

3. Find the distance flown for the leg. In this case it is 90 NM. The flight log shows the L/O point as the FSD 048° radial at 90 NM.

4. Find the ground speed for the leg from L/O to FSD using a flight computer:

> Wind direction 281° (calculated in Step 1).
> Wind speed 89 knots (given in the flight log).
> Course 228° (L/O point is on the FSD 048° radial).
> TAS 456 knots (see Step 2).

> Calculated GS is 396.9 knots.

5. Compute the time en route for the leg from L/O to FSD:

> Distance 90 NM (determined in Step 3).
> Ground speed 396.9 (calculated in Step 4).

> Calculated leg time is 13 minutes, 36 seconds.

6. Since the next question asks for the fuel required for the flight, calculate the fuel burned on this leg:

> ETE is :13:36 (calculated in Step 5).
> Fuel flow is 9,026 PPH (in note at the bottom of the flight log).

> Fuel burned is 2,045.9 pounds.

7. Repeat steps for the subsequent legs to fill in the flight log:

FROM	TO	CRS	TAS	GS	NM	ETE	FUEL
MSP	L/O	—	—	—	90	:19:00*	4,170.0*
L/O	FSD	228	456	396.9	90	:13:36	2,045.9
FSD	OBH	198	456	436.5	153	:21:02	3,163.6
OBH	LBF	249	456	390.1	110	:16:55	2,545.2
LBF	MODES	250	456	389.3	104	:16:02	2,411.3
MODES	AMWAY	218	456	423.5	11	:01:34	234.5
AMWAY	DEN	—	—	—	97	:25:00*	3,107.0*
						1:53:09	17,677.5

(given)

(PLT012) — FAA-H-8083-15

Answers
9628 [B]   9642 [A]

ATM, ATS, DSP
9643. (Refer to Figures 190, 191, 192, 193, 193A, 194, 195 and 195A.) The required fuel that should be onboard PIL 10 at MSP is

A— 28,053 pounds.
B— 29,057 pounds.
C— 29,960 pounds.

In this question, the regulation-required fuel must be calculated using the summary box at the bottom of the flight plan.

1. *Compute the fuel required to fly the flight:*

    Fuel required is 17,677.5 pounds (see flight plan in Question 9643).

2. *Compute the required reserve fuel (see Question 9643, Step 6):*

    Time required is 45 minutes (§121.639).
    Fuel flow is 7,688 PPH (given at bottom of flight plan in FAA Figure 190).

    Reserve fuel is 5,766.0 pounds.

3. *Determine ETE to alternate:*

    ETE to alternate is 36 minutes (given in the flight log).

4. *Compute fuel burn to alternate (see Question 9642, Step 6):*

    Time to alternate is :36:00 (from Step 3).
    Fuel flow is 7,688 PPH (given in flight log).

    Fuel burn to alternate is 4,612.8 pounds.

5. *Add the totals of Steps 1 through 4:*

    FUEL
17,677.5	En route
5,766.0	Reserve
+ 4,612.8	Alternate
28,056.3	Total

(PLT012) — FAA-H-8083-15

ATM, ATS, DSP
8795. (Refer to Figure 103.) What CAS should be used to maintain the fixed TAS at the proposed altitude?

A— 157 knots.
B— 167 knots.
C— 172 knots.

The required CAS (Calibrated Airspeed) can be computed given TAS, pressure altitude, and OAT. The filed TAS from the flight plan in FAA Figure 103 is 233 knots. The OAT is -31°C, and the pressure altitude is 22,000 feet. Using a flight computer, the CAS is 167 knots. (PLT012) — FAA-H-8083-15

ATM, ATS, DSP
8835. (Refer to Figures 115, 116, and 117.) Due to traffic, LAX Center radar vectored PTL 130 to TRM, then cleared the flight to PHX via J169 BLH, direct to Arlin Intersection. What approximate indicated Mach should be maintained to arrive over the BLH VORTAC 8 minutes after passing TRM VORTAC?

A— .84 Mach.
B— .82 Mach.
C— .86 Mach.

1. *Compute the ground speed:*

    Distance between TRM VORTAC and BLH VORTAC is 70 NM (from FAA Figure 117).
    Time enroute is 8 minutes (given in question).

    Therefore, ground speed is 525 knots.

2. *Compute the required true airspeed:*

    Wind is 285° (300° – 15° variation) at 43 knots (from FAA Figure 115).
    Magnetic course is 078° (from FAA Figure 117).
    Ground speed is 525 knots (from Step 1).

    Therefore, required TAS is 487.1 knots.

3. *Compute required Mach number:*

    TAS is 487.1 knots (from Step 2).
    OAT is -41°C (ISA at FL270 is -2° = -41°C, from FAA Figure 115).

    Therefore, required Mach number is .82.

(PLT012) — FAA-H-8083-15

Answers

9643 [A]	8795 [B]	8835 [B]

RTC

9566. (Refer to Figures 108, 109, 110, and 112.) What is the ETE from DFW to landing at IAH?

A— 1 hour 55 minutes.
B— 1 hour 59 minutes.
C— 2 hours 03 minutes.

To answer this question, complete the flight log in FAA Figure 108, using the information given in the problem:

1. *Change the winds aloft at 7,000 from true to magnetic, using the variation from the Chart Supplements U.S.. Winds at BILEE are 220° True at 36 knots.*

    220° True
    – 08° East variation
    212° Magnetic

2. *Find the distance flown for the leg. In this case it is 84 NM. The sum of the distances from DFW to BILEE is 107 NM, and 23 NM of that is used by the climb. Distances for subsequent legs must be determined by referring to the enroute charts and the CUGAR Four Arrival (FAA Figures 110 and 112).*

3. *Find the ground speed for the leg from L/O to BILEE using a flight computer:*

    Wind direction 212° (calculated in Step 1).
    Wind speed 36 knots (given on the flight log).
    Magnetic course 154° (V369 is on the DFW 154° radial).
    TAS 115 knots (given in the flight plan on FAA Figure 108).

    Calculated GS is 91.8 knots.

4. *Compute the time en route for the leg from L/O to BILEE:*

    Distance 84 NM (determined in Step 2).
    Ground speed 91.8 (calculated in Step 3).

    Calculated leg time is 54 minutes, 54 seconds.

5. *Since the next question asks for the fuel required for the flight, calculate the fuel burned on this leg:*

    ETE is :54:54 (calculated in Step 4).
    Fuel flow is 165 PPH (in note at the bottom of the flight log).

    Fuel burned is 151.0 pounds.

6. *Repeat steps for the subsequent legs to fill in the flight log:*

FROM	TO	CRS	TAS	GS	NM	ETE	FUEL
DFW	L/O	—	—	—	23	:14:00*	123.0*
L/O	BILEE	154	115	91.8	84	:54:54	151.0
BILEE	T/P*	154	115	91.8	34	:22:13	61.1
T/P**	CUGAR	125	115	107.4	13	:07:16	20.0
CUGAR	T/D	125	115	107.4	9	:05:02	13.8
T/D	IAH	—	—	—	37	:16:00*	140.0*
						1:59:25	508.9

*(given)

**Note: *Split the leg from BILEE to CUGAR into two legs at 34 NM SE of BILEE. The 29° turn will affect the GS and the ETE and leg fuel will change as well.*

(PLT012) — FAA-H-8083-15

RTC

9567. (Refer to Figures 108, 109, 110, and 112.) What is the total fuel required for the flight from DFW to IAH?

A— 693 pounds.
B— 595 pounds.
C— 638 pounds.

In this question, the regulation-required fuel must be calculated using the summary box at the bottom of the flight plan.

1. *Compute the fuel required to fly the flight:*

    Fuel required is 508.9 pounds (see flight plan in Question 9566).

2. *Compute the required reserve fuel (see Question 9566, Step 5):*

    Time required is 30 minutes (§135.223).
    Fuel flow is 172 PPH (given at bottom of flight plan in FAA Figure 108).

    Reserve fuel is 86 pounds.

3. *Determine ETE to alternate:*

    ETE to alternate is 15 minutes (given in the flight log).

4. *Compute fuel burn to alternate (see Question 9566, Step 5):*

    Time to alternate is :15:00 (from previous step).
    Fuel flow is 172 PPH (given in flight log).

    Fuel burn to alternate is 43.0 pounds.

5. *Add any additional fuel required for a missed approach at the destination. In this case add 55 pounds (given at the bottom of the flight log).*

Answers

9566 **[B]**   9567 **[A]**

6. Add the totals of Steps 1 through 5.

FUEL

508.9	En route
86.0	Reserve
+ 98.0	Alternate (43.0 + 55)
692.9	Total

(PLT012) — FAA-H-8083-15

RTC
9568. (Refer to Figures 108, 109, 110, and 112.) What TAS should be maintained to arrive at Cugar Four Arrival initial point 1 hour 6 minutes after level-off?

A— 140 knots.
B— 143 knots.
C— 146 knots.

Compute the distance and enroute time from the flight log used in Question 9567. Using the time and distance, compute the average ground speed at 115 TAS. The difference between the ground speed 115 knots and the required ground speed to travel the computed distance in 1 hour and 6 minutes will equal the change in TAS needed:

FROM	TO	GS	DISTANCE	TIME
L/O	BILEE	91.8	84	:54:54
BILEE	X	91.8	34	:22:13
x	CUGAR	107.4	13	:07:16
			131	1:24:23

131 / 1:06:00 = 119.1 (required)
131 / 1:24:23 = – 93.1 (at 115 TAS)
$\overline{26}$
+ 115.0 (TAS)
$\overline{141}$ (required)

(PLT012) — FAA-H-8083-15

RTC
9574. (Refer to Figures 113 and 114.) What is the ETE for the IFR helicopter flight from Baker Airport to LAX?

A— 1 hour 32 minutes.
B— 1 hour 35 minutes.
C— 1 hour 38 minutes.

To answer this question, complete the flight log in FAA Figure 113, using the information given in the problem:

1. *Change the winds aloft at 12,000 from true to magnetic, using the variation from the Chart Supplements U.S. entries for Baker and LAX. Winds at DAG are 290° True at 36 knots.*

290°	True
– 15°	East variation
275°	Magnetic

2. *Find the distance flown for the leg. In this case it is 15 NM, given in the flight log.*

3. *Find the ground speed for the leg from L/O to DAG using a flight computer:*

   Wind direction 275° (calculated in Step 1).
   Wind speed 36 knots (given on the flight log).
   Course 211° (V394).
   TAS 110 knots (given in the flight plan on FAA Figure 113).

   Calculated GS is 89.4 knots.

4. *Compute the time en route for the leg from L/O to DAG:*

   Distance 15 NM (determined in Step 2).
   Ground speed 89.4 (calculated in Step 3).

   Calculated leg time is 10 minutes, 4 seconds.

5. *Since the next question asks for the fuel required for the flight, calculate the fuel burned on this leg:*

   ETE is :10:04 (calculated in Step 4).
   Fuel flow is 1,045 PPH (in note at the bottom of the flight log).

   Fuel burned is 175.4 pounds.

6. *Repeat steps for the subsequent legs to fill in the flight log:*

FROM	TO	CRS	TAS	GS	NM	ETE	FUEL
O02	L/O	—	—	—	8	:10:00*	250.0*
L/O	DAG	211	110	89.4	15	:10:04	175.4
DAG	POM	214	110	87.9	80	:54:35	950.6
POM	PIRRO	225	110	83.3	5	:03:36	62.7
PIRRO	LAX	—	—	—	29	:17:00*	348.0*
						1:35:15	1,786.7

*(given)

(PLT012) — FAA-H-8083-15

RTC
9575. (Refer to Figures 113 and 114.) What is the total fuel required for the IFR helicopter flight from Baker Airport to LAX, with LGB as an alternate?

A— 2,625 pounds.
B— 2,536 pounds.
C— 2,335 pounds.

In this question, the regulation-required fuel must be calculated using the summary box at the bottom of the flight plan.

Continued

Answers

1. Compute the fuel required to fly the flight:

   Fuel required is 1,786.7 pounds (see flight plan in Question 9574).

2. Compute the required reserve fuel (see Question 9574, Step 5):

   Time required is 30 minutes (§135.223).
   Fuel flow is 1,095 PPH (given at bottom of flight plan in FAA Figure 113).

   Reserve fuel is 547.5 pounds.

3. Determine ETE to alternate:

   ETE to alternate is 11 minutes (given in the flight log).

4. Compute fuel burn to alternate (see Question 9574, Step 5):

   Time to alternate is :11:00 (from Step 3).
   Fuel flow is 1,095 PPH (given in flight log).

   Fuel burn to alternate is 200.7 pounds.

5. Add any additional fuel required for a missed approach at the destination. In this case add 89 pounds (given at the bottom of the flight log).

6. Add the totals of Steps 1 through 5:

   FUEL

1,786.7	En route
547.5	Reserve
+ 289.7	Alternate (200.7 + 89)
2,623.9	Total

(PLT012) — FAA-H-8083-15

RTC

9621. (Refer to Figures 174, 175, 176, 177, 177A, and 178.) The estimated time enroute from LWS to HQM, for Sea Hawk 1 is

A— 2 hours 31 minutes.
B— 2 hours 34 minutes.
C— 2 hours 37 minutes.

To answer this question, complete the flight log in FAA Figure 174, using the information given in the problem:

1. Change the winds aloft at 12,000 feet from true to magnetic, using the variation from the Chart Supplements U.S. entries for the LWS and HQM VORTACs. Winds at ALW are 340° True at 40 knots.

340°	True
– 20°	East variation
320°	Magnetic

2. Calculate the TAS for existing temperature:

   ISA temperature at 12,000 feet is -9°C
   ((12 x (-2°)) + 15°).
   ISA -8°= -17°C

   Using a flight calculator, determine that a CAS of 132 knots gives a TAS of 155.6. Note that the temperature and altitude changes many times in flight log.

3. Find the distance flown for the leg. In this case it is 43 NM. FAA Figure 175 shows a distance of 43 NM from CLOVA Int. to ALW. The flight log shows the first cruise leg to be from MQG to ALW, but this an apparent misprint. The mileage shown in the climb leg agrees with the SID distance to CLOVA (FAA Figure 177A). The time and fuel calculations only work out if CLOVA is substituted for MQG in the flight log.

4. Find the ground speed for the leg from CLOVA to ALW using a flight computer:

   Wind direction 320° (calculated in Step 1).
   Wind speed 40 knots (given on the flight log).
   Course 234° (V520 is the MQG 234 radial).
   TAS 155.6 knots (calculated in Step 2).

   Calculated GS is 147.6 knots.

5. Compute the time en route for the leg from CLOVA to ALW:

   Distance 43 NM (determined in Step 3).
   Ground speed 147.6 (calculated in Step 4).

   Calculated leg time is 17 minutes, 29 seconds.

6. Since the next question asks for the fuel required for the flight, calculate the fuel burned on this leg:

   ETE is :17:29 (calculated in Step 5).
   Fuel flow is 525 PPH (in note at the bottom of the flight log).

   Fuel burned is 152.9 pounds.

7. Repeat steps for the subsequent legs to fill in the flight log:

FROM	TO	CRS	TAS	GS	NM	ETE	FUEL
LWS	CLOVA	—	—	—	15	:15:00*	191.0*
CLOVA	ALW	234	155.6	147.6	43	:17:29	152.9
ALW	PSC	267	157.1	129.9	36	:16:39	145.6
PSC	YKM	268	157.1	126.4	58	:27:33	241.0
YKM	SEA	283	158.3	129.4	93**	:43:08	377.4
SEA	ULESS	228	139.9	134.0	64	:28:40	250.8
ULESS	HQ	—	—	—	—	:02:00*	16.0*
HQ	HQM	—	—	—	—	:04:00*	32.0*
						2:34:29	1,406.7

*(given)

**Caution: the 78 NM shown in the box on V4 is the distance from SEA to the compulsory reporting point TITON. It is another 15 NM from TITON to YKM.

(PLT012) — FAA-H-8083-15

RTC

9607. (Refer to Figures 162, 163, 163A, 164, 165, 166A and 167.) What is the ETE for the IFR helicopter flight from Tucson/Ryan to Albuquerque/Double Eagle II?

A— 2 hours 14 minutes.
B— 2 hours 16 minutes.
C— 2 hours 18 minutes.

To answer this question, complete the flight log in FAA Figure 162, using the information given in the problem:

1. *Change the winds aloft at 11,000 feet from true to magnetic, using the variation from the Chart Supplements U.S. entries for the TUS and ABQ VORTACs. Winds at CIE are 240° True at 31 knots.*

    240°   *True*
    – 12°   *East variation*
    228°   *Magnetic*

2. *Calculate the TAS for existing temperature:*

    ISA temperature at 11,000 feet is -7°C
       ((11 x (-2°)) + 15°).
    ISA -6° = -13°C

    Using a flight calculator, determine that a CAS of 125 knots gives a TAS of 145.7. Note that the temperature changes three times in flight log.

3. *Find the distance flown for the leg. In this case it is 38 NM. FAA Figure 164 shows a distance of 38 NM from MESCA Int. to CIE.*

4. *Find the ground speed for the leg from MESCA to CIE using a flight computer:*

    Wind direction 228° (calculated in Step 1).
    Wind speed 31 knots (given in the flight log).
    *Course 065° (MESCA is on the CIE
       245° radial).*
    TAS 145.7 knots (calculated in Step 2).

    Calculated GS is 175.1 knots.

5. *Compute the time en route for the leg from MESCA to CIE:*

    Distance 38 NM (determined in Step 3).
    Ground speed 175.1 (calculated in Step 4).

    Calculated leg time is 13 minutes, 1 second.

6. *Since the next question asks for the fuel required for the flight, calculate the fuel burned on this leg:*

    ETE is :13:01 (calculated in Step 5).
    Fuel flow is 523 PPH (in note at the bottom of the flight log).

    Fuel burned is 113.5 pounds.

7. *Repeat steps for the subsequent legs to fill in the flight log:*

FROM	TO	CRS	TAS	GS	NM	ETE	FUEL
RYN	MESCA	—	—	—	38	:17:00*	180.0*
MESCA	CIE	065	145.7	175.1	38	:13:01	113.5
CIE	SSO	048	145.7	176.7	29	:09:51	85.8
SSO	DMN	077	147.1	172.4	84	:29:14	254.9
DMN	TCS	003	147.1	160.9	62	:23:07	201.5
TCS	T/P**	015	147.9	179.9	39	:13:00	113.4
T/P**	ONM	356	147.9	174.9	29	:09:57	86.7
ONM	ABQ	347	147.9	171.2	42	:14:43	128.3
ABQ	AEG	—	—	—	6	:06:00*	49.0*
						2:15:53	1,213.1

*(given)

**Note: The leg from TCS to ONM should be split in two (39 NM from TCS) due to the turn in the airway. This results in more accurate time and fuel burn numbers.

(PLT012) — FAA-H-8083-15

RTC

9608. (Refer to Figures 162, 163, 164, 165, and 167.) What is the total estimated fuel required for this IFR helicopter flight from RYN to AEG with ABQ as an alternate?

A— 1,462 pounds.
B— 1,503 pounds.
C— 1,543 pounds.

In this question, the regulation-required fuel must be calculated using the summary box at the bottom of the flight plan.

1. *Compute the fuel required to fly the flight:*

    Fuel required is 1,213.1 pounds (see flight plan in Question 9607).

2. *Compute the required reserve fuel (see Step 5 in Question 9607):*

    Time required is 30 minutes (§135.223).
    Fuel flow is 1,898 PPH (given at bottom of flight plan in FAA Figure 113).

    Reserve fuel is 497 pounds.

Continued

Answers

9607   [B]   9608   [C]

3. Determine ETE to alternate:

ETE to alternate is 5 minutes (given in the flight log).

4. Compute fuel burn to alternate (see Step 5 in Question 9607):

Time to alternate is :05:00 (computed in previous step).
Fuel flow is 497 PPH (given in flight log).

Fuel burn to alternate is 41.4 pounds.

5. Add any additional fuel required for a missed approach at the destination. In this case add 40 pounds (given at the bottom of the flight log).

6. Add the totals of Steps 1 through 5:

FUEL

1,213.1	En route
248.5	Reserve
+ 81.4	Alternate (41.4 + 40)
1,543.0	Total

(PLT012) — FAA-H-8083-15

RTC

9639. (Refer to Figures 184, 186, 187, and 188A.) What is the ETE for Hoss 1 from Las Vegas to Provo?

A— 1 hour 31 minutes.
B— 1 hour 33 minutes.
C— 1 hour 35 minutes.

To answer this question, complete the flight log in FAA Figure 184, using the information given in the problem:

1. Change the winds aloft at 15,000 feet from true to magnetic, using the variation from the Chart Supplements U.S. entries for the LAS and PVU VORTACs. Winds at MMM are 210° True at 71 knots.

210° True
− 15° East variation
195° Magnetic

2. Calculate the TAS for existing temperature:

ISA temperature at 15,000 feet is -15°C
((15 x (-2°)) + 15°).
ISA -10° = -25°C

Using a flight calculator, determine that a CAS of 135 knots gives a TAS of 166.1.

3. Find the distance flown for the leg. In this case it is 43 NM. FAA Figure 186 shows a distance of 43 NM from ACLAM Int. to MMM.

4. Find the ground speed for the leg from ACLAM to MMM using a flight computer:

Wind direction 195° (calculated in Step 1).
Wind speed 71 knots (given on the flight log).
Course 360° (V8 is the MMM 180° radial).
TAS 166.1 knots (calculated in Step 2).

Calculated GS is 233.7 knots.

5. Compute the time en route for the leg from ACLAM to MMM:

Distance 43 NM (determined in Step 3).
Ground speed 233.7 (calculated in Step 4).

Calculated leg time is 11 minutes, 2 seconds.

6. Since the next question asks for the fuel required for the flight, calculate the fuel burned on this leg:

ETE is :11:02 (calculated in Step 5).
Fuel flow is 496 PPH (in note at the bottom of the flight log).

Fuel burned is 91.3 pounds.

7. Repeat steps for the subsequent legs to fill in the flight log. Although the leg from MMM to REEKA is shown on one line on the flight log, each segment should be calculated separately to get the most accurate time and fuel.

FROM	TO	CRS	TAS	GS	NM	ETE	FUEL
LAS	ACLAM	—	—	—	31	:15:00*	152.0*
ACLAM	MMM	360	166.1	233.7	43	:11:02	91.3
MMM	MLF	016	166.1	237.1	113	:28:36	236.4
MLF	DTA	007	166.1	236.1	61	:15:13	125.8
DTA	REEKA	008	166.1	236.4	50	:12:42	105.0
REEKA	PVU	—	—	—	19	:10:00*	87.0*
						1:32:50	797.5

*(given)

(PLT012) — FAA-H-8083-15

RTC

9640. (Refer to Figures 184, 186, 187, 188, and 188A.) What is the minimum fuel required under 14 CFR Part 135 for this IMC helicopter flight from LAS to PVU? The visibility is forecast to be 15 SM over the entire route.

A— 1,304 pounds.
B— 985 pounds.
C— 1,224 pounds.

In this question, the regulation-required fuel must be calculated using the summary box at the bottom of the flight plan.

Answers

9639 [B]   9640 [C]

1. Compute the fuel required to fly the flight:

   Fuel required is 797.5 pounds (see flight plan in Question 9639).

2. Compute the required reserve fuel (see Question 9639, Step 5):

   Time required is 30 minutes (§135.223).
   Fuel flow is 480 PPH (given at bottom of flight plan in FAA Figure 113).
   Reserve fuel is 240.0 pounds.

3. Determine ETE to alternate:

   ETE to alternate is 17 minutes, 20 seconds.

4. Compute fuel burn to alternate (see Question 9639, Step 5):

   Time to alternate is :17:20 (from Step 3).
   Fuel flow is 480 PPH (given in flight log).

   Fuel burn to alternate is 138.7 pounds.

5. Add any additional fuel required for a missed approach at the destination. In this case add 40 pounds (given at the bottom of the flight log).

6. Add the totals of Steps 1 through 5:

   FUEL
7,97.5	En route
240.0	Reserve
+ 178.7	Alternate (138.7 + 40)
1,216.2	Total

(PLT012) — FAA-H-8083-15

RTC

9652. (Refer to Figures 197, 199, and 200.) What is the ETE for the IFR helicopter flight from Eagle County Regional to Salt Lake City Intl? (PUC to FFU should read "14,000" for altitude. Use PUC magnetic variation for entire problem.)

A— 1 hour 28 minutes.
B— 1 hour 35 minutes.
C— 1 hour 31 minutes.

To answer this question, complete the flight log in FAA Figure 197, using the information given in the problem:

1. Change the winds aloft at 14,000 feet from true to magnetic, using the variation for PUC given in the remarks of the flight plan. Winds at JNC are 100° true at 41 knots.

100°	True
– 12°	East variation
088°	Magnetic

2. Calculate the TAS for existing temperature:

   ISA temperature at 14,000 feet is -13°C ((14 x (-2°)) + 15°).
   ISA +20° = 7°C. Notice the wind and temperature change at FFU.

   Using a flight calculator, determine that a CAS of 139 Kts gives a TAS of 178.1.

3. Find the distance flown for the leg. In this case it is 91 NM. FAA Figure 199 shows a distance of 91 NM from DBL to JNC.

4. Find the ground speed for the leg from DBL to JNC using a flight computer:

   Wind direction 088° (calculated in Step 1).
   Wind speed 41 knots (given in the flight log).
   Course 242° (V134).
   TAS 178.1 knots (calculated in Step 2).

   Calculated GS is 214.5 knots.

5. Compute the time en route for the leg from DBL to JNC:

   Distance 91 NM (determined in Step 3).
   Ground speed 214.5 (calculated in Step 4).

   Calculated leg time is 25 minutes, 28 seconds.

6. Since the next question asks for the fuel required for the flight, calculate the fuel burned on this leg:

   ETE is :25:28 (calculated in Step 5).
   Fuel flow is 495 PPH (in note at the bottom of the flight log).

   Fuel burned is 210.0 pounds.

7. Repeat steps for the subsequent legs to fill in the flight log:

FROM	TO	CRS	TAS	GS	NM	ETE	FUEL
EGE	DBL	—	—	—	13	:10:00*	101.0*
DBL	JNC	242	178.1	214.5	91	:25:28	210.0
JNC	PUC	275	178.1	218.5	97	:26:38	219.7
PUC	FFU	291	176.2	210.1	68	:19:25	160.2
FFU	JAURN	341	176.2	193.5	12	:03:43	30.7
JAURN	SLC	—	—	—	18	:10:00*	92.0*
						1:35:14	813.6

*(given)

(PLT012) — FAA-H-8083-15

RTC
9653. (Refer to Figures 197, 199, and 200.) What is the total estimated fuel required for this IFR helicopter flight from EGE to SLC with OGD as an alternate?

A— 1,152 pounds.
B— 1,119 pounds.
C— 1,049 pounds.

In this question, the regulation-required fuel must be calculated using the summary box at the bottom of the flight plan.

1. *Compute the fuel required to fly the flight:*

    Fuel required is 813.6 pounds (see flight plan in Question 9652).

2. *Compute the required reserve fuel (see Question 9652, Step 5):*

    Time required is 30 minutes (§135.223).
    Fuel flow is 469 PPH (given at bottom of flight plan in FAA Figure 113).

    Reserve fuel is 234.5 pounds.

3. *Determine ETE to alternate:*

    ETE to alternate is 9 minutes.

4. *Compute fuel burn to alternate (see Question 9652, Step 5):*

    Time to alternate is :09:00 (from Step 3).
    Fuel flow is 469 PPH (given in flight log).

    Fuel burn to alternate is 70.3 pounds.

5. *Add any additional fuel required for a missed approach at the destination. In this case add 33 pounds (given at the bottom of the flight log).*

6. *Add the totals of Steps 1 through 5:*

    FUEL
813.6	En route
234.5	Reserve
+ 103.3	Alternate (70.3 + 33)
1,151.4	Total

(PLT012) — FAA-H-8083-15

Chapter 5
Weight and Balance

Center of Gravity Computation

Note applicable to Chapters 4 and 5: The ATP Single-engine exam (ATS) focuses on the Cessna 208 and the ATP Multi-engine exam (ATM) focuses on the Bombardier CRJ200 and Q400.

The start of the solution to any weight and balance problem is the calculation of the total weight of the aircraft (gross weight) and the total moment. All weight and balance problems on the ATP test use a moment index rather than the actual moment. The moment index is the actual moment divided by 1,000.

Basic Operating Weight (BOW) is defined as the empty weight of the aircraft plus the weight of the required crew, their baggage and other standard items such as meals and potable water. The BOW and the Basic Operating Index (Moment/1,000) are the same for all questions.

The Moment Index (MOM/1,000) is calculated by using the formula:

Weight x Arm/1,000 = MOM/1,000

The Center of Gravity (CG) in inches aft of the Datum line can be determined by using the formula:

CG = Total Moment / Total Weight

Since some FAA questions use a Moment Index instead of Moment, for these it is necessary to modify this formula by multiplying the (Total Moment/Total Weight) by the reduction factor (1,000). The formula then becomes:

CG = (Total Moment Index / Total Weight) x 1,000

ATM, DSP
8697. (Refer to Figures 405 through 416.) (Note: Applicants may request a printed copy of the chart(s) or graph(s) for use while computing the answer. All printed pages must be returned to test proctor.) With the load weights shown in Figure 414, you fill the fuel tanks to the maximum fuel to remain under maximum gross weight and compute the center of gravity. Your computations indicate

A— at a CG of 200.1, your loading is satisfactory for flight operations.
B— at a CG of 180.19, you need to redistribute your loads.
C— at a CG of 190.27, you only need to change the cargo pod loading.

1. *On Figure 405, note the maximum gross weight of 8,785 lbs.*

2. *On Figure 410, note the 200-pound pilot yields a 27.1 moment.*

3. *Using Figure 411, using maximum fuel at a weight of 2,224 lbs, the moment is 451.7.*

4. *On Figure 414, using the pilot weight of 200 lbs and 27.1 moment, and the fuel of 2,224 and moment of 451.7, the calculated ramp weight is 7,429 lbs. Adding all the moments together yields 1408.2.*

5. *The CG is calculated by taking the total moment (1,408.2 x 1,000) and dividing by aircraft weight. 14,082,000 ÷ 7,429 lbs = 189.6.*

6. *On Figure 415, note the aircraft is out of CG, but can be brought into CG by changing the cargo pad loading.*

(PLT003) — FAA-H-8083-25

Answers
8697   [C]

ATM, ATS, DSP

8698. (Refer to Figures 405 through 416.) What is the CG in inches from datum under the following loading conditions?

	Weight (lbs.)
Basic empty weight	5,005
Pilot	185
Cargo	
Zone 1	200
Zone 2	240
Zone 3	500
Zone 4	400
Zone 5	200
Zone 6	50
Cargo Pod	
Zone A	0
Zone B	0
Zone C	0
Zone D	0
Fuel	275 gallons

A— Station 202.6.
B— Station 198.5.
C— Station 205.6.

1. Use Figure 410 to calculate the weight and moment for the pilot. The arm is 135.5 inches, so multiply 185 x 135.5 to get a moment of 25,067.5. Record these numbers under "Your Airplane" in the Figure 414 worksheet.

2. Use Figure 412 to calculate the cargo weights at each zone by multiplying the weight by the arm, to get the following results:

	Weight	x Arm	= Moment
Zone 1	200	172.1	34,420
Zone 2	240	217.8	52,272
Zone 3	500	264.4	132,200
Zone 4	400	294.5	117,800
Zone 5	200	319.5	63,900
Zone 6	50	344	17,200

Record these in the Figure 414 worksheet.

3. Using Figure 411, calculate the weight and moment of 275 gallons of fuel and find 1,843 pounds, and a moment of 374,500. Record in Figure 414 worksheet.

4. Add all the items from the Figure 414 worksheet, including the basic empty weight and moment:

	Weight	Moment
Basic empty weight	5,005	929,400
Pilot	185	25,067.5
Zone 1	200	34,420
Zone 2	240	52,272
Zone 3	500	132,200
Zone 4	400	117,800
Zone 5	200	63,900
Zone 6	50	17,200
Zone A	0	
Zone B	0	
Zone C	0	
Zone D	0	
Fuel	1,843	374,500
Total	8,623 lbs	1,746,760 in-lbs

5. Divide the total moment by the total weight to get a CG of 202.6 inches. (PLT121) — FAA-H-8083-1

Answers

8698 [A]

ATM, ATS, DSP
8699. (Refer to Figures 405 through 416.) What is the CG in inches from datum under the following loading conditions?

Weight (lbs.)

Basic empty weight..5,005
    Pilot..190
    Front seat passenger......................................200
Cargo
    Zone 1 180
    Zone 2 505
    Zone 3 198
    Zone 4 600
    Zone 5 0
    Zone 6 60
Cargo Pod
    Zone A 100
    Zone B 80
    Zone C 200
    Zone D 180
Fuel...180 gallons

A— 196.4 inches aft of datum.
B— 200.4 inches aft of datum.
C— 204.1 inches aft of datum.

1. Use Figure 410 to calculate the weight and moment for the pilot and passenger. The arm is 135.5 inches, so multiply 390 x 135.5 to get a moment of 52,845. Record these numbers under "Your Airplane" in the Figure 414 worksheet.

2. Use Figure 412 to calculate the cargo weights at each zone by multiplying the weight by the arm, to get the following results:

	Weight	x Arm	= Moment
Zone 1	180	172.1	30,978
Zone 2	505	217.8	109,989
Zone 3	198	264.4	52,351.2
Zone 4	600	294.5	176,700
Zone 5	0	319.5	0
Zone 6	60	344	20,640
Zone A	100	132.4	13,240
Zone B	80	182.1	14,568
Zone C	200	233.4	46,680
Zone D	180	287.6	51,768

Record these in the Figure 414 worksheet.

3. Using Figure 411, calculate the weight and moment of 180 gallons of fuel and find 1,206 pounds, and a moment of 245,200. Record in Figure 414 worksheet.

4. Add all the items from the Figure 414 worksheet, including the basic empty weight and moment:

	Weight	Moment
Basic empty weight	5,005	929,400
Pilot	190	25,745
Front Passenger	200	27,100
Zone 1	180	30,978
Zone 2	505	109,989
Zone 3	198	52,351.2
Zone 4	600	176,700
Zone 5	0	0
Zone 6	60	20,640
Zone A	100	13,240
Zone B	80	14,568
Zone C	200	46,680
Zone D	180	51,768
Fuel	1206	245,200
Total	8,704 lbs	1,744,359 in-lbs

5. Divide the total weight to arrive at a CG of 200.4 inches. (PLT121) — FAA-H-8083-1

Answers

8699   [B]

ATM, DSP
8623. (Refer to Figures 53 and 55.) What is the STAB TRIM setting for Operating Conditions R-1?

A— 8 ANU.
B— 7-5/8 ANU.
C— 7-3/4 ANU.

CG (inches aft of LEMAC) = 635.7" – 625.0" = 10.7"
CG (% of MAC) = 10.7"/134.0" = 8.0%
Stab Trim = 7-3/4 ANU

(PLT010) — FAA-H-8083-25

ATM, DSP
8624. (Refer to Figures 53 and 55.) What is the STAB TRIM setting for Operating Conditions R-2?

A— 5-3/4 ANU.
B— 7 ANU.
C— 6-3/4 ANU.

CG (inches aft of LEMAC) = 643.8" – 625.0" = 18.8"
CG (% of MAC) = 18.8"/134.0" = 14.0%
Stab Trim = 6-3/4 ANU

(PLT010) — FAA-H-8083-25

ATM, DSP
8625. (Refer to Figures 53 and 55.) What is the STAB TRIM setting for Operating Conditions R-3?

A— 3 ANU.
B— 4-1/2 ANU.
C— 5 ANU.

CG (inches aft of LEMAC) = 665.2" – 625.0" = 40.2"
CG (% of MAC) = 40.2"/134.0" = 30.0%
Stab Trim = 3 ANU

(PLT010) — FAA-H-8083-25

ATM, DSP
8626. (Refer to Figures 53 and 55.) What is the STAB TRIM setting for Operating Conditions R-4?

A— 4-1/4 ANU.
B— 4-1/2 ANU.
C— 5 ANU.

CG (inches aft of LEMAC) = 657.2" – 625.0" = 32.2"
CG (% of MAC) = 32.2"/134.0" = 24.0%
Stab Trim = 4-1/2 ANU

(PLT010) — FAA-H-8083-25

ATM, DSP
8627. (Refer to Figures 53 and 55.) What is the STAB TRIM setting for Operating Conditions R-5?

A— 6-3/4 ANU.
B— 8 ANU.
C— 7-1/2 ANU.

CG (inches aft of LEMAC) = 638.4" – 625.0" = 13.4"
CG (% of MAC) = 13.4"/134.0" = 10.0%
Stab Trim = 7-1/2 ANU

(PLT010) — FAA-H-8083-25

Stabilizer Trim Setting

The correct horizontal stabilizer trim setting is very critical for proper takeoff performance of jet aircraft. The main determinants are the CG location and possibly the flap setting. Some aircraft, such as the DC-9, have their stabilizer trim indicators calibrated in percent of MAC, so it is necessary to calculate the CG to know the trim setting. Other aircraft (such as the B-737 and B-727) have their trim indicators marked off in units of nose up trim. In such cases it is necessary to refer to the trim table to determine the proper setting for a given CG. *See FAA Figure 55.*

The **Stab Trim Setting** Table at the bottom left side of FAA Figure 55 is used to determine the takeoff trim setting for a B-737. CG location in percent of MAC is used to determine the setting. For example, if the CG is at 8.0% of MAC, the stab trim setting is 7-3/4 units ANU (Airplane Nose Up).

The Stab Trim Setting Table at the left side of FAA Figure 83 is used to determine the takeoff trim setting for a B-727. Flap setting and CG location in percent of MAC are used to determine the setting. For example, if the CG is at 28% of MAC and the flaps are set at 15°, the stab trim setting is 4-1/2 units ANU.

Answers

8623 [C]	8624 [C]	8625 [A]	8626 [B]	8627 [C]

DSP

8588. (Refer to Figures 45, 46, and 47.) What is the STAB TRIM setting for Operating Conditions A-1?

A— 29 percent MAC.
B— 32 percent MAC.
C— 36 percent MAC.

Using FAA Figure 45, calculate the CG in inches and % of MAC:

$$CG \text{ (inches aft of LEMAC)} = 590.2" - 549.13" = 41.07"$$
$$CG \text{ (\% of MAC)} = 41.07"/141.5" = 29.0\%$$

(PLT010) — FAA-H-8083-25

DSP

8589. (Refer to Figures 45, 46, and 47.) What is the STAB TRIM setting for Operating Conditions A-2?

A— 26 percent MAC.
B— 20 percent MAC.
C— 22 percent MAC.

Using FAA Figure 45, convert CG from index arm to inches aft of datum:

$$CG \text{ (inches aft of Datum)} = 580.0" - 3.1" = 576.9"$$
$$CG \text{ (inches aft of LEMAC)} = 576.9" - 549.13" = 27.77"$$
$$CG \text{ (\% of MAC)} = 27.77"/141.5" = 19.6\%$$

(PLT010) — FAA-H-8083-25

DSP

8590. (Refer to Figures 45, 46, and 47.) What is the STAB TRIM setting for Operating Conditions A-3?

A— 18 percent MAC.
B— 20 percent MAC.
C— 22 percent MAC.

Using FAA Figure 45 calculate the CG in inches and % of MAC:

$$CG \text{ (inches aft of LEMAC)} = 580.3" - 549.13" = 31.17"$$
$$CG \text{ (\% of MAC)} = 31.17"/141.5" = 22.0\%$$

(PLT010) — FAA-H-8083-25

DSP

8591. (Refer to Figures 45, 46, and 47.) What is the STAB TRIM setting for Operating Conditions A-4?

A— 26 percent MAC.
B— 22 percent MAC.
C— 18 percent MAC.

Using FAA Figure 45, convert CG from index arm to inches aft of datum:

$$CG \text{ (inches aft of Datum)} = 580.0" + 5.9" = 585.9"$$
$$CG \text{ (inches aft of LEMAC)} = 585.9" - 549.13" = 36.77"$$
$$CG \text{ (\% of MAC)} = 36.77"/141.5" = 26.0\%$$

(PLT010) — FAA-H-8083-25

DSP

8592. (Refer to Figures 45, 46, and 47.) What is the STAB TRIM setting for Operating Conditions A-5?

A— 26 percent MAC.
B— 30 percent MAC.
C— 32 percent MAC.

Using FAA Figure 45, calculate the CG in inches and % of MAC:

$$CG \text{ (inches aft of LEMAC)} = 594.4" - 549.13" = 45.27"$$
$$CG \text{ (\% of MAC)} = 45.27"/141.5" = 32.0\%$$

(PLT010) — FAA-H-8083-25

Answers

8588   [A]   8589   [B]   8590   [C]   8591   [A]   8592   [C]

Changing Loading Conditions

Whenever weight is either added to or subtracted from a loaded airplane, both the gross weight and the center of gravity location will change. The solution to such a calculation is really a simplified loading problem. Instead of calculating a weight and moment for every section of the aircraft, it is only necessary to compute the original weight and moment—then, the *effect* of the change in weight. Often in these problems, the original CG is expressed in percent of MAC and it is necessary to convert this to an arm for the entire aircraft.

For example, if an aircraft's total weight was 8,600 pounds, and you shifted 100 pounds from station (or, arm) 100 to arm 150, a simple weight shift formula can be applied:

$$\frac{\text{Weight to be Shifted (100 pounds)}}{\text{Total Weight (8,600 pounds)}} = \frac{\text{Change in CG}}{\text{Distance CG Shifted (50 inches)}}$$

This is solved easily by cross-multiplying: 50 x 100 ÷ 8,600 = .06 inches. Therefore, the CG shifts .06 inches aft.

ATM, ATS, DSP

8700. (Refer to Figures 405 through 416.) What is the old and new CG if 300 pounds of cargo is moved from Zone 2 to Zone 3 given the following conditions?

	Weight (lbs.)
Basic empty weight	5,005
Pilot	190
Front seat passenger	200
Cargo	
Zone 1	180
Zone 2	505
Zone 3	198
Zone 4	600
Zone 5	0
Zone 6	60
Cargo Pod	
Zone A	100
Zone B	80
Zone C	200
Zone D	180
Fuel	180 gallons

A— 200.2 and 198.6.
B— 196.4 and 199.2.
C— 200.4 and 202.

First, calculate the old CG by using the following procedure:

1. *Use Figure 410 to calculate the weight and moment for the pilot and passenger. The arm is 135.5 inches, so multiply 390 x 135.5 to get a moment of 52,845. Record these numbers under "Your Airplane" in the Figure 414 worksheet.*

2. *Use Figure 412 to calculate the cargo weights at each zone by multiplying the weight by the arm, to get the following results:*

	Weight	**x Arm**	**= Moment**
Zone 1	180	172.1	30,978
Zone 2	505	217.8	109,989
Zone 3	198	264.4	52,351.2
Zone 4	600	294.5	176,700
Zone 5	0	319.5	0
Zone 6	60	344	20,640
Zone A	100	132.4	13,240
Zone B	80	182.1	14,568
Zone C	200	233.4	46,680
Zone D	180	287.6	51,768

Record these in the Figure 414 worksheet.

3. *Using Figure 411, calculate the weight and moment of 180 gallons of fuel and find 1,206 pounds, and a moment of 245,200. Record in Figure 414 worksheet.*

Answers

8700   [C]

4. Add all the items from the Figure 414 worksheet, including the basic empty weight and moment:

	Weight	**Moment**
Basic empty weight	5,005	929,400
Pilot	190	25,745
Front Passenger	200	27,100
Zone 1	180	30,978
Zone 2	505	109,989
Zone 3	198	52,351.2
Zone 4	600	176,700
Zone 5	0	0
Zone 6	60	20,640
Zone A	100	13,240
Zone B	80	14,568
Zone C	200	46,680
Zone D	180	51,768
Fuel	1206	245,200
Total	8,704 lbs	1,744,359 in-lbs

5. Divide the total moment by the total weight to arrive at a CG of 200.4 inches. This is the old CG.

6. You are moving 300 pounds from Zone 2 (arm 217.8) to Zone 3 (arm 264.4). This is a distance of (264.4 − 217.8) 46.6 inches. The formula for weight shift is given as:

$$\frac{\text{Weight to be shifted}}{\text{Total weight}} = \frac{\text{Change in CG}}{\text{Distance CG is shifted}}$$

$$\frac{300}{8,704} = \frac{\text{Change in CG}}{46.6}$$

Using cross-multiplication, 46.6 x 300 ÷ 8,704 equals 1.6 inches. Since Zone 3 is aft of Zone 2, the CG also shifts aft and the new CG is 200.4 + 1.6 = 202 inches. (PLT121) — FAA-H-8083-1

DSP
8578. (Refer to Figure 44.) What is the new CG if the weight is removed from the forward compartment under Loading Conditions WS 1?

A— 27.1 percent MAC.
B— 26.8 percent MAC.
C— 30.0 percent MAC.

1. Calculate original CG in inches aft of datum:

CG (inches aft of LEMAC) = (22.5% / 100%)
× 141.5" = 31.84"
CG (inches aft of Datum) = 549.13" + 31.84"
= 580.97"

2. Use the original weight and the CG to calculate the original Moment/1,000. Next use the weight change and station to determine the Moment/1,000 change:

	Weight	**Moment/1,000**
Original Weight	90,000	52,287.08
Weight Change	− 2,500	− 880.25
New Weight	87,500	51,406.83

3. Determine the new CG:

CG = (51,406.83/87,500) × 1,000 = 587.51"

4. Convert CG to percent of MAC:

CG (inches aft of LEMAC) = 587.51" − 549.13" = 38.38"
CG (% of MAC) = (38.38/141.5) = 27.1%

(PLT021) — FAA-H-8083-1

DSP
8579. (Refer to Figure 44.) Where is the new CG if the weight is added to the aft compartment under Loading Conditions WS 2?

A— +17.06 index arm.
B— +14.82 index arm.
C— +12.13 index arm.

1. Calculate original CG in inches aft of datum:

CG (inches aft of LEMAC) = (28.4% / 100%)
× 141.5" = 40.19"
CG (inches aft of Datum) = 549.13" + 40.19"
= 589.32"

2. Use the original weight and the CG to calculate the original Moment/1,000. Next use the weight change and station to determine the Moment/1,000 change:

	Weight	**Moment/1,000**
Original Weight	85,000	50,091.87
Weight Change	+ 1,800	+ 1,304.82
New Weight	86,800	51,396.69

3. Determine the new CG:

CG = (51,396.69/86,800) × 1,000 = 592.13"

4. Convert to Index Arm (0 Index Arm = 580.0"):

CG (Index Arm) = 592.13" − 580" = +12.13"

(PLT021) — FAA-H-8083-1

Answers

8578   [A]   8579   [C]

DSP

8580. (Refer to Figure 44.) What is the new CG if the weight is added to the forward compartment under Loading Conditions WS 3?

A— 11.4 percent MAC.
B— 14.3 percent MAC.
C— 14.5 percent MAC.

1. Calculate original CG in inches aft of datum:

CG (inches aft of LEMAC) = (19.8% / 100%)
    × 141.5" = 28.02"
CG (inches aft of Datum) = 549.13" + 28.02"
    = 577.15"

2. Use the original weight and the CG to calculate the original Moment/1,000. Next use the weight change and station to determine the Moment/1,000 change:

	Weight	Moment/1,000
Original Weight	84,500	48,768.92
Weight Change	+ 3,000	+ 1,056.30
New Weight	87,500	49,825.22

3. Determine the new CG:

CG = (49,825.22/87,500) x 1,000 = 569.43

4. Convert CG to percent of MAC:

CG (inches aft of LEMAC) = 569.43" – 549.13" =
    20.3"
CG (% of MAC) = (20.3"/141.5") x 100%
    = 14.3%

(PLT021) — FAA-H-8083-1

DSP

8581. (Refer to Figure 44.) Where is the new CG if the weight is removed from the aft compartment under Loading Conditions WS 4?

A— +15.53 index arm.
B— +8.50 index arm.
C— -93.51 index arm.

1. Calculate original CG in inches aft of datum:

CG (inches aft of LEMAC) = (30.3% / 100%)
    x 141.5" = 42.87"
CG (inches aft of Datum) = 549.13" + 42.87"
    = 592.00"

2. Use the original weight and the CG to calculate the original Moment/1,000. Next use the weight change and station to determine the Moment/1,000 change:

	Weight	Moment/1,000
Original Weight	81,700	48,366.40
Weight Change	– 2,100	– 1,522.29
New Weight	79,600	46,844.11

3. Determine the new CG:

CG = (46,844.11/79,600) x 1,000 = 588.49"

4. Convert to Index Arm:

CG (Index Arm) = 588.49" – 580" = +8.50"

(PLT021) — FAA-H-8083-1

DSP

8582. (Refer to Figure 44.) What is the new CG if the weight is removed from the forward compartment under Loading Conditions WS 5?

A— 31.9 percent MAC.
B— 19.1 percent MAC.
C— 35.2 percent MAC.

1. Calculate original CG in inches aft of datum:

CG (inches aft of LEMAC) = (25.5% / 100%)
    x 141.5" = 36.08"
CG (inches aft of Datum) = 549.13" + 36.08"
    = 585.21"

2. Use the original weight and the CG to calculate the original Moment/1,000. Next use the weight change and station to determine the Moment/1,000 change:

	Weight	Moment/1,000
Original Weight	88,300	51,674.04
Weight Change	– 3,300	– 1,161.93
New Weight	85,000	50,512.11

3. Determine the new CG:

CG = (50,512.11 ÷ 85,000) × 1,000 = 594.26"

4. Convert CG to percent of MAC:

CG (inches aft of LEMAC) = 594.26" – 549.13" =
    45.13"
CG(% of MAC) = (45.13"/141.5") x 100% = 31.9%

(PLT021) — FAA-H-8083-1

Answers

8580   [B]   8581   [B]   8582   [A]

DSP

8573. (Refer to Figure 44.) What is the new CG if the weight is shifted from the forward to the aft compartment under Loading Conditions WS 1?

A— 15.2 percent MAC.
B— 29.8 percent MAC.
C— 30.0 percent MAC.

Change in CG = (2,500 lbs x 372.8)/90,000 lbs = +10.4"
Change in CG (% of MAC) = (10.4"/141.5") × 100% = 7.35%
New CG = 22.5% + 7.35% = 29.85%

(PLT021) — FAA-H-8083-1

DSP

8574. (Refer to Figure 44.) What is the new CG if the weight is shifted from the aft to the forward compartment under Loading Conditions WS 2?

A— 26.1 percent MAC.
B— 20.5 percent MAC.
C— 22.8 percent MAC.

Change in CG = (1,800 lbs × (-372.8))/85,000 lbs = -7.89"
Change in CG (% of MAC) = (-7.89"/141.5") × 100% = -5.6%
New CG = 28.4% − 5.6% = 22.8%

(PLT021) — FAA-H-8083-1

DSP

8575. (Refer to Figure 44.) What is the new CG if the weight is shifted from the forward to the aft compartment under Loading Conditions WS 3?

A— 29.2 percent MAC.
B— 33.0 percent MAC.
C— 28.6 percent MAC.

Change in CG = (3,000 lbs x 372.8")/84,500 lbs = 13.24"
Change in CG (% of MAC) = (13.24"/141.5") x 100% = 9.4%
New CG = 19.8% + 9.4% = 29.2%

(PLT021) — FAA-H-8083-1

DSP

8576. (Refer to Figure 44.) What is the new CG if the weight is shifted from the aft to the forward compartment under Loading Conditions WS 4?

A— 37.0 percent MAC.
B— 23.5 percent MAC.
C— 24.1 percent MAC.

Change in CG = (2,100 lbs × (-372.8")/81,700 lbs = -9.58"
Change in CG (% of MAC) = (-9.58"/141.5") x 100% = -6.8%
New CG = 30.3% − 6.8% = 23.5%.

(PLT021) — FAA-H-8083-1

DSP

8577. (Refer to Figure 44.) Where is the new CG if the listed weight is shifted from the forward to the aft compartment under Loading Conditions WS 5?

A— +19.15 index arm.
B— +13.93 index arm.
C— -97.92 index arm.

CG (inches aft of LEMAC) = (25.5%/100%) x 141.5 = 36.08"
CG (inches aft of Datum) = 549.13" + 36.08" = 585.21"
CG (Index Arm) = 585.21" − 580" = +5.21"
Change in CG = (3,300 lbs x 372.8")/88,300 lbs = 13.93"
New CG (Index Arm) = +5.21" + 13.93" = 19.14"

(PLT021) — FAA-H-8083-1

Answers

8573 [B]   8574 [C]   8575 [A]   8576 [B]   8577 [A]

C208 Weight and Balance

Note: By definition, "basic empty weight" does not include crew weight, so you must include crew in the calculation. By definition, "basic operating weight" includes crew weight so you do not include crew in the calculation.

The other key to C208 weight and balance is to use the actual arms listed (FAA Figure 405) for each position. You can use the charts and pre-calculated moments as depicted in FAA Figure 412, but the actual calculation is more accurate and probably quicker. The only exception to this is fuel, as the arm changes based upon fuel weight, therefore the chart in FAA Figure 411 should be used.

ATS, DSP

8049. The weight and CG of an aircraft used in 135 operations must have been calculated from those values established by actual weighing of the aircraft within what period of time?

A— Multiengine aircraft, preceding 36 calendar months.
B— Multiengine and single-engine aircraft, preceding 36 calendar months.
C— Multiengine aircraft, last 36 calendar months; single-engine, last 24 calendar months.

No person may operate a multi-engine aircraft unless the current empty weight and center of gravity are calculated from values established by actual weighing of the aircraft within the preceding 36 calendar months. (PLT454) — 14 CFR §135.185

ATS, DSP

8067. What are the empty weight and balance currency requirements for aircraft used in 135 operations?

A— The empty weight and CG of multiengine and single-engine aircraft must have been calculated from an actual weighing within the previous 36 calendar months.
B— The empty weight and CG must have been calculated from an actual weighing within the previous 24 calendar months unless the original Airworthiness Certificate was issued within the previous 36 calendar months.
C— The empty weight and CG of multiengine aircraft must have been calculated from an actual weighing within the previous 36 calendar months.

No person may operate a multi-engine aircraft unless the current empty weight and center of gravity are calculated from values established by actual weighing of the aircraft within the preceding 36 calendar months. (PLT454) — 14 CFR §135.185

Answers

8049 [A]   8067 [C]

Beech 1900 Weight and Balance

Note: By definition, "Basic Empty Weight" does not include crew weight, so you must include crew in the calculation. By definition, "Basic Operating Weight" includes crew weight so you do not include crew in the calculation.

DSP

8434. (Refer to Figures 3, 6, 8, 9, 10, and 11.) What is the CG in inches from datum under Loading Conditions BE-1?

A— Station 290.3.
B— Station 285.8.
C— Station 291.8.

	Weight	Moment/100
Basic Empty Wt.	9,226	25,823
Crew	360	464
Row 1	350	700
Row 2	260	598
Row 3	200	520
Row 4	340	986
Row 5	120	384
Row 6	400	1,400
Row 7	120	456
Row 8	250	1,025
Row 9	—	—
Baggage		
Nose	60	39
FWD Cabin	250	409
Aft (FWD Sec)	500	2,418
Aft (Aft Sec)	—	—
Fuel (Jet B @ 6.6)	+ 2,442	+ 7,299
Total	14,878	42,521

CG = (42,521 ÷ 14,878) x 100 = 285.8"

(PLT021) — FAA-H-8083-1

DSP

8435. (Refer to Figures 3, 6, 8, 9, 10, and 11.) What is the CG in inches from datum under Loading Conditions BE-2?

A— Station 295.2.
B— Station 292.9.
C— Station 293.0.

	Weight	Moment/100
Basic Empty Wt.	9,226	25,823
Crew	340	439
Row 1	300	600
Row 2	250	575
Row 3	190	494
Row 4	170	493
Row 5	190	608
Row 6	340	1,190
Row 7	190	722
Row 8	—	—
Row 9	—	—
Baggage		
Nose	—	—
FWD Cabin	100	164
Aft (FWD Sec)	200	967
Aft (Aft Sec)	600	3,198
Fuel (Jet A @ 6.8)	+ 2,652	+ 7,924
Total	14,748	43,197

CG = (43,197 ÷ 14,748) x 100 = 292.9"

(PLT021) — FAA-H-8083-1

Answers

8434 [B]   8435 [B]

DSP

8436. (Refer to Figures 3, 6, 8, 9, 10, and 11.) What is the CG in inches from datum under Loading Conditions BE-3?

A— Station 288.2.
B— Station 285.8.
C— Station 290.4.

	Weight	Moment/100
Basic Empty Wt.	9,226	25,823
Crew	350	452
Row 1	120	240
Row 2	340	782
Row 3	350	910
Row 4	300	870
Row 5	170	544
Row 6	—	—
Row 7	—	—
Row 8	—	—
Row 9	—	—
Baggage		
Nose	80	52
FWD Cabin	120	197
Aft (FWD Sec)	250	1,209
Aft (Aft Sec)	500	2,665
Fuel (Jet B @ 6.7)	+ 2,680	+ 8,007
Total	14,486	41,751

$CG = (41,751 \div 14,486) \times 100 = 288.2''$

(PLT021) — FAA-H-8083-1

DSP

8437. (Refer to Figures 3, 6, 8, 9, 10, and 11.) What is the CG in inches from datum under Loading Conditions BE-4?

A— Station 297.4.
B— Station 299.6.
C— Station 297.7.

	Weight	Moment/100
Basic Empty Wt.	9,226	25,823
Crew	340	439
Row 1	—	—
Row 2	370	851
Row 3	400	1,040
Row 4	290	841
Row 5	200	640
Row 6	170	595
Row 7	210	798
Row 8	190	779
Row 9	420	1,848
Baggage		
Nose	—	—
FWD Cabin	—	—
Aft (FWD Sec)	800	3,868
Aft (Aft Sec)	—	—
Fuel (Jet A @ 6.8)	+ 1,972	+ 5,912
Total	14,588	43,434

$CG = (43,434 \div 14,588) \times 100 = 297.7''$

(PLT021) — FAA-H-8083-1

Answers

8436   [A]   8437   [C]

DSP
8438. (Refer to Figures 3, 6, 8, 9, 10, and 11.) What is the CG in inches from datum under Loading Conditions BE-5?

A— Station 288.9.
B— Station 290.5.
C— Station 289.1.

	Weight	Moment/100
Basic Empty Wt.	9,226	25,823
Crew	360	464
Row 1	—	—
Row 2	—	—
Row 3	170	442
Row 4	200	580
Row 5	290	928
Row 6	400	1,400
Row 7	370	1,406
Row 8	340	1,394
Row 9	430	1,892
Baggage		
Nose	100	66
FWD Cabin	200	327
Aft (FWD Sec)	—	—
Aft (Aft Sec)	—	—
Fuel (Jet B @ 6.5)	+ 2,210	+ 6,610
Total	14,296	41,332

CG = (41,332 ÷ 14,296) x 100 = 289.1"

(PLT021) — FAA-H-8083-1

DSP
8439. (Refer to Figures 3, 6, 8, 9, 10, and 11.) What is the CG shift if the passengers in row 1 are moved to seats in row 9 under Loading Conditions BE-1?

A— 1.5 inches aft.
B— 5.6 inches aft.
C— 6.2 inches aft.

	Weight	Moment/100
Basic Empty Wt.	9,226	25,823
Crew	360	464
Row 1	350	700
Row 2	260	598
Row 3	200	520
Row 4	340	986
Row 5	120	384
Row 6	400	1,400
Row 7	120	456
Row 8	250	1,025
Row 9	—	—
Baggage		
Nose	60	39
FWD Cabin	250	409
Aft (FWD Sec)	500	2,418
Aft (Aft Sec)	—	—
Fuel (Jet B @ 6.6)	+ 2,442	+ 7,299
Total	14,878	42,521

Change in CG = 350 lbs x 240" ÷ 14,878 lbs = 5.6 aft

(PLT021) — FAA-H-8083-1

Answers

8438 [C]   8439 [B]

DSP
8440. (Refer to Figures 3, 6, 8, 9, 10, and 11.) What is the CG shift if the passengers in row 1 are moved to row 8, and the passengers in row 2 are moved to row 9 under Loading Conditions BE-2?

A— 9.2 inches aft.
B— 5.7 inches aft.
C— 7.8 inches aft.

	Weight	Moment/100
Basic Empty Wt.	9,226	25,823
Crew	340	439
Row 1	300	600
Row 2	250	575
Row 3	190	494
Row 4	170	493
Row 5	190	608
Row 6	340	1,190
Row 7	190	722
Row 8	—	—
Row 9	—	—
Baggage		
Nose	—	—
FWD Cabin	100	164
Aft (FWD Sec)	200	967
Aft (Aft Sec)	600	3,198
Fuel (Jet A @ 6.6)	+ 2,652	+ 7,924
Total	14,748	43,197

Change in CG = 550 lbs x 210" ÷ 14,748 lbs = 7.8" aft

(PLT021) — FAA-H-8083-1

DSP
8441. (Refer to Figures 3, 6, 8, 9, 10, and 11.) What is the CG shift if four passengers weighing 170 pounds each are added; two to seats in row 6 and two to seats in row 7 under Loading Conditions BE-3?

A— 3.5 inches aft.
B— 2.2 inches forward.
C— 1.8 inches aft.

Use the following steps:

1. Compute the CG position prior to changes:

	Weight	Moment/100
Basic Empty Wt.	9,226	25,823
Crew	350	452
Row 1	120	240
Row 2	340	782
Row 3	350	910
Row 4	300	870
Row 5	170	544
Row 6	—	—
Row 7	—	—
Row 8	—	—
Row 9	—	—
Baggage		
Nose	80	52
FWD Cabin	120	197
Aft (FWD Sec)	250	1,209
Aft (Aft Sec)	500	2,665
Fuel (Jet B @ 6.7)	+ 2,680	+ 8,007
Total	14,486	41,751

CG = (41,751 ÷ 14,486) x 100 = 288.2"

2. Calculate the weight additions:

	Weight	Moment/100
Original Wt.	14,486	41,751
2 pax in row 6	+ 340	+ 1,190
2 pax in row 7	+ 340	+ 1,292
New Total	15,166	44,233

3. CG = (44,233 ÷ 15,166) x 100 = 291.7"

4. The CG moved from station 288.2 to station 291.7, a movement of 3.5 inches aft.

(PLT021) — FAA-H-8083-1

Answers

8440   [C]   8441   [A]

DSP

8442. (Refer to Figures 3, 6, 8, 9, 10, and 11.) What is the CG shift if all passengers in rows 2 and 4 are deplaned under Loading Conditions BE-4?

A— 2.5 inches aft.
B— 2.5 inches forward.
C— 2.0 inches aft.

Use the following steps:

1. *Compute the CG position prior to changes:*

	Weight	**Moment/100**
Basic Empty Wt.	*9,226*	*25,823*
Crew	*340*	*439*
Row 1	*—*	*—*
Row 2	*370*	*851*
Row 3	*400*	*1,040*
Row 4	*290*	*841*
Row 5	*200*	*640*
Row 6	*170*	*595*
Row 7	*210*	*798*
Row 8	*190*	*779*
Row 9	*420*	*1,848*
Baggage		
Nose	*—*	*—*
FWD Cabin	*—*	*—*
Aft (FWD Sec)	*800*	*3,868*
Aft (Aft Sec)	*—*	*—*
Fuel (Jet A @ 6.8)	*+1,972*	*+ 5,912*
Total	*14,588*	*43,434*

   CG = (43,434 ÷ 14,588) x 100 = 297.7"

2. *Calculate the weight reductions:*

	Weight	**Moment/100**
Original Wt.	*14,588*	*43,434*
2 pax in row 2	*– 370*	*– 851*
2 pax in row 4	*– 290*	*– 841*
New Total	*13,928*	*41,742*

3. *Calculate the new CG:*

   CG = (41,742 ÷ 13,928) × 100 = 299.7"

4. *The CG moved from station 297.7 to station 299.7, a movement of 2.0 inches aft.*

(PLT021) — FAA-H-8083-1

DSP

8443. (Refer to Figures 3, 6, 8, 9, 10, and 11.) What is the CG shift if the passengers in row 8 are moved to row 2, and the passengers in row 7 are moved to row 1 under Loading Conditions BE-5?

A— 1.0 inches forward.
B— 8.9 inches forward.
C— 6.5 inches forward.

	Weight	**Moment/100**
Basic Empty Wt.	*9,226*	*25,823*
Crew	*360*	*464*
Row 1	*—*	*—*
Row 2	*—*	*—*
Row 3	*170*	*442*
Row 4	*200*	*580*
Row 5	*290*	*928*
Row 6	*400*	*1,400*
Row 7	*370*	*1,406*
Row 8	*340*	*1,394*
Row 9	*430*	*1,892*
Baggage		
Nose	*100*	*66*
FWD Cabin	*200*	*327*
Aft (FWD Sec)	*—*	*—*
Aft (Aft Sec)	*—*	*—*
Fuel (Jet B @ 6.5)	*+ 2,210*	*+ 6,610*
Total	*14,296*	*41,332*

Change in CG = 710 lbs x 180" ÷ 14,296 lbs = 8.9" forward

(PLT021) — FAA-H-8083-1

DSP
8444. (Refer to Figures 4, 7, 9, 10, and 11.) What is the CG in inches from datum under Loading Conditions BE-6?

A— Station 300.5.
B— Station 296.5.
C— Station 300.8.

	Weight	Moment/100
Basic Operating Wt.	9,005	25,934
Sec A	500	1,125
Sec B	500	1,275
Sec C	550	1,567.5
Sec D	550	1,732.5
Sec E	600	2,070
Sec F	600	2,250
Sec G	450	1,822.5
Sec H	—	—
Sec J	350	1,627.5
Sec K	—	—
Sec L	—	—
Fuel (Jet B @ 6.5)	+2,210	+ 6,610
Total	15,315	46,014

CG = (46,014 ÷ 15,315) x 100 = 300.5"

(PLT021) — FAA-H-8083-1

DSP
8445. (Refer to Figures 4, 7, 9, 10, and 11.) What is the CG in inches from datum under Loading Conditions BE-7?

A— Station 296.0.
B— Station 297.8.
C— Station 299.9.

	Weight	Moment/100
Basic Operating Wt.	9,005	25,934
Sec A	—	—
Sec B	400	1,020
Sec C	450	1,282.5
Sec D	600	1,890
Sec E	600	2,070
Sec F	600	2,250
Sec G	500	2,025
Sec H	—	—
Sec J	—	—
Sec K	—	—
Sec L	—	—
Fuel	+ 2,442	+ 7,299
Total	14,597	43,770.5

CG = (43,770.5 ÷ 14,597) x 100 = 299.9"

(PLT021) — FAA-H-8083-1

DSP
8446. (Refer to Figures 4, 7, 9, 10, and 11.) What is the CG in inches from datum under Loading Conditions BE-8?

A— Station 297.4.
B— Station 298.1.
C— Station 302.0.

	Weight	Moment/100
Basic Operating Wt.	9,005	25,934
Sec A	600	1,350
Sec B	200	510
Sec C	400	1,140
Sec D	400	1,260
Sec E	200	690
Sec F	200	750
Sec G	200	810
Sec H	200	870
Sec J	300	1,395
Sec K	250	1,248.75
Sec L	100	533
Fuel	+ 2,652	+ 7,924
Total	14,707	44,414.75

CG = (44,414.75 ÷ 14,707) x 100 = 302.0"

(PLT021) — FAA-H-8083-1

DSP
8447. (Refer to Figures 4, 7, 9, 10, and 11.) What is the CG in inches from datum under Loading Conditions BE-9?

A— Station 296.7.
B— Station 297.1.
C— Station 301.2.

	Weight	Moment/100
Basic Operating Wt.	9,005	25,934
Sec A	600	1,350
Sec B	600	1,530
Sec C	600	1,710
Sec D	600	1,890
Sec E	550	1,897.5
Sec F	350	1,312.5
Sec G	250	1,012.5
Sec H	250	1,087.5
Sec J	150	697.5
Sec K	200	999
Sec L	100	533
Fuel (Jet A @ 6.8)	+ 1,972	+ 5,912
Total	15,227	45,865.5

CG = (45,865.5 ÷ 15,227) x 100 = 301.2"

(PLT021) — FAA-H-8083-1

Answers

8444 [A]	8445 [C]	8446 [C]	8447 [C]

DSP

8448. (Refer to Figures 4, 7, 9, 10, and 11.) What is the CG in inches from datum under Loading Conditions BE-10?

A— Station 298.4.
B— Station 298.1.
C— Station 293.9.

	Weight	Moment/100
Basic Operating Wt.	9,005	25,934
Sec A	350	787.5
Sec B	450	1,147.5
Sec C	450	1,282.5
Sec D	550	1,732.5
Sec E	550	1,897.5
Sec F	600	2,250
Sec G	600	2,430
Sec H	—	—
Sec J	—	—
Sec K	—	—
Sec L	—	—
Fuel (Jet B @ 6.7)	+ 2,680	+ 8,007
Total	15,235	45,468.5

CG = (45,468.5 ÷ 15,235) x 100 = 298.4"

(PLT021) — FAA-H-8083-1

DSP

8449. (Refer to Figures 4, 7, 9, 10, and 11.) What is the CG shift if 300 pounds of cargo in section A is moved to section H under Loading Conditions BE-6?

A— 4.1 inches aft.
B— 3.5 inches aft.
C— 4.0 inches aft.

	Weight	Moment/100
Basic Operating Wt.	9,005	25,934
Sec A	500	1,125
Sec B	500	1,275
Sec C	550	1,567.5
Sec D	550	1,732.5
Sec E	600	2,070
Sec F	600	2,250
Sec G	450	1,822.5
Sec H	—	—
Sec J	350	1,627.5
Sec K	—	—
Sec L	—	—
Fuel (Jet B @ 6.5)	+ 2,210	+ 6,610
Total	15,315	46,014

Change in CG = 300 lbs x 210" ÷ 15,315 lbs = 4.1" aft

(PLT021) — FAA-H-8083-1

DSP

8450. (Refer to Figures 4, 7, 9, 10, and 11.) What is the CG shift if the cargo in section F is moved to section A, and 200 pounds of the cargo in section G is added to the cargo in section B, under Loading Conditions BE-7?

A— 7.5 inches forward.
B— 8.0 inches forward.
C— 8.2 inches forward.

	Weight	Moment/100
Basic Operating Wt.	9,005	25,934
Sec A	—	—
Sec B	400	1,020
Sec C	450	1,282.5
Sec D	600	1,890
Sec E	600	2,070
Sec F	600	2,250
Sec G	500	2,025
Sec H	—	—
Sec J	—	—
Sec K	—	—
Sec L	—	—
Fuel	+ 2,442	+ 7,299
Total	14,597	43,770.5

CG change moving weight from F to A is:
  600 x 150 ÷ 14,597 = 6.2 inches forward
CG change moving weight from G to B is:
  200 x 150 ÷ 14,597 = 2.1 inches forward
Total change:
  6.2 inches + 2.1 inches = 8.3 inches forward

(PLT021) — FAA-H-8083-1

Answers

8448   [A]   8449   [A]   8450   [C]

DSP

8451. (Refer to Figures 4, 7, 9, 10, and 11.) What is the CG if all cargo in sections A, B, J, K, and L are off-loaded under Loading Conditions BE-8?

A— Station 292.7.
B— Station 297.0.
C— Station 294.6.

Calculate the weight and CG accounting for the off-loaded items:

	Weight	Moment/100
Basic Operating Wt.	9,005	25,934
Sec A	—	—
Sec B	—	—
Sec C	400	1,140
Sec D	400	1,260
Sec E	200	690
Sec F	200	750
Sec G	200	810
Sec H	200	870
Sec J	—	—
Sec K	—	—
Sec L	—	—
Fuel	+ 2,652	+ 7,924
Total	13,257	39,378

$CG = (39,378 \div 13,257) \times 100 = 297.0''$

(PLT021) — FAA-H-8083-1

DSP

8452. (Refer to Figures 4, 7, 9, 10, and 11.) What is the CG if cargo is loaded to bring sections F, G, and H to maximum capacity under Loading Conditions BE-9?

A— Station 307.5.
B— Station 305.4.
C— Station 303.5.

Use the following steps:

1. Calculate the weight and CG prior to weight changes:

	Weight	Moment/100
Basic Operating Wt.	9,005	25,934
Sec A	600	1,350
Sec B	600	1,530
Sec C	600	1,710
Sec D	600	1,890
Sec E	550	1,897.5
Sec F	350	1,312.5
Sec G	250	1,012.5
Sec H	250	1,087.5
Sec J	150	697.5
Sec K	200	999
Sec L	100	533
Fuel (Jet A @ 6.8)	+ 1,972	+ 5,912
Total	15,227	45,865.5

$CG = (45,865.5 \div 15,227) \times 100 = 301.2''$

2. 250 pounds can be added to Section F, 350 pounds to Section G and 350 pounds to Section H. Apply these weight additions to the previously calculated weight and Moment/100, then calculate the new CG:

	Weight	Moment/100
Original Wt.	15,227	45,865.5
Sec F	250	937.5
Sec G	350	1,417.5
Sec H	+ 350	+1,522.5
New Wt.	16,177	49,743

$CG = (49,743 \div 16,177) \times 100 = 307.5''$

(PLT021) — FAA-H-8083-1

Answers

8451 [B]   8452 [A]

DSP

8453. (Refer to Figures 4, 7, 9, 10, and 11.) What is the CG shift if the cargo in section G is moved to section J under Loading Conditions BE-10?

A— 2.7 inches aft.
B— 2.4 inches aft.
C— 3.2 inches aft.

	Weight	Moment/100
Basic Operating Wt.	9,005	25,934
Sec A	350	787.5
Sec B	450	1,147.5
Sec C	450	1,282.5
Sec D	550	1,732.5
Sec E	550	1,897.5
Sec F	600	2,250
Sec G	600	2,430
Sec H	—	—
Sec J	—	—
Sec K	—	—
Sec L	—	—
Fuel (Jet B @ 6.7)	+ 2,680	+ 8,007
Total	15,235	45,468.5

Change in CG = 600 lbs x 60" ÷ 15,235 lbs = 2.4" aft

(PLT021) — FAA-H-8083-1

DSP

8454. (Refer to Figures 5, 7, 9, and 11.) What limit is exceeded under Operating Conditions BE-11?

A— ZFW limit is exceeded.
B— Aft CG limit is exceeded at takeoff weight.
C— Aft CG limit is exceeded at landing weight.

Use the following steps:

1. Calculate the Zero Fuel Weight (ZWF) using Operating Conditions BE-11:

	Weight	Moment/100
Basic Empty Wt.	9,225	25,820
Crew	340	439
Pax & Bags	+ 4,200	+ 15,025
Zero Fuel Wt.	13,765	41,284

2. Determine the Takeoff Weight:

	Weight	Moment/100
Zero Fuel Wt.	13,765	41,284
T/O Fuel (340 gal)	+ 2,312	+ 6,915
Takeoff Wt.	16,077	48,199

3. Calculate the Takeoff CG:

CG = (48,199 ÷ 16,077) x 100 = 299.8

4. Determine the Landing Weight:

	Weight	Moment/100
Zero Fuel Wt.	13,765	41,284
Land Fuel (100 gal)	+ 680	+ 2,068
Land Wt.	14,445	43,352

5. Calculate the Landing Weight CG. Refer to CG = (43,352 ÷ 14,445) x 100 = 300.1

This exceeds the aft CG limit (300.0) at landing.

(PLT021) — FAA-H-8083-1

DSP

8455. (Refer to Figures 5, 7, 9, and 11.) What limit(s) is(are) exceeded under Operating Conditions BE-12?

A— ZFW limit is exceeded.
B— Landing aft CG limit is exceeded.
C— ZFW and maximum takeoff weight limits are exceeded.

Use the following steps:

1. Calculate the Zero Fuel Weight using Operating Conditions BE-12:

	Weight	Moment/100
Basic Empty Wt.	9,100	24,990
Crew	380	490
Pax & Bags	+ 4,530	+ 16,480
Zero Fuel Wt.	14,010	41,960

2. Determine the Takeoff Weight:

	Weight	Moment/100
Zero Fuel Wt.	14,010	41,960
T/O Fuel (300 gal)	+ 2,040	+ 6,112
Takeoff Wt.	16,050	48,072

3. Calculate the Takeoff CG:

CG = (48,172 ÷ 16,050) x 100 = 299.5

4. Determine the Landing Weight:

	Weight	Moment/100
Zero Fuel Wt.	14,010	41,960
Land Fuel (160 gal)	+ 1,088	+ 3,303
Land Wt.	15,098	45,263

5. Calculate the Landing Weight CG. Refer to CG = (45,263 ÷ 15,098) x 100 = 299.8

This exceeds the maximum Zero Fuel Weight.

(PLT021) — FAA-H-8083-1

Answers

8453   [B]   8454   [C]   8455   [A]

DSP
8456. (Refer to Figures 5, 7, 9, and 11.) What limit, if any, is exceeded under Operating Conditions BE-13?

A— Takeoff forward CG limit is exceeded.
B— No limit is exceeded.
C— Landing aft CG limit is exceeded.

Use the following steps:

1. *Calculate the Zero Fuel Weight using Operating Conditions BE-13:*

	Weight	Moment/100
Basic Empty Wt.	9,000	24,710
Crew	360	464
Pax & Bags	+ 4,630	+ 16,743
Zero Fuel Wt.	13,990	41,917

2. *Determine the Takeoff Weight:*

	Weight	Moment/100
Zero Fuel Wt.	13,990	41,917
T/O Fuel (330 gal)	+ 2,244	+ 6,713
Takeoff Wt.	16,234	48,630

3. *Calculate the Takeoff CG:*

$$CG = (48,630 \div 16,234) \times 100 = 299.6$$

4. *Determine the Landing Weight:*

	Weight	Moment/100
Zero Fuel Wt.	13,990	41,917
Land Fuel (140 gal)	+ 952	+ 2,893
Land Wt.	14,942	44,810

5. *Calculate the Landing Weight CG. Refer to CG = (44,810 ÷ 14,942) x 100 = 299.9*

No limits are exceeded.

(PLT021) — FAA-H-8083-1

DSP
8457. (Refer to Figures 5, 7, 9, and 11.) What limit(s) is(are) exceeded under Operating Conditions BE-14?

A— Maximum ZFW limit is exceeded.
B— Takeoff forward CG limit is exceeded.
C— Maximum landing weight and landing forward CG limits are exceeded.

Use the following steps:

1. *Calculate the Zero Fuel Weight using Operating Conditions BE-14:*

	Weight	Moment/100
Basic Empty Wt.	8,910	24,570
Crew	400	516
Pax & Bags	+ 4,690	+ 13,724
Zero Fuel Wt.	14,000	38,810

2. *Determine the Takeoff Weight:*

	Weight	Moment/100
Zero Fuel Wt.	14,000	38,810
T/O Fuel (290 gal)	+ 1,972	+ 5,912
Takeoff Wt.	15,972	44,722

3. *Calculate the Takeoff CG:*

$$CG = (44,722 \div 15,972) \times 100 = 280.0$$

The forward takeoff CG limit is exceeded.

(PLT021) — FAA-H-8083-1

DSP
8458. (Refer to Figures 5, 7, 9, and 11.) What limit(s) is(are) exceeded under Operating Conditions BE-15?

A— Maximum takeoff weight limit is exceeded.
B— Maximum ZFW and takeoff forward CG limits are exceeded.
C— Maximum takeoff weight and takeoff forward CG limits are exceeded.

Use the following steps:

1. *Calculate the Zero Fuel Weight using Operating Conditions BE-15:*

	Weight	Moment/100
Basic Empty Wt.	9,150	25,240
Crew	370	477
Pax & Bags	+ 4,500	+ 13,561
Zero Fuel Wt.	14,020	39,278

2. *Determine the Takeoff Weight:*

	Weight	Moment/100
Zero Fuel Wt.	14,020	39,278
T/O Fuel (380 gal)	+ 2,584	+ 7,722
Takeoff Wt.	16,604	47,000

3. *Calculate the Takeoff CG:*

$$CG = (47,000 \div 16.604) \times 100 = 283.1$$

This exceeds the maximum takeoff gross weight of 16,600.

(PLT021) — FAA-H-8083-1

Answers

8456	[B]	8457	[B]	8458	[A]

Helicopter Weight and Balance

RTC
8419. What is the result of loading a helicopter so that the CG is aft of the rearward limit?

A— Insufficient aft cyclic control to decelerate properly during an approach.
B— Inability of the pilot to recognize this dangerous condition when hovering in a strong headwind.
C— Insufficient forward cyclic control to fly in the upper allowable airspeed range.

If the center of gravity is too far aft of the mast, the helicopter hangs with the nose tilted up. If flight is attempted in this condition, the pilot may find it impossible to fly in the upper allowable airspeed range due to insufficient forward cyclic displacement to maintain a nose low attitude. (PLT240) — FAA-H-8083-21

RTC
8513. (Refer to Figures 29, 31, 32, and 33.) Where is the longitudinal CG located under Operating Conditions BL-1?

A— Station 214.3.
B— Station 235.6.
C— Station 237.8.

Condition	BL-1	Weight	Moment
Empty		9,387.5	2,327,105
Crew		340.0	39,780
Pax Row	1	700.0	109,830
	2	830.0	154,546
	3	800.0	172,320
	4	—	—
Baggage	Center	500.0	148,500
	L & R	200.0	59,040
Fuel		+ 2,040.0	+ 475,400
Total		14,797.5	3,486,521

Total Moment ÷ Total Weight = Longitudinal CG

$$\frac{3,486,521}{14,797.5} = 235.6$$

(PLT021) — FAA-H-8083-1

RTC
8514. (Refer to Figures 29, 31, 32, and 33.) Where is the longitudinal CG located under Operating Conditions BL-2?

A— Station 237.6.
B— Station 238.5.
C— Station 262.3.

Condition	BL-2	Weight	Moment
Empty		9387.5	2,327,105
Crew		400.0	46,800
Pax Row	1	620.0	97,278
	2	700.0	130,340
	3	680.0	146,472
	4	400.0	97,840
Baggage	Center	550.0	163,350
	L & R	250.0	73,800
Fuel		+ 1,625.0	+ 389,400
Total		14,612.5	3,472,385

Total Moment ÷ Total Weight = Longitudinal CG

$$\frac{3,472,385}{14,612.5} = 237.6$$

(PLT021) — FAA-H-8083-1

RTC
8515. (Refer to Figures 29, 31, 32, and 33.) Where is the longitudinal CG located under Operating Conditions BL-3?

A— Station 223.4.
B— Station 239.0.
C— Station 240.3.

Condition	BL-3	Weight	Moment
Empty		9,387.5	2,327,105
Crew		360.0	42,120
Pax Row	1	—	—
	2	750.0	139,650
	3	810.0	174,474
	4	650.0	158,990
Baggage	Center	300.0	89,100
	L & R	—	—
Fuel		+ 2,448.0	+ 583,900
Total		14,705.5	3,515,339

Total Moment ÷ Total Weight = Longitudinal CG

$$\frac{3,515,339}{14,705.5} = 239.05$$

(PLT021) — FAA-H-8083-1

Answers

8419 [C]	8513 [B]	8514 [A]	8515 [B]

RTC
8516. (Refer to Figures 29, 31, 32, and 33.) Where is the longitudinal CG located under Operating Conditions BL-4?

A— Station 238.1.
B— Station 220.4.
C— Station 236.5.

Condition	BL-4	Weight	Moment
Empty		9,387.5	2,327,105
Crew		380.0	44,460
Pax Row	1	180.0	28,242
	2	800.0	148,960
	3	720.0	155,088
	4	200.0	48,920
Baggage	Center	200.0	59,400
	L & R	100.0	29,520
Fuel		+ 2,600.0	+ 627,400
Total		14,567.5	3,469,095

Total Moment ÷ Total Weight = Longitudinal CG

$$\frac{3,469,095}{14,567.5} = 238.14$$

(PLT021) — FAA-H-8083-1

RTC
8517. (Refer to Figures 29, 31, 32, and 33.) Where is the longitudinal CG located under Operating Conditions BL-5?

A— Station 232.0.
B— Station 235.4.
C— Station 234.9.

Condition	BL-5	Weight	Moment
Empty		9,387.5	2,327,105
Crew		370.0	43,290
Pax Row	1	680.0	106,692
	2	950.0	176,890
	3	850.0	183,090
	4	500.0	122,300
Baggage	Center	450.0	133,650
	L & R	—	—
Fuel		+ 1,768.0	+ 420,000
Total		14,955.5	3,513,017

Total Moment ÷ Total Weight = Longitudinal CG

$$\frac{3,513,017}{14,955.5} = 234.9$$

(PLT021) — FAA-H-8083-1

Helicopter Weight and Balance: CG Shifts

These questions require a re-computation of CG based on a shift of weight only, i.e., CG will change but total weight does not change. AC 91-23A, Chapter 5 gives us a formula for working this type of problem.

$$\frac{\text{Weight Shifted}}{\text{Total Weight}} = \frac{\text{Change of CG}}{\text{Distance of Shift}}$$

These problems may also be worked with a flight computer as shown in AC 91-23A, Chapter 5 in the following manner:

1. Set Weight Shifted (mile scale) over Total Weight (minute scale).

2. Find the Change in CG on the mile scale over the distance shifted on the minute scale.

Question 8518 is solved using both methods.

Answers

8516 [A]   8517 [C]

RTC
8518. (Refer to Figures 29, 31, 32, and 33.) What is the CG shift if all passengers in row 1 are moved to row 4 under Operating Conditions BL-1?

A— 5.0 inches aft.
B— 4.1 inches aft.
C— 0.19 inch aft.

Using FAA Figure 29:
Weight shifted = 700 lbs, Total weight = 14,797.5
The distance shifted is the difference between Row 4 (Station 244.6) and Row 1 (Station 156.9):

$$244.6 - 156.9 = 87.7$$

To find the CG shift:

$$\frac{700}{14,797.5} = \frac{CG\ Shift}{87.7}$$

The shift from Row 1 to Row 4 is 4.15 aft.

or:

On the E6-B, set 700 (miles scale) over 14,797.5 (round it out: 14,800) on the minutes scale. Find 87.7 on the minutes scale and read 4.15 above it.

(PLT021) — FAA-H-8083-1

RTC
8519. (Refer to Figures 29, 31, 32, and 33.) What is the CG shift if one passenger weighing 150 pounds in row 2 is moved to row 4 under Operating Conditions BL-2?

A— 0.1 inch aft.
B— 0.6 inch aft.
C— 1.1 inches aft.

$$\frac{Weight\ Shifted\ (150)}{Total\ Weight\ (14,612.5)} = \frac{CG\ Shift}{Distance\ of\ Shift\ (58.4)}$$

$$= .60\ aft$$

(PLT021) — FAA-H-8083-1

RTC
8520. (Refer to Figures 29, 31, 32, and 33.) What is the CG shift if all passengers in row 4 are moved to row 1 under Operating Conditions BL-3?

A— 3.7 inches forward.
B— 0.4 inch forward.
C— 3.9 inches forward.

$$\frac{Weight\ Shifted\ (650)}{Total\ Weight\ (14,705.5)} = \frac{CG\ Shift}{Distance\ of\ Shift\ (87.7)}$$

$$= -3.88\ FWD$$

(PLT021) — FAA-H-8083-1

RTC
8521. (Refer to Figures 29, 31, 32, and 33.) What is the CG shift if the passengers in row 1 are moved to row 4 under Operating Conditions BL-4?

A— 1.1 inches aft.
B— 1.6 inches aft.
C— 0.2 inch aft.

$$\frac{Weight\ Shifted\ (180)}{Total\ Weight\ (14,567.5)} = \frac{CG\ Shift}{Distance\ of\ Shift\ (87.7)}$$

$$= 1.08\ aft$$

(PLT021) — FAA-H-8083-1

RTC
8522. (Refer to Figures 29, 31, 32, and 33.) What is the CG shift if one passenger, weighing 100 pounds, seated in row 1 is moved to row 3 under Operating Conditions BL-5?

A— 1.0 inch aft.
B— 0.4 inch aft.
C— 1.3 inches aft.

$$\frac{Weight\ Shifted\ (100)}{Total\ Weight\ (14,955.5)} = \frac{CG\ Shift}{Distance\ of\ Shift\ (58.5)}$$

$$= .39\ aft$$

(PLT021) — FAA-H-8083-1

Answers

| 8518 | [B] | 8519 | [B] | 8520 | [C] | 8521 | [A] | 8522 | [B] |

Helicopter Weight and Balance: Load Limits

In these questions, it will be necessary to compute both a takeoff and a landing weight and balance. Since the stations (CG) for fuel vary with weight, the most simple method of solving these problems is to compute the zero fuel weight for the given conditions, then perform a separate weight and balance for takeoff and landing. Some moments are given; others are not and therefore must be computed. Also, the fuel is stated in gallons, not pounds, which can be converted using the Jet A Table (FAA Figure 33).

RTC
8523. (Refer to Figures 30, 32, 33, and 35.) What limits are exceeded under Loading Conditions BL-6?

A— Aft CG limits are exceeded at takeoff and landing.
B— Takeoff aft CG and landing forward CG limits are exceeded.
C— Maximum takeoff weight and takeoff aft CG limits are exceeded.

Condition BL-6	Weight	Moment
Empty/basic	10,225	2,556,250
Crew	340	39,780
Passengers	3,280	672,250
Baggage Center	+ 700	+ 207,900
Zero Fuel wt.	14,545	3,476,180

Takeoff	Weight	Moment
Zero fuel wt.	14,545	3,476,180
Fuel 435 gal.	+ 2,958	+ 719,900
Total	17,503	4,196,080

Landing	Weight	Moment
Zero fuel wt.	14,545	3,476,180
Fuel 80 gal.	+ 544	+ 125,600
Total	15,089	3,601,780

CG = 4,196,080 ÷ 17,503 = 239.73
CG = 3,601,780 ÷ 15,089 = 238.7

Checking the longitudinal CG envelope (FAA Figure 35), we find that at takeoff, the aircraft is both over maximum gross weight and out of aft CG. (PLT021) — FAA-H-8083-1

RTC
8524. (Refer to Figures 30, 32, 33, and 35.) What limit, if any, is exceeded under Loading Conditions BL-7?

A— No limit is exceeded.
B— Forward CG limit is exceeded at landing only.
C— Forward CG limit is exceeded at takeoff and landing.

Condition BL-7	Weight	Moment
Empty/basic	9,450	2,323,600
Crew	380	44,460
Passengers	2,880	541,860
Baggage (center)	+ 600	+ 178,200
Zero Fuel	13,310	3,088,120

Takeoff	Weight	Moment
Zero fuel wt.	13,310	3,088,120
Fuel 290 gal.	+ 1,972	+ 457,900
Total	15,282	3,546,020

Takeoff CG = 3,546,020 ÷ 15,282 = 232.04

Original fuel load (Fig 30) is 290 gal. Trip fuel burn is indicated at 190 gal. Fuel upon landing is 100 gal. 100 gal x 6.8 lbs/gal = 680 lbs. Figure 33 shows the CG for 680 lbs is 228.2. 680 x 228.2 = 155,176.

Landing	Weight	Moment
Zero fuel wt.	13,310	3,088,120
Fuel 100 gal.	+ 680	+ 155,176
Total	13,990	3,243,296

CG = 3,243,296 ÷ 13,990 = 231.82

Checking the longitudinal CG envelope (FAA Figure 35), we find that at landing only, the forward CG limit is exceeded. (PLT021) — FAA-H-8083-1

RTC
8525. (Refer to Figures 30, 32, 33, and 35.) What limit, if any, is exceeded under Loading Conditions BL-8?

A— No limit is exceeded.
B— Forward CG limit is exceeded at landing only.
C— Forward CG limit is exceeded at takeoff and landing.

Condition BL-8	Weight	Moment
Empty/basic	9,000	2,202,050
Crew	410	47,970
Passengers	3,150	642,580
Bags center	+ 300	+ 89,100
Zero Fuel	12,860	2,981,700

Answers

8523 [C]   8524 [B]   8525 [A]

Takeoff	Weight	Moment
Zero fuel wt.	12,860	2,981,700
Fuel 220 gal.	+ 1,496	+ 369,400
Total	14,356	3,351,100

Takeoff CG = 3,351,100 ÷ 14,356 = 233.43

Original fuel load (Fig 30) is 220 gal. Trip fuel burn is indicated at 190 gal. Fuel upon landing is 30 gal. 30 gal x 6.8 lbs/gal = 204 lbs. Figure 33 shows the CG for 204 lbs is 244.4. 204 x 244.4 = 49,857.6.

Landing	Weight	Moment
Zero fuel wt.	12,860	2,981,700
Fuel 30 gal.	+ 204	+ 49,857.6
Total	13,064	3,031,557

Landing CG = 3,031,557 ÷ 13,064 = 232.05

Checking the longitudinal CG envelope (FAA Figure 35), we find that no limits are exceeded. (PLT021) — FAA-H-8083-1

RTC
8526. (Refer to Figures 30, 32, 33, and 35.) What limit, if any, is exceeded under Loading Conditions BL-9?

A— No limit is exceeded.
B— Aft CG limit is exceeded at takeoff only.
C— Aft CG limit is exceeded at takeoff and landing.

Condition BL-9	Weight	Moment
Empty/basic	9,510	2,349,990
Crew	360	42,120
Passengers	2,040	473,220
Bags center	+ 550	+ 163,350
Zero Fuel	12,460	3,028,680

Takeoff	Weight	Moment
Zero fuel wt.	12,460	3,028,680
Fuel 435 gal.	+ 2,958	+ 719,900
Total	15,418	3,748,580

Landing	Weight	Moment
Zero fuel wt.	12,460	3,028,680
Fuel 110 gal.	+ 748	+ 170,900
Total	13,208	3,199,580

CG = 3,748,580 ÷ 15,418 = 243.13
CG = 3,199,580 ÷ 13,208 = 242.24

Checking the longitudinal CG envelope (FAA Figure 35), we find that aft CG is exceeded at takeoff only. (PLT021) — FAA-H-8083-1

RTC
8527. (Refer to Figures 30, 32, 33, and 35.) What limit, if any, is exceeded under Loading Conditions BL-10?

A— No limit is exceeded.
B— Aft CG limit is exceeded at takeoff.
C— Forward CG limit is exceeded at landing.

Condition BL-10	Weight	Moment
Empty/basic	9,375	2,329,680
Crew	400	46,800
Passengers	2,400	456,070
Baggage (center)	+ 650	+ 193,050
Zero Fuel	12,825	3,025,600

Note: For this problem, it is easier to compute the landing data by subtracting the weight and moment of the fuel used from the takeoff data.

Takeoff	Weight	Moment
Zero fuel wt.	12,825	3,025,600
Fuel 380 gal.	+ 2,584	+ 620,200
Total	15,409	3,645,800

Landing	Weight	Moment
Takeoff	15,409	3,645,800
Fuel 330 gal.	− 2,244	− 529,600
Total	13,165	3,116,200

CG = 3,645,800 ÷ 15,409 = 236.6
CG = 3,116,200 ÷ 13,165 = 236.7

Checking the longitudinal CG envelope (FAA Figure 35), we find that no limits are exceeded. (PLT021) — FAA-H-8083-1

Answers

8526   [B]   8527   [A]

Helicopter Weight and Balance: Lateral CG

These questions are answered by using the formula given in AC 91-23A.

1. For shifted weight:

$$\frac{\text{Weight Shifted (WS)}}{\text{Total Weight (TW)}} = \frac{\text{CG Shift (CS)}}{\text{Distance Shifted (DS)}}$$

2. For added/removed weight (WA or WR):

$$\frac{\text{(WA or WR)}}{\text{New Total Weight (NTW)}} = \frac{\text{CG Shift (CS)}}{\text{Distance shifted (DS)}}$$

Refer to answers to Questions 8523 through 8527 for total weights.

RTC

8528. (Refer to Figures 30, 31, 32, 33, and 34.) Given Loading Conditions BL-6, what is the effect on lateral CG if the outside passengers from each row on the left side are deplaned? Deplaned passenger weights are 170 pounds each.

A— CG shifts 1.5 inches right, out of limits.
B— CG shifts 1.4 inches right, within limits.
C— CG shifts 1.6 inches left, out of limits.

1. Total weight for BL-6 = 17,503 (from Question 8523)

2. Weight removed = 170 x 4 = 680

3. New total weight = 17,503 – 680 = 16,823

4. Distance shifted = the average arm of the four outboard seats (34 + 35.4 + 35.4 + 39.4) ÷ 4 = 36.05.

$$\frac{WR}{NTW} = \frac{CS}{DS}$$

(Very close to 1.5 inches.)

Since the deplaned passengers were all on the left, CG shift is to the right. Referring to FAA Figure 34, at our new weight of 16,823, the lateral CG is out of limits to the right. (PLT021) — FAA-H-8083-1

RTC

8529. (Refer to Figures 30, 31, 32, 33, and 34.) Given Loading Conditions BL-7, what is the effect on lateral CG if additional passengers, each weighing 200 pounds, are seated, one in each outside right seat of rows 1, 2, 3, and 4?

A— CG shifts 1.5 inches left, out of limits.
B— CG shifts 0.2 inch right, within limits.
C— CG shifts 1.8 inches right, out of limits.

1. Total weight for BL-7 = 15,282 (from Question 8524)

2. Weight added = 800

3. New total weight = 15,282 + 800 = 16,082

4. Distance shifted = the average arm of the four outboard seats (34 + 35.4 + 35.4 + 39.4) ÷ 4 = 36.05.

$$\frac{WA}{NTW} = \frac{CS}{DS}$$

CG shifts right 1.79 inches, out of limits.

(PLT021) — FAA-H-8083-1

RTC

8530. (Refer to Figures 30, 31, 32, 33, and 34.) Given Loading Conditions BL-8, what is the effect on lateral CG if a passenger weighing 200 pounds is added to the outer left seat of row 1, and a passenger weighing 220 pounds is added to the outer left seat of row 4?

A— CG shifts 1.5 inches left, out of limits.
B— CG shifts 1.2 inches left, within limits.
C— CG shifts 1.0 inch left, within limits.

1. Total weight for BL-8 = 14,356 (from Question 8525)

2. Weight added = 420

3. New total weight = 14,356 + 420 = 14,776

4. Distance shifted = the average arm of Row 1 and Row 4 (34 + 39.4) ÷ 2 = 36.7

$$\frac{WA}{NTW} = \frac{CS}{DS}$$

CG shifts left 1.04 inches, within limits.

(PLT021) — FAA-H-8083-1

Answers

8528 [A]	8529 [C]	8530 [C]

RTC

8531. (Refer to Figures 30, 31, 32, 33, and 34.) Given Loading Conditions BL-9, what is the effect on lateral CG if passengers, each weighing 160 pounds, are added to the outer left seats of rows 1 and 2; and passengers, each weighing 180 pounds, are added to the outer right seats of rows 3 and 4?

A— CG shifts 0.14 inch left.
B— CG shifts 0.15 inch right.
C— CG does not shift.

It is obvious without doing the math, considering the weights and arms involved, that answer B is the only possible answer. However:

1. *Total weight for BL-9 = 15,418 (from Question 8526)*

2. *Weight added = 680*

3. *New total weight = 15,418 + 680 = 16,098*

4. *Distance shifted = the difference between the average left and right arms. If we consider the left side as negative, then distance shifted = [-(34 + 35.4) ÷ 2] + (35.4 + 39.4) ÷ 2 = -34.7 + 37.4 = + 2.7 inches.*

$$\frac{WA}{NTW} = \frac{CS}{DS}$$

CG shifts .11 inches right.

(PLT021) — FAA-H-8083-1

RTC

8532. (Refer to Figures 30, 31, 32, 33, and 34.) Given Loading Conditions BL-10, what is the effect on lateral CG if a passenger, weighing 240 pounds, is shifted from the outer right seat of row 4 to the outer left seat of row 1?

A— CG shifts 1.1 inches left, within limits.
B— CG shifts 1.5 inches left, out of limits.
C— CG shifts 1.7 inches left, out of limits.

1. *Total weight for BL-10 = 15,409 (from Question 8527)*

2. *Weight Shifted = 240*

3. *Distance shifted = the distance between Row 1 and Row 4 (34 + 39.4) = 73.4*

$$\frac{WS}{NTW} = \frac{CS}{DS}$$

CG shifts left 1.14 inches, within limits.

(PLT021) — FAA-H-8083-1

Floor Loading Limits

In addition to ensuring that an aircraft is loaded within its weight and balance limits, it is important to make sure that the floor of a cargo compartment is not overloaded. The load limit of a floor is stated in pounds per square foot. The questions on the test require you to determine the maximum load that can be placed on a pallet of certain dimensions.

For example: what is the maximum weight that may be carried on a pallet which has the dimensions of 37 x 39 inches, when the floor load limit is 115 pounds per square foot, the pallet weight is 37 pounds, and the weight of the tiedown devices is 21 pounds?

The first step is to determine the area of the floor (in square feet) covered by the pallet. This is done by multiplying the given dimensions (which calculates the area in square inches) and dividing by 144 (which converts the area to square feet):

37 inches x 39 inches ÷ 144 square inches = 10.02 square feet.

The next step is to determine the total weight that the floor under the pallet can support, by multiplying the area times the floor load limit given in the question:

10.02 square feet x 115 pounds per square foot = 1,152.39 pounds.

The final step is to determine the maximum weight which can be placed on the pallet by subtracting the weight of the pallet and the tiedown devices from the total load limit:

Continued

Answers

8531 [B]   8532 [A]

1,152.39 pounds – 58 pounds = 1,094.39 pounds.

The weight on the pallet must be equal to or less than this number (1,094.39, in this example). If it is more than this number, the combination of cargo, pallet, and tiedown weight would exceed the floor load limit. A review of the test questions reveals that the closest answer choice is always equal to or slightly less than the floor limit. All the calculations in this section were performed with a calculator carrying all digits to the right of the decimal point forward for the next step of the problem. The explanations show only two places to the right of the decimal.

A variation of the pallet loading problem is to determine the minimum floor load limit (in pounds per square foot) required to carry a particular loaded pallet. For example: what is the minimum floor load limit to carry a pallet of cargo with a pallet dimension of 78.9 inches x 98.7 inches, and a combination weight of pallet, cargo, and tiedown devices of 9,896.5 pounds?

The first step is to determine the floor area, multiplying the dimensions and dividing by 144 (78.9 x 98.7 ÷ 144 = 54.08 square feet). The second step is to determine the minimum required floor limit by dividing the total weight of the pallet, cargo, and tiedowns by the pallet area (9,896.5 ÷ 54.08 = 183.00 pounds). The correct answer must be at or *above* this weight (183.00 pounds, in this example).

ALL
8769. What is the maximum allowable weight that may be carried on a pallet which has the dimensions of 33.5 x 48.5 inches?

    Floor load limit — 76 lb/sq ft
    Pallet weight — 44 lb
    Tiedown devices — 27 lb

A— 857.4 pounds.
B— 830.4 pounds.
C— 786.5 pounds.

1. Determine the area.

    33.5 x 48.5 ÷ 144 = 11.28 square feet.

2. Determine the floor load limit.

    11.28 x 76 = 857.51 pounds.

3. Subtract the weight of the pallet and tiedown devices.

    857.51 – 71 = 786.51 pounds.

(PLT121) — FAA-H-8083-1

ALL
8770. What is the maximum allowable weight that may be carried on a pallet which has the dimensions of 36.5 x 48.5 inches?

    Floor load limit — 112 lb/sq ft
    Pallet weight — 45 lb
    Tiedown devices — 29 lb

A— 1,331.8 pounds.
B— 1,302.8 pounds.
C— 1,347.8 pounds.

1. Determine the area.

    36.5 x 48.5 ÷ 144 = 12.29 square feet.

2. Determine the floor load limit.

    12.29 x 112 = 1,376.86 pounds.

3. Subtract the weight of the pallet and tiedown devices.

    1,376.86 – 74 = 1,302.86 pounds.

(PLT121) — FAA-H-8083-1

ALL
8771. What is the maximum allowable weight that may be carried on a pallet which has the dimensions of 42.6 x 48.7 inches?

    Floor load limit — 121 lb/sq ft
    Pallet weight — 47 lb
    Tiedown devices — 33 lb

A— 1,710.2 pounds.
B— 1,663.2 pounds.
C— 1,696.2 pounds.

1. Determine the area.

    42.6 x 48.7 ÷ 144 = 14.41 square feet.

2. Determine the floor load limit.

    14.41 x 121 = 1,743.25 pounds.

3. Subtract the weight of the pallet and tiedown devices.

    1,743.25 – 80 = 1,663.25 pounds.

(PLT121) — FAA-H-8083-1

Answers

8769 [C]   8770 [B]   8771 [B]

ALL

8772. What is the maximum allowable weight that may be carried on a pallet which has the dimensions of 24.6 x 68.7 inches?

>   Floor load limit — 85 lb/sq ft
>   Pallet weight — 44 lb
>   Tiedown devices — 29 lb

A— 924.5 pounds.
B— 968.6 pounds.
C— 953.6 pounds.

1. *Determine the area.*

   24.6 x 68.7 ÷ 144 = 11.74 square feet.

2. *Determine the floor load limit.*

   11.74 x 85 = 997.58 pounds.

3. *Subtract the weight of the pallet and tiedown devices.*

   997.58 – 73 = 924.58 pounds.

(PLT121) — FAA-H-8083-1

ALL

8773. What is the maximum allowable weight that may be carried on a pallet which has the dimensions of 34.6 x 46.4 inches?

>   Floor load limit — 88 lb/sq ft
>   Pallet weight — 41 lb
>   Tiedown devices — 26 lb

A— 914.1 pounds.
B— 940.1 pounds.
C— 981.1 pounds.

1. *Determine the area.*

   34.6 x 46.4 ÷ 144 = 11.15 square feet.

2. *Determine the floor load limit.*

   11.15 x 88 = 981.10 pounds.

3. *Subtract the weight of the pallet and tiedown devices.*

   981.10 – 67 = 914.10 pounds.

(PLT121) — FAA-H-8083-1

ALL

8776. What is the maximum allowable weight that may be carried on a pallet which has the dimensions of 33.5 x 48.5 inches?

>   Floor load limit — 66 lb/sq ft
>   Pallet weight — 34 lb
>   Tiedown devices — 29 lb

A— 744.6 pounds.
B— 681.6 pounds.
C— 663.0 pounds.

1. *Determine the area.*

   33.5 x 48.5 ÷ 144 = 11.28 square feet.

2. *Determine the floor load limit.*

   11.28 x 66 = 744.68 pounds.

3. *Subtract the weight of the pallet and tiedown devices.*

   744.68 – 63 = 681.68 pounds.

(PLT121) — FAA-H-8083-1

ALL

8777. What is the maximum allowable weight that may be carried on a pallet which has the dimensions of 36.5 x 48.5 inches?

>   Floor load limit — 107 lb/sq ft
>   Pallet weight — 37 lb
>   Tiedown devices — 33 lb

A— 1,295.3 pounds.
B— 1,212.3 pounds.
C— 1,245.3 pounds.

1. *Determine the area.*

   36.5 x 48.5 ÷ 144 = 12.29 square feet.

2. *Determine the floor load limit.*

   12.29 x 107 = 1,315.39 pounds.

3. *Subtract the weight of the pallet and tiedown devices.*

   1,315.39 – 70 = 1,245.39 pounds.

(PLT121) — FAA-H-8083-1

Answers

8772   [A]   8773   [A]   8776   [B]   8777   [C]

ALL

8778. What is the maximum allowable weight that may be carried on a pallet which has the dimensions of 42.6 x 48.7 inches?

Floor load limit — 117 lb/sq ft
Pallet weight — 43 lb
Tiedown devices — 31 lb

A— 1,611.6 pounds.
B— 1,654.6 pounds.
C— 1,601.6 pounds.

1. Determine the area.

42.6 x 48.7 ÷ 144 = 14.41 square feet.

2. Determine the floor load limit.

14.41 x 117 = 1,685.63 pounds.

3. Subtract the weight of the pallet and tiedown devices.

1,685.63 – 74 = 1,611.63 pounds.

(PLT121) — FAA-H-8083-1

ALL

8781. What is the maximum allowable weight that may be carried on a pallet which has the dimensions of 143 x 125.2 inches?

Floor load limit — 209 lb/sq ft
Pallet weight — 197 lb
Tiedown devices — 66 lb

A— 25,984.9 pounds.
B— 25,787.9 pounds.
C— 25,721.9 pounds.

1. Determine the area.

143 x 125.2 ÷ 144 = 124.33 square feet.

2. Determine the floor load limit.

124.33 x 209 = 25,985.09 pounds.

3. Subtract the weight of the pallet and tiedown devices.

25,985.09 – 263 = 25,722.09 pounds.

(PLT121) — FAA-H-8083-1

ALL

8779. What is the maximum allowable weight that may be carried on a pallet which has the dimensions of 24.6 x 68.7 inches?

Floor load limit — 79 lb/sq ft
Pallet weight — 43 lb
Tiedown devices — 27 lb

A— 884.1 pounds.
B— 857.1 pounds.
C— 841.1 pounds.

1. Determine the area.

24.6 x 68.7 ÷ 144 = 11.74 square feet.

2. Determine the floor load limit.

11.74 x 79 = 927.16 pounds.

3. Subtract the weight of the pallet and tiedown devices.

927.16 – 70 = 857.16 pounds.

(PLT121) — FAA-H-8083-1

ALL

8787. What is the maximum allowable weight that may be carried on a pallet which has the dimensions of 138.5 x 97.6 inches?

Floor load limit — 235 lb/sq ft
Pallet weight — 219 lb
Tiedown devices — 71 lb

A— 21,840.9 pounds.
B— 21,769.9 pounds.
C— 22,059.9 pounds.

1. Determine the area.

138.5 x 97.6 ÷ 144 = 93.87 square feet.

2. Determine the floor load limit.

93.87 x 235 = 22,059.97 pounds.

3. Subtract the weight of the pallet and tiedown devices.

22,059.97 – 290 = 21,769.97 pounds.

(PLT121) — FAA-H-8083-1

Answers

8778   [A]   8779   [B]   8781   [C]   8787   [B]

ALL

8788. What is the maximum allowable weight that may be carried on a pallet which has the dimensions of 96.1 x 133.3 inches?

> Floor load limit — 249 lb/sq ft
> Pallet weight — 347 lb
> Tiedown devices — 134 lb

A— 21,669.8 pounds.
B— 21,803.8 pounds.
C— 22,120.8 pounds.

1. Determine the area.

   96.1 x 133.3 ÷ 144 = 88.96 square feet.

2. Determine the floor load limit.

   88.96 x 249 = 22,150.85 pounds.

3. Subtract the weight of the pallet and tiedown devices.

   22,150.85 – 481 = 21,669.85 pounds.

(PLT121) — FAA-H-8083-1

ALL

8789. What is the maximum allowable weight that may be carried on a pallet which has the dimensions of 87.7 x 116.8 inches?

> Floor load limit — 175 lb/sq ft
> Pallet weight — 137 lb
> Tiedown devices — 49 lb

A— 12,262.4 pounds.
B— 12,448.4 pounds.
C— 12,311.4 pounds.

1. Determine the area.

   87.7 x 116.8 ÷ 144 = 71.13 square feet.

2. Determine the floor load limit.

   71.13 x 175 = 12,448.52 pounds.

3. Subtract the weight of the pallet and tiedown devices.

   12,448.52 – 186 = 12,262.52 pounds.

(PLT121) — FAA-H-8083-1

ALL

8790. What is the maximum allowable weight that may be carried on a pallet which has the dimensions of 98.7 x 78.9 inches?

> Floor load limit — 183 lb/sq ft
> Pallet weight — 161 lb
> Tiedown devices — 54 lb

A— 9,896.5 pounds.
B— 9,735.5 pounds.
C— 9,681.5 pounds.

1. Determine the area.

   98.7 x 78.9 ÷ 144 = 54.08 square feet.

2. Determine the floor load limit.

   54.08 x 183 = 9,896.53 pounds.

3. Subtract the weight of the pallet and tiedown devices.

   9,896.53 – 215 = 9,681.53 pounds.

(PLT121) — FAA-H-8083-1

ALL

8791. What minimum floor load limit must an aircraft have to carry the following pallet of cargo?

> Pallet size is 78.9 wide and 98.7 long
> Pallet weight — 161 lb
> Tiedown devices — 54 lb
> Cargo weight — 9,681.5 lb

A— 182 lb/sq ft.
B— 180 lb/sq ft.
C— 183 lb/sq ft.

1. Determine the area.

   78.9 x 98.7 ÷ 144 = 54.08 square feet.

2. Determine the total weight.

   9,681.5 + 54 + 161 = 9,896.5

3. Determine the minimum floor load limit.

   9,896.5 ÷ 54.08 = 183.00 lbs/sq ft.

(PLT121) — FAA-H-8083-1

Answers

8788   [A]   8789   [A]   8790   [C]   8791   [C]

ALL

8844. What is the minimum floor load limit that an aircraft must have to carry the following pallet of cargo?

> Pallet dimensions are 39 x 37 inches.
> Pallet weight — 37 lbs.
> Tiedown devices — 21 lbs
> Cargo weight — 1,094.3 lbs.

A— 115 lbs/sq ft.
B— 112 lbs/sq ft.
C— 109 lbs/sq ft.

1. Determine the area.

   39 x 37 ÷ 144 = 10.02 sq ft.

2. Determine the total weight.

   1,094.3 + 21 + 37 = 1,152.3

3. Determine the minimum floor load limit.

   1,152.3 ÷ 10.02 = 114.99 lbs/sq ft.

(PLT121) — FAA-H-8083-1

ALL

8845. What is the minimum floor load limit that an aircraft must have to carry the following pallet of cargo?

> Pallet dimensions are 37.5 x 35 inches.
> Pallet weight — 34 lbs.
> Tiedown devices — 23 lbs.
> Cargo weight — 1,255.4 lbs.

A— 152 lbs/sq ft.
B— 148 lbs/sq ft.
C— 144 lbs/sq ft.

1. Determine the area.

   37.5 x 35 ÷ 144 = 9.12 sq ft.

2. Determine the total weight.

   1,255.4 + 23 + 34 = 1,312.4

3. Determine the minimum floor load limit.

   1,312.4 ÷ 9.12 = 143.99 lbs/sq ft.

(PLT121) — FAA-H-8083-1

ALL

8846. What is the minimum floor load limit that an aircraft must have to carry the following pallet of cargo?

> Pallet dimensions are 48.5 x 33.5 inches.
> Pallet weight — 44 lbs.
> Tiedown devices — 27 lbs.
> Cargo weight — 786.5 lbs.

A— 79 lbs/sq ft.
B— 76 lbs/sq ft.
C— 73 lbs/sq ft.

1. Determine the area.

   48.5 x 33.5 ÷ 144 = 11.28 sq ft.

2. Determine the total weight.

   786.5 + 27 + 44 = 857.5

3. Determine the minimum floor load limit.

   857.5 ÷ 11.28 = 76.00 lbs/sq ft.

(PLT121) — FAA-H-8083-1

ALL

8847. What is the minimum floor load limit that an aircraft must have to carry the following pallet of cargo?

> Pallet dimensions are 116.8 x 87.7 inches
> Pallet weight — 137 lbs.
> Tiedown devices — 49 lbs.
> Cargo weight — 12,262.4 lbs.

A— 172 lbs/sq ft.
B— 176 lbs/sq ft.
C— 179 lbs/sq ft.

1. Determine the area.

   116.8 x 87.7 ÷ 144 = 71.13 sq ft.

2. Determine the total weight.

   12,262.4 + 49 + 137 = 12,448.4

3. Determine the minimum floor load limit.

   12,448.4 ÷ 71.13 = 175.00 lbs/sq ft.

(PLT121) — FAA-H-8083-1

Answers

8844 [A]   8845 [C]   8846 [B]   8847 [B]

ALL

8848. What is the minimum floor load limit that an aircraft must have to carry the following pallet of cargo?

> Pallet dimensions are 78.9 x 98.7 inches
> Pallet weight — 161 lbs.
> Tiedown devices — 54 lbs.
> Cargo weight — 9,681.5 lbs.

A— 180 lbs/sq ft.
B— 186 lbs/sq ft.
C— 183 lbs/sq ft.

1. *Determine the area.*

   78.9 x 98.7 ÷ 144 = 54.08 sq ft.

2. *Determine the total weight.*

   9,681.5 + 54 + 161 = 9,896.5

3. *Determine the minimum floor load limit.*

   9,896.5 ÷ 54.08 = 183.00 lbs/sq ft.

(PLT121) — FAA-H-8083-1

ATM, ATS, DSP

8431. What is the maximum allowable weight that may be carried on a pallet which has the dimensions of 36 x 48 inches?

Floor load limit ....169 lbs/sq ft
Pallet weight ....47 lbs
Tiedown devices ....33 lbs

A— 1,948.0 pounds.
B— 1,995.0 pounds.
C— 1,981.0 pounds.

Pallet area = (36 x 48)/144 = 12 sq ft
Floor load limit = 12 sq ft x 169 lbs/sq ft = 2,028 lbs
Allowable weight = 2,028 lbs – 80 lbs = 1,948 lbs

(PLT121) — FAA-H-8083-1

ATM, ATS, DSP

8432. What is the maximum allowable weight that may be carried on a pallet which has the dimensions of 76 x 74 inches?

Floor load limit ....176 lbs/sq ft
Pallet weight ....77 lbs
Tiedown devices ....29 lbs

A— 6,767.8 pounds.
B— 6,873.7 pounds.
C— 6,796.8 pounds.

Floor load limit – 176 lbs/sq ft
Pallet weight – 77 lbs
Tiedown devices – 29 lbs
Pallet area = (76" x 74")/144 = 39.1 sq ft
Floor load limit = 39.1 sq ft x 176 lbs/sq ft = 6,873.8 lbs
Allowable weight = 6,873.8 lbs – 106 lbs = 6,767.8 lbs

(PLT121) — FAA-H-8083-1

ATM, ATS, DSP

8433. What is the maximum allowable weight that may be carried on a pallet which has the dimensions of 81 x 83 inches?

Floor load limit ....180 lbs/sq ft
Pallet weight ....82 lbs
Tiedown devices ....31 lbs

A— 8,403.7 pounds.
B— 8,321.8 pounds.
C— 8,290.8 pounds.

Floor load limit – 180 lbs/sq ft
Pallet weight – 82 lbs
Tiedown devices – 31 lbs
Pallet area = (81" x 83")/144 = 46.7 sq ft
Floor load limit = 46.7 sq ft x 180 lbs/sq ft = 8,403.8 lbs
Allowable weight = 8,403.8 lbs – 113 lbs = 8,290.8 lbs

(PLT121) — FAA-H-8083-1

Answers

8848   [C]   8431   [A]   8432   [A]   8433   [C]

Chapter 6
Flight Operations

Airspace

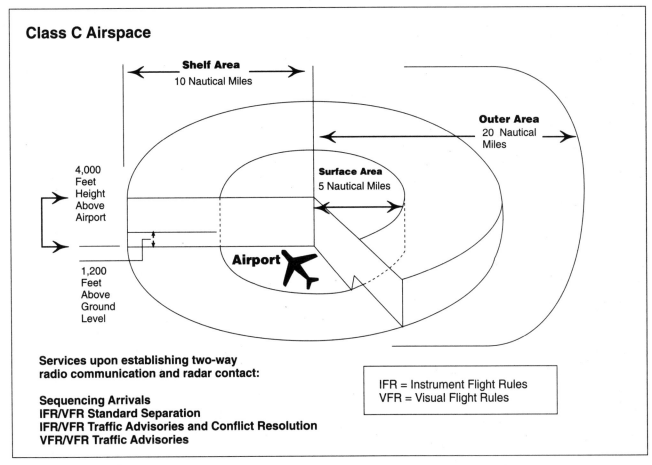

Figure 6-1. Class C airspace

Figure 6-2. Airspace

Figure 6-3. Minimum in-flight visibility and distance from clouds

A turbine-powered airplane or a large airplane must enter **Class D airspace** at an altitude of at least 1,500 feet AGL and maintain that altitude in the traffic pattern until a lower altitude is necessary for a safe landing. When taking off, the pilot of a turbine-powered airplane or a large airplane must climb as rapidly as practicable to an altitude of 1,500 feet AGL.

No person may operate an aircraft within **Class B airspace** unless a proper authorization from ATC has been received prior to entry. An IFR clearance is not necessarily required. Unless otherwise authorized by ATC, every person flying a large turbine-engine-powered airplane to or from the primary airport in Class B airspace must operate at or above the floor of Class B airspace.

All **Class C airspace** has the same dimensions with minor site variations. They are composed of two circles both centered on the primary airport. The surface area has a radius of 5 nautical miles and extends from the surface up to 4,000 feet above the airport. The shelf area has a radius of 10 nautical miles and extends vertically from 1,200 feet AGL up to 4,000 feet above the primary airport. In addition to the Class C airspace proper, there is an outer area with a radius of 20 nautical miles and vertical coverage from the lower limits of the radio/radar coverage up to the top of the approach control facility's delegated airspace.

The only equipment requirements for an aircraft to operate within Class C airspace are a two-way radio and a transponder. No specific pilot certification is required.

The following services are provided within Class C airspace:

- Sequencing of all arriving aircraft to the primary airport.
- Standard IFR separation between IFR aircraft.
- Between IFR and VFR aircraft — traffic advisories and conflict resolution so that radar targets do not touch, or 500 feet vertical separation.
- Between VFR aircraft, traffic advisories and as appropriate, safety alerts.

The same services are provided in the outer area when two-way radio and radar contact is established. There is no requirement for VFR participation in the outer area.

No one may operate an aircraft below 10,000 feet MSL at an indicated speed greater than 250 knots. No one may operate an aircraft within Class D airspace at an indicated airspeed of more than 200 knots. There is no special speed limit for operations within Class B airspace other than the 250-knot limit when below 10,000 feet MSL. When operating beneath the lateral limits of Class B airspace, the indicated airspeed cannot exceed 200 knots. If the minimum safe airspeed for any particular operation is greater than the maximum speed prescribed by 14 CFR §91.117, the aircraft may be operated at that minimum speed.

Warning Areas are so designated because they are located in international (and therefore uncontrolled) airspace and have invisible hazards to flight. The purpose of a **Military Operating Area (MOA)** is to separate IFR traffic from military training activities. Normally, ATC will not clear an IFR flight into an MOA if it is in use by the military. In an MOA, the individual pilots are responsible for collision avoidance. **VR** Military Training Routes which extend above 1,500 feet AGL, and **IR** Training Routes are depicted on IFR Enroute Low Altitude Charts.

When a flight is to penetrate an **Air Defense Identification Zone (ADIZ)**, it must be on either an IFR or a DVFR flight plan. The flight must penetrate the ADIZ within ±5 minutes of the flight plan estimate and within 10 miles when over land or within 20 miles when over water. These were formerly referred to as domestic and coastal ADIZs in the AIM.

A **VFR-On-Top** clearance is an IFR authorization to fly the cleared route at the VFR altitude of the pilot's choice. To request VFR-On-Top, the flight must be able to maintain the minimum VFR visibility and cloud clearances appropriate for the airspace and altitude. This may be done above, below or between the clouds, if any. While the pilot is expected to comply with all IFR rules, ATC will provide traffic advisories only. VFR-On-Top will not be authorized in Class A airspace. VFR weather minimums must be observed when operating under a VFR-On-Top clearance.

An air carrier flight may conduct day Over-the-Top operations below the minimum IFR altitude if the following are observed:

- The flight must be at least 1,000 feet above the top of a broken or overcast layer.
- The top of the clouds are generally uniform and level.
- The flight visibility is at least five miles.
- The base of any higher ceiling is at least 1,000 feet above the minimum IFR altitude.

OROCA is an off-route altitude which provides obstruction clearance with a 1,000-foot buffer in nonmountainous terrain areas, and a 2,000-foot buffer in designated mountainous areas within the U.S. **Minimum Vectoring Altitudes (MVAs)** are established for use by ATC when radar is exercised; MVA charts are prepared by air traffic facilities at locations where there are many different minimum IFR altitudes. **Minimum Safe/Sector Altitudes (MSA)** are published for emergency use on IAP charts; they are expressed in MSL and normally have a 25 NM radius; however, this radius may be expanded to 30 NM if necessary to encompass the airport landing surfaces.

ALL
8881. (Refer to Figure 127.) Which altitude is appropriate for circle 4 (top of Class G airspace)?

A— 700 feet AGL.
B— 1,200 feet AGL.
C— 1,500 feet AGL.

Circle 4 corresponds to 1,200 feet, the floor of controlled airspace or the ceiling of Class G airspace in this area. (PLT040) — AIM ¶3-2-1

Answer (A) is incorrect because 700 feet AGL is the base of Class E airspace when used in conjunction with an instrument approach that has been prescribed, as in circle 6. Answer (C) is incorrect because 1,500 feet AGL is not an altitude which defines a certain airspace.

ALL
8882. (Refer to Figure 127.) Which altitude is normally appropriate for circle 5 (top of Class D airspace)?

A— 1,000 feet AGL.
B— 2,500 feet AGL.
C— 3,000 feet AGL.

Circle 5 corresponds to the ceiling of Class D airspace which is normally at 2,500 feet AGL. There will be variations to suit special conditions. (PLT040) — AIM ¶3-2-5

Answer (A) is incorrect because 1,000 feet AGL is the normal traffic pattern altitude for piston aircraft, not the ceiling of Class D airspace. Answer (C) is incorrect because 3,000 feet AGL is not an altitude which defines a certain airspace.

ALL
8883. (Refer to Figure 127.) Which altitude is appropriate for circle 6 (top of Class G airspace)?

A— 700 or 2,500 feet AGL.
B— 500 or 2,000 feet AGL.
C— 700 or 1,200 feet AGL.

Circle 6 corresponds to the floor of the Class G airspace, which could be 700 or 1,200 feet AGL, depending on whether an instrument approach is present. (PLT040) — AIM ¶3-2-1

ALL
8884. (Refer to Figure 127.) Which altitude is appropriate for circle 1 (top of Class E airspace)?

A— 14,000 feet MSL.
B— 14,500 feet MSL.
C— 18,000 feet MSL.

Circle 1 corresponds to 18,000 feet MSL, the ceiling of the Class E airspace. (PLT040) — AIM ¶3-2-1

Answer (A) is incorrect because 14,000 feet MSL is not an altitude which defines a certain airspace. Answer (B) is incorrect because 14,500 MSL is the base of Class E airspace when it is not set lower.

ALL
8885. (Refer to Figure 127.) Which altitude is appropriate for circle 2 (top of Class C airspace)?

A— 3,000 feet AGL.
B— 4,000 feet AGL.
C— 3,500 feet MSL.

Circle 2 indicates the ceiling of Class C airspace, generally 4,000 AGL. (PLT040) — AIM ¶3-2-4

Answers (A) and (C) are incorrect because neither 3,000 feet AGL nor 3,500 feet MSL are altitudes which define a certain airspace.

ALL
8886. (Refer to Figure 127.) Which altitude is appropriate for circle 3 (top of Class A airspace)?

A— FL 600.
B— FL 450.
C— FL 500.

Circle 3 indicates the upper limits of Class A airspace which is FL600. (PLT040) — AIM ¶3-2-1

Answers (B) and (C) are incorrect because neither FL450 nor FL500 are altitudes which define a certain airspace.

ALL
8888. (Refer to Figure 127.) What is the base of the Class A airspace?

A— 12,000 feet AGL.
B— 14,500 feet MSL.
C— FL 180.

The base of Class A airspace is 18,000 feet MSL. (PLT040) — AIM ¶3-2-1

Answer (A) is incorrect because 12,000 feet AGL is not an altitude which defines a certain airspace. Answer (B) is incorrect because 14,500 MSL is the base of Class E airspace when it is not set lower.

Answers

8881 [B]	8882 [B]	8883 [C]	8884 [C]	8885 [B]	8886 [A]
8888 [C]					

ALL

9409. In what altitude structure is a transponder required when operating in controlled airspace?

A— Above 12,500 feet MSL, excluding the airspace at and below 2,500 feet AGL.
B— Above 10,000 feet MSL, excluding the airspace at and below 2,500 feet AGL.
C— Above 14,500 feet MSL, excluding the airspace at and below 2,500 feet AGL.

A transponder is required at and above 10,000 feet MSL and below the floor of Class A airspace, excluding the airspace at and below 2,500 feet AGL. (PLT429) — 14 CFR §91.215

Answer (A) is incorrect because 12,500 feet MSL was the old altitude above which a transponder was needed; it is now 10,000 feet MSL. Answer (C) is incorrect because 14,500 feet MSL is the base of Class E airspace when it is not set lower.

ALL

9424. Pilots should state their position on the airport when calling the tower for takeoff

A— from a runway intersection.
B— from a runway intersection, only at night.
C— from a runway intersection, only during instrument conditions.

Pilots should state their position on the airport when calling the tower for takeoff from a runway intersection. (PLT434) — AIM ¶4-3-10

Answers (B) and (C) are incorrect because this rule applies to all operations.

ALL

9780. When flying in the airspace underlying Class B airspace, the maximum speed authorized is

A— 200 knots.
B— 230 knots.
C— 250 knots.

No person may operate an aircraft in the airspace underlying Class B airspace at a speed of more than 200 knots. (PLT161) — 14 CFR §91.117

ALL

8889. What restriction applies to a large, turbine-powered airplane operating to or from a primary airport in Class B airspace?

A— Must not exceed 200 knots within Class B airspace.
B— Must operate above the floor when within lateral limits of Class B airspace.
C— Must operate in accordance with IFR procedures regardless of weather conditions.

Unless otherwise authorized by ATC, each person operating a large turbine-engine-powered airplane to or from a primary airport in Class B airspace shall operate at or above the designated floors while within the lateral limits of the Class B airspace. (PLT161) — AIM ¶3-2-3

Answer (A) is incorrect because the speed limit within a Class B airspace is 250 knots for all aircraft. Answer (C) is incorrect because VFR is permitted in Class B airspace; i.e., an IFR clearance is not required as it is at FL180 and above.

ALL

8872. (Refer to Figure 126.) What is the normal radius from the airport of the outer area, B?

A— 10 miles.
B— 20 miles.
C— 25 miles.

The normal radius of the outer area of Class C airspace is 20 NM. (PLT040) — AIM ¶3-2-4

Answer (A) is incorrect because 10 NM is the radius of the outer circle of Class C airspace. Answer (C) is incorrect because 25 NM does not pertain to any set radius of Class C airspace.

ALL

8873. (Refer to Figure 126.) What is the usual radius from the airport of the inner circle (now called surface area), C?

A— 5 miles.
B— 7 miles.
C— 10 miles.

The usual radius from the airport of the surface area is 5 NM in Class C airspace. (PLT040) — AIM ¶3-2-4

Answer (B) is incorrect because 7 NM is not established as the radius for any portion of Class C airspace. Answer (C) is incorrect because 10 NM is the radius of the outer circle of Class C airspace.

Answers

9409 [B]	9424 [A]	9780 [A]	8889 [B]	8872 [B]	8873 [A]

ALL
8874. (Refer to Figure 126.) What is the radius from the airport of the outer circle (now called shelf area), A?

A— 5 miles.
B— 10 miles.
C— 15 miles.

The radius of the shelf area is 10 NM in Class C airspace. (PLT040) — AIM ¶3-2-4

Answer (A) is incorrect because 5 NM is the radius of the surface area of Class C airspace. Answer (C) is incorrect because 15 NM is not established as the radius for any area of Class C airspace.

ALL
8875. (Refer to Figure 126.) Which altitude (box 2) is applicable to the base of the outer circle (now called shelf area)?

A— 700 feet AGL.
B— 1,000 feet AGL.
C— 1,200 feet AGL.

The base of the shelf area is 1,200 feet AGL. (PLT040) — AIM ¶3-2-4

Answer (A) is incorrect because 700 feet AGL is not applicable to Class C airspace (it is the base of some Class E airspace). Answer (B) is incorrect because 1,000 feet AGL is not applicable to Class C airspace (it is the normal traffic pattern altitude for propeller airplanes).

ALL
8876. (Refer to Figure 126.) Which altitude (box 1) is applicable to the vertical extent of the inner and outer circles (now called surface and shelf areas)?

A— 3,000 feet AGL.
B— 3,000 feet above airport.
C— 4,000 feet above airport.

The vertical extent of the surface and shelf areas is 4,000 feet above the airport. (PLT040) — AIM ¶3-2-4

Answers (A) and (B) are incorrect because 3,000 feet AGL does not define an airspace.

ALL
8877. What minimum aircraft equipment is required for operation within Class C airspace?

A— Two-way communications.
B— Two-way communications and transponder.
C— Transponder and DME.

An encoding transponder and two-way radio is required in order to operate within Class C airspace. (PLT040) — AIM ¶3-2-4

Answer (A) is incorrect because a Mode C transponder is also required. Answer (C) is incorrect because two-way communications are also required and DME is not required.

ALL
8878. What service is provided for aircraft operating within the outer area of Class C airspace?

A— The same as within Class C airspace when communications and radar contact is established.
B— Radar vectors to and from secondary airports within the outer area.
C— Basic radar service only when communications and radar contact is established.

The same services are provided for aircraft operating within the outer area, as within the Class C airspace, when two-way communication and radar contact are established. (PLT161) — AIM ¶3-2-4

Answer (B) is incorrect because providing radar vectors to and from secondary airports within the outer circle is not a mandated service of ATC. Answer (C) is incorrect because the same services are provided in the outer area as within Class C airspace, once two-way communications and radar contact are established.

ALL
8879. What services are provided for aircraft operating within Class C airspace?

A— Sequencing of arriving aircraft, separation of aircraft (except between VFR aircraft), and traffic advisories.
B— Sequencing of arriving aircraft (except VFR aircraft), separation between all aircraft, and traffic advisories.
C— Sequencing of all arriving aircraft, separation between all aircraft, and traffic advisories.

ATC services within an Class C airspace include:

1. *Sequencing of all arriving aircraft to the primary Class C airport,*

2. *Standard IFR separation between IFR aircraft,*

3. *Between IFR and VFR aircraft — traffic advisories and conflict resolution so that radar targets do not touch, or 500 feet vertical separation, and*

4. *Between VFR aircraft — traffic advisories and as appropriate, safety alerts.*

(PLT161) — AIM ¶3-2-4

Answer (B) is incorrect because the services in the Class C airspace provide sequencing of all aircraft to the primary/Class C airspace airport. Answer (C) is incorrect because the services in the Class C airspace do not provide separation between VFR aircraft, only traffic advisories and safety alerts.

Answers

| 8874 [B] | 8875 [C] | 8876 [C] | 8877 [B] | 8878 [A] | 8879 [A] |

ALL

8880. What pilot certification and aircraft equipment are required for operating in Class C airspace?

A— No specific certification but a two-way radio.
B— At least a Private Pilot Certificate and two-way radio.
C— At least a Private Pilot Certificate, two-way radio, and a TSO-C74b transponder.

No specific pilot certification is required for operation within Class C airspace. The aircraft must be equipped with a two-way radio for operations within Class C airspace. (PLT161) — AIM ¶3-2-4

Answers (B) and (C) are incorrect because there is no specific pilot certificate required, although two-way radio and transponder are required.

ALL

9399. What is the maximum indicated airspeed a turbine-powered aircraft may be operated below 10,000 feet MSL?

A— 288 knots.
B— 250 knots.
C— 230 knots.

Unless otherwise authorized by the Administrator, no person may operate an aircraft below 10,000 feet MSL at an indicated airspeed of more than 250 knots (288 MPH). (PLT161) — 14 CFR §91.117

ALL

8890. Why are certain areas that start 3 nautical miles from the coastline of the U.S. and extend outward, classified as Warning Areas?

A— To inform pilots of participating aircraft to maintain extreme vigilance while conducting flight within the area.
B— To warn all aircraft pilots that flying within the area may be extremely hazardous to aircraft and occupants.
C— To warn pilots of nonparticipating aircraft of a potential danger within the area.

A Warning Area is airspace of defined dimensions, extending from three nautical miles outward from the coast of the United States, that contains activity that may be hazardous to nonparticipating aircraft. The purpose of such warning areas is to warn nonparticipating pilots of the potential danger. A warning area may be located over domestic or international waters or both. (PLT161) — AIM ¶3-4-4

ALL

8891. What is the purpose of MOAs?

A— To protect military aircraft operations from civil aircraft.
B— To separate military training activities from IFR traffic.
C— To separate military training activities from both IFR and VFR traffic.

Military Operations Areas (MOAs) consist of airspace of defined vertical and lateral limits established for the purpose of separating certain military training activities from IFR traffic. (PLT161) — AIM ¶3-4-5

Answer (A) is incorrect because MOAs are to separate (not protect) military training activities from IFR traffic. Answer (C) is incorrect because MOAs are established for the purpose of separating IFR traffic from military training activities.

ALL

8892. Who is responsible for collision avoidance in an MOA?

A— Military controllers.
B— ATC controllers.
C— Each pilot.

Pilots operating under VFR should exercise extreme caution while flying within an MOA when military activity is being conducted. (PLT162) — AIM ¶3-4-5

ALL

9049. Which aeronautical chart depicts Military Training Routes (MTR) above 1,500 feet?

A— IFR Low Altitude En Route Chart.
B— IFR High Altitude En Route Chart.
C— IFR Planning Chart.

The IFR Enroute Low Altitude Chart depicts all Military Training Routes (MTR) that accommodate operations above 1,500 feet AGL. (PLT100) — AIM ¶3-5-2

Answer (B) is incorrect because IFR High Altitude Enroute Charts do not depict MTRs. Answer (C) is incorrect because VFR Planning Charts depict MTRs.

Answers

| 8880 [A] | 9399 [B] | 8890 [C] | 8891 [B] | 8892 [C] | 9049 [A] |

ALL

9100. What is the maximum acceptable position tolerance for penetrating a domestic ADIZ over land?

A— Plus or minus 10 miles; plus or minus 10 minutes.
B— Plus or minus 20 miles; plus or minus 5 minutes.
C— Plus or minus 10 miles; plus or minus 5 minutes.

The aircraft position tolerances over land in a domestic ADIZ is within ±5 minutes from the estimated time over a reporting point or point of penetration and within 10 NM from the centerline of an intended track over an estimated reporting point or penetration point. (PLT161) — AIM ¶5-6-1

Answer (A) is incorrect because penetration of an ADIZ within 10 minutes is not an acceptable tolerance for either over water or land. Answer (B) is incorrect because the maximum acceptable tolerance for penetrating over water (a coastal ADIZ) is within 20 NM of the intended track and within 5 minutes of the estimated penetration time.

ALL

9741. What is the maximum acceptable position tolerance for penetrating a domestic ADIZ over water?

A— Plus or minus 10 miles; plus or minus 10 minutes.
B— Plus or minus 10 miles; plus or minus 5 minutes.
C— Plus or minus 20 miles; plus or minus 5 minutes.

The aircraft position tolerances over water in a domestic ADIZ is plus or minus five minutes from the estimated time over a reporting point or point of penetration and within 20 NM from the centerline of the intended track over an estimated reporting point or point of penetration. (PLT161) — AIM ¶5-6-1

ALL

9046. Under what conditions may a pilot on an IFR flight plan comply with authorization to maintain "VFR on Top"?

A— Maintain IFR flight plan but comply with visual flight rules while in VFR conditions.
B— Maintain VFR altitudes, cloud clearances, and comply with applicable instrument flight rules.
C— Maintain IFR altitudes, VFR cloud clearances, and comply with applicable instrument flight rules.

When operating in VFR conditions with an ATC authorization to "maintain VFR-On-Top" pilots on IFR flight plans must:

1. Fly an appropriate VFR altitude,

2. Comply with VFR visibility and distance from cloud criteria, and

3. Comply with instrument flight rules that are applicable to the flight.

(PLT370) — AIM ¶5-5-13

Answer (A) is incorrect because not only will a pilot remain on the IFR flight plan and comply with VFR altitudes, visibility, and cloud clearances, he/she must also comply with applicable IFR rules, e.g., position reporting, minimum IFR altitudes. Answer (C) is incorrect because, while operating on a "VFR-On-Top" clearance, a pilot must maintain VFR altitudes.

ALL

9047. What cloud clearance must be complied with when authorized to maintain "VFR on Top"?

A— May maintain VFR clearance above, below, or between layers.
B— Must maintain VFR clearance above or below.
C— May maintain VFR clearance above or below, but not between layers.

ATC authorization to "maintain VFR-On-Top" is not intended to restrict pilots so that they must operate only above an obscuring meteorological formation. Instead, it permits operations above, below, between or in areas where there is no meteorological obstruction. (PLT370) — AIM ¶5-5-13

ALL

9048. In what airspace will ATC not authorize "VFR on Top"?

A— Class C airspace.
B— Class B airspace.
C— Class A airspace.

ATC will not authorize VFR or VFR-On-Top operations in Class A airspace. (PLT161) — AIM ¶5-5-13

ALL

9093. What separation or service by ATC is afforded pilots authorized "VFR on Top"?

A— The same afforded all IFR flights.
B— 3 miles horizontally instead of 5.
C— Traffic advisories only.

Pilots operating VFR-On-Top may receive traffic information from ATC on other pertinent IFR or VFR aircraft. (PLT172) — AIM ¶5-5-13

Answer (A) is incorrect because separation will be provided for all IFR flights except those operating with a VFR-On-Top clearance. In that case, only traffic advisories may be provided. Answer (B) is incorrect because, when radar is employed for separation of aircraft at the same altitude, a minimum of 3 miles separation is provided between airplanes operating within 40 miles of the radar antenna site, and 5 miles between aircraft operating beyond 40 miles from the antenna site.

Answers

| 9100 | [C] | 9741 | [C] | 9046 | [B] | 9047 | [A] | 9048 | [C] | 9093 | [C] |

ALL

9018. A minimum instrument altitude for enroute operations off of published airways which provides obstruction clearance of 1,000 feet in nonmountainous terrain areas and 2,000 feet in designated mountainous areas within the United States is called

A— Minimum Obstruction Clearance Altitude (MOCA).
B— Off-Route Obstruction Clearance Altitude (OROCA).
C— Minimum Safe/Sector Altitude (MSA).

OROCA is an off-route altitude which provides obstruction clearance with a 1,000-foot buffer in nonmountainous terrain areas, and a 2,000-foot buffer in designated mountainous areas within the U.S. (PLT162) — AIM ¶4-4-9

Answer (A) is incorrect because MOCAs provide the lowest published altitude in effect between radio fixes on VOR airways, off-airway routes, or route segments which meets obstacle clearance requirements for the entire route segment and which ensures acceptable navigational signal coverage only within 25 SM (22 NM) of a VOR. Answer (C) is incorrect because MSAs are published for emergency use on IAP charts; they are expressed in feet above mean sea level and normally have a 25 NM radius; however, this radius may be expanded to 30 NM if necessary to encompass the airport landing surfaces.

ALL

8893. What is the required flight visibility and distance from clouds if you are operating in Class E airspace at 9,500 feet with a VFR-on-Top clearance during daylight hours?

A— 3 statute miles, 1,000 feet above, 500 feet below, and 2,000 feet horizontal.
B— 5 statute miles, 500 feet above, 1,000 feet below, and 2,000 feet horizontal.
C— 3 statute miles, 500 feet above, 1,000 feet below, and 2,000 feet horizontal.

A pilot receiving authorization for VFR-On-Top must comply with VFR visibility, distance from cloud criteria, and minimum IFR altitudes. When operating at more than 1,200 feet AGL but less than 10,000 feet MSL, pilots are required to maintain flight visibility of 3 statute miles and a distance from clouds of 1,000 feet above, 500 feet below, and 2,000 feet horizontal. (PLT163) — 14 CFR §91.155

Answer (B) is incorrect because the visibility requirement is 3 miles (not 5 miles) and the distances from clouds above and below are reversed. They should be 1,000 feet above and 500 feet below. Answer (C) is incorrect because the distances from clouds above and below are reversed. They should be 1,000 feet above and 500 feet below.

ALL

8894. (Refer to Figure 128.) What is the minimum in-flight visibility and distance from clouds required for a VFR-on-Top flight at 9,500 feet MSL (above 1,200 feet AGL) during daylight hours for the circle 3 area?

A— 2,000 feet; (E) 1,000 feet; (F) 2,000 feet; (H) 500 feet.
B— 5 miles; (E) 1,000 feet; (F) 2,000 feet; (H) 500 feet.
C— 3 miles; (E) 1,000 feet; (F) 2,000 feet; (H) 500 feet.

When operating at more than 1,200 feet AGL but less than 10,000 feet MSL during the day in controlled airspace, pilots are required to maintain a flight visibility of 3 statute miles and a distance of 1,000 feet above, 500 feet below, and 2,000 feet horizontally from clouds. (PLT163) — 14 CFR §91.155

ALL

8895. (Refer to Figure 128.) A flight is to be conducted in VFR-on-Top conditions at 12,500 feet MSL (above 1,200 feet AGL). What is the in flight visibility and distance from clouds required for operations during daylight hours for the circle 1 area?

A— 5 miles; (A) 1,000 feet; (B) 2,000 feet; (D) 500 feet.
B— 5 miles; (A) 1,000 feet; (B) 1 mile; (D) 1,000 feet.
C— 3 miles; (A) 1,000 feet; (B) 2,000 feet; (D) 1,000 feet.

A pilot on an IFR flight plan requesting and receiving authorization to operate VFR-On-Top must comply with instrument flight rules as well as VFR visibilities and distances from clouds. When operating at more than 1,200 feet AGL and at or above 10,000 feet MSL, pilots are required to maintain flight visibility of 5 statute miles and distances of 1,000 feet above, 1,000 feet below, and 1 mile horizontally from clouds. (PLT163) — 14 CFR §91.155

Answer (A) is incorrect because the distance from cloud requirements listed are for below 10,000 feet MSL. Answer (C) is incorrect because the visibility requirement is 5 miles and the horizontal separation from clouds requirement is 1 mile.

Answers

9018	[B]	8893	[A]	8894	[C]	8895	[B]

ALL

8896. (Refer to Figure 128.) What is the minimum in-flight visibility and distance from clouds required in VFR conditions above clouds at 13,500 feet MSL (above 1,200 feet AGL) during daylight hours for the circle 2 area?

A— 5 miles; (A) 1,000 feet; (C) 2,000 feet; (D) 500 feet.

B— 3 miles; (A) 1,000 feet; (C) 1 mile; (D) 1,000 feet.

C— 5 miles; (A) 1,000 feet; (C) 1 mile; (D) 1,000 feet.

The minimum flight visibility in Class G airspace during daylight hours in VFR conditions above clouds at 13,500 feet MSL (above 1,200 feet AGL) is 5 statute miles. The distance from clouds required is 1,000 feet below, 1,000 feet above, and 1 mile horizontally. (PLT163) — 14 CFR §91.155

Answer (A) is incorrect because 1,000 feet above, 2,000 feet horizontal, and 500 feet below are the minimum cloud distances for VFR in Class G airspace above 1,200 feet AGL and below 10,000 feet MSL. Answer (B) is incorrect because visibility minimum is 5 miles.

ALL

8897. (Refer to Figure 128.) What in-flight visibility and distance from clouds is required for a flight at 8,500 feet MSL (above 1,200 feet AGL) in VFR conditions during daylight hours for the circle 4 area?

A— 1 mile; (E) 1,000 feet; (G) 2,000 feet; (H) 500 feet.

B— 3 miles; (E) 1,000 feet; (G) 2,000 feet; (H) 500 feet.

C— 5 miles; (E) 1,000 feet; (G) 1 mile; (H) 1,000 feet.

At 8,500 feet MSL (above 1,200 feet AGL) in Class G airspace in VFR conditions during daylight hours the visibility is 1 statute mile and distance from clouds required is 500 feet below, 1,000 feet above, and 2,000 feet horizontally. (PLT163) — 14 CFR §91.155

Answer (B) is incorrect because these are the VFR weather minimums for Class E airspace below 10,000 feet MSL and above 1,200 feet AGL. Answer (C) is incorrect because these are the VFR weather minimums for Class E and Class G airspace above 10,000 feet MSL.

ALL

8898. (Refer to Figure 128.) What is the minimum in-flight visibility and distance from clouds required for an airplane operating less than 1,200 feet AGL during daylight hours in the circle 6 area?

A— 3 miles; (I) 1,000 feet; (K) 2,000 feet; (L) 500 feet.

B— 1 mile; (I) clear of clouds; (K) clear of clouds; (L) clear of clouds.

C— 1 mile; (I) 500 feet; (K) 1,000 feet; (L) 500 feet.

When operating outside Class E airspace at less than 1,200 feet AGL during daylight hours, pilots are required to maintain flight visibility of 1 statute mile and operate clear of clouds. (PLT163) — 14 CFR §91.155

Answer (A) is incorrect because 3 miles visibility, 1,000 feet above, 500 feet below, and 2,000 feet horizontal are the VFR weather minimums for a flight in airspace above 1,200 feet AGL and below 10,000 feet MSL at night. Answer (C) is incorrect because no such combination of requirements exists in any airspace.

ALL

8899. (Refer to Figure 128.) What is the minimum in-flight visibility and distance from clouds required for an airplane operating less than 1,200 feet AGL under special VFR during daylight hours in the circle 5 area?

A— 1 mile; (I) 2,000 feet; (J) 2,000 feet; (L) 500 feet.

B— 3 miles; (I) clear of clouds; (J) clear of clouds; (L) 500 feet.

C— 1 mile; (I) clear of clouds; (J) clear of clouds; (L) clear of clouds.

When operating under special VFR during daylight hours, pilots are required to maintain flight visibility of 1 statute mile and operate clear of clouds. (PLT163) — 14 CFR §91.157

Answers (A) and (B) are incorrect because special VFR permits operation just clear of clouds and with a minimum visibility of 1 mile.

ALL

8900. What is the minimum flight visibility and distance from clouds for flight at 10,500 feet, in Class E airspace, with a VFR-on-Top clearance during daylight hours?

A— 3 statute miles, 1,000 feet above, 500 feet below, and 2,000 feet horizontal.

B— 5 statute miles, 1,000 feet above, 1,000 feet below, and 1 mile horizontal.

C— 5 statute miles, 1,000 feet above, 500 feet below, and 1 mile horizontal.

Answers

8896 [C]   8897 [A]   8898 [B]   8899 [C]   8900 [B]

A pilot on an IFR flight plan requesting and receiving authorization to operate VFR-On-Top must comply with instrument flight rules as well as VFR visibilities and distances from clouds. When operating at more than 1,200 feet AGL and at or above 10,000 feet MSL pilots are required to maintain flight visibility of 5 statute miles and distances of 1,000 feet above, 1,000 feet below, and 1 mile horizontally from clouds. (PLT163) — 14 CFR §91.155

Answer (A) is incorrect because it presents the VFR weather minimums for below 10,000 feet MSL. Answer (C) is incorrect because the vertical separation from clouds is 1,000 feet both above and below.

ATM, DSP

8253. Which in-flight conditions are required by a supplemental air carrier to conduct a day, over-the-top flight below the specified IFR minimum en route altitude?

A— The flight must remain clear of clouds by at least 1,000 feet vertically and 1,000 feet horizontally and have at least 3 miles flight visibility.

B— The flight must be conducted at least 1,000 feet above an overcast or broken cloud layer, any higher broken/overcast cloud cover is a minimum of 1,000 feet above the IFR MEA, and have at least 5 miles flight visibility.

C— The height of any higher overcast or broken layer must be at least 500 feet above the IFR MEA.

A person may conduct day Over-the-Top operations in an airplane at flight altitudes lower than the minimum enroute IFR altitudes if—

1. The operation is conducted at least 1,000 feet above the top of lower broken or overcast cloud cover;

2. The top of the lower cloud cover is generally uniform and level;

3. Flight visibility is at least 5 miles; and

4. The base of any higher broken or overcast cloud cover is generally uniform and level, and is at least 1,000 feet above the minimum enroute IFR altitude for that route segment.

(PLT468) — 14 CFR §121.657

Answer (A) is incorrect because the flight must remain at least 1,000 feet above the cloud layer with a flight visibility of at least 5 miles. Answer (C) is incorrect because the height of any higher ceiling must be at least 1,000 feet above the IFR MEA.

ATM, ATS, DSP

9395. At what minimum altitude is a turbine-engine-powered, or large airplane, required to enter Class D airspace?

A— 1,500 feet AGL.
B— 2,000 feet AGL.
C— 2,500 feet AGL.

When operating to an airport with an operating control tower, each pilot of a turbine-powered airplane or a large airplane shall, unless otherwise required by the applicable distance from cloud criteria, enter Class D airspace at an altitude of at least 1,500 feet above the surface of the airport. (PLT161) — 14 CFR §91.129

ATM, ATS, DSP

9401. A pilot of a turbine-powered airplane should climb as rapidly as practicable after taking off to what altitude?

A— 1,000 feet AGL.
B— 1,500 feet AGL.
C— 5,000 feet AGL.

When taking off from an airport with an operating control tower, each pilot of a turbine-powered airplane shall climb to an altitude of 1,500 feet above the surface as rapidly as practicable. (PLT459) — 14 CFR §91.129

ATM, ATS, DSP

9396. What is the maximum indicated airspeed a reciprocating-engine-powered airplane may be operated within Class B airspace?

A— 180 knots.
B— 230 knots.
C— 250 knots.

Unless otherwise authorized by the Administrator, no person may operate an aircraft below 10,000 feet MSL at an indicated airspeed of more than 250 knots (288 MPH). There is no specific speed restriction which applies to operation within Class B airspace. (PLT161) — 14 CFR §91.117

Answer (A) is incorrect because 180 knots is the old maximum airspeed for turbine-powered aircraft while operating within Class D airspace (it is now 200 knots). Answer (B) is incorrect because 230 knots is the maximum authorized holding speed for all civil turbojet aircraft while operating from the minimum holding altitude to 14,000 feet. It is not an airspeed limitation in Class B airspace.

Answers

| 8253 | [B] | 9395 | [A] | 9401 | [B] | 9396 | [C] |

ATM, ATS, DSP

8887. The maximum indicated airspeed that an aircraft may be flown in Class B airspace, after departing the primary airport, while at 1,700 feet AGL and 3.5 nautical miles from the airport is

A— 200 knots.
B— 230 knots.
C— 250 knots.

Unless otherwise authorized by the Administrator, no person may operate an aircraft below 10,000 feet MSL at an indicated airspeed of more than 250 knots (288 MPH). (PLT161) — 14 CFR §91.117

ATM, ATS, DSP

9397. At what maximum indicated airspeed can a B-727 operate within Class B airspace without special ATC authorization?

A— 230 knots.
B— 250 knots.
C— 275 knots.

Unless otherwise authorized by the Administrator, no person may operate an aircraft below 10,000 feet MSL at an indicated airspeed of more than 250 knots (288 MPH). There is no specific speed restriction which applies to operation within Class B airspace. (PLT161) — 14 CFR §91.117

Answer (A) is incorrect because 230 knots is not an airspeed limitation in Class B airspace. Answer (C) is incorrect because 275 knots is not an established maximum speed for any type of operation.

ATM, ATS, DSP

9398. At what maximum indicated airspeed may a reciprocating-engine-powered airplane be operated within Class D airspace?

A— 156 knots.
B— 180 knots.
C— 200 knots.

Unless otherwise authorized or required by ATC, no person may operate an aircraft within Class D airspace at an indicated airspeed of more than 200 knots. (PLT161) — 14 CFR §91.117

Answer (A) is incorrect because 156 knots was the old maximum authorized airspeed for reciprocating aircraft in Class D airspace (it is now 200 knots). Answer (B) is incorrect because 180 knots was the old maximum authorized airspeed for turbine-powered aircraft in Class D airspace (it is now 200 knots).

ATM, ATS, DSP

9400. At what maximum indicated airspeed can a reciprocating-engine airplane operate in the airspace underlying Class B airspace?

A— 180 knots.
B— 200 knots.
C— 230 knots.

No person may operate an aircraft in the airspace underlying Class B airspace at an indicated airspeed of more than 200 knots (230 MPH). (PLT161) — 14 CFR §91.117

Answer (A) is incorrect because 180 knots was the old published maximum airspeed for turbine-powered aircraft in Class D airspace (it is now 200 knots). Answer (C) is incorrect because the limitation is 200 knots or 230 MPH, not 230 knots.

NOTAMs (NOtices To AirMen)

Notices to Airmen (NOTAMs) provide the most current information available. They provide time-critical information on airports and changes that affect the national airspace system and are of concern to instrument flight rule (IFR) operations. NOTAM information is classified into five categories: NOTAM (D) or distant, Flight Data Center (FDC) NOTAMs, pointer NOTAMs, Special Activity Airspace (SAA) NOTAMs, and military NOTAMs.

NOTAM (D)s are attached to hourly weather reports and are available at flight service stations (AFSS/FSS). FDC NOTAMs are issued by the National Flight Data Center and contain regulatory information, such as temporary flight restrictions or an amendment to instrument approach procedures.

Pointer NOTAMs highlight or point out another NOTAM, such as an FDC or NOTAM (D). This type of NOTAM will assist pilots in cross-referencing important information that may not be found under an airport or NAVAID identifier. Military NOTAMs pertain to U.S. Air Force, Army, Marine, and Navy NAVAIDs/airports that are part of the NAS.

Answers

8887 [C]	9397 [B]	9398 [C]	9400 [B]

SAA NOTAMs are issued when Special Activity Airspace will be active outside the published schedule times and when required by the published schedule. Pilots and other users are still responsible to check published schedule times for Special Activity Airspace as well as any NOTAMs for that airspace.

NOTAM (D)s and FDC NOTAMs are contained in the Notices to Airmen publication, which is issued every 28 days. Prior to any flight, pilots should check for any NOTAMs that could affect their intended flight.

ALL
9086. What are FDC NOTAMs?

A— Conditions of facilities en route that may cause delays.

B— Time critical aeronautical information of a temporary nature from distant centers.

C— Regulatory amendments to published IAPs and charts not yet available in normally published charts.

FDC NOTAMs contain such things as amendments to published IAPs and other current aeronautical charts and other information which is considered regulatory in nature. (PLT323) — AIM ¶5-1-3

Answer (A) is incorrect because NOTAM (D) contains information on navigational facilities en route that may cause delays. Answer (B) is incorrect because time critical aeronautical information of a temporary nature from distant centers will be included in a NOTAM (D) ("distant").

ALL
9087. What type information is disseminated by NOTAM (D)s?

A— Status of navigation aids, ILSs, radar service available, and other information essential to planning.

B— Airport or primary runway closings, runway and taxiway conditions, and airport lighting aids outages.

C— Temporary flight restrictions, changes in status in navigational aids, and updates on equipment such as VASI.

NOTAM (D) information is disseminated for all navigational facilities that are part of the national airspace system, all IFR airports with approved instrument approaches, and those VFR airports annotated with the NOTAM service symbol (§) in the Chart Supplements U.S. (previously A/FD). NOTAM (D) information could affect a pilot's decision to make a flight. It includes such information as airport or primary runway closures, changes in the status of navigational aids, ILS's, radar service availability, and other information essential to planned en route, terminal or landing operations. (PLT323) — AIM ¶5-1-3

ALL
9089. How often are NOTAMs broadcast to pilots on a scheduled basis?

A— 15 minutes before and 15 minutes after the hour.

B— Between weather broadcasts on the hour.

C— Hourly, appended to the weather broadcast.

NOTAM (D) information is appended to the hourly weather reports via the Service A (ATC/FSS) telecommunications system. (PLT323) — AIM ¶5-1-3

Answer (A) is incorrect because SIGMETs and AIRMETs are broadcast by FSS's and/or by the Hazardous In-flight Weather Advisory Service (HIWAS) to pilots 15 minutes before and 15 minutes after the hour during the valid period. Answer (B) is incorrect because NOTAM (D)s are appended to the hourly weather broadcast, not a separate broadcast between weather reports.

Answers

9086 [C]   9087 [A]   9089 [C]

Items on the Flight Plan

An IFR flight plan should be filed at least 30 minutes prior to the departure time, and pilots should request their IFR clearance no more than 10 minutes prior to taxi.

If the flight is to be flown on established airways, the route should be defined using the airways or jet routes with transitions. Intermediate VORs and fixes on an airway need not be listed. If filing for an off-airway direct route, list all the radio fixes over which the flight will pass. Pilots of appropriately equipped aircraft may file for random RNAV routes. The following rules must be observed:

- Radar monitoring by ATC must be available along the entire proposed route.
- Plan the random route portion to begin and end over appropriate departure and arrival transition fixes or navigation aids appropriate for the altitude structure used for the flight. Use of DPs and STARs, where available, is recommended.
- Define the random route by waypoints. Use degree-distance fixes based on navigational aids appropriate for the altitude structure used. Above FL390 latitude/longitude fixes may be used to define the route.
- List at least one waypoint for each Air Route Traffic Control Center through which the flight will pass. The waypoint must be within 200 NM of the preceding Center's boundary.

A pilot may file a flight plan to an airport containing a special or privately-owned instrument approach procedure only upon approval of the owner.

Air ambulance flights and air carrier flights responding to medical emergencies will receive expedited handling by ATC when necessary. When appropriate, the word "Lifeguard" should be entered in the remarks section of the flight plan. It should also be used in the flight's radio call sign as in, "Lifeguard Delta Thirty-Seven."

ALL

9031. What is the suggested time interval for filing and requesting an IFR flight plan?

A— File at least 30 minutes prior to departure and request the clearance not more than 10 minutes prior to taxi.

B— File at least 30 minutes prior to departure and request the clearance at least 10 minutes prior to taxi.

C— File at least 1 hour prior to departure and request the clearance at least 10 minutes prior to taxi.

Pilots should file IFR flight plans at least 30 minutes prior to the estimated time of departure to preclude possible delay in receiving a departure clearance from ATC. Pilots should call clearance delivery or ground control for their IFR clearance not more than 10 minutes before the proposed taxi time. (PLT224) — AIM ¶5-1-8, 5-2-1

ALL

9032. How should the route of flight be defined on an IFR flight plan?

A— A simplified route via airways or jet routes with transitions.

B— A route via airways or jet routes with VORs and fixes used.

C— A route via airways or jet routes with only the compulsory reporting points.

Pilots are requested to file via airways or jet routes established for use at the altitude or flight level planned. If the flight is to be conducted via designated airways or jet routes, describe the route by indicating the type and number designators of the airway(s) or jet route(s) requested. If more than one airway or jet route is to be used, clearly indicate points of transition. (PLT224) — AIM ¶5-1-8

Answer (B) is incorrect because, to simplify the route, all VORs and fixes are not used to define a route on an IFR flight plan. Answer (C) is incorrect because compulsory reporting points might not define the transitions between airways or jet routes.

ALL

9033. How should an off-airway direct flight be defined on an IFR flight plan?

A— The initial fix, the true course, and the final fix.
B— All radio fixes over which the flight will pass.
C— The initial fix, all radio fixes which the pilot wishes to be compulsory reporting points, and the final fix.

Any portions of the route which will not be flown on the radials or courses of established airways or routes, such as direct route flights, must be clearly defined by indicating the radio fixes over which the flight will pass. (PLT225) — AIM ¶5-1-8

Answer (A) is incorrect because true course is not an item that is reported on an IFR flight plan. The initial fix and the final fix are listed as radio fixes that define the start and finish points of a flight. Answer (C) is incorrect because initial and final fixes are required to define random RNAV (not direct flight) routes. All radio fixes that define the route of a direct flight automatically become compulsory reporting points, not just those the pilot chooses.

ALL

9026. How are random RNAV routes below FL 390 defined on the IFR flight plan?

A— Define route waypoints using degree-distance fixes based on appropriate navigational aids for the route and altitude.
B— List the initial and final fix with at least one waypoint each 200 NM.
C— Begin and end over appropriate arrival and departure transition fixes or navigation aids for the altitude being flown, define the random route waypoints by using degree-distance fixes based on navigation aids appropriate for the altitude being flown.

Pilots of aircraft equipped with operational area navigation equipment may file for random RNAV routes throughout the national airspace system, where radar monitoring by ATC is available, in accordance with the following:

1. File airport-to-airport flight plans prior to departure.

2. File the appropriate RNAV capability suffix in the flight plan.

3. Plan the random route portion of the flight plan to begin and end over appropriate arrival and departure fixes.

4. Define the random route by waypoints. File route description waypoints by using degree/distance fixes based on navigation aids which are appropriate to the altitude.

5. File a minimum of one route description waypoint for each ARTCC through whose area the random route will be flown. These waypoints must be located within 200 NM of the preceding center's boundary. (PLT224) — AIM ¶5-1-8

Answer (A) is incorrect because RNAV routes defined on an IFR flight plan must also begin and end over an established radio fix. Answer (B) is incorrect because RNAV waypoints have no established distance requirement. A minimum of one waypoint must be filed for each ARTCC through which the route is planned, and this must be located within 200 NM of the preceding center's boundary.

ALL

9027. What is one limitation when filing a random RNAV route on an IFR flight plan?

A— The waypoints must be located within 200 NM of each other.
B— The entire route must be within radar environment.
C— The waypoints may only be defined by degree-distance fixes based on appropriate navigational aids.

Random RNAV routes can only be approved in a radar environment. Aircraft operating at or above FL390 may file waypoints based on latitude/longitude fixes, under some circumstances. (PLT225) — AIM ¶5-1-8

Answer (A) is incorrect because VOR/VORTAC facilities must be within 200 NM of each other when operating above FL450 to define a direct route. Answer (C) is incorrect because random RNAV waypoints may be defined by degree-distance fixes based on appropriate navigational aids, of latitude/longitude coordinate navigation, independent of VOR/TACAN references, operating at and above FL390 in the conterminous U.S.

ALL

9040. Under what condition may a pilot file an IFR flight plan containing a special or privately owned IAP?

A— Upon approval of ATC.
B— Upon approval of the owner.
C— Upon signing a waiver of responsibility.

Pilots planning flights to locations served by special IAPs should obtain advance approval from the owner of the procedure. Approval by the owner is necessary because special procedures are for the exclusive use of the single interest unless otherwise authorized by the owner. Controllers assume a pilot has obtained approval and is aware of any details of the procedure if he/she files an IFR flight plan to that airport. (PLT083) — AIM ¶5-4-7

Answer (A) is incorrect because ATC is not required to question pilots to determine whether they have the owner's permission to use the procedure. Answer (C) is incorrect because a pilot is responsible for the safe operation of the airplane. To sign a waiver of responsibility is contrary to a pilot's duty.

Answers

9033	[B]	9026	[C]	9027	[B]	9040	[B]

ALL

9053. To assure expeditious handling of a civilian air ambulance flight, the word "LIFEGUARD" should be entered in which section of the flight plan?

A— Aircraft type/special equipment block.
B— Pilot's name and address block.
C— Remarks block.

When expeditious handling is necessary because of a medical emergency, add the word "LIFEGUARD" in the remarks section of the flight plan. (PLT225) — AIM ¶4-2-4

Answer (A) is incorrect because only the airplane's designator or manufacturer's name and the transponder DME and/or RNAV equipment code is entered in the aircraft type/special equipment block. Answer (B) is incorrect because the complete name, address, and telephone number of the pilot-in-command are entered in the pilot's name and address block. Sufficient information is listed here to identify home base, airport, or operator. This information would be essential in the event of a search and rescue operation.

ALL

9809. Before requesting RVSM clearance, each person

A— shall correctly annotate the flight plan.
B— must file an ICAO RVSM flight plan.
C— should file for odd altitudes only.

Each person requesting a clearance to operate within reduced vertical separate minimum (RVSM) airspace shall correctly annotate the flight plan filed with air traffic control with regard to RVSM approval. (PLT367) — AIM ¶4-6-4

Alternate Airport Planning

An airport may not be available for alternate use if the airport NAVAID is unmonitored, is GPS-based, or if it does not have weather-reporting capabilities.

For an airport to be used as an alternate, the forecast weather at that airport must meet certain qualifications at the estimated time of arrival. Standard alternate minimums for a precision approach are a 600-foot ceiling and 2 SM visibility. For a nonprecision approach, the minimums are an 800-foot ceiling and 2 SM visibility. Standard alternate minimums apply unless higher alternate minimums are listed for an airport.

Alternate Airport for Destination — Domestic Air Carriers: Unless the weather at the destination meets certain criteria, an alternate must be listed in the dispatch release (and flight plan) for each destination airport. If the weather at the first listed alternate is marginal (as defined by the operations specifications) at least one additional alternate must be listed.

Alternate Airport for Destination — Flag Carriers: An alternate airport must be listed in the dispatch release (and flight plan) for all flag air carrier flights longer than 6 hours. An alternate is not required for a flag air carrier flight if it is scheduled for less than 6 hours and the weather forecast for the destination meets certain criteria. For the period from 1 hour before to 1 hour after the estimated time of arrival:

• The ceiling must be forecast to be at least 1,500 feet above the lowest minimums or 2,000 feet, whichever is higher; and

• The visibility must be forecast to be 3 miles, or 2 miles greater than the lowest applicable visibility minimum, whichever is greater.

Alternate Airport for Destination — Supplemental Air Carriers and Commercial Operators: Except for certain operations, a supplemental air carrier or commercial operator must always list an alternate airport regardless of existing or forecast weather conditions.

An airport cannot be listed as an alternate in the dispatch or flight release unless the appropriate weather reports and forecasts indicate that the weather conditions will be at or above the alternate

Answers

9053   [C]   9809   [A]

Chapter 6 **Flight Operations**

weather minimums specified in the certificate holder's operations specifications for that airport, when the flight arrives. Alternate weather minimums are for planning purposes only and do not apply to actual operations. If an air carrier flight actually diverts to an alternate airport, the crew may use the actual weather minimums shown on the IAP (Instrument Approach Procedure) Chart for that airport.

If the weather conditions at the departure airport are below landing minimums in the airline's operations specifications, a departure alternate must be listed in the dispatch or the flight release. Weather at alternate airports must meet the conditions for alternates in the operations specifications. The maximum distance to the departure alternate for a two-engine airplane cannot be more than 1 hour from the departure airport in still air with one engine operating. The distance to the departure alternate for an airplane with three or more engines cannot be more than 2 hours from the departure airport in still air with one engine inoperative.

ALL

9394-1. When proceeding to the alternate airport, which minimums apply?

A— The IFR alternate minimums section in front of the NOAA IAP book.

B— 2000-3 for at least 1 hour before until 1 hour after the ETA.

C— The actual minimums shown on the IAP chart for the airport.

When the approach procedure being used provides for and requires the use of a DH or MDA, the authorized decision height or authorized minimum descent altitude is the DH or MDA prescribed by the approach procedure, the DH or MDA prescribed for the pilot-in-command, or the DH or MDA for which the aircraft is equipped, whichever is highest.

Note: The alternate airport minimums are used only during preflight planning to determine the suitability of an airport as an IFR alternate. They impose no additional restrictions should a flight actually divert to the filed alternate. (PLT421) — 14 CFR §91.175

Answer (A) is incorrect because the alternate minimums listed in the NOAA IAP (National Oceanic and Atmospheric Administration Instrument Approach Procedure) book refer to the ceiling and visibility requirements for that airport in order to file it as an alternate, not the ceiling and visibility required to execute an instrument approach. Answer (B) is incorrect because 2000-3 minimums apply to the destination airport. If your destination airport has a forecast ceiling of at least 2,000 feet and a visibility of at least 3 miles, an alternate airport need not be filed in the flight plan.

ALL

9394-2. An airport may not be qualified for alternate use if

A— the airport has AWOS-3 weather reporting.

B— the airport is located next to a restricted or prohibited area.

C— the NAVAIDs used for the final approach are unmonitored.

Not all airports can be used as an alternate. An airport may not be qualified for alternate use if the airport NAVAID is unmonitored, is GPS-based, or if it does not have weather reporting capability. (PLT379) — FAA-H-8083-16

Answer (A) is incorrect because an airport can qualify for alternate use if it has any weather reporting capability. Answer (B) is incorrect because an airport can qualify for alternate use even if it is located in a restricted or prohibited area.

ALL

9770. When planning to use RNAV equipment with GPS input for an instrument approach at a destination airport, any required alternate airport must have an available instrument approach procedure that does not

A— require the use of GPS except when the RNAV system has a WAAS input.

B— require the use of GPS except when the RNAV system has an IRU input.

C— require the use of GPS except when dual, independent GPS receivers are installed.

Aircraft using GPS navigation equipment under IFR for domestic en route, terminal operations, and certain IAPs must be equipped with an approved and operational alternate means of navigation appropriate to the flight. However, a required alternate airport may be selected if it uses an RNAV system with WAAS equipment. (PLT420) — FAA-H-8083-15

Answers

9394-1   [C]   9394-2   [C]   9770   [A]

ATM, DSP

8247. When the forecast weather conditions for a destination and alternate airport are considered marginal for a domestic air carrier's operation, what specific action should the dispatcher or pilot in command take?

A— List an airport where the forecast weather is not marginal as the alternate.
B— Add 1 additional hour of fuel based on cruise power settings for the airplane in use.
C— List at least one additional alternate airport.

When weather conditions forecast for the destination and first alternate airport are marginal, at least one additional alternate must be designated. (PLT379) — 14 CFR §121.619

ATM, DSP

8256. Which dispatch requirement applies to a flag air carrier that is scheduled for a 7-hour IFR flight?

A— No alternate airport is required if the forecast weather at the ETA at the destination airport is at least 1,500 feet and 3 miles.
B— An alternate airport is not required if the ceiling will be at least 1,500 feet above the lowest circling MDA.
C— An alternate airport is required.

All flag air carrier flights over 6 hours require an alternate airport. (PLT379) — 14 CFR §121.621

Answers (A) and (B) are incorrect because whenever the scheduled flight exceeds 6 hours, a flag air carrier must list an alternate regardless of the weather.

ATM, DSP

8262. An alternate airport is not required to dispatch a flag air carrier airplane for a flight of less than 6 hours when the visibility for at least 1 hour before and 1 hour after the ETA at the destination airport is forecast to be

A— 2 miles or greater.
B— at least 3 miles, or 2 miles more than the lowest applicable minimum.
C— 3 miles.

An alternate airport need not be listed if the destination weather, from an hour before to an hour after the ETA, is forecast to have the required ceiling criteria and the visibility is forecast to be at least 3 miles, or 2 miles more than the lowest visibility minimums, whichever is greater, for the instrument approach procedures to be used at the destination airport. (PLT379) — 14 CFR §121.621

ATM, DSP

8251. When is a supplemental air carrier, operating under IFR, required to list an alternate airport for each destination airport within the 48 contiguous United States?

A— When the forecast weather indicates the ceiling will be less than 1,000 feet and visibility less than 2 miles at the estimated time of arrival.
B— On all flights, an alternate is required regardless of existing or forecast weather conditions at the destination.
C— When the flight is scheduled for more than 6 hours en route.

A supplemental air carrier must declare an alternate airport for all IFR operations. (PLT379) — 14 CFR §121.623

ATM, DSP

8254. Prior to listing an airport as an alternate airport in the dispatch or flight release, weather reports and forecasts must indicate that weather conditions will be at or above authorized minimums at that airport

A— for a period 1 hour before or after the ETA.
B— during the entire flight.
C— when the flight arrives.

No person may list an airport as an alternate airport in the dispatch release or flight release unless the appropriate weather reports or forecasts, or any combination thereof, indicate that the weather conditions will be at or above the alternate weather minimums specified in the certificate holder's operations specifications for that airport when the flight arrives. (PLT380) — 14 CFR §121.625

ATM, DSP

8255. The minimum weather conditions that must exist for an airport to be listed as an alternate in the dispatch release for a domestic air carrier flight are

A— those listed in the NOAA IAP charts for the alternate airport, at the time the flight is expected to arrive.
B— those specified in the certificate holder's Operations Specifications for that airport, when the flight arrives.
C— those listed in the NOAA IAP charts for the alternate airport, from 1 hour before or after the ETA for that flight.

Answers

8247 [C]	8256 [C]	8262 [B]	8251 [B]	8254 [C]	8255 [B]

No person may list an airport as an alternate airport in the dispatch release or flight release unless the appropriate weather reports or forecasts, or any combination thereof, indicate that the weather conditions will be at or above the alternate weather minimums specified in the certificate holder's operations specifications for that airport when the flight arrives. (PLT380) — 14 CFR §121.625

Answers (A) and (C) are incorrect because, although the alternate minimums in IAP charts may coincide with the air carrier's operation specifications, it is the operations specifications that determine alternate weather minimums.

ATM, DSP

8248. An alternate airport for departure is required

A— if weather conditions are below authorized landing minimums at the departure airport.
B— when the weather forecast at the ETD is for landing minimums only at the departure airport.
C— when destination weather is marginal VFR (ceiling less than 3,000 feet and visibility less than 5 SM).

If the weather conditions at the airport of takeoff are below the landing minimums in the certificate holder's operations specifications for that airport, no person may dispatch or release an aircraft from that airport unless the dispatch or flight release specifies an alternate airport located within the following distances from the airport of takeoff.

1. Aircraft having two engines: Not more than 1 hour from the departure airport at normal cruising speed in still air with one engine inoperative.

2. Aircraft having three or more engines: Not more than 2 hours from the departure airport at normal cruising speed in still air with one engine inoperative.

(PLT379) — 14 CFR §121.617

ATM, DSP

8249. What is the maximum distance that a departure alternate airport may be from the departure airport for a two-engine airplane?

A— 1 hour at normal cruise speed in still air with both engines operating.
B— 1 hour at normal cruise speed in still air with one engine operating.
C— 2 hours at normal cruise speed in still air with one engine operating.

If the weather conditions at the airport of takeoff are below the landing minimums in the certificate holder's operations specifications for that airport, no person may dispatch or release an aircraft from that airport unless the dispatch or flight release specifies an alternate airport located within the following distances from the airport of takeoff.

1. Aircraft having two engines: Not more than 1 hour from the departure airport at normal cruising speed in still air with one engine inoperative.

2. Aircraft having three or more engines: Not more than 2 hours from the departure airport at normal cruising speed in still air with one engine inoperative.

(PLT379) — 14 CFR §121.617

Answer (A) is incorrect because the maximum distance is determined with one engine operating. Answer (C) is incorrect because 2 hours is the limit for airplanes with three or more engines with one engine inoperative.

ATM, DSP

8250. If a four-engine air carrier airplane is dispatched from an airport that is below landing minimums, what is the maximum distance that a departure alternate airport may be located from the departure airport?

A— Not more than 2 hours at cruise speed with one engine inoperative.
B— Not more than 2 hours at normal cruise speed in still air with one engine inoperative.
C— Not more than 1 hour at normal cruise speed in still air with one engine inoperative.

If the weather conditions at the airport of takeoff are below the landing minimums in the certificate holder's operations specifications for that airport, no person may dispatch or release an aircraft from that airport unless the dispatch or flight release specifies an alternate airport located within the following distances from the airport of takeoff.

1. Aircraft having two engines: Not more than 1 hour from the departure airport at normal cruising speed in still air with one engine inoperative.

2. Aircraft having three or more engines: Not more than 2 hours from the departure airport at normal cruising speed in still air with one engine inoperative.

(PLT396) — 14 CFR §121.617

Answers

8248 [A]   8249 [B]   8250 [B]

ATM, DSP

8252. When a departure alternate is required for a three-engine air carrier flight, it must be located at a distance not greater than

A— 2 hours from the departure airport at normal cruising speed in still air with one engine not functioning.

B— 1 hour from the departure airport at normal cruising speed in still air with one engine inoperative.

C— 2 hours from the departure airport at normal cruising speed in still air.

If the weather conditions at the airport of takeoff are below the landing minimums in the certificate holder's operations specifications for that airport, no person may dispatch or release an aircraft from that airport unless the dispatch or flight release specifies an alternate airport located within the following distances from the airport of takeoff.

1. *Aircraft having two engines: Not more than 1 hour from the departure airport at normal cruising speed in still air with one engine inoperative.*

2. *Aircraft having three or more engines: Not more than 2 hours from the departure airport at normal cruising speed in still air with one engine inoperative.*

(PLT379) — 14 CFR §121.617

Answer (B) is incorrect because 1 hour is correct for a two-engine airplane. Answer (C) is incorrect because it does not contain the words "with one engine inoperative."

ATC Clearances

No one may operate an aircraft in Class A, B, C, D or E airspace under Instrument Flight Rules (IFR) unless he/she has filed an IFR flight plan and received an appropriate ATC clearance. No flight plan or clearance is required for IFR operations in Class G airspace.

IFR clearances always contain:

• A clearance limit (usually the destination);
• Route of flight;
• Altitude assignment; and
• Departure instructions (could be a DP).

The words "cleared as filed" replace only the route of flight portion of a normal clearance. The controller will still state the destination airport, the enroute altitude (or initial altitude and expected final altitude) and DP if appropriate. If a STAR is filed on the flight plan, it is considered part of the enroute portion of the flight plan and is included in the term "cleared as filed."

When an ATC clearance has been received, you may not deviate from it (except in an emergency) unless an amended clearance is received. If you are uncertain of the meaning of an ATC clearance or the clearance appears to be contrary to a regulation, you should immediately request a clarification. When you receive a clearance you should always read back altitude assignments, altitude restrictions, and vectors. A Departure Procedure (DP) may contain these elements but they need not be included in the readback unless the ATC controller specifically states them.

At airports with pretaxi clearance delivery, a pilot should call for the clearance 10 minutes prior to the desired taxi time. After receiving clearance on the clearance delivery frequency, the pilot should call ground control for taxi when ready.

Occasionally, an aircraft with an IFR release will be held on the ground for traffic management reasons. The traffic may be too heavy or weather may be causing ATC delays. If this happens to an aircraft waiting for takeoff, it will be given a hold for release instruction.

Answers

8252 [A]

When ATC can anticipate long delays for IFR aircraft, they will establish gate hold procedures. The idea is to hold aircraft at the gate rather than cause congestion and unnecessary fuel burn on the taxiways while waiting for an IFR release. Ground control will instruct aircraft when to start engines. ATC expects that turbine-powered aircraft will be ready for takeoff as soon as they reach the runway after having been released from gate hold.

When departing uncontrolled airports, IFR flights will often receive a void time with their clearance. The void time is a usually a 30-minute window of time during which the aircraft must takeoff for its IFR clearance to be valid. If unable to comply with the void time, a pilot must receive another clearance with an amended void time.

The flight plan of an airborne IFR aircraft may only be canceled when the aircraft is in VFR weather conditions and outside of Class A airspace.

ALL
9374. A pilot is operating in Class G airspace. If existing weather conditions are below those for VFR flight, an IFR flight plan must be filed and an ATC clearance received prior to

A— takeoff if weather conditions are below IFR minimums.
B— entering controlled airspace.
C— entering IFR weather conditions.

No person may operate an aircraft in Class A, B, C, D or E airspace under IFR unless an IFR flight plan has been filed and an appropriate ATC clearance has been received. (PLT162) — 14 CFR §91.173

Answers (A) and (C) are incorrect because an IFR flight plan and an ATC clearance are not required to fly in IMC (instrument meteorological conditions) in Class G airspace.

ALL
9006. What minimum information does an abbreviated departure clearance "cleared as filed" include?

A— Clearance limit and en route altitude.
B— Clearance limit, transponder code, and DP, if appropriate.
C— Destination airport, en route altitude, transponder code, and DP, if appropriate.

The following apply to "cleared as filed" clearances:

1. *The clearance as issued will include the destination airport filed in the flight plan. "Cleared to (destination) as filed."*

2. *The controller will state the DP name and number.*

3. *STARs, when filed in a flight plan, are considered a part of the filed route of flight and will not normally be stated in an initial clearance.*

4. *An enroute altitude will be stated in the clearance or the pilot will be advised to expect an assigned or filed altitude within a given time frame or at a certain point after departure. This may be done verbally in the departure clearance or stated in the DP.*

(PLT370) — AIM ¶5-2-5

Answer (A) is incorrect because a clearance limit may be a fix, point, or location. An abbreviated clearance will be a clearance to the destination airport. In some cases, a clearance is issued to a fix (limit) from which another clearance limit will be issued. DPs are stated in all IFR departure clearances when appropriate. Answer (B) is incorrect because a clearance will state the destination airport's name, not a clearance limit.

ALL
9439. An ATC "instruction"

A— is the same as an ATC "clearance."
B— is a directive issued by ATC for the purpose of requiring a pilot to take a specific action.
C— must be "read back" in full to the controller and confirmed before becoming effective.

Instructions are directives issued by air traffic control for the purpose of requiring a pilot to take specific actions; e.g., "Turn left heading two five zero," "Go around," "Clear the runway." (PLT370) — Pilot/Controller Glossary

Answer (A) is incorrect because an ATC clearance is not the same as an ATC instruction. Answer (C) is incorrect because an ATC instruction does not have to be read back in full to the controller and confirmed before becoming effective.

Answers
9374 [B]   9006 [C]   9439 [B]

9402. What action should a pilot take when a clearance is received from ATC that appears to be contrary to a regulation?

A— Read the clearance back in its entirety.
B— Request a clarification from ATC.
C— Do not accept the clearance.

If a pilot is uncertain of the meaning of an ATC clearance, he/she shall immediately request clarification from ATC. (PLT444) — 14 CFR §91.123

Answer (A) is incorrect because reading the clearance back in its entirety does not inform ATC of the possible conflict to a regulation. A pilot should actively seek clarification if there is any doubt. Answer (C) is incorrect because not accepting a clearance is not the proper procedure to use when, in a pilot's opinion, it would conflict with a regulation. First, a pilot should receive a clarification from ATC, then ask for an amended clearance, if necessary.

9045. What is the pilot's responsibility for clearance or instruction readback?

A— Except for SIDs, acknowledge altitude assignments, altitude restrictions, and vectors.
B— If the clearance or instruction is understood, an acknowledgment is sufficient.
C— Read back the entire clearance or instruction to confirm the message is understood.

Pilots of airborne aircraft should read back those parts of ATC clearances and instructions containing altitude assignments or vectors. Altitudes contained in charted procedures such as DPs, instrument approaches, etc., should not be read back unless they are specifically stated by the controller. (PLT370) — AIM ¶4-4-7

Answer (B) is incorrect because the best way to know that the clearance or instruction is understood is to read back the "numbers" as a double-check between the pilot and ATC. This reduces the kinds of communication errors that occur when a number is either misheard or is incorrect. Answer (C) is incorrect because the pilot's responsibility is to read back the clearances and instructions containing altitude assignments, altitude restrictions, and vectors, not the entire clearance or instruction.

9008. What is the normal procedure for IFR departures at locations with pretaxi clearance programs?

A— Pilots request IFR clearance when ready to taxi. The pilot will receive taxi instruction with clearance.
B— Pilots request IFR clearance when ready to taxi. Pilots will receive taxi clearance, then receive IFR clearance while taxiing or on runup.
C— Pilots request IFR clearance 10 minutes or less prior to taxi, then request taxi clearance from ground control.

When operating at airports with pretaxi clearance delivery, participating pilots should call clearance delivery or ground control not more than 10 minutes before taxi. When the IFR clearance is received on clearance delivery frequency, pilots should call ground control when ready to taxi. (PLT370) — AIM ¶5-2-1

Answers (A) and (B) are incorrect because the pilot will first be given the IFR clearance, then the taxi instruction or clearance.

9009. What is the purpose of the term "hold for release" when included in an IFR clearance?

A— A procedure for delaying departure for traffic volume, weather, or need to issue further instructions.
B— When an IFR clearance is received by telephone, the pilot will have time to prepare for takeoff prior to being released.
C— Gate hold procedures are in effect and the pilot receives an estimate of the time the flight will be released.

ATC may issue "hold for release" instructions in a clearance to delay an aircraft's departure for traffic management reasons (i.e., weather, traffic volume, etc.). (PLT370) — AIM ¶5-2-6

Answer (B) is incorrect because, when a pilot receives an IFR clearance via telephone, it is normally because he/she is departing from an uncontrolled airport. In this case, ATC would issue a clearance void time, not a hold for release. Answer (C) is incorrect because gate hold procedures are in effect whenever departure delays exceed (or are expected to exceed) 15 minutes. This procedure is not a way for ATC to delay an airplane's departure.

Answers

9402 [B]   9045 [A]   9008 [C]   9009 [A]

ALL

9056. What action should the pilot take when "gate hold" procedures are in effect?

A— Contact ground control prior to starting engines for sequencing.
B— Taxi into position and hold prior to requesting clearance.
C— Start engines, perform pretakeoff check, and request clearance prior to leaving the parking area.

When gate hold procedures are in effect, pilots should contact ground control or clearance delivery prior to starting engines, because departure delays are expected to exceed 15 minutes. (PLT434) — AIM ¶4-3-15

Answer (B) is incorrect because taxi into position means that the pilot is on the active runway and ready for takeoff. This is not a position where ATC would issue an IFR clearance. Answer (C) is incorrect because pilots should contact ground control for sequencing before starting engines.

ALL

9057. What special consideration is given for turbine-powered aircraft when "gate hold" procedures are in effect?

A— They are given preference for departure over other aircraft.
B— They are expected to be ready for takeoff when they reach the runway or warmup block.
C— They are expected to be ready for takeoff prior to taxi and will receive takeoff clearance prior to taxi.

Even with gate holds in effect, the tower controller will consider that pilots of turbine-powered aircraft are ready for takeoff when they reach the runway or warm up block unless advised otherwise. (PLT149) — AIM ¶4-3-15

Answer (A) is incorrect because, when gate hold procedures are in effect, sequencing of all airplanes is based on the initial call-up to ground control or clearance delivery. Answer (C) is incorrect because a pilot of any airplane should be ready to taxi prior to requesting taxi, and takeoff clearance is received prior to takeoff.

ALL

9007. Under what condition does a pilot receive a "void time" specified in the clearance?

A— On an uncontrolled airport.
B— When "gate hold" procedures are in effect.
C— If the clearance is received prior to starting engines.

If operating from an airport not served by a control tower, the pilot may receive a clearance containing a provision that if the flight has not departed by a specific time, the clearance is void. (PLT370) — AIM ¶5-2-6

Answer (B) is incorrect because gate hold procedures are in effect whenever departure delays exceed or are anticipated to exceed 15 minutes. Answer (C) is incorrect because clearances can be issued before starting the airplane's engine(s).

ALL

9005. Under what condition may a pilot cancel an IFR flight plan prior to completing the flight?

A— Anytime it appears the clearance will cause a deviation from FARs.
B— Anytime within controlled airspace by contacting ARTCC.
C— Only if in VFR conditions in other than Class A airspace.

An IFR flight plan may be canceled anytime the flight is operating in VFR conditions outside Class A airspace. (PLT224) — AIM ¶5-1-14

Answer (A) is incorrect because anytime a clearance appears to deviate from a regulation, the pilot should request clarification from ATC and an amended clearance. Answer (B) is incorrect because all aircraft in Class A airspace (above FL180) or when operating in IMC in Class B, C, D or E must be operating under an IFR flight plan.

Answers

9056 [A]   9057 [B]   9007 [A]   9005 [C]

ALL

9737. (Refer to Runway Incursion Figure.) You have requested taxi instructions for takeoff using Runway 16. The controller issues the following taxi instructions: "N123, Taxi to runway 16." Where are you required to stop in order to be in compliance with the controller's instructions?

Runway Incursion

A— 5 (Five).
B— 6 (Six).
C— 9 (Nine).

When ATC clears an aircraft to "taxi to" an assigned takeoff runway, the absence of holding instructions does not authorize the aircraft to "cross" all runways which the taxi route intersects except the assigned takeoff runway. A clearance must be obtained prior to crossing any runway. It does not include authorization to "taxi onto" or "cross" the assigned takeoff runway at any point. You should taxi and hold short of runway 16, which is position 5. (PLT141) — AIM 4-3-18

Answer (B) is incorrect because "taxi to" does not authorize the aircraft to "taxi onto" the assigned takeoff runway. Answer (C) is incorrect because the airplane should taxi the most direct route to the assigned runway unless instructed otherwise; position 9 would not be encountered for the airplane at the west ramp to taxi to runway 16.

ALL

9788. As you call for taxi instructions, the key words to understand are

A— cleared to runway.
B— hold short of or "cross."
C— taxi to and "expedite."

When issuing taxi instructions to any point other than an assigned takeoff runway, ATC will specify the point to taxi to, issue taxi instructions, and state any hold short instructions or runway crossing clearances if the taxi route will cross a runway. (PLT149) — AIM ¶4-3-18

Answer (A) is incorrect because ATC will not use the word "cleared" in conjunction with authorization for aircraft to taxi. Answer (C) is incorrect because "expedite" is not as critical as being told to hold short or cross.

ALL

9789. You received these ATC taxi instructions: "Taxi to Runway 30 via Lima and hold short of Runway 25L". Your airplane is on the ramp by the terminal and NWS on the east side of the airport. Your taxi route

A— requires crossing of Runway 25L at Lima.
B— involves transiting HS 4.
C— requires crossing Runway 34R en route to the assigned runway.

When assigned a takeoff runway, ATC will first specify the runway, issue taxi instructions, and state any hold short instructions or runway crossing clearances if the taxi route will cross a runway. (PLT149) — AIM ¶4-3-18

ALL

9790. As you rolled out long on Runway 30 after landing at Long Beach (LGB) (figures 241 and 242), you slowed and turned left on very wide pavement and now see Taxiway D signs on both sides of your pavement. You notice your heading is about 250°. Tower is urging you to turn left on D, cross 16R/34L, then taxi to G and hold short of Runway 30. You now know you

A— exited onto Runway 25R and transited HS 2.
B— exited onto Taxiway G.
C— exited at Taxiway J and transited HS 4.

The very wide pavement and taxiway D signs on both sides of the pavement indicate you are now on runway 25R in the HS1 and HS2 region. (PLT149) — AIM ¶4-3-18

Answers

9737 [A]   9788 [B]   9789 [A]   9790 [A]

ALL
9818. When should an aircraft depart if issued an EDCT?

A— No earlier than 5 minutes before and no later than 5 minutes after the EDCT.
B— No later than 5 minutes before and no earlier than 5 minutes after the EDCT.
C— No earlier than 15 minutes before and no later than 15 minutes after the EDCT.

The EDCT is the runway release time assigned to an aircraft included in traffic management programs. Aircraft are expected to depart no earlier than 5 minutes before, and no later than 5 minutes after the EDCT. (PLT080) — AIM ¶5-2-6

Takeoff Procedures

Unless otherwise authorized by the FAA, an air carrier flight may not takeoff unless the weather meets the prescribed takeoff minimums for that airport. If takeoff minimums are not published for the airport, the following visibility is required for takeoff:

• For aircraft having two engines or less: 1 statute mile visibility.
• For aircraft having three or more engines: 1/2 statute mile visibility.

If an air carrier flight is going to takeoff from an airport that is not listed in its operations specifications, the pilot must observe the takeoff weather minimums published for that airport. If no takeoff weather minimums are published for that airport, then the pilot must be sure that the ceiling and visibility meet a sliding scale requirement of 800-2 or 900-1-1/2 or 1,000-1.

V_1 is the critical engine failure speed or decision speed. Engine failure below this speed shall result in an aborted takeoff; above this speed the takeoff run should be continued.

V_R is defined as the speed at which the rotation of the aircraft should be initiated to takeoff attitude. Rotation speed (V_R) cannot be less than V_1. If it is greater than V_1 and it is found that, at V_R, rotation cannot be achieved, a subsequent rejected take off may not be possible within the remaining runway length and is likely to result in a Runway Excursion.

ATM, ATS, DSP
9370. When takeoff minimums are not prescribed for a civil airport, what are the takeoff minimums under IFR for a three-engine airplane?

A— 1 SM.
B— 1/2 SM.
C— 300 feet and 1/2 SM.

If takeoff minimums are not prescribed under 14 CFR Part 97, the takeoff minimums under IFR for aircraft having more than two engines are 1/2 statute mile visibility. (PLT421) — 14 CFR §91.175

Answer (A) is incorrect because 1 SM visibility is for aircraft, other than helicopters, having two engines or less. Answer (C) is incorrect because minimum ceilings are not specified for takeoff minimums.

ATM, DSP
8257. An airport is not listed in a domestic Air Carrier's Operations Specifications and does not have the prescribed takeoff weather minimums. What are the minimum weather conditions required for takeoff?

A— 800-2.
B— 900-1.
C— 1000-1/2.

When departing from an alternate airport within the United States which is not listed in the operations specifications, an air carrier must use the 14 CFR Part 97 takeoff minimums. When no takeoff minimums are specified, the air carrier must use a ceiling and visibility of 800-2, 900-1-1/2, or 1,000-1. (PLT398) — 14 CFR §121.637

Answer (B) is incorrect because a 900-foot ceiling requires 1.5 miles visibility. Answer (C) is incorrect because a 1,000-foot ceiling requires 1 mile visibility.

Answers

9818   [A]   9370   [B]   8257   [A]

ATM, DSP

8261. The weather conditions that meet the minimum requirements for a flag air carrier to take off from an alternate airport that is not listed in the Operations Specifications are

A— 800-2, 900-1-1/2, or 1000-1.
B— 800-1/2, 900-1, or 1000-2.
C— 800-1, 900-2, or 1000-3.

When departing from an alternate airport within the United States which is not listed in the operations specifications, an air carrier must use the 14 CFR Part 97 takeoff minimums. When no takeoff minimums are specified, the air carrier must use a ceiling and visibility of 800-2, 900-1-1/2, or 1,000-1. (PLT380) — 14 CFR §121.637

ATM, DSP

8263. The minimum weather conditions that must exist for a domestic air carrier flight to take off from an airport that is not listed in the Air Carrier's Operations Specifications (takeoff minimums are not prescribed for that airport) is

A— 800-2, 1,100-1, or 900-1-1/2.
B— 1,000-1, 900-1-1/4, or 800-2.
C— 1,000-1, 900-1-1/2, or 800-2.

When departing from an alternate airport within the United States which is not listed in the operations specifications, an air carrier must use the 14 CFR Part 97 takeoff minimums. When no takeoff minimums are specified, the air carrier must use a ceiling and visibility of 800-2, 900-1-1/2, or 1,000-1. (PLT459) — 14 CFR §121.637

ATM, DSP

8264. When an alternate airport outside the United States has no prescribed takeoff minimums and is not listed in a Flag Air Carrier's Operations Specifications, the minimum weather conditions that will meet the requirements for takeoff is

A— 800-1-1/2.
B— 600-2.
C— 900-1-1/2.

When departing from an alternate airport outside the United States which is not listed in the operations specifications, an air carrier must use the takeoff minimums approved by the government of the country in which the airport is located. When no takeoff minimums are specified, the air carrier must use a ceiling and visibility of 800-2, 900-1-1/2, or 1,000-1. (PLT380) — 14 CFR §121.637

ALL

9826. (Refer to Figure 177A.) An air carrier is going to depart LWS from RWY 8. There are no special company procedures for this airport. As pilot-in-command you know that at 180 knots ground speed you must be able to climb at

A— 270 feet per minute with one engine inoperative with visibility of 2 miles.
B— 1000 feet per minute with both engines operating with visibility of 1 mile.
C— 810 feet per minute with one engine inoperative with visibility of 2 miles.

The Note in the plan view of the DP requires 900 FPM/200K. 900 FPM at 200K IAS = 810 FPM at 180 knots. (900 FPM / 200K IAS = X FPM / 180 knots; X = 810) To depart on RWY 8 at 180 knots ground speed, you must be able to climb at 810 feet per minute. (PLT380) — FAA-H-8083-15

ALL

9827. (Refer to Figure 177A.) An air carrier is going to depart LWS from RWY 29. There are no special company procedures for this airport. As pilot-in-command you know that at 180 knots ground speed you must be able to climb at

A— 900 fpm with one engine inoperative.
B— 300 fpm with one engine inoperative.
C— 750 fpm with one engine inoperative.

The Note in the plan view of the DP requires 1000 FPM/200K. 1000 FPM at 200K IAS = 900 FPM at 180 knots (1000 FPM / 200K IAS = X FPM / 180 knots; X = 900). To depart on RWY 29 at 180 knots ground speed, you must be able to climb at 900 feet per minute. (PLT380) — FAA-H-8083-15

Answers

8261 [A]	8263 [C]	8264 [C]	9826 [C]	9827 [A]

ATM, DSP

9827-1. You are rolling on takeoff in a 14 CFR Part 25 certified jet and you see an engine oil pressure caution light as you approach V_1. You should

A— continue the takeoff as briefed and handle the illumination as an inflight emergency.

B— promptly abort the takeoff and plan on only having asymmetrical reverse thrust.

C— abort the takeoff and plan for a maximum reverse thrust for deceleration.

V_1 is the critical engine failure speed or decision speed. Engine failure below this speed shall result in an aborted takeoff; above this speed the takeoff run should be continued. (PLT208) — FAA-H-8083-25

ATM, DSP

9827-2. You are rolling on takeoff in a 14 CFR Part 25 certified jet and you see an engine oil pressure caution light as you pass V_1. You should

A— continue the takeoff as briefed and handle the illumination as an inflight emergency.

B— promptly abort the takeoff and plan on only having asymmetrical reverse thrust.

C— abort the takeoff and plan for a maximum reverse thrust for deceleration.

V_1 is the critical engine failure speed or decision speed. Engine failure below this speed shall result in an aborted takeoff; above this speed the takeoff run should be continued. (PLT208) — FAA-H-8083-25

ATM, DSP

9827-3. During takeoff roll with runway remaining, you receive a master caution light after V_R. What action should you take?

A— Reject the takeoff.

B— Hold the nose down to takeoff speed.

C— Continue the takeoff.

V_R is defined as the speed at which the rotation of the aircraft should be initiated to takeoff attitude. V_R or rotation speed cannot be less than V_1. If it is greater than V_1 and it is found that, at V_R, rotation cannot be achieved, a subsequent rejected takeoff may not be possible within the remaining runway length and is likely to result in a runway excursion. In these circumstances (after V_R, runway remaining), you should continue the takeoff. (PLT208) — FAA-H-8083-3

Instrument Approaches

This section is limited to rules and procedures common to most, or all approaches, or procedures that may be used in connection with published instrument approaches.

Contact and visual approaches are both IFR authorizations to proceed to an airport visually. A **visual approach** may be authorized by ATC to reduce pilot or controller workload and to expedite traffic by shortening flight paths to the airport. The weather must be VFR and the pilot must report either the airport or the preceding aircraft in sight. Either the pilot or ATC may initiate a visual approach. A **contact approach** may be initiated only by the pilot. The weather need not be VFR but the aircraft must be clear of the clouds, have at least 1 mile visibility and be able to proceed to the landing airport visually.

When an airport has ILS or MLS approaches to parallel runways at least 4,300 feet apart, ATC may conduct approaches to both runways simultaneously. The pilots will be informed if simultaneous approaches are in progress. To ensure safe separation between aircraft, radar monitoring is provided on the tower frequency. A pilot must report any malfunctioning aircraft receivers if he/she has been informed that simultaneous approaches are in progress.

Occasionally, a pilot will be asked to fly an instrument approach to a runway and then fly a visual "sidestep" maneuver to land on a parallel runway. This sidestep maneuver should be executed as soon as possible after the runway environment is in sight.

Continued

Answers

9827-1   [B]   9827-2   [A]   9827-3   [C]

If a pilot is being radar vectored when an approach clearance is received, he/she must maintain the last assigned altitude until the aircraft is established on a segment of a published route or approach procedure unless a different altitude is assigned by ATC. If a flight is being radar vectored to the final approach course and intercepts a published portion of the course, the pilot may not descend to the published altitudes until cleared for the approach. If a flight has not been cleared for approach while on a radar vector and it becomes apparent that the current vector will take it across the final approach course, the pilot should advise ATC of the situation. Do not turn to intercept the approach course unless cleared to do so.

Unless ATC issues a clearance otherwise, no pilot may make a procedure turn on an instrument approach if any of the following apply:

- The flight is radar vectored to the final approach course or fix
- The flight makes a timed approach from a holding fix
- The approach procedure specifies "No PT"

When the approach procedure involves a procedure turn, a maximum speed of not greater than 200 KIAS should be observed from first overheading the course reversal IAF through the procedure turn maneuver, to ensure containment with the obstruction clearance area.

Except for Category II and III approaches, if RVR minimums for takeoff or landing are prescribed in an instrument approach procedure, but the RVR is not reported for the runway intended, the ground visibilities may be substituted. These may be found in FAA Legend 7.

A pilot may not continue an approach past the final approach fix or on to the final approach segment unless the latest weather report for the airport indicates that the visibility is equal to, or greater than, the visibility required for the approach procedure. If a pilot has begun the final approach segment and then receives a report of below minimum conditions, he/she may continue the approach to the DH or MDA.

To descend below the published DH or MDA on an instrument approach, one of the following must be distinctly visible and identifiable to the pilot:

- Approach light system, except that the pilot may not descend below 100 feet above the touchdown zone elevation using the approach lights as a reference unless the red terminating bars or red side row bars are also distinctly visible and identifiable.
- Threshold
- Threshold markings
- Threshold lights
- Runway end identifier lights
- Visual approach slope indicator
- Touchdown zone or touchdown zone markings
- Touchdown zone lights
- Runway or runway markings
- Runway lights

A pilot must initiate a missed approach from an ILS upon arrival at the DH on the glide slope if none of the required visual references is distinctly visible. If visual contact is lost anytime after descending below the DH but before touchdown, the pilot must start a missed approach.

If a pilot loses visual reference while circling to land from an instrument approach, he/she should follow the missed approach procedure published for the approach used. The pilot should make an initial climbing turn toward the landing runway to establish the aircraft on the missed approach course.

An **Airport Surveillance Radar (ASR)** approach is one in which an ATC radar controller provides directional guidance and distance to the runway information to the pilot. The only airborne equipment required is an operating radio receiver. The controller will tell the pilot when the aircraft is at the missed approach point and give missed approach instructions as required. If the pilot desires to execute a missed approach prior to the missed approach point, he/she should inform the controller, who will then issue missed approach instructions.

Precision Runway Monitor (PRM) is a high update-rate radar surveillance system, certified to provide simultaneous independent approaches to closely-spaced parallel runways.

If there is penetration of the obstacle identification surfaces (OIS), the published approach visibility can be no lower than 3/4 SM.

ALL

9091. What is the difference between a visual and a contact approach?

A— A visual approach is an IFR authorization while a contact approach is a VFR authorization.

B— A visual approach is initiated by ATC while a contact approach is initiated by the pilot.

C— Both are the same but classified according to the party initiating the approach.

Visual approaches are initiated by ATC to reduce pilot/controller workload and expedite traffic. Pilots operating on IFR flight plans may request a contact approach if the appropriate weather conditions exist. (PLT170) — AIM ¶5-4-22, 5-4-24

Answer (A) is incorrect because both a visual and contact approach are initiated from an IFR flight plan. Answer (C) is incorrect because a visual approach is one in which the pilot has a preceding aircraft or the airport in sight and can maintain basic VFR weather minimums. A contact approach is used by a pilot in lieu of conducting a standard or special instrument approach to an airport.

ALL

8953. When simultaneous approaches are in progress, how does each pilot receive radar advisories?

A— On tower frequency.

B— On approach control frequency.

C— One pilot on tower frequency and the other on approach control frequency.

Whenever simultaneous approaches are in progress, radar advisories will be provided on the tower frequency. (PLT420) — AIM ¶5-4-15

Answer (B) is incorrect because pilots will be advised to monitor the tower (not approach control) frequency to receive radar advisories and instructions. Answer (C) is incorrect because both pilots would receive radar advisories on the tower frequency.

ALL

8955. When simultaneous ILS approaches are in progress, which of the following should approach control be advised of immediately?

A— Any inoperative or malfunctioning aircraft receivers.

B— If a simultaneous ILS approach is desired.

C— If radar monitoring is desired to confirm lateral separation.

When advised that simultaneous ILS approaches are in progress, pilots shall advise approach control immediately of malfunctioning or inoperative receivers or if simultaneous approach is not desired. (PLT170) — AIM ¶5-4-15

Answer (B) is incorrect because simultaneous approaches are issued at any time according to ATC needs, and it is not the responsibility of the pilot to request such an approach. Answer (C) is incorrect because radar monitoring is always provided during simultaneous approaches.

ALL

8954. When cleared to execute a published side-step maneuver, at what point is the pilot expected to commence this maneuver?

A— At the published DH.

B— At the MDA published or a circling approach.

C— As soon as possible after the runway environment is in sight.

Pilots are expected to execute the side-step maneuver as soon as possible after the runway or runway environment is in sight. (PLT083) — AIM ¶5-4-19

Answers (A) and (B) are incorrect because the side-step maneuver can only be performed and should be performed as soon as possible after the runway or runway environment is in sight.

Answers

| 9091 | [B] | 8953 | [A] | 8955 | [A] | 8954 | [C] |

ALL

9438. When cleared to execute a published side-step maneuver for a specific approach and landing on the parallel runway, at what point is the pilot expected to commence this maneuver?

A— At the published minimum altitude for a circling approach.

B— As soon as possible after the runway or runway environment is in sight.

C— At the localizer MDA minimums and when the runway is in sight.

Pilots are expected to execute the side-step maneuver as soon as possible after the runway or runway environment is in sight. (PLT170) — AIM ¶5-4-19

Answers (A) and (C) are incorrect because the maneuver should be started as soon as the runway environment is in sight not at a DH or MDA of an approach.

ALL

9037. While being vectored to the final approach course of an IFR approach, when may the pilot descend to published altitudes?

A— Anytime the flight is on a published leg of an approach chart.

B— When the flight is within the 10-mile ring of a published approach.

C— Only when approach control clears the flight for the approach.

When operating on an unpublished route or while being radar vectored, the pilot, when approach clearance is received, in addition to complying with the minimum altitudes for IFR operations, shall maintain the last assigned altitude unless a different altitude is assigned by ATC, or until the aircraft is established on a segment of published route or IAP. This implies that even if a radar vector should happen to put a flight on a published route, the pilot may not descend until cleared for the approach. (PLT420) — AIM ¶5-4-7

Answer (A) is incorrect because you may only descend if cleared. Answer (B) is incorrect because the 10-mile ring has nothing to do with descent clearance.

ALL

9383. What action should be taken when a pilot is "cleared for approach" while being radar vectored on an unpublished route?

A— Descend to minimum vector altitude.

B— Remain at last assigned altitude until established on a published route segment.

C— Descend to initial approach fix altitude.

When operating on an unpublished route or while being radar vectored, the pilot, when an approach clearance is received, shall maintain the last altitude assigned until the aircraft is established on a segment of a published route or instrument approach procedure, unless a different altitude is assigned by ATC. (PLT421) — 14 CFR §91.175

Answer (A) is incorrect because a pilot should maintain the last altitude assigned by ATC and should use the minimum vector altitude only during lost communication procedures. Answer (C) is incorrect because a pilot should maintain the last altitude assigned by ATC.

ALL

9385. What altitude is a pilot authorized to fly when cleared for an ILS approach? The pilot

A— may begin a descent to the procedure turn altitude.

B— must maintain the last assigned altitude until established on a published route or segment of the approach with published altitudes.

C— may descend from the assigned altitude only when established on the final approach course.

When operating on an unpublished route or while being radar vectored, the pilot, when an approach clearance is received, shall maintain the last altitude assigned until the aircraft is established on a segment of a published route or instrument approach procedure, unless a different altitude is assigned by ATC. (PLT421) — 14 CFR §91.175

Answer (A) is incorrect because descent to the procedure turn altitude can be commenced only when you are established on that route segment or instrument approach. Answer (C) is incorrect because the pilot does not have to be established on the final approach course to descend from the last assigned altitude, if established on a published route segment with a specified lower minimum altitude than the last assigned altitude.

Answers

9438 [B]   9037 [C]   9383 [B]   9385 [B]

ALL

9036. What action(s) should a pilot take if vectored across the final approach course during an IFR approach?

A— Continue on the last heading issued until otherwise instructed.
B— Contact approach control, and advise that the flight is crossing the final approach course.
C— Turn onto final, and broadcast in the blind that the flight has proceeded on final.

Aircraft will normally be informed when it is necessary to vector across the final approach course for spacing or other reasons. If approach course crossing is imminent and the pilot has not been informed that he will be vectored across the final approach course, he should query the controller. (PLT420) — AIM ¶5-4-3

Answer (A) is incorrect because the pilot should maintain last heading issued, but should also advise approach control that the flight is crossing the final approach course. Answer (C) is incorrect because a pilot should broadcast in the blind that the flight has turned onto final when operating VFR at an uncontrolled airport.

ALL

9369. If being radar vectored to the final approach course of a published instrument approach that specifies "NO PT," the pilot should

A— advise ATC that a procedure turn will not be executed.
B— not execute the procedure turn unless specifically cleared to do so by ATC.
C— execute a holding-pattern type procedure turn.

In the case of a radar vector to a final approach course or fix, a timed approach from a holding fix, or an approach for which the approach procedure specifies "NoPT," no pilot may make a procedure turn unless cleared to do so by ATC. (PLT420) — 14 CFR §91.175

Answer (A) is incorrect because a procedure turn is not authorized or expected to be executed for this instrument approach; therefore, advising ATC of your intention to omit a procedure turn is not necessary. Answer (C) is incorrect because if the published instrument approach specifies "NoPT," you should follow the published procedure rather than automatically reverting to a holding-pattern-type procedure turn.

ALL

9021. When the approach procedure involves a procedure turn the maximum speed that should be observed from first overheading the course reversal IAF through the procedure turn is

A— 180 knots IAS.
B— 200 knots TAS.
C— 200 knots IAS.

When the approach procedure involves a procedure turn, a maximum speed of not greater than 200 knots (IAS) should be observed from first overheading the course reversal IAF through the procedure turn maneuver, to ensure containment within the obstruction clearance area. (PLT420) — AIM ¶5-4-9

ALL

9391. What minimum ground visibility may be used instead of a prescribed visibility criteria of RVR 16 when that RVR value is not reported?

A— 1/4 SM.
B— 3/4 SM.
C— 1/2 SM.

RVR minimum may be converted to ground visibility using FAA Legend 7. (PLT420) — 14 CFR §91.175

ALL

9392. The prescribed visibility criteria of RVR 32 for the runway of intended operation is not reported. What minimum ground visibility may be used instead of the RVR value?

A— 3/8 SM.
B— 5/8 SM.
C— 3/4 SM.

RVR minimum may be converted to ground visibility using FAA Legend 7. (PLT420) — 14 CFR §91.175

ALL

9393. The visibility criteria for a particular instrument approach procedure is RVR 40. What minimum ground visibility may be substituted for the RVR value?

A— 5/8 SM.
B— 3/4 SM.
C— 7/8 SM.

RVR minimum may be converted to ground visibility using FAA Legend 7. (PLT420) — 14 CFR §91.175

Answers

9036 [B]	9369 [B]	9021 [C]	9391 [A]	9392 [B]	9393 [B]

ALL

9384. Under which condition, if any, may a pilot descend below DH or MDA when using the ALSF-1 approach light system as the primary visual reference for the intended runway?

A— Under no condition can the approach light system serve as a necessary visual reference for descent below DH or MDA.
B— Descent to the intended runway is authorized as long as any portion of the approach light system can be seen.
C— The approach light system can be used as a visual reference, except that descent below 100 feet above TDZE requires that the red light bars be visible and identifiable.

A pilot may descend below the MDA or DH using the approach light system as the sole visual reference. However, the pilot may not descend below 100 feet above touchdown zone elevation (TDZE) using the approach lights as a reference unless the red terminating bars or the red side row bars are also distinctly visible and identifiable. (PLT420) — 14 CFR §91.175

Answer (A) is incorrect because approach lighting systems can be used as a reference below the DH or MDA up to 100 feet above the TDZE, at which point the red terminating bars must be in sight. Answer (B) is incorrect because the approach lighting system can only be used to within 100 feet of the TDZE, at which point the red side row bars must be in sight.

ALL

8726. (Refer to Figure 310.) What is the required minimum reported weather to initiate the ILS Rwy 9L approach at PHL in your CAT C turbine-powered airplane with no MEL items?

A— Ceiling at least 200 feet and RVR 2400.
B— Ceiling 300 feet minimum.
C— Visibility 1800 RVR.

The approach plates notes a minimum RVR of 1800 in the top left portion of the approach plate. (PLT420) — Instrument Approach Procedures

ALL

9368. When must the pilot initiate a missed approach procedure from an ILS approach?

A— At the DA/DH when the runway is not clearly visible.
B— When the time has expired after reaching the DA/DH and the runway environment is not clearly visible.
C— At the DA/DH, if the visual references for the intended runway are not distinctly visible or anytime thereafter that visual reference is lost.

A pilot must initiate a missed approach procedure from an ILS approach at the DA/DH, if the required visual references for intended runway are not distinctly visible or anytime thereafter if visual reference is lost. (PLT420) — 14 CFR §91.175

Answer (A) is incorrect because the runway itself does not have to be visible at the DA/DH to continue with the approach; a pilot may use the required visual references. Answer (B) is incorrect because as soon as the DA/DH is reached on an ILS approach, regardless of the elapsed time, a missed approach procedure should be executed if visual references are not obtained, or any time thereafter that visual reference is lost.

ALL

9382. Assuming that all ILS components are operating and the required visual references are not acquired, the missed approach should be initiated upon

A— arrival at the DH on the glide slope.
B— arrival at the visual descent point.
C— expiration of the time listed on the approach chart for missed approach.

A pilot must initiate a missed approach procedure from an ILS approach at the DH, if the required visual references for intended runway are not distinctly visible or any time thereafter if visual reference is lost. (PLT356) — 14 CFR §91.175

Answer (B) is incorrect because a visual descent point is a point in which an aircraft operating visually can descend from a specified altitude to the runway and land. If on an ILS approach and no visual flight is encountered, a missed approach should be executed at the DH. Answer (C) is incorrect because time listed on the approach chart is used only if the glide slope were to fail. If the aircraft reaches the DH prior to the time listed on the chart, the pilot should execute a missed approach.

Answers

9384   [C]   8726   [C]   9368   [C]   9382   [A]

ALL

9041. When may a pilot execute a missed approach during an ASR approach?

A— Anytime at the pilot's discretion.
B— Only at the MAP.
C— Only when advised by the controller.

Controllers will terminate guidance on an ASR approach and instruct the pilot to execute a missed approach unless at the MAP, the pilot has the runway or airport in sight. Also, if at any time during an ASR approach the controller considers that safe guidance for the remainder of the approach cannot be provided, he will terminate the approach and instruct the pilot to execute a missed approach. A missed approach will also be effected upon pilot request. (PLT420) — AIM ¶5-4-10

Answer (B) is incorrect because the controller will instruct the pilot to execute a missed approach at the MAP or anytime during the approach that the controller considers that safe guidance cannot be provided. Answer (C) is incorrect because a missed approach will be effected upon pilot request.

ALL

9090-1. If visual reference is lost while circling to land from an instrument approach, what action(s) should the pilot take?

A— Make a climbing turn toward the landing runway until established on the missed approach course.
B— Turn toward the landing runway maintaining MDA, and if visual reference is not regained, perform missed approach.
C— Make a climbing turn toward the VOR/NDB, and request further instructions.

If visual reference is lost while circling to land from an instrument approach, the missed approach specified for that particular procedure must be followed. To become established on the prescribed missed approach course, the pilot should make an initial climbing turn toward the landing runway and continue the turn until he is established on the missed approach course. (PLT170) — AIM ¶5-4-21

Answer (B) is incorrect because while turning toward the runway, a climbing turn should be established. Answer (C) is incorrect because a pilot should make a climbing turn toward the runway to ensure obstacle clearance while becoming established on the missed approach course.

ALL

9090-2. Precision Runway Monitoring (PRM) is

A— an airborne RADAR system for monitoring approaches to two runways.
B— a RADAR system for monitoring approaches to closely spaced parallel runways.
C— a high update rate RADAR system for monitoring multiple aircraft ILS approaches to a single runway.

Precision Runway Monitoring (PRM) is a high update-rate radar surveillance system, certified to provide simultaneous independent approaches to closely spaced parallel runways. (PLT172) — FAA-H-8083-16

Answer (A) is incorrect because PRM is not an airborne radar system; it is ground based. Answer (C) is incorrect because PRM monitors simultaneous approaches to two closely spaced parallel runways.

ALL

9760. Precision runway monitoring requires

A— pilot responsibility to monitor 2 simultaneous radios.
B— pilot responsibility to monitor 2 ILS receivers.
C— detailed performance during the "decision region": 1/3 dot localizer and 1/2 dot glideslope.

The aircraft flying the ILS/PRM or LDA/PRM approach must have the capability of enabling the pilots to listen to two communications frequencies simultaneously. (PLT172) — AIM ¶5-4-16

Answers

| 9041 | [A] | 9090-1 | [A] | 9090-2 | [B] | 9760 | [A] |

ALL

9090-3. How can the pilot determine, for an ILS runway equipped with MALSR, that there may be penetration of the obstacle identification surfaces (OIS), and care should be taken in the visual segment to avoid any obstacles?

A— The runway has a visual approach slope indicator (VASI).
B— The published visibility for the ILS is no lower than 3/4 SM.
C— The approach chart has a visual descent point (VDP) published.

The visibility published on an approach chart is dependent on many variables, including the height above touchdown for straight-in approaches, or height above airport elevation for circling approaches. Other factors include the approach light system coverage, and type of approach procedure, such as precision, nonprecision, circling or straight-in. Another factor determining the minimum visibility is the penetration of the 34:1 and 20:1 surfaces. These surfaces are inclined planes that begin 200 feet out from the runway and extend outward to 10,000 feet. If there is a penetration of the 34:1 surface, the published visibility can be no lower than 3/4 SM. If there is penetration of the 20:1 surface, the published visibility can be no lower than 1 SM with a note prohibiting approaches to the affected runway at night (both straight-in and circling). Pilots should be aware of these penetrating obstacles when entering the visual and/or circling segments of an approach and take adequate precautions to avoid them. (PLT170) — FAA-H-8083-16

Answers (A) and (C) are incorrect because a VASI or VDP are not indicators to a possible penetration of the OIS.

ALL

9738. To conduct a localizer performance with vertical guidance (LPV) RNAV (GPS) approach, the aircraft must be furnished with

A— a GPS/WAAS receiver approved for an LPV approach by the AFM supplement.
B— a GPS (TSO-129) receiver certified for IFR operations.
C— an IFR approach-certified system with required navigation performance (RNP) of 0.5.

"LPV" is the acronym for localizer performance with vertical guidance. LPV identifies the APV minimums with electronic lateral and vertical guidance. The lateral guidance is equivalent to localizer, and the protected area is considerably smaller than the protected area for the present LNAV and LNAV/VNAV lateral protection. Aircraft can fly this minima line with a statement in the Aircraft Flight Manual that the installed equipment supports LPV approaches. This includes Class 3 and 4 TSO-C146 WAAS equipment, and future LAAS equipment. (PLT354) — AIM ¶5-4-5

ALL

9744. Pilots are not authorized to fly a published RNAV or RNP procedure unless it is retrievable by the procedure name from

A— the aircraft navigation database, or manually loaded with each individual waypoint in the correct sequence.
B— the aircraft navigation database, or manually loaded with each individual waypoint and verified by the pilot(s).
C— the aircraft navigation database.

Pilots are not authorized to fly a published RNAV or RNP procedure (instrument approach, departure, or arrival procedure) unless it is retrievable by the procedure name from the aircraft navigation database and conforms to the charted procedure. (PLT354) — AIM ¶5-5-16

ALL

9744-1. GBAS approaches are

A— flown using the same techniques as an ILS once selected and identified.
B— flown the same as an LDA with glide slope tuning and identification.
C— automatically tuned and displayed after selection of the three character procedure identifier.

GBAS is a ground-based augmentation to GPS that focuses its service on the airport area (approximately a 20-30 mile radius) for precision approach, departure procedures, and terminal area operations. GBAS is the ICAO term for Local Area Augmentation System (LAAS). LAAS was developed as an "ILS look-alike" system from the pilot perspective. (PLT354) — AIM ¶1-1-21

Answers

9090-3 [B]   9738 [A]   9744 [C]   9744-1 [A]

ALL

9773. Pilots are responsible for knowing

A— if they can conduct an RNP approach with an arc at a designated airspeed.

B— if the RNP missed approach is normal or reduced.

C— if the RNP registration is complete.

Some RNP approaches have a curved path, also called a radius-to-a-fix (RF) leg. Since not all aircraft have the capability to fly these arcs, pilots are responsible for knowing whether or not they can conduct an RNP approach with an arc. (PLT300) — AIM ¶5-4-18

ATM, DSP

8279. Under what conditions may an air carrier pilot continue an instrument approach to the DH, after receiving a weather report indicating that less than minimum published landing conditions exist at the airport?

A— If the instrument approach is conducted in a radar environment.

B— When the weather report is received as the pilot passes the FAF.

C— When the weather report is received after the pilot has begun the final approach segment of the instrument approach.

If a pilot has begun the final approach segment of an instrument approach procedure with the reported weather at or above landing minimums and later receives a report indicating below minimum conditions, he may continue the approach to DH or MDA. The pilot may land from that approach if he discovers that the visibility is at least that required by the approach, he/she has the required visual references in sight and a normal descent and landing can be made. (PLT420) — 14 CFR §121.651

ALL

9817. When executing a stabilized approach, you should use

A— no more than 1000 FPM rate of descent for a non-precision or precision approach from 1,000 feet above the airport or TDZE.

B— no more than 1000 FPM for a precision approach or 1200 FPM for a non-precision approach.

C— no more than 800 FPM for a non-precision approach or 1000 FPM for a precision approach.

For all straight-in-instrument approaches in IFR weather conditions, the approach must be stabilized (descent rate of less than 1,000 fpm) before descending below 1,000 feet above the airport or TDZE. (PLT420) — FAA-H-8083-16

ALL

8736. (Refer to Figure 1.) What does the 20:1 ratio represent?

A— Displaced threshold.

B— Final approach fix.

C— Obstacle clearance surface (OCS).

The obstacle clearance surface (OCS). The OCS used to evaluate the missed approach is a 20:1 inclined plane. This surface is twice as steep for the helicopter as the OCS used to evaluate the airplane missed approach segment. (PLT170) — FAA-H-8083-16

Answers

9773 [A]   8279 [C]   9817 [A]   8736 [C]

Landing

Except for emergencies, the landing priority of aircraft arriving at a tower controlled airport is on "first-come, first-served" basis. When landing at a tower controlled airport, an aircraft should exit the runway at the first suitable taxiway and remain on the tower frequency until instructed to do otherwise. The aircraft should not turn onto any other taxiway unless a clearance to do so has been received.

If a flight is making an IFR approach at an uncontrolled airport, radar service will be terminated when the aircraft lands or when the controller tells the pilot to change to advisory frequency. After changing to the advisory frequency, the pilot should broadcast his/her intentions and continually update position reports. The advisory frequency will be an FSS frequency, or if there is no FSS on the field, a UNICOM frequency.

ATC furnishes pilots' braking action reports using the terms good, good to medium, medium, medium to poor, or nil. If you give a braking action report to ATC, you should use the same terminology.

ALL

9092. Except during an emergency, when can a pilot expect landing priority?

A— When cleared for an IFR approach.
B— When piloting a large, heavy aircraft.
C— In turn, on a first-come, first-serve basis.

Air Traffic Control towers handle all aircraft, regardless of the type of flight plan, on a "first-come, first-served" basis. (PLT170) — AIM ¶5-4-25

Answer (A) is incorrect because a clearance for an IFR approach does not mean landing priority will be given over other traffic. Answer (B) is incorrect because a large, heavy aircraft will be sequenced for landing on a first-come, first-served basis, with no special priority over other traffic.

ALL

9044. What action is expected of an aircraft upon landing at a controlled airport?

A— Continue taxiing in the landing direction until advised by the tower to switch to ground control frequency.
B— Exit the runway at the nearest suitable taxiway and remain on tower frequency until instructed otherwise.
C— Exit the runway at the nearest suitable taxiway and switch to ground control upon crossing the taxiway holding lines.

After landing, unless otherwise instructed by the control tower, continue to taxi in the landing direction, proceed to the nearest suitable taxiway and exit the runway without delay. Do not turn on another runway or make a 180° turn to taxi back on an active runway or change to ground control frequency while on the active runway without authorization from the tower. A pilot who has just landed should not change from the tower frequency to the ground control frequency until he is directed to do so by the controller. (PLT434) — AIM ¶4-3-20

Answer (A) is incorrect because upon landing, the pilot should exit the runway at the nearest suitable taxiway to clear the runway for other traffic. Answer (C) is incorrect because while the crossing of the taxiway hold lines indicates clearing of the active runway, a pilot should not switch to ground control until directed to do so by the controller. Switching without permission may be confusing to ATC.

ALL

9038. When is radar service terminated while vectored for an IFR approach at an uncontrolled airport?

A— Only upon landing or advised to change to advisory frequency.
B— When aligned on the final approach course.
C— When cleared for the approach.

Whether aircraft are vectored to the appropriate final approach course or provide their own navigation on published routes to it, radar service is automatically terminated when the landing is completed or when instructed to change to advisory frequency at uncontrolled airports, whichever occurs first. (PLT420) — AIM ¶5-4-3

Answer (B) is incorrect because when established on the final approach course, radar separation will be maintained and the pilot is expected to complete the approach utilizing the approach aid designated in the clearance (ILS, VOR, etc.). Answer (C) is incorrect because when cleared for the approach, approach control will continue to maintain radar separation and the pilot is expected to complete the approach utilizing the approach aid designated in the clearance (ILS, VOR, etc.).

Answers

9092   [C]   9044   [B]   9038   [A]

ALL

9039. When cleared for an IFR approach to an uncontrolled airport with no FSS, what precaution should the pilot take after being advised to change to advisory frequency?

A— Monitor ATC for traffic advisories as well as UNICOM.

B— Broadcast position and intentions on the Common Traffic Advisory Frequency and monitor the frequency.

C— Wait until visual contact is made with the airport and then broadcast position and intentions to land on UNICOM.

When making an IFR approach to an airport not served by a tower or FSS, after the ATC controller advises, "CHANGE TO ADVISORY FREQUENCY APPROVED" you should broadcast your intentions, including the type of approach being executed, your position, and when you are over the outer marker or final approach fix. Continue to monitor the appropriate frequency (UNICOM, etc.) for reports from other pilots. (PLT170) — AIM ¶5-4-4

Answer (A) is incorrect because after ATC advises the pilot to change to advisory frequency, ATC will no longer be able to provide traffic advisories. Answer (C) is incorrect because a pilot should always broadcast intentions and continually update position reports on UNICOM, not wait until visual contact is made with airport.

ALL

9055. How should a pilot describe braking action?

A— 00 percent, 50 percent, 75 percent, or 100 percent.

B— Zero-zero, fifty-fifty, or normal.

C— Good, good to medium, medium, medium to poor, or nil.

Pilots should describe the quality of braking action by using the terms good, good to medium, medium, medium to poor, or nil. (PLT144) — AIM ¶4-3-8

ATM, ATS, DSP

9005-1. A landing weight increase of 10% will result in a landing distance increase of approximately

A— 7%.

B— 10%.

C— 15%.

The minimum landing distance will vary directly as the gross weight varies. For example, a 10% increase in gross weight at landing would cause a 5% increase in landing velocity and a 10% increase in landing distance. (PLT247) — ANA

ATM, ATS, DSP

9005-2. A landing weight increase of 10% will result in

A— 7% increase in kinetic energy.

B— 21% increase in kinetic energy.

C— 33% increase in kinetic energy.

As an example of measuring the effectiveness of aircraft brakes, a 30,000-pound aircraft landing at 175 knots has a kinetic energy of 41,000,000 ft-lbs at the instant of touchdown. While a 10% increase in landing weight causes a 5% higher landing speed and a 10% greater landing distance, it also produces a 21% increase in the kinetic energy of the airplane to be dissipated during the landing roll. (PLT247) — ANA

Communications

The "Sterile Cockpit" Rule: Regulations say only those duties required for the safe operation of the aircraft are allowed during critical phases of flight. Critical phases of flight are defined as climb and descent when below 10,000 feet, taxi, takeoff, and landing. Excluded from the definition of critical phase of flight are any operations at or above 10,000 feet and cruise flight below 10,000 feet. Activities which are prohibited during critical phases of flight include filling out logs, ordering galley supplies, making passenger announcements or pointing out sights of interest. Activities such as eating meals or engaging in nonessential conversations are also prohibited.

The following should be reported without ATC request:

• Vacating a previously assigned altitude for a newly assigned one.

• An altitude change when operating under a VFR-On-Top clearance.

• When unable to climb or descend at a rate of at least 500 feet per minute.

Continued

Answers

9039 [B]	9055 [C]	9005-1 [B]	9005-2 [B]

- When an approach has been missed.
- A change in cruising true airspeed of 10 knots or 5%, whichever is greater.
- The time and altitude (or Flight Level) upon reaching a holding fix or clearance limit.
- When leaving an assigned holding fix or point.
- The malfunction of navigation, approach or communication equipment.
- Any information pertaining to the safety of flight.

In addition to the reports listed above, when not in radar contact a pilot must report:
- When over designated compulsory reporting points.
- When leaving the final approach fix inbound on an instrument approach.
- When it becomes apparent that an estimate of arrival time over a fix is in error by more than 3 minutes.

Occasionally an ATC controller will query a pilot about the aircraft's altitude or course. For example, a controller says "Verify 9000," meaning he/she wants confirmation that the aircraft is at 9,000 feet altitude. If the aircraft is not at that altitude, the pilot should reply, "Negative, maintaining 8,000 as assigned." No climb or descent should be started unless specifically assigned by the controller.

Pilots should notify controllers on initial contact that they have received the ATIS broadcast by repeating the alphabetical code used appended to the broadcast. For example, "Information Sierra received."

ALL
8854. What report should the pilot make at a clearance limit?

A— Time and altitude/flight level arriving or leaving.
B— Time, altitude/flight level, and expected holding speed.
C— Time, altitude/flight level, expected holding speed, and inbound leg length.

Pilots should report to ATC the time and altitude/flight level at which the aircraft reaches the clearance limit, and report when leaving the clearance limit. (PLT171) — AIM ¶5-3-2

Answer (B) is incorrect because ATC does not need the expected holding speed reported since it will be below the maximum holding airspeed. For all aircraft between MHA and 6,000 feet MSL, holding speed is 200 KIAS; for all aircraft between 6,001 and 14,000 feet MSL, holding speed is 230 KIAS; for all aircraft 14,001 feet MSL and above, holding speed is 265 KIAS. For turbojet airplanes, the maximum holding airspeed is 230 knots IAS from minimum holding altitude to 14,000 feet. Answer (C) is incorrect because inbound leg lengths are set by time or DME distance. At or below 14,000 feet MSL there is a 1-minute inbound leg. Above 14,000 feet MSL the inbound leg is 1-1/2 minutes.

ALL
9014. Where are position reports required on an IFR flight on airways or routes?

A— Over all designated compulsory reporting points.
B— Only where specifically requested by ARTCC.
C— When requested to change altitude or advise of weather conditions.

A position report is required by all flights regardless of altitude over each designated compulsory reporting point along the route being flown.

Note: When the controller states "radar contact," this requirement is removed. However, the question states nothing about being in "radar contact." (PLT421) — AIM ¶5-3-2

Answer (B) is incorrect because the "on request" reporting point is indicated on enroute charts by an open triangle. Reports passing an "on request" reporting point are only necessary when requested by ARTCC. Answer (C) is incorrect because pilots in IFR are expected to report weather conditions which have not been forecast, or hazardous conditions which have been forecast.

Answers

8854   [A]   9014   [A]

ALL

9015. Which reports are required when operating IFR in radar environment?

A— Position reports, vacating an altitude, unable to climb 500 ft/min, and time and altitude reaching a holding fix or point to which cleared.

B— Position reports, vacating an altitude, unable to climb 500 ft/min, time and altitude reaching a holding fix or point to which cleared, and a change in average true airspeed exceeding 5 percent or 10 knots.

C— Vacating an altitude, unable to climb 500 ft/min, time and altitude reaching a holding fix or point to which cleared, a change in average true airspeed exceeding 5 percent or 10 knots, and leaving any assigned holding fix or point.

The following reports should be made to ATC or FSS facilities without specific ATC request:

1. *Vacating any previously assigned altitude.*

2. *Making an altitude change when VFR-On-Top.*

3. *Unable to climb or descend at least 500 feet per minute.*

4. *Making a missed approach.*

5. *Changing true airspeed from flight plan by 5% or 10 knots (whichever is greater).*

6. *Time and altitude of reaching a clearance holding fix or point.*

7. *Leaving any holding fix.*

(PLT171) — AIM ¶5-3-3

Answers (A) and (B) are incorrect because position reports are not required in a radar environment.

ALL

9016. Which reports are always required when on an IFR approach not in radar contact?

A— Leaving FAF inbound or outer marker inbound and missed approach.

B— Leaving FAF inbound, leaving outer marker inbound or outbound, and missed approach.

C— Leaving FAF inbound, leaving outer marker inbound or outbound, procedure turn outbound and inbound, and visual contact with the runway.

The following reports should be made when not in radar contact:

1. *When over designated compulsory reporting points*

2. *When leaving the final approach fix inbound*

3. *When it becomes apparent that an ETA is in error by more than 3 minutes.*

(PLT171) — AIM ¶5-3-3

Answer (B) is incorrect because a pilot is required to report leaving the outer marker inbound on final approach. Answer (C) is incorrect because a pilot is not required to report leaving the outer marker outbound, the execution of a procedure turn, and/or visual contact with the runway.

ALL

9013. What action should a pilot take if asked by ARTCC to "VERIFY 9,000" and the flight is actually maintaining 8,000?

A— Immediately climb to 9,000.

B— Report climbing to 9,000.

C— Report maintaining 8,000.

At times controllers will ask pilots to verify that they are at a particular altitude. Pilots should confirm that they are at the altitude stated. If this is not the case, they should inform the controller of the actual altitude being maintained. Pilots should not take action to change their actual altitude to the altitude stated in the controller's verification request unless the controller specifically authorizes a change. (PLT171) — AIM ¶5-3-1

Answers (A) and (B) are incorrect because pilots should not take action to change their actual altitude to the altitude stated in the controller's verification request unless the controller specifically authorizes a change.

ALL

9022. Pilots should notify controllers on initial contact that they have received the ATIS broadcast by

A— stating "Have Numbers".

B— stating "Have Weather".

C— repeating the alphabetical code word appended to the broadcast.

Pilots should notify controllers on initial contact that they have received the ATIS broadcast by repeating the alphabetical code word appended to the broadcast. For example, "Information Sierra received." (PLT196) — AIM ¶4-1-13

Answers

9015 [C]   9016 [A]   9013 [C]   9022 [C]

ALL

9022-1. While holding short for an intersection takeoff runway 36 at taxiway C, tower clears you to "line up and wait runway 36." You should

A— line up and wait for takeoff on taxiway C.
B— line up and wait on runway 36 at intersection C for departure.
C— hold short and advise tower that you are at intersection C short of runway 36.

"Line up and wait" is an ATC phrase used to instruct pilots to taxi onto the departure runway, line up, and wait for imminent departure. (PLT171) — AIM Chapter 5

ATM, DSP

8297. Below what altitude, except when in cruise flight, are non-safety related cockpit activities by flight crewmembers prohibited?

A— 10,000 feet.
B— 14,500 feet.
C— FL 180.

No certificate holder shall require, nor may any flight crewmember perform, any duties during a critical phase of flight except those duties required for the safe operation of the aircraft. For purposes of this section, critical phases of flight include all ground operations involving taxi, takeoff and landing, and all other flight operations conducted below 10,000 feet, except cruise flight. (PLT430) — 14 CFR §121.542

ATM, DSP

8298. With regard to flight crewmember duties, which of the following operations are considered to be in the "critical phase of flight"?

A— Taxi, takeoff, landing, and all other operations conducted below 10,000 feet MSL, including cruise flight.
B— Descent, approach, landing, and taxi operations, irrespective of altitudes MSL.
C— Taxi, takeoff, landing, and all other operations conducted below 10,000 feet, excluding cruise flight.

No certificate holder shall require, nor may any flight crewmember perform, any duties during a critical phase of flight except those duties required for the safe operation of the aircraft. For purposes of this section, critical phases of flight include all ground operations involving taxi, takeoff and landing, and all other flight operations conducted below 10,000 feet, except cruise flight. (PLT029) — 14 CFR §121.542

Answer (A) is incorrect because critical phase of flight includes all operations (except cruise flight) below 10,000 feet. Answer (B) is incorrect because 14,500 feet is the base of Class E airspace (if not set lower).

Speed Adjustments

ATC controllers often issue speed adjustments to radar controlled aircraft to achieve or maintain the desired separation. The following minimum speeds are usually observed:

• Turbine-powered aircraft below 10,000 feet: 210 knots.

• Turbine-powered aircraft departing an airport: 230 knots.

If an ATC controller assigns a speed which is too fast or too slow for the operating limitations of the aircraft under the existing circumstances, the pilot should advise ATC of the speed that will be used. The controller will then issue instructions based on that speed.

Because of the great differences in speed and operating characteristics of helicopters and airplanes, they are usually assigned different routing. Occasionally, larger/faster helicopters are integrated with fixed-wing aircraft. These situations could occur on IFR flights, routes that avoid noise-sensitive areas, or when the helicopter is assigned runways or taxiways to avoid downwash in congested areas.

Answers

9022-1   [B]   8297   [A]   8298   [C]

ALL

9094. When a speed adjustment is necessary to maintain separation, what minimum speed may ATC request of a turbine-powered aircraft operating below 10,000 feet?

A— 200 knots.
B— 210 knots.
C— 250 knots.

When a speed adjustment is necessary to maintain separation, the minimum airspeed for a turbine-powered aircraft operated below 10,000 feet is 210 knots. (PLT161) — AIM ¶4-4-12

Answer (A) is incorrect because 200 knots is the maximum airspeed of any airplane operating within Class C or D airspace, a VFR-designated corridor through Class B airspace, or in airspace underlying Class B airspace. Answer (C) is incorrect because 250 knots is the maximum airspeed of any airplane operating below 10,000 feet MSL.

ALL

9095. When a speed adjustment is necessary to maintain separation, what minimum speed may ATC request of a turbine-powered aircraft departing an airport?

A— 188 knots.
B— 210 knots.
C— 230 knots.

When a speed adjustment is necessary to maintain separation, the minimum airspeed for a turbine-powered aircraft on departure is 230 knots. (PLT161) — AIM ¶4-4-12

Answer (A) is incorrect because 188 knots is not an applicable airspeed for any ATC operation. All airspeeds used by ATC/regulations are expressed in 10-knot increments. Answer (B) is incorrect because it is the minimum airspeed that ATC can request of a turbine-powered airplane operating below 10,000 feet, excluding departing airplanes.

ALL

9096. If ATC requests a speed adjustment that is not within the operating limits of the aircraft, what action must the pilot take?

A— Maintain an airspeed within the operating limitations as close to the requested speed as possible.
B— Attempt to use the requested speed as long as possible, then request a reasonable airspeed from ATC.
C— Advise ATC of the airspeed that will be used.

The pilots retain the prerogative of rejecting the application of speed adjustment by ATC if the minimum safe airspeed for any particular operation is greater than the speed adjustment. In such cases, the pilots are expected to advise ATC of the speed that will be used. (PLT172) — AIM ¶4-4-12

Answer (A) is incorrect because while a pilot should maintain at least the minimum safe airspeed for any particular operation, a pilot is expected to advise ATC of the airspeed being used when it differs from ATC's requested speed adjustment. Answer (B) is incorrect because a pilot who uses an airspeed that is not within the operating limits of the airplane is not only in violation of regulations, but is also risking the safety of all on board the airplane. A pilot must operate the airplane in a safe manner and advise ATC of the airspeed that will be used.

RTC

9042. Under what situations are faster/larger helicopters integrated with fixed-wing aircraft?

A— IFR flights, noise avoidance routes, and use of runways or taxiways.
B— Use of taxiways, sequencing for takeoff and landing, and use of the same traffic patterns.
C— Use of taxiways, sequencing for takeoff and landing, and use of the same loading ramps.

There will be situations where faster/larger helicopters may be integrated with fixed-wing aircraft. These include IFR flights, avoidance of noise-sensitive areas, or use of runway/taxiways to minimize the hazardous effects of rotor downwash in congested areas. (PLT434) — AIM ¶4-3-17

Answers

9094 [B]	9095 [C]	9096 [C]	9042 [A]

Holding

Holding may be necessary when ATC is unable to clear a flight to its destination. VORs, nondirectional beacons, airway intersections, and DME fixes may all be used as holding points. Flying a holding pattern involves two turns and two straight-and-level legs as shown in Figure 6-4.

At and below 14,000 feet MSL (no wind), the aircraft flies the specified course inbound to the fix, turns to the right 180°, flies a parallel course outbound for 1 minute, again turns 180° to the right, and flies 1 minute inbound to the fix. Above 14,000 feet MSL, the inbound leg length is 1-1/2 minutes. If a nonstandard pattern is to be flown, ATC will specify left turns.

When 3 minutes or less from the holding fix, the pilot is expected to start a speed reduction so as to cross the fix at or below the maximum holding airspeed. For all aircraft between MHA (minimum holding altitude) and 6,000 feet MSL, holding speed is 200 KIAS. For all aircraft between 6,001 and 14,000 feet MSL, holding speed is 230 KIAS. For all aircraft 14,001 feet MSL and above, holding speed is 265 KIAS. Exceptions to these speeds will be indicated by an icon.

The aircraft is in a holding pattern as of the initial time of arrival over the fix, and that time should be reported to ATC. The initial outbound leg is flown for 1 minute at or below 14,000 feet MSL. Subsequently, timing of the outbound leg should be adjusted as necessary to arrive at the proper inbound leg length. Timing of the outbound leg begins over or abeam the fix, whichever occurs later. If the abeam position cannot be determined, start timing when the turn to outbound is completed. The same entry and holding procedures apply to DME holding, except distance in nautical miles are used to establish leg length.

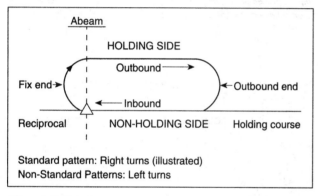

Standard pattern: Right turns (illustrated)
Non-Standard Patterns: Left turns

Figure 6-4

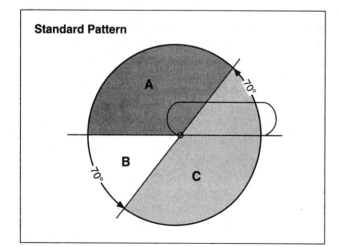

Figure 6-5

The FAA has three recommended methods for entering a holding pattern, as shown in Figure 6-5. An aircraft approaching from within sector (A) would fly a parallel entry by turning left to parallel the outbound course, making another left turn to remain in protected airspace, and returning to the holding fix. Aircraft approaching from sector (B) would fly a teardrop entry, by flying outbound on a track of 30° or less to the holding course, and then making a right turn to intercept the holding course inbound to the fix. Those approaching from within sector (C) would fly a direct entry by turning right to fly the pattern.

If the holding pattern is charted, the controller may omit all holding instructions, except the holding direction and the statement "as published." Pilots are expected to hold in the pattern depicted even if it means crossing the clearance limit. If the holding pattern to be used is not depicted on charts, ATC will issue general holding instructions. The holding clearance will include the following information: direction of holding from the fix in terms of the eight cardinal compass points; holding fix; radial, course, bearing, airway, or route on which the aircraft is to hold; leg length in miles if DME or RNAV is to be used; direction of turn if left turns are to be made; time to expect further clearance and any pertinent additional delay information.

ALL

8853. What action should a pilot take if within 3 minutes of a clearance limit and further clearance has not been received?

A— Assume lost communications and continue as planned.

B— Plan to hold at cruising speed until further clearance is received.

C— Start a speed reduction to holding speed in preparation for holding.

When an aircraft is 3 minutes or less from a clearance limit and a clearance beyond the fix has not been received, the pilot is expected to start a speed reduction so that he will cross the fix, initially, at or below the maximum holding airspeed. (PLT296) — AIM ¶5-3-7

Answer (A) is incorrect because if two-way communications are lost, the pilot is required to hold at the clearance limit in a standard pattern on the course that was used to approach the fix. If an expected further clearance time was received, plan on leaving the fix at that time. If none was given and the fix is an IAF, plan your arrival as close as possible to the estimated time of arrival. Answer (B) is incorrect because cruising speed may be greater than maximum holding speed.

ALL

8855. The maximum speed a propeller-driven airplane may hold at is

A— 265 knots.

B— 230 knots.

C— 156 knots.

For all aircraft between MHA and 6,000 feet MSL, holding speed is 200 KIAS. For all aircraft between 6,001 and 14,000 feet MSL, holding speed is 230 KIAS. For all aircraft 14,000 feet MSL and above, holding speed is 265 KIAS. Exceptions to these speeds will be indicated by an icon. Since this question does not specify what altitude the airplane is holding at, both answers (A) and (B) are correct. Choosing either of these will result in a correct response. (PLT296) — AIM ¶5-3-7

ALL

8856. Maximum holding speed for a turbojet airplane above 14,000 feet is

A— 210 knots.

B— 230 knots.

C— 265 knots.

For all aircraft between MHA (minimum holding altitude) and 6,000 feet MSL, holding speed is 200 KIAS. For all aircraft between 6,001 and 14,000 feet MSL, holding speed is 230 KIAS. For all aircraft 14,000 feet MSL and above, holding speed is 265 KIAS. Exceptions to these speeds will be indicated by an icon. (PLT296) — AIM ¶5-3-7

ALL

8857. Maximum holding speed for a civil turbojet aircraft at a joint use airport (civil/Navy) between 7,000 and 14,000 feet is

A— 265 knots.

B— 230 knots.

C— 200 knots.

The following are exceptions to the maximum holding airspeeds: Holding patterns at Navy fields only 230 KIAS maximum, unless otherwise depicted. (PLT296) — AIM ¶5-3-7

ALL

9418. What is the maximum holding speed for a civil turbojet holding at a civil airport at 15,000 feet MSL, unless a higher speed is required due to turbulence or icing and ATC is notified?

A— 265 knots.

B— 230 knots.

C— 250 knots.

For all aircraft between MHA (minimum holding altitude) and 6,000 feet MSL, holding speed is 200 KIAS. For all aircraft between 6,001 and 14,000 feet MSL, holding speed is 230 KIAS. For all aircraft 14,000 feet MSL and above, holding speed is 265 KIAS. Exceptions to these speeds will be indicated by an icon. (PLT296) — AIM ¶5-3-7

Answers

| 8853 | [C] | 8855 | [A] or [B] | 8856 | [C] | 8857 | [B] | 9418 | [A] |

ALL

9419. Civil aircraft holding at an altitude of 14,000 feet at a military or joint civil/military use airports should expect to operate at which holding pattern airspeed?

A— 250 knots.
B— 260 knots.
C— 230 knots.

Aircraft holding at military or joint civil/military use airports should expect to operate at a maximum holding pattern airspeed of 230 knots up to and including 14,000 feet. (PLT296) — AIM ¶5-3-7

ALL

8858. When using a flight director system, what rate of turn or bank angle should a pilot observe during turns in a holding pattern?

A— 3° per second or 25° bank, whichever is less.
B— 3° per second or 30° bank, whichever is less.
C— 1-1/2° per second or 25° bank, whichever is less.

When making turns in the holding pattern, use whichever of the following requires the least angle of bank:

1. 3° per second;

2. 30° bank angle; or

3. 25° bank provided a flight director system is used.

(PLT047) — AIM ¶5-3-7

ALL

8859. When holding at an NDB, at what point should the timing begin for the second leg outbound?

A— Abeam the holding fix or when the wings are level after completing the turn to the outbound heading, whichever occurs first.
B— At the end of a 1-minute standard rate turn after station passage.
C— When abeam the holding fix.

Outbound leg timing begins over or abeam the holding fix, whichever occurs later. If the abeam position cannot be determined, start timing when the turn to outbound is complete. (PLT296) — AIM ¶5-3-7

Answer (A) is incorrect because the pilot should start the timing when the turn is complete, only when a position abeam the fix cannot be determined. Answer (B) is incorrect because abeam the fix is preferable and should be used rather than at the completion of a standard rate turn, especially if turn completion occurs before coming abeam the fix.

ALL

8860. When entering a holding pattern above 14,000 feet, the initial outbound leg should not exceed

A— 1 minute.
B— 1-1/2 minutes.
C— 1-1/2 minutes or 10 NM, whichever is less.

Inbound leg time should not exceed 1 minute when holding at or below 14,000 feet, or 1-1/2 minutes when holding above 14,000 feet. The outbound leg should be flown for 1 minute or 1-1/2 minutes as appropriate on the first leg and then adjusted on subsequent legs to get the correct time on the inbound leg. (PLT296) — AIM ¶5-3-7

Answer (A) is incorrect because an initial outbound leg of 1 minute should be used only when below 14,000 feet. Answer (C) is incorrect because a DME distance is issued only by the specified controller for aircraft equipped with DME capability. A DME distance is not required unless specified by the controller.

Answers

9419 [C]   8858 [A]   8859 [C]   8860 [B]

ALL

8861. (Refer to Figure 123.) You receive this ATC clearance:

"…HOLD EAST OF THE ABC VORTAC ON THE ZERO NINER ZERO RADIAL, LEFT TURNS…"

What is the recommended procedure to enter the holding pattern?

A— Parallel only.
B— Direct only.
C— Teardrop only.

Determine the holding pattern by placing your pencil on the holding fix and dragging it on the holding radial given by ATC, then returning back to the fix. Then draw the pattern from the fix with turns in the direction specified. Holding east on the 090° radial with left turns means you will be south of R-090.

The entry procedure is based on the aircraft's heading. To determine which entry procedure to use, draw a line at a 70° angle from the holding fix, and cutting the outbound leg at about one-third its length. With a heading of 055°, we are in the middle-size piece of pie, so a parallel entry would be used. See the figure below. (PLT296) — AIM ¶5-3-7

Answer (B) is incorrect because a direct entry would be appropriate if you were coming in on R-340 to R-160. Answer (C) is incorrect because a teardrop entry would be appropriate if you were coming in from R-270 to R-340.

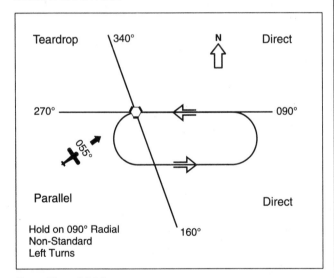

Question 8861

ALL

8862. (Refer to Figure 123.) You receive this ATC clearance:

"…CLEARED TO THE ABC VORTAC. HOLD SOUTH ON THE ONE EIGHT ZERO RADIAL…"

What is the recommended procedure to enter the holding pattern?

A— Teardrop only.
B— Direct only.
C— Parallel only.

Determine the holding pattern by placing your pencil on the holding fix and dragging it on the holding radial given by ATC, then returning back to the fix. Then draw the pattern from the fix with turns in the direction specified. Holding south on the 180° radial with right turns means you will be east of R-180.

The entry procedure is based on the aircraft's heading. To determine which entry procedure to use, draw a line at a 70° angle from the holding fix, and cutting the outbound leg at about one-third its length. With a heading of 055°, we are in the largest piece of pie, so a direct entry would be used. See the figure below. (PLT087) — AIM ¶5-3-7

Answer (A) is incorrect because a teardrop entry would be appropriate only from R-290 to R-360. Answer (C) is incorrect because a parallel entry would only be appropriate from R-360 to R-110.

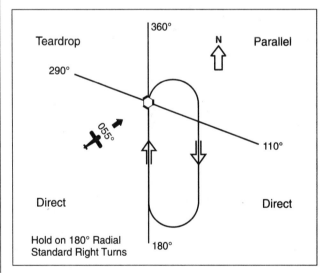

Question 8862

ALL
8863. (Refer to Figure 123.) You receive this ATC clearance:

"...CLEARED TO THE XYZ VORTAC. HOLD NORTH ON THE THREE SIX ZERO RADIAL, LEFT TURNS..."

What is the recommended procedure to enter the holding pattern?

A— Parallel only.
B— Direct only.
C— Teardrop only.

Determine the holding pattern by placing your pencil on the holding fix and dragging it on the holding radial given by ATC, then returning back to the fix. Then draw the pattern from the fix with turns in the direction specified. Holding north on the 360° radial with left turns means you will be east of R-090.

The entry procedure is based on the aircraft's heading. To determine which entry procedure to use, draw a line at a 70° angle from the holding fix, and cutting the outbound leg at about one-third its length. With a heading of 055°, we are in the smallest piece of pie, so a teardrop entry would be used. See the figure below. (PLT296) — AIM ¶5-3-7

Answer (A) is incorrect because a parallel entry would be appropriate only from R-070 to R-180. Answer (B) is incorrect because a direct entry would only be appropriate from R-250 to R-070.

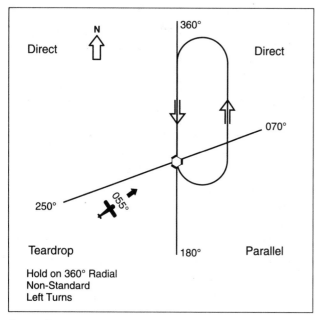

Question 8863

ALL
8864. (Refer to Figure 123.) You receive this ATC clearance:

"...CLEARED TO THE ABC VORTAC. HOLD WEST ON THE TWO SEVEN ZERO RADIAL..."

What is the recommended procedure to enter the holding pattern?

A— Parallel only.
B— Direct only.
C— Teardrop only.

Determine the holding pattern by placing your pencil on the holding fix and dragging it on the holding radial given by ATC, then returning back to the fix. Then draw the pattern from the fix with turns in the direction specified. Holding west on the 270° radial with right turns means you will be south of R-090.

The entry procedure is based on the aircraft's heading. To determine which entry procedure to use, draw a line at a 70° angle from the holding fix, and cutting the outbound leg at about one-third its length. With a heading of 055°, we are in the largest piece of pie, so a direct entry would be used. See the figure below. (PLT296) — AIM ¶5-3-7

Answer (A) is incorrect because a parallel entry would be appropriate only from R-090 to R-200. Answer (C) is incorrect because a teardrop entry would only be appropriate from R-020 to R-090.

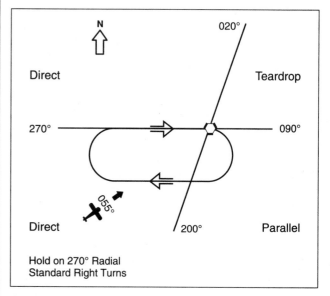

Question 8864

Answers

8863 [C]   8864 [B]

ALL
8865. (Refer to Figure 124.) A pilot receives this ATC clearance:

"...CLEARED TO THE ABC VORTAC. HOLD WEST ON THE TWO SEVEN ZERO RADIAL..."

What is the recommended procedure to enter the holding pattern?

A— Parallel or teardrop.
B— Parallel only.
C— Direct only.

Determine the holding pattern by placing your pencil on the holding fix and dragging it on the holding radial given by ATC, then returning back to the fix. Then draw the pattern from the fix with turns in the direction specified. Holding west on the 270° radial with right turns means you will be south of R-090.

The entry procedure is based on the aircraft's heading. To determine which entry procedure to use, draw a line at a 70° angle from the holding fix, and cutting the outbound leg at about one-third its length. With a heading of 155°, we are in the largest piece of pie, so a direct entry would be used. See the figure below. (PLT296) — AIM ¶5-3-7

Answer (A) is incorrect because the parallel or teardrop entries are alternatives only when approaching on R-090. Answer (B) is incorrect because a parallel entry would only be appropriate when approaching from R-090 to R-200.

Question 8865

ALL
8866. (Refer to Figure 124.) A pilot receives this ATC clearance:

"...CLEARED TO THE XYZ VORTAC. HOLD NORTH ON THE THREE SIX ZERO RADIAL, LEFT TURNS..."

What is the recommended procedure to enter the holding pattern?

A— Teardrop only.
B— Parallel only.
C— Direct.

Determine the holding pattern by placing your pencil on the holding fix and dragging it on the holding radial given by ATC, then returning back to the fix. Then draw the pattern from the fix with turns in the direction specified. Holding north on the 360° radial with left turns means you will be east of R-360.

The entry procedure is based on the aircraft's heading. To determine which entry procedure to use, draw a line at a 70° angle from the holding fix, and cutting the outbound leg at about one-third its length. With a heading of 155°, we are in the largest piece of pie, so a direct entry would be used. See the figure below. (PLT296) — AIM ¶5-3-7

Answer (A) is incorrect because a teardrop entry would be appropriate only from R-180 to R-250. Answer (B) is incorrect because, if you were approaching on R-070 to R-180, you would make a parallel entry.

Question 8866

Answers

8865 [C]   8866 [C]

ALL

8867. (Refer to Figure 124.) A pilot receives this ATC clearance:

"...CLEARED TO THE ABC VORTAC. HOLD SOUTH ON THE ONE EIGHT ZERO RADIAL..."

What is the recommended procedure to enter the holding pattern?

A— Teardrop only.
B— Parallel only.
C— Direct only.

Determine the holding pattern by placing your pencil on the holding fix and dragging it on the holding radial given by ATC, then returning back to the fix. Then draw the pattern from the fix with turns in the direction specified. Holding south on the 180° radial with right turns means you will be east of R-360.

The entry procedure is based on the aircraft's heading. To determine which entry procedure to use, draw a line at a 70° angle from the holding fix, and cutting the outbound leg at about one-third its length. With a heading of 155°, we are in the smallest piece of pie, so a teardrop entry would be used. See the following figure. (PLT296) — AIM ¶5-3-7

Answer (B) is incorrect because a parallel entry would be appropriate only from R-360 to R-110. Answer (C) is incorrect because a direct entry would only be appropriate from R-110 to R-290.

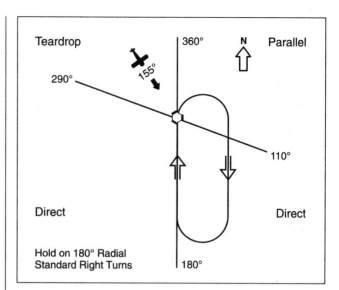

Teardrop 360° N Parallel
290° 155°
110°
Direct Direct
Hold on 180° Radial
Standard Right Turns 180°

Question 8867

Charts

The pilot-in-command must ensure that the appropriate aeronautical charts are on board the aircraft for each flight.

There are a number of questions that require reference to a segment of the *Chart Supplements U.S.* (previously A/FD). The legend for this publication is available in the FAA Legends 13 through 19.

Most of the questions concerning interpretation of Approach Charts, DPs and STARs can be answered by referring to the appropriate legend. These legends are available during the test in FAA Legend 40.

There are a few questions that require you to interpret the symbology on Enroute Charts. Unlike the other charts, no legend is available in the test book.

Departure Procedures (DPs) are depicted in one of two basic forms. Pilot Navigation (Pilot NAV) DPs are established where the pilot is primarily responsible for navigation on the DP route. Vector DPs are established where ATC will provide radar navigational guidance to an assigned route or fix. A vector DP will often include procedures to be followed in the event of a two-way communication radio failure.

Standard Terminal Arrival Routes (STARs) are ATC-coded IFR arrival routes established for certain airports. STARs purpose is to simplify clearance delivery procedures. ATC will assign a STAR to a civil aircraft whenever they deem it appropriate.

The Jet Route system consists of jet routes established from 18,000 feet MSL to FL450 inclusive.

The GPS Approach Overlay Program permits pilots to use GPS avionics under IFR for flying existing instrument approach procedures, except localizer (LOC), localizer directional aid (LDA), and simplified directional facility (SDF) procedures. Aircraft navigating by GPS are considered to be RNAV aircraft. Therefore, the appropriate equipment suffix must be included in the ATC flight plan. The word "or" in the approach title indicates that approach is in Phase III of the GPS Overlay Program. This allows the approach to be flown without reference of any kind to the ground-based NAVAIDs associated with the approach. When using GPS for the approach at the destination airport, the alternate must be an approach other than a GPS.

ALL

9012. In what way are SIDs depicted in plan view?

A— "Vectors" provided for navigational guidance or "Pilot NAV" with courses the pilot is responsible to follow.

B— "Vectors" and "Pilot NAV" for pilots to use at their discretion.

C— Combined textual and graphic form which are mandatory routes and instructions.

Pilot navigation (Pilot NAV) DPs (previously called SIDs) are established where the pilot is primarily responsible for navigation on the DP route. Vector DPs are established where ATC will provide radar navigational guidance to a filed/assigned route or to a fix depicted on the DP. (PLT201) — AIM ¶5-2-8

Answer (B) is incorrect because DPs are departure procedures and must be followed as depicted (not at the pilot's discretion). If a pilot does not wish to use a DP, then he/she must notify ATC. Answer (C) is incorrect because a NOS DP does not list the textual description in the plan view. The plan view depicts a DP as either a "pilot nav" or "vector" to signify if navigation is provided by the pilot or by radar vectors.

ALL

9034. What is the primary purpose of a STAR?

A— Provide separation between IFR and VFR traffic.

B— Simplify clearance delivery procedures.

C— Decrease traffic congestion at certain airports.

A STAR is an ATC-coded IFR arrival route established for application to arriving IFR aircraft destined for certain airports. Its purpose is to simplify clearance delivery procedures. (PLT170) — AIM ¶5-4-1

Answer (A) is incorrect because separation between IFR and VFR traffic is provided by Stage III radar service, not a STAR. Answer (C) is incorrect because controlled airspace, e.g., Class B, Class C, can be used to decrease traffic congestion at some airports by allowing ATC to regulate traffic flow and volume.

Answers

9012   [A]   9034   [B]

ALL
9035. When does ATC issue a STAR?

A— Only when ATC deems it appropriate.
B— Only to high priority flights.
C— Only upon request of the pilot.

Pilots of IFR civil aircraft destined to locations for which STARs have been published may be issued a clearance containing a STAR whenever ATC deems it appropriate. (PLT170) — AIM ¶5-4-1

Answer (B) is incorrect because any type of IFR flight can be issued a STAR. High priority flights will normally be handled in an expeditious manner by ATC. Answer (C) is incorrect because a STAR is a clearance delivery procedure that is issued by ATC. A pilot has the responsibility to accept or refuse that clearance. A pilot can list a STAR in the flight plan, but·ATC will issue one only if appropriate.

ALL
9549. (Refer to Figures 94, 95, and 96.) What action should be taken by the pilot, if communications are lost, while IMC, after takeoff on RWY 13L at Chicago Midway Airport?

A— Return and land immediately at Chicago Midway Airport.
B— Complete initially assigned turn south of DPA R-096, maintain 3,000 feet or lower if assigned. Then 10 minutes after departure, climb to FL 190, direct to GIJ, then flight plan route.
C— Complete initially assigned turn within 4 DME of Midway and maintain 3,000 feet or lower, if· assigned. Then 10 minutes after departure, climb to FL 190, direct to GIJ, and then flight plan route.

If a two-way radio communications failure occurs while in IFR conditions, the pilot of a flight should comply with the route and altitude listed.
Route:

1. By the route assigned in the last IFR clearance.

2. If being radar vectored, by the direct route from the point of failure to the fix, route, or airway specified in the vector clearance.

3. In the absence of an assigned route, by the route that ATC has advised may be expected in a further clearance.

4. If there is no assigned or expected route, by the route in the flight plan.

The pilot should maintain the highest of the following altitudes for the route segment flown:

1. The altitude or flight level in the last clearance.

2. The minimum altitude for IFR operations (i.e., MEA).

3. The altitude or flight level that ATC has advised may be expected in a further clearance.

(PLT052) — 14 CFR §91.185

Answer (A) is incorrect because the pilot is in IFR conditions, and therefore must continue the flight according to the route and altitude assigned in the last clearance. Answer (B) is incorrect because these are the actions for a non-DME equipped aircraft, and the question deals with an aircraft which has DME.

ALL
9613. (Refer to Figures 168, 353, and 354.) What action should be taken by the pilot if communications are lost after departure from RWY 16 at PWK if VMC?

A— Continue the flight under VMC and land as soon as practicable.
B— Climb to 3,000 feet; after 3 minutes, turn direct to PMM and climb to FL 190.
C— Start right turn within 1 mile of the departure end of RWY, remain east of ORD VOR/DME R-345, and maintain 3,000 feet; 3 minutes after departure, turn direct to PMM, and climb to FL 190.

If a radio failure occurs in VFR conditions, or if VFR conditions are encountered after the failure, each pilot shall continue the flight under VFR and land as soon as practicable. (PLT078) — 14 CFR §91.185

ALL
9616. (Refer to Figure 169A.) What action should be taken by the PIC of PTZ 70 if the communication radios fail after takeoff from RWY 16 at PWK while in IMC conditions?

A— Climb to 3,000 feet on RWY heading; after 3 minutes, turn direct to PMM and climb to FL 190.
B— Start right turn within 1 mile of the departure end of RWY 16 and remain east of the 345 radial of the ORD VOR/DME while climbing to 3,000 feet; after 3 minutes, turn direct to PMM and climb to FL 190.
C— Set 7600 in Mode 3 of the transponder, turn direct to Northbrook (the IAF), climb to 2,700 feet, and fly the ILS RWY 16 to land at PWK.

If a two-way radio communications failure occurs while in IFR conditions, the pilot of a flight should comply with the route and altitude listed.
Route:

1. By the route assigned in the last IFR clearance.

Answers

| 9035 | [A] | 9549 | [C] | 9613 | [A] | 9616 | [B] |

2. If being radar vectored, by the direct route from the point of failure to the fix, route, or airway specified in the vector clearance.

3. In the absence of an assigned route, by the route that ATC has advised may be expected in a further clearance.

4. If there is no assigned or expected route, by the route in the flight plan.

The pilot should maintain the highest of the following altitudes for the route segment flown:

1. The altitude or flight level in the last clearance.

2. The minimum altitude for IFR operations (i.e., MEA).

3. The altitude or flight level that ATC has advised may be expected in a further clearance.

(PLT391) — 14 CFR §91.185

ALL

9550. (Refer to Figure 97.) In the profile view of the RNAV or GPS RWY 32 approach to Buffalo Intl, between CYUGA and the MAP, the following appears: ∠ 2 91°. What is it?

A— The required pitch attitude change at CYUGA, to ensure arriving at 1,220 feet and 1.5 miles at the same time.

B— It indicates that 2.91° below level is recommended on the attitude indicator.

C— The Final Approach Angle for Vertical Path Computers.

The symbol in the profile section of a nonprecision approach is used to designate the Final Approach Path Angle for Vertical Path Computers (RNAV Descent). (PLT083) — Instrument Approach Procedures

Answer (A) is incorrect because it is the vertical path from CYUGA to the runway, not the vertical path from CYUGA to arrive at 1,220 feet and 1.5 miles at the same time. Answer (B) is incorrect because it must indicate 2.91° below the level flight attitude indication on the attitude indicator which may or may not be 2.91° below the horizon on the attitude indicator.

ALL

9551. (Refer to Figure 97A.) Greater Buffalo Intl was closed upon N60JB's arrival and was not expected to be open for 4 hours, for snow removal. N60JB received clearance to ROC. Upon arrival at ROC, the flight was cleared for the ILS RWY 28. To fly the ILS RWY 28 at ROC, the aircraft must have the following navigation equipment:

A— Radar and VOR/DME.

B— VOR/DME and ADF.

C— Radar and VOR/ILS/DME.

The remarks listed in the bottom left-hand corner of the instrument approach procedure (FAA Figure 97) indicates ADF is required for this approach. (PLT083) — Instrument Approach Procedures

ALL

9552. (Refer to Figure 97.) How can the FAF on the RNAV RWY 32 approach at BUF be identified?

A— The RNAV receiver will indicate 175.1° and 2.5 DME miles from BUF VORTAC.

B— The RNAV receiver will indicate a change from TO to FROM and 0 deflection of the course needle.

C— Two flashes/second on the OM beacon light.

The FAF (CYUGA waypoint) is indicated by a Maltese Cross in the profile view of the chart. When passing CYUGA, the RNAV receiver will either indicate station passage by changing from TO to FROM, or by changing the active waypoint to the missed approach point. The RNAV displays navigational information to the pilot with reference to the active waypoint and not to the NAVAIDs that define the waypoint. (PLT083) — Instrument Approach Procedures

Answer (A) is incorrect because the waypoint would be set as the BUF 175.1° at 2.5 DME; thus at the waypoint, the indication would change from TO to FROM without any right or left deflection of the course line. Answer (C) is incorrect because the approach chart does not indicate that there is a marker beacon at the FAF.

Answers

9550 [C]   9551 [B]   9552 [B]

ALL

9553. (Refer to Figure 97.) Which of the following will define the position of the RNAV MAP for Greater Buffalo Intl?

A— 116.4 BUF 286.9°, -3.5 NM.
B— 42°56.44'N - 78°38.48'W.
C— 42°56.26'N - 78°43.57'W.

The MAP waypoint identification box lists the coordinates as N42°56.29' W78°43.54', with a frequency of 116.4. The identifier is BUF, and the radial-distance (facility to waypoint) is 286.9° – 3.5NM. (PLT083) — Instrument Approach Procedures

Answers (B) and (C) are incorrect because they are the wrong coordinates for the MAP waypoint.

ALL

9554. (Refer to Figure 259.) When performing the LOC RWY 33R approach and sidestep, at what point would you initiate the missed approach?

A— anytime after the FAF.
B— 4.5 NM after JOLTE.
C— IAH DME 1.0.

The FAF to MAP for the LOC approach is listed in the bottom left corner of the approach plate. FAF to MAP is 4.5 NM. (PLT083) — Instrument Approach Procedures

ALL

9555. (Refer to Figures 97A, 97B, and 97C.) N60JB desired to list ROC as an alternate for BUF. The active RWY at ROC was expected to be RWY 28. What weather forecast was required at Greater Rochester Intl, for N60JB to list it as an alternate?

A— Nonprecision approach 800-2, precision approach 800-2.
B— Nonprecision approach 800-2, precision approach 600-2.
C— Nonprecision approach 800-2 1/4, precision approach 600-2.

The A in the triangle in the bottom left-hand corner of the approach chart indicates that Rochester has non-standard alternate minimums. FAA Figure 97C lists all the approaches at Rochester which have nonstandard alternate minimums. Assuming that N60JB is in approach category A or B, the minimums for the ILS 28 approach are 800-2. Since no nonstandard minimums are listed for a nonprecision approach to runway 28 in a category A or B aircraft, we can assume that standard alternate

minimums (800-2) apply. The standard alternate minimums are listed at the top of FAA Figure 97B. (PLT083) — Instrument Approach Procedures

Answers (B) and (C) are incorrect because the lowest minimums for a precision approach in any category aircraft is 800-2.

ALL

9565. (Refer to Legends 43 and 43A and Figure 103.) The RWYs at LAX are closed and expected to remain closed for 2 hours when N91JB arrives. N91JB requests 4,000 feet, Tower Enroute Control (TEC) with radar vectors to BUR. What altitude can N91JB expect based upon the type aircraft?

A— 4,000 feet.
B— 5,000 feet.
C— 6,000 feet.

Aircraft types (J, M, P, and Q) are given for each city pair and should be used with the route of flight filed. M = Turbo Props/Special (cruise speed 190 knots or greater). Not all city pairs are depicted; however, geographic areas connected by tower enroute control are shown. The closest paring given is the Coast Tracon to Burbank (BUR). N91JB has filed the Downe Three Arrival, which terminates with vectors to final approach course for runways 6 and 7 at Los Angeles International (LAX). This indicates that LAX is landing to the East, therefore the CSTJ2 route should be used. The altitude for CSTJ2 is 5,000 feet (JM50PQ40). (PLT073) — Chart Supplement U.S.

ALL

9563. (Refer to Figures 103 and 104.) If communications are lost soon after takeoff on RWY 11R at Tucson Intl, what altitude restrictions apply, in IMC conditions?

A— Fly assigned heading for vectors to intercept appropriate transition, maintain 17,000 feet to GBN, then climb to assigned altitude.
B— Fly assigned heading for vectors to intercept the Gila Bend transition; climb to 17,000 feet or lower assigned altitude; climb to FL 220, 10 minutes after departure.
C— Fly assigned heading for vectors to intercept the Gila Bend transition; climb to 17,000 feet; 10 minutes after departure, climb to FL 220.

If a two-way radio communications failure occurs while in IFR conditions, the pilot of a flight should comply with the route and altitude listed.
Route:

Answers

| 9553 [A] | 9554 [B] | 9555 [A] | 9565 [B] | 9563 [B] |

1. By the route assigned in the last IFR clearance.

2. If being radar vectored, by the direct route from the point of failure to the fix, route, or airway specified in the vector clearance.

3. In the absence of an assigned route, by the route that ATC has advised may be expected in a further clearance.

4. If there is no assigned or expected route, by the route in the flight plan.

The pilot should maintain the highest of the following altitudes for the route segment flown:

1. The altitude or flight level in the last clearance.

2. The minimum altitude for IFR operations (i.e., MEA).

3. The altitude or flight level that ATC has advised may be expected in a further clearance.

See FAA Figure 104, DP Route Description. (PLT052) — 14 CFR §91.185

Answers (A) and (C) are incorrect because the statement "or assigned lower altitude" omits an important altitude restriction. The pilot would be required to maintain the lower assigned altitude until 10 minutes after the departure before climbing to the filed flight level.

ALL
9564. (Refer to Figure 104.) What are the takeoff minimums for RWY 11R at Tucson Intl that apply to N91JB?

A— 1 SM.
B— 800/1.
C— 4,000/3.

See FAA Figure 104, and reference the first note in the DP plan view that says, "Rwys 3, 11L/R ... require a ceiling of 4,000 and 3 miles visibility." or you must be able to meet the minimum climb requirements of 250 feet per NM to 6,500 feet. Figure 103 identifies N91JB as a BE1900. The standard takeoff minimum for a BE1900 (2 engines or less) is 1 SM, as long as the minimum climb of 250 ft/min can be performed. (PLT052) — Departure Procedure (DP) Chart

ALL
9569. (Refer to Figures 110 and 112.) In addition to VOR and DME, what other avionics equipment is required to be operational, at takeoff, to fly the VOR/DME RWY 32R approach at IAH?

A— Altitude alerting system.
B— Standby VOR and DME receivers.
C— VHF communications and transponder equipment.

The charts and the Chart Supplements U.S. (previously A/FD) indicate Houston Intercontinental Airport is a Class II TCA. TCAs have been redesignated as Class B airspace. To operate in Class B airspace, an aircraft must be equipped with a VOR, two-way radio, and a transponder. (PLT083) — 14 CFR §91.131

ALL
9571. (Refer to Figure 259.) Which approach lighting is available for RWY 33R?

A— MALSR and RAIL.
B— MIRL.
C— TDZ and CL.

The A$_5$ inside the circle with the dot indicates that runway 33R has MALSR approach lights with RAIL. See FAA Legend 5. (PLT083) — Instrument Approach Procedures

Answer (B) is incorrect because MIRL indicates Medium Intensity Runway Lights. Answer (C) is incorrect because TDZ and CL lighting is not available for RWY 33R and it is in-runway, not approach lighting.

ALL
9573. (Refer to Figure 112.) At what point must the missed approach be initiated on the VOR/DME RWY 32R approach at IAH, if still IMC?

A— Anytime after the FAF.
B— IAH 1.3 DME.
C— IAH 1 DME.

The profile view of the approach chart shows the change from the procedure track to the missed approach track at the IAH 1.0 DME fix. (PLT083) — Instrument Approach Procedures

Answer (A) is incorrect because the question asks what is the latest point at which you must initiate the missed approach. Answer (B) is incorrect because it is the VDP, not the MAP.

Answers

9564 [A]	9569 [C]	9571 [A]	9573 [C]

ALL

9587. (Refer to Figure 118C.) What instrument approach light system or RWY lighting system is available for the LOC BC RWY 26L approach at Phoenix Sky Harbor Intl?

A— HIRL and REIL.
B— MALS and REIL.
C— SALS and ODALS.

The Chart Supplements U.S. (previously A/FD) indicates that runway 26L has HIRL and REIL. (PLT078) — Chart Supplements U.S.

ALL

9588. (Refer to Figure 273.) The touchdown zone elevation of the ILS RWY 25L approach at Phoenix Sky Harbor Intl is

A— 1,126 feet.
B— 1,135 feet.
C— 1,458 feet.

The notation "TDZE 1126" indicates the touchdown zone elevation on runway 25L is 1,126 feet MSL. See FAA Legend 4. (PLT049) — Instrument Approach Procedures

ALL

9590. (Refer to Figure 118A.) What is the HAT a Category B aircraft may descend to if the pilot has identified HADEN INT on the LOC BC RWY 26L approach at Phoenix Sky Harbor Intl?

A— 510 feet.
B— 667 feet.
C— 670 feet.

The Height Above Touchdown (HAT) for a Category B airplane with HADEN DME is 510 feet. See FAA Legend 7. (PLT083) — Instrument Approach Procedures

Answer (B) is incorrect because this is the HAT for the Category B circling approach without HADEN INT. Answer (C) is incorrect because this is the HAT for straight-in approach RWY 26L without HADEN.

ALL

9596. (Refer to Figure 121, upper panel.) On the airway J220 (BUF R-158) SE of Buffalo, the MAA is 39,000 feet. What is the MAA on J547 between BUF and PMM (lower panel)?

A— 60,000 feet.
B— 43,000 feet.
C— 45,000 feet.

The Maximum Authorized Altitude is the maximum usable altitude or flight level on an airway or jet route for which an MEA is published. FL450 is the upper limit of all jet routes. (PLT055) — Pilot/Controller Glossary

Answer (A) is incorrect because this is the upper limit of Class A airspace, but the jet route system stops above 45,000 feet. Answer (B) is incorrect because the upper limit of the jet route system includes FL450 unless marked otherwise.

ALL

9599. (Refer to Figure 161.) To receive the DME information from the facility labeled "DME Chan 22" at La Guardia requires that

A— N711JB be equipped with a UHF NAV radio, which is tuned to channel 22.
B— a military TACAN tuned to channel 22.
C— the VHF NAV radio be tuned to the ILS (108.5) frequency.

VOR/ILS frequencies are paired with TACAN channels so that the VHF and UHF facilities can be tuned together. FAA Legend 21 indicates that DME channel 22 is paired with LOC frequency 108.5. (PLT202) — FAA-H-8083-15

ALL

9600. (Refer to Figure 293.) The La Guardia weather goes below minimums and New York Approach Control issues a clearance to N711JB, via radar vectors, to ASALT Intersection. As N711JB is approaching ASALT, Approach Control clears the aircraft to fly the VOR RWY 13L/13R approach. What is the distance from ASALT Intersection to RWY 13L?

A— 11.2 NM
B— 12.2 NM.
C— 8.6 NM.

The profile view indicates that the distance from ASALT INT to CRI VOR is 6.0 NM, CRI VOR to MAP is 2.6 NM. On the plan view it is noted that from MAP to Rwy 13L is 3.6NM. 6 + 2.6 + 3.6 = 12.2 (PLT083) — Instrument Approach Procedures

Answers

| 9587 [A] | 9588 [A] | 9590 [A] | 9596 [C] | 9599 [C] | 9600 [B] |

ALL

9601. (Refer to Figure 293.) The La Guardia weather goes below minimums and New York Approach Control issues a clearance to N711JB, via radar vectors, to ASALT Intersection. What is the lowest altitude that Approach Control may clear N711JB to cross ASALT Intersection?

A— 3,000 feet.
B— 2,500 feet.
C— 2,000 feet.

The profile view shows a mandatory altitude of 3,000 feet at ASALT unless advised by ATC, then 2,000 feet is the minimum. (PLT049) — Instrument Approach Procedures

ALL

9602. (Refer to Figure 293.) For landing on RWY 13R at JFK, how much RWY is available?

A— 12,468 feet.
B— 14,511 feet.
C— 9,095.

The runway landing distance for 13R is listed in the upper center left portion of the approach plate and is 12,468. (PLT083) — Instrument Approach Procedures

Answer (B) is incorrect because 14,511 is the overall length of runway 13R/31L. Answer (C) is incorrect because 9,905 is the runway landing distance for 13L.

ALL

9603. (Refer to Figure 293.) What must be operational for N711JB to execute the VOR RWY 13L/13R approach to JFK?

A— DME or radar.
B— LDIN and VOR.
C— VOR, LDIN, and DME or radar.

VOR is required, as indicated by the approach title. The plan view indicates that DME or radar is required. The notes section at the top of the chart shows that the lead-in light system must be operational to execute the procedure. (PLT083) — Instrument Approach Procedures

ALL

9604. (Refer to Figure 293.) The distance from Canarsie (CRI) to RWY 13R at JFK is

A— 5.2 NM.
B— 6.2 NM.
C— 8.6 NM.

The profile view indicates that the distance from CRI VOR to MAP is 2.6 NM and the distance from the MAP to Rwy 13R is 2.6 NM. (PLT083) — Instrument Approach Procedures

ALL

9614. (Refer to Figure 169A.) The PIC of PTZ 70 will use 25° of bank during the turn after departing RWY 16 at PWK. What is the maximum TAS that the aircraft may maintain during the turn and remain east of the ORD VOR/DME R-345 under a no wind condition?

A— 160 knots.
B— 162 knots.
C— 164 knots.

The table at the top of the plan view shows the maximum TAS for various bank angles. (PLT052) — Instrument Approach Procedures

ALL

9615. (Refer to Figure 169A.) To remain east of the ORD VOR/DME R-345, while flying the PAL-WAUKEE TWO DEPARTURE, requires a turn radius of

A— over 5,000 feet.
B— 5,000 feet.
C— less than 5,000 feet.

The note in the bottom left corner of the plan view states that a turn radius of less than 5,000 feet is required. (PLT052) — Instrument Approach Procedures

ALL

9617. (Refer to Figure 172A.) The airport diagram of Greater Buffalo Intl Airport has a symbol (appears to be a triangle balanced on top of another triangle) located close to the end of RWYs 14 and 32. What do these symbols indicate?

A— Helicopter landing areas.
B— That special takeoff and landing minimums apply to RWYs 14 and 32.
C— RWY Radar Reflectors.

The double triangle symbol in the airport diagram indicates runway radar reflectors. See FAA Legend 4. (PLT083) — Instrument Approach Procedures

ALL

9619. (Refer to Figure 301.) During the approach (ILS RWY 10 at SYR) while maintaining an on glide slope indication with a groundspeed of 110 knots, what was the approximate rate of descent for PTZ 70?

A— 475 feet per minute.
B— 585 feet per minute.
C— 690 feet per minute.

The profile view indicates that the final approach angle is 3.0°. The table in FAA Legend 9 shows that a 555 fpm descent rate is required for 105 knots, and 635 fpm is required for 120 knots. 585 is the only answer choice to fall within these limits. (PLT049) — FAA-H-8083-15, Chapter 7

ALL

9620. (Refer to Figure 171, top panel.) The facility (Kankakee) that is located 9 miles NE of Chicago Midway or 27 miles SSE of Northbrook (OBK) is a/an

A— Aeronautical Radio Inc. (AIRINC) transmitter.
B— Automated Weather Observing System (AWOS-ASOS) with frequency.
C— Flight Service, Remote Communications Outlet.

This is the symbol for a Remote Communication Outlet (RCO). The remoted FSS and frequency are shown. (PLT058) — Enroute Low Altitude Chart Legend

ALL

9623. (Refer to Figure 175.) Four airways (V298, V25, V448 and V204) near YKM have a series of dots that overlay the airway. What do these dots indicate?

A— That the airways penetrate a Prohibited and Restricted Airspace.
B— That 2 miles either side of the airway, where shaded, is a Controlled Firing Area.
C— That the airways penetrate a Military Operations Area (MOA) and a special clearance must be received from ATC.

A series of dots overlaying an airway segment indicates that it penetrates restricted or prohibited airspace. (PLT058) — Enroute Low Altitude Chart Legend

ALL

9629. (Refer to Figure 182A.) EAB 90 is a "CAT B" aircraft and received a clearance to fly the LOC RWY 09R approach, to circle to land RWY 27R. The Baldn fix was received. What are the minimums?

A— 540-1.
B— 600-1.
C— 680-1.

The note in the plan view shows category B circling minimums of 600-1 if the BALDN fix is received. (PLT083) — Instrument Approach Procedures

ALL

9630. (Refer to Figure 182A.) EAB 90 is a "CAT B" aircraft and received a clearance to fly the LOC RWY 09R, to land RWY 09R. The Baldn fix was received. What are the minimums?

A— 520/24.
B— 600/24.
C— 680/24.

The note in the plan view shows category A and B LOC 9R minimums of 520-24 when the BALDN fix is received. (PLT083) — Instrument Approach Procedures

ALL

9631. (Refer to Figure 182A.) EAB 90 is a "CAT B" aircraft and received a clearance to fly the LOC RWY 09R to sidestep and land RWY 09L. The Baldn fix was received. What are the minimums?

A— 680-1.
B— 520/24.
C— 600-1.

The note in the plan view shows category B sidestep 9L minimums are 600-1 when BALDN is received. (PLT083) — Instrument Approach Procedures

Answer (A) is incorrect because it is the sidestep minimums without BALDN fix. Answer (B) is incorrect because it is the LOC minimums with the BALDN fix.

ALL

9644. (Refer to Figure 192.) On the airway J10 between OBH and LBF, the MAA is 41,000 feet. What is the MAA on J197 between FSD and OBH?

A— 43,000 feet.
B— 45,000 feet.
C— 60,000 feet.

Answers

| 9619 | [B] | 9620 | [C] | 9623 | [A] | 9629 | [B] | 9630 | [A] | 9631 | [C] |
| 9644 | [B] | | | | | | | | | | |

The Maximum Authorized Altitude is the maximum usable altitude or flight level on an airway or jet route which has a published MEA. FL450 is the upper limit of all jet routes. (PLT100) — Pilot/Controller Glossary

Answer (A) is incorrect because the upper limit of the jet route system includes FL450 unless marked otherwise. Answer (C) is incorrect because this is the upper limit of Class A airspace, but the jet route system stops above 45,000 feet.

ALL
9645. (Refer to Figure 373.) Inbound to DEN from Dallas/Fort Worth (DFW), Center gives you a vector and a frequency for Denver Approach Control, but you miss-copy the frequency. You determine you probably were assigned

A— 119.3 and should expect a tower frequency of 124.3.
B— 120.35 and should expect a tower frequency of 132.35.
C— 120.35 and should expect a tower frequency of 124.3.

Approaching Denver from Dallas, you will use the Denver Approach Center designed for "South" which is 120.35, and 132.35 for Denver tower. (PLT049) — Instrument Approach Procedures

ALL
9645-1. (Refer to Figure 374.) Inbound to DEN from Dallas/Fort Worth (DFW), Center gives you a vector and a frequency for Denver Approach Control, but you miss-copy the frequency. You determine you probably were assigned

A— 119.3 and should expect a tower frequency of 124.3.
B— 120.35 and should expect a tower frequency of 124.3.
C— 120.35 and should expect a tower frequency of 132.35.

Approaching Denver from Dallas, you will use the Denver Approach Center designed for "South" which is 120.35, and 124.3 for Denver tower. (PLT049) — Instrument Approach Procedures

ALL
9647. (Refer to Figures 193, 193A, and 194.) The entry points for the (NORTHEAST GATE) LANDR ONE and SAYGE ONE arrivals are approximately

A— 11 NM apart.
B— 12 NM apart.
C— 13 NM apart.

The Arrival Overview in the upper left-hand corner of FAA Figure 194 states that entry points for parallel arrivals are approximately 12 NM apart. (PLT080) — Instrument Approach Procedures

ALL
9648. (Refer to Figures 195, 195A, 196, and 196A.) When PIL 10 becomes visual, at 3.8 NM from the end of Runway 35R, if the aircraft is on glide slope and on course, what should the pilot see for a Visual Glideslope Indicator?

A— Two white and two red lights on the left side of the runway, in a row.
B— One white and one red light on the left or right side of the runway, in a row.
C— Two red and two white lights, in a row, on the right side of the runway.

FAA Figure 196A indicates Runway 35R has PAPI(P4R), which means the visual glide slope indicators are 4 identical light units placed on the right side of the runway. See FAA Legend 17. (PLT147) — Chart Supplements U.S.

ALL
9649. (Refer to Figures 195, 195A, 196, and 196A.) All of the runways at Denver Intl have what type of Visual Glideslope Indicators?

A— PVASI.
B— PAPI.
C— APAP.

The airport diagrams display the P inside the circle at both end of all runways. FAA Legend 6 indicates this symbol means the runway has Precision Approach Path Indicator (PAPI) approach lighting system. (PLT147) — Instrument Approach Procedures

ALL

9654. (Refer to Figure 198A.) The highest terrain shown in the planview section of the LOC-B approach to Eagle County Regional is

A— 11,275 feet.
B— 11,573 feet.
C— 12,354 feet.

The highest terrain is indicated by a large dot in the plan view. In this case, the large dot is in the upper left corner above Denver Center. (PLT083) — Instrument Approach Procedures

ALL

9655. (Refer to Figures 201 and 201A.) What type of weather information would normally be expected to be available from the Weather Data Source at Ogden-Hinckley?

A— Cloud height, weather, obstructions to vision, temperature, dewpoint, altimeter, surface winds, and any pertinent remarks.
B— Cloud bases/tops, obstructions to vision, altimeter, winds, precipitation, and the intensity of the precipitation.
C— Cloud height, obstructions to vision, temperature, dewpoint, altimeter, wind data, and density altitude.

The Chart Supplements U.S. (previously A/FD) indicates the weather source for Ogden-Hinckley is LAWRS (Limited Aviation Weather Reporting Station). Observers report cloud height, weather, obstructions to vision, temperature and dew point (in most cases), surface wind, altimeter, and pertinent remarks. See FAA Legend 18. (PLT078) — Chart Supplements U.S.

Answer (B) is incorrect because it does not report cloud bases or tops, nor precipitation and intensity. Answer (C) is incorrect because it does not report wind data and density altitude.

ALL

9658. (Refer to Figure 185A.) The maximum gross weight that an L1011 can be operated on RWY 07R/25L at McCarran Intl is

A— 521,000 pounds.
B— 633,000 pounds.
C— 620,000 pounds.

The runway weight limit for a dual tandem gear airplane on runway 07R-25L is listed as 633,000 pounds. However, the remarks section states the maximum weight for an L1011 is 521,000 pounds. (PLT078) — Chart Supplements U.S.

ALL

9659. (Refer to Figures 185 and 185A.) The threshold of RWY 07L at McCarran Intl is displaced

A— 874 feet, due to a pole.
B— 2,133 feet, due to a hangar.
C— 1,659 feet, due to a pole.

The Chart Supplements U.S. (previously A/FD) listing for runway 07L states the threshold is displaced 2,133 feet for a hangar. (PLT078) — Chart Supplements U.S.

ALL

9660. (Refer to Figures 203 and 203A.) PTL 55 will be unable to cross the Oasis Intersection at 9,500 feet. What should the crew do?

A— Enter holding on R-211 LAS at 15 DME, right-hand turns, advise Departure Control, climb to 9,500 prior to Oasis.
B— Advise Las Vegas Departure Control and request radar vectors.
C— Continue the climb on LAS R-211 to 9,500 feet, then turn right to 260°.

The note on the plan view states that aircraft on the Beatty transition which are unable to cross OASIS at 9,500 feet should continue the climb on the LAS R-211 until reaching 9,500 feet and then turn right to 260°. (PLT052) — Instrument Approach Procedures

ALL

9661. (Refer to Figures 205 and 206.) What is the maximum weight that PTL 55 may weigh for landing at San Francisco Intl (SFO)?

A— 710,000 pounds.
B— 715,000 pounds.
C— 720,000 pounds.

The remarks section of the Chart Supplements U.S. (previously A/FD) states that the maximum weight for a B-747 is 710,000 pounds. (PLT078) — Chart Supplements U.S.

ALL

9666. (Refer to Figures 205 and 206A.) At San Francisco Intl (SFO), the runway hold position signs are

A— all on the left-hand side of the taxiways.
B— all on the right-hand side of the taxiways.
C— on either side of the taxiways.

Answers

9654 [C]   9655 [A]   9658 [A]   9659 [B]   9660 [C]   9661 [A]
9666 [C]

The note on the airport diagram states that several runway hold position signs are on the right rather than the left side of the taxiways. (PLT083) — Instrument Approach Procedures

ALL
9667. (Refer to Figures 207 and 207A.) Due to weather PTL 55 was unable to land at SFO. PTL 55 was given radar vectors to COMMO Intersection and clearance to fly the ILS RWY 11 approach at Oakland Intl. What frequencies will PTL 55 use for Oakland Tower and Oakland Ground Control?

A— 118.3 and 121.75.
B— 127.2 and 121.75.
C— 127.2 and 121.9.

The frequency listing on the plan view of the approach chart lists the runway 11-29 tower frequency as 127.2 and the ground control frequency as 121.75. The Chart Supplements U.S. lists these frequencies for the south complex, which is runway 11-29. (PLT083) — Instrument Approach Procedures

ALL
9670. (Refer to Figure 210.) The route between FIS (near Key West) and MTH, which is labeled B646, is an example of a

A— LF/MF Airway.
B— LF/MF Oceanic Route.
C— Military Training Route.

The brown color and airway designation (Blue 646) indicate it is a LF/MF airway. A solid narrow line indicates that it is an Oceanic route. A domestic LF/MF airway would be represented by a broader, shaded line. (PLT058) — Enroute Low Altitude Chart Legend

ALL
9675. (Refer to Figure 210.) The Miami ARTCC remote site located near Pahokee has a discrete VHF frequency of

A— 123.45.
B— 133.55.
C— 135.35.

The Miami ARTCC remote site communication box is the light blue scalloped box southwest of the Pahokee VOR-TAC. (PLT058) — Enroute Low Altitude Chart Legend

ALL
9686. (Refer to Figure 215A.) The airport diagram of Bradley Intl Airport has a symbol (appears to be a triangle balanced on top of another triangle) located close to the approach end of RWY 19. What does this symbol indicate?

A— Runway Radar Reflectors.
B— Practice hover area for the Army National Guard helicopters.
C— Two course lights, back to back, which flash beams of light along the course of an airway.

The double triangle symbol in the airport diagram stands for runway radar reflectors. See FAA Legend 4. (PLT083) — Instrument Approach Procedures

ALL
9691. The GPS Approach Overlay Program permits pilots to use GPS avionics when IFR for flying existing instrument approach procedures, except

A— LOC, LDA and ADF.
B— LDA, TAC and SDF.
C— SDF, LOC and LDA.

The GPS Approach Overlay Program permits pilots to use GPS avionics under IFR for flying existing instrument approach procedures, except localizer (LOC), localizer directional aid (LDA), and simplified directional facility (SDF) procedures. (PLT354) — AIM ¶1-1-19

ALL
9692. Aircraft navigating by GPS are considered, on the flight plan, to be

A— RNAV equipped.
B— in compliance with ICAO Annex 10.
C— FMS/EFIS equipped.

Aircraft navigating by GPS are considered to be RNAV aircraft. Therefore, the appropriate equipment suffix must be included in the ATC flight plan. (PLT354) — Pilot/Controller Glossary

Answers

| 9667 | [B] | 9670 | [B] | 9675 | [B] | 9686 | [A] | 9691 | [C] | 9692 | [A] |

ALL

9693. The Instrument Approach Procedure Chart top margin identification is VOR or GPS RWY 25, AL-5672 (FAA), LUKACHUKAI, ARIZONA. In what phase of the approach overlay program is this GPS approach?

A— Phase I.
B— Phase III.
C— Phase II.

The word "or" in the approach title indicates that approach is in Phase III of the GPS Overlay Program. This allows the approach to be flown without reference of any kind to the ground-based NAVAIDs associated with the approach. (PLT354) — AIM ¶1-1-19

ALL

9694. The weather forecast requires an alternate for LUKACHUKAI (GPS RWY 25) ARIZONA. The alternate airport must have an approved instrument approach procedure, which is anticipated to be operational and available at the estimated time of arrival, other than

A— GPS or VOR.
B— ILS or GPS.
C— GPS.

When using GPS for the approach at the destination airport, the alternate must be an approach other than a GPS. (PLT354) — AIM ¶1-1-19

ALL

8793. (Refer to Figure 104.) Determine the DEP CON frequency for the TUS3.GBN SID after takeoff from RWY 11R at Tucson Intl.

A— 125.1 MHz.
B— 118.5 MHz.
C— 128.5 MHz.

The Chart Supplements U.S. (previously A/FD) indicates that the Departure Control Frequency for runway 11, departures on bearings 090° through 285° from the airport, is 125.1 Mhz. (PLT078) — Chart Supplements U.S.

Answer (B) is incorrect because 118.5 MHz is for departures from RWY 11 with a departure heading between 286° to 089°. Answer (C) is incorrect because 128.5 is the general approach/departure control frequency.

ALL

8794. (Refer to Figure 104.) Using an average ground-speed of 140 knots, what minimum indicated rate of climb must be maintained to meet the required climb rate (feet per NM) to 9,000 as specified on the SID?

A— 349 ft/min.
B— 560 ft/min.
C— 584 ft/min.

The DP (previously called SID) requires a 250 foot per NM climb gradient to 9,000 feet. FAA Legend 10 indicates that at 140 knots, a rate of climb of 583 feet per minute is required to meet this climb gradient. (PLT052) — DP Chart

ALL

8796. (Refer to Figure 104.) How can the pilot receive the latest NOTAMs for the TUS LAX flight?

A— Monitor ATIS on 123.8 MHz.
B— Contact the FSS on 122.2 MHz.
C— Request ADCUS on any FSS or Tower frequency.

NOTAMs can be received through the FSS located on the airport. The standard FSS frequency is 122.2 MHz. (PLT078) — Chart Supplements U.S.

ALL

8797. (Refer to Figure 348.) What distance is available for takeoff on RWY 11R at Tucson Intl?

A— 6,998 feet.
B— 8,408 feet.
C— 10,996 feet.

Runway 11R-29L is 8,408 feet long. The displaced threshold does not reduce takeoff distance. (PLT078) — Chart Supplements U.S.

Answer (A) is incorrect because 6,998 feet is the length of the runway without the displaced threshold. Answer (C) is incorrect because 10,996 feet is the length of RWY 11L-29R.

Answers

9693 [B]	9694 [C]	8793 [A]	8794 [C]	8796 [B]	8797 [B]

ALL

8798. (Refer to Figure 348.) What effect on the takeoff run can be expected on RWY 11R at Tucson Intl?

A— Takeoff length shortened to 6,986 feet by displaced threshold.

B— Takeoff run shortened by 0.7 percent runway slope to the SE.

C— Takeoff run will be lengthened by the 0.7 percent upslope of the runway.

There is a 0.7% upslope to the southeast on runway 11R-29L. (PLT078) — Chart Supplements U.S.

Answer (A) is incorrect because a displaced threshold will shorten the usable runway but has no effect on an airplane's required takeoff distance. Answer (B) is incorrect because the takeoff run is lengthened due to the 0.7% upslope to the southeast.

ALL

8782. (Refer to Figures 99 and 101.) Which frequency should be selected to check airport conditions and weather prior to departure at DFW Intl?

A— 117.0 MHz.

B— 134.9 MHz.

C— 135.5 MHz.

The departure ATIS for DFW airport is listed as 135.5 Mhz. (PLT078) — Chart Supplements U.S.

Answer (A) is incorrect because 117.0 MHz is the listed ATIS frequency for arriving airplanes. Answer (B) is incorrect because 134.9 MHz is also a listed ATIS frequency for arriving airplanes.

ALL

8783. (Refer to Figures 99, 100, and 101.) The frequency change from departure control to ARTCC after departing DFW Intl for IAH is

A— 135.5 to 126.0 MHz.

B— 118.55 to 127.95 MHz.

C— 127.75 to 127.95 MHz.

The Chart Supplements U.S. (previously A/FD) lists 127.75 MHz as the southbound Departure Control frequency for DFW. That would be most appropriate for V369. The "postage stamp" symbol just above and to the right of KILLR INT in FAA Figure 100 indicates that the Fort Worth Center frequency in that area is 127.95 Mhz. (PLT078) — Chart Supplements U.S.

Answer (A) is incorrect because 135.5 MHz is the ATIS frequency for departing airplanes and 126.0 MHz is the ARTCC discrete frequency for northwest of DFW. Answer (B) is incorrect because 118.55 MHz is the departure control frequency for eastbound traffic from DFW.

ALL

8784. (Refer to Figure 100.) Where is the VOR changeover point on V369 between DFW Intl and TNV?

A— Ft. Worth/Houston ARTCC boundary.

B— 81 NM from DFW Intl.

C— TORNN Int.

The distance on V369 between DFW and TNV is 162 NM. Since there is no VOR changeover symbol on the chart, the changeover point is halfway (81 NM from DFW). (PLT058) — Enroute Low Altitude Chart Legend

Answer (A) is incorrect because the Ft. Worth/Houston ARTCC boundary would indicate a radio communication frequency change, not a navigational frequency change. Answer (C) is incorrect because TORNN intersection is 85 NM from DFW VORTAC. Even though a DME distance fix is shown for TORNN, there is no special VOR changeover indicator that designates TORNN as a COP, thus the midway point (81 NM) should be used.

ALL

8785. (Refer to Figure 100 or 101.) What is the magnetic variation at both DFW Intl and IAH?

A— 08 E.

B— 0.

C— 08 W.

The Magnetic Variation for the DFW VOR is 8° East. (PLT078) — Chart Supplements U.S.

ALL

8786. (Refer to Figures 100 and 102.) How should the pilot identify the position to leave V369 for the Cugar Four Arrival?

A— Intercept R-305 of IAH.

B— 21 DME miles from TNV.

C— 141 DME miles from DFW.

The CUGAR4 STAR begins at BILEE INT but the initial course is inbound on the TNV 334° radial which is the same as V369. This is the course to be flown until intercepting the IAH 305° radial. (PLT080) — Enroute Low Altitude Chart Legend

Answer (B) is incorrect because there is no DME fix for 21 DME miles from TNV VORTAC on either the STAR or the IFR Enroute Chart. Answer (C) is incorrect because a pilot should have changed over to TNV VORTAC, and there is no 141 DME fix from DFW on V369.

Answers

8798 [C]	8782 [C]	8783 [C]	8784 [B]	8785 [A]	8786 [A]

ALL
8824. (Refer to Figure 114.) The changeover point on V394 between DAG VORTAC and POM VORTAC is

A— halfway.
B— 38 DME miles from DAG VORTAC.
C— 64 DME miles from DAG VORTAC.

There is a changeover point marked on the enroute chart at 64 NM from DAG VORTAC and 16 NM from POM VORTAC. (PLT058) — Enroute Low Altitude Chart

Answer (A) is incorrect because when the changeover point is not located at the midway point, aeronautical charts will depict the location and give mileage to the radio aids. Answer (B) is incorrect because 38 DME miles from DAG VORTAC is APLES INT (not the change-over point).

ALL
8825. (Refer to Figure 114.) The minimum crossing altitude at APLES INT southwest bound on V394 is

A— 7,500 feet.
B— 9,100 feet.
C— 11,500 feet.

There is a Minimum Crossing Altitude (MCA) of 9,100 feet at APLES INT when southwest bound on V394. (PLT058) — Enroute Low Altitude Chart Legend

Answer (A) is incorrect because 7,500 feet is the minimum enroute altitude (MEA) from DAG VORTAC to APLES INT on V394, not the MCA at APLES INT. Answer (C) is incorrect because 11,500 feet is the minimum enroute altitude after APLES INT, not the MCA at APLES INT.

ALL
8826. (Refer to Figure 114, lower panel.) What is the minimum enroute altitude on V210, when crossing the POM VORTAC southwest bound and continuing on the same airway?

A— 10,700 feet.
B— 10,300 feet.
C— 5,300 feet.

The Minimum Enroute Altitude (MEA) approaching POM VORTAC southwest bound is 5,300 feet. Absent an MCA, this is the minimum crossing altitude at the VORTAC. There is no published MCA for V210 Southwest bound crossing POM. (PLT058) — Enroute Low Altitude Chart Legend

Answer (A) is incorrect because 10,700 feet is the MEA from MEANT INT to CALBE INT when southwest bound on V210. Answer (B) is incorrect because 10,300 feet is the MCA on V210 northeast bound.

ALL
8810. (Refer to Figures 110 and 112.) How should the pilot identify the position to leave V369 for the Cugar Four Arrival?

A— Intercept R-305 of IAH.
B— 21 DME miles from TNV.
C— 141 DME miles from DFW.

The CUGAR4 STAR begins at BILEE INT but the initial course is inbound on the TNV 334° radial which is the same as V369. This is the course to be flown until intercepting the IAH 305° radial. (PLT080) — Enroute Chart

Answer (B) is incorrect because the pilot should leave V369 when he/she intercepts R-305 of IAH, not 21 DME miles from TNV. Answer (C) is incorrect because the pilot should have switched to TNV VORTAC for V369 course guidance before BILEE INT and should not be using DFW VORTAC for any navigational guidance.

ALL
8811. (Refer to Figure 112.) What action should the pilot take if communications were lost during the Cugar Four Arrival, after turning on the 305 radial of IAH?

A— Proceed direct to IAH VORTAC, then outbound on the IAH R-125 for a procedure turn for final approach.
B— From BANTY INT, proceed to the IAF on the IAH R-290, then continue on the IAH 10 DME Arc to final approach.
C— Proceed direct to IAH VORTAC, then to either IAF on the IAH 10 DME Arc to final approach.

In the event of a two-way radio failure, the pilot should fly the cleared route to the clearance limit. If the clearance limit is not a fix from which an approach begins, he/she should leave the clearance limit (if no EFC has been received) upon arrival at the limit and proceed to a fix from which an approach begins. Then, commence descent and approach as close as possible to the estimated time of arrival. (PLT208) — 14 CFR §91.185(c)

Answer (A) is incorrect because there is no procedure turn indicated for the VOR/DME RWY 32R approach; thus, no procedure turn can be made to reverse course. Answer (B) is incorrect because the pilot would proceed to the IAH VORTAC, then to either IAF on the IAH 10 DME arc to final approach.

Answers

| 8824 [C] | 8825 [B] | 8826 [C] | 8810 [A] | 8811 [C] |

ALL

8812. (Refer to Figure 112.) The Cugar Four Arrival ends

A— at BANTY INT.
B— at IAH VORTAC.
C— when cleared to land.

The text portion of the STAR says to expect radar vectors to final after BANTY INT. (PLT080) — STAR Chart

Answer (B) is incorrect because the arrival ends at BANTY INT. Answer (C) is incorrect because a clearance to land will be given during the instrument approach procedure, which is after the end of the Cugar Four Arrival.

ALL

8816. (Refer to Figure 112.) What effect on approach minimums, if any, does an inoperative MALSR have for an aircraft with an approach speed of 120 knots at IAH?

A— None.
B— Increases RVR to 5,000 feet.
C— Increases RVR to 6,000 feet.

A 120-knot approach speed makes this a Category B aircraft for approach minimum purposes. When MALSR is inoperative on a VOR/DME approach, 1/2 mile must be added to the required visibility. The published Category B minimums are 2,400 RVR (1/2 mile). The higher minimums are therefore 1 mile or 5,000 RVR. (PLT082) — FAA Legend 11

Answer (A) is incorrect because, with an inoperative MALSR, there is no change to the MDA, but an increase of 1/2 mile to the required visibility. Answer (C) is incorrect because an airplane with an approach speed of 141-165 knots (Category D) or greater would have the visibility increased to RVR of 6,000 feet.

ALL

8817. (Refer to Figure 112.) When is the earliest time the pilot may initiate a descent from 460 feet MSL to land at IAH?

A— Anytime after GALES INT if the runway environment is visible.
B— Only after the IAH 1.3 DME if the runway environment is visible.
C— Only after the IAH 1 DME if the runway environment is visible.

The "v" symbol in the profile view at the 1.3 DME fix is a Visual Descent Point (VDP). If able to receive the VDP, a pilot may not begin descent below the MDA until reaching the VDP. (PLT083) — FAA Legend 3

Answer (A) is incorrect because GALES INT is the final approach fix (FAF) which indicates the point at which a pilot may initiate a descent to the MDA. Answer (C) is incorrect because, at the IAH, 1 DME is the MAP which must be initiated if the runway environment is not in sight. The earliest time the pilot may initiate a descent from the MDA of 460 feet at IAH is at the VDP.

ALL

8818. (Refer to Figure 112.) How should the pilot identify the MAP on the IAH VOR/DME RWY 32R?

A— After time has elapsed from FAF.
B— IAH 1.3 DME.
C— IAH 1 DME.

The IAH 1 DME fix is designated as the MAP. (PLT083) — IFR Approach Plate

Answer (A) is incorrect because timing from the FAF is used on non-precision approaches that are not VOR/DME procedures, or when the facility is on the airport and the facility is the MAP. Answer (B) is incorrect because IAH 1.3 DME is the VDP.

ALL

8849. (Refer to Figure 122.) What is the lowest altitude at which the glide slope may be intercepted when authorized by ATC?

A— 2,500 feet.
B— 3,000 feet.
C— 4,000 feet.

The lowest altitude at which the glide slope may be intercepted when authorized by ATC is 2,500 feet as indicated by the number 2500 with a solid line below the altitude next to the FAF. (PLT083) — FAA-H-8083-15

Answer (B) is incorrect because 3,000 feet is the minimum altitude at GRETI, which is prior to the FAF unless ATC authorizes a descent to 2,500 feet. Answer (C) is incorrect because 4,000 feet is the minimum altitude at KITTS (not the FAF), unless ATC authorizes a descent to 2,500 feet.

Answers

| 8812 | [A] | 8816 | [B] | 8817 | [B] | 8818 | [C] | 8849 | [A] |

ALL

8850. (Refer to Figure 122.) What would be the DME reading at the lowest altitude at which the glide slope may be intercepted when authorized by ATC?

A— 12.4 miles.
B— 9.4 miles.
C— 7.7 miles.

The DME reading at the lowest altitude for glide slope intercept is at the FAF marker which indicates altitude of 2500 at 7.7 DME. See FAA Figure 122 around Jockey LOM. (PLT083) — Instrument Approach Procedure

Answer (A) is incorrect because 12.4 NM is the DME reading at KITTS. Answer (B) is incorrect because 9.4 NM is the DME reading at GRETI.

ALL

8851. (Refer to Figure 122.) At what altitude and indicated airspeed would you expect to cross PIVOT INT on the approach to ORD?

A— FL 200 and 300 KIAS.
B— 10,000 feet and 250 KIAS.
C— 12,000 feet and 200 KIAS.

You would expect to cross PIVOT intersection at 10,000 feet and 250 KIAS as indicated by the vertical navigation planning information on the upper left-hand corner of the STAR. (PLT083) — STAR Chart

Answer (A) is incorrect because turbojet arrivals should expect a clearance to cross PMM VORTAC at FL200. Answer (C) is incorrect because 12,000 feet and 200 KIAS is not an expected clearance for either a turbojet or turboprop aircraft using the Pullman Two Arrival to ORD.

ALL

8852. (Refer to Figure 279 and Legend 9.) What is the approximate rate of descent required (for planning purposes) to maintain the electronic glide slope at 120 KIAS with a reported headwind component of 15 knots?

A— 635 ft/min.
B— 650 ft/min.
C— 555 ft/min.

The ILS RWY 32L approach into Chicago-O'Hare has a 3° glide slope as indicated within the profile section of the approach chart. Using FAA Legend 9 along with a ground speed of 105 (120 KIAS – 15K headwind component) the rate of descent is 555 feet per minute. (PLT083) — IFR Approach Procedures

Answer (A) is incorrect because a rate of descent of 635 fpm is appropriate for the indicated airspeed of 120 knots. Answer (B) is incorrect because a rate of descent of 650 fpm is appropriate for a 3.5° glide slope angle.

ALL

8799. (Refer to Figures 106 and 107.) Which approach control frequency is indicated for the TNP.DOWNE3 Arrival with LAX as the destination?

A— 128.5 MHz.
B— 124.9 MHz.
C— 124.5 MHz.

FAA Figure 106 lists the approach frequency as 124.5 for the TNP.DOWNE3 arrival. (PLT080) — Chart Supplements U.S.

Answers (A) and (B) are incorrect because the Chart Supplements U.S. frequencies do not apply when using the TNP.DOWNE3 arrival.

ALL

8800. (Refer to Figures 106 and 107.) At what point does the flight enter the final approach phase of the ILS RWY 25L at LAX?

A— FUELR INT.
B— HUNDA INT.
C— Intercept of glide slope.

The "Lightning Bolt" symbol indicates that 3,500 feet is the glide slope interception altitude. An aircraft is considered to be on the final approach segment past this point when on an ILS approach. (PLT083) — Instrument Approach Procedure

Answer (A) is incorrect because FUELR INT is an initial approach fix (IAF) and does not mark the point at which the flight enters the final approach phase. Answer (B) is incorrect because HUNDA INT is a fix at which the pilot should intercept the glide slope, but the intersection itself does not mark the point at which the airplane enters the final approach phase.

ALL

8801. (Refer to Figures 106 and 107.) What is the DH for the ILS RWY 25L at LAX if the pilot has completed the initial Category II certification within the preceding 6 months, but has flown no CAT II approaches?

A— 201 feet.
B— 251 feet.
C— 301 feet.

The IAP minimums section shows DHs of 251 and 201 MSL, which represent 150-foot and 100-foot DHs respectively. Regulations restrict a pilot who has completed initial CAT II qualification to the 150-foot DH until he/she has completed 3 approaches to that minimum within the previous 6 months. (PLT420) — 14 CFR §61.13

Answer (A) is incorrect because a DH of 201 feet is available once the initial Category II limitation is removed. Answer (C) is incorrect because a DH of 150 feet is the limitation placed upon an original issue for Category II operations.

Answers

8850 [C]	8851 [B]	8852 [C]	8799 [C]	8800 [C]	8801 [B]

ALL

8802. (Refer to Figures 106 and 107.) The radio altimeter indication for the DH at the inner marker on the ILS RWY 25L approach at LAX is

A— 101.
B— 111.
C— 201.

The RA height at the IM is also the DH for the 100-foot minimums. At this point, the radio altimeter will indicate 111 feet. (PLT083) — Instrument Approach Procedure

Answer (A) is incorrect because 101 feet is the touchdown zone elevation (TDZE). Answer (C) is incorrect because 201 feet is the height above touchdown (HAT) at the inner marker.

ALL

8803. (Refer to Figure 257A.) If the glide slope indication is lost upon passing LIMMA INT on the ILS RWY 25L approach at LAX, what action should the pilot take?

A— Continue to the MAP, and execute the missed approach as indicated.
B— Continue the approach as an LOC, and add 100 feet to the DH.
C— Immediately start the missed approach left turn to CATLY INT.

Obstacle clearance on a missed approach is predicated on the assumption that the abort is initiated at the MAP and not lower than the DH or MDA. When an early missed approach is executed, pilots should, unless otherwise authorized by ATC, fly the instrument approach procedure to the MAP at or above the DH or MDA before executing any turning maneuver. (PLT083) — AIM ¶5-5-5

Answer (B) is incorrect because the LOC minimums for this approach are 540 feet MDA and 24 RVR. Answer (C) is incorrect because protected obstacle clearance areas for missed approaches are made on the assumption that the abort is made at the MAP. No consideration is made for an abnormally early turn, unless otherwise directed by ATC.

ALL

8804. (Refer to Figures 106 and 107.) What approach lights are available for the ILS RWY 25L approach at LAX?

A— ALSF-2 with sequenced flashing lights.
B— MALSR with a displayed threshold.
C— HIRL and TDZ/CL.

The "A" in the circle next to runway 25L on the Airport Diagram indicates that ALSF-2 approach lights are available. The dot at the top of the circle indicates that sequenced flashing lights are part of the system. See FAA Legend 5. (PLT078) — Chart Supplements U.S.

Answer (B) is incorrect because RWY 25R has an out of service (see Remarks) MALSR and a displaced threshold. Answer (C) is incorrect because high intensity runway lights (HIRL), touchdown zone lights (TDZ), and centerline lights (CL) are runway lighting systems.

ALL

8805. (Refer to Figures 106 and 107.) How can DOWNE INT be identified?

A— ILAX 15 DME.
B— LAX 15 DME.
C— LAX R-249 and SLI R-327.

DOWNE INT can be identified by the SLI 327° radial crossing the localizer or by the I-LAX 15 DME. (PLT083) — Instrument Approach Procedure

Answer (B) is incorrect because LAX 15 DME defines a circle, not an intersection. The correct answer would be LAX R-068, 15 DME. Answer (C) is incorrect because DOWNE INT is located on the ILS localizer, not on a radial from the LAX VORTAC.

ALL

8806. (Refer to Figure 107.) How should the IFR flight plan be closed upon landing at LAX?

A— Contact Hawthorne FSS on 123.6 MHz.
B— Phone Hawthorne FSS on 644-1020.
C— LAX tower will close it automatically.

If operating IFR to an airport with a functioning control tower, the flight plan is automatically closed upon landing. (PLT224) — AIM ¶5-1-14

Answer (A) is incorrect because an IFR flight plan would be closed with a flight service station only if there is no operating tower. According to the Chart Supplement U.S. (previously A/FD) in Figure 107, 123.6 MHz is not a frequency on which to contact Hawthorne FSS.

ALL

8950. (Refer to Figure 134.) What are the required weather minimums to execute the CONVERGING ILS RWY 9R approach procedure?

A— Ceiling 700 feet and 2-1/2 miles visibility.
B— At least 1,000 feet and 3 miles visibility.
C— Ceiling 800 feet and 2 miles visibility.

The required weather minimums are listed as 721–2-1/2 700 (700–2-1/2). The 721 refers to DH in MSL. The 2-1/2 refers to visibility in miles. The 700 refers to height of DH above touchdown zone. The minimums in parentheses apply only to military pilots. (PLT083) — FAA-H-8083-15

Answer (B) is incorrect because 1,000 feet and 3 miles visibility defines the minimums required for VFR flight in Class D or E airspace for an airport. Answer (C) is incorrect because 800 feet and 2 miles visibility with a nonprecision approach are alternate minimums.

Answers

8802 [B] 8803 [A] 8804 [A] 8805 [A] 8806 [C] 8950 [A]

ALL

8951. (Refer to Figure 134.) What is the final approach fix for the CONVERGING ILS RWY 9R approach procedure?

A— BWINE INT and 3,000 feet MSL.
B— KELEE INT.
C— 1,800 feet MSL and glide slope interception.

The final approach fix is designated on government charts by the Maltese Cross symbol for nonprecision approaches and the lightning bolt symbol for precision approaches. The lightning bolt symbol on the descent profile portion of the chart indicates the FAF as 1,800 feet MSL. See Legend 3. (PLT083) — Pilot/Controller Glossary

Answer (A) is incorrect because by looking at the plan view of the chart (Figure 6-38), BWINE Intersection is labeled as an IAF or initial approach fix (not a final approach fix). Answer (B) is incorrect because KELEE Intersection only identifies the outer marker. Note that the lightning bolt arrow is depicted just prior to KELEE Intersection.

ALL

8952. (Refer to Figure 134.) What is the MINIMUM airborne equipment required to execute the CONVERGING ILS RWY 9R approach procedure?

A— Localizer and DME.
B— Localizer and glide slope.
C— Localizer only.

Neither the chart title nor the missed approach procedure specifies DME. The category minimums specify "NA" (not authorized) for localizer only and circling approaches. (PLT083) — AIM ¶5-5-4

ALL

8836. (Refer to Figure 118A.) Straight-in minimums for a Category B aircraft equipped with DME on the LOC BC RWY 26L approach are

A— 1,800/1.
B— 700/1.
C— 1,640/1.

The straight in minimums for the LOC 26L approach are an MDA of 1,640 and visibility of 1 mile if the HADEN DME fix is identified. (PLT083) — Instrument Approach Procedure

Answer (A) is incorrect because 1,800/1 are the straight-in minimums without DME. Answer (B) is incorrect because 700/1 are military minimums without operating DME.

ALL

8837. (Refer to Figure 118A.) How is course reversal accomplished when outbound on the LOC BC RWY 26L approach at Phoenix Sky Harbor Intl?

A— Radar vector only.
B— Procedure turn beyond 10 NM.
C— Holding pattern entry beyond 10 NM.

The absence of the procedure turn barb in the plan view indicates that a procedure turn is not authorized for that procedure. (PLT083) — AIM ¶5-4-9

Answer (B) is incorrect because no procedure turn is depicted on the IAP chart, and when radar is used for vectoring, no pilot may make a procedure turn unless he/she requests and is issued a clearance by ATC. Answer (C) is incorrect because no holding pattern is depicted on the IAP chart and it may not be used as a course reversal.

ALL

8839. (Refer to Figure 118A.) Identify the final approach fix on the LOC BC RWY 26L approach at Phoenix Sky Harbor Intl.

A— Upon intercepting the glide slope beyond I PHX 5 DME.
B— When crossing I-PHX 5 DME at 3,000 feet.
C— When crossing the SRP VORTAC on the glide slope.

The "Maltese Cross" symbol indicates the final approach fix for the LOC 26L approach is at the I-PHX 5 DME fix. The minimum altitude for crossing that fix is 3,000 feet MSL. See FAA Legend 3. (PLT083) — Instrument Approach Procedure

Answers (A) and (C) are incorrect because an LOC approach is a nonprecision approach that does not provide glide slope information. On the back course a glide slope indication may be indicated, but it must be ignored.

ATM, ATS

8704. (Refer to Figure 263.) You are flying a turbojet cleared for the RIICE THREE arrival, IAH landing to the west. ATC tells you to cross RIICE at 12,000 feet and 220 knots until BRKMN. What airspeed should you fly after passing BRKMN?

A— 200 knots.
B— 220 knots.
C— 250 knots.

The chart notes, "TURBOJETS: Landing west at IAH expect clearance to cross RIICE at 12000, cross BRKMN at 250kts." (PLT083) — Instrument Approach Procedures

Answers

| 8951 | [C] | 8952 | [B] | 8836 | [C] | 8837 | [A] | 8839 | [B] | 8704 | [C] |

ATM, DSP

8242. Assuring that appropriate aeronautical charts are aboard an aircraft is the responsibility of the

A— aircraft dispatcher.
B— first officer.
C— pilot-in-command.

The pilot-in-command shall ensure that appropriate aeronautical charts containing adequate information concerning navigation aids and instrument approach procedures are aboard the aircraft for each flight. (PLT444) — 14 CFR §121.549

Answer (A) is incorrect because the dispatcher may be hundreds of miles from the origination of the flight, e.g., in a central dispatch office. Answer (B) is incorrect because although a first officer may be assigned the task of carrying aeronautical charts, the pilot-in-command is responsible for ensuring that adequate charts are aboard the aircraft.

RTC

9572. (Refer to Figures 111 and 112.) While N131JB was flying the VOR/DME RWY 32R approach to Houston Intercontinental, approach control told them to contact copter control, at GALES. Approach control did not tell them what frequency, and did not respond when N131JB asked what frequency. What frequency should N131JB use for copter control?

A— 118.1.
B— 121.5.
C— 135.15.

The frequency for copter control at Houston Intercontinental is found under the tower listing in the Chart Supplements U.S. (previously A/FD). (PLT078) — Chart Supplements U.S.

Answers

8242 [C]   9572 [C]

Chapter 7
Emergencies, Hazards, and Flight Physiology

Flight Emergencies and Hazards

The Pilot/Controller Glossary divides emergencies into two categories: **distress** and **urgency**. Distress is a condition of being threatened by serious and/or imminent danger and of requiring immediate assistance. Distress conditions include fire, mechanical failure or structural damage. An urgency condition is one of being concerned about safety and of requiring timely but not immediate assistance. At least an urgency condition exists the moment a pilot becomes doubtful about position, fuel endurance, weather or any other condition that could adversely affect the safety of flight. A pilot should declare an emergency when either an urgency or a distress condition exists.

When a distress or urgency condition exists, the pilot should set the radar beacon transponder to code 7700. If an aircraft is being hijacked or illegally interfered with, the pilot can alert ATC to that fact by setting the transponder to code 7500. If an aircraft has experienced a two-way communications radio failure, the pilot should set the transponder to code 7600. The pilot should also conform to the radio failure procedures of 14 CFR §91.185 (IFR operations: Two-way radio communications failure). In order to avoid false alarms, pilots should take care not to inadvertently switch through codes 7500, 7600 and 7700 when changing the transponder.

If a two-way radio failure occurs in VFR conditions, or if VFR conditions are encountered after the failure, the pilot must continue the flight under VFR and land as soon as practicable. If IFR conditions prevail, the pilot must follow the rules listed below for route, altitude and time to leave a clearance limit:

Route to be Flown

- The route assigned in the last ATC clearance received.
- If being radar vectored, fly by the direct route from the point of the radio failure to the fix, route or airway specified in the vector clearance.
- In the absence of an assigned route, fly by the route that ATC has advised may be expected in a further clearance.
- In the absence of an assigned route or expected further routing, fly by the route filed in the flight plan.

Altitude

Fly the highest of the following altitudes or flight levels for the route segment being flown:

- The altitude or flight level assigned in the last ATC clearance received.
- The minimum IFR altitude for the route segment being flown (MEA).
- The altitude or flight level that ATC has advised may be expected in a further clearance.

When to Leave a Clearance Limit

- When the clearance limit is a fix from which an approach begins, commence descent or descent and approach as close as possible to the expect further clearance (EFC) time if one has been received; or if one has not been received, as close as possible to the estimated time of arrival (ETA) as calculated from the filed or amended estimated time en route.
- If the clearance limit is not a fix from which an approach begins, leave the clearance limit at the expect further clearance (EFC) time if one has been received; or if none has been received, upon arrival over the clearance limit, and proceed to a fix from which an approach begins and commence descent or descent and approach as close as possible to the estimated time of arrival (ETA) as calculated from the filed or amended time en route.

Continued

A near midair collision is defined as an occurrence in which the possibility of a collision existed as the result of two aircraft coming within 500 feet or less of each other.

A minimum fuel advisory is used by a pilot to inform ATC that the fuel supply has reached a state where the pilot cannot accept any undue delay upon arrival at the destination. The minimum fuel advisory is not a declaration of an emergency, nor is it a request for priority. It does indicate that an emergency situation may develop if any undue delay occurs during the rest of the flight.

Some airports have a number of wind indicators located around the perimeter of the field as well as a center field windsock. When there is a significant difference in speed or direction between the center field windsock and one or more of the boundary wind indicators, the tower can report that a wind shear condition exists.

A safety alert will be issued to pilots being controlled by ATC in either of two circumstances. A controller will issue a safety alert when, in the controller's opinion, the aircraft's altitude will put it in unsafe proximity to the surface or an obstacle. A controller will also issue an alert if he/she becomes aware of another aircraft, not controlled by him/her, that will put both aircraft in an unsafe proximity to each other.

The **wake turbulence** developed by large aircraft can present a significant flight hazard to other aircraft that encounter them. The main component of wake turbulence is **wing-tip vortices**. These are twin vortices of air trailing behind an aircraft in flight. The **vortex** is a by-product of lift. The pressure under each wing is greater than the pressure above it and this induces a flow of air outward, upward and around the wing tip. This leaves two counter-rotating spirals of air trailing behind the aircraft. *See* Figure 7-1.

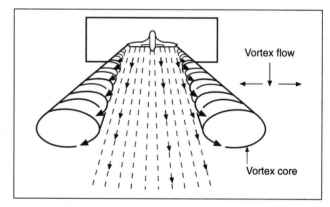

Figure 7-1

The characteristics of a vortex can be altered by changing the aircraft's configuration. The most intense vortices will be produced by an airplane that is heavy, flying slowly, and with the landing gear and flaps retracted.

The vortices generated by a large aircraft will slowly sink below its flight path and dissipate by the time they have descended about 1,000 feet. They will also tend to drift away from each other at a speed of about five knots. In a light crosswind, the upwind vortex will tend to stay over the same position on the ground while the downwind vortex will move away at about twice its normal rate. It is good wake turbulence avoidance technique to stay above and on the upwind side of the flight path of a preceding large airplane.

If the vortices reach the ground before dissipating, they will move away from each other as noted above. In a light crosswind, the upwind vortex can remain on the runway long after a large airplane has taken off or landed. The most hazardous situation is a light quartering tailwind, which not only keeps a vortex on the runway but also inhibits its dissipation.

If you plan to take off behind a large airplane, try to rotate prior to that airplane's point of rotation and climb out above and on the upwind side of the other airplane's flight path. If you plan to takeoff from a runway on which a large airplane has just landed, try to plan your lift-off point to be beyond the point where that aircraft touched down. *See* Figure 7-2.

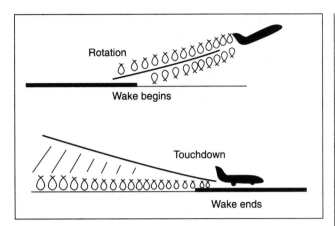

Figure 7-2

ALL
9097. What minimum condition is suggested for declaring an emergency?

A— Anytime the pilot is doubtful of a condition that could adversely affect flight safety.
B— When fuel endurance or weather will require an en route or landing priority.
C— When distress conditions such as fire, mechanical failure, or structural damage occurs.

An aircraft is in an emergency condition the moment the pilot becomes doubtful about position, fuel endurance, weather or any other condition that could adversely affect flight safety. (PLT394) — AIM ¶6-1-2

Answer (B) is incorrect because, if fuel endurance or weather will require an en route or landing priority, this is beyond an urgency situation and is now a distress condition. Answer (C) is incorrect because this is the step after an urgency condition, one that has the potential to become a distress condition.

ALL
9051. What is the hijack code?

A— 7200.
B— 7500.
C— 7777.

Only nondiscrete transponder code 7500 will be decoded as the hijack code. (PLT497) — AIM ¶4-1-20

Answer (A) is incorrect because 7200 is a code that is used for normal operating procedures. Answer (C) is incorrect because code 7777 is reserved for military interceptor operations.

ALL
9052. Which range of codes should a pilot avoid switching through when changing transponder codes?

A— 0000 through 1000.
B— 7200 and 7500 series.
C— 7500, 7600, and 7700 series.

When making routine transponder code changes, pilot should avoid inadvertent selection of codes 7500, 7600 or 7700 thereby causing momentary false alarms at automated ground facilities. (PLT497) — AIM ¶4-1-20

Answer (A) is incorrect because codes 0000 through 1000 are acceptable codes that may be used during normal operations. Answer (B) is incorrect because the 7200 series can be used during normal operations, while 7500 should be avoided except in the case of a hijack.

ALL
9362. After experiencing two-way radio communications failure en route, when should a pilot begin the descent for the instrument approach?

A— Upon arrival at any initial approach fix for the instrument approach procedure but not before the flight plan ETA as amended by ATC.
B— Upon arrival at the holding fix depicted on the instrument approach procedure at the corrected ETA, plus or minus 3 minutes.
C— At the primary initial approach fix for the instrument approach procedure at the ETA shown on the flight plan or the EFC time, whichever is later.

During a two-way radio communications failure, if the clearance limit is a fix from which an approach begins, commence descent or descent and approach as close as possible to the expect further clearance (EFC) time, if one has been received. If no EFC time has been received, commence descent and approach as close as possible to the estimated time of arrival as calculated from the filed or amended (with ATC) estimated time en route. (PLT391) — 14 CFR §91.185

Answer (B) is incorrect because an approach should begin at the initial approach fix, not at a holding fix, as close as possible to the ETA. Answer (C) is incorrect because an EFC time supersedes a flight plan ETA and should be used if one has been received (no matter if the EFC is sooner or later than the flight plan ETA).

Answers

9097   [A]   9051   [B]   9052   [C]   9362   [A]

ALL

9363. If a pilot is being radar vectored in IFR conditions and loses radio communications with ATC, what action should be taken?

A— Fly directly to the next point shown on the IFR flight plan and continue the flight.

B— Squawk 7700 and climb to VFR on Top.

C— Fly direct to a fix, route, or airway specified in the vector clearance.

If a two-way radio communication failure occurs while in IFR conditions the pilot should continue the flight by the following route:

1. By the route assigned in the last ATC clearance;

2. If being radar vectored, by the direct route from the point of the radio failure to the fix, route or airway specified in the vector clearance;

3. In the absence of an assigned route, by the route that ATC has advised may be expected in a further clearance; or

4. In the absence of an assigned route or a route that ATC has advised may be expected in a further clearance, by the route filed in the flight plan.

(PLT406) — 14 CFR §91.185

Answer (A) is incorrect because the route shown on the flight plan should be the last route to be used and only if an assigned route, vector, or expected route has not been received. Answer (B) is incorrect because a climb should only be initiated in order to establish the highest of either the assigned, MEA, or expected altitude. The squawk of 7700 is no longer correct.

ALL

9364. A pilot is flying in IFR weather conditions and has two-way radio communications failure. What altitude should be used?

A— Last assigned altitude, altitude ATC has advised to expect, or the MEA, whichever is highest.

B— An altitude that is at least 1,000 feet above the highest obstacle along the route.

C— A VFR altitude that is above the MEA for each leg.

A pilot should maintain the highest altitude or flight level of the following for each route segment:

1. The altitude or flight level assigned in the last ATC clearance received;

2. The minimum altitude or flight level for IFR operations (MEA); or

3. The altitude that ATC has advised may be expected in a further clearance.

(PLT391) — 14 CFR §91.185

Answer (B) is incorrect because 1,000 feet above the highest obstacle along the route is what a MOCA, (minimum obstruction clearance altitude) provides. Answer (C) is incorrect because VFR altitudes or regulations should never be used while flying in IFR weather conditions.

ALL

9365. A pilot is holding at an initial approach fix after having experienced two-way radio communications failure. When should that pilot begin descent for the instrument approach?

A— At the EFC time, if this is within plus or minus 3 minutes of the flight plan ETA as amended by ATC.

B— At flight plan ETA as amended by ATC.

C— At the EFC time as amended by ATC.

During a two-way radio communications failure, if the clearance limit is a fix from which an approach begins, commence descent or descent and approach as close as possible to the expect further clearance (EFC) time, if one has been received. If no EFC time has been received, commence descent and approach as close as possible to the estimated time of arrival as calculated from the filed or amended (with ATC) estimated time enroute. (PLT391) — 14 CFR §91.185

Answer (A) is incorrect because the approach should begin at the EFC time, regardless of whether it is close to the planned ETA or not; ETA is only used if an EFC has not been received. Answer (B) is incorrect because a pilot who is holding at an initial approach fix after having experienced a two-way radio communication failure without an EFC time should begin descent for the instrument approach so that the arrival will coincide as closely as possible with the ETA.

ALL

9389. What altitude and route should be used if the pilot is flying in IFR weather conditions and has two-way radio communications failure?

A— Continue on the route specified in the clearance and fly the highest of the following: the last assigned altitude, altitude ATC has informed the pilot to expect, or to the MEA.

B— Descend to MEA and, if clear of clouds, proceed to the nearest appropriate airport. If not clear of clouds, maintain the highest of the MEAs along the clearance route.

C— Fly the most direct route to the destination, maintaining the last assigned altitude or MEA, whichever is higher.

Answers

9363 [C]   9364 [A]   9365 [C]   9389 [A]

If a two-way radio communication failure occurs while in IFR conditions the pilot should continue the flight by the following route:

1. *By the route assigned in the last ATC clearance;*

2. *If being radar vectored, by the direct route from the point of the radio failure to the fix, route or airway specified in the vector clearance;*

3. *In the absence of an assigned route, by the route that ATC has advised may be expected in a further clearance; or*

4. *In the absence of an assigned route or a route that ATC has advised may be expected in a further clearance, by the route filed in the flight plan.*

A pilot should maintain the highest altitude or flight level of the following for each route segment:

1. *The altitude or flight level assigned in the last ATC clearance received;*

2. *The minimum altitude or flight level for IFR operations (MEA); or*

3. *The altitude that ATC has advised may be expected in a further clearance.*

(PLT391) — 14 CFR §91.185

Answer (B) is incorrect because the highest of either the MEA, expected altitude, or assigned altitude should be used. Answer (C) is incorrect because, if ATC advises you may expect an altitude after reaching a clearance limit, and it is higher than the published MEA or assigned altitude, the expected altitude should be used. The route to be used should be the one assigned by ATC, as specified in a vector clearance, by the route ATC has advised may be expected, or in the absence of all of these, the route as filed in the flight plan, not the most direct route.

ALL

9390. While in IFR conditions, a pilot experiences two-way radio communications failure. Which route should be flown in the absence of an ATC assigned route or a route ATC has advised to expect in a further clearance?

A— The most direct route to the filed alternate airport.
B— An off-airway route to the point of departure.
C— The route filed in the flight plan.

If a two-way radio communication failure occurs while in IFR conditions the pilot should continue the flight by the following route:

1. *By the route assigned in the last ATC clearance;*

2. *If being radar vectored, by the direct route from the point of the radio failure to the fix, route or airway specified in the vector clearance;*

3. *In the absence of an assigned route, by the route that ATC has advised may be expected in a further clearance; or*

4. *In the absence of an assigned route or a route that ATC has advised may be expected in a further clearance, by the route filed in the flight plan.*

(PLT391) — 14 CFR §91.185

ALL

9098. It is the responsibility of the pilot and crew to report a near midair collision as a result of proximity of at least

A— 50 feet or less to another aircraft.
B— 500 feet or less to another aircraft.
C— 1,000 feet or less to another aircraft.

A near midair collision is defined as an incident associated with the operation on an aircraft in which a possibility of collision occurs as a result of proximity of less than 500 feet to another aircraft, or a report is received from a pilot or flight crewmember stating that a collision hazard existed between two or more aircraft. (PLT366) — AIM ¶7-6-3

ALL

9010. Under what condition should a pilot on IFR advise ATC of minimum fuel status?

A— When the fuel supply becomes less than that required for IFR.
B— If the remaining fuel suggests a need for traffic or landing priority.
C— If the remaining fuel precludes any undue delay.

A pilot should advise ATC of his/her minimum fuel status when the fuel supply has reached a state where, upon reaching destination, he/she cannot accept any undue delay. It indicates a possible future emergency, but does not declare one and does not get priority handling. (PLT318) — AIM ¶5-5-15

Answer (A) is incorrect because a pilot must ensure the minimum amount of fuel is on board the airplane for the planned IFR flight and alternatives, if needed, during the flight planning phase. Answer (B) is incorrect because, if the remaining fuel suggests a need for traffic or landing priority, the pilot should declare an emergency (not minimum fuel status), and report fuel remaining in minutes.

ALL

9011. What does the term "minimum fuel" imply to ATC?

A— Traffic priority is needed to the destination airport.

B— Emergency handling is required to the nearest suitable airport.

C— Advisory that indicates an emergency situation is possible should an undue delay occur.

A pilot should advise ATC of his/her minimum fuel status when the fuel supply has reached a state where, upon reaching destination, he/she cannot accept any undue delay. It indicates a possible future emergency, but does not declare one and does not get priority handling. (PLT318) — AIM ¶5-5-15

Answer (A) is incorrect because a pilot should declare an emergency and report fuel remaining in minutes if traffic priority is needed to the destination airport. Answer (B) is incorrect because emergency handling to the nearest suitable airport would be required in a distress or urgent type of emergency.

ALL

9420. You should advise ATC of minimum fuel status when your fuel supply has reached a state where, upon reaching your destination, you cannot accept any undue delay.

A— This will ensure your priority handling by ATC.

B— ATC will consider this action as if you had declared an emergency.

C— If your remaining usable fuel supply suggests the need for traffic priority to ensure a safe landing, declare an emergency due to low fuel and report fuel remaining in minutes.

If the remaining usable fuel supply suggests the need for traffic priority to ensure a safe landing, you should declare an emergency due to low fuel and report fuel remaining in minutes. (PLT318) —AIM ¶5-5-15

Answer (A) is incorrect because minimum fuel advisory does not imply a need for a traffic priority. Answer (B) is incorrect because minimum fuel advisory is not an emergency situation, but merely an advisory that indicates an emergency situation is possible should any undue delay occur.

ALL

9054. What airport condition is reported by the tower when more than one wind condition at different positions on the airport is reported?

A— Light and variable.

B— Wind shear.

C— Frontal passage.

The Low-Level Wind Shear Alert System (LLWAS) is a computerized system which detects low level wind shear by continuously comparing the winds measured by sensors installed around the periphery of an airport with the wind measured at the center field location. When a significant difference exists, the tower controller will provide aircraft with an advisory of the situation which includes the center field wind plus the remote site location and wind. (PLT518) — AIM ¶4-3-7

Answer (A) is incorrect because "light and variable" is used to report the wind conditions when wind speed is less than 5 knots. Answer (C) is incorrect because a frontal passage is normally indicated by a change in wind direction, but it is usually not reported by the tower.

ALL

9050. Under what condition does ATC issue safety alerts?

A— When collision with another aircraft is imminent.

B— If the aircraft altitude is noted to be in close proximity to the surface or an obstacle.

C— When weather conditions are extreme and wind shear or large hail is in the vicinity.

A safety alert will be issued to pilots of aircraft being controlled by ATC if the controller is aware the aircraft is at an altitude which, in the controller's judgment, places the aircraft in unsafe proximity to terrain, obstructions or other aircraft. (PLT172) — AIM ¶4-1-16

Answer (A) is incorrect because a safety alert is issued to a pilot if ATC believes that his/her airplane is at an altitude which would place it in unsafe proximity to another airplane. Answer (C) is incorrect because, when weather conditions are extreme and wind shear or large hail is in the vicinity, a Convective SIGMET would be broadcast.

ALL

9119. Which flight conditions of a large jet airplane create the most severe flight hazard by generating wingtip vortices of the greatest strength?

A— Heavy, slow, gear and flaps up.

B— Heavy, slow, gear and flaps down.

C— Heavy, fast, gear and flaps down.

The greatest vortex strength occurs when the generating aircraft is heavy, clean (gear and flaps up) and slow. (PLT509) — AIM ¶7-3-3

Answers

| 9011 | [C] | 9420 | [C] | 9054 | [B] | 9050 | [B] | 9119 | [A] |

ALL
9120. Hazardous vortex turbulence that might be encountered behind large aircraft is created only when that aircraft is

A— developing lift.
B— operating at high airspeeds.
C— using high power settings.

Lift is generated by the creation of a pressure differential over the wing surface. The lowest pressure occurs over the upper wing surface and the highest pressure under the wing. This pressure differential triggers the roll up of the airflow aft of the wing resulting in swirling air masses trailing downstream of the wing tips. (PLT509) — AIM ¶7-3-2

Answer (B) is incorrect because hazardous vortex turbulence is created only when the aircraft is developing lift, which can be while operating at low or high airspeeds. A slow, heavy, and clean airplane will generate the most hazardous vortex turbulence. Answer (C) is incorrect because most takeoff rolls are at high power settings, but the generation of vortices does not occur until lift is produced. Landing approaches are also conducted at lower power settings; vortex turbulence is produced whenever an airplane is producing lift.

ALL
9121. Wingtip vortices created by large aircraft tend to

A— sink below the aircraft generating the turbulence.
B— rise from the surface to traffic pattern altitude.
C— accumulate and remain for a period of time at the point where the takeoff roll began.

Flight tests have shown that the vortices from large aircraft sink at a rate of several hundred feet per minute. They tend to level off at a distance about 900 feet below the flight path of the generating aircraft. (PLT509) — AIM ¶7-3-4

Answer (B) is incorrect because vortices created by large aircraft tend to sink from (not rise into) the traffic pattern altitude. Answer (C) is incorrect because wing-tip vortices are not generated until the aircraft's wings develop lift, so no wing-tip vortices are generated at the point where the takeoff roll begins.

ALL
9122. How does the wake turbulence vortex circulate around each wingtip?

A— Inward, upward, and around the wingtip.
B— Counterclockwise when viewed from behind the aircraft.
C— Outward, upward, and around the wingtip.

The vortex circulation is outward, upward and around the wing tips when viewed from either ahead or behind the aircraft. (PLT509) — AIM ¶7-3-4

ALL
9123. Which statement is true concerning the wake turbulence produced by a large transport aircraft?

A— Vortices can be avoided by flying 300 feet below and behind the flightpath of the generating aircraft.
B— The vortex characteristics of any given aircraft may be altered by extending the flaps or changing the speed.
C— Wake turbulence behind a propeller-driven aircraft is negligible because jet engine thrust is a necessary factor in the formation of vortices.

The strength of the vortex is governed by the weight, speed and shape of the wing of the generating aircraft. The vortex characteristics of a given aircraft can be changed by extension of flaps or other wing configuring devices as well as by a change in speed. (PLT509) — AIM ¶7-3-3

Answer (A) is incorrect because the vortices generated by large transport aircraft tend to sink below and behind, thus vortices can be expected by flying 300 feet below and behind the flight path of the generating aircraft. Answer (C) is incorrect because wake turbulence vortices are generated by lift produced by any airplane. It does not matter whether the airplane is powered by propeller or jet engines.

ALL
9124. What effect would a light crosswind have on the wingtip vortices generated by a large airplane that has just taken off?

A— The upwind vortex will tend to remain on the runway longer than the downwind vortex.
B— A crosswind will rapidly dissipate the strength of both vortices.
C— The downwind vortex will tend to remain on the runway longer than the upwind vortex.

A crosswind will decrease the lateral movement of the upwind vortex and increase the movement of the downwind vortex. Thus, a light wind of 3 to 7 knots could result in the upwind vortex remaining in the touchdown zone for a period of time and hasten the drift of the downwind vortex toward another runway. (PLT509) — AIM ¶7-3-4

Answer (B) is incorrect because a crosswind will hold the upwind vortex in the vicinity of the runway. Answer (C) is incorrect because the downwind vortex moves away at a faster rate than the upwind vortex.

Answers

9120 [A]	9121 [A]	9122 [C]	9123 [B]	9124 [A]

ALL

9125. To avoid the wingtip vortices of a departing jet airplane during takeoff, the pilot should

A— lift off at a point well past the jet airplane's flightpath.
B— climb above and stay upwind of the jet airplane's flightpath.
C— remain below the flightpath of the jet airplane.

When departing behind a large aircraft, note its rotation point and rotate prior to that point. During the climb, stay above and upwind of the large aircraft's climb path until turning clear of its wake. (PLT509) — AIM ¶7-3-4

Answer (A) is incorrect because, if you rotate beyond the jet's rotation point, you will have to fly up into the jet's vortices. Answer (C) is incorrect because the jet's vortices will sink. If you stay below the jet's flight path, you will fly in the area of the vortices.

ALL

9126. What wind condition prolongs the hazards of wake turbulence on a landing runway for the longest period of time?

A— Direct tailwind.
B— Light quartering tailwind.
C— Light quartering headwind.

A crosswind will decrease the lateral movement of the upwind vortex and increase the movement of the downwind vortex. Thus a light wind of 3 to 7 knots could result in the upwind vortex remaining in the touchdown zone for a period of time and hasten the drift of the downwind vortex toward another runway. Similarly, a tailwind condition can move the vortices of the preceding aircraft forward into the touchdown zone. The light, quartering tailwind requires maximum caution. (PLT509) — AIM ¶7-3-4

Answer (A) is incorrect because, even though a direct tailwind can move the vortices of a preceding aircraft forward into the touchdown zone, it is not as hazardous because both vortices would move to the sides (and not remain on the runway). Answer (C) is incorrect because a light quartering headwind would move the vortices toward the runway threshold, away from (not into) the touchdown zone on a landing runway.

ALL

9127. If you take off behind a heavy jet that has just landed, you should plan to lift off

A— prior to the point where the jet touched down.
B— beyond the point where the jet touched down.
C— at the point where the jet touched down and on the upwind edge of the runway.

When departing behind a large aircraft which has just landed, note the aircraft's touchdown point and rotate past that point on the runway. (PLT509) — AIM ¶7-3-6

Answer (A) is incorrect because a lift-off prior to the point where the jet touched down would force you to climb through the jet's vortices. Answer (C) is incorrect because lift-off should be planned beyond the point of touchdown to ensure that you avoid the vortices, and you should remain on the center of the runway during takeoff.

ALL

9715. To allow pilots of in-trail lighter aircraft to make flight path adjustments to avoid wake turbulence, pilots of heavy and large jet aircraft should fly

A— below the established glidepath and slightly to either side of the on-course centerline.
B— on the established glidepath and on the approach course centerline or runway centerline extended.
C— above the established glidepath and slightly downwind of the on-course centerline.

Pilots of aircraft that produce strong wake vortices should make every attempt to fly on the established glidepath, and as closely as possible to the approach course centerline or to the extended centerline of the runway of intended landing. (PLT509) — AIM ¶7-3-8

ALL

9858. Which phase of flight has the greatest occurrence of fatal accidents?

A— Takeoff.
B— Landing.
C— Approach.

The pilot's work requirements vary depending on the mode of flight. The tasks increase significantly during the landing phase, creating greater risk to the pilot and warranting actions that require greater precision and attention, but the greatest percentage of fatal accidents occurs during the approach phase of flight. (PLT509) — FAA-H-8083-2

Answers

| 9125 | [B] | 9126 | [B] | 9127 | [B] | 9715 | [B] | 9858 | [C] |

Flight Physiology

Even small amounts of alcohol have an adverse effect on reaction and judgment. This effect is magnified as altitude increases. No one may serve as a crewmember on a civil aircraft:

- Within 8 hours of the consumption of any alcoholic beverage.
- While having a blood alcohol level of .04% or higher.

Runway width illusion — A runway that is narrower than usual can create the illusion that the aircraft is higher than it really is. This can cause an unwary pilot to descend too low on approach. A wide runway creates an illusion of being too low on glide slope.

Featureless terrain illusion — An absence of ground feature, as when landing over water, darkened areas and terrain made featureless by snow can create the illusion that the aircraft is higher than it really is.

Autokinesis — In the dark, a static light will appear to move about when stared at for a period of time.

An effective scan pattern is necessary to ensure that a pilot will see other aircraft in time to avoid potential midair collisions. This means that 2/3 to 3/4 of a pilot's time should be spent scanning outside the aircraft. The best method would be to look outside for about 15 seconds and then inside for about 5 seconds. It is much easier to see an aircraft which is moving relative to the observer. Unfortunately, aircraft which present a collision hazard are usually on the horizon with little or no apparent horizontal or vertical movement. The image only grows larger as the threat aircraft gets closer. Special vigilance must be exercised for this type of situation. A pilot's most acute night vision is off-center in his/her peripheral vision. When looking for other aircraft at night, scan slowly to allow sufficient time for this off-center viewing.

All pilots who fly in instrument conditions or at night are subject to spatial disorientation. This occurs when body sensations are used to interpret flight attitudes, and there is no visual reference to the horizon. The only reliable way to overcome this disorientation is to rely entirely on the indications of the flight instruments. Some types of vertigo include:

The leans — An abrupt correction of a banked angle can create the illusion of banking in the opposite direction.

Coriolis illusion — An abrupt head movement during a constant rate turn can create the illusion of rotation in an entirely different axis. This illusion can be overwhelming and so rapid head movements in turns should be avoided.

Inversion illusion — An abrupt change from a climb to straight and level flight can create the illusion of tumbling backwards.

Somatogravic illusion — A rapid acceleration during takeoff can create the illusion of being in a nose up attitude.

Hypoxia is caused by insufficient oxygen reaching the brain. The most usual reason is the low partial pressure of oxygen encountered at altitude. Carbon monoxide poisoning is similar to hypoxia in that it causes too little oxygen to reach the brain. Carbon monoxide (usually from an exhaust leak) binds with the hemoglobin in the blood, preventing its usual oxygen-carrying function. The symptoms of both are similar and include dizziness, tingling of the hands, feet and legs, loss of higher thought processes, and unconsciousness. The sufferer may not notice or react to any of the symptoms due to his degraded mental faculties. Hyperventilation is caused by a reduction of carbon dioxide in the blood, usually due to rapid breathing in a stressful situation. The symptoms of hyperventilation are similar to hypoxia, but recovery is rapid once the rate of breathing is brought under control.

ALL

9354. A person may not act as a crewmember of a civil aircraft if alcoholic beverages have been consumed by that person within the preceding

A— 8 hours.
B— 12 hours.
C— 24 hours.

No person may act or attempt to act as a crewmember of a civil aircraft within 8 hours after the consumption of any alcoholic beverage. (PLT463) — 14 CFR §91.17

ALL

9354-1. A pilot should be aware the alcohol in one beer can be detected for as long as

A— minimum of 60 minutes.
B— 2 hours.
C— 3 hours.

As little as one ounce of liquor, one bottle of beer or four ounces of wine can impair flying skills, with the alcohol consumed in these drinks being detectable in the breath and blood for at least 3 hours. (PLT104) — AIM ¶8-1-1

ALL

9111. What is the effect of alcohol consumption on functions of the body?

A— Alcohol has an adverse effect, especially as altitude increases.
B— Small amounts of alcohol in the human system increase judgment and decision-making abilities.
C— Alcohol has little effect if followed by an ounce of black coffee for every ounce of alcohol.

The adverse effect of alcohol is greatly multiplied when a person is exposed to altitude. Two drinks on the ground are equivalent to three or four at altitude. (PLT205) — AIM ¶8-1-1

Answer (B) is incorrect because even small amounts of alcohol impair judgment and decision-making abilities. Answer (C) is incorrect because there is no way to increase the body's metabolism of alcohol or to alleviate a hangover (including drinking black coffee).

ALL

9111-1. Pilot performance can be seriously degraded by

A— prescribed and over-the-counter medications.
B— prescription medications only.
C— over-the-counter medications only.

Pilot performance can be seriously degraded by both prescribed and over-the-counter medications, as well as by the medical conditions for which they are taken. Many medications have primary effects that may impair judgment, memory, alertness, coordination, vision, and the ability to make calculations. Others have side effects that may impair the same critical functions. Any medication that depresses the nervous system, such as a sedative, tranquilizer or antihistamine, can make a pilot much more susceptible to hypoxia. Pilots are prohibited from performing crewmember duties while using any medication that affects the faculties in any way contrary to safety. (PLT354) — AIM ¶8-1-1

ALL

9107. When making an approach to a narrower-than-usual runway, without VASI assistance, the pilot should be aware that the approach

A— altitude may be higher than it appears.
B— altitude may be lower than it appears.
C— may result in leveling off too high and landing hard.

An approach to a narrower-than-usual runway can create the illusion that the aircraft is higher than it actually is. (PLT280) — AIM ¶8-1-5

Answer (A) is incorrect because wider-than-usual runways may result in higher than desired approaches. Answer (C) is incorrect because leveling off too high is not affected by the runway width, but rather by the pilot's landing proficiency.

ALL

9107-1. You have just touched down hard in the rain on a narrower-than-usual runway at night. You realize you have just experienced

A— runway length illusion.
B— an atmospheric height illusion.
C— ground lighting illusion.

An approach to a narrower-than-usual runway can create the illusion that the aircraft is higher than it actually is. (PLT280) — AIM ¶8-1-5

Answers

| 9354 | [A] | 9354-1 | [C] | 9111 | [A] | 9111-1 | [A] | 9107 | [B] | 9107-1 | [B] |

ALL

9109. In the dark, a stationary light will appear to move when stared at for a period of time. This illusion is known as

A— somatogravic illusion.
B— ground lighting illusion.
C— autokinesis.

In the dark, a stationary light will appear to move about when stared at for many seconds. This illusion is known as Autokinesis. (PLT280) — AIM ¶8-1-5

Answer (A) is incorrect because somatogravic illusion occurs with a rapid acceleration during takeoff, creating the illusion of being in a nose-up attitude. Answer (B) is incorrect because a ground lighting illusion refers to lights on a straight path such as a road being mistaken by a pilot for runway or approach lights.

ALL

9110. When making a landing over darkened or featureless terrain such as water or snow, a pilot should be aware of the possibility of illusion. The approach may appear to be too

A— high.
B— low.
C— shallow.

An absence of ground features, when landing over water, darkened areas and terrain made featureless by snow, can create the illusion that the aircraft is at a higher altitude than it actually is. (PLT280) — AIM ¶8-1-5

ALL

9110-1. You have just touched down on the runway faster than planned in the haze at night. You realize that you have just experienced

A— an atmospheric distance illusion.
B— a gravotopic height illusion.
C— the elevator illusion.

An absence of ground features, when landing over water, darkened areas and terrain made featureless by snow, can create the illusion that the aircraft is at a higher altitude than it actually is. (PLT280) — AIM ¶8-1-5

ALL

9108. The illusion of being in a noseup attitude which may occur during a rapid acceleration takeoff is known as

A— inversion illusion.
B— autokinesis.
C— somatogravic illusion.

A rapid acceleration during takeoff can create the illusion of being in a nose-up attitude. This is known as a Somatogravic Illusion. (PLT280) — AIM ¶8-1-5

Answer (A) is incorrect because the inversion illusion results from an abrupt change from climb to straight-and-level flight which can create an illusion of tumbling backwards. Answer (B) is incorrect because autokinesis refers to a stationary light appearing to move about when stared at for many seconds in the dark.

ALL

9114. What is the most effective way to use the eyes during night flight?

A— Look only at far away, dim lights.
B— Scan slowly to permit offcenter viewing.
C— Concentrate directly on each object for a few seconds.

One should scan slowly at night to permit off-center viewing of dim objects. (PLT099) — FAA-H-8083-3

Answer (A) is incorrect because pilots must look at their gauges and instruments, which are about 2 feet in front of them. Answer (C) is incorrect because peripheral (off-center) vision is more effective at night.

ALL

9116. Which observed target aircraft would be of most concern with respect to collision avoidance?

A— One which appears to be ahead and moving from left to right at high speed.
B— One which appears to be ahead and moving from right to left at slow speed.
C— One which appears to be ahead with no lateral or vertical movement and is increasing in size.

Any aircraft that appears to have no relative motion and stays in one scan quadrant is likely to be on a collision course. If a target shows no lateral or vertical motion, but increases in size, take evasive action. (PLT099) — AIM ¶8-1-8

Answers (A) and (B) are incorrect because an airplane which is ahead of you and moving from left to right, or from right to left, should pass in front of you.

Answers

9109 [C]	9110 [A]	9110-1 [A]	9108 [C]	9114 [B]	9116 [C]

ALL

9117. Scanning procedures for effective collision avoidance should constitute

A— looking outside for 15 seconds, then inside for 5 seconds, then repeat.

B— 1 minute inside scanning, then 1 minute outside scanning, then repeat.

C— looking outside every 30 seconds except in radar contact when outside scanning is unnecessary.

Studies show that the time a pilot spends on visual tasks inside the cabin should represent no more than 1/4 to 1/3 of the scan time outside, or no more than 4 to 5 seconds on the instrument panel for every 16 seconds outside. (PLT099) — AIM ¶8-1-6

Answer (B) is incorrect because pilots should spend the majority of scan time outside the airplane when in VFR conditions. Answer (C) is incorrect because pilots should spend the majority of scan time outside the airplane, and outside scanning is necessary when in radar contact in VFR conditions.

ALL

9118. When using the Earth's horizon as a reference point to determine the relative position of other aircraft, most concern would be for aircraft

A— above the horizon and increasing in size.

B— on the horizon with little relative movement.

C— on the horizon and increasing in size.

Any aircraft that appears to have no relative motion and stays in one scan quadrant is likely to be on a collision course. If a target shows no lateral or vertical motion, but increases in size, take evasive action. (PLT099) — AIM ¶8-1-8

Answer (A) is incorrect because an airplane above the horizon is probably at a higher altitude. Answer (B) is incorrect because an airplane on the horizon without movement may be traveling in the same direction as you.

ALL

9112. A pilot is more subject to spatial disorientation when

A— ignoring or overcoming the sensations of muscles and inner ear.

B— eyes are moved often in the process of cross-checking the flight instruments.

C— body sensations are used to interpret flight attitudes.

When seated on an unstable moving platform at altitude with your vision cut off from the earth, horizon or other fixed reference, you are susceptible to misinterpreting certain body sensations caused by angular accelerations. (PLT334) — AIM ¶8-1-5

Answer (A) is incorrect because ignoring or overcoming the sensations of muscles and inner ear is a means of avoiding (not becoming subject to) spatial disorientation. Answer (B) is incorrect because rapid eye movements have little or no impact on spatial disorientation and vision reference to reliable flight instruments helps avoid spatial disorientation.

ALL

9113. Which procedure is recommended to prevent or overcome spatial disorientation?

A— Reduce head and eye movement to the greatest possible extent.

B— Rely on the kinesthetic sense.

C— Rely entirely on the indications of the flight instruments.

The best method to prevent or overcome spatial disorientation is to rely entirely on the indications of the flight instruments. (PLT334) — AIM ¶8-1-5

Answer (A) is incorrect because head and eye movement have little effect on spatial disorientation. Answer (B) is incorrect because relying on the kinesthetic sense encourages (not prevents) spatial disorientation.

ALL

9115. While making prolonged constant rate turns under IFR conditions, an abrupt head movement can create the illusion of rotation on an entirely different axis. This is known as

A— autokinesis.

B— Coriolis illusion.

C— the leans.

An abrupt head movement while making a prolonged constant rate turn, can produce a strong sensation of rotation or movement in an entirely different axis. The phenomenon is known as Coriolis Illusion. (PLT280) — AIM ¶8-1-5

Answer (A) is incorrect because Autokinesis refers to a stationary light appearing to move about when stared at for many seconds in the dark. Answer (C) is incorrect because the "leans" refer to an abrupt correction of a banked attitude which can create the illusion of bank in the opposite direction.

Answers

| 9117 | [A] | 9118 | [C] | 9112 | [C] | 9113 | [C] | 9115 | [B] |

ALL

9433. Haze can give the illusion that the aircraft is

A— closer to the runway than it actually is.
B— farther from the runway than it actually is.
C— the same distance from the runway as when there is no restriction to visibility.

Atmospheric haze can create an illusion of being at a greater distance from the runway than you actually are. (PLT280) — AIM ¶8-1-5

ALL

9434. Sudden penetration of fog can create the illusion of

A— pitching up.
B— pitching down.
C— leveling off.

Penetration of fog can create an illusion of pitching up. (PLT280) — AIM ¶8-1-5

ALL

9435. What illusion, if any, can rain on the windscreen create?

A— Does not cause illusions.
B— Lower than actual.
C— Higher than actual.

Rain on the windscreen can create an illusion of being at a higher altitude than you are. (PLT280) — AIM ¶8-1-5

ALL

9101. What is a symptom of carbon monoxide poisoning?

A— Rapid, shallow breathing.
B— Pain and cramping of the hands and feet.
C— Dizziness.

Carbon monoxide poisoning produces the same symptoms as hypoxia, which include dizziness. (PLT097) — AIM ¶8-1-4

Answer (A) is incorrect because rapid breathing can result in hyperventilation, but it is not a symptom of carbon monoxide poisoning. Answer (B) is incorrect because tingling in the extremities (not pain and cramping) is one symptom of hyperventilation (not carbon monoxide poisoning).

ALL

9102. Which would most likely result in hyperventilation?

A— A stressful situation causing anxiety.
B— The excessive consumption of alcohol.
C— An extremely slow rate of breathing and insufficient oxygen.

You are most likely to hyperventilate when under stress or at high altitudes. (PLT332) — AIM ¶8-1-3

Answer (B) is incorrect because excessive consumption of alcohol results in intoxication, not hyperventilation. Answer (C) is incorrect because a slow rate of breathing is the cure for hyperventilation, and insufficient oxygen is the cause of hypoxia, not hyperventilation.

ALL

9103. What causes hypoxia?

A— Excessive carbon dioxide in the atmosphere.
B— An increase in nitrogen content of the air at high altitudes.
C— A decrease of oxygen partial pressure.

Low partial pressure of oxygen causes hypoxia. (PLT330) — AIM ¶8-1-2

Answer (A) is incorrect because the percentage of carbon dioxide and oxygen in the atmosphere remains constant with changes in altitude, but there is less pressure as you increase in altitude. Answer (B) is incorrect because relative nitrogen content also remains constant at high altitudes, but there is less pressure.

ALL

9104. Which is a common symptom of hyperventilation?

A— Tingling of the hands, legs, and feet.
B— Increased vision keenness.
C— Decreased breathing rate.

Symptoms of hyperventilation include dizziness, tingling of the extremities, sensation of body heat, rapid heart rate, blurring of vision, muscle spasm and, finally, unconsciousness. (PLT332) — AIM ¶8-1-3

Answer (B) is incorrect because hyperventilation distorts one's abilities. Answer (C) is incorrect because decreasing the breathing rate overcomes hyperventilation and is not a symptom of it.

ALL

9105. Loss of cabin pressure may result in hypoxia because as cabin altitude increases

A— the percentage of nitrogen in the air is increased.
B— the percentage of oxygen in the air is decreased.
C— oxygen partial pressure is decreased.

Low partial pressure of oxygen causes hypoxia. (PLT330) — AIM ¶8-1-2

Answers (A) and (B) are incorrect because the percentage of nitrogen, carbon dioxide and oxygen in the atmosphere remains constant with changes in altitude, but there is less pressure as you increase in altitude.

ALL

9106. Hypoxia is the result of which of these conditions?

A— Insufficient oxygen reaching the brain.
B— Excessive carbon dioxide in the bloodstream.
C— Limited oxygen reaching the heart muscles.

Hypoxia is a result of too little oxygen reaching the brain. (PLT330) — AIM ¶8-1-2

Answer (B) is incorrect because excessive carbon dioxide in the blood stream causes hyperventilation. Answer (C) is incorrect because it is the result of insufficient oxygen to the brain.

ALL

9856. Human behavior

A— rarely results in accidents unless deliberate actions are performed.
B— is responsible for three out of four accidents.
C— is well understood, so behavioral induced accidents are exceedingly rare occurrences.

Three out of four accidents result from improper human performance. The human element is the most flexible, adaptable, and valuable part of the aviation system, but it is also the most vulnerable to influences that can adversely affect its performance. (PLT104) — FAA-H-8083-2

ALL

9778. An experienced pilot trying to meet a schedule

A— can expect the flight crew to alert them to problems or areas of concern.
B— will always err on the side of caution.
C— can fail to perceive operational pitfalls.

Although more experienced pilots are likely to make more automatic decisions, there are tendencies or operational pitfalls that come with the development of pilot experience. These are classic behavioral traps into which pilots have been known to fall. More experienced pilots (as a rule) try to complete a flight as planned, please passengers, and meet schedules. The desire to meet these goals can have an adverse effect on safety and contribute to an unrealistic assessment of piloting skills. (PLT104) — FAA-H-8083-25

ALL

9778-1. Automatic Decision-Making is

A— a reflexive type of decision-making.
B— an impulsive type of decision-making.
C— an internalized type of decision-making.

Automatic decision-making is a reflexive type of decision-making anchored in training and experience and is most often used in times of emergency when there is no time to practice analytical decision-making. (PLT104) — FAA-H-8083-2

ALL

9804. The crew monitoring function is essential,

A— particularly during high altitude cruise flight modes to prevent CAT issues.
B— particularly during approach and landing to prevent CFIT.
C— during RNAV departures in class B airspace.

Effective monitoring and cross-checking can be the last line of defense that prevents an accident because detecting an error or unsafe situation may break the chain of events leading to an accident. This monitoring function is always essential, and particularly so during approach and landing when controlled flight into terrain (CFIT) accidents are most common. (PLT104) — AC 120-71A

Answers

9105 [C]	9106 [A]	9856 [B]	9778 [C]	9778-1 [A]	9804 [B]

ALL
9804-1. In order to achieve the highest level of safety,

A— each flight crewmember must carefully monitor the aircraft's flight path.
B— the crewmembers must continually monitor their seat dependent tasks.
C— the captain's judgment must not be questioned.

The FAA expects the flight crew to monitor the aircraft's flight path. (PLT354) — AC 120-71A

ALL
9805. CRM training refers to

A— the two components of flight safety and resource management, combined with mentor feedback.
B— the three components of initial indoctrination awareness, recurrent practice and feedback, and continual reinforcement.
C— the five components of initial indoctrination awareness, communication principles, recurrent practice and feedback, coordination drills, and continual reinforcement.

The critical components of effective crew resource management (CRM) training include initial indoctrination awareness, recurrent practice and feedback, and continual reinforcement. (PLT104) — AC120-51

ALL
9805-1. CRM error management includes

A— effective use of all available resources: human resources, hardware, and information.
B— error callout and error guidance training.
C— error prevention, error detection, and recovery from the error.

It is now understood that pilot errors cannot be entirely eliminated. It is important, therefore, that pilots develop appropriate error management skills and procedures. It is certainly desirable to prevent as many errors as possible, but since they cannot all be prevented, detection and recovery from errors should be addressed in training. Evaluation of pilots should also consider error management (error prevention, detection, and recovery). (PLT104) — AC 120-51

ALL
9805-2. CRM is defined as

A— application of team management in the flight deck environment.
B— the use of human factors principles in the aviation environment.
C— a human error avoidance approach to aviation management in the flight deck.

Crew resource management (CRM) is the application of team management concepts in the flight deck environment. It was initially known as cockpit resource management, but as CRM programs evolved to include cabin crews, maintenance personnel, and others, the phrase "crew resource management" was adopted. (PLT104) — FAA-H-8083-2

ALL
9805-3. Cultural issues in CRM

A— are not appropriate subjects for effective CRM training in any population.
B— must be addressed for each training population.
C— can be discussed if the training syllabus allows training time for those topics.

While individuals and even teams of individuals may perform well under many conditions, they are subject to the influence of at least three cultures: the professional cultures of the individuals themselves, the cultures of their organizations, and the national cultures surrounding the individuals and their organizations. If not recognized and addressed, factors related to culture may degrade crew performance. Hence, effective CRM training must address culture issues, as appropriate in each training population. (PLT104) — AC 120-51

ALL
9805-4. Crew resource management (CRM) is

A— a dilution of the captain's authority.
B— the only method of accident avoidance and error prevention.
C— one way to make good decisions.

CRM refers to the effective use of all available resources: human resources, hardware, and information. CRM training is one way of addressing the challenge of optimizing the human/machine interface and accompanying interpersonal activities, including decisionmaking. (PLT104) — AC 120-51

Answers

9804-1　[A]　　　9805　[B]　　　9805-1　[C]　　　9805-2　[A]　　　9805-3　[B]　　　9805-4　[C]

ALL

9805-5. Risk management, as part of the aeronautical decision making (ADM) process, relies on which features to reduce the risks associated with each flight?

A— Application of stress management and risk element procedures.

B— Situational awareness, problem recognition, and good judgment.

C— The mental process of analyzing all information in a particular situation and making a timely decision on what action to take.

Risk management is the part of the decision making process which relies on situational awareness, problem recognition, and good judgment to reduce risks associated with each flight. (PLT104) — FAA-H-8083-2

ALL

9806. The error management evaluation process

A— should recognize not all errors can be prevented.

B— may include error evaluation that should have been prevented.

C— must count errors as disqualifying.

It is certainly desirable to prevent as many errors as possible, but since they cannot all be prevented, detection and recovery from errors should be addressed in training. Error management (error prevention, detection, and recovery) should be considered in the evaluation of pilots, as well as the fact that since not all errors can be prevented, it is important that errors be managed properly. (PLT104) — AC120-51

ALL

9816. An experienced pilot mistakes the runway heading for the instructed heading for departure. What kind of error is this?

A— Experience error.

B— Detection error.

C— Insight detection.

Problem detection is the first step in the decision-making process. It begins with recognizing that a change occurred or that an expected change did not occur. A problem is perceived first by the senses and then it is determined through insight and experience. These same abilities, as well as an objective analysis of all available information, are used to determine the nature and severity of the problem. Therefore, incorrectly detecting the problem to begin with is an error that is critical during a decision-making process. (PLT104) — FAA-H-8083-25A

ALL

9816-1. An experienced, current, and proficient pilot fails to notice the landing gear is not extended for landing. This is an example of

A— systems training.

B— problem detection.

C— procedures knowledge.

Problem detection is the first step in the decision-making process. It begins with recognizing that a change occurred or that an expected change did not occur. A problem is perceived first by the senses and then it is determined through insight and experience. These same abilities, as well as an objective analysis of all available information, are used to determine the nature and severity of the problem. Therefore, incorrectly detecting a problem to begin with is an error that is critical during a decision-making process. (PLT104) — FAA-H-8083-25

ALL

9832. Accident-prone pilots tend to

A— have disdain toward rules.

B— follow methodical information gathering techniques.

C— excessively utilize outside resources.

One of the primary characteristics exhibited by accident-prone pilots was their disdain toward rules. (PLT103) — FAA-H-8083-2

Answers

9805-5 [B]   9806 [A]   9816 [B]   9816-1 [B]   9832 [A]

ALL

9815. When a recently certificated pilot decides to not wait any longer for the fog and low ceilings to burn off, this pilot may be exhibiting the hazardous

A— resigned attitude.
B— macho attitude.
C— impulsive attitude.

ADM addresses the following five hazardous attitudes: Antiauthority (don't tell me!), Impulsivity (do something quickly!), Invulnerability (it won't happen to me), Macho (I can do it), Resignation (what's the use?). This pilot is exhibiting an impulsive attitude by departing before conditions warrant. (PLT103) — FAA-H-8083-2

ALL

9815-1. When an aircraft pilot takes off as ordered in the afternoon when embedded thunderstorms are indicated on radar and NOAA is broadcasting weather watches, it might be described as an example of

A— the resigned effect.
B— an anti-authority attitude.
C— an impulsive attitude.

ADM addresses the following five hazardous attitudes: Antiauthority (don't tell me!), Impulsivity (do something quickly!), Invulnerability (it won't happen to me), Macho (I can do it), and Resignation (what's the use?). This pilot is exhibiting a resigned attitude by leaving the departure decision up to others. Pilots who think, "What's the use?" will leave the action to others and may even go along with unreasonable requests. (PLT103) — FAA-H-8083-25

Answer (B) is incorrect because the question involves an example of the pilot following the authority to a fault. Answer (C) is incorrect because the question involves an example of a pilot following orders; the impulsive attitude is demonstrated when the pilot does not select the best alternative and they do the first thing that comes to mind.

ALL

9833. An air carrier crew fixated on completing the last flight of a four day trip often may exhibit

A— get-there-itis.
B— staged decision-making.
C— naturalistic decision-making.

There are a number of classic behavioral traps into which pilots have been known to fall. These dangerous tendencies or behavior patterns, which must be identified and eliminated, include: peer pressure, mind set, get-there-itis, duck-under syndrome, scud running, continuing visual flight rules into instrument conditions, getting behind the aircraft, loss of positional or situation awareness, operating without adequate fuel reserves, descent below the minimum enroute altitude, flying outside the envelope, neglect of flight planning, preflight inspections, checklists, etc. (PLT104) — FAA-H-8083-2

ALL

9834. An air carrier aircraft flown into the ground while troubleshooting a landing gear fault is an example of

A— neglect and reliance on memory.
B— loss of situational awareness.
C— lack of aviation experience.

Instances of human factor accidents include operational errors that relate to loss of situational awareness and flying outside the envelope. These can be termed as operational pitfalls. (PLT104) — FAA-H-8083-2

Answers

9815 [C]   9815-1 [A]   9833 [A]   9834 [B]

Chapter 8
Meteorology and Weather Services

The Atmosphere

The primary cause of all the Earth's weather is the variation in solar radiation received at the surface. When the surface is warmed by the sun, the air next to it is, in turn, heated and it expands. This creates a low pressure area where the air rises and, at altitude, expands outward. Air from regions of relatively high pressure descends and then moves away from the center of the high toward the lower pressure areas. On both a global and local scale, this movement of air sets off an immensely complex process that generates all the Earth's weather. *See* Figure 8-1.

Another major influence in the pattern of the weather is a phenomenon known as **Coriolis effect**. This is an apparent force, caused by the Earth's rotation, acting on any movement of air. If the Earth did not rotate, air would move directly from areas of high pressure to areas of low pressure. Coriolis force bends the track of the air over the ground to right in the northern hemisphere and to the left in the southern hemisphere. Viewed from above (as on a weather map) this makes air rotate clockwise around high pressure areas in the northern hemisphere and counterclockwise around lows. In the southern hemisphere, the rotation around highs and lows is just the opposite. In the northern hemisphere, the rotation of air around a low pressure area is called a cyclone and that around a high is called an anticyclone.

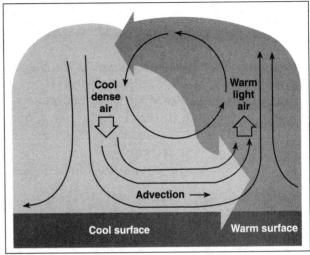

Figure 8-1. Circulation of air due to uneven surface heating

The strength of the Coriolis force is determined by wind speed and the latitude. Coriolis has the least effect at the equator and the most at the poles. It is also reduced in effect when wind speed decreases. Air moving near the Earth's surface is slowed by friction. This reduces the Coriolis force. However, the gradient pressure causing the air to move remains the same. The reduced Coriolis allows air to spiral out away from the center of a high and in toward the center of a low, and at an angle to winds aloft which are out of the friction level.

If the Earth did not rotate, air would move from the poles to the equator at the surface and from the equator to the poles at altitude. Because the Earth does rotate, Coriolis force and the pressure gradients tend to form three bands of prevailing winds in each hemisphere. Weather systems tend to move from east to west in the subtropical regions on the "trade winds." In the mid latitudes, the prevailing westerlies move weather systems from west to east. *See* Figure 8-2.

All air carrier flights take place in the two lowest levels of the atmosphere. These are the **troposphere** and the **stratosphere**. The troposphere starts at the surface and extends vertically to roughly 35,000 feet. The thickness of the troposphere varies with latitude, being thicker over the equator than over the poles and with the season of the year (thicker in the summer than in the winter). The stratosphere extends from the top of the

Figure 8-2. Global wind systems

troposphere to about 26 to 29 miles altitude. *See* Figure 8-3. The main characteristic that distinguishes the troposphere from the stratosphere is the temperature lapse rate. In the troposphere, the temperature decreases with increasing altitude at an average rate of two degrees Celsius per one thousand feet of altitude. In the stratosphere, there is little or no change in temperature with altitude. In fact, in some regions the temperature increases with increasing altitude causing temperature inversions.

The thin boundary layer between the troposphere and the stratosphere is called the **tropopause**. The height of the tropopause is of great interest to the pilots of jet aircraft for two reasons. First, there is an abrupt change in the temperature lapse rate at the tropopause and that has a significant effect on jet engine performance. Second, maximum winds (the jet stream) and narrow zones of wind shear are found at the tropopause.

The **jet stream** is a few thousand feet thick and a few hundred miles wide. By arbitrary definition, it has wind speeds of fifty knots or greater. The highest wind speeds can be found on the polar side of the jet core. *See* Figure 8-4. There may be two or more jet streams in existence at one time. The jet stream is always found at a vertical break in the tropopause where the tropical and polar tropopauses meet. In addition to the high speed horizontal winds, the jet stream contains a circular rotation with rising air on the tropical side and descending air on the polar side. Because of the rising air, cirrus clouds will sometimes form on the equatorial side of the jet.

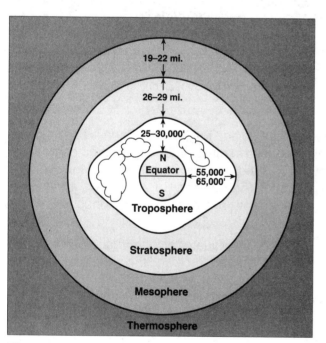

Figure 8-3. Levels of atmosphere

Figure 8-4. Cross-section of the jet stream

ALL
9152. What is the primary cause of all changes in the Earth's weather?

A— Variations of solar energy at the Earth's surface.
B— Changes in air pressure over the Earth's surface.
C— Movement of air masses from moist areas to dry areas.

Every physical process of weather is accompanied by or is the result of a heat exchange. Differences in solar energy create temperature variations. These temperature variations create forces that drive the atmosphere in its endless motion. (PLT510) — AC 00-6

Answer (B) is incorrect because changes in air pressure are due to temperature variations. Answer (C) is incorrect because movement of air masses is a result of varying temperatures and pressures.

Answers

9152 [A]

ALL
9160. Where is the usual location of a thermal low?

A— Over the arctic region.
B— Over the eye of a hurricane.
C— Over the surface of a dry, sunny region.

A dry, sunny region can become quite warm from intense surface heating, thus generating a surface low-pressure area. This is called a thermal low. (PLT511) — AC 00-6

Answer (A) is incorrect because thermal lows develop over dry, sunny regions, not in the arctic. Answer (B) is incorrect because the eye of a hurricane marks the center of a well-developed tropical cyclone.

ALL
9159. What is a feature of air movement in a high pressure area?

A— Ascending from the surface high to lower pressure at higher altitudes.
B— Descending to the surface and then outward.
C— Moving outward from the high at high altitudes and into the high at the surface.

Air in a high pressure system (in the northern hemisphere) tends to descend to the surface and then spiral out from the center of the high. (PLT173) — AC 00-6

ALL
9157. At lower levels of the atmosphere, friction causes the wind to flow across isobars into a low because the friction

A— decreases windspeed and Coriolis force.
B— decreases pressure gradient force.
C— creates air turbulence and raises atmospheric pressure.

Frictional force slows wind speed near the surface and Coriolis force is decreased. The stronger pressure gradient force turns the wind at an angle across the isobars toward lower pressure until the three forces (Coriolis, pressure gradient, and friction) are in balance. (PLT173) — AC 00-6

Answer (B) is incorrect because friction does not affect the pressure gradient force. Answer (C) is incorrect because of surface obstructions.

ALL
9176. At which location does Coriolis force have the least effect on wind direction?

A— At the poles.
B— Middle latitudes (30° to 60°).
C— At the Equator.

Coriolis force varies with latitude from zero at the Equator to a maximum at the poles. (PLT510) — AC 00-6

ALL
9177. How does Coriolis force affect wind direction in the Southern Hemisphere?

A— Causes clockwise rotation around a low.
B— Causes wind to flow out of a low toward a high.
C— Has exactly the same effect as in the Northern Hemisphere.

Coriolis force deflects air flow to the right causing winds above the friction level to flow parallel to the isobars. In the northern hemisphere, winds flow clockwise around high-pressure areas and counterclockwise around low-pressure areas. In the southern hemisphere, Coriolis force causes a counterclockwise flow around highs and a clockwise flow around lows. (PLT516) — AC 00-6

Answer (B) is incorrect because the wind flows from a high to a low (not a low to a high) in both the northern and southern hemispheres. Answer (C) is incorrect because the Coriolis force deflects air to the left in the southern hemisphere, which is the opposite effect from the northern hemisphere.

ALL
9178. Which weather condition is defined as an anticyclone?

A— Calm.
B— High pressure area.
C— COL.

The clockwise flow of air around a high-pressure area in the northern hemisphere is called an anticyclone. (PLT173) — AC 00-6

Answer (A) is incorrect because calm is defined as the absence of wind or of apparent motion of the air. Answer (C) is incorrect because COL is the neutral area between two highs or two lows. It is also the intersection of a trough and a ridge.

ALL
9178-1. A cyclone is

A— a hurricane force storm in the Indian Ocean.
B— a tropical depression with sustained winds of 63 knots.
C— a tropical depression with a barometric pressure in the center of the feature that is 35 mb lower than pressure outside the weather feature.

The low pressure and its wind system is a cyclone. Strong tropical cyclones are known by different names in different regions of the world. A tropical cyclone in the Atlantic and eastern Pacific is a "hurricane"; in the western Pacific, "typhoon"; near Australia, "willy-willy"; and in the Indian Ocean, simply "cyclone." (PLT517) — AC 00-6

ALL
9156. Which area or areas of the Northern Hemisphere experience a generally east to west movement of weather systems?

A— Arctic only.
B— Arctic and subtropical.
C— Subtropical only.

Polar easterlies carry storms from east to west. The northeasterly trade winds carry tropical storms from east to west. The prevailing westerlies drive mid-latitude storms generally from west to east. (PLT510) — AC 00-6

ALL
9233. Summer thunderstorms in the arctic region will generally move

A— northeast to southwest in polar easterlies.
B— southwest to northeast with the jetstream flow.
C— directly north to south with the low-level polar airflow.

Arctic thundershowers, usually circumnavigable, move generally from northeast to southwest in the polar easterlies which is opposite from the general movement in mid-latitudes. (PLT495) — AC 00-6

ALL
9151. What is a characteristic of the troposphere?

A— It contains all the moisture of the atmosphere.
B— There is an overall decrease of temperature with an increase of altitude.
C— The average altitude of the top of the troposphere is about 6 miles.

The troposphere is the layer of atmosphere from the surface to an average altitude of 7 miles. It is characterized by an overall decrease of temperature with increasing altitude. (PLT203) — AC 00-6

Answer (A) is incorrect because moisture can be found in the stratosphere, as evidenced by some of the largest thunderstorms. Answer (C) is incorrect because the average altitude of the top of the troposphere is about 7 miles.

ALL
9240. What weather feature occurs at altitude levels near the tropopause?

A— Maximum winds and narrow wind shear zones.
B— Abrupt temperature increase above the tropopause.
C— Thin layers of cirrus (ice crystal) clouds at the tropopause level.

Maximum winds generally occur at levels near the tropopause. These strong winds create narrow zones of wind shear which often generate hazardous turbulence. (PLT203) — AC 00-6

Answer (B) is incorrect because temperature is fairly constant above the tropopause. Answer (C) is incorrect because thin layers of cirrus (ice crystal) clouds can develop at altitudes below the tropopause level and extend into the lower stratosphere.

ALL
9209. Which feature is associated with the tropopause?

A— Absence of wind and turbulence.
B— Absolute upper limit of cloud formation.
C— Abrupt change of temperature lapse rate.

An abrupt change in the temperature lapse rate characterizes the tropopause. (PLT203)—AC 00-6

Answer (A) is incorrect because the jet stream (wind) and clear air turbulence are found extensively in the tropopause. Answer (B) is incorrect because clouds can be present into the stratosphere, as in very large thunderstorms and cirrus clouds made up of ice crystals.

ALL
9168. Where is a common location for an inversion?

A— At the tropopause.
B— In the stratosphere.
C— At the base of cumulus clouds.

Inversions are common in the stratosphere. (PLT203) — AC 00-6

Answer (A) is incorrect because a common location for an inversion is in the stratosphere, not at the tropopause. Answer (C) is incorrect because the base of cumulus clouds is where the dew point lapse rate and the dry adiabatic lapse rate converge. It is not a common location for an inversion.

Answers

9178-1 [A]	9156 [B]	9233 [A]	9151 [B]	9240 [A]	9209 [C]
9168 [B]					

ALL
9241. Where are jetstreams normally located?

A— In areas of strong low pressure systems in the stratosphere.
B— In a break in the tropopause where intensified temperature gradients are located.
C— In a single continuous band, encircling the Earth, where there is a break between the equatorial and polar tropopause.

The jet stream is usually associated with a break in the tropopause where intensified temperature gradients are located. (PLT302) — AC 00-6

Answer (A) is incorrect because a jet stream is located in a break in the tropopause, not in the stratosphere. Answer (C) is incorrect because there may be more than one jet stream at any time; up to three at one time are not uncommon.

ALL
9779. The tropopause is generally found when the free air temperatures are

A— between -55°C and -65°C.
B— between -40°C and -55°C.
C— colder than -60°C.

In the absence of other information, the tropopause will generally have a temperature of between -55°C and -65°C. (PLT302) — AC 00-30

ALL
9229. Which type clouds may be associated with the jetstream?

A— Cumulonimbus cloud line where the jetstream crosses the cold front.
B— Cirrus clouds on the equatorial side of the jetstream.
C— Cirrostratus cloud band on the polar side and under the jetstream.

When high-level moisture is present, cirriform clouds form on the equatorial side of the jet stream. (PLT302) — AC 00-6

Answer (A) is incorrect because cirriform, not cumulonimbus, clouds are associated with the jet stream. Answer (C) is incorrect because cirriform clouds form on the equatorial side of the jet stream.

ALL
9229-1. When high level moisture is available, cirrus clouds form on the

A— polar side of the jet stream.
B— equatorial side of the jet stream.
C— acute angle side of the jet stream.

When high-level moisture is present, cirriform clouds form on the equatorial side of the jet stream. (PLT226) — AC 00-6

ALL
9238. Where do the maximum winds associated with the jetstream usually occur?

A— In the vicinity of breaks in the tropopause on the polar side of the jet core.
B— Below the jet core where a long straight stretch of the jetstream is located.
C— On the equatorial side of the jetstream where moisture has formed cirriform clouds.

Maximum winds in a jet stream occur near a break in the tropopause and on the polar side. (PLT302) — AC 00-6

Answer (B) is incorrect because in the jet stream, the maximum winds are found in, not below, the core. Answer (C) is incorrect because when moisture is available, cirriform clouds will form on the upward motion of air of the jet stream on the equatorial side. This will occur in the slower winds of the jet stream.

ALL
9238-1. The rate of decrease in wind speed from the jet stream core is considerably greater on the

A— equatorial side.
B— polar side.
C— acute angle side.

The rate of decrease of wind speed is considerably greater on the polar side than on the equatorial side; hence, the magnitude of wind shear is greater on the polar side than on the equatorial side. (PLT226) — AC 00-6

ALL
9810. Large areas of land

A— tend to increase temperature variations.
B— do not influence the troposhere.
C— minimize temperature variations.

Land and water surfaces underlying the atmosphere greatly affect cloud and precipitation development. (PLT512) — AC 00-6

Answers

| 9241 | [B] | 9779 | [A] | 9229 | [B] | 9229-1 | [B] | 9238 | [A] | 9238-1 | [B] |
| 9810 | [A] |

ALL

8710. For a flight to an airport in the vicinity of the coast, land surface cooling means you can expect to encounter

A— sea breezes.
B— land breezes.
C— a chinook wind.

During the day, the sun heats up both the ocean surface and the land. However, water heats up much more slowly than land and so the air above the land will be warmer compared to the air over the ocean. The warm air over the land will rise throughout the day, causing low pressure at the surface. Over the water, high surface pressure will form because of the colder air. To compensate, the air will sink over the ocean. The wind will blow from the higher pressure over the water to lower pressure over the land causing the sea breeze. The opposite occurs at night, with land surface cooling causing a land breeze. (PLT512) — AC 00-6

Answer (A) is incorrect because a sea breeze is cause by land surface warming. Answer (C) is incorrect because a chinook wind is associated with mountainous terrain.

Weather Systems

When air masses of different temperature or moisture content collide, they force air aloft along the area where they meet. An elongated line of low pressure is referred to as a trough.

A **front** is defined as the boundary between two different air masses. The formation of a front is called frontogenesis. When a front dissipates, the area experiences frontolysis. All fronts lie in troughs. This means that winds flow around a front more or less parallel to the front, and in a counterclockwise direction. As an aircraft flies toward a front in the northern hemisphere, the pilot will notice a decreasing pressure and a wind from the left of the aircraft. After passing through the front, the pilot will note a wind shift to the right and increasing air pressure.

A front is usually the boundary between air masses of different temperatures. If cold air is displacing warm air, it is called a cold front. When warm air displaces cold air, it is a warm front. The speed of movement of the front is determined by the winds aloft. A cold front will move at about the speed of the wind component perpendicular to the front just above the friction level. It is harder for warm air to displace cold air and so warm fronts move at about half the speed of cold fronts under the same wind conditions.

A stationary front is one with little or no movement. Stationary fronts or slow moving cold fronts can form frontal waves and low pressure areas. A small disturbance can cause a bend in the frontal line that induces a counterclockwise flow of air around a deepening low pressure area. The wave forms into a warm front followed by a cold front. The cold front can then overtake the warm front and force the warm air between the two aloft. This is called an occluded front or an occlusion.

Most fronts mark the line between two air masses of different temperature. However, this is not always the case. Sometimes, air masses with virtually the same temperatures will form a front. The only difference between the two is the moisture content. The front formed in such conditions is called a dew point front or a dry line.

The surface position of a front often marks the line where an arctic and a tropical air mass meet at the surface. The jet stream is located in the area where these air masses meet at the altitude of the tropopause. There is often a rough correlation between the surface position of a front and the location of the jet stream. Generally speaking, the jet stream will lie to the north of the surface position of a front. As a frontal wave forms, the jet will move toward the center of the deepening low pressure area. If an occluded front forms, the jet stream will often cross the front near the point of the occlusion.

Answers

8710 [B]

ALL
9165. What term describes an elongated area of low pressure?

A— Trough.
B— Ridge.
C— Hurricane or typhoon.

A trough is an elongated area of low pressure with the lowest pressure along a line marking maximum anticyclonic curvature. (PLT173) — AC 00-6

Answer (B) is incorrect because a ridge is an elongated area of high pressure. Answer (C) is incorrect because a hurricane or typhoon is a tropical cyclone (low) with highest sustained winds of 65 knots or greater.

ALL
9165-1. Low pressure areas are areas of

A— stagnant air.
B— descending air.
C— ascending air.

At the surface when air converges into a low, it cannot go outward against the pressure gradient, nor can it go downward into the ground; it must go upward. Therefore, a low or trough is an area of rising air. (PLT173) — AC 00-6

ALL
9191. What is a feature of a stationary front?

A— The warm front surface moves about half the speed of the cold front surface.
B— Weather conditions are a combination of strong cold front and strong warm front weather.
C— Surface winds tend to flow parallel to the frontal zone.

The opposing forces exerted by adjacent air masses in a stationary front are such that the frontal surface between them shows little or no movement. In such cases, the surface winds tend to blow parallel to the frontal zone. (PLT511) — AC 00-6

Answer (A) is incorrect because the movement of a warm front surface in comparison to a cold front surface has nothing to do with a stationary front. Answer (B) is incorrect because weather conditions that are a combination of strong cold front and strong warm front weather are a feature of an occluded front.

ALL
9192. Which event usually occurs after an aircraft passes through a front into the colder air?

A— Temperature/dewpoint spread decreases.
B— Wind direction shifts to the left.
C— Atmospheric pressure increases.

A front lies in a pressure trough, and pressure generally is higher in the cold air. Thus, when crossing a front directly into colder air, the pressure will usually rise abruptly. (PLT511) — AC 00-6

Answer (A) is incorrect because the temperature/dew point spread usually differs across a front. But it might not decrease if you fly in to a cold, dry air mass. Answer (B) is incorrect because in the northern hemisphere the wind always shifts to the right due to the Coriolis force.

ALL
9213. If the winds aloft are blowing parallel to the front,

A— the front can be expected to move with the upper winds.
B— the winds aloft can be expected to turn at the frontal boundary.
C— the front moves slowly if at all.

The upper winds will dictate to a great extent the movement of the front, along with the amount of cloudiness and rain accompanying the frontal system. If winds aloft parallel a front, the front moves slowly if at all. If winds aloft blow across a front it tends to move with the wind. (PLT511) — AC 00-6

ALL
9215. Which atmospheric factor causes rapid movement of surface fronts?

A— Upper winds blowing across the front.
B— Upper low located directly over the surface low.
C— The cold front overtaking and lifting the warm front.

Cold fronts move at about the speed of the wind component perpendicular to the front just above the frictional layer. (PLT511) — AC 00-6

Answer (B) is incorrect because an upper low located directly over a surface low would be a factor in how extensive the weather would be, not in how fast it would move. Answer (C) is incorrect because a cold front overtaking and lifting the warm front is a characteristic of an advancing cold front.

Answers

| 9165 | [A] | 9165-1 | [C] | 9191 | [C] | 9192 | [C] | 9213 | [C] | 9215 | [A] |

ALL

9215-1. Dew point fronts result from

A— air density differences due to the humidity levels.
B— air density due to temperature.
C— temperatures aloft.

During a considerable part of the year, dew point fronts are common in Western Texas and New Mexico northward over the Plains States. Moist air flowing north from the Gulf of Mexico abuts the drier and therefore slightly denser air flowing from the southwest. Except for moisture differences, there is seldom any significant air mass contrast across this "front"; therefore, it is commonly called a "dry line." Nighttime and early morning fog and low level clouds often prevail on the moist side of the line while generally clear skies mark the dry side. (PLT511) — AC 00-6

ALL

9216. In which meteorological conditions can frontal waves and low pressure areas form?

A— Warm fronts or occluded fronts.
B— Slow-moving cold fronts or stationary fronts.
C— Cold front occlusions.

Frontal waves and cyclones (areas of low pressure) usually form on slow moving cold fronts or on stationary fronts. (PLT511) — AC 00-6

Answer (A) is incorrect because occluded fronts are formed by frontal waves and areas of low pressure which cause a cold front to close together with a warm front. Frontal waves and low pressure areas normally form on slow-moving cold fronts. Answer (C) is incorrect because a cold front occlusion occurs when the air behind the cold front is colder than the air in advance of the warm front, lifting the warm front aloft.

ALL

9217. What weather difference is found on each side of a "dry line"?

A— Extreme temperature difference.
B— Dewpoint difference.
C— Stratus versus cumulus clouds.

A dew point front or "dry line" is formed when two air masses of similar density and temperature meet. Except for the moisture differences, there is little contrast across the front. (PLT511) — AC 00-6

Answer (A) is incorrect because except for moisture (not extreme temperature) difference, there is seldom any significant air mass contrast across the "dry line." Answer (C) is incorrect because the side with moisture may have clouds, while generally clear skies mark the dry side.

ALL

9227. Where is the normal location of the jetstream relative to surface lows and fronts?

A— The jetstream is located north of the surface systems.
B— The jetstream is located south of the low and warm front.
C— The jetstream is located over the low and crosses both the warm front and the cold front.

Development of a surface low is usually south of the jet stream. As the low deepens, it moves nearer the jet center. When a low occludes, the jet stream usually crosses the frontal system at the point of the occlusion. (PLT302) — AC 00-6

Answer (B) is incorrect because the jet stream is located to the north of the low and warm front. Answer (C) is incorrect because the jet stream crosses the occlusion of the warm and cold front at the point of occlusion.

ALL

9228. Which type frontal system is normally crossed by the jetstream?

A— Cold front and warm front.
B— Warm front.
C— Occluded front.

Development of a surface low is usually south of the jet stream. As the low deepens, it moves nearer the jet center. When a low occludes, the jet stream usually crosses the frontal system at the point of the occlusion. (PLT302) — AC 00-6

ALL

9228-1. Steep frontal surfaces are usually associated with

A— fast moving warm front.
B— fast moving cold front.
C— dry lines.

The leading edge of an advancing cold air mass is a cold front. Warm fronts on the surface are seldom as well marked as cold fronts, and they usually move about half as fast when the general wind flow is the same in each case. (PLT511) — AC 00-6

Answers

| 9215-1 | [A] | 9216 | [B] | 9217 | [B] | 9227 | [A] | 9228 | [C] | 9228-1 | [B] |

ALL
9228-2. If a sample of air is forced upward and it is colder than the surrounding air, it

A—sinks until it reaches denser air.
B—gets energy from surrounding air and remains in place.
C—warms from the surrounding air and rises to expansion.

If the upward moving air becomes colder than surrounding air, it sinks; but if it remains warmer it is accelerated upward as a convective current. Whether it sinks or rises depends on the ambient or existing temperature lapse rate. (PLT511) — AC 00-6

ALL
9776. A jet stream is a narrow, shallow, meandering river of maximum winds extending around the globe in a wavelike pattern with speeds of

A— 50 knots or greater.
B— 71 knots or greater.
C— 100 knots or greater.

The concentrated winds, by arbitrary definition, must be 50 knots or greater to be classified as a jet stream. (PLT302) — AC 00-6

ALL
9820. (Refer to Figure 153.) What areas does the jet stream overlie?

A— Central portion of Texas.
B— North of Washington and Idaho.
C— South of Montana and North Dakota.

The concentrated winds, by arbitrary definition, must be 50 knots or greater to classify it as a jet stream. Strong, long trajectory jet streams usually are associated with well-developed surface lows and frontal systems beneath deep upper troughs or lows. (PLT302) — AC 00-6

ALL
9821. (Refer to Figure 154.) What areas does the jet stream overlie?

A— North of California and Nevada.
B— South of the low pressure system in Canada.
C— North of the low pressure system in Canada.

The concentrated winds, by arbitrary definition, must be 50 knots or greater to classify it as a jet stream. Strong, long trajectory jet streams usually are associated with well-developed surface lows and frontal systems beneath deep upper troughs or lows. (PLT302) — AC 00-6

ALL
9822. (Refer to Figure 155.) What areas does the jet stream overlie?

A— South of the high pressure system located in Texas.
B— Southern California and central Nevada.
C— South of the low pressure system in Canada.

The concentrated winds, by arbitrary definition, must be 50 knots or greater to classify it as a jet stream. Strong, long trajectory jet streams usually are associated with well-developed surface lows and frontal systems beneath deep upper troughs or lows. (PLT302) — AC 00-6

Stability and Instability of Air

When a parcel of air is forced to rise it expands because its pressure decreases. Air that is forced to descend is compressed. When the pressure and volume change, so does the temperature. When air expands, it cools and when it is compressed, it warms. This cooling or heating is referred to as being **adiabatic**, meaning that no heat was removed from or added to the air.

When unsaturated air is forced to rise or descend it cools or heats at a rate of about 3°C per 1,000 feet of altitude change. This called the dry adiabatic rate. The saturated adiabatic rate is normally much lower.

When moist air is forced upward, the temperature and the dew point converge on each other at a rate of about 2.5°C per 1,000 feet. At the altitude where the dew point lapse rate and the dry adiabatic rate meet, cloud bases will form. Once the condensation starts taking place the adiabatic rate slows considerably because the process of condensation releases latent heat into the air and partially offsets the expansional cooling.

Continued

Answers

9228-2   [A]   9776   [A]   9820   [C]   9821   [B]   9822   [C]

Saturated air flowing downward will also warm at less than the dry adiabatic rate because vaporization of water droplets uses heat. Once the air is no longer saturated it will heat at the normal dry rate. An example of this is the "katabatic wind" which becomes warmer and dryer as it flows downslope.

The adiabatic rate should not be confused with the actual (ambient) lapse rate. The actual lapse rate is the rate at which the air temperature varies with altitude when air is not being forced to rise or descend. The actual lapse averages about 2°C per 1,000 feet, but that is highly variable. When a parcel of air is forced to rise, the adiabatic rate may be different than the ambient rate.

When a parcel of air becomes colder (and more dense) than the air around it, it will tend to sink back toward its original altitude. If the parcel becomes warmer than the surrounding air, it will tend to rise convectively even though the original lifting force may have disappeared. If this happens, the air is said to be unstable. When a parcel of air resists convective movement through it, it is said to be stable.

The best indication of the stability or instability of an air mass is the ambient temperature lapse rate. If the temperature drops rapidly as the altitude increases, the air is unstable. If the temperature remains unchanged or decreases only slightly as altitude is increased, the air mass is stable. If the temperature actually increases as altitude increases, a temperature inversion exists. This is the most stable of weather conditions.

ALL
9170. Which term applies when the temperature of the air changes by compression or expansion with no heat added or removed?

A— Katabatic.
B— Advection.
C— Adiabatic.

When air expands, it cools; and when compressed, it warms. These changes are adiabatic, meaning that no heat is removed from or added to the air. (PLT024) — AC 00-6

Answer (A) is incorrect because katabatic is a wind blowing down an incline caused by cold, heavier air spilling down the incline displacing warmer, less dense air. Answer (B) is incorrect because advection is the horizontal flow in a convective current, i.e., wind.

ALL
9186. Which process causes adiabatic cooling?

A— Expansion of air as it rises.
B— Movement of air over a colder surface.
C— Release of latent heat during the vaporization process.

When air expands, it cools; and when compressed, it warms. These changes are adiabatic, meaning that no heat is removed from or added to the air. (PLT024) — AC 00-6

Answer (B) is incorrect because adiabatic cooling means that no heat is removed from the air, as would be the case if the air was moved over a colder surface. Answer (C) is incorrect because adiabatic cooling is the process in which no heat is removed from or added to the air.

ALL
9158. Which type wind flows downslope becoming warmer and dryer?

A— Land breeze.
B— Valley wind.
C— Katabatic wind.

A katabatic wind is any wind blowing down an incline when the incline is influential in causing the wind. Any katabatic wind originates because cold, heavy air spills down sloping terrain displacing warmer, less dense air ahead of it. Air is heated and dried as it flows downslope. (PLT516) — AC 00-6

Answer (A) is incorrect because a land breeze is a wind that flows from the cooler land toward warmer water. Answer (B) is incorrect because a valley wind is wind flowing up out of a valley because colder, denser air settles downward and forces the warmer air near the ground up a mountain slope.

ALL
9171. What is the approximate rate unsaturated air will cool flowing upslope?

A— 3°C per 1,000 feet.
B— 2°C per 1,000 feet.
C— 4°C per 1,000 feet.

Unsaturated air moving upward and downward cools and warms at about 3.0°C (5.4°F) per 1,000 feet. (PLT024) — AC 00-6

Answers (B) and (C) are incorrect because unsaturated air will cool flowing upslope at 3°C per 1,000 feet.

Answers

9170   [C]   9186   [A]   9158   [C]   9171   [A]

ALL

9182. What is the result when water vapor changes to the liquid state while being lifted in a thunderstorm?

A— Latent heat is released to the atmosphere.
B— Latent heat is transformed into pure energy.
C— Latent heat is absorbed from the surrounding air by the water droplet.

When water vapor condenses to liquid water or sub-limates directly to ice, energy originally used in the evaporation reappears as heat and is released to the atmosphere. This energy is "latent heat." (PLT512) — AC 00-6

Answer (B) is incorrect because latent heat cannot create pure energy. Latent heat is returned to the surrounding atmosphere. Answer (C) is incorrect because this is the process of latent heat in vaporization, which is changing liquid water to vapor.

ALL

9185. What weather condition occurs at the altitude where the dewpoint lapse rate and the dry adiabatic lapse rate converge?

A— Cloud bases form.
B— Precipitation starts.
C— Stable air changes to unstable air.

Unsaturated air in a convective current cools at about 5.4°F (3°C) per 1,000 feet. The dew point decreases at about 1°F (5/9°C) per 1,000 feet. When the temperature and dew point converge, cloud bases will form. (PLT512) — AC 00-6

Answer (B) is incorrect because precipitation starts when precipitation particles have grown to a size and weight that the atmosphere can no longer suspend, and the particles fall as precipitation. Answer (C) is incorrect because air stability depends on the ambient or existing temperature lapse rate, not the convergence of the dew point lapse rate and the dry adiabatic lapse rate.

ALL

9185-1. Adiabatic warming is also described as

A— chronographic warming.
B— expansional heating.
C— compressional heating.

The adiabatic process is the change of the temperature of air without transferring heat. In an adiabatic process, compression results in warming, and expansion results in cooling. (PLT512) — AC 00-6

ALL

9187. When saturated air moves downhill, its temperature increases

A— at a faster rate than dry air because of the release of latent heat.
B— at a slower rate than dry air because vaporization uses heat.
C— at a slower rate than dry air because condensation releases heat.

The saturated adiabatic rate of heating is slower than the dry rate because vaporization uses heat. (PLT024) — AC 00-6

Answer (A) is incorrect because when saturated air moves downhill, its temperature increases at a slower rate than dry air because of the absorption of latent heat. Answer (C) is incorrect because as air moves downhill, its temperature increases at a slower rate than dry air because vaporization uses heat, not because of the release of heat through condensation.

ALL

9154. What feature is associated with a temperature inversion?

A— A stable layer of air.
B— An unstable layer of air.
C— Air mass thunderstorms.

A temperature inversion is defined as an increase in temperature with increasing altitude, or a negative temperature lapse rate. Stable air masses have a low or negative lapse rate. (PLT301) — AC 00-6

Answer (B) is incorrect because instability occurs when the temperature decreases (not increases as in a temperature inversion) with an increase in altitude, and the rising air continues to rise. Answer (C) is incorrect because air mass thunderstorms result from instability. They do not occur when there is a temperature inversion.

ALL

9184. What is indicated about an air mass if the temperature remains unchanged or decreases slightly as altitude is increased?

A— The air is unstable.
B— A temperature inversion exists.
C— The air is stable.

A mass of air in which the temperature decreases rapidly with height favors instability. Air tends to be stable if the temperature changes little or not at all with altitude. (PLT512) — AC 00-6

Answer (A) is incorrect because unstable air would have a uniform decrease (approaching 3°C/1,000 feet) in temperature with an increase in altitude. Answer (B) is incorrect because in a temperature inversion, the temperature increases with increases in altitude.

Answers

9182 [A]	9185 [A]	9185-1 [C]	9187 [B]	9154 [A]	9184 [C]

ALL

9188. Which condition is present when a local parcel of air is stable?

A— The parcel of air resists convection.
B— The parcel of air cannot be forced uphill.
C— As the parcel of air moves upward, its temperature becomes warmer than the surrounding air.

A parcel of air which resists convection when forced upward is called stable. (PLT173) — AC 00-6

Answer (B) is incorrect because stable air can be forced uphill to form a mountain wave. Answer (C) is incorrect because rising air, warmer than the surrounding air, describes unstable air.

ALL

9195. How can the stability of the atmosphere be determined?

A— Ambient temperature lapse rate.
B— Atmospheric pressure at various levels.
C— Surface temperature/dewpoint spread.

A mass of air in which the temperature decreases rapidly with height favors instability. Air tends to be stable if the temperature changes little or not at all with altitude. The rate of temperature decrease with altitude is referred to as the temperature lapse rate. (PLT173) — AC 00-6

Answer (B) is incorrect because the difference between ambient temperature and adiabatic lapse rate, not atmospheric pressure at various levels, determines stability. Answer (C) is incorrect because the surface temperature/dew point spread is used to indicate probability of fog, not atmospheric stability.

Fog and Rain

Fog is a surface-based cloud that always forms in stable air conditions. The three main types are radiation fog, advection fog and upslope fog.

Radiation fog occurs when there is a surface-based temperature inversion. On a clear, relatively calm night the surface rapidly cools by radiating heat into space. This in turn cools the air within a few hundred feet of the surface and leaves warmer air aloft. If the temperature drops to the dew point, fog will form. Since the minimum temperature during the day occurs just after sunrise, this type of fog often forms then. This fog will dissipate when the air warms up enough to raise the temperature above the dew point again. However, if the inversion persists, visibility can remain limited due to lingering fog and haze. Wind or any significant movement of air will disperse both radiation fog and haze.

Advection fog and **upslope fog** both require wind to form. Advection fog forms when warm moist air flows over a colder surface. The temperature of the air drops to the dew point and fog forms. This commonly occurs over bodies of water such as lakes or oceans. The fog can drift over land on the leeward (downwind) side of the body of water lowering visibility at nearby airports. If the wind increases to over about 15 knots, the fog will tend to lift into low stratus clouds.

Upslope fog forms when moist, stable air is gradually moved over higher ground by the wind. As the air rises, it cools adiabatically and fog forms. This type of fog is common in mountainous areas.

All clouds are composed of tiny droplets of water (or ice crystals). As these drops of water collide with each other, they form larger drops until they precipitate out as rain. As a general rule, clouds need to be at least 4,000 feet thick to produce precipitation reported as light or greater intensity.

ALL

9153. What characterizes a ground-based inversion?

A— Convection currents at the surface.
B— Cold temperatures.
C— Poor visibility.

Inversions can occur in warm and cold temperatures in stable air, and usually trap particles in the air causing poor visibility. (PLT301) — AC 00-6

Answer (A) is incorrect because convective currents at the surface do not occur when there is a ground-based inversion. Answer (B) is incorrect because when the temperature is cold, it is difficult for the earth to radiate enough heat to become colder than the overlying air.

Answers

9188 [A]	9195 [A]	9153 [C]

ALL

9155. When does minimum temperature normally occur during a 24-hour period?

A— After sunrise.
B— About 1 hour before sunrise.
C— At midnight.

At night, solar radiation ceases, but terrestrial radiation continues and cools the surface. Cooling continues after sunrise until solar radiation again exceeds terrestrial radiation. Minimum temperature usually occurs after sunrise, sometimes as much as 1 hour after. (PLT512) — AC 00-6

Answer (B) is incorrect because the minimum temperature normally occurs after sunrise. Answer (C) is incorrect because the minimum temperature normally occurs after sunrise, not at midnight.

ALL

9169. What condition produces the most frequent type of ground- or surface-based temperature inversion?

A— The movement of colder air under warm air or the movement of warm air over cold air.
B— Widespread sinking of air within a thick layer aloft resulting in heating by compression.
C— Terrestrial radiation on a clear, relatively calm night.

An inversion often develops near the ground on clear, cool nights when the wind is light. The ground radiates and cools much faster than the overlying air. Air in contact with the ground becomes cold while the temperature a few hundred feet above changes very little. Thus, temperature increases with height. (PLT301) — AC 00-6

Answer (A) is incorrect because the movement of colder air under warm air is what happens when a cold front is advancing, and the movement of warm air over cold air is the process of an advancing warm front. Answer (B) is incorrect because widespread sinking of air describes compressional or adiabatic heating.

ALL

9208. How are haze layers cleared or dispersed?

A— By convective mixing in cool night air.
B— By wind or the movement of air.
C— By evaporation similar to the clearing of fog.

Haze or smoke must be dispersed by movement of air. (PLT510) — AC 00-6

Answer (A) is incorrect because convective mixing would be caused by heating during the day, not by the cool night air. Answer (C) is incorrect because haze must be dispersed by movement of air, it cannot evaporate in a similar manner to the clearing of fog.

ALL

9206. You are planning a flight to a coastal area which is currently below published weather minimums for the ILS approach due to fog. The winds are forecast to increase to 20 knots from the west at your scheduled arrival time. What weather should you expect?

A— Surface ice.
B— Advection fog thickening as the winds increase to 20 knots.
C— A low layer of stratus or stratocumulus clouds.

Advection fog is most common along coastal areas and will develop into a layer of stratus of stratocumulus clouds with winds speeds in excess of 15 knots. (PLT226) — AC 00-6

ALL

9207. Which conditions are necessary for the formation of upslope fog?

A— Moist, stable air being moved over gradually rising ground by a wind.
B— A clear sky, little or no wind, and 100 percent relative humidity.
C— Rain falling through stratus clouds and a 10- to 25-knot wind moving the precipitation up the slope.

Upslope fog forms as a result of moist, stable air being cooled adiabatically as it moves up sloping terrain. (PLT226) — AC 00-6

Answer (B) is incorrect because these are conditions necessary for the formation of radiation fog which usually occurs at night. Answer (C) is incorrect because upslope fog is formed by moist air being moved gradually over rising ground, not by rain falling through stratus clouds and not by a wind blowing the precipitation up the slope.

ALL

9207-1. Precipitation induced fog

A— results from relatively warm rain or drizzle falling through cooler air.
B— results from relatively cooler rain or drizzle falling through warmer air.
C— is usually of short duration.

When relatively warm rain or drizzle falls through cool air, evaporation from the precipitation saturates the cool air and forms fog. (PLT226) — AC 00-6

Answers

9155 [A]	9169 [C]	9208 [B]	9206 [C]	9207 [A]	9207-1 [A]

Airline Transport Pilot Test Prep ASA **8–15**

ALL
9207-2. You are approaching an airport to land in 20 minutes. The METAR reports temperature 10°C, dew point 10°C, winds 310/04, scattered clouds and rain. You expect

A— radiation fog.
B— deepening fog.
C— clearing conditions.

Conditions favorable for radiation fog are clear sky, little or no wind, and small temperature-dew point spread. (PLT226) — AC 00-6

ALL
9194. Which condition produces weather on the lee side of a large lake?

A— Warm air flowing over a colder lake may produce fog.
B— Cold air flowing over a warmer lake may produce advection fog.
C— Warm air flowing over a cool lake may produce rain showers.

When warm air flows over a colder lake, the air may become saturated by evaporation from the water while also becoming cooler in the low levels by contact with the cool water. Fog often becomes extensive and dense to the lee (downwind) side of the lake. (PLT226) — AC 00-6

Answer (B) is incorrect because cold air flowing over a warmer lake may produce rain showers, not advection fog, on the lee side of the lake. Answer (C) is incorrect because warm air flowing over a cool lake may produce fog, not rain showers, on the lee side of the lake.

ALL
9193. What minimum thickness of cloud layer is indicated if precipitation is reported as light or greater intensity?

A— 4,000 feet thick.
B— 2,000 feet thick.
C— A thickness which allows the cloud tops to be higher than the freezing level.

When arriving at or departing from a terminal reporting precipitation of light or greater intensity, expect clouds to be more than 4,000 feet thick. (PLT192) — AC 00-6

Answer (B) is incorrect because to produce significant precipitation (light or greater intensity), clouds are normally at least 4,000 feet thick. Answer (C) is incorrect because a cloud thickness resulting in cloud tops above the freezing level means ice droplets and supercooled water will develop.

ALL
8723. A flight is scheduled at daybreak. The current conditions are rainy, but conditions are expected to clear. The forecast temperature is 10°C, dew point 10°C, with winds 330° at 5 knots. What weather conditions can you expect?

A— The conditions are favorable for radiation fog.
B— Dense fog which will deepen during the day.
C— Severe ground icing.

Conditions favorable for radiation fog are clear sky, little or no wind, and small temperature/dew point spread (high relative humidity). Radiation fog is restricted to land because water surfaces cool little from nighttime radiation. (PLT226) — AC 00-6

Answer (B) is incorrect because as the temperature rises with sunrise, fog will tend to burn off. Answer (C) is incorrect because the temperature and dew point are not favorable for icing conditions.

Thunderstorms

Thunderstorms are always generated in very unstable conditions. Warm, moist air is forced upward either by heating from below or by frontal lifting, and becomes unstable. When the rising air cools to its dew point, a cumulus cloud forms. This "cumulus stage" is the first of three in a thunderstorm's life. It is characterized by a continuous updraft as the cloud builds. As the raindrops and ice pellets in the cloud grow larger, their weight begins to overpower the lifting force of the updrafts. As the drops fall through the cloud, they cool the air making it more dense than in the surrounding updrafts. This process causes downdrafts to form within the cloud.

When the **downdrafts** become strong enough to allow the first precipitation to reach the surface, the mature stage of the thunderstorm has begun. Eventually, the downdrafts cut off the updrafts and the storm loses the source of warm air that is its driving force. When the storm is characterized predominantly by downdrafts, it is in the dissipating stage.

Answers

9207-2 [A]   9194 [A]   9193 [A]   8723 [A]

Air mass thunderstorms are associated with local surface heating. On a clear, sunny day, local hot spots form that are capable of making the air over them unstable enough to generate a thunderstorm. Because the downdrafts in an air mass thunderstorm shut off the updrafts fairly quickly, this type of storm is relatively short-lived.

Steady-state thunderstorms are usually associated with weather systems. Fronts, converging winds and troughs aloft force upward motion. In a steady-state storm the precipitation falls outside the updraft allowing the storm to continue without abating for several hours.

The most violent type of steady-state thunderstorms are those generated by cold fronts or by squall lines. A **squall line** is a non-frontal instability line that often forms ahead of a fast moving cold front. Thunderstorms generated under these conditions are the most likely to develop cumulonimbus mamma clouds, funnel clouds and tornadoes. A severe thunderstorm is one which has surface winds of 50 knots or more, and/or has hail 3/4-inch or more in diameter.

Pressure usually falls rapidly with the approach of a thunderstorm, then rises sharply with onset of the first gust and arrival of the cold downdraft and heavy rain showers. As the storm passes on, the pressure returns to normal.

Even though thunderstorms are cumulus clouds formed in unstable air they can sometimes penetrate overlying bands of stratiform clouds. These are known as "**embedded thunderstorms.**" Because these thunderstorms are obscured by other clouds and it is impossible for a pilot to visually detour around them, they present a particular hazard to IFR flight.

When they can, most pilots prefer to visually avoid thunderstorms by flying around them or, if they can maintain a high enough altitude, by flying over the storm. If you are going to fly over the top of a thunderstorm, a good rule of thumb to follow is that the cloud should be overflown by at least 1,000 feet for each 10 knots of wind speed. Radar is a very useful tool in thunderstorm avoidance, especially at night or in IFR weather. The radar displays an area of precipitation size rain drops as a bright spot on the screen. Since thunderstorms often contain large water drops, they usually show up on the radar screen. A dark area on the screen is one in which no precipitation drops are detected. Areas of clouds may or may not be displayed depending on the size of the drops that make up the clouds. *See* Figure 8-5.

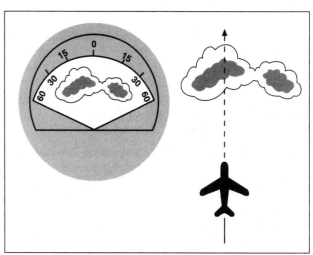

Figure 8-5. Radar display of a thunderstorm

9196. Which weather phenomenon signals the beginning of the mature stage of a thunderstorm?

A— The appearance of an anvil top.
B— The start of rain at the surface.
C— Growth rate of the cloud is at its maximum.

Precipitation beginning to fall from the cloud base is the indication that a downdraft has developed and a thunderstorm cell has entered the mature stage. (PLT495) — AC 00-6

Answer (A) is incorrect because the appearance of an anvil top occurs during the dissipating stage. Answer (C) is incorrect because the growth rate of a thunderstorm is at its greatest during the cumulus stage.

Answers
9196   [B]

ALL
9197. During the life cycle of a thunderstorm, which stage is characterized predominately by downdrafts?

A— Cumulus.
B— Dissipating.
C— Mature.

Downdrafts characterize the dissipating stage of the thunderstorm. (PLT495) — AC 00-6

Answer (A) is incorrect because the cumulus stage is the building stage characterized by updrafts. Answer (C) is incorrect because the mature stage has both updrafts and downdrafts, which create strong wind shears.

ALL
9198. What feature is normally associated with the cumulus stage of a thunderstorm?

A— Beginning of rain at the surface.
B— Frequent lightning.
C— Continuous updraft.

The key feature of the cumulus stage is a continuous updraft. (PLT495) — AC 00-6

Answer (A) is incorrect because the beginning of rain at a surface marks the beginning of the mature stage. Answer (B) is incorrect because frequent lightning occurs after the downdrafts have developed and produce the static electricity which causes lightning.

ALL
9203. Why are downdrafts in a mature thunderstorm hazardous?

A— Downdrafts are kept cool by cold rain which tends to accelerate the downward velocity.
B— Downdrafts converge toward a central location under the storm after striking the surface.
C— Downdrafts become warmer than the surrounding air and reverse into an updraft before reaching the surface.

Precipitation beginning to fall from the cloud base is the indication that a downdraft has developed and a thunderstorm cell has entered the mature stage. Cold rain in the downdraft retards compressional heating, and the downdraft remains cooler than surrounding air. Therefore, its downward speed is accelerated and may exceed 2,500 feet per minute. (PLT495) — AC 00-6

Answer (B) is incorrect because after striking the ground the downdrafts will move away from the storm's center. Answer (C) is incorrect because downdrafts remain colder than the surrounding air and accelerate downward into an updraft.

ALL
9200. Where do squall lines most often develop?

A— In an occluded front.
B— Ahead of a cold front.
C— Behind a stationary front.

A squall line is a non-frontal, narrow band of active thunderstorms. Often it develops ahead of a cold front in moist, unstable air. (PLT475) — AC 00-6

Answer (A) is incorrect because squall lines most often develop ahead of a cold front, not in an occluded front. Answer (C) is incorrect because squall lines most often develop ahead of a cold front, not behind a stationary front.

ALL
9204. What is a difference between an air mass thunderstorm and a steady-state thunderstorm?

A— Air mass thunderstorms produce precipitation which falls outside of the updraft.
B— Air mass thunderstorm downdrafts and precipitation retard and reverse the updrafts.
C— Steady-state thunderstorms are associated with local surface heating.

Air mass thunderstorms most often result from surface heating. When the storm reaches the mature stage, rain falls through or immediately beside the updraft. Falling precipitation induces frictional drag, retards the updraft and reverses it to a downdraft. Such a self-destructive cell usually has a life cycle of 20 minutes to 1-1/2 hours. In a steady-state thunderstorm, the precipitation falls outside the downdraft and so the cell can last several hours. (PLT495) — AC 00-6

Answer (A) is incorrect because steady-state, not air mass, thunderstorms produce precipitation which falls outside the updraft. Answer (C) is incorrect because air mass, not steady-state, thunderstorms are associated with local surface heating.

ALL
9205. Which type storms are most likely to produce funnel clouds or tornadoes?

A— Air mass thunderstorms.
B— Cold front or squall line thunderstorms.
C— Storms associated with icing and supercooled water.

Tornadoes occur with isolated thunderstorms at times, but much more frequently, they form with steady-state thunderstorms associated with cold fronts or squall lines. (PLT495) — AC 00-6

Answers

9197 [B]	9198 [C]	9203 [A]	9200 [B]	9204 [B]	9205 [B]

Answer (A) is incorrect because even though air mass thunderstorms may produce funnel clouds or tornadoes, they are most likely to occur with steady-state thunderstorms. Answer (C) is incorrect because all thunderstorms that have updrafts and carry water above the freezing level can produce icing and supercooled water. But thunderstorms associated with cold fronts and squall lines are most likely to produce funnel clouds or tornadoes.

ALL

9210. Which type cloud is associated with violent turbulence and a tendency toward the production of funnel clouds?

A— Cumulonimbus mammatus.
B— Standing lenticular.
C— Stratocumulus.

Frequently, cumulonimbus mammatus clouds occur in connection with violent thunderstorms and tornadoes. (PLT501) — AC 00-6

Answer (B) is incorrect because standing lenticular clouds mark mountain waves that are the product of stable air flowing over an obstruction. Answer (C) is incorrect because stratocumulus sometimes form from the breaking up of stratus or the spreading out of cumulus, and they are associated with some turbulence and possible icing at subfreezing levels.

ALL

9214. Which weather condition is an example of a nonfrontal instability band?

A— Squall line.
B— Advective fog.
C— Frontogenesis.

An instability line is a narrow, nonfrontal line or band of convective activity. If the activity is fully developed thunderstorms, the line is a squall line. (PLT511) — AC 00-6

Answer (B) is incorrect because advective fog occurs when warm moist air moves over a cool surface. It forms in stable air. Answer (C) is incorrect because frontogenesis is the generation of a frontal zone.

ALL

9706. A severe thunderstorm is one in which the surface wind is

A— 58 MPH or greater and/or surface hail is 3/4 inch or more in diameter.
B— 50 knots or greater and/or surface hail is 1/2 inch or more in diameter.
C— 45 knots or greater and/or surface hail is 1 inch or more in diameter.

A severe thunderstorm is one which has surface winds of 50 knots (58 MPH) or more, and/or has hail 3/4 inch or more in diameter. (PLT495) — AC 00-45

ALL

9708. A squall is a sudden increase of at least 15 knots in average wind speed to a sustained speed of

A— 24 knots or more for at least 1 minute.
B— 22 knots or more for at least 1 minute.
C— 20 knots or more for at least 1 minute.

A squall (SQ) means there has been a sudden increase in wind speed of at least 15 knots to a speed of 20 knots or more, and it lasted at least one minute. (PLT475) — AC 00-6

ALL

9708-1. Shear turbulence from a thunderstorm has been encountered

A— 10 miles from the severe thunderstorm.
B— 15 miles from the severe thunderstorm.
C— 20 miles from the severe thurnderstorm.

*Hazardous turbulence is present in **all** thunderstorms; and in a severe thunderstorm, it can damage an airframe. Strongest turbulence within the cloud occurs with shear between updrafts and downdrafts. Outside the cloud, shear turbulence has been encountered several thousand feet above and 20 miles laterally from a severe storm. (PLT475) — AC 00-6*

ALL

9202. Atmospheric pressure changes due to a thunderstorm will be at the lowest value

A— during the downdraft and heavy rain showers.
B— when the thunderstorm is approaching.
C— immediately after the rain showers have stopped.

Pressure usually falls rapidly with the approach of a thunderstorm, then rises sharply with the onset of the first gust and the arrival of the cold downdraft and heavy rain showers, falling back to normal as the storm moves on. (PLT495) — AC 00-6

Answer (A) is incorrect because during the downdraft and heavy rain showers the pressure rises sharply. Answer (C) is incorrect because immediately after the rain showers have stopped the pressure will return to normal.

Answers

9210 [A]	9214 [A]	9706 [A]	9708 [C]	9708-1 [C]	9202 [B]

ALL

9189. Convective clouds which penetrate a stratus layer can produce which threat to instrument flight?

A— Freezing rain.
B— Clear air turbulence.
C— Embedded thunderstorms.

A layer of stratiform clouds may sometimes form in a mildly stable layer while a few convective clouds penetrate the layer thus merging stratiform with cumuliform. Under the right conditions, the cumuliform clouds can become thunderstorms which are completely obscured by the surrounding stratus clouds. (PLT192) — AC 00-6

Answer (A) is incorrect because the formation of freezing rain is dependent on rain falling through colder air. Convective clouds that penetrate a stratus layer may or may not produce precipitation. Answer (B) is incorrect because clear air turbulence is turbulence encountered in air where no clouds are present.

ALL

9199. What is indicated by the term "embedded thunderstorms"?

A— Severe thunderstorms are embedded in a squall line.
B— Thunderstorms are predicted to develop in a stable air mass.
C— Thunderstorms are obscured by other types of clouds.

A layer of stratiform clouds may sometimes form in a mildly stable layer while a few convective clouds penetrate the layer, thus merging stratiform with cumuliform. Under the right conditions, the cumuliform clouds can become thunderstorms which are completely obscured by the surrounding stratus clouds. (PLT495) — AC 00-6

Answer (A) is incorrect because a squall line consists of severe thunderstorms which can always be seen. Answer (B) is incorrect because thunderstorms do not occur in stable air masses.

ALL

9211. A clear area in a line of thunderstorm echoes on a radar scope indicates

A— the absence of clouds in the area.
B— an area of no convective turbulence.
C— an area where precipitation drops are not detected.

Airborne weather radar detects only precipitation size raindrops and hail. Absence of a radar return does indicate an area free of clouds or turbulence. (PLT495) — AC 00-6

Answer (A) is incorrect because weather radar detects only precipitation drops, not clouds. Answer (B) is incorrect because convective turbulence, which would not be detected by radar, could be found under cumulus clouds. Radar does not detect turbulence.

ALL

9212. When flying over the top of a severe thunderstorm, the cloud should be overflown by at least

A— 1,000 feet for each 10 knots windspeed.
B— 2,500 feet.
C— 500 feet above any moderate to severe turbulence layer.

When flying over the top of a severe thunderstorm, clear the top by 1,000 feet for each 10 knots of wind at the cloud top. (PLT495) — AC 00-6

Answer (B) is incorrect because the cloud should be overflown by at least 1,000 feet for each 10 knots wind speed, which would normally be greater than 2,500 feet with a severe thunderstorm. Answer (C) is incorrect because the exact location of a turbulence layer will not usually be known.

ALL

9835. A steady state thunderstorm is associated with

A— surface heating.
B— weather systems.
C— mature stage.

Steady state thunderstorms usually are associated with weather systems. Fronts, converging winds, and troughs aloft force upward motion spawning these storms which often form into squall lines. Afternoon heating intensifies them. (PLT495) — AC 00-6

Answers

| 9189 | [C] | 9199 | [C] | 9211 | [C] | 9212 | [A] | 9835 | [B] |

Wind Shear

Normally we think of changes in wind speed or direction as having an effect only on an aircraft's ground speed and track. However, when there is a very rapid shift in wind speed or direction there is a noticeable change in the aircraft's indicated airspeed as well.

In a situation where there is a sudden increase in headwind (or decrease in tailwind) the aircraft's momentum keeps it moving through space at the same ground speed as before. This means that the aircraft will be moving through the air faster than before and there will be an increase in its indicated airspeed. The aircraft will react to this increase by pitching up and by tending to climb (or descend more slowly). When there is a sudden increase in a tailwind (or decrease in the headwind), just the opposite occurs. There will be a loss of indicated airspeed accompanied by a tendency to pitch down and descend.

Wind shear is defined as any rapid change in wind direction or velocity. Often, there is little or no turbulence associated with wind shear. Severe wind shear is defined as a rapid change in wind direction or velocity causing airspeed changes greater than 15 knots or vertical speed changes greater than 500 feet per minute.

Wind shear may be associated with either a wind shift or a wind speed gradient at any level in the atmosphere. Three common generators of wind shear conditions are thunderstorms, temperature inversions and jet stream winds. Thunderstorms generate a very significant wind shear hazard for two reasons. The shear from thunderstorms is usually encountered close to the ground where there is little time or altitude to recover. The magnitude of the shear is often very severe, especially in situations involving microbursts, which we will discuss shortly. Wind shear can be encountered on all sides and directly under the thunderstorm cell. Often, in a low altitude temperature inversion the winds are very light but just above the inversion layer the wind is much stronger. When an aircraft either climbs or descends through the top of the inversion it can encounter significant wind shear because of the change in wind speed. A jet stream is a narrow "river" of wind where the speed can change a great deal over a very short distance. This is the very definition of wind shear.

Microbursts are a very localized, but very dangerous, wind shear condition. They can occur anywhere that convective weather conditions exist. This includes rain showers, virga and thunderstorms. It is believed that about five percent of thunderstorms produce a microburst.

A microburst is a very narrow downdraft of very high speed wind. The downdraft is typically a few hundred to 3,000 feet across with vertical speeds up to 6,000 feet per minute. When the downdraft approaches the surface, the wind flows outward from the core in all directions. Not only are these outflow winds very strong (up to 45 knots) but their effect is doubled when an aircraft flies through the shear. For example, a 45 knot headwind approaching the microburst will be a 45 knot tailwind flying out the other side — a change of 90 knots. This is usually a short-lived phenomena, seldom lasting more than 15 minutes from the time the burst strikes the ground until it dissipates.

An aircraft approaching a microburst will first experience an increasing headwind as it encounters the outflow. The increasing headwind shear causes the indicated airspeed to increase and gives the aircraft a tendency to pitch up and climb. This increase in performance without an increase in power might induce an unwary pilot into reducing power to maintain airspeed and flight path. As the aircraft flies into the core of the microburst the headwind shifts to a downdraft. The sudden loss of headwind will cause indicated airspeed to drop and cause the aircraft to pitch down and descend. The strong downdraft increases the tendency to descend and the aircraft can quickly get into the situation of having low airspeed and a very high rate of descent. As the aircraft flies out the backside of the microburst, it encounters an increasing tailwind shear that further reduces indicated airspeed and performance.

Continued

There are some wind shear conditions that exceed the performance capability of typical air carrier aircraft. For this reason it is imperative that pilots avoid situations where severe wind shear is either reported or is likely to exist. At this time only a couple of airports in the United States have experimental Doppler radar units capable of detecting wind shear. Many airports have the less sophisticated Low-Level Wind Shear Alert System (LLWAS), which is used to alert pilots to the possibility of wind shear on or near the airport. This system consists of wind sensors located around the perimeter of the airport as well as a center field wind sensor. When there is a significant difference in speed or direction between any of these sensors and the center field sensor, the tower will broadcast the difference. A typical tower transmission would be:

"SOUTH BOUNDARY WIND ONE SIX ZERO AT TWO FIVE, WEST BOUNDARY WIND TWO FOUR ZERO AT THREE FIVE."

The greatest danger from a wind shear encounter at low altitude is that the aircraft will pick up such a high rate of descent that the pilots will be unable to stop it before hitting the ground. The technique to be used during a wind shear encounter essentially involves trading airspeed for altitude. The exact procedures vary from one aircraft to another but if an aircraft encounters severe wind shear, the pilot should maintain or increase the pitch attitude, increase power to the maximum available and accept lower than normal airspeed indications. If this does not arrest the descent, the pilot should continue to pitch up until the descent does stop or until "stick shaker" is encountered.

ALL
9139. Which is a definition of "severe wind shear"?

A— Any rapid change of horizontal wind shear in excess of 25 knots; vertical shear excepted.
B— Any rapid change in wind direction or velocity which causes airspeed changes greater than 15 knots or vertical speed changes greater than 500 ft/min.
C— Any change of airspeed greater than 20 knots which is sustained for more than 20 seconds or vertical speed changes in excess of 100 ft/min.

Severe wind shear is defined as any rapid change in wind direction or velocity which causes airspeed changes greater than 15 knots or vertical speed changes greater than 500 feet per minute. (PLT518) — AC 00-54

Answer (A) is incorrect because a severe wind shear can be caused to both horizontal and vertical shears. Answer (C) is incorrect because a severe wind shear causes airspeed changes greater than 15 knots or vertical speed changes greater than 500 fpm.

ALL
9220. In comparison to an approach in a moderate headwind, which is an indication of a possible wind shear due to a decreasing headwind when descending on the glide slope?

A— Less power is required.
B— Higher pitch attitude is required.
C— Lower descent rate is required.

When a headwind shears to calm or a tailwind, the aircraft tends to lose airspeed, get low, and pitch nose down. The aircraft will require more power and a higher pitch attitude to stay on glide slope. (PLT518) — AC 00-54

Answer (A) is incorrect because as airspeed decreases, more power is required. Answer (C) is incorrect because as the headwind decreases, ground speed will increase, requiring a higher descent rate.

ALL
9133. Which INITIAL cockpit indications should a pilot be aware of when a headwind shears to a calm wind?

A— Indicated airspeed decreases, aircraft pitches up, and altitude decreases.
B— Indicated airspeed increases, aircraft pitches down, and altitude increases.
C— Indicated airspeed decreases, aircraft pitches down, and altitude decreases.

With a headwind shearing to a calm wind there is a loss of lift as airspeed decreases, the aircraft pitches down, and the aircraft drops below glide slope (altitude decreases). Responding promptly by adding power and pitching up, a pilot may overshoot the glide slope and airspeed target but then recover. (PLT518) — AC 00-54

Answer (A) is incorrect because the aircraft will pitch down due to the relatively small angle of attack used during the headwind and the sudden decrease in the airflow over the wing when the wind shears to calm. Answer (B) is incorrect because less power is required to maintain an indicated airspeed in a headwind than in calm air because of ram air; thus, a shear from a headwind to calm would be indicated by a decrease in airspeed and a decrease in altitude.

Answers

9139 [B]   9220 [B]   9133 [C]

ALL

9134. Which condition would INITIALLY cause the indicated airspeed and pitch to increase and the sink rate to decrease?

A— Sudden decrease in a headwind component.
B— Tailwind which suddenly increases in velocity.
C— Sudden increase in a headwind component.

An increase in headwind component (which could also be caused by a tailwind shearing to calm) causes airspeed and pitch to increase, sink rate to decrease. (PLT518) — AC 00-54

Answer (A) is incorrect because a sudden decrease in a headwind component would decrease aircraft performance and would be indicated by a decrease in airspeed, pitch, and altitude. Answer (B) is incorrect because an increase in tailwind velocity would decrease performance and be indicated by a decrease in airspeed, pitch, and altitude.

ALL

9135. Which INITIAL cockpit indications should a pilot be aware of when a constant tailwind shears to a calm wind?

A— Altitude increases; pitch and indicated airspeed decrease.
B— Altitude, pitch, and indicated airspeed decrease.
C— Altitude, pitch, and indicated airspeed increase.

When a tailwind on final shears to calm (or headwind), descent rate decreases. The closest answer suggests altitude decreases, which is still true when one considers the ground speed decreases in this situation. Indicated airspeed and pitch increase. An overshoot can result from insufficient power reduction. (PLT518) — AC 00-54

Answer (A) is incorrect because pitch and indicated airspeed also increase. Answer (B) is incorrect because altitude, pitch, and indicated airspeed decrease when a headwind (not tailwind) shears to a calm wind.

ALL

9135-1. Which initial cockpit indications should a pilot be aware of when a constant headwind shears to a calm wind?

A— Altitude increases; pitch and indicated airspeed decrease.
B— Altitude, pitch, and indicated airspeed decrease.
C— Altitude, pitch, and indicated airspeed increase.

An increasing tailwind (or decreasing headwind) shear will decrease indicated airspeed and performance capability. Due to airspeed loss, the airplane may tend to pitch down to regain trim speed. (PLT518) — AC 00-54

ALL

9137. Which wind-shear condition results in a loss of airspeed?

A— Decreasing headwind or tailwind.
B— Decreasing headwind and increasing tailwind.
C— Increasing headwind and decreasing tailwind.

Decreasing headwind by itself or with a shear to a tailwind will result in loss of indicated airspeed. (PLT518) — AC 00-54

Answer (A) is incorrect because in a decreasing tailwind condition, airspeed initially increases. Answer (C) is incorrect because an increasing headwind and a decreasing tailwind both initially increase airspeed.

ALL

9138. Which wind-shear condition results in an increase in airspeed?

A— Increasing tailwind and decreasing headwind.
B— Increasing tailwind and headwind.
C— Decreasing tailwind and increasing headwind.

A headwind increasing against the pitot and airframe will result in an airspeed increase. (PLT518) — AC 00-54

Answers (A) and (B) are incorrect because when a headwind shears to a tailwind, increasing tailwind component and decreasing headwind component, the reduction of the ram air pressure on the pitot tube causes an initial reduction of indicated airspeed. The reduced headwind component will also cause a pitch down moment and a decrease in altitude.

ALL

9141. Which airplane performance characteristics should be recognized during takeoff when encountering a tailwind shear that increases in intensity?

A— Loss of, or diminished, airspeed performance.
B— Decreased takeoff distance.
C— Increased climb performance immediately after takeoff.

When a tailwind is encountered at liftoff, airspeed will decrease. The pilot must overcome the instinct to lower pitch attitude to recover airspeed or the aircraft may sink beyond recovery limits. Use all available performance by commanding a higher-than-normal pitch attitude and accepting the lower airspeed. (PLT518) — AC 00-54

Answer (B) is incorrect because as a tailwind shear increases, takeoff distance is increased because more power or distance is required to attain lift-off speed. Answer (C) is incorrect because as a tailwind shear increases during climb-out, the climb performance will decrease.

Answers

9134 [C]	9135 [C]	9135-1 [B]	9137 [B]	9138 [C]	9141 [A]

ALL

9142. Thrust is being managed to maintain desired indicated airspeed and the glide slope is being flown. Which characteristics should be observed when a tailwind shears to a constant headwind?

A— PITCH ATTITUDE: Increases. VERTICAL SPEED: Increases. INDICATED AIRSPEED: Decreases, then increases to approach speed.

B— PITCH ATTITUDE: Increases. VERTICAL SPEED: Decreases. INDICATED AIRSPEED: Increases, then decreases.

C— PITCH ATTITUDE: Decreases. VERTICAL SPEED: Decreases. INDICATED AIRSPEED: Decreases, then increases to approach speed.

Shearing to a headwind will create an increased airspeed condition, causing a pitch up with a vertical speed decrease. (PLT518) — AC 00-54

Answer (A) is incorrect because indicated airspeed will initially increase. Answer (C) is incorrect because pitch and indicated airspeed will both initially increase.

ALL

9166. What is an important characteristic of wind shear?

A— It is primarily associated with the lateral vortices generated by thunderstorms.

B— It usually exists only in the vicinity of thunderstorms, but may be found near a strong temperature inversion.

C— It may be associated with either a wind shift or a windspeed gradient at any level in the atmosphere.

Wind shear may be associated with either a wind shift or a wind speed gradient at any level in the atmosphere. (PLT518) — AC 00-6

Answer (A) is incorrect because wind shear can be vertical (as well as lateral) in thunderstorm clouds between the updrafts and downdrafts, as well as in other areas such as frontal zones and low-level temperature inversions. Answer (B) is incorrect because wind shear can be encountered in areas other than thunderstorms; e.g., within a frontal zone, in and near the jet stream, low level inversions.

ALL

9201. Where can the maximum hazard zone caused by wind shear associated with a thunderstorm be found?

A— In front of the thunderstorm cell (anvil side) and on the southwest side of the cell.

B— Ahead of the roll cloud or gust front and directly under the anvil cloud.

C— On all sides and directly under the thunderstorm cell.

Wind shear can be found on all sides of a thunderstorm cell and in the downdraft directly under the cell. (PLT495) — AC 00-54

Answer (A) is incorrect because the wind shear associated with a thunderstorm is on all sides and directly under the cell, not just in the front and on the southwest side. Answer (B) is incorrect because the wind shear associated with a thunderstorm is on all sides and directly under the cell. A roll cloud is not present on all thunderstorms, and when present it marks the eddies of the shear zone between the downdraft and surrounding air.

ALL

9225. Which is a necessary condition for the occurrence of a low-level temperature inversion wind shear?

A— The temperature differential between the cold and warm layers must be at least 10°C.

B— A calm or light wind near the surface and a relatively strong wind just above the inversion.

C— A wind direction difference of at least 30° between the wind near the surface and the wind just above the inversion.

When taking off or landing in calm wind under clear skies within a few hours before or after sunrise, a pilot should be prepared for a temperature inversion near the ground. A shear zone in the inversion is relatively certain if the wind at 2,000 to 4,000 is 25 knots or more. (PLT501) — AC 00-6

Answer (A) is incorrect because magnitude of temperature differential in the inversion is not important; the wind shear is caused by the variation in wind speed. Answer (C) is incorrect because surface wind and a relatively strong wind just above the inversion, not a wind direction difference of at least 30°, are needed to form a low-level temperature inversion wind shear. The wind shear is caused by wind speed variation, not variation in wind direction.

ALL

9701. The horizontal wind shear, critical for turbulence (moderate or greater) per 150 miles is

A— 18 knots or less.

B— greater than 18 knots.

C— not a factor, only vertical shear is a factor.

Horizontal wind shear can be determined from the spacing of isotachs. The horizontal wind shear critical for turbulence (moderate or greater) is greater than 18 knots per 150 miles. 150 nautical miles is equal to 2-1/2 degrees latitude. (PLT263) — AC 00-45

Answers

| 9142 | [B] | 9166 | [C] | 9201 | [C] | 9225 | [B] | 9701 | [B] |

ALL

9130. What is the expected duration of an individual microburst?

A— Two minutes with maximum winds lasting approximately 1 minute.
B— One microburst may continue for as long as 2 to 4 hours.
C— Seldom longer than 15 minutes from the time the burst strikes the ground until dissipation.

Wind speeds intensify for about 5 minutes after a microburst initially contacts the ground. An encounter during the initial stage of microburst development may not be considered significant, but an airplane following may experience an airspeed change two to three times greater. Microbursts typically dissipate within 10 to 20 minutes after ground contact. (PLT317) — AIM ¶7-1-25

ALL

9131. Maximum downdrafts in a microburst encounter may be as strong as

A— 8,000 ft/min.
B— 7,000 ft/min.
C— 6,000 ft/min.

The downdrafts can be as strong as 6,000 feet per minute. Horizontal winds near the surface can be as strong as 45 knots resulting in a 90-knot shear across the microburst. (PLT317) — AIM ¶7-1-25

ALL

9814. Maximum downdrafts in a microburst encounter are strong and may include horizontal winds near the surface as strong as

A— 34 knots.
B— 20 knots.
C— 45 knots.

Microburst downdrafts can be as strong as 6,000 feet per minute. Horizontal winds near the surface can be as strong as 45 knots resulting in a 90-knot shear across the microburst. (PLT317) — AIM ¶7-1-25

ALL

9132. An aircraft that encounters a headwind of 40 knots, within a microburst, may expect a total shear across the microburst of

A— 40 knots.
B— 80 knots.
C— 90 knots.

With a headwind of 40 knots, the pilot may expect a total shear of 80 knots across the microburst. (PLT317) — AIM ¶7-1-25

Answers (A) and (C) are incorrect because the total shear is the total headwind to tailwind change of a traversing airplane, thus a 40-knot headwind would shear 80 knots to a 40-knot tailwind.

ALL

9140. Doppler wind measurements indicate that the windspeed change a pilot may expect when flying through the peak intensity of a microburst is approximately

A— 15 knots.
B— 25 knots.
C— 45 knots.

The downdrafts can be as strong as 6,000 feet per minute. Horizontal winds near the surface can be as strong as 45 knots resulting in a 90-knot shear across the microburst. (PLT317) — AIM ¶7-1-25

ALL

9143. Maximum downdrafts in a microburst encounter may be as strong as

A— 8,000 ft/min.
B— 7,000 ft/min.
C— 6,000 ft/min.

The downdrafts can be as strong as 6,000 feet per minute. Horizontal winds near the surface can be as strong as 45 knots resulting in a 90-knot shear across the microburst. (PLT317) — AIM ¶7-1-25

ALL

9144. An aircraft that encounters a headwind of 45 knots, within a microburst, may expect a total shear across the microburst of

A— 40 knots.
B— 80 knots.
C— 90 knots.

With a headwind of 45 knots, the pilot may expect a total shear of 90 knots across the microburst. (PLT317) — AIM ¶7-1-25

Answer (A) is incorrect because the total shear is the total headwind to tailwind change of a traversing airplane, thus a 45-knot headwind would shear 90 knots, not 40 knots, to a 45-knot tailwind. Answer (B) is incorrect because the total shear is the total headwind to tailwind change of a traversing airplane, thus a 45-knot headwind would shear 90 knots, not 80 knots, to a 45-knot tailwind.

Answers

9130 [C]	9131 [C]	9814 [C]	9132 [B]	9140 [C]	9143 [C]
9144 [C]					

ALL
9145. (Refer to Figure 144.) If involved in a microburst encounter, in which aircraft positions will the most severe downdraft occur?

A— 4 and 5.
B— 2 and 3.
C— 3 and 4.

An airplane flying through the microburst as depicted in FAA Figure 144 would encounter increasing performance in position 1, followed by a decreasing headwind in position 2. At position 3 the aircraft would encounter the strong downdraft followed by a strong tailwind at position 4. Position 5 represents the situation just before ground contact. (PLT317) — AIM ¶7-1-25

Answer (A) is incorrect because position 5 has significantly less downdraft even though it has considerably more tailwind. Answer (B) is incorrect because position 2 has not as significant a downdraft as 3 and 4, but it contains a significant headwind even though it is decreasing.

ALL
9146. (Refer to Figure 144.) When penetrating a microburst, which aircraft will experience an increase in performance without a change in pitch or power?

A— 3.
B— 2.
C— 1.

An airplane flying through the microburst as depicted in FAA Figure 144 would encounter increasing performance in position 1, followed by a decreasing headwind in position 2. At position 3 the aircraft would encounter the strong downdraft followed by a strong tailwind at position 4. Position 5 represents the situation just before ground contact. (PLT317) — AIM ¶7-1-25

Answer (A) is incorrect because position 3 indicates where the most severe downdraft occurs, which results in a decrease in performance. Answer (B) is incorrect because position 2 does not have as significant a headwind component as position 1, and thus performance is less than at position 1.

ALL
9147. (Refer to Figure 144.) What effect will a microburst encounter have upon the aircraft in position 3?

A— Decreasing headwind.
B— Increasing tailwind.
C— Strong downdraft.

An airplane flying through the microburst as depicted in FAA Figure 144 would encounter increasing performance in position 1, followed by a decreasing headwind in position 2. At position 3 the aircraft would encounter the strong downdraft followed by a strong tailwind at position 4. Position 5 represents the situation just before ground contact. (PLT317) — AIM ¶7-1-25

Answer (A) is incorrect because at position 2, not 3, the airplane encounters decreasing headwind. Answer (B) is incorrect because at position 5 the airplane encounters an increasing tailwind and it may result in an extreme situation as pictured, i.e., just before impact.

ALL
9148. (Refer to Figure 144.) What effect will a microburst encounter have upon the aircraft in position 4?

A— Strong tailwind.
B— Strong updraft.
C— Significant performance increase.

An airplane flying through the microburst as depicted in FAA Figure 144 would encounter increasing performance in position 1, followed by a decreasing headwind in position 2. At position 3 the aircraft would encounter the strong downdraft followed by a strong tailwind at position 4. Position 5 represents the situation just before ground contact. (PLT317) — AIM ¶7-1-25

Answer (B) is incorrect because updrafts will occur in thunderstorms, not in microbursts from thunderstorms. Answer (C) is incorrect because the significant increase in performance occurs at position 1 where the headwind component is the greatest.

ALL
9149. (Refer to Figure 144.) How will the aircraft in position 4 be affected by a microburst encounter?

A— Performance increasing with a tailwind and updraft.
B— Performance decreasing with a tailwind and downdraft.
C— Performance decreasing with a headwind and downdraft.

An airplane flying through the microburst as depicted in FAA Figure 144 would encounter increasing performance in position 1, followed by a decreasing headwind in position 2. At position 3 the aircraft would encounter the strong downdraft followed by a strong tailwind at position 4. Position 5 represents the situation just before ground contact. (PLT317) — AIM ¶7-1-25

Answer (A) is incorrect because performance will decrease with a tailwind, and thunderstorms (not microbursts) will have updrafts. Answer (C) is incorrect because the airplane at position 2 indicates where performance will decrease due to a headwind and downdraft.

Answers

| 9145 | [C] | 9146 | [C] | 9147 | [C] | 9148 | [A] | 9149 | [B] |

ALL

9150. What is the expected duration of an individual microburst?

A— Two minutes with maximum winds lasting approximately 1 minute.
B— One microburst may continue for as long as 2 to 4 hours.
C— Seldom longer than 15 minutes from the time the burst strikes the ground until dissipation.

An individual microburst will seldom last longer than 15 minutes from the time it strikes the ground until dissipation. The horizontal winds continue to increase during the first 5 minutes with the maximum intensity winds lasting approximately 2 to 4 minutes. (PLT317) — AIM ¶7-1-25

Answer (A) is incorrect because microbursts last 15, not 2 minutes, and maximum winds last 2 to 4 minutes, not 1 minute. Answer (B) is incorrect because the maximum winds last 2 to 4 minutes, not 2 to 4 hours, and the microburst is usually limited to about 15 minutes.

ALL

9167. What information from the control tower is indicated by the following transmission?

"SOUTH BOUNDARY WIND ONE SIX ZERO AT TWO FIVE, WEST BOUNDARY WIND TWO FOUR ZERO AT THREE FIVE."

A— A downburst is located at the center of the airport.
B— Wake turbulence exists on the west side of the active runway.
C— There is a possibility of wind shear over or near the airport.

The Low-Level Wind Shear Alert System (LLWAS) is a computerized system which detects the presence of a possible hazardous low-level wind shear by continuously comparing the winds measured by sensors installed around the periphery on an airport with the wind measured at the center field location. If the difference between the center field wind sensor and peripheral sensor becomes excessive, a thunderstorm or thunderstorm gust front wind shear is probable. When this condition exists, the tower controller will provide arrival and departure aircraft with an advisory of the situation which includes the center field wind plus the remote location and wind. The broadcast quoted in the question is an example of this type of advisory. (PLT044) — AIM ¶4-3-7

Answer (A) is incorrect because a downburst is a vertical movement of air which is not measured by the LLWAS until it has horizontal movement. Also the wind direction is toward the center of the airport, not away from it. Answer (B) is incorrect because wake turbulence does not produce wind. It is generated by an aircraft that is producing lift, which could be on either side of the active runway.

ALL

9136. What is the recommended technique to counter the loss of airspeed and resultant lift from wind shear?

A— Lower the pitch attitude and regain lost airspeed.
B— Avoid overstressing the aircraft, "pitch to airspeed," and apply maximum power.
C— Maintain, or increase, pitch attitude and accept the lower-than-normal airspeed indications.

Pitch attitude must be maintained or increased even when lower-than-normal airspeed indications are required. (PLT518) — AC 00-54

Answer (A) is incorrect because lowering the pitch attitude to regain lost airspeed is a result of past training emphasis on airspeed control, not recovering from a wind shear. Answer (B) is incorrect because the recommended technique to recover from a wind shear is to maintain or increase pitch attitude and not "pitch to airspeed," which may decrease pitch to regain lost airspeed.

Answers

9150 [C]   9167 [C]   9136 [C]

Frost and Ice

No person may dispatch or release an aircraft, continue to operate en route, or land when in the opinion of the pilot-in-command or aircraft dispatcher, icing conditions are expected or met that might adversely affect the safety of the flight. No person may takeoff when frost, snow or ice is adhering to the wings, control surfaces or propellers of the aircraft.

Deicing is a procedure in which frost, ice, or snow is removed from the aircraft in order to provide clean surfaces. Anti-icing is a process that provides some protection against the formation of frost or ice for a limited period of time.

The equipment most commonly used for **deicing** and **anti-icing** airplanes on the ground is the truck-mounted mobile deicer/anti-icer. The two basic types of fluids used are Type 1 (unthickened) fluids and Type 2 (thickened) fluids. Type 1 fluids have a minimum 80% glycol content and a relatively low viscosity, except at very low temperatures. The viscosity of Type 1 fluids depends only on temperature. The holdover time is relatively short for Type 1 fluids. Type 2 fluids have a significantly higher holdover time. Type 2 fluids have a minimum glycol content of 50% with 45% to 50% water plus thickeners and inhibitors. Water decreases the freeze point. The freeze point should be no greater than 20°F below ambient or surface temperature, whichever is less.

There is a one-step process and a two-step process for deicing and anti-icing. The one-step process uses heated fluid to remove snow, ice and frost. The primary advantage of this process is that it is quick and uncomplicated. However, where large deposits of snow or ice must be flushed off, fluid usage will be greater than with the two-step process. The two-step process consists of separate deicing and anti-icing steps. A diluted fluid, usually heated, is used to deice and a more concentrated fluid (either 100% or diluted, depending on the weather), usually cold, is used to anti-ice. Type 1 or 2 fluids can be used for both steps, or Type 1 for step 1 and Type 2 for step 2.

Two precautions to observe when using this equipment are:

1. Do not spray deice/anti-ice fluid at or into pitot inlets, TAT probes, or static ports; and

2. Apply deice/anti-ice fluid on pressure relief doors, lower door sills, and bottom edges of doors prior to closing for flight.

Icing

For ice to form, there must be moisture present in the air and the air must be cooled to a temperature of 0°C (32°F) or less. Aerodynamic cooling can lower the temperature of an airfoil to 0°C even though the ambient temperature is a few degrees warmer.

Ice is identified as clear, rime, or mixed. *Rime ice* forms if the droplets are small and freeze immediately when contacting the aircraft surface. This type of ice usually forms on areas such as the leading edges of wings or struts. It has a somewhat rough looking appearance and is a milky white color. *Clear ice* is usually formed from larger water droplets or freezing rain that can spread over a surface. This is the most dangerous type of ice since it is clear, hard to see, and can change the shape of the airfoil. *Mixed ice* is a mixture of clear ice and rime ice. It has the bad characteristics of both types and can form rapidly.

There are two kinds of icing that are significant to aviation: structural icing and induction icing. *Structural icing* refers to the accumulation of ice on the exterior of the aircraft; *induction icing* affects the powerplant operation. Structural icing occurs on an aircraft whenever supercooled droplets of water make contact with any part of the aircraft that is also at a temperature below freezing.

One inflight condition necessary for structural icing is visible moisture (clouds or raindrops). *Freezing rain* always occurs in a temperature inversion. As the rain falls through air that is below freezing, its temperature begins to fall below freezing yet it does not freeze solid — i.e., freezing rain. The process requires the temperature of the rain to be above freezing before it becomes supercooled. Eventually, the water drops will freeze into ice pellets. Any encounter with ice pellets in flight indicates that there is freezing rain at a higher altitude.

Aircraft structural ice will most likely have the highest accumulation in freezing rain; therefore, an operational consideration if you fly into rain which freezes on impact is that temperatures are above freezing at some higher altitude.

Hazards of Structural Icing

The most hazardous aspect of structural icing is its aerodynamic effects. Ice can alter the shape of an airfoil. This can cause control problems, change the angle of attack at which the aircraft stalls, and cause the aircraft to stall at a significantly higher airspeed. Ice can reduce the amount of lift that an airfoil will produce and increase the amount of drag by several times. It can partially block or limit control surfaces, which will limit or make control movements ineffective. If the extra weight caused by ice accumulation is too great, the aircraft might not be able to become airborne, and if in flight, might not be able to maintain altitude.

For this reason, regulations prohibit takeoff when snow, ice, or frost is adhering to wings, propellers, or control surfaces of an aircraft. Yet another hazard of structural icing is the possible uncommanded and uncontrolled roll phenomenon referred to as "roll upset," which is associated with severe inflight icing. Therefore, pilots flying airplanes certificated for flight in known icing conditions should be aware that severe icing is a condition that is outside of the airplane's certificated icing envelope.

Structural icing can also cause tailplane (empennage) stall. The tail can collect ice faster than the wing and because it is not visible to the pilot inflight, the situation could go undetected. A tailplane stall occurs when, same as with the wing, the critical angle of attack is exceeded. Since the horizontal stabilizer counters the natural nose-down tendency caused by the center of lift of the main wing, the airplane will react by pitching down, sometimes uncontrollably, when the tailplane is stalled. Application of flaps can aggravate or initiate the stall.

Because of this, the pilot should use caution when applying flaps during an approach if there is the possibility of icing on the tailplane. Ice buildup will cause the airplane to require more power to maintain cruise airspeed. Ice on the tailplane can cause diminished nose-up pitch control and heavy elevator forces, and the aircraft may buffet if flaps are applied. Ice on the rudder or ailerons can cause control oscillations or vibrations.

For an airplane to be approved for flight into icing conditions, the airplane must be equipped with systems that will adequately protect various components. Not all airplanes with these components are approved for flight into known icing; check your POH to know if your airplane has been certificated to operate in known icing conditions.

Frost Formation

Frost is described as ice deposits formed by sublimation on a surface when the temperature of the collecting surface is at or below the dew point of the adjacent air and the dew point is below freezing. Frost causes early airflow separation on an airfoil resulting in a loss of lift. Therefore, all frost should be removed from the lifting surfaces of an airplane before flight or it may prevent the airplane from becoming airborne.

Continued

Snow always forms in colder than freezing temperatures by the process of sublimation. This is when water goes straight from its vapor state into ice without ever being a liquid. Wet snow occurs when it falls to altitudes with above freezing temperatures and begins to melt.

Test data indicate that ice, snow, or frost formations having a thickness and surface roughness similar to medium or course sandpaper on the leading edge and upper surface of a wing can reduce wing lift by as much as 30% and increase drag by 40%.

ALL
9440. Which is an effect of ice, snow, or frost formation on an airplane?

A— Increased stall speed.
B— Increased pitchdown tendencies.
C— Increased angle of attack for stalls.

Aircraft with ice, snow, or frost on the wings may experience increased stall speed, decreased angle of attack for stalls, and increased pitchup tendencies. (PLT493) — AC 20-117

ALL
9440-1. Frozen dew is

A— white and opaque.
B— hard and opaque.
C— hard and transparent.

Frost forms in much the same way as dew. The difference is that the dew point of surrounding air must be colder than freezing. Water vapor then sublimates directly as ice crystals or frost rather than condensing as dew. Sometimes dew forms and later freezes; however, frozen dew is easily distinguished from frost. Frozen dew is hard and transparent while frost is white and opaque. (PLT493) — AC 00-6

ALL
9449. Clear ice generally forms in outside temperature ranges of

A— -15 to -25°C.
B— 0 to -10°C.
C— colder than -25°C.

Temperatures close to the freezing point, large amounts of liquid water, high aircraft velocities, and large droplets are conducive to the formation of clear ice. (PLT493) — AC 91-51

ALL
9451. Test data indicate that ice, snow, or frost having a thickness and roughness similar to medium or coarse sandpaper on the leading edge and upper surface of a wing can

A— reduce lift by as much as 40 percent and increase drag by 30 percent.
B— increase drag and reduce lift by as much as 40 percent.
C— reduce lift by as much as 30 percent and increase drag by 40 percent.

Test data indicate that ice, snow, or frost formations having a thickness and surface roughness similar to medium or coarse sandpaper on the leading edge and upper surface of a wing can reduce wing lift by as much as 30 percent and increase drag by 40 percent. (PLT128) — AC 120-58

ALL
9695. The adverse effects of ice, snow, or frost on aircraft performance and flight characteristics include decreased lift and

A— increased thrust.
B— a decreased stall speed.
C— an increased stall speed.

Ice, frost, or snow on an aircraft can cause decreased lift, increased stall speed, and loss of thrust. (PLT493) — AC 120-58

ALL
9302. Even a small amount of frost, ice, or snow may

A— increase takeoff performance.
B— hinder lift production to a point where takeoff will be impossible.
C— decrease takeoff ground run.

Aircraft that have ice, snow, or frost on their surfaces must be carefully cleaned prior to beginning a flight because of the possible airflow disruption and loss of lift. (PLT128) — FAA-H-8083-25

Answers

| 9440 | [A] | 9440-1 | [C] | 9449 | [B] | 9451 | [C] | 9695 | [C] | 9302 | [B] |

ALL

9441. Which is a disadvantage of the one-step over the two-step process when deicing/anti-icing an airplane?

A— It is more complicated.
B— The holding time is increased.
C— More fluid is used with the one-step method when large deposits of ice and snow must be flushed off airplane surfaces.

Use the two-stage process to remove ice deposits with hot water or a mix of FPD (Freezing Point Depressant) and water. This reduces the amount of fluid required. (PLT108) — AC 120-58

Answer (A) is incorrect because the one-step process is less complicated. Answer (B) is incorrect because one of the advantages of the one-step process is increased holding time.

ALL

9442. The purpose of diluting ethylene glycol deicing fluid with water in non-precipitation conditions is to

A— raise the eutectic point.
B— decrease the freeze point.
C— increase the minimum freezing point (onset of crystallization).

Pure ethylene glycol will freeze at warmer temperatures than aqueous solutions of ethylene glycol. (PLT108) — AC 20-117

Answer (A) is incorrect because diluting ethylene glycol lowers the eutectic point. Answer (C) is incorrect because diluting ethylene glycol decreases the minimum freezing point (onset of crystallization).

ALL

9443. Which procedure increases holding time when deicing/anti-icing an airplane using a two-step process?

A— Heated Type 1 fluid followed by cold Type 2 fluid.
B— Cold Type 2 fluid followed by hot Type 2 fluid.
C— Heated Type 1 or 2 fluid followed by cold Type 1 fluid.

Type 2 fluid is applied cold to increase its thickness and increase holding time. (PLT108) — AC 120-58

Answer (B) is incorrect because cold Type 2 would not be an effective deicer. Answer (C) is incorrect because step 2 should be Type 2.

ALL

9444. Which of the following will decrease the holding time during anti-icing using a two-step process?

A— Apply heated Type 2 fluid.
B— Decrease the water content.
C— Increase the viscosity of Type 1 fluid.

Heating fluids increases their deicing effectiveness; however, in the anti-icing process, unheated fluids are more effective. (PLT108) — AC 120-58

Answer (B) is incorrect because decreasing the water content will increase the holding time. Answer (C) is incorrect because increasing the viscosity of Type 1 fluid will increase the holding time.

ALL

9753. When icing is detected, particularly while operating an aircraft without deicing equipment, the pilot should

A— fly to an area with liquid precipitation.
B— fly to a lower altitude.
C— leave the area of precipitation or go to an altitude where the temperature is above freezing.

When icing is detected, a pilot should do one of two things, particularly if the aircraft is not equipped with deicing equipment: leave the area of precipitation or go to an altitude where the temperature is above freezing. This "warmer" altitude may not always be a lower altitude. Proper preflight action includes obtaining information on the freezing level and the above-freezing levels in precipitation areas. (PLT493) — FAA-H-8083-15

Answer (A) is incorrect because pilots should leave the area of any precipitation; even liquid precip can result in an icing scenario. Answer (B) is incorrect because a "warmer" altitude may not always be a lower altitude.

Answers

9441 [C]	9442 [B]	9443 [A]	9444 [A]	9753 [C]

ALL

9756. If icing is suspected on an airplane equipped with deicing equipment, the pilot should

A— first confirm ice with the ice light prior to deploying the pneumatic boots.
B— operate the pneumatic deicing system several times to clear the ice.
C— operate the pneumatic deicing system once to allow time for the ice removal.

Pneumatic boots are one method capable of removing ice from an aircraft surface. This system is commonly used on smaller aircraft and usually provides ice removal for the wing and tail section by inflating a rubber boot. (PLT493) — FAA-H-8083-15

Answer (A) is incorrect because the deicing system should be used as soon as icing is suspected. Answer (C) is incorrect because the pneumatic boots should be inflated/deflated several times to try to remove the ice.

ALL

9445. What should the deice/anti-ice fluid temperature be during the last step of a two-phase process?

A— Hot.
B— Warm.
C— Cold.

The two-step procedure involves both deicing and anti-icing. Deicing is accomplished with hot water or a hot mixture of FPD and water. The ambient weather conditions and the type of accumulation to be removed from the aircraft must be considered when determining which type of deicing fluid to use. The second (anti-icing) step involves applying a mixture of SAE or ISO Type 2 and water to the critical surfaces of the aircraft. (PLT108) — AC 120-58

Answers (A) and (B) are incorrect because heated fluids are used during the first step of a two-phase process.

ALL

9446. What is the minimum glycol content of Type 1 deicing/anti-icing fluid?

A— 30 percent.
B— 50 percent.
C— 80 percent.

SAE and ISO Type 1 fluids in the concentrated form contain a minimum of 80 percent glycols and are considered "unthickened" because of their relatively low viscosity. (PLT108) — AC 120-58

ALL

9447. What is the minimum glycol content of Type 2 deicing/anti-icing fluid?

A— 30 percent.
B— 50 percent.
C— 80 percent.

SAE and ISO Type 2 fluids contain a minimum of 50 percent glycols and are considered "thickened" because of added thickening agents that enable the fluid to be deposited in a thicker film and to remain on the aircraft surfaces until the time for takeoff. (PLT108) — AC 120-58

ALL

9448. Anti-icing fluid should provide freezing point protection to

A— -20°F ambient temperature.
B— +32°F outside temperature or below.
C— a freezing point no greater than 20°F below the ambient or airplane surface temperature.

In any case the freezing point of residual fluids (water, FPD fluids or mixtures) should not be greater than 20°F below ambient or surface temperature, whichever is less. (PLT108) — AC 20-117

Answers (A) and (B) are incorrect because anti-icing fluid should protect from icing to a freezing point no greater than 20°F below the ambient or aircraft surface temperature.

ALL

9450. Freezing Point Depressant (FPD) fluids used for deicing

A— provide ice protection during flight.
B— are intended to provide ice protection on the ground only.
C— on the ground, cause no performance degradation during takeoff.

FPD fluids are used to aid the ground deicing process and provide a protective film to delay formations of frost, snow, or other ice. (PLT108) — AC 120-58

Answer (A) is incorrect because FPD does not provide inflight protection. Answer (C) is incorrect because some large aircraft experience performance degradation and may require weight or other compensation.

Answers

| 9756 | [B] | 9445 | [C] | 9446 | [C] | 9447 | [B] | 9448 | [C] | 9450 | [B] |

ALL

9452. Snow on top of deicing or anti-icing fluids

A— need not be considered as adhering to the aircraft.
B— must be considered as adhering to the aircraft.
C— must be considered as adhering to the aircraft, but a safe takeoff can be made as it will blow off.

FPD fluids are highly soluble in water; however, ice is slow to absorb FPD or to melt when in contact with it. If frost, ice, or snow is adhering to an aircraft surface, the formation may be melted by repeated application of proper quantities of FPD fluid. This process can be significantly accelerated by thermal energy from heated fluids. As the ice melts, the FPD mixes with the water thereby diluting the FPD. As dilution occurs, the resulting mixture may begin to run off. If all the ice is not melted, additional applications of FPD become necessary until the fluid penetrates to the aircraft surface. When all the ice has melted, the remaining liquid residue is a mixture of water and FPD. The resulting film could freeze (begin to crystallize) with only a slight temperature decrease. (PLT108) — AC 120-58

Answer (A) is incorrect because snow (ice) needs to be considered as adhering to the aircraft (see explanation). Answer (C) is incorrect because snow may not necessarily blow off during takeoff.

ALL

9453. Freezing Point Depressant (FPD) fluids are highly soluble in water; however,

A— ice is slow to absorb it but fast to melt when in contact with FPD.
B— ice absorbs it very fast but is slow to melt when in contact with it.
C— ice is slow to absorb it, and to melt when in contact with it.

FPD fluids are highly soluble in water; however, ice is slow to absorb FPD or to melt when in contact with it. (PLT108) — AC 120-58

Answer (A) is incorrect because FPD fluids are slow to melt. Answer (B) is incorrect because FPD fluids are slow to absorb.

ALL

9454. Freezing Point Depressant (FPD) fluid residue on engine fan or compressor blades

A— can increase performance and cause stalls or surges.
B— could cause FPD vapors to enter the aircraft but would have no affect on engine thrust or power.
C— can reduce engine performance and cause surging and/or compressor stalls.

Fluid residue on engine fan or compressor blades can reduce engine performance or cause stall or surge. (PLT108) — AC 120-58

Answer (A) is incorrect because fluid residue would cause a decrease in performance. Answer (B) is incorrect because fluid residue would have an affect on engine thrust or power.

ALL

9698. The practice developed and accepted by the North American air carrier industry using traditional North American fluids is to ensure that the freeze point of the remaining film is below ambient temperature by at least

A— 10°F.
B— 20°F.
C— 20°C.

As it is applied, deicing fluid is often diluted by melted snow and ice. It is standard practice to ensure that the remaining film of diluted fluid has a freeze point at least 20°F below the ambient temperature. (PLT108) — AC 120-58

ALL

9700. What is the effect of Freezing Point Depressant (FPD) fluid residue on engine fan or compressor blades?

A— could cause FPD vapors to enter the aircraft but would have no affect on engine thrust or power.
B— It can increase performance and cause stalls or surges.
C— It can reduce engine performance and cause surging and/or compressor stalls.

Fluid residue on engine fan or compressor blades can reduce engine performance or cause stall or surge. In addition, this could increase the possibility of, or the quantity of, glycol vapors entering the aircraft through the engine bleed air system. (PLT108) — AC 120-58

Answers

9452 [B]	9453 [C]	9454 [C]	9698 [B]	9700 [C]

ALL
9183. What is a feature of supercooled water?

A— The water drop sublimates to an ice particle upon impact.
B— The unstable water drop freezes upon striking an exposed object.
C— The temperature of the water drop remains at 0°C until it impacts a part of the airframe, then clear ice accumulates.

Rain or drizzle is always formed in temperatures which are above freezing. Rain falling through colder air may become supercooled, freezing on impact as freezing rain. (PLT512) — AC 00-6

Answer (A) is incorrect because sublimation is the process of changing water vapor to ice crystals (not liquid water to ice). Answer (C) is incorrect because supercooled water temperature is below 0°C.

ALL
9221. What condition is necessary for the formation of structural icing in flight?

A— Supercooled water drops.
B— Water vapor.
C— Visible water.

For structural icing to form, the aircraft must be flying through visible moisture and the temperature where the moisture strikes the aircraft must 0°C or colder. Note that the moisture does not need to be supercooled. (PLT274) — AC 00-6

Answer (A) is incorrect because supercooled water drops increase the rate of icing, but are not a condition necessary for the formation of structural icing. Answer (B) is incorrect because water must be visible, not in a gaseous (vapor) state.

ALL
9224. Which type of icing is associated with the smallest size of water droplet similar to that found in low-level stratus clouds?

A— Clear ice.
B— Frost ice.
C— Rime ice.

Rime ice forms when drops are small, such as those in stratified clouds or light drizzle. (PLT274) — AC 00-6

Answer (A) is incorrect because clear ice forms when drops are large, not small, as found in rain or cumuliform clouds. Answer (B) is incorrect because frost is not a structural icing condition found in flight; it happens to airplanes parked on the ground as well.

ALL
9161. Freezing rain encountered during climb is normally evidence that

A— a climb can be made to a higher altitude without encountering more than light icing.
B— a layer of warmer air exists above.
C— ice pellets at higher altitudes have changed to rain in the warmer air below.

Rain or drizzle is always formed in temperatures which are above freezing. Rain falling through colder air may become supercooled, freezing on impact as freezing rain. (PLT512) — AC 00-6

Answer (A) is incorrect because freezing rain only means that a layer of warmer air exists above; it does not indicate the amount of icing that may be encountered during a climb. Answer (C) is incorrect because freezing rain is formed by rain falling through colder air, not from ice pellets melting through warmer air.

ALL
9223. Which type precipitation is an indication that supercooled water is present?

A— Wet snow.
B— Freezing rain.
C— Ice pellets.

Rain or drizzle is always formed in temperatures which are above freezing. Rain falling through colder air may become supercooled, freezing on impact as freezing rain. (PLT344) — AC 00-6

Answer (A) is incorrect because wet snow is an indication that temperature is above freezing at the present level. Answer (C) is incorrect because ice pellets indicate that water has frozen, not that is has become supercooled.

ALL
9180. What condition is indicated when ice pellets are encountered during flight?

A— Thunderstorms at higher levels.
B— Freezing rain at higher levels.
C— Snow at higher levels.

Rain or drizzle is always formed in temperatures which are above freezing. Rain falling through colder air may become supercooled, freezing on impact as freezing rain. As it continues to fall in the freezing temperature, it will form into ice pellets. (PLT493) — AC 00-6

Answer (A) is incorrect because ice pellets always indicate freezing rain, not thunderstorms, at higher altitudes. Answer (C) is incorrect because freezing rain, not snow, is indicated at higher altitude when ice pellets are encountered.

Answers

9183 [B]   9221 [C]   9224 [C]   9161 [B]   9223 [B]   9180 [B]

ALL

9774. The most likely condition in which to experience severe inflight icing with the ambient temperature below 0°C is

A— rain.
B— visible moisture.
C— fog.

For structural icing to occur two conditions must be present: The aircraft must be flying through visible water such as rain or cloud droplets and temperature at the point where the moisture strikes the aircraft must be 0° or colder. (PLT274) — AC 00-6

ALL

9775. Which of the following weather conditions are conducive to inflight icing?

A— Visible rain with temperatures below 0°C.
B— Visible rain with temperatures below 10°C.
C— Visible moisture with temperatures below 5°C.

The following weather conditions may be conducive to severe in-flight icing: visible rain at temperatures below 0°C ambient air temperature; droplets that splash or splatter on impact at temperatures below 0°C ambient air temperature. (PLT274) — AC 91-51

ALL

9162. What temperature condition is indicated if precipitation in the form of wet snow occurs during flight?

A— The temperature is above freezing at flight altitude.
B— The temperature is above freezing at higher altitudes.
C— There is an inversion with colder air below.

Snowflakes are formed by sublimation in below-freezing temperatures. If the snow falls into an area of above-freezing temperatures it will start to melt, become wet snow and eventually turn into rain. (PLT493) — AC 00-6

Answer (B) is incorrect because wet snow indicates above-freezing temperature at flight level, not at higher altitudes. The temperature was below freezing at the altitudes where the snow formed. Answer (C) is incorrect because wet snow indicates falling snow that has begun to melt due to above-freezing temperature at flight level. An inversion may or may not be the cause of the warmer air.

ALL

9179. Which conditions result in the formation of frost?

A— The temperature of the collecting surface is at or below freezing and small droplets of moisture are falling.
B— Dew collects on the surface and then freezes because the surface temperature is lower than the air temperature.
C— Temperature of the collecting surface is below the dewpoint and the dewpoint is also below freezing.

Frost forms when both the temperature and the dew point of the collecting surface are below freezing. When this occurs, water vapor sublimates directly into frost. This condition most often occurs on clear nights with little or no wind. (PLT493) — AC 00-6

Answer (A) is incorrect because moisture that falls on a collecting surface that is at or below freezing will form ice. Answer (B) is incorrect because frozen dew is hard and transparent, while frost is the sublimation of vapor into ice, and is white and opaque.

ALL

9748. When flying in the rain and an air temperature of 1°C, a pilot should

A— not expect icing until the air temperature is 0°C or less.
B— Use autopilot in icing to lower the work load.
C— be aware of the possibility of airframe icing.

Pilots should be vigilant and aware of icing possibilities, particularly when flying in conditions between -5 and +2 degrees C. (PLT274) — AC 91-74

ALL

9181. When will frost most likely form on aircraft surfaces?

A— On clear nights with stable air and light winds.
B— On overcast nights with freezing drizzle precipitation.
C— On clear nights with convective action and a small temperature/dewpoint spread.

Frost forms when both the temperature and the dew point of the collecting surface are below freezing. When this occurs, water vapor sublimates directly into frost. This condition most often occurs on clear nights with little or no wind. (PLT493) — AC 00-6

Answer (B) is incorrect because freezing drizzle would produce ice on the aircraft surfaces, not frost. Answer (C) is incorrect because stable air is required. Convective action requires unstable conditions.

Answers

9774 [A]	9775 [A]	9162 [A]	9179 [C]	9748 [C]	9181 [A]

ALL

9736. During an IFR cross-country flight you picked up rime icing which you estimate is 1/2" thick on the leading edge of the wings. You are now below the clouds at 2000 feet AGL and are approaching your destination airport under VFR. Visibility under the clouds is more than 10 miles, winds at the destination airport are 8 knots right down the runway, and the surface temperature is 3 degrees Celsius. You decide to:

A— use a faster than normal approach and landing speed.
B— approach and land at your normal speed since the ice is not thick enough to have any noticeable effect.
C— fly your approach slower than normal to lessen the "wind chill" effect and break up the ice.

Ice will accumulate unevenly on the airplane. It will add weight and drag, and decrease thrust and lift. With ice accumulations, landing approaches should be made with a minimum wing flap setting and with an added margin of airspeed. Sudden and large configuration and airspeed changes should be avoided. (PLT274) — FAA-H-8083-3

Answer (B) is incorrect because ice having a thickness similar to sandpaper on the leading edge and upper surface of a wing can reduce wing lift by as much as 30% and increase drag by 40%. Answer (C) is incorrect because ice will increase drag, requiring additional lift (airspeed); "wind chill" effect cannot be relied upon to melt/remove the ice that has already accumulated; flying slower than normal increases the possibility of a stall due to the decreased lift.

ATM, DSP

8258. The pilot in command of an airplane en route determines that icing conditions can be expected that might adversely affect safety of the flight. Which action is appropriate?

A— The pilot in command may continue to the original destination airport, after climbing to a higher altitude.
B— The pilot in command shall not continue flight into the icing conditions.
C— The flight may continue to the original destination airport, provided all anti-icing and deicing equipment is operational and is used.

No person may dispatch or release an aircraft, continue to operate an aircraft en route, or land an aircraft when, in the opinion of the pilot-in-command or aircraft dispatcher, icing conditions are expected or met that might adversely affect the safety of flight. (PLT379) — 14 CFR §121.629

ATM, DSP

8265. What action is required prior to takeoff if snow is adhering to the wings of an air carrier airplane?

A— Sweep off as much snow as possible and the residue must be polished smooth.
B— Assure that the snow is removed from the airplane.
C— Add 15 knots to the normal VR speed as the snow will blow off.

No person may take off in an aircraft when frost, snow, or ice is adhering to the wings, control surfaces, or propellers of the aircraft. (PLT493) — 14 CFR §121.629

Answer (A) is incorrect because all of the snow must be removed prior to takeoff. Answer (C) is incorrect because there is no V-speed adjustment authorized to compensate for snow on the wings; it must be removed prior to takeoff.

ATS

9696. A pretakeoff contamination check for snow, ice or frost is required by 14 CFR Part 135. This check is required to

A— be made within 2 minutes of starting the takeoff roll.
B— be completed within 5 minutes prior to beginning the taxi to the runway.
C— see that the aircraft is clean, therefore, a safe takeoff can be made during the next 5 minutes.

A pre-takeoff inspection for ice, snow, or frost must be completed no more than 5 minutes prior to takeoff anytime conditions require it. (PLT108) — 14 CFR §135.227

ATS

9697. Deicing procedures and equipment developed for large transport airplanes

A— will not be appropriate for the smaller aircraft, used under 14 CFR Part 135.
B— will be appropriate for all of the smaller aircraft, used under 14 CFR Part 135.
C— may not be appropriate for some of the smaller aircraft, used under 14 CFR Part 135.

Deicing procedures developed for large transport aircraft may not be appropriate for smaller, slower aircraft. (PLT108) — AC 120-58

Answers

9736 [A]	8258 [B]	8265 [B]	9696 [C]	9697 [C]

Turbulence

Light chop causes slight, rapid and somewhat erratic bumpiness without appreciable changes in altitude or attitude. Light turbulence causes momentary slight erratic changes in altitude and/or attitude. Light chop causes rapid bumps or jolts without appreciable changes in aircraft altitude or attitude. Moderate turbulence is similar to light turbulence, but of greater intensity. Changes in altitude or attitude occur but the aircraft remains in positive control at all times. It usually causes variations in indicated airspeed. Severe turbulence causes large, abrupt changes in altitude or attitude. It usually causes large variations in indicated airspeed. The aircraft may be momentarily out of control. In extreme turbulence the aircraft is violently tossed about and is practically impossible to control. Extreme turbulence may cause structural damage.

Turbulence that occurs less than 1/3 of the time should be reported as occasional. Turbulence that occurs 1/3 to 2/3 of the time is intermittent. Turbulence that occurs more than 2/3 of the time is continuous. High altitude turbulence (normally above 15,000 feet MSL) not associated with cumuliform cloudiness should be reported as **CAT (Clear Air Turbulence)**.

Strong winds across mountain crests can cause turbulence for 100 or more miles downwind of the mountains and to altitudes as high as 5,000 feet above the tropopause. If there is enough moisture in the air, a mountain wave can be marked by standing lenticular clouds. These clouds mark the crest of each wave. Under the right conditions, several lenticulars can form one above another. A rotor current forms below the crest of a mountain wave. This is sometimes marked by a rotor cloud which will be the lowest of a group of stationary clouds. *See* Figure 8-6.

The jet stream is a common source of CAT. The strong winds and steep wind gradients will almost always produce some turbulence. The most likely place to find turbulence is on the polar side of the stream in an upper trough. The strongest turbulence will be found in a curving jet stream associated with such a trough. If you encounter turbulence in the jet stream and you have a direct headwind or tailwind you should change course or altitude. With the wind parallel to your heading, you are likely to remain in the jet and the turbulence for a considerable distance. If you approach a jet stream from the polar side the temperature will drop. When you approach it from the tropical side, the temperature rises. Recall that there is a downdraft on the polar side and an updraft on the tropical side. Therefore, to avoid jet stream turbulence descend if the temperature is falling and climb if the temperature is rising as you approach the stream.

Fronts often have turbulence due to the wind shift associated with a sharp pressure trough. Try to cross the front at right angles to minimize the time you are exposed to this turbulence.

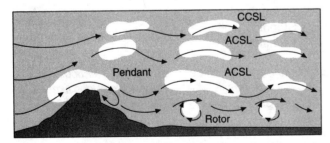

Figure 8-6. Mountain wave and associated clouds

ALL

9262. What type turbulence should be reported when it causes slight, rapid, and somewhat rhythmic bumpiness without appreciable changes in attitude or altitude, less than one-third of the time?

A— Occasional light chop.
B— Moderate turbulence.
C— Moderate chop.

This description meets the criteria for occasional light chop. (PLT501) — AC 00-45

Answer (B) is incorrect because moderate turbulence causes a change in the aircraft's attitude and/or altitude. Answer (C) is incorrect because moderate chop causes rapid, not rhythmic, bumps or jolts, which are not "slight."

ALL

9263. What type turbulence should be reported when it causes changes in altitude and/or attitude more than two-thirds of the time, with the aircraft remaining in positive control at all times?

A— Continuous severe chop.
B— Continuous moderate turbulence.
C— Intermittent moderate turbulence.

This description meets the criteria for continuous moderate turbulence. (PLT501) — AC 00-45

Answer (A) is incorrect because severe chop is not a turbulence reporting term. Answer (C) is incorrect because intermittent means that turbulence is occurring from one-third to two-thirds of the time.

ALL

9264. What type turbulence should be reported when it momentarily causes slight, erratic changes in altitude and/or attitude, one-third to two-thirds of the time?

A— Occasional light chop.
B— Moderate chop.
C— Intermittent light turbulence.

This description meets the criteria for intermittent light turbulence. (PLT501) — AC 00-45

Answer (A) is incorrect because light chop does not cause any appreciable changes in altitude and/or attitude, and occasional is less than one-third of the time. Answer (B) is incorrect because moderate chop does not cause any appreciable changes in altitude and/or attitude.

ALL

9235. Turbulence encountered above 15,000 feet AGL, not associated with cloud formations, should be reported as

A— convective turbulence.
B— high altitude turbulence.
C— clear air turbulence.

High-level turbulence (normally above 15,000 feet AGL) not associated with cumuliform cloudiness, including thunderstorms, should be reported as CAT (Clear Air Turbulence). (PLT501) — AC 00-45

Answer (A) is incorrect because convective turbulence is normally associated with cumuliform clouds and is reported as turbulence. Answer (B) is incorrect because turbulence above 15,000 feet AGL, not associated with clouds, is termed clear air turbulence, not high altitude turbulence.

ALL

9190. Which type clouds are indicative of very strong turbulence?

A— Nimbostratus.
B— Standing lenticular.
C— Cirrocumulus.

Standing lenticular clouds form at the crests of waves created by barriers to the wind flow. Though the clouds do not move, they are indicative of strong winds and possible turbulence. (PLT192) — AC 00-6

Answer (A) is incorrect because nimbostratus is a gray or dark massive cloud layer, diffused by continuous rain, snow, or ice pellets. The stratus feature indicates very little turbulence. Answer (C) is incorrect because cirrocumulus are thin clouds appearing as small white flakes or patches of cotton. Their presence indicates some turbulence and possible icing.

ALL

9226. What is the lowest cloud in the stationary group associated with a mountain wave?

A— Rotor cloud.
B— Standing lenticular.
C— Low stratus.

Mountain waves can generate standing lenticular clouds and rotor clouds. Of these, the rotor cloud is likely to be the lowest. (PLT501) — AC 00-6

Answer (B) is incorrect because the standing lenticular clouds mark the crest, or the top, of each standing wave. Answer (C) is incorrect because low stratus clouds are not associated with a mountain wave.

Answers

9262   [A]   9263   [B]   9264   [C]   9235   [C]   9190   [B]   9226   [A]

ALL

9232. Clear air turbulence (CAT) associated with a mountain wave may extend as far as

A— 1,000 miles or more downstream of the mountain.
B— 5,000 feet above the tropopause.
C— 100 miles or more upwind of the mountain.

Mountain wave CAT may extend from the mountain crests to as high as 5,000 feet above the tropopause, and can range 100 miles or more downwind from the mountains. (PLT501) — AC 00-6

Answer (A) is incorrect because mountain wave CAT can range 100, not 1,000, miles or more downstream of the mountain. Answer (C) is incorrect because mountain wave CAT is downwind of the mountain.

ALL

9777. Clear air turbulence associated with a jet stream is

A— most commonly found in temperatures between -40 and -50 degrees C.
B— most commonly found in the vicinity of the tropopause.
C— similar to that associated with a tropical maritime front.

Maximum winds generally occur at levels near the tropopause. These strong winds create narrow zones of wind shear which often generate hazardous turbulence. (PLT501) — AC 00-6

Answer (A) is incorrect because temperatures are not a primary factor for CAT. Answer (C) is incorrect because CAT is associated with the tropopause, not a tropical maritime front.

ALL

9777-1. The threshold wind speed in the jet stream for clear air turbulence is generally considered to be

A— 100 kts.
B— 110 kts.
C— 120 kts.

The threshold wind speed in the jet stream for CAT is generally considered to be 110 knots. Wind speed in jet streams can be much stronger than 110 knots and the probability of encountering CAT increases proportionally with the wind speed and the wind shear it generates. It is not the wind speed itself that causes CAT; it is the wind shear or difference in wind speed from one level or point to another that causes the wave motion or overturning in the atmosphere that is turbulence to an aircraft. (PLT501) — AC 00-30B

ALL

9237. What is a likely location of clear air turbulences?

A— In an upper trough on the polar side of a jetstream.
B— Near a ridge aloft on the equatorial side of a high pressure flow.
C— Downstream of the equatorial side of a jetstream.

A likely location of CAT is in an upper trough on the cold (polar) side of the jet stream. (PLT302) — AC 00-6

Answer (B) is incorrect because CAT is likely to occur on the polar side of the jet stream in an upper trough. Answer (C) is incorrect because CAT is likely on the polar, not equatorial, side of a jet stream.

ALL

9239. Which type jetstream can be expected to cause the greater turbulence?

A— A straight jetstream associated with a high pressure ridge.
B— A jetstream associated with a wide isotherm spacing.
C— A curving jetstream associated with a deep low pressure trough.

A frequent CAT location is along the jet stream where it curves north and northeast of a rapidly deepening surface low. (PLT302) — AC 00-6

Answer (A) is incorrect because greater turbulence is expected in a curved, not a straight jet stream. Answer (B) is incorrect because greater turbulence is more pronounced when isotherm spacing is narrow.

ALL

9230. Which action is recommended if jetstream turbulence is encountered with a direct headwind or tailwind?

A— Increase airspeed to get out of the area quickly.
B— Change course to fly on the polar side of the jetstream.
C— Change altitude or course to avoid a possible elongated turbulent area.

If jet stream turbulence is encountered with direct tailwinds or headwinds, a change of flight level or course should be initiated since these turbulent areas are elongated with the wind, and are shallow and narrow. (PLT263) — AC 00-30, Appendix 1

Answer (A) is incorrect because an increase in airspeed may overstress the airplane in turbulent conditions. Normally, a reduction in airspeed is required for turbulent air penetration. Answer (B) is incorrect because CAT is normally on the polar side of the jet stream, so you would be flying into more turbulent weather.

Answers

| 9232 | [B] | 9777 | [B] | 9777-1 | [B] | 9237 | [A] | 9239 | [C] | 9230 | [C] |

ALL

9231. Which action is recommended regarding an altitude change to get out of jetstream turbulence?

A— Descend if ambient temperature is falling.
B— Descend if ambient temperature is rising.
C— Maintain altitude if ambient temperature is not changing.

If you want to traverse an area of CAT more quickly, watch the temperature gauge for a minute or two. If the temperature is rising—climb; if the temperature is falling—descend. Application of these rules will prevent you from following the sloping tropopause and staying in the turbulent area. If the temperature remains constant, the flight is probably close to the level of the core, so either climb or descend as is convenient. (PLT263) — AC 00-30, Appendix 1

Answer (B) is incorrect because to get out of jet stream turbulence with a rising ambient temperature you would climb, not descend. Answer (C) is incorrect because you would need to make an altitude change due to jet stream turbulence, and there should be a temperature change due to a sloping tropopause.

ALL

9219. What action is recommended when encountering turbulence due to a wind shift associated with a sharp pressure trough?

A— Establish a straight course across the storm area.
B— Climb or descend to a smoother level.
C— Increase speed to get out of the trough as soon as possible.

If turbulence is encountered in an abrupt wind shift associated with a sharp pressure storm area, establish a straight course across the storm area rather than parallel to it. A change in flight level is not likely to alleviate the bumpiness. (PLT501) — AC 00-30, Appendix 1

Answer (B) is incorrect because there is no indication to identify in which direction the turbulence is stronger. A change in altitude will normally remove the aircraft from the turbulent zone. Answer (C) is incorrect because speed should be decreased to the recommended airspeed for rough air. This will avoid overstressing the airplane.

Arctic and Tropical Weather Hazards

"Whiteout" is a visibility restricting phenomenon that occurs in the Arctic when a layer of cloudiness of uniform thickness overlies a snow or ice covered surface. Parallel rays of the sun are broken up and diffused when passing through the cloud layer so that they strike the snow surface from many angles. The diffused light then reflects back and forth between the clouds and the snow eliminating all shadows. The result is a loss of depth perception that makes takeoff or landing on snow-covered surfaces very dangerous.

"Tropical Cyclone" is the term for any low that originates over tropical oceans. Tropical cyclones are classified according to their intensity based on average one minute wind speeds. These classifications are:

Tropical Depression — highest sustained winds up to 34 knots.

Tropical Storm — highest sustained winds of 35 knots through 64 knots.

Hurricane or Typhoon — highest sustained winds of 65 knots or more.

The movement of hurricanes is erratic and very difficult to predict with any degree of precision. As a general rule, hurricanes in the northern hemisphere tend to move to the northwest while they are in the lower latitudes and under the influence of the trade winds. Once they move far enough north to come under the influence of the prevailing westerlies of the mid-latitudes their track tends to curve back to the northeast.

Answers

9231   [A]   9219   [A]

ALL

9234. Which arctic flying hazard is caused when a cloud layer of uniform thickness overlies a snow or ice covered surface?

A— Ice fog.
B— Whiteout.
C— Blowing snow.

"Whiteout" is a visibility restricting phenomenon that occurs in the Arctic when a layer of cloudiness of uniform thickness overlies a snow or ice covered surface. The result is a loss of depth perception. (PLT512) — AC 00-6

Answer (A) is incorrect because ice fog forms in moist air during extremely cold conditions. It is not formed by a cloud layer overlying a snow-covered surface. Answer (C) is incorrect because blowing snow is snow that is blown by light or greater winds, causing decreased visibility. It is not formed by a cloud layer overlying a snow-covered surface.

ALL

9259. Which weather condition is present when the tropical storm is upgraded to a hurricane?

A— Highest windspeed, 100 knots or more.
B— A clear area or hurricane eye has formed.
C— Sustained winds of 65 knots or more.

Tropical cyclone international classifications are:

1. *Tropical depression — highest sustained winds up to 34 knots;*

2. *Tropical storm — highest sustained winds of 35 through 64 knots;*

3. *Hurricane or typhoon — highest sustained winds of 65 knots or more.*

(PLT511) — AC 00-6

Answer (A) is incorrect because tropical cyclones are classified based on the sustained winds, not the highest wind speed. Answer (B) is incorrect because a clear area, or eye, usually forms in the tropical storm stage and continues through the hurricane stage.

ALL

9260. What is the general direction of movement of a hurricane located in the Caribbean or Gulf of Mexico region?

A— Northwesterly curving to northeasterly.
B— Westerly, until encountering land, then easterly.
C— Counterclockwise over open water, then dissipating outward over land.

Hurricanes located in the Caribbean or Gulf of Mexico move northwesterly in the lower latitudes curving to northeasterly in the higher latitudes. (PLT068) — AC 00-6

Answer (B) is incorrect because a hurricane will curve easterly because of prevailing winds, not because of land. Answer (C) is incorrect because the windflow in the hurricane is counterclockwise, not the general movement of the hurricane itself.

Answers

9234   [B]   9259   [C]   9260   [A]

Aviation Routine Weather Report (METAR)

Weather reports (METAR) and forecasts (TAF) follow the format shown in Figure 8-7.

Key to Aerodrome Forecast (TAF) and Aviation Routine Weather Report (METAR)

TAF	KPIT 091730Z 0918/1024 15005KT 5SM HZ FEW020 WS010/31022KT
	FM091930 30015G25KT 3SM SHRA OVC015
	TEMPO 0920/0922 1/2SM +TSRA OVC008CB
	FM100100 27008KT 5SM SHRA BKN020 OVC040
	PROB30 1004/1007 1SM -RA BR
	FM101015 18005KT 6SM -SHRA OVC020
	BECMG 1013/1015 P6SM NSW SKC

Note: Users are cautioned to confirm *DATE* and *TIME* of the TAF.
For example FM**100000** is 0000Z on the **10th.** Do not confuse with *1000Z!*

METAR KPIT 091955Z COR 22015G25KT 3/4SM R28L/2600FT TSRA OVC010CB
18/16 A2992 RMK SLP045 T01820159

Forecast	Explanation	Report
TAF	Message type: TAF: routine or TAF AMD: amended forecast; METAR: hourly; SPECI: special or TESTM: noncommissioned ASOS report	METAR
KPIT	ICAO location indicator	KPIT
091730Z	Issuance time: ALL times in UTC "Z", 2-digit date, 4-digit time	091955Z
0918/1024	Valid period: Either 24 hours or 30 hours. The first two digits of EACH four-digit number indicate the date of the valid period, the final two digits indicate the time (valid from 18Z on the 9th to 24Z on the 10th).	
	In U.S. METAR; CORrected ob; or AUTOmated ob for automated report with no human intervention; omitted when observer logs on.	COR
15005KT	Wind: 3-digit true-north direction, nearest 10 degrees (or VaRiaBle); next 2–3 digits for speed and unit, KT (KMH or MPS); as needed, Gust and maximum speed; 00000KT for calm; for METAR, if direction varies 60 degrees or more, Variability appended, e.g., 180V260	22015G25KT
5SM	Prevailing visibility: In U.S., Statute Miles and fractions; above 6 miles in TAF Plus6SM. (Or, 4-digit minimum visibility in meters and as required, lowest value with direction.)	3/4SM
	Runway Visual Range: R; 2-digit runway designator Left, Center, or Right as needed; "/"; Minus or Plus in U.S., 4-digit value, FeeT in U.S. (usually meters elsewhere); 4-digit value Variability, 4-digit value (and tendency Down, Up or No change)	R28L/2600FT
HZ	Significant present, forecast and recent weather: See table (to the right)	TSRA
FEW020	Cloud amount, height and type: SKy Clear 0/8, FEW >0/8-2/8, SCaTtered 3/8-4/8, BroKeN 5/8-7/8, OVerCast 8/8; 3-digit height in hundreds of feet; Towering CUmulus or CumulonimBus in METAR; in TAF, only CB. Vertical Visibility for obscured sky and height "VV004". More than 1 layer may be reported or forecast. In automated METAR reports only, CLeaR for "clear below 12,000 feet."	OVC010CB
	Temperature: Degrees Celsius; first 2 digits, temperature "/" last 2 digits, dewpoint temperature; Minus for below zero, e.g., M06	18/16
	Altimeter setting: Indicator and 4 digits; in U.S., A: inches and hundredths; (Q: hectoPascals, e.g., Q1013)	A2992
		Continued

Key to Aerodrome Forecast (TAF) and Aviation Routine Weather Report (METAR)

Forecast	Explanation	Report
WS010/ 31022KT	In U.S. TAF, nonconvective low-level (≤2,000 feet) Wind Shear; 3-digit height (hundreds of feet); "/"; 3-digit wind direction and 2–3 digit wind speed above the indicated height, and unit, KT	
	In METAR, ReMarK indicator and remarks. For example: Sea-Level Pressure in hectoPascals and tenths, as shown: 1004.5 hPa; Temp/dewpoint in tenths °C, as shown: temp. 18.2°C, dewpoint 15.9°C	RMK SLP045 T01820159
FM091930	FroM: Changes are expected at: 2-digit date, 2-digit hour, and 2-digit minute beginning time: indicates significant change. Each FM starts on a new line, indented 5 spaces	
TEMPO 0920/0922	TEMPOrary: Changes expected for <1 hour and in total, < half of the period between the 2-digit date and 2-digit hour beginning, and 2-digit date and 2-digit hour ending time	
PROB30 1004/1007	PROBability and 2-digit percent (30 or 40): Probable condition in the period between the 2-digit date and 2-digit hour beginning time, and the 2-digit date and 2-digit hour ending time	
BECMG 1013/1015	BECoMinG: Change expected in the period between the 2-digit date and 2-digit hour beginning time, and the 2-digit date and 2-digit hour ending time	

Table of Significant Present, Forecast and Recent Weather—Grouped in categories and used in the order listed below; or as needed in TAF, No Significant Weather

QUALIFIERS
Intensity or Proximity
"–" = Light   **No sign** = Moderate   "+" = Heavy

"VC" = Vicinity, but not at aerodrome. In the U.S. METAR, 5 to 10 SM from the point of observation. In the U.S. TAF, 5 to 10 SM from the center of the runway complex. Elsewhere, within 8000m.

Descriptor
| BC | Patches | BL | Blowing | DR | Drifting | FZ | Freezing |
| MI | Shallow | PR | Partial | SH | Showers | TS | Thunderstorm |

WEATHER PHENOMENA
Precipitation
DZ	Drizzle	GR	Hail	GS	Small hail or snow pellets	
IC	Ice crystals	PL	Ice pellets	RA	Rain	SG	Snow grains
SN	Snow	UP	Unknown precipitation in automated observations		

Obscuration
| BR | Mist (≥5/8SM) | DU | Widespread dust | FG | Fog (<5/8SM) | FU | Smoke |
| HZ | Haze | PY | Spray | SA | Sand | VA | Volcanic ash |

Other
| DS | Dust storm | FC | Funnel cloud | +FC | Tornado or waterspout | |
| PO | Well-developed dust or sand whirls | SQ | Squall | SS | Sandstorm |

- Explanations in parentheses "( )" indicate different worldwide practices.
- Ceiling is not specified; defined as the lowest broken or overcast layer, or the vertical visibility.
- NWS TAFs exclude BECMG groups and temperature forecasts, NWS TAFs do not use PROB in the first 9 hours of a TAF; NWS METARs exclude trend forecasts. U.S. Military TAFs include Turbulence and Icing groups.

Figure 8-7. TAF/METAR weather card

ALL

9266. (Refer to Figure 145.) What was the local Central Standard Time of the Aviation Routine Weather Report at Austin (KAUS)?

A— 11:53 a.m.
B— 5:53 p.m.
C— 10:53 p.m.

"131753Z" indicates that this METAR report is for the thirteenth day of the month, at 1753 Coordinated Universal Time (UTC). Central Standard Time is UTC minus 6 hours (1753 – 6 = 1153). (PLT059) — AC 00-45

ALL

9267. (Refer to Figure 145.) What type of report is listed for Lubbock (KLBB) at 1818Z?

A— An Aviation selected special weather report.
B— A special report concerning very low station pressure.
C— A Special METAR weather observation, concerning significant weather changes.

The designation "SPECI" means that this is a special weather observation. (PLT059) — AC 00-45

Answers

9266 [A]   9267 [A]

ALL

9268. (Refer to Figure 146.) What method was used to obtain the METAR at Tyler (KTYR) at 1753Z?

A— Automated Surface Observing System (ASOS), having a precipitation discriminator.

B— Automatic Meteorological Observing Station (AMOS), with a precipitation discriminator.

C— Automated Weather Observing System (AWOS), without a precipitation discriminator.

The word "AUTO" after the date-time group indicates that this is an automated weather report. The "A02" in the remarks section indicate that it was made by an unattended Automated Surface Observing System (ASOS). The ASOS will automatically report precipitation amounts. (PLT059) — AC 00-45

ALL

9269. (Refer to Figure 145.) What condition is reported at Childress (KCDS)?

A— Light rain showers.

B— Heavy rain showers began 42 minutes after the hour.

C— The ceiling is solid overcast at an estimated 1,800 feet above sea level.

"-SHRA" indicates an observation of light rain showers. (PLT059) — AC 00-45

Answer (B) is incorrect because the remark "RERAB42" means an observed recent weather event was that rain began at 42 minutes past the previous hour. Answer (C) is incorrect because the abbreviation "OVC180" indicated the base of an overcast layer is at 18,000 feet above the station.

ALL

9270. (Refer to Figure 145.) What condition is reported at Dallas (KDAL)?

A— The tops of the overcast is 10,000 feet.

B— Temperature/dewpoint spread is 8°F.

C— Altimeter setting is 30.07.

"A3007" indicates an altimeter setting of 30.07" Hg. (PLT059) — AC 00-45

Answer (A) is incorrect because "OVC100" indicates the base of the overcast layer is 10,000 feet above the station. Answer (B) is incorrect because the reported temperature/dew point are given in degrees Celsius, not Fahrenheit.

ALL

9272. SPECI KGLS 131802Z 10012G21KT 060V140 2SM +SHRA SCT005 BKN035 OVC050CB 24/23 A2980 RMK RAB57 WS TKO RW09L WSHFT 58 FROPA.

This SPECI report at Galveston (KGLS) indicates which condition?

A— Wind steady at 100° magnetic at 12 knots, gusts to 21.

B— Precipitation started at 1757.

C— 5,000 feet overcast with towering cumulus.

The remarks "RAB57" indicates rain began at 57 minutes past the hour. (PLT059) — AC 00-45

Answer (A) is incorrect because "10012G21KT 060V140" indicates the wind was from 100° at 12 knots with gusts to 21 knots; however, the wind direction was variable between 60-140°, and wind direction in written reports and forecasts are referenced to true north. Answer (C) is incorrect because "OVC050CB" indicates there was an overcast cumulonimbus cloud at 5,000 feet. Towering cumulus is abbreviated "TCU."

ALL

9273. (Refer to Figure 145.) What weather improvement was reported at Lubbock (KLBB) between 1750 and 1818 UTC?

A— The wind shift and frontal passage at 1812Z.

B— The vertical visibility improved by 2,000 feet.

C— The temperature and dew point spread improved.

At 1750Z, the vertical visibility was 1,000 feet (VV010). At 1818Z, the vertical visibility had improved to 3,000 feet (VV030). (PLT059) — AC 00-45

Answer (A) is incorrect because even though the description of the events is correct, it is not an improvement since the wind speed increased and the visibility decreased. Answer (C) is incorrect because the temperature and dew point actually converged. At 1750Z, the spread was 4°C (03/M01), but by 1818Z, there was a 0° spread (M01/M01).

Answers

9268 [A]   9269 [A]   9270 [C]   9272 [B]   9273 [B]

ALL
8735. What hazard should you expect for a morning departure from KPDX, based on this METAR?

KPDX 271154Z 00000KT 9SM CLR -10/-10 A2979.

A— Wind shear.
B— Frost on the aircraft.
C— Sea breeze.

On calm clear nights with little-to-no wind, and a temperature at or below the dew point, you should expect dew or frost. Because the temperature and dew point are both -10 there is a high likelihood of the presence of frost on the aircraft surfaces. (PLT059) — AC 00-6

Answers (A) and (C) are incorrect because the wind is calm.

ALL
9274. METAR KMAF 131756Z 02020KT 12SM BKN025 OVC250 27/18 A3009 RMK RAE44.

Which weather condition is indicated by this METAR report at Midland (KMAF)?

A— Rain of unknown intensity ended 16 minutes before the hour.
B— The ceiling was at 25,000 feet MSL.
C— Wind was 020° magnetic at 20 knots.

"RAE44" indicates the rain ended 44 minutes past the hour, which is the same thing as 16 minutes before the hour. (PLT059) — AC 00-45

Answer (B) is incorrect because a ceiling is the lowest broken or overcast layer. "BKN025" indicates a broken layer (not a ceiling) at 2,500 feet. The base of the higher overcast layer is at 25,000 feet above the station (not sea level). Answer (C) is incorrect because the winds are 020° true at 20 knots.

ALL
9275. METAR KSPS 131757Z 09014KT 6SM -RA SCT025 OVC090 24/22 A3005.
SPECI KSPS 131820Z 01025KT 3SM +RA FC OVC015 22/21 A3000.

Which change took place at Wichita Falls (KSPS) between 1757 and 1820 UTC?

A— The rain became lighter.
B— Atmospheric pressure increased.
C— A funnel cloud was observed.

"FC" in the 1820Z report indicates that a funnel cloud/tornado/waterspout was observed. (PLT059) — AC 00-45

Answer (A) is incorrect because the rain increased in intensity. At 1757Z, the abbreviation "-RA" indicated light rain; at 1820Z, "+RA" indicates heavy rain. Answer (B) is incorrect because the atmospheric pressure is decreased. The altimeter went from 30.05" Hg (A3005) at 1757Z, to 30.00" Hg (A3000) at 1820Z.

ALL
9276. (Refer to Figure 146.) What was the ceiling at Walnut Ridge (KARG)?

A— 1,000 feet AGL.
B— 2,400 feet AGL.
C— 1,000 feet MSL.

"OVC010" indicates an overcast layer with bases at 1,000 feet AGL. (PLT059) — AC 00-45

Answer (B) is incorrect because 2,400 feet is the RVR for runway 28 at Walnut Ridge airport. Answer (C) is incorrect because the sky condition is reported in feet above the ground.

ALL
9277. METAR KHRO 131753Z 09007KT 7SM FEW020 BKN040 30/27 A3001.
SPECI KHRO 131815Z 13017G26KT 3SM +TSRA SCT020 BKN045TCU 29/24 A2983 RMK RAB12 WS TKO LDG RW14R FRQ LTGICCG VC.

What change has taken place between 1753 and 1815 UTC at Harrison (KHRO)?

A— The ceiling lowered and cumulonimbus clouds developed.
B— Thundershowers began at 12 minutes past the hour.
C— Visibility reduced to IFR conditions.

At 1815Z, the station was reporting heavy thunderstorms and rain (+TSRA). "RAB12" indicates that the rain began at 12 minutes past the hour. (PLT059) — AC 00-45

ALL
9824. In this METAR excerpt, "SLP993 SNINCR 1/10" means

A— 0.1" of snow on the runway land zone during the last hour.
B— 1" of snow in the last 10 hours.
C— 1" and a total of 10" of snow is on the ground with 1" in the last hour.

At designated stations, the "snow increasing rapidly" remark is reported in the next METAR whenever the snow depth increases by 1 inch or more in the past hour. The remark is coded in the following format: the remark indicator SNINCR, the depth increase in the past hour, and the total depth on the ground, separated from each other by a "/". (PLT059) — AC 00-45

Answers

8735 [B]   9274 [A]   9275 [C]   9276 [A]   9277 [B]   9824 [C]

ALL

9704. Data that may be added (manual weather augmentation) to the Automated Weather Observing System (AWOS) report is limited to

A— the precipitation accumulation report, an automated variable visibility, and wind direction remark.

B— thunderstorms (intensity and direction), precipitation (type and intensity), and obstructions to visibility (dependent on the visibility being 3 miles or less).

C— density Altitude, NOTAMs, and reported slant range visibility.

In addition to the information automatically included in an AWOS report, information can be manually added. The remarks are limited to thunderstorms (type and intensity), and obstructions to vision when the visibility is 3 SM or less. Augmentation is identified in the observation as "observer weather." (PLT515) — AIM ¶7-1-11

ALL

9716. The prevailing visibility in the following METAR is

METAR KFSM 131756Z AUTO 00000KT M1/4SM
  R25/0600V1000FT -RA FG VV004 06/05
A2989 RMK AO2 $

A— less than 1/4 statute mile.

B— measured 1/4 statute mile.

C— a mean (average) of 1/4 statute mile.

The prevailing visibility is less than 1/4 statute miles, indicated by the "M1/4SM." (PLT059) — AIM ¶7-1-11

ALL

9717. The symbol ($) at the end of the following METAR indicates that

METAR KFSM 131756Z AUTO 00000KT M1/4SM
  R25/0600V1000FT -RA FG VV004 06/05
A2989 RMK AO2 $

A— the latest information is transmitted over a discrete VHF frequency at KFSM.

B— the latest information is broadcast on the voice portion of a local navaid at KFSM.

C— maintenance is needed on the system.

The dollar symbol ($) indicates the system may need maintenance. (PLT059) — AIM ¶7-1-11

ALL

9718. The VV001 in the following METAR indicates

METAR KFSM 131756Z AUTO 00000KT M1/4SM
  R25/0600V1000FT -RA FG VV001
A2989 RMK AO2 VIS 3/4 RWY19 CHINO RWY19 $

A— an observer reported the vertical visibility as 100 feet.

B— a 100 foot indefinite ceiling.

C— the variability value is 100 feet.

The height into an indefinite ceiling is preceded by "VV" and followed by three digits indicating the vertical visibility in hundreds of feet. This layer indicates total obscuration. The indefinite ceiling is 100 feet. (PLT059) — AIM ¶7-1-11

ALL

9242. METAR KFSO 030900Z VRB02KT 7SM MIFG SKC 15/14 A3012 RMK SLP993 6///// T01500139 56012

In the above METAR, the "SLP993 6/////" indicates

A— sea-level pressure 999.3 hectopascals which in the last 6 hours has dropped .4 hectopascals.

B— sea-level pressure 999.3 hectopascals and an indeterminable amount of precipitation has occurred over the last 3 hours.

C— sea-level pressure 999.3 hectopascals and in the last 6 hours that four-tenths of an inch of precipitation has fallen.

The "SLP993 6/////" in the Remarks section of the METAR indicates sea-level pressure 999.3 hectopascals and an indeterminable amount of precipitation has occurred over the last 3 hours. (PLT059) — AC 00-45

Answers

9704 [B]	9716 [A]	9717 [C]	9718 [B]	9242 [B]

The Terminal Aerodrome Forecast (TAF)

TAFs use the same code used in the METAR weather reports. (*See* Figure 8-7.)

ALL
9244. Which primary source contains information regarding the expected weather at the destination airport, at the ETA?

A— Low-Level Prog Chart.
B— Weather Depiction Charts.
C— Terminal Aerodrome Forecast.

A Terminal Aerodrome Forecast (TAF) is a concise statement of the expected meteorological conditions at an airport during a specified period (usually 24 hours). (PLT288) — AC 00-45

Answer (A) is incorrect because a Low-Level Prog Chart is a forecast of significant weather for the United States, not a forecast for a specific destination. Answer (B) is incorrect because Weather Depiction Charts are national weather maps of observed weather at a specific time; they do not provide specific information about a particular destination.

ALL
9245. Weather conditions expected to occur in the vicinity of the airport, but not at the airport, are denoted by the letters "VC." When VC appears in a Terminal Aerodrome Forecast, it covers a geographical area of

A— a 5 to 10 statute mile radius from the airport.
B— a 5-mile radius of the center of a runway complex.
C— 10 miles of the station originating the forecast.

Proximity applies to weather conditions expected to occur in the vicinity of the airport (between a 5 to 10 mile radius of the airport), but not at the airport itself. It is denoted by the letters "VC." (PLT288) — AC 00-45

ALL
9248. What weather is predicted by the term VCTS in a Terminal Aerodrome Forecast?

A— Thunderstorms are expected in the vicinity.
B— Thunderstorms may occur over the station and within 50 miles of the station.
C— Thunderstorms are expected between 5 and 25 miles of the runway complex.

"VC" applies to weather conditions expected to occur in the vicinity of the airport (between a 5 to 10 statute mile radius of the airport), but not at the airport itself. "TS" denotes thunderstorms. Therefore, "VCTS" in a Terminal Aerodrome Forecast indicates thunderstorms are expected between a 5 to 10 mile radius of the airport, but not at the airport itself. (PLT288) — AC 00-45

ALL
9246. Which are the only cloud types forecast in the Terminal Aerodrome Forecast?

A— Altocumulus
B— Cumulonimbus
C— Stratocumulus

If cumulonimbus clouds are expected at the airport, the contraction "CB" is appended to the cloud layer which represents the base of the cumulonimbus cloud(s). Cumulonimbus clouds are the only cloud type forecast in TAFs. (PLT288) — AC 00-45

ALL
9278. A PROB40 (PROBability) HHhh group in an International Terminal Aerodrome Forecast (TAF) indicates the probability of

A— thunderstorms or other precipitation.
B— precipitation or low visibility.
C— thunderstorms or high wind.

A PROB40 (PROBability) HHhh group in a TAF indicates the probability of occurrence of thunderstorms or other precipitation events. (PLT288) — AC 00-45

ALL
9279. (Refer to Figure 147.) At which time is IFR weather first predicted at Lubbock (KLBB)?

A— 0100Z.
B— 2100Z.
C— 0400Z.

"PROB40 0103 06025G35KT 1/8SM +SHRASNPE OVC003" indicates there is a 40% probability between 0100 and 0300Z that the visibility will drop to 1/8 SM in heavy rain showers, snow and ice pellets, and the ceiling will be 300 feet overcast. Consequently, the first prediction of IFR would be at 0100Z. (PLT072) — AC 00-45

Answers

| 9244 | [C] | 9245 | [A] | 9248 | [A] | 9246 | [B] | 9278 | [A] | 9279 | [A] |

ALL

9280. (Refer to Figure 147.) What type conditions can be expected for a flight scheduled to land at San Angelo (KSJT) at 1500Z?

A— Chance of 1 statute mile visibility and cumulonimbus clouds.

B— IFR conditions due to low visibility, rain, and mist.

C— IFR conditions due to low ceilings, rain, and fog.

The last line of the forecast includes 1500Z. "FM0900 17020G34KT 2SM RA BR OVC010CB" means that from 0900Z on, the forecast is for winds from 170° at 20 knots with gusts to 34 knots. The visibility will be two statute miles. There will be a 1,000 foot overcast ceiling, with cumulonimbus clouds along with rain (RA) and mist (BR). (PLT072) — AC 00-45

ALL

9707. On the constant pressure analysis chart, satellite and aircraft observations are used in the analysis, over areas of sparse data. A satellite observation plotted using

A— a station circle at the cloud top location.

B— a square at the cloud top location.

C— a star at the cloud top location.

A star identifies satellite wind estimates made from cloud types. (PLT283) — AC 00-45

Answer (A) is incorrect because a station circle is used for the weather stations which send up radiosondes. Answer (B) is incorrect because a square at the aircraft location is used to signify an aircraft report.

ALL

9709. A calm wind that is forecast, in the International Terminal Aerodrome Forecast (TAF) is encoded as

A— VRB00KT.

B— 00000KT.

C— 00003KT.

A forecast of "00000KT" (calm) on a TAF means winds are expected at 3 knots or less. (PLT288) — AC 00-45

ALL

9710. In the International Terminal Aerodrome Forecast (TAF), a variable wind direction is noted by "VRB" where the three digit direction usually appears. A calm wind appears in the TAF as

A— 00003KT.

B— VRB00KT.

C— 00000KT.

Calm wind forecasts in a TAF are entered as "00000KT." (PLT288) — AC 00-45

ALL

9711. On the constant pressure analysis chart, aircraft and satellite observations are used in the analysis over areas of sparse data. An aircraft observation is plotted using

A— a station circle at the aircraft location.

B— a square at the aircraft location.

C— a star at the aircraft location.

A square is used to signify an aircraft report. (PLT283) — AC 00-45

Answer (A) is incorrect because a station circle is used for the weather stations which send up radiosondes. Answer (C) is incorrect because a star identifies satellite wind estimates made from cloud tops.

Answers

9280 [B]	9707 [C]	9709 [B]	9710 [C]	9711 [B]

Enroute Forecasts

Winds and temperatures aloft are forecast for various stations around the country. Wind directions are always relative to true north and the speed is in knots. Temperatures, in degrees Celsius, are forecast for all altitudes except for 3,000 feet. At altitudes where the wind or temperature is not forecast, a blank space is used to signify the omission. At 30,000 feet and above the minus sign is deleted from the temperature to save space.

When winds are light and variable the notation 9900 is used. When wind speeds exceed 99 knots, fifty is added to the wind direction and only the last two digits of the wind speed is printed. For example, an FB (previously FD) forecast of "731960" at FL390 is 230° true (73 − 50 = 23) at 119 knots with a temperature of -60°C. When winds exceed 199 knots they are indicated as a forecast speed of 199 knots. For example, winds from 280° at 205 knots are coded as 7899.

The temperature in the tropopause (36,000 feet and above) is approximately -56°C. ISA at sea level is 15°C and decreases at a rate of 2°/1,000 feet up to 36,000 feet MSL.

Forecast winds and temperatures aloft for international flights may be obtained by consulting wind and temperature aloft charts prepared by a Regional Area Forecast Center (RAFC).

ALL

9281. Constant Pressure Analysis Charts contain contours, isotherms and some contain isotachs. The contours depict

A— ridges, lows, troughs and highs aloft.
B— highs, lows, troughs, and ridges on the surface.
C— highs, lows, troughs, and ridges corrected to MSL.

Heights of the specified pressure for each station are analyzed through the use of solid lines called contours. This contour analysis gives the charts a height pattern. The contours depict highs, lows, troughs, and ridges, and all heights are given as pressure altitude. (PLT283) — AC 00-45

ALL

9283. Vertical wind shear can be determined by comparing winds on vertically adjacent constant pressure charts. The vertical wind shear that is critical for probability of turbulence is

A— 4 knots or greater per 1,000 feet.
B— 6 knots or more per 1,000 feet.
C— greater than 8 knots per 1,000 feet.

Vertical wind shear can be identified by comparing winds on vertically adjacent constant pressure charts. The vertical shear critical for probable turbulence is 6 knots per 1,000 feet. (PLT518) — AC 00-45

ALL

9287. (Refer to Figure 149.) What approximate wind direction, speed, and temperature (relative to ISA) are expected for a flight over OKC at FL 370?

A— 265° true; 27 knots; ISA +1°C.
B— 260° true; 27 knots; ISA +6°C.
C— 260° magnetic; 27 knots; ISA +10°C.

The Winds Aloft forecast (FD) for OKC at 34,000 feet shows a wind of 250° at 27 knots and a temperature of -43°C. At 39,000 feet the winds are 270° at 27 knots with a temperature of -54°C. Interpolation of these forecasts yields a forecast for 37,000 feet of winds from 260° at 27 knots with a temperature of -50°C. The ISA temperature at 37,000 feet is -56°C. All wind directions on a FD are relative to true north. (PLT076) — AC 00-45

Answer (A) is incorrect because the direction is rounded to the nearest 10° and temperature is ISA +6°C. Answer (C) is incorrect because winds are in degrees true, not magnetic.

ALL

9288. (Refer to Figure 149.) What approximate wind direction, speed, and temperature (relative to ISA) are expected for a flight over TUS at FL 270?

A— 347° magnetic; 5 knots; ISA -10°C.
B— 350° true; 5 knots; ISA +5°C.
C— 010° true; 5 knots; ISA +13°C.

Answers

9281   [A]   9283   [B]   9287   [B]   9288   [C]

The FD forecast of TUS at 24,000 feet is 050° at 5 knots with a temperature of -17°C. At 30,000 feet, the winds are 330° at 5 knots with a temperature of -33°C. Interpolation of these forecasts yields a forecast for 27,000 feet of winds from 010° at 5 knots with a temperature of -25°C. ISA temperature at 27,000 feet is -39°C. All wind directions on a FD are referenced to true north. (PLT076) — AC 00-45

Answer (A) is incorrect because wind direction is degrees true (not magnetic). Answer (B) is incorrect because wind direction is 010° true, not 350° true.

ALL

9289. (Refer to Figure 149.) What will be the wind and temperature trend for an SAT ELP TUS flight at 16,000 feet?

A— Temperature decrease slightly.
B— Windspeed decrease.
C— Wind direction shift from southwest to east.

SAT — Winds 196° at 8 knots, temperature -2°C.
ELP — Winds 026° at 14 knots, temperature -1°C.
TUS — Winds 080° at 11 knots, temperature 0°C.

(PLT076) — AC 00-45

Answer (A) is incorrect because temperatures increase slightly. Answer (B) is incorrect because wind speed increases between SAT and ELP, but decreases from ILP to TUS.

ALL

9290. (Refer to Figure 149.) What will be the wind and temperature trend for an STL MEM MSY flight at FL 330?

A— Windspeed decrease.
B— Wind shift from west to north.
C— Temperature increase 5°C.

Interpolation of the FD forecasts for 30,000 and 34,000 feet yield a forecast at 33,000 feet of:

STL — Wind 260° at 56 knots, temperature -42°C.
MEM — Wind 260° at 20 knots, temperature -41°C.
MSY — Wind light and variable (9900), temperature -41°C.

(PLT076) — AC 00-45

Answer (B) is incorrect because the wind direction remains westerly and becomes light and variable (not shifting to the north). Answer (C) is incorrect because temperature increases 1°C.

ALL

9291. (Refer to Figure 149.) What will be the wind and temperature trend for a DEN ICT OKC flight at 11,000 feet?

A— Temperature decrease.
B— Windspeed increase slightly.
C— Wind shift from calm to a westerly direction.

Interpolation of the FD forecasts for 9,000 and 12,000 feet yield a forecast at 11,000 feet of:

DEN — Wind light and variable (9900), temperature +6°C.
ICT — Wind 060° at 2 knots, temperature +5°C.
OKC — Wind 110° at 2 knots, temperature +6°C.

(PLT076) — AC 00-45

Answer (A) is incorrect because the temperature increases at OKC to a temperature higher than DEN. Answer (C) is incorrect because the wind shifts from calm to an easterly direction.

ALL

9292. (Refer to Figure 149.) What will be the wind and temperature trend for a DSM LIT SHV flight at 12,000 feet?

A— Windspeed decrease.
B— Temperature decrease.
C— Wind direction shift from northwest to southeast.

The FB forecasts for 12,000 feet are:

DSM — Wind 300° at 22 knots, temperature 0°C.
LIT — Wind 280° at 8 knots, temperature +6°C.
SHV — Wind 210° at 6 knots, temperature +6°C.

(PLT076) — AC 00-45

Answer (B) is incorrect because the temperature increases en route. Answer (C) is incorrect because the wind direction shifts from northwest to southwest.

ALL

9293. (Refer to Figure 149.) What is the forecast temperature at ATL for the 3,000-foot level?

A— +6°C.
B— +6°F.
C— Not reported.

Temperatures are not forecast on the FB at the 3,000 feet level when within 2,500 of the surface. (PLT076) — AC 00-45

Answer (A) is incorrect because no temperature is reported at the 3,000-foot level or for a level within 2,500 feet of station elevation. Answer (B) is incorrect because no temperature is reported at the 3,000-foot level, and temperatures are depicted in degrees Celsius, not Fahrenheit. The 06 indicates wind velocity of 6 knots.

Answers

9289 [C]   9290 [A]   9291 [B]   9292 [A]   9293 [C]

ALL

9294. (Refer to Figure 149.) What approximate wind direction, speed, and temperature (relative to ISA) are expected for a flight over MKC at FL 260?

A— 260° true; 43 knots; ISA +10°C.
B— 260° true; 45 knots; ISA -10°C.
C— 260° magnetic; 42 knots; ISA +9°C.

The FB forecast for MKC at 24,000 feet is winds of 260° at 38 knots with a temperature of -21°C. At 30,000 feet, the winds are forecast to be 260° at 50 knots with a temperature of -36°C. Interpolation for 26,000 feet yields a forecast of 260° at 42 knots with a temperature of -26°C. ISA temperature for 26,000 feet is -36°C. All wind directions on a FD are referenced to true north. (PLT076) — AC 00-45

Answer (B) is incorrect because forecast temperature is warmer than ISA. Answer (C) is incorrect because wind direction is degrees true, not magnetic.

ALL

9295. What wind direction and speed aloft are forecast by this WINDS AND TEMPERATURE ALOFT FORE-CAST (FD) for FL390 — "750649"?

A— 350° at 64 knots.
B— 250° at 106 knots.
C— 150° at 6 knots.

For FB forecasts of wind speeds from 100 knots through 199 knots, subtract 50 from the wind direction code and add 100 to the speed code. The forecast of 750649 decodes as a wind of 250° (75 – 50 = 25) at 106 knots (100 + 06 = 106) with a temperature of –49°C (temperatures above FL240 are always negative). (PLT076) — AC 00-45

Answer (A) is incorrect because direction is the first two, not three, digits, and 50 must be subtracted from the first two digits. Speed is the second group of digits, not the fourth and fifth digits. Answer (C) is incorrect because 50 must be subtracted from the first two digits and 100 added to the second two digits, because the wind speed is forecast to be greater than 100 knots.

ALL

9296. What wind direction and speed aloft are forecast by this WINDS AND TEMPERATURE ALOFT FORE-CAST (FD) for FL390 — "731960"?

A— 230° at 119 knots.
B— 131° at 96 knots.
C— 073° at 196 knots.

FB forecasts of wind speeds from 100 knots through 199 knots have 50 added to the wind direction code and 100 subtracted from the speed. The forecast of 731960 decodes as a wind of 230° at 119 knot with a temperature of -60°C. (PLT076) — AC 00-45

Answer (B) is incorrect because coded directions with wind speed over 100 knots range from 51 through 86. The direction is 230° (not 131°) at 119 knots (not 96 knots). Answer (C) is incorrect because 50 must be subtracted from the first two digits and 100 added to the second two digits. The last two digits are the temperature.

ALL

9251. Forecast winds and temperatures aloft for an international flight may be obtained by consulting

A— Area Forecasts published by the departure location host country.
B— The current International Weather Depiction Chart appropriate to the route.
C— Wind and Temperature Aloft Charts prepared by the U.S. National Centers of Environmental Prediction (NCEP).

Computer-generated forecast charts of winds and temperatures aloft are available for international flights at specified levels. The U.S. National Centers for Environmental Prediction (NCEP), near Washington D.C., prepares and supplies to users charts of forecast winds, temperatures, and significant weather. (PLT284) — AC 00-45

Answer (A) is incorrect because Area Forecasts are forecasts of general weather conditions over an area of several states and do not contain forecasts of the winds and temperatures aloft. Answer (B) is incorrect because the International Weather Depiction Chart indicates current weather and does not forecast winds and temperatures aloft.

ALL

9255. A station is forecasting wind and temperature aloft to be 280° at 205 knots; temperature -51°C at FL390. How would this data be encoded in the FD?

A— 780051.
B— 789951.
C— 280051.

FB forecasts of wind speeds from 100 knots through 199 knots have 50 added to the wind direction code and 100 subtracted from the speed code. Winds over 200 knots are coded as 199 knots. A wind of 280° at 205 knots with a temperature of -51°C is coded as "789951." (PLT076) — AC 00-45

Answer (A) is incorrect because it indicates a wind at 280° at 100 knots. The minus sign is to be omitted above 24,000 feet MSL. Answer (C) is incorrect because if the wind is 0 knots, the direction and wind group is coded "9900."

Answers

9294 [A]   9295 [B]   9296 [A]   9251 [C]   9255 [B]

Surface Analysis and Constant Pressure Charts

The Surface Analysis Chart shows pressure patterns, fronts and information on individual reporting stations. The pressure patterns are shown by lines called **isobars**. The isobars on a surface weather map represent lines of equal pressure reduced to sea level.

Constant pressure charts are similar in many ways to the surface analysis chart in that they show the pressure patterns and some weather conditions for reporting stations. These charts show conditions at one of five pressure levels from 850 millibars to 200 millibars. These pressure levels correspond roughly with altitudes from 5,000 feet MSL to 39,000 feet MSL. The chart is for a pressure level rather than an altitude. The altitude (in meters) of the pressure level is shown by height contours. In addition to the height contour lines, constant pressure charts can contain lines of equal temperature (isotherms) and lines of equal wind speed (isotachs). Since these are both dotted lines, be careful not to get them confused when looking at a chart. Six items of information are shown on the charts for reporting stations. These are the wind, temperature, temperature/dew point spread, height of the pressure level and the change of the height level over the previous 12 hours.

These charts can be used to locate the jet stream and its associated turbulence and wind shear. When there is a large change in wind speed over a short distance, as indicated by closely spaced isotachs, the probability of turbulence is greatly increased. Since the jet stream is associated with discontinuities in the temperature lapse rate at breaks in the tropopause, closely spaced isotherms indicate the possibility of turbulence or wind shear.

Charts can be used together to get a three dimensional view of the weather. For example, lows usually slope to the west with increasing height. If a low stops moving, it will extend almost vertically. This type of low is typical of a slow moving storm that may cause extensive and persistent cloudiness, precipitation, and generally adverse flying weather.

ALL

9175. Isobars on a surface weather chart represent lines of equal pressure

A— at the surface.
B— reduced to sea level.
C— at a given atmospheric pressure altitude.

Sea level pressures are plotted on a surface weather chart and lines are drawn connecting lines of equal pressure. These lines of equal pressure are called isobars. (PLT287) — AC 00-45

Answer (A) is incorrect because the isobars are depicted at the sea level pressure pattern at 4 MB intervals, not just at the surface. Answer (C) is incorrect because the isobars are reduced to sea level pressure, not any given atmospheric pressure altitude.

ALL

9218. Under what conditions would clear air turbulence (CAT) most likely be encountered?

A— When constant pressure charts show 20-knot isotachs less than 150 NM apart.
B— When constant pressure charts show 60-knot isotachs less than 20 NM apart.
C— When a sharp trough is moving at a speed less than 20 knots.

Clear Air Turbulence (CAT) is likely in areas where the vertical wind shear exceeds 6 knots per 1,000 feet or horizontal shear exceeds 40 knots per 150 miles. (PLT501) — AC 00-6

Answer (B) is incorrect because when constant pressure charts show 20-knot isotachs less than 60 NM, CAT is most likely to be encountered, and "60-knot isotachs" do not exist. Answer (C) is incorrect because CAT can be expected upwind of the base of a deep upper trough, not because a sharp trough is moving.

Answers

9175   [B]   9218   [A]

ALL

9236. A strong wind shear can be expected

A— on the low pressure side of a 100-knot jetstream core.
B— where the horizontal wind shear is 15 knots, in a distance equal to 2.5° longitude.
C— if the 5°C isotherms are spaced 100 NM or closer together.

Jet streams stronger than 110 knots are apt to have significant turbulence in them in the sloping tropopause above the core, in the jet stream front below the core and on the low-pressure side of the core. (PLT518) — AC 00-30, Appendix 1

ALL

9310. (Refer to Figure 154.) What is the height of the 300-millibar level at the low pressure center in Canada?

A— 9,120 meters MSL.
B— 18,000 meters MSL.
C— 11,850 meters MSL.

The "912" just below the "L" symbol indicates an altitude of 9,120 meters. (PLT043) — AC 00-45

Answer (B) is incorrect because the height of the 300-mb level of the low-pressure center is 9,120 meters MSL. Answer (C) is incorrect because it is the 200 MB (not 300 MB) pressure chart. The "185" below the "L" indicates the height of the 200 MB low-pressure center to be 18,500 meters MSL.

ALL

9311. (Refer to Figures 153, 154, and 155.) Interpret the path of the jetstream.

A— Southern California, Nevada, Utah, Nebraska/Kansas, and then southeastward.
B— Oregon, Idaho, Wyoming, Nebraska, Iowa, and across the Great Lakes.
C— The Alaska area, across Canada to Montana, South Dakota, then across the Great Lakes area.

The strongest winds shown on the 300 MB and 200 MB charts indicate the jet stream flows from Alaska, across Canada to Montana, etc. Hatching indicates winds of 70 to 110 knots. (PLT042) — AC 00-45

Answer (A) is incorrect because the isotachs in southern California area are between 30 to 50 knots Answer (B) is incorrect because Oregon has isotachs between 10 to 30 knots.

ALL

9312. (Refer to Figure 153.) What type weather system is approaching the California Coast from the west?

A— LOW.
B— HIGH.
C— Cold front.

The counterclockwise flow around the system indicates that it is a low-pressure area. (PLT043) — AC 00-45

Answer (B) is incorrect because the height contours would increase for a high. Answer (C) is incorrect because pressure systems, not fronts, are depicted on a Constant Pressure Chart.

ALL

9313. (Refer to Figures 153, 154, and 155.) What type weather is inferred by the almost vertical extent of the LOW in Canada?

A— A rapid-moving system with little chance of developing cloudiness, precipitation, and adverse flying conditions.
B— A slow-moving storm which may cause extensive and persistent cloudiness, precipitation, and generally adverse flying weather.
C— A rapid-moving storm, leaning to west with altitude, which encourages line squalls ahead of the system with a potential of severe weather.

An old, non-developing low-pressure system tilts little with height. The low becomes almost vertical and is clearly evident on both surface and upper air maps. Upper winds encircle the surface low rather than blow across it. Thus, the storm moves very slowly and usually causes extensive and persistent cloudiness, precipitation, and generally adverse flying weather. (PLT042) — AC 00-45

Answer (A) is incorrect because the wind aloft is encircling the low which means it is a slow moving system. Answer (C) is incorrect because the low is leaning very little, and the winds are encircling the low, which means it is a slow moving system.

ALL

9314. (Refer to Figures 153 through 155.) What is the approximate temperature for a flight from southern California to central Kansas at FL 350?

A— -16°C.
B— -39°C.
C— -41°C.

Temperatures at the 300 MB level are in the -30°C range, and the temperatures at the 200 MB level are in the -52°C range. (PLT043) — AC 00-45

Answers

9236 [A]   9310 [A]   9311 [C]   9312 [A]   9313 [B]   9314 [C]

Answer (A) is incorrect because -16°C is the approximate tempera-ture at FL230 (not FL350) from southern CA to central KS. Answer (B) is incorrect because -39°C is the approximate temperature at FL340 (not FL350).

ALL
9315. (Refer to Figures 153 through 155.) Determine the approximate wind direction and velocity at FL 240 over the station in central Oklahoma.

A— 280° at 10 knots.
B— 320° at 10 knots.
C— 330° at 13 knots.

The 500 MB chart shows a wind of WNW at 10 knots. The 300 MB chart shows a north wind at 10 knots. (PLT043) — AC 00-45

Answer (A) is incorrect because 280° at 10 knots is the wind direc-tion and speed at the 500 MB pressure level (FL180). Answer (C) is incorrect because 330° at 13 knots is the interpolation between the 200 and 300 MB Charts, not the 300 and 500 MB Charts.

ALL
9316. (Refer to Figures 153 through 155.) What is the relative moisture content of the air mass approaching the California coast?

A— Dry.
B— Moist enough for condensation.
C— Very wet with high potential for clouds and precipitation.

The 500 MB chart shows either dry air or high tempera-ture/dewpoint spreads for stations at the leading edge of the air mass. (PLT043) — AC 00-45

Answer (B) is incorrect because there is very little moisture, as depicted by the wide temperature/dewpoint spread. Answer (C) is incorrect because the air mass is dry, not wet.

Reports and Forecasts of Hazardous Weather

A **Convective Outlook (AC)** describes the prospects for general thunderstorm activity during the fol-lowing 24 hours. Areas in which there is a high, moderate or slight risk of severe thunderstorms are included as well as areas where thunderstorms may approach severe limits.

The **Severe Weather Outlook Chart** is a preliminary 24-hour outlook for thunderstorms presented in two panels. A line with an arrowhead delineates an area of probable general thunderstorm activity. An area labeled APCHG indicates probable general thunderstorm activity may approach severe intensity. "Approaching" means winds of 35 to 50 knots or hail 1/2 to 3/4 of an inch in diameter.

AIRMETs and **SIGMETs** are issued to alert pilots to potentially hazardous weather. They are broadcast by the FSS upon issue and at H+15 and H+45 while they are in effect. ARTCC facilities will announce that a SIGMET is in effect and the pilot can then contact the nearest FSS for the details.

AIRMET forecast:
- Moderate icing
- Moderate turbulence
- Sustained winds of 30 knots or more at the surface
- Widespread areas of ceilings less than 1,000 feet or visibilities of less than 3 miles
- Extensive mountain obscurement

SIGMET forecast:
- Severe and extreme turbulence
- Severe icing
- Widespread dust storms, sandstorms or volcanic ash lowering visibility to below three miles

Continued

Answers

9315 [B]   9316 [A]

Convective SIGMETs cover the following:

- Tornadoes
- Lines of thunderstorms
- Embedded thunderstorms
- Thunderstorm areas greater than or equal to intensity level 4
- Hail greater than 3/4 of an inch in diameter

Convective SIGMETs are each valid for one hour and are removed at H+40. They are reissued as necessary. On an hourly basis, an outlook is made up for each of the WST regions. This outlook covers the prospects for 2 to 6 hours.

Telephone Information Briefing Service (TIBS) is provided by automated flight service stations (AFSS). It is a continuous recording of meteorological and aeronautical information, available by telephone by calling 1-800-WX-BRIEF. Each AFSS provides at least four route and/or area briefings. In addition, airspace procedures and special announcements (if applicable) concerning aviation interests may also be available. Depending on user demand, other items may be provided, such as METAR observations, terminal aerodrome forecasts, wind/temperatures aloft forecasts, etc. TIBS is not intended to substitute for specialist-provided preflight briefings. It is, however, recommended for use as a preliminary briefing, and often will be valuable in helping you to make a "go or no go" decision.

ALL

9305. What information is provided by a Convective Outlook (AC)?

A— It describes areas of probable severe icing and severe or extreme turbulence during the next 24 hours.

B— It provides prospects of both general and severe thunderstorm activity during the following 24 hours.

C— It indicates areas of probable convective turbulence and the extent of instability in the upper atmosphere (above 500 mb).

A Convective Outlook (AC) describes the prospects for general and severe thunderstorm activity during the following 24 hours. Use the outlook primarily for planning (or canceling) flights later in the day. (PLT514) — AC 00-45

Answer (A) is incorrect because severe icing and severe or extreme turbulence are the subjects of SIGMETs. Answer (C) is incorrect because it describes a 500-mb Constant Pressure Analysis Chart.

ALL

9252. How will an area of thunderstorm activity, that may grow to severe intensity, be indicated on the Severe Weather Outlook Chart?

A— SLGT within cross-hatched areas.
B— APCHG within any area.
C— SVR within any area.

On a Severe Weather Outlook Chart, an area labeled "APCHG" indicates that probable general thunderstorm activity may approach severe intensity. (PLT518) — AC 00-45

Answer (A) is incorrect because a cross-hatched area identifies a tornado watch area. Answer (C) is incorrect because the term SVR is not used on the Severe Weather Outlook Chart.

ALL

9578. When are severe weather watch bulletins (WW) issued?

A— Every 12 hours as required.
B— Every 24 hours as required.
C— Unscheduled and issued as required.

A severe weather watch bulletin (WW) defines areas of possible severe thunderstorms or tornado activity. They are unscheduled and are issued as required. (PLT316) — AC 00-45

Answers

9305   [B]   9252   [B]   9578   [C]

ALL

9705. The Hazardous Inflight Weather Advisory Service (HIWAS) is a continuous broadcast over selected VORs of

A— SIGMETs, CONVECTIVE SIGMETs, AIRMETs, Severe Weather Forecast Alerts (AWW), and Center Weather Advisories (CWA).

B— SIGMETs, CONVECTIVE SIGMETs, AIRMETs, Wind Shear Advisories, and Severe Weather Forecast Alerts (AWW).

C— Wind Shear Advisories, Radar Weather Reports, SIGMETs, CONVECTIVE SIGMETs, AIRMETs, and Center Weather Advisories (CWA).

HIWAS broadcasts include SIGMETs, Convective SIGMETs, AIRMETs, Severe Weather Forecast Alerts, and Center Weather Advisories. (PLT515) — AC 00-45

ALL

9256. At what time are current AIRMETs broadcast in their entirety by the Hazardous Inflight Weather Advisory Service (HIWAS)?

A— 15 and 45 minutes after the hour during the first hour after issuance, and upon receipt.

B— Every 15 minutes until the AIRMET is canceled.

C— There is a continuous broadcast over selected VORs of Inflight Weather Advisories.

The Hazardous Inflight Weather Advisory Service (HIWAS) is a continuous broadcast service over selected VORs of In-Flight Weather Advisories; i.e. SIGMETs, CONVECTIVE SIGMETs, AIRMETs, Severe Weather Forecast Alerts (AWW), and Center Weather Advisories (CWA). (PLT515) — AC 00-45

ALL

9257. If a SIGMET alert is announced, how can information contained in the SIGMET be obtained?

A— ATC will announce the hazard and advise when information will be provided in the FSS broadcast.

B— By contacting a weather watch station.

C— By contacting the nearest flight service.

SIGMETs, CWAs, and AIRMETs are broadcast by FSS's upon receipt and at 30-minute intervals at H+15 and H+45 for the first hour after issuance. Thereafter, a summarized alert notice will be broadcast at H+15 and H+45 during the valid period of the advisories. If a pilot has not previously received the SIGMET, etc., he/she should call the nearest FSS. (PLT290) — AC 00-45

Answer (A) is incorrect because ATC does not advise when to listen to an FSS broadcast, rather they tell you to contact FSS. Answer (B) is incorrect because the pilot may monitor an FSS broadcast or contact any FSS. "Weather watch station" is a nonexistent term.

ALL

9249. If squalls are reported at the destination airport, what wind conditions existed at the time?

A— Sudden increases in windspeed of at least 15 knots, to a sustained wind speed of 20 knots, lasting for at least 1 minute.

B— A sudden increase in wind speed of at least 16 knots, the speed rising to 22 knots or more for 1 minute or longer.

C— Rapid variation in wind direction of at least 20° and changes in speed of at least 10 knots between peaks and lulls.

A squall (SQ) is a sudden increase in wind speed of at least 16 knots, the speed rising to 22 knots or more, and lasting at least 1 minute. (PLT475) — AC 00-45

ALL

9284. (Refer to Figure 148.) Which system in the Convective SIGMET listing has the potential of producing the most severe storm?

A— The storms in Texas and Oklahoma.

B— The storms in Colorado, Kansas, and Oklahoma.

C— The isolated storm 50 miles northeast of Memphis (MEM).

Convective SIGMET 44C forecasts level 5 thunderstorms 50 miles northeast of MEM. (PLT067) — AC 00-45

ALL

9285. When you hear a SIGMET on an ATC frequency forecasting severe icing conditions on the route to your destination, you plan for

A— the installed transport category airplane ice protection system protecting against all types and levels of icing as designed.

B— very little airframe icing because of an OAT of -10°C or colder, the moisture is already frozen and cannot adhere to airplane surfaces.

C— the possibility of freezing rain and freezing drizzle that can accumulate on and beyond the limits of any deicing/anti-icing equipment.

Severe icing means the rate of accumulation is such that deicing/anti-icing equipment fails to reduce or control the hazard. Immediate diversion is necessary. (PLT274) — AC 00-45

Answers

9705 [A]	9256 [C]	9257 [C]	9249 [B]	9284 [C]	9285 [C]

ALL

9286. Which type weather conditions are covered in the Convective SIGMET?

A— Embedded thunderstorms, lines of thunderstorms, and thunderstorms with 3/4-inch hail or tornadoes.
B— Cumulonimbus clouds with tops above the tropopause and thunderstorms with 1/2-inch hail or funnel clouds.
C— Any thunderstorm with a severity level of VIP 2 or more.

Convective SIGMET forecast:

1. *Severe thunderstorms which have either surface winds greater than 50 knots, hail equal to or greater than 3/4 inches in diameter, or tornadoes;*

2. *Embedded thunderstorms;*

3. *Lines of thunderstorms; or*

4. *Thunderstorms equal to or greater than VIP level 4 affecting 40% or more of an area at least 3,000 square miles.*

(PLT290) — AC 00-45

Answer (B) is incorrect because cumulonimbus clouds with tops above the tropopause is not a weather condition covered in a Convective SIGMET. Answer (C) is incorrect because thunderstorms must be at least VIP level 4.

ALL

9747. The Telephone Information Briefing Service (TIBS) recordings are provided by selected Automated Flight Service Stations and

A— are updated on the hour.
B— are designed to replace the standard briefing given by a flight service specialist.
C— contain area briefings encompassing a 50 NM radius.

TIBS provides continuous telephone recordings of meteorological and aeronautical information, specifically area and route briefings, as well as airspace procedures and special announcements, if applicable. It is designed to be a preliminary briefing tool and is not intended to replace a standard briefing from a flight service specialist. TIBS is available 24 hours a day by calling 1-800-WX-BRIEF and is updated when conditions change. As a minimum, area briefings encompass a 50 NM radius. (PLT515) — AIM ¶7-1-7

ALL

9747-1. All ATC facilities using radar weather processors with the ability to determine precipitation intensities will describe the intensity as

A— light, moderate, heavy, intense, extreme, or severe.
B— light, moderate, heavy, extreme, severe.
C— light, moderate, heavy, extreme.

All ATC facilities using radar weather processors with the ability to determine precipitation intensity describes the intensity to pilots as: "LIGHT" (< 30 dBZ), "MODERATE" (30 to 40 dBZ), "HEAVY" (>40 to 50 dBZ), or "EXTREME" (>50 dBZ). (PLT515) — FAA-H-8083-15

ALL

9747-2. Maximum turbulence potential charts (GTG-2) are issued

A— every morning at 0400.
B— two times a day.
C— hourly.

The Graphical Turbulence Guidance (GTG-2) graphics are computer-generated four-dimensional forecasts of information related to the likelihood of encountering Clear Air Turbulence (CAT) associated with upper-level fronts and jet streams. The GTG-2 product consists of a 00, 01, 02, and 03 hour forecast, which are updated every hour, and a 06, 09, and 12 hour forecast, which are updated every three hours starting at 00Z. GTG-2 graphics are "snapshot" graphics, intended to depict forecasted clear air turbulence conditions at the valid time (for example, at 1200Z), not for a valid time range (for example, from 1200Z to 1300Z). (PLT515) — AC 00-45

Answers

9286 [A]   9747 [C]   9747-1 [C]   9747-2 [C]

PIREPs

A pilot weather report (PIREP) is often the most timely source of information about such weather conditions as icing and multiple cloud layers. While area forecasts and freezing level charts can give the pilot a good idea of the potential for icing, only a PIREP can let the pilot know what is happening currently. A typical PIREP appended to an SA is:

FTW UA /OV DFW 18005/TM1803/FL095/TP PA 30/SK 036 OVC 060/070 OVC 075/OVC ABV

The translation is:

FTW / UA — PIREP from reporting station FTW.

OV DFW 18005 — location is the DFW 180° radial at 5 miles.

TM 1803 — time of the report is 1803.

FL095 — altitude is 9,500 feet.

TP PA 30 — Type of aircraft is a PA 30.

SK 036 OVC 060/070 OVC 075/OVC ABV — Sky condition. The base of an overcast layer is at 3,600 feet with top at 6,000 feet. A second overcast layer has its base at 7,000 feet and its top is 7,500 feet. There is another overcast layer above the aircraft's altitude of 9,500 feet.

ALL

9247. What sources reflect the most accurate information on current and forecast icing conditions?

A— Low-Level Sig Weather Prog Chart, RADATs, and the Area Forecast.
B— PIREPs, Area Forecast, and the Freezing Level Chart.
C— AIRMET Zulus.

AIRMET Zulu describes moderate icing and provides freezing level heights. (PLT294) — AC 00-45

Answer (A) is incorrect because Low-Level Sig Weather Prog Charts do not forecast icing conditions but do forecast freezing levels. Answer (B) is incorrect because although the Freezing Level Panel of the Composite Moisture Stability Chart gives you the lowest observed freezing level, it does not indicate the presence of clouds or precipitation, which must be present for icing to occur.

ALL

9250. Which type of weather can only be directly observed during flight and then reported in a PIREP?

A— Turbulence and structural icing.
B— Jetstream-type winds and icing.
C— Level of the tropopause and turbulence.

Aircraft in flight are the only means of directly observing cloud tops, icing and turbulence. (PLT061) — AC 00-45

Answer (B) is incorrect because a pilot would not be able to determine from observation if jet stream type winds or other CAT were encountered. Answer (C) is incorrect because the level of the tropopause is determined by radiosondes released by ground weather observing stations. It is not a type of weather that can be directly observed by a pilot during flight.

ALL

9271. (Refer to Figure 145.) The peak wind at KAMA was reported to be from 320° true at 39 knots,

A— which occurred at 1743Z.
B— with gusts to 43 knots.
C— with .43 of an inch liquid precipitation since the last report.

"PK WND 32039/43" indicates that the peak wind was reported to be from 320° true at 39 knots, which occurred at 43 minutes past the hour. (PLT059) — AC 00-45

ALL

9713. KFTW UA/OV DFW/TM 1645/FL100/TP PA30/ SK SCT031-TOP043/BKN060-TOP085/OVC097- TOPUNKN/WX FV00SM RA/TA 07.

This pilot report to Fort Worth (KFTW) indicates

A— the aircraft is in light rain.
B— that the top of the ceiling is 4,300 feet.
C— the ceiling at KDFW is 6,000 feet.

"BKN060-TOP085" indicates the ceiling (defined as the lowest broken or overcast layer aloft) is broken at 6,000 feet with tops at 8,500 feet. (PLT061) — AC 00-45

Answer (A) is incorrect because "WX FV00SM RA" indicates the flight visibility is 0 statute miles due to moderate rain. Answer (B) is incorrect because the scattered layer has tops at 4,300 feet, but this does not constitute a ceiling.

Answers

9247 [C]	9250 [A]	9271 [A]	9713 [C]

Cross-Reference A
Question Number and Page Number

The following list of the numbered questions included in this ASA Test Prep is given in sequential order; however, as a result of our ongoing review of FAA test question databases, some question numbers may have been removed due to changes in the database. **All currently existing questions are accounted for in this list**. For more information about the questions included in ASA Test Preps, please read Pages v–vi in the front matter for this book.

Question Number	Page Number	Question Number	Page Number	Question Number	Page Number	Question Number	Page Number
8001	1–80	8050	1–79	8099	1–25	8148	2–15
8002	1–93	8051	1–79	8100	1–18	8149	2–22
8003	1–38	8052	1–84	8101	1–25	8150	2–14
8004	1–82	8053	1–77	8102	1–25	8151	2–15
8005	1–80	8054	1–77	8103	1–19	8152	2–22
8006	1–82	8055	1–70	8104	1–26	8153	1–52
8007	1–54	8056	1–70	8105	1–26	8154	2–15
8008	1–54	8057	1–86	8106	1–26	8155	1–64
8009	1–54	8058	1–85	8107	1–19	8156	1–64
8010	1–80	8059	1–85	8108	1–19	8157	1–63
8011	1–80	8060	1–85	8109	1–20	8158	1–63
8012	1–82	8061	1–85	8110	1–20	8159	1–62
8013	1–81	8062	1–85	8111	1–20	8160	1–62
8014	1–83	8063	1–87	8112	1–82	8161	1–62
8015	1–83	8064	1–87	8113	1–26	8162	1–62
8016	1–83	8065	1–87	8114	1–89	8163	1–69
8017	1–83	8066	1–87	8115	1–78	8164	1–66
8018	1–22	8067	5–12	8116	1–78	8165	1–78
8019	1–82	8068	1–87	8117	4–51	8166	1–66
8020	1–70	8069	1–77	8118	4–51	8167	1–66
8021	1–71	8070	1–86	8119	4–51	8168	1–66
8022	1–70	8071	1–86	8120	4–51	8169	1–66
8023	1–71	8072	1–70	8121	4–52	8170	1–67
8024	1–72	8073	1–71	8122	4–52	8171	1–67
8025	1–72	8074	1–71	8123	4–52	8172	1–67
8026	1–22	8075	1–77	8124	4–52	8173	1–63
8027	1–22	8076	1–24	8125	4–52	8174	1–65
8028	1–22	8077	1–86	8126	4–53	8175	1–53
8029	1–23	8078	1–86	8127	4–53	8176	1–61
8030	1–72	8079	1–86	8128	4–53	8177	1–61
8031	1–72	8080	1–71	8129	4–53	8178	1–63
8032	1–54	8081	1–72	8130	4–54	8179	1–63
8033	1–81	8082	1–18	8131	1–50	8180	1–65
8034	1–23	8083	1–18	8132	1–51	8181	1–51
8035	1–23	8084	1–88	8133	4–35	8182	1–65
8036	1–23	8085	1–88	8134	4–12	8183	1–64
8037	1–83	8086	1–88	8135	2–17	8184	1–64
8038	1–81	8087	1–88	8136	1–51	8185	1–65
8039	1–55	8088	1–78	8137	1–50	8186	1–65
8040	1–55	8089	1–78	8138	1–53	8187	1–64
8041	1–56	8090	1–89	8139	1–52	8188	1–9
8042	1–56	8091	1–89	8140	2–15	8189	1–8
8043	1–56	8092	1–89	8141	2–16	8190	1–8
8044	1–23	8093	1–82	8142	2–16	8191	1–7
8045	1–83	8094	1–18	8143	2–16	8192	1–9
8046	1–84	8095	1–24	8144	1–62	8193	1–9
8047	1–84	8096	1–24	8145	2–21	8194	1–36
8048	1–84	8097	1–24	8146	2–22	8195	2–21
8049	5–12	8098	1–25	8147	2–22	8195-1	2–21

Question Number	Page Number	Question Number	Page Number	Question Number	Page Number	Question Number	Page Number
8196	2–29	8257	6–27	8337	3–22	8394	4–5
8197	2–29	8258	8–36	8338	3–21	8394-2	3–16
8198	1–67	8259	1–41	8339	3–22	8395	3–15
8199	2–30	8260	1–41	8340	3–22	8396	3–10
8200	1–68	8261	6–28	8341	3–20	8397	3–6
8201	1–9	8262	6–20	8342	3–19	8398	4–31
8202	1–10	8263	6–28	8343	3–19	8399	3–6
8203	2–49	8264	6–28	8344	4–39	8400	4–25
8204	1–68	8265	8–36	8345	3–11	8401	4–31
8205	1–14	8266	1–41	8345-1	3–11	8402	3–25
8206	2–10	8267	1–41	8345-2	3–11	8403	3–25
8207	1–14	8268	1–46	8346	3–5	8404	3–25
8208	1–15	8269	1–46	8347	3–9	8405	3–25
8209	1–15	8270	1–47	8348	3–5	8406	3–25
8210	1–15	8271	1–46	8349	3–9	8407	4–9
8211	1–31	8272	1–46	8350	3–9	8408	3–26
8212	1–8	8273	1–47	8351	3–10	8409	3–26
8213	1–8	8274	1–48	8352	3–11	8410	3–26
8214	1–15	8275	1–48	8353	3–10	8411	3–26
8215	1–14	8276	1–47	8354	3–10	8412	3–26
8216	1–14	8277	1–47	8355	3–25	8413	3–26
8217	1–14	8278	2–4	8356	3–20	8414	4–9
8218	1–68	8279	6–37	8357	3–7	8415	4–9
8219	1–31	8280	1–40	8358	3–7	8416	4–9
8220	1–30	8281	1–44	8359	3–8	8417	3–27
8221	1–31	8282	1–44	8360	3–8	8418	3–27
8222	1–31	8283	1–40	8361	3–8	8419	5–23
8223	1–31	8284	1–40	8362	3–8	8420	3–27
8224	1–32	8285	1–17	8363	3–8	8421	3–27
8225	1–51	8286	1–42	8364	3–8	8422	3–27
8226	1–41	8287	1–42	8365	3–12	8423	3–27
8227	1–30	8288	1–42	8366	3–12	8424	3–28
8228	1–30	8289	1–16	8367	3–13	8425	3–28
8229	1–32	8290	1–39	8368	3–6	8426	4–10
8230	1–17	8291	1–42	8369	4–44	8427	4–10
8231	1–32	8292	1–39	8370	4–45	8428	4–10
8232	1–41	8293	1–40	8371	4–45	8429	1–38
8233	1–52	8294	1–40	8372	3–12	8430	1–38
8234	1–52	8295	1–43	8373	3–12	8431	5–35
8235	1–63	8296	1–42	8374	4–33	8432	5–35
8236	1–68	8297	6–42	8375	3–6	8433	5–35
8237	1–68	8298	6–42	8376	3–13	8434	5–13
8238	1–32	8317	1–76	8377	3–4	8435	5–13
8239	1–69	8318	1–76	8378	3–5	8436	5–14
8240	1–69	8319	1–76	8379	3–7	8437	5–14
8241	1–68	8320	1–76	8380	3–13	8438	5–15
8242	6–69	8321	1–76	8381	4–31	8439	5–15
8243	1–39	8322	1–76	8382	3–6	8440	5–16
8244	1–52	8323	1–76	8383	4–31	8441	5–16
8245	1–67	8324	3–19	8384	3–23	8442	5–17
8246	1–69	8325	3–19	8385	3–23	8443	5–17
8247	6–20	8326	3–18	8386	3–24	8444	5–18
8248	6–21	8327	3–18	8387	3–15	8445	5–18
8249	6–21	8328	3–22	8388	3–15	8446	5–18
8250	6–21	8329	3–22	8389	3–15	8447	5–18
8251	6–20	8330	3–21	8390	3–15	8448	5–19
8252	6–22	8331	3–23	8391	3–16	8449	5–19
8253	6–13	8332	3–19	8391-1	3–16	8450	5–19
8254	6–20	8333	3–19	8391-2	3–16	8451	5–20
8255	6–20	8334	3–23	8392	3–15	8452	5–20
8256	6–20	8336	3–19	8393	3–16	8453	5–21

Question Number	Page Number	Question Number	Page Number	Question Number	Page Number	Question Number	Page Number
8695	4–38	8790	5–33	8851	6–66	8921	2–53
8696	4–38	8791	5–33	8852	6–66	8922	2–46
8697	5–3	8792	1–79	8853	6–45	8923	2–46
8698	5–4	8793	6–62	8854	6–40	8924	2–46
8699	5–5	8794	6–62	8855	6–45	8925	2–47
8700	5–8	8795	4–99	8856	6–45	8926	2–47
8701	2–52	8796	6–62	8857	6–45	8927	2–47
8702	4–85	8797	6–62	8858	6–46	8928	2–47
8710	8–8	8798	6–63	8859	6–46	8929	2–47
8711	2–12	8799	6–66	8860	6–46	8930	2–47
8712	4–22	8800	6–66	8861	6–47	8931	2–47
8713	4–22	8801	6–66	8862	6–47	8932	2–48
8714	4–22	8802	6–67	8863	6–48	8933	4–34
8715	4–22	8803	6–67	8864	6–48	8934	4–35
8716	4–22	8804	6–67	8865	6–49	8935	4–34
8717	4–17	8805	6–67	8866	6–49	8936	4–34
8718	4–17	8806	6–67	8867	6–50	8937	4–35
8719	4–17	8807	1–89	8872	6–7	8938	4–34
8720	4–17	8808	1–89	8873	6–7	8939	4–35
8721	4–18	8809	1–90	8874	6–8	8950	6–67
8727	4–41	8810	6–64	8875	6–8	8951	6–68
8728	4–42	8811	6–64	8876	6–8	8952	6–68
8729	4–42	8812	6–65	8877	6–8	8953	6–31
8730	4–42	8813	1–90	8878	6–8	8954	6–31
8731	4–42	8814	1–90	8879	6–8	8955	6–31
8732	4–42	8815	1–90	8880	6–9	8956	2–34
8733	4–42	8816	6–65	8881	6–6	8957	2–34
8734	4–42	8817	6–65	8882	6–6	8958	2–33
8735	8–44	8818	6–65	8883	6–6	8959	2–33
8736	6–37	8819	1–90	8884	6–6	8960	2–33
8742	4–36	8820	1–91	8885	6–6	8961	2–32
8743	4–36	8821	1–91	8886	6–6	8962	2–33
8744	4–36	8822	4–78	8887	6–14	8963	2–35
8745	4–36	8823	4–78	8888	6–6	8965	2–36
8746	4–37	8824	6–64	8889	6–7	8966	2–32
8750	4–37	8825	6–64	8890	6–9	8967	2–36
8753	4–37	8826	6–64	8891	6–9	8968	2–34
8756	4–37	8827	1–91	8892	6–9	8969	2–34
8767	1–38	8828	1–91	8893	6–11	8970	2–34
8768	1–39	8829	1–91	8894	6–11	8971	2–35
8769	5–30	8830	1–91	8895	6–11	8972	2–35
8770	5–30	8831	1–79	8896	6–12	8973	2–35
8771	5–30	8832	1–79	8897	6–12	8974	4–7
8772	5–31	8833	1–80	8898	6–12	8975	1–95
8773	5–31	8834	1–92	8899	6–12	8984	2–25
8774	4–12	8835	4–99	8900	6–12	8985	2–25
8775	4–13	8836	6–68	8901	2–45	8986	2–25
8776	5–31	8837	6–68	8902	2–45	8987	2–26
8777	5–31	8838	1–92	8903	2–46	8988	2–26
8778	5–32	8839	6–68	8904	2–46	8989	2–26
8779	5–32	8840	1–92	8905	2–43	8990	2–26
8780	4–13	8841	1–92	8906	2–44	8991	2–26
8781	5–32	8842	1–80	8907	2–46	8992	2–27
8782	6–63	8843	1–92	8908	2–53	8993	2–27
8783	6–63	8844	5–34	8909	2–54	8994	2–27
8784	6–63	8845	5–34	8910	2–54	8995	2–27
8785	6–63	8846	5–34	8911	2–53	8996	2–28
8786	6–63	8847	5–34	8912	2–53	8997	2–28
8787	5–32	8848	5–35	8913	2–53	8998	2–28
8788	5–33	8849	6–65	8914	2–48	8999	2–24
8789	5–33	8850	6–66	8915	2–48	9000	2–24

Question Number	Page Number	Question Number	Page Number	Question Number	Page Number	Question Number	Page Number
9001	2–24	9063	4–8	9118	7–14	9176	8–5
9002	2–24	9064	4–6	9119	7–8	9177	8–5
9003	2–25	9065	4–6	9120	7–9	9178	8–5
9004	2–25	9066	4–6	9121	7–9	9178-1	8–6
9005	6–25	9067	4–7	9122	7–9	9179	8–35
9005-1	6–39	9068	4–5	9123	7–9	9180	8–34
9005-2	6–39	9068-1	4–5	9124	7–9	9181	8–35
9006	6–23	9069	4–8	9125	7–10	9182	8–13
9007	6–25	9070	4–7	9126	7–10	9183	8–34
9008	6–24	9071	4–7	9127	7–10	9184	8–13
9009	6–24	9072	4–5	9128	4–43	9185	8–13
9010	7–7	9073	4–5	9129	4–40	9185-1	8–13
9011	7–8	9074	4–33	9130	8–25	9186	8–12
9012	6–51	9074-1	4–33	9131	8–25	9187	8–13
9013	6–41	9075	4–13	9132	8–25	9188	8–14
9014	6–40	9076	4–13	9133	8–22	9189	8–20
9015	6–41	9077	4–31	9134	8–23	9190	8–38
9016	6–41	9078	4–31	9135	8–23	9191	8–9
9018	6–11	9079	4–33	9135-1	8–23	9192	8–9
9019	2–19	9080	2–8	9136	8–27	9193	8–16
9020	2–19	9081	2–9	9137	8–23	9194	8–16
9021	6–33	9082	2–9	9138	8–23	9195	8–14
9022	6–41	9083	4–13	9139	8–22	9196	8–17
9022-1	6–42	9084	4–34	9140	8–25	9197	8–18
9023	2–21	9085	4–13	9141	8–23	9198	8–18
9024	2–21	9086	6–15	9142	8–24	9199	8–20
9026	6–17	9087	6–15	9143	8–25	9200	8–18
9027	6–17	9089	6–15	9144	8–25	9201	8–24
9031	6–16	9090-1	6–35	9145	8–26	9202	8–19
9032	6–16	9090-2	6–35	9146	8–26	9203	8–18
9033	6–17	9090-3	6–36	9147	8–26	9204	8–18
9034	6–51	9091	6–31	9148	8–26	9205	8–18
9035	6–52	9092	6–38	9149	8–26	9206	8–15
9036	6–33	9093	6–10	9150	8–27	9207	8–15
9037	6–32	9094	6–43	9151	8–6	9207-1	8–15
9038	6–38	9095	6–43	9152	8–4	9207-2	8–16
9039	6–39	9096	6–43	9153	8–14	9208	8–15
9040	6–17	9097	7–5	9154	8–13	9209	8–6
9041	6–35	9098	7–7	9155	8–15	9210	8–19
9042	6–43	9099	2–7	9156	8–6	9211	8–20
9043	1–93	9100	6–10	9157	8–5	9212	8–20
9044	6–38	9101	7–15	9158	8–12	9213	8–9
9045	6–24	9102	7–15	9159	8–5	9214	8–19
9046	6–10	9103	7–15	9160	8–5	9215	8–9
9047	6–10	9104	7–15	9161	8–34	9215-1	8–10
9048	6–10	9105	7–16	9162	8–35	9216	8–10
9049	6–9	9106	7–16	9163	2–8	9217	8–10
9050	7–8	9107	7–12	9164	2–7	9218	8–51
9051	7–5	9107-1	7–12	9165	8–9	9219	8–40
9052	7–5	9108	7–13	9165-1	8–9	9220	8–22
9053	6–18	9109	7–13	9166	8–24	9221	8–34
9054	7–8	9110	7–13	9167	8–27	9222	2–9
9055	6–39	9110-1	7–13	9168	8–6	9223	8–34
9056	6–25	9111	7–12	9169	8–15	9224	8–34
9057	6–25	9111-1	7–12	9170	8–12	9225	8–24
9058	4–5	9112	7–14	9171	8–12	9226	8–38
9059	4–7	9113	7–14	9172	2–8	9227	8–10
9060	4–6	9114	7–13	9173	2–7	9228	8–10
9061	4–7	9115	7–14	9173-1	2–7	9228-1	8–10
9061-1	4–8	9116	7–13	9174	2–7	9228-2	8–11
9062	4–8	9117	7–14	9175	8–51	9229	8–7

Question Number	Page Number	Question Number	Page Number	Question Number	Page Number	Question Number	Page Number
9229-1	8–7	9295	8–50	9360	4–46	9418	6–45
9230	8–39	9296	8–50	9361	4–46	9419	6–46
9231	8–40	9302	8–30	9362	7–5	9420	7–8
9232	8–39	9305	8–54	9363	7–6	9421	2–44
9233	8–6	9310	8–52	9364	7–6	9421-1	2–44
9234	8–41	9311	8–52	9365	7–6	9421-2	2–44
9235	8–38	9312	8–52	9366	1–94	9421-3	2–44
9236	8–52	9313	8–52	9367	1–94	9422	2–44
9237	8–39	9314	8–52	9368	6–34	9423	2–49
9238	8–7	9315	8–53	9369	6–33	9423-1	2–49
9238-1	8–7	9316	8–53	9370	6–27	9424	6–7
9239	8–39	9317	4–12	9371	1–95	9425	2–14
9240	8–6	9318	3–28	9372	1–95	9426	2–14
9241	8–7	9319	4–12	9373	1–95	9427	2–14
9242	8–45	9320	4–40	9374	6–23	9427-1	2–14
9244	8–46	9321	4–39	9375	2–19	9428	2–13
9245	8–46	9322	4–33	9376	2–20	9429	2–38
9246	8–46	9323	4–33	9377	2–20	9430	2–38
9247	8–57	9324	4–12	9378	2–52	9431	2–39
9248	8–46	9325	1–6	9379	1–61	9432	2–39
9249	8–55	9326	1–38	9380	2–3	9433	7–15
9250	8–57	9327	4–12	9381	2–3	9434	7–15
9251	8–50	9328	1–5	9382	6–34	9435	7–15
9252	8–54	9329	1–5	9383	6–32	9436	2–50
9255	8–50	9329-1	1–5	9384	6–34	9437	2–51
9256	8–55	9329-2	1–5	9385	6–32	9438	6–32
9257	8–55	9330	1–5	9386	2–4	9439	6–23
9258	2–17	9331	1–5	9387	2–4	9440	8–30
9259	8–41	9332	1–6	9388	1–61	9440-1	8–30
9260	8–41	9333	1–7	9389	7–6	9441	8–31
9262	8–38	9334	1–12	9390	7–7	9442	8–31
9263	8–38	9335	1–6	9391	6–33	9443	8–31
9264	8–38	9336	1–93	9392	6–33	9444	8–31
9266	8–42	9337	1–93	9393	6–33	9445	8–32
9267	8–42	9338	1–94	9394-1	6–19	9446	8–32
9268	8–43	9339	1–11	9394-2	6–19	9447	8–32
9269	8–43	9340	1–7	9395	6–13	9448	8–32
9270	8–43	9341	1–94	9396	6–13	9449	8–30
9271	8–57	9342	1–12	9397	6–14	9450	8–32
9272	8–43	9342-1	1–12	9398	6–14	9451	8–30
9273	8–43	9342-2	1–12	9399	6–9	9452	8–33
9274	8–44	9343	1–7	9400	6–14	9453	8–33
9275	8–44	9344	1–12	9401	6–13	9454	8–33
9276	8–44	9345	1–13	9402	6–24	9546	4–85
9277	8–44	9346	1–13	9403	2–34	9547	4–86
9278	8–46	9347	1–13	9404	2–20	9548	4–86
9279	8–46	9348	1–13	9405	2–19	9549	6–52
9280	8–47	9349	1–6	9406	2–20	9550	6–53
9281	8–48	9350	1–4	9407	2–3	9551	6–53
9283	8–48	9350-1	1–4	9408	2–20	9552	6–53
9284	8–55	9351	1–6	9409	6–7	9553	6–54
9285	8–55	9352	2–29	9410	2–13	9554	6–54
9286	8–56	9353	2–29	9411	2–35	9555	6–54
9287	8–48	9354	7–12	9412	2–36	9556	4–86
9288	8–48	9354-1	7–12	9413	2–36	9557	4–87
9289	8–49	9355	4–45	9414	1–95	9558	4–87
9290	8–49	9355-1	4–45	9415	1–95	9559	4–88
9291	8–49	9356	2–13	9416	2–51	9560	4–88
9292	8–49	9357	2–13	9416-1	2–49	9561	4–89
9293	8–49	9358	4–45	9416-2	2–49	9563	6–54
9294	8–50	9359	4–46	9417	2–50	9564	6–55

Question Number	Page Number	Question Number	Page Number	Question Number	Page Number	Question Number	Page Number
9816-1	7−18	9836	1−77	9855	2−11	9901	4−58
9817	6−37	9837	1−32	9856	7−16	9902	4−58
9818	6−27	9838	1−32	9857	2−11	9903	4−59
9819	1−73	9839	1−33	9858	7−10	9904	4−62
9820	8−11	9840	1−33	9864	4−20	9905	4−62
9821	8−11	9841	1−33	9865	4−20	9906	4−63
9822	8−11	9842	1−34	9866	4−20	9907	4−68
9823	3−10	9843	1−34	9867	4−20	9908	4−68
9824	8−44	9844	1−34	9868	4−20	9909	4−68
9826	6−28	9845	1−34	9874	4−22	9910	4−69
9827	6−28	9846	1−34	9875	4−28	9911	4−69
9827-1	6−29	9847	1−35	9876	4−29	9912	4−69
9827-2	6−29	9847-1	1−35	9877	4−29	9913	4−69
9827-3	6−29	9848	1−35	9894	4−56	9914	4−70
9830	2−11	9849	1−35	9895	4−56	9915	4−83
9831	3−28	9850	1−35	9896	4−57	9916	4−83
9832	7−18	9851	1−35	9897	4−57	9917	2−41
9833	7−19	9852	1−36	9898	4−57		
9834	7−19	9853	2−11	9899	4−57		
9835	8−20	9854	2−11	9900	4−57		

Cross-Reference B
Learning Statement Code and Question Number

The expression "learning statement," as used in FAA airman testing, refers to measurable statements about the knowledge a student should be able to demonstrate following a certain segment of training. When you take the applicable airman knowledge test required for an airman pilot certificate or rating, you will receive an Airman Knowledge Test Report. The test report will list the learning statement codes for questions you have answered incorrectly. Match the codes given on your test report to the ones in the official FAA Learning Statement Codes (listed in this cross-reference). Use Cross-Reference A in this book to find the page number for the question numbers listed in the table beginning on the next page.

Your instructor is required to provide instruction on each of the areas of deficiency listed on your Airman Knowledge Test Report (as LSCs), and give you an endorsement for this instruction. The Airman Knowledge Test Report must be presented to the examiner conducting your practical test. During the oral portion of the practical test, the examiner is required to evaluate the noted areas of deficiency.

The FAA's learning statement codes are a hierarchical sequence of classification codes that places a knowledge item in a unique category, which can then be used for reference to source textbooks and study material. The LSCs are assigned to all FAA test questions in order to categorize them for placement on a given Knowledge Exam. This classification code system uses the following hierarchy (which is further detailed in the cross-reference table):

- *Topic* — this is the overall subject matter topic code, the highest classification of overall subject matter a knowledge test item was developed to assess (for example, "Aerodynamics").

- *Content* — the secondary level subject matter code (for example, "Airspeed").

- *Specific* — the basic hierarchical classification code the subject matter for a knowledge test item (for example, "Thrust").

If you received a code on your Airman Test Report that is not listed in this cross-reference, email ASA at **cfi@asa2fly.com**. We will provide the definition so you can review that subject area.

The FAA appreciates testing experience feedback. You can contact the branch responsible for the FAA Knowledge Exams directly at:

Federal Aviation Administration
AFS-630, Airman Testing Standards Branch
PO Box 25082
Oklahoma City, OK 73125
Email: AFS630comments@faa.gov

Learning Statement Code	FAA Reference	Subject Description (or *Topic* 〉 *Content* 〉 *Specific* classification) Question Numbers
PLT002	FAA-H-8083-25	Aircraft Performance 〉 Computations 〉 Airspeeds *8563, 8564, 8565, 8566, 8567, 8696*
PLT003	FAA-H-8083-25	Aircraft Performance 〉 Computations 〉 Center of Gravity *8697*
PLT004	FAA-H-8083-25	Aircraft Performance 〉 Charts 〉 Climb; Engine Out Performance *8382, 8474, 8475, 8476, 8477, 8478, 8480, 8481, 8482, 8553, 8554, 8555, 8556, 8557, 8558, 8559, 8560, 8561, 8562, 8593, 8594, 8595, 8596, 8597, 8598, 8599, 8600, 8601, 8602, 8628, 8629, 8630, 8631, 8632, 8635, 8636, 8637, 8682, 8683, 8684, 8685, 8686, 9875, 9876, 9877*
PLT005	AC 00-6 FAA-H-8083-25	Aircraft Performance 〉 Computations 〉 Density Altitude *9813*
PLT006	FAA- H-8083-3	Calculate aircraft performance — glide *8381*
PLT007	FAA-H-8083-25	Aircraft Performance 〉 Charts 〉 Holding; Landing; Takeoff *8615, 8616, 8617, 8638, 8639, 8640, 8641, 8642-1, 8668, 8669, 8670, 8671, 8672, 8687, 8688, 8689, 8690, 8691, 8763, 9874*
PLT008	FAA-H-8083-25	Aircraft Performance 〉 Charts 〉 Landing *8117, 8118, 8119, 8120, 8121, 8122, 8123, 8124, 8125, 8126, 8129, 8504, 8505, 8506, 8507, 8508, 8509, 8510, 8511, 8512, 8608, 8609, 8610, 8611, 8612, 8692, 8742, 8743, 8744, 8745, 8750, 8753, 8756, 9907, 9908, 9909, 9910, 9911, 9912, 9913, 9914*
PLT009	FAA-H-8083-21	Aircraft Performance 〉 Charts 〉 Power Check; Turbine Engine *8533, 8534, 8535, 8536, 8537, 8604*
PLT010	FAA-H-8083-25	Aircraft Performance 〉 Charts 〉 Takeoff *8588, 8589, 8590, 8591, 8592, 8623, 8624, 8625, 8626, 8627*
PLT011	FAA-H-8083-25	Aircraft Performance 〉 Charts 〉 Takeoff *8115, 8116, 8466, 8467, 8468, 8469, 8470, 8471, 8472, 8743, 8479, 8548, 8549, 8550, 8551, 8552, 8568, 8569, 8570, 8571, 8572, 8603, 8613, 8614, 8618, 8619, 8620, 8642-4, 8712, 8713, 8714, 8715, 8716, 8717, 8718, 9076, 9797, 9797-1, 9797-2, 9864, 9865, 9866, 9867, 9868, 9899, 9900, 9901, 9902, 9903*
PLT012	FAA-H-8083-15 FAA-H-8083-25	Aircraft Performance 〉 Computations 〉 ETE; Fuel; Mach; Preflight Planning Aircraft Performance 〉 Charts 〉 Alternate; Cruise Navigation 〉 Radio 〉 VOR *8483, 8489, 8490, 8491, 8492, 8493, 8494, 8495, 8496, 8497, 8498, 8499, 8500, 8605, 8606, 8607, 8621, 8622, 8633, 8634, 8643, 8644, 8645, 8646, 8647, 8648, 8649, 8650, 8651, 8652, 8658, 8659, 8660, 8661, 8662, 8663, 8664, 8665, 8666, 8667, 8673, 8674, 8675, 8676, 8677, 8693, 8694, 8695, 8702, 8720, 8721, 8795, 8822, 8823, 8835, 9546, 9547, 9548, 9556, 9557, 9558, 9559, 9560, 9561, 9566, 9567, 9568, 9574, 9575, 9578, 9579, 9581, 9582, 9583, 9584, 9585, 9591, 9592, 9594, 9595, 9597, 9598, 9607, 9608, 9610, 9611, 9612, 9621, 9627, 9628, 9639, 9640, 9642, 9643, 9652, 9653, 9904, 9905, 9906, 9915, 9916*
PLT013	FAA-H-8083-25	Aircraft Performance 〉 Charts 〉 Takeoff *8727*

Learning Statement Code	FAA Reference	Subject Description (or Topic) Content) Specific classification) Question Numbers
PLT015	ANA FAA-H-8083-25	Aerodynamics) Performance) Normal Flight Aircraft Performance) Computations) Specific Range: NAM/1000# Fuel Aircraft Performance) Limitations) Best Range *8397, 9077, 9078, 9580, 9593*
PLT016	FAA-H-8083-1	Aircraft Performance) Computations) Fuel Dump *8678, 8679, 8680, 8681*
PLT018	FAA-H-8083-25	Aerodynamics) Load Factor) Angle of Bank *8354, 8728*
PLT020	FAA-H-8083-25	Aircraft Performance) Charts) Turbulent Air Penetration *8653, 8654, 8655, 8656, 8657*
PLT021	FAA-H-8083-1 FAA-H-8083-25	Aircraft Performance) Charts) Climb; Landing Weight and Balance) Aircraft Loading) Weight/Moment Indexes Weight and Balance) Center of Gravity) Computations; Shifting Weight *8434, 8435, 8436, 8437, 8438, 8439, 8440, 8441, 8442, 8443, 8444, 8445, 8446, 8447, 8448, 8449, 8450, 8451, 8452, 8453, 8454, 8455, 8456, 8457, 8458, 8513, 8514, 8515, 8516, 8517, 8518, 8519, 8520, 8521, 8522, 8523, 8524, 8525, 8526, 8527, 8528, 8529, 8530, 8531, 8532, 8573, 8574, 8575, 8576, 8577, 8578, 8579, 8580, 8581, 8582*
PLT023	AC 00-6	Navigation) Instrument) Altimeter *9164, 9172, 9173, 9173-1*
PLT024	AC 00-6	Meteorology) Atmosphere) Stability *9170, 9171, 9186, 9187*
PLT029	14 CFR 121 FAA-H-8083-16	Regulations) 14 CFR Part 121) Flight Crewmember Duties *8106, 8298*
PLT032	FAA-H-8083-25	Aerodynamics) Airspeed) Mach *8387*
PLT034	14 CFR 121	Regulations) 14 CFR Part 121) Takeoff Minimums *8134*
PLT040	14 CFR 71 AIM	Navigation) Airspace) Class B Regulations) 14 CFR Part 91) Airspace *8872, 8873, 8874, 8875, 8876, 8877, 8881, 8882, 8883, 8884, 8885, 8886, 8888*
PLT042	AC 00-45	Weather) Aeronautical Weather Reports) Constant Pressure Analysis Charts *9311, 9313*
PLT043	AC 00-45	Weather) Aeronautical Weather Reports) Constant Pressure Analysis Charts *9310, 9312, 9314, 9315, 9316*
PLT044	AIM	Air Traffic Control Procedures) Arrival) After Landing Air Traffic Control Procedures) Departure) Speed Adjustments; Takeoff Air Traffic Control Procedures) En Route) Speed Adjustments Air Traffic Control Procedures) Ground) Ground Hold Delays *9167, 9388*
PLT045	FAA-H-8083-25	Aircraft Performance) Charts) Descent *8501, 8502, 8503, 9749*

Learning Statement Code	FAA Reference	Subject Description (or **Topic** ⟩ **Content** ⟩ **Specific** classification) Question Numbers
PLT047	AIM	Navigation ⟩ Avionics ⟩ Airborne Equipment *8858*
PLT048	FAA-H-8083-21	Aircraft Performance ⟩ Charts ⟩ Hovering *8538, 8539, 8540, 8541, 8542, 8543, 8544, 8545, 8546, 8547*
PLT049	14 CFR 61 14 CFR 91 AC 00-45 AIM U.S. Terminal Procedures	Navigation ⟩ Avionics ⟩ Airborne Equipment Navigation ⟩ Flight Operations ⟩ Approach Chart Navigation ⟩ Radio ⟩ ILS; Instrument Approach; Non-precision approach *8972, 9588, 9601, 9619, 9645, 9645-1*
PLT052	14 CFR 21 AIM U.S. Terminal Procedures	Instrument Procedures ⟩ Instrument Departures ⟩ SID Regulations ⟩ 14 CFR Part 121/135 ⟩ Performance Requirements *8794, 9549, 9563, 9564, 9614, 9615, 9660*
PLT055	AIM IFR Enroute High Altitude Chart	Air Traffic Control Procedures ⟩ En Route ⟩ Airways and Route Systems Navigation ⟩ Flight Operations ⟩ IFR En Route Charts *9596*
PLT058	FAA-H-8083-15 FAA-H-8083-16 IFR Enroute Low Altitude Chart	Instrument Procedures ⟩ En Route ⟩ Chart Interpretation Publications ⟩ Aeronautical Charts ⟩ IFR En Route *8784, 8824, 8825, 8826, 9620, 9623, 9670, 9675*
PLT059	AC 00-45	Weather ⟩ Aeronautical Weather Reports ⟩ Aviation Routine Weather Reports (METAR); Aviation Selected Special Report (SPECI); Aviation Weather Reports *8735, 9242, 9266, 9267, 9268, 9269, 9270, 9271, 9272, 9273, 9274, 9275, 9276, 9277, 9716, 9717, 9718, 9824*
PLT061	AC 00-45	Weather ⟩ Aeronautical Weather Reports ⟩ PIREPS *9250, 9713*
PLT065	FAA-H-8083-25	Aircraft Performance ⟩ Charts ⟩ Engine Out Performance *8484, 8485, 8486, 8487, 8488*
PLT067	AC 00-45	Weather ⟩ Aeronautical Weather Forecasts ⟩ Inflight Aviation Weather Advisories; SIGMETS *9284*
PLT068	AC 00-45	Weather ⟩ Aeronautical Weather Reports ⟩ Significant Weather Prognostic Charts *9260*
PLT069	FAA-H-8083-25	Aircraft Performance ⟩ Charts ⟩ Takeoff *8642-3*
PLT072	AC 00-45	Weather ⟩ Aeronautical Weather Forecasts ⟩ TAF *9279, 9280*
PLT073	Chart Supplements U.S.	Air Traffic Control Procedures ⟩ En Route ⟩ Tower Enroute *9565*
PLT076	AC 00-45	National Weather Service (NWS) ⟩ Functions ⟩ Aeronautical Weather Forecasts Weather ⟩ Aeronautical Weather Forecasts ⟩ Winds/Temperatures Aloft Forecasts *9255, 9287, 9288, 9289, 9290, 9291, 9292, 9293, 9294, 9295, 9296*

Learning Statement Code	FAA Reference	Subject Description (or **Topic** 〉 **Content** 〉 **Specific** classification) / Question Numbers
PLT078	Chart Supplements U.S. U.S. Terminal Procedures	Air Traffic Control Procedures 〉 Communications 〉 Pilot Procedures Air Traffic Control Procedures 〉 Ground 〉 Taxi National Weather Service 〉 Functions 〉 Aeronautical Weather Reports; Weather Outlets Navigation 〉 Flight Operations 〉 Airport; Communications; Runway *8782, 8783, 8785, 8793, 8796, 8797, 8798, 8804, 9572, 9587, 9613, 9625, 9637, 9655, 9658, 9659, 9661, 9782*
PLT080	AIM U.S. Terminal Procedures	Air Traffic Control Procedures 〉 Arrival 〉 Approach Control Air Traffic Control Procedures 〉 Communications 〉 ATC Communications; Clearances Navigation 〉 Flight Operations 〉 Arrivals Navigation 〉 Radio 〉 STAR *8786, 8799, 8810, 8812, 9647, 9818*
PLT082	U.S. Terminal Procedures	Regulations 〉 14 CFR Parts 121/135 〉 Flight Planning *8816, 8842, 9618*
PLT083	AIM FAA-H-8083-15 U.S. Terminal Procedures	Air Traffic Control Procedures 〉 Arrival 〉 Instrument Approach Procedures; Missed Approach Navigation 〉 Flight Operations 〉 Approach Chart Navigation 〉 Radio 〉 DME; ILS *8704, 8800, 8802, 8803, 8805, 8817, 8818, 8836, 8837, 8839, 8849, 8850, 8851, 8852, 8950, 8951, 8952, 8954, 9040, 9550, 9551, 9552, 9553, 9554, 9555, 9569, 9571, 9573, 9586, 9589, 9590, 9600, 9602, 9603, 9604, 9617, 9629, 9630, 9631, 9654, 9666, 9667, 9686*
PLT085	FAA-H-8083-25	Aircraft Performance 〉 Charts 〉 Takeoff *8642-2*
PLT087	FAA-H-8083-15	Navigation 〉 Radio 〉 DME; Holding *8862*
PLT089	FAA-H-8083-25	Aircraft Performance 〉 Charts 〉 Takeoff *8719*
PLT094	ANA	Aerodynamics 〉 Stalls/Spins 〉 Angle of Attack *8391-1, 8391-2, 8394-2*
PLT097	AIM	Human Factors 〉 Aeromedical Factors 〉 Physiological *9101*
PLT099	AIM	Human Factors 〉 Aeromedical Factors 〉 Flight Illusions; Physiological *9114, 9116, 9117, 9118*
PLT100	AIM IFR Enroute Low Altitude Chart	Recall aeronautical charts — IFR En Route Low Altitude *9049, 9644*
PLT103	FAA-H-8083-25	Aeronautical Decision Making 〉 Judgment 〉 Hazardous; Training *9832, 9815, 9815-1*
PLT104	FAA-H-8083-25	Aeronautical Decision Making (ADM), CRM 〉 Judgment 〉 Automatic Decisions Aeronautical Decision Making (ADM), CRM 〉 Risk Management 〉 Phase of Flight Human Factors 〉 Aeronautical Decision Making (ADM), CRM 〉 Problem Detection *8711, 9354-1, 9778, 9778-1, 9804, 9805, 9805-1, 9805-2, 9805-3, 9805-4, 9805-5, 9806, 9816, 9816-1, 9830, 9833, 9834, 9853, 9854, 9855, 9856, 9857*

Learning Statement Code	FAA Reference	Subject Description (or Topic) Content) Specific classification) Question Numbers
PLT108	AC 120-58 AC 135-17	Aerodynamics) Powerplant) Turbine Meteorology) Hazardous) Icing *9441, 9442, 9443, 9444, 9445, 9446, 9447, 9448, 9450, 9452, 9453, 9454, 9696, 9697, 9698, 9700*
PLT112	AIM	Recall aircraft controls — proper use / techniques *9043*
PLT121	FAA-H-8083-1	Weight and Balance) Aircraft Loading) Limitations *8431, 8432, 8433, 8698, 8699, 8700, 8729, 8730, 8746, 8769, 8770, 8771, 8772, 8773, 8776, 8777, 8778, 8779, 8781, 8787, 8788, 8789, 8790, 8791, 8844, 8845, 8846, 8847, 8848*
PLT123	FAA-H-8083-25	Aircraft Performance) Charts) Takeoff *8583, 8584, 8585, 8586, 8587*
PLT124	FAA-H-8083-25	Aircraft Performance) Atmospheric Effects) Instrumentation Error *8374, 8404, 8405, 8417, 8418, 9767*
PLT127	FAA-8083-3	Aerodynamics) Powerplant) Turbine; Turboprop Aircraft Performance) Atmospheric Effects) Density Altitue *9059, 9061, 9061-1, 9062, 9063*
PLT128	AC 91-74 AC 120-58 AC 135-17	Aerodynamics) Flight Characteristics) Flight Hazards Meteorology) Hazards) Icing *9080, 9302, 9451*
PLT129	FAA-H-8083-25	Aircraft Performance) Charts) Runway *9083*
PLT130	FAA-H-8083-25	Recall aircraft performance — fuel *9071*
PLT131	FAA-H-8083-25	Aerodynamics) Principles of Flight) Ground Effect *8375, 8379*
PLT132	FAA-H-8083-25	Navigation) Instrumentation) Airspeed Indicator *8364, 9321*
PLT134	ANA	Recall aircraft performance — takeoff *9075, 9801, 9802*
PLT139	14 CFR 121 ANA	Aerodynamics) Stall/Spins) Stall Warning Devices Regulations) 14 CFR Part 121 Subpart K) Navigation Equipment *8069, 8070, 8071, 8154*
PLT140	AIM	Recall airport operations — LAHSO *9731, 9732, 9733, 9734*
PLT141	AIM	Air Traffic Control Procedures) Ground) Landing Roll Out Navigation) Flight Operations) Airport; Heliport; Runway Navigation) Pilotage) Runway Markings; Runway Signs; Taxiway Markings; Taxiway Signs *8722, 8903, 8904, 8905, 8906, 8907, 8922, 8923, 8924, 8925, 8926, 8927, 8928, 8929, 8930, 8931; 8932, 9416, 9416-1, 9416-2, 9417, 9421, 9421-1, 9421-2, 9422, 9423, 9423-1, 9436, 9437, 9735, 9735-1, 9735-2, 9735-3, 9737, 9764, 9785, 9785-1, 9786, 9786-1, 9798, 9799*

Learning Statement Code	FAA Reference	Subject Description (or Topic ⟩ Content ⟩ Specific classification) / Question Numbers
PLT143	Chart Supplements U.S.	Navigation ⟩ Flight Operations ⟩ Airport *9636, 9668, 9669, 9690*
PLT144	AIM FAA-H-8083-3	Air Traffic Control Procedures ⟩ Ground ⟩ Braking Action Aircraft Performance ⟩ Atmospheric Effects ⟩ Braking Action Aircraft Performance ⟩ Limitations ⟩ Braking Action *8133, 8933, 8934, 8935, 8936, 8937, 8938, 8939, 9055*
PLT145	AIM	Navigation ⟩ Flight Operations ⟩ Runway *8914, 8915*
PLT147	AIM U.S. Terminal Procedures	Navigation ⟩ Flight Operations ⟩ Airport; Runway *8705, 8908, 8909, 8910, 8911, 8912, 8913, 8921, 9378, 9648, 9649*
PLT148	AIM Chart Supplements U.S.	Navigation ⟩ Flight Operations ⟩ Runway Navigation ⟩ Pilotage ⟩ Approach Lights *8901, 8902*
PLT149	AIM	Air Traffic Control Procedures ⟩ Communications ⟩ Gate Hold Procedures; Pilot Procedures *8203, 8701, 9057, 9258, 9421-3, 9783, 9784, 9787, 9788, 9789, 9790*
PLT161	14 CFR 91 AIM	Air Traffic Control Procedures ⟩ Communications ⟩ Airspace Requirements Air Traffic Control Procedures ⟩ En Route ⟩ ADIZ Navigation ⟩ 14 CFR Part 91 ⟩ Airspace; Equipment/Instrument/Certificate Requirement; Flight Rules *8878, 8879, 8880, 8887, 8889, 8890, 8891, 9048, 9094, 9095, 9100, 9395, 9396, 9397, 9398, 9399, 9400, 9741, 9780*
PLT162	14 CFR 91 AIM	Air Traffic Control Procedures ⟩ Communications ⟩ Traffic Alert/Collision Avoidance Air Traffic Control Procedures ⟩ En Route ⟩ MOA Air Traffic Control Procedures ⟩ Services ⟩ Outer Class C Regulations ⟩ 14 CFR Part 91 ⟩ Flight Rules *8892, 9018, 9374, 9381*
PLT163	14 CFR 91 14 CFR 121	Regulations ⟩ 14 CFR Part 91 ⟩ Enroute Regulations ⟩ 14 CFR Part 121 ⟩ Flight Rules *8114, 8893, 8894, 8895, 8896, 8897, 8898, 8899, 8900*
PLT166	AC 00-6	Navigation ⟩ Instrumentation ⟩ Altimeter *9099, 9163, 9174*
PLT168	FAA-H-8083-25	Recall angle of attack — characteristics/forces/principles *8378*
PLT169	FAA-H-8083-25	Recall antitorque system — components/functions *8459, 8460, 8461, 8462, 8463, 8464, 8465, 9894, 9895, 9896, 9897, 9898*
PLT170	FAA-H-8083-3 FAA-H-8083-16	Aerodynamics ⟩ Performance ⟩ Brakes Navigation ⟩ Flight Operations ⟩ Approach *8402, 8403, 8736, 8955, 8969, 9034, 9035, 9039, 9074, 9074-1, 9084, 9090-1, 9090-3, 9091, 9092, 9438, 9791, 9792, 9793*

Learning Statement Code	FAA Reference	Subject Description (or Topic 〉 Content 〉 Specific classification) Question Numbers
PLT171	AIM	Air Traffic Control Procedures 〉 En Route 〉 Reporting Air Traffic Control Procedures 〉 Communications 〉 Pilot Procedures; Radio Procedures *8854, 9013, 9015, 9016, 9022-1*
PLT172	AIM	Air Traffic Control Procedures 〉 Approach 〉 Priority Air Traffic Control Procedures 〉 Arrival 〉 Approach Control; Uncontrolled Field Air Traffic Control Procedures 〉 Communications 〉 ATC Altitude Alerts Air Traffic Control Procedures 〉 Services 〉 Class C; IFR Flight Plans; Weather Radar *9050, 9090-2, 9093, 9096, 9760*
PLT173	AC 00-6	Meteorology 〉 Atmosphere 〉 Pressure; Stability; Temperature *9157, 9159, 9165, 9165-1, 9178, 9188, 9195*
PLT192	AC 00-6	Meteorology 〉 Clouds 〉 Turbulence *9189, 9190, 9193*
PLT195	AIM	Air Traffic Control Procedures 〉 Communications 〉 Traffic Alert/Collision Avoidance System *9425, 9426, 9427, 9427-1, 9428*
PLT196	AIM	Recall communications — ATIS broadcasts *9022*
PLT197	FAA-H-8083-21	Aerodynamics 〉 Principles of Flight 〉 Forces Acting on Rotary Wing *8420*
PLT201	FAA-H-8083-16	Navigation 〉 Radio 〉 Departure Obstruction Clearance *9012*
PLT202	FAA-H-8083-15	Navigation 〉 Radio 〉 DME *9023, 9024, 9570, 9599*
PLT203	AC 00-6	Meteorology 〉 Atmosphere 〉 Temperature; Troposphere *9151, 9168, 9209, 9240*
PLT205	AIM	Human Factors 〉 Aeromedical Factors 〉 Alcohol *9111*
PLT208	14 CFR 91 14 CFR 121	Navigation 〉 Flight Operations 〉 Communications Regulations 〉 14 CFR Part 121 〉 Crew Equipment/Publications/Checklists *8360, 8369, 8406, 8811, 9827-1, 9827-2, 9827-3*
PLT213	FAA-H-8083-25	Aerodynamics 〉 Stability/Control 〉 Static *8366, 8372*
PLT214	FAA-H-8083-3 FAA-H-8083-25	Aerodynamics 〉 Flight Controls 〉 Normal Flight Aerodynamics 〉 Principles of Flight 〉 Forces Acting on Aircraft; Lift *8368, 8388, 8389, 8390, 8391, 8392, 8393, 8395*
PLT219	FAA-H-8083-3 FAA-H-8083-21	Flight Operations 〉 Maneuvers 〉 Basics *9831*
PLT223	FAA-H-8083-3	Aerodynamics 〉 Airspeed 〉 V_Y Aerodynamics 〉 Principles of Flight 〉 Drag *8051, 8241, 8357, 8359, 8370*

Learning Statement Code	FAA Reference	Subject Description (or Topic ⟩ Content ⟩ Specific classification) Question Numbers
PLT224	AIM	Air Traffic Control Procedures ⟩ Preflight ⟩ Flight Plan *8806, 9005, 9026, 9031, 9032*
PLT225	AIM	Air Traffic Control Procedures ⟩ Preflight ⟩ Flight Plan *9027, 9033, 9053*
PLT226	AC 00-6	Meteorology ⟩ Clouds ⟩ Fog *8723, 9194, 9206, 9207, 9207-1, 9207-2, 9229-1, 9238-1*
PLT234	FAA-H-8083-15	Recall forces acting on aircraft — 3 axis intersect *9740*
PLT236	FAA-H-8083-25	Recall forces acting on aircraft — airfoil/center of pressure/mean camber line *8365, 8367, 8373, 8376*
PLT237	ANA	Aerodynamics ⟩ Load Factor ⟩ Lift *8345-1, 8345-2, 8421*
PLT240	FAA-H-8083-25	Weight and Balance ⟩ Center of Gravity ⟩ Effect of Load Distribution *8380, 8419*
PLT242	FAA-H-8083-3 FAA-H-8083-25	Aerodynamics ⟩ Airspeed ⟩ General Aerodynamics ⟩ Principles of Flight ⟩ Forces Acting on Wing; Lift *8377, 8383*
PLT244	FAA-H-8083-25	Recall forces acting on aircraft — stability/controllability *9079*
PLT245	FAA-H-8083-25	Aerodynamics ⟩ Load Factor ⟩ Lift *8344*
PLT247	ANA	Aerodynamics ⟩ Normal Flight ⟩ Landing *9005-1, 9005-2, 9793-1*
PLT248	FAA-H-8083-3 FAA-H-8083-25	Aerodynamics ⟩ Principles of Flight ⟩ Forces Acting on Aircraft; Load Factor *8345, 8352, 8353, 8422, 8423*
PLT263	AC 00-6 AC 00-45	Weather ⟩ Meteorology ⟩ Icing; Moisture Windshear/Turbulence ⟩ Clear Air Turbulence ⟩ Jet Stream; Windshear *9230, 9231, 9701*
PLT266	ANA FAA-H-8083-25	Aerodynamics ⟩ Performance ⟩ Normal Flight Aerodynamics ⟩ Principles of Flight ⟩ Lift *8341, 8356, 8384, 8385, 8386, 9759, 9766, 9771, 9803*
PLT268	FAA-H-8083-25	Aerodynamics ⟩ Principles of Flight ⟩ Forces Acting on Aircraft *8409*
PLT274	AC 00-6 AC 91-74	Meteorology ⟩ Hazardous ⟩ Icing Meteorology ⟩ Icing ⟩ Freezing Rain *9221, 9224, 9285, 9736, 9748, 9774, 9775*
PLT276	FAA-H-8083-15	Navigation ⟩ Radio ⟩ VOR *8968, 8971, 8973, 8984, 8985, 8986, 8987, 8988, 8989*
PLT277	FAA-H-8083-15	Navigation ⟩ Radio ⟩ ILS *8959, 8960, 8962, 8970*

Learning Statement Code	FAA Reference	Subject Description (*or* **Topic** 〉 **Content** 〉 **Specific** classification) Question Numbers
PLT280	AIM	Human Factors 〉 Aeromedical Factors 〉 Flight Illusions; Spatial Disorientation *9107, 9107-1, 9108, 9109, 9110, 9110-1, 9115, 9433, 9434, 9435*
PLT282	14 CFR 121	Regulations 〉 14 CFR Part 121 〉 Dispatch/Redispatch *8004, 8005, 8011, 8019, 8068, 8093*
PLT283	AC 00-45	Weather 〉 Aeronautical Weather Reports 〉 Constant Pressure Analysis Charts *9281, 9707, 9711*
PLT284	AC 00-06	Recall information on a Forecast Winds and Temperatures Aloft (FD) *9251*
PLT287	AC 00-45	Meteorology 〉 Air Masses and Fronts 〉 Pressure *9175*
PLT288	AC 00-45	Weather 〉 Aeronautical Weather Forecasts 〉 Aviation Weather Forecasts; TAF *9244, 9245, 9246, 9248, 9278, 9709, 9710*
PLT290	AC 00-45	National Weather Service (NWS) 〉 Functions 〉 Aeronautical Weather Forecasts; Aeronautical Weather Reports Weather 〉 Aeronautical Weather Forecasts 〉 SIGMETS *9257, 9286*
PLT294	AC 00-45 AIM	National Weather Service (NWS) 〉 Functions 〉 Aeronautical Weather Forecasts; En Route Flight Advisory Service *9247*
PLT296	AIM FAA-H-8083-15	Navigation 〉 Radio 〉 ADF/NDB; Holding; Instrument Approach *8853, 8855, 8856, 8857, 8859, 8860, 8861, 8863, 8864, 8865, 8866, 8867, 9418, 9419*
PLT300	AIM	Recall instrument/navigation system checks/inspections — limits/tuning/identifying/logging *9019, 9020, 9773*
PLT301	AC 00-6	Meteorology 〉 Atmosphere 〉 Temperature *9153, 9154, 9169*
PLT302	AC 00-6	Meteorology 〉 High Altitude 〉 Jet Stream Windshear/Turbulence 〉 Clear Air Turbulence 〉 High Altitude *9227, 9228, 9229, 9237, 9238, 9239, 9241, 9776, 9779, 9820, 9821, 9822*
PLT303	ANA FAA-H-8083-3 FAA-H-8083-25	Recall L/D ratio *8346, 8398, 8399, 8400, 8401*
PLT309	FAA-H-8083-25	Aerodynamics 〉 Load Factor 〉 Angle of Bank *8396*
PLT310	FAA-H-8083-25	Aerodynamics 〉 Load Factor 〉 Lift *8347, 8355*
PLT314	FAA-H-8083-3	Recall longitudinal axis — aerodynamics/center of gravity/direction of motion *8362*
PLT316	AC 00-45	Weather 〉 Hazardous 〉 Thunderstorms *9758*

Learning Statement Code	FAA Reference	Subject Description (or Topic 〉 Content 〉 Specific classification) Question Numbers
PLT317	AC 00-54 AIM	Weather/Turbulence 〉 Microbursts 〉 Performance; Windshear *9130, 9131, 9132, 9140, 9143, 9144, 9145, 9146, 9147, 9148, 9149, 9150, 9814*
PLT318	AIM	Air Traffic Control Procedures 〉 Arrival 〉 Low Fuel Air Traffic Control Procedures 〉 Communications 〉 Pilot Procedures *9010, 9011, 9420*
PLT322	14 CFR 121	Regulations 〉 14 CFR Part 121 Subpart K 〉 Navigation Equipment *8145, 8147*
PLT323	14 CFR 121 AIM	Air Traffic Control Procedures 〉 Preflight 〉 NOTAMS Regulations 〉 14 CFR Part 121 〉 Crew Equipment/Publications/Checklists *8283, 9086, 9087, 9089*
PLT325	49 CFR 830	Recall operations manual — transportation of prisoner *8132, 8136*
PLT328	FAA-H-8083-25	Recall performance planning, aircraft loading *8733, 8734*
PLT330	AIM FAA-H-8083-25	Human Factors 〉 Aeromedical Factors 〉 Physiological *9103, 9105, 9106*
PLT332	AIM	Human Factors 〉 Aeromedical Factors 〉 Fitness for Flight; Physiological *9102, 9104*
PLT334	AIM	Human Factors 〉 Aeromedical Factors 〉 Flight Illusions *9112, 9113*
PLT337	AC 91-43	Navigation 〉 Instrumentation 〉 Airspeed Indicator *9081, 9082, 9222*
PLT343	14 CFR 1 FAA-H-8083-25	Aerodynamics 〉 Powerplant 〉 Reciprocating *9064, 9065, 9066, 9067, 9072, 9073*
PLT344	AC 00-6	Meteorology 〉 Hazardous 〉 Icing *9223*
PLT346	AC 65-15	Aerodynamics 〉 Flight Characteristics 〉 Normal Flight Aerodynamics 〉 Flight Controls 〉 Primary; Secondary *8324, 8325, 8326, 8337, 8342, 8343*
PLT347	ANA FAA-H-8083-3	Recall principles of flight — critical engine *8361, 9085*
PLT348	FAA-H-8083-3	Aerodynamics 〉 Principles of Flight 〉 Forces Acting on Wing *8349, 8350, 8351, 9823*
PLT354	AIM Instrument Approach Procedure Charts U.S. Terminal Procedures	Air Traffic Control Procedures 〉 Preflight 〉 Flight Plan Navigation 〉 Avionics 〉 Airborne Equipment; GPS Navigation 〉 Flight Operations 〉 Approach Chart; Preflight Planning/Calculations Navigation 〉 Radio 〉 GPS; Non-precision Approach *8703, 9111-1, 9429, 9430, 9431, 9432, 9691, 9692, 9693, 9694, 9722, 9723, 9725, 9726, 9727, 9728, 9729, 9729-1, 9730, 9738, 9739, 9743, 9744, 9744-1, 9794, 9795, 9796, 9796-1, 9804-1, 9812, 9812-1, 9917*

Learning Statement Code	FAA Reference	Subject Description (or Topic ⟩ Content ⟩ Specific classification) Question Numbers
PLT355	FAA-H-8083-15	Navigation ⟩ Radio ⟩ HSI; ILS 8990, 8991, 8992, 8993, 8994, 8995, 8996, 8997, 8998, 8999, 9000, 9001, 9002, 9003, 9004
PLT356	AIM	Navigation ⟩ Radio ⟩ ILS 8956, 8957, 8958, 8963, 8966, 8967, 8975, 9380, 9382, 9403, 9412
PLT358	AIM	Navigation ⟩ Radio ⟩ ILS 8961
PLT361	FAA-H-8083-15	Navigation ⟩ Radio ⟩ SDF 8965
PLT362	AC 120-74	Recall radio — VHF/Direction Finding 9783-1
PLT365	FAA-H-8083-25	Recall reciprocating engine — components/operating principles/characteristics 9068, 9068-1, 9069
PLT366	49 CFR 830	Regulations ⟩ NTSB Part 830 ⟩ Definitions; Reports/Reporting 8233, 8236, 8246, 8317, 8318, 8322, 8323, 8725, 9098
PLT367	14 CFR 91 14 CFR 121 14 CFR 135	Regulations ⟩ 14 CFR Part 91 ⟩ Limitations Regulations ⟩ 14 CFR Part 121 ⟩ Aircraft Equipment Regulations ⟩ 14 CFR Part 135 ⟩ Aircraft Equipment 8061, 8062, 9355, 9355-1, 9358, 9359, 9360, 9361, 9809
PLT370	14 CFR 91 AIM	Air Traffic Control Procedures ⟩ Communications ⟩ ATC Communications; Clearances Air Traffic Control Procedures ⟩ Departure ⟩ Clearances Air Traffic Control Procedures ⟩ En Route ⟩ Speed Adjustments Regulations ⟩ 14 CFR Part 91 ⟩ Flight Rules 9006, 9007, 9008, 9009, 9045, 9046, 9047, 9439
PLT373	14 CFR 121	Regulations ⟩ 14 CFR Part 121 ⟩ Flight Crewmember Duties 9745, 9807
PLT374	14 CFR 121 14 CFR 135	Recall regulations — aircraft owner/operator responsibilities 8006, 8199, 8200
PLT375	14 CFR 135	Regulations ⟩ 14 CFR Part 135 Subpart B ⟩ Records Keeping 8012
PLT379	14 CFR 121	Regulations ⟩ 14 CFR Part 121 ⟩ Flight Release 8063, 8064, 8086, 8247, 8248, 8249, 8251, 8252, 8256, 8258, 8262, 9394-2
PLT380	14 CFR 121	Regulations ⟩ 14 CFR Part 121 ⟩ Alternate/Weather/Fuel/Requirements 8087, 8254, 8255, 8261, 8264, 9826, 9827
PLT382	14 CFR 121 U.S. Terminal Procedures	Navigation ⟩ Radio ⟩ VOR Regulations ⟩ 14 CFR Part 121 ⟩ Landing Minimums 9721
PLT383	14 CFR 121	Regulations ⟩ 14 CFR Part 121 ⟩ Icing Conditions 9379
PLT384	14 CFR 121	Regulations ⟩ 14 CFR Part 121 ⟩ Seat Belts/Cabin Announcements 8027, 8029, 8225

Learning Statement Code	FAA Reference	Subject Description (or Topic 〉 Content 〉 Specific classification) Question Numbers
PLT385	14 CFR 121	Regulations 〉 14 CFR Part 121 〉 Cargo *8032, 8038, 8039, 8040, 8041, 8042, 8138, 8139, 8175, 8832*
PLT388	14 CFR 91 14 CFR 121	Regulations 〉 14 CFR Part 91 〉 Equipment/Instrument/Certificate Rating; Limitations Regulations 〉 14 CFR Part 121 Subpart K 〉 FDR *8047, 8141, 8142, 8143, 8833, 9356, 9357, 9410*
PLT389	14 CFR 119 AIM	Navigation 〉 Radio 〉 GPS Regulations 〉 14 CFR Part 119 〉 Definitions *8003, 8192, 8193, 8196, 8197, 8201, 8202, 8430, 8767, 8768, 9724*
PLT390	14 CFR 121 AIM	Air Traffic Control Procedures 〉 En Route 〉 Reporting Regulations 〉 14 CFR Part 121 〉 Communications *8135*
PLT391	14 CFR 91	Regulations 〉 14 CFR Part 91 〉 Instrument Flight Rules *9362, 9364, 9365, 9389, 9390, 9616*
PLT392	14 CFR 135	Regulations 〉 14 CFR Part 135 〉 Operator/Control/Manual(s) *8010*
PLT393	14 CFR 91	Regulations 〉 14 CFR Part 91 〉 Flight Rules *9352, 9353*
PLT394	14 CFR 121 AIM	Recall regulations — declaration of an emergency *8239, 9097*
PLT395	14 CFR 1 14 CFR 119	Regulations 〉 14 CFR Part 1 〉 General Definitions Regulations 〉 14 CFR Part 119 〉 Definitions *8319, 8320, 8429, 9324, 9325, 9327, 9837*
PLT396	14 CFR 121	Regulations 〉 14 CFR Part 121 〉 Takeoff Minimums *8250*
PLT398	14 CFR 121	Navigation 〉 Flight Operations 〉 Preflight Planning/Calculations Regulations 〉 14 CFR Part 121 〉 Dispatch/Redispatch Regulations 〉 14 CFR Part 121 Subpart E 〉 ETOPS *8257, 8259, 8260, 8266, 8267, 8280, 8284, 9746-2*
PLT400	14 CFR 121	Regulations 〉 14 CFR Part 121 〉 Dispatch/Redispatch *8007, 8226, 8286, 8292, 8296*
PLT402	14 CFR 121	Regulations 〉 14 CFR Part 121 〉 Emergency Equipment/Survival *8171*
PLT403	14 CFR 121	Regulations 〉 14 CFR Part 121 〉 Emergency Authority/Actions/Reports *8240, 8245*
PLT404	14 CFR 121	Regulations 〉 14 CFR Part 121 〉 Emergency Equipment/Survival Regulations 〉 14 CFR Part 121 Subpart K 〉 Emergency Equipment *8058, 8059, 8060, 8144, 8157, 8159, 8163, 8164, 8165, 8167, 8168, 8170, 8172, 8177, 8834*
PLT405	14 CFR 91 14 CFR 121	Regulations 〉 14 CFR Part 91 〉 Equipment/Instrument/Certificate Requirement Regulations 〉 14 CFR Part 121 〉 Crew Equipment/Publications/Checklists; Dispatch/Redispatch *8045, 8046, 8053, 8054, 8140, 8146, 8235, 8808, 9407, 9414, 9415*

Learning Statement Code	FAA Reference	Subject Description (or Topic 〉 Content 〉 Specific classification) Question Numbers
PLT406	14 CFR 91	Regulations 〉 14 CFR Part 91 〉 Equipment/Instrument/Certificate Requirement; Flight Rules *8237, 9363, 9386, 9387*
PLT407	14 CFR 61 14 CFR 121	Regulations 〉 14 CFR Part 61 〉 Limitations Regulations 〉 14 CFR Part 121 〉 Landing Minimums; Line-Oriented Simulator Training Course; Training/Currency *8034, 8103, 8108, 8109, 8110, 8111, 8205, 8207, 8215, 8216, 8217, 8218, 8820, 8821, 8827, 8829, 9346, 9347, 9618, 9632, 9720, 9847-1*
PLT408	14 CFR 121	Regulations 〉 14 CFR Part 121 〉 Emergency Equipment/Survival *8176*
PLT409	14 CFR 61 14 CFR 121	Regulations 〉 14 CFR Part 61 〉 Limitations Regulations 〉 14 CFR Part 121 〉 Flight Time/Duty/Rest/Requirements *8002, 8104, 8189, 8211, 8219, 8220, 8221, 8222, 8223, 8224, 8227, 8228, 8229, 8231, 8238, 8706, 8707, 8708, 8709, 8724, 8814, 8815, 9342, 9714, 9838, 9839, 9840, 9841, 9842, 9843, 9844, 9845, 9846, 9847, 9848, 9849, 9850, 9851, 9852*
PLT412	14 CFR 121	Regulations 〉 14 CFR Part 121 〉 Flight Release *8293, 8294, 8295*
PLT413	14 CFR 121	Regulations 〉 14 CFR Part 121 〉 Alternate/Weather/Fuel/Requirements *8088, 8089, 8268, 8269, 8270, 8271, 8272, 8273, 8274, 8275, 8276, 8277*
PLT416	49 CFR 830	Regulations 〉 NTSB Part 830 〉 Reports/Reporting *8321*
PLT417	14 CFR 121	Regulations 〉 14 CFR Part 121 Subpart K 〉 Emergency Equipment *8166, 8169*
PLT420	14 CFR 91	Regulations 〉 14 CFR Part 91 〉 Instrument Flight Rules *8092, 8279, 8726, 8801, 8953, 9021, 9036, 9037, 9038, 9041, 9348, 9368, 9369, 9384, 9391, 9392, 9393, 9411, 9413, 9742, 9770, 9817*
PLT421	14 CFR 91 AIM	Recall regulations — instrument flight rules *9014, 9370, 9383, 9385, 9394-1*
PLT424	14 CFR 135	Regulations 〉 14 CFR Part 135 〉 Aircraft Equipment; Flight Operations Regulations 〉 14 CFR Part 135 Subpart B 〉 Flight/Crewmember Duties *8013, 8014, 8015, 8016, 8017, 8037, 8102*
PLT425	14 CFR 135	Regulations 〉 14 CFR Part 135 Subpart B 〉 Records Keeping *9746, 9746-1, 9761, 9762*
PLT427	14 CFR 61	Regulations 〉 14 CFR Part 61 〉 Limitations *9333, 9335, 9340, 9343, 9349, 9811*
PLT428	14 CFR 135	Regulations 〉 14 CFR Part 135 〉 MEL/CDL; Operator/Control/Manual(s)/ Operation Specs *8052, 8731, 8732, 8807*
PLT429	14 CFR 121	Regulations 〉 14 CFR Part 121 Subpart K 〉 Navigation Equipment *8149, 8152, 8195, 8195-1, 9408, 9409*
PLT430	14 CFR 91	Regulations 〉 14 CFR Part 91 〉 Instrument Flight Rules *8297, 9366, 9367, 9373*

Learning Statement Code	FAA Reference	Subject Description (or Topic 〉 Content 〉 Specific classification) Question Numbers
PLT432	14 CFR 1	Regulations 〉 14 CFR Part 1 〉 General Definitions *9326*
PLT434	AIM	Airport Operations 〉 Taxiing 〉 Airport Taxi Modes; Taxiing After Landing Airport Operations 〉 Tower Controlled 〉 ATC Procedures *9042, 9044, 9056, 9424*
PLT436	14 CFR 121	Regulations 〉 14 CFR Part 121 〉 Crew Equipment/Publications/Checklists; Enroute *8198, 8278*
PLT437	14 CFR 135	Regulations 〉 14 CFR Part 135 〉 Aircraft Equipment; Performance Requirements *8050, 8078, 8079, 8838, 8840, 8841*
PLT438	14 CFR 121	Regulations 〉 14 CFR Part 121 〉 Supplemental; Oxygen for Sustenance: Turbine Engine Regulations 〉 14 CFR Part 121 Subpart K 〉 Emergency Equipment *8020, 8021, 8022, 8023, 8024, 8025, 8028, 8030, 8031, 8055, 8056, 8072, 8073, 8074, 8080, 8081, 8156, 8173, 8174, 8180, 8181, 8182, 8183, 8184, 8185, 8186, 8187, 9576, 9577, 9605, 9606, 9638, 9650, 9651, 9819*
PLT440	14 CFR 121	Regulations 〉 14 CFR Part 121 Subpart M 〉 Flight Engineer Requirements *8008, 8009, 8026, 8033, 8043, 8113, 8155, 8188, 8190, 8212, 8213*
PLT442	14 CFR 61 14 CFR 121 14 CFR 135	Regulations 〉 14 CFR Part 61 〉 Instrument Currency Regulations 〉 14 CFR Part 121 〉 Recent Experience; Training Currency Regulations 〉 14 CFR Part 135 〉 Crew Requirements *8095, 8096, 8097, 8098, 8099, 8100, 8101, 8105, 8208, 8209, 8210, 8809, 8830, 9329, 9329-2, 9334, 9336, 9337, 9338, 9339, 9341, 9344, 9345*
PLT443	14 CFR 61 14 CFR 121	Regulations 〉 14 CFR Part 61 〉 Type Rating Regulations 〉 14 CFR Part 121 〉 Flight Time/Duty/Rest/Requirements Regulations 〉 14 CFR Part 121 Subpart M 〉 Flight Engineer Requirements *8035, 8036, 8044, 8082, 8083, 8107, 8112, 8191, 8289, 9328, 9329-1, 9350, 9633, 9634, 9646, 9663*
PLT444	14 CFR 121	Regulations 〉 14 CFR Part 121 〉 Crew Equipment/Publications/Checklists; Emergency Authority/Actions/ Reports; Operational Control/ Flight Release *8018, 8234, 8242, 8243, 8244, 8281, 8282, 8285, 8819, 9402*
PLT447	14 CFR 61	Regulations 〉 14 CFR Part 61 〉 Limitations *9351*
PLT449	14 CFR 121	Regulations 〉 14 CFR Part 121 〉 Training/Currency *8214*
PLT450	14 CFR 63 14 CFR 121	Regulations 〉 14 CFR Part 63 〉 Experience Requirements Regulations 〉 14 CFR Part 121 〉 Flight Time/Duty/Rest Requirements Regulations 〉 14 CFR Part 121 Subpart P 〉 Dispatcher Duty Limitations *8194, 8230, 9342-1, 9342-2, 9350-1*
PLT452	14 CFR 121	Recall regulations — re-dispatch *8232*
PLT453	14 CFR 121	Regulations 〉 14 CFR Part 121 〉 Records Keeping *8287, 8288*

Learning Statement Code	FAA Reference	Subject Description (or **Topic** ⟩ **Content** ⟩ **Specific** classification) Question Numbers
PLT454	14 CFR 135	Regulations ⟩ 14 CFR Part 135 ⟩ Aircraft Equipment *8001, 8049, 8067*
PLT455	14 CFR 121	Regulations ⟩ 14 CFR Part 121 ⟩ Dispatch/Redispatch *8290, 8291*
PLT456	14 CFR 121	Regulations ⟩ 14 CFR Part 121 ⟩ Landing Minimums *8094, 8127, 8128, 8130, 8831*
PLT459	14 CFR 91 14 CFR 121	Regulations ⟩ 14 CFR Part 91 ⟩ Instrument Flight Rules Regulations ⟩ 14 CFR Part 121 ⟩ Takeoff Minimums *8057, 8065, 8066, 8085, 8090, 8091, 8158, 8263, 8358, 8363, 8843, 9371, 9372, 9401*
PLT460	14 CFR 121 14 CFR 135	Regulations ⟩ 14 CFR Part 121 ⟩ Training/Currency Regulations ⟩ 14 CFR Part 121/135 ⟩ Training *8204, 8828, 9330, 9331*
PLT462	14 CFR 121 14 CFR 135	Regulations ⟩ 14 CFR Part 121 Subpart K ⟩ Emergency Equipment Regulations ⟩ 14 CFR Part 121/135 ⟩ Aircraft Equipment *8048, 8160, 8161, 8162, 8178, 8179, 8792*
PLT463	14 CFR 61 14 CFR 121	Regulations ⟩ 14 CFR Part 61 ⟩ Limitations Regulations ⟩ 14 CFR Part 121 ⟩ Passenger/Flight Events/Disturbances *8813, 9332, 9354,*
PLT464	14 CFR 135	Regulations ⟩ 14 CFR 135 ⟩ Aircraft Equipment Regulations ⟩ 14 CFR Part 135 Subpart B ⟩ Flight/Crewmember Duties *8075, 8076, 8077*
PLT465	14 CFR 121	Regulations ⟩ 14 CFR Part 121 ⟩ Seat Belts/Cabin Announcements *8153*
PLT466	FAA-H-8083-3	Weight and Balance ⟩ Center of Gravity ⟩ Limitations *8371, 8775, 8780, 9317, 9318, 9319, 9320, 9322, 9323*
PLT468	14 CFR 121	Recall regulations — Visual Meteorological Conditions (VMC) *8253*
PLT469	14 CFR 121	Regulations ⟩ 14 CFR Part 121 Subpart K ⟩ Navigation Equipment *8148, 8150, 8151*
PLT470	ANA	Aerodynamics ⟩ Flight Characteristics ⟩ Flight Limitations; Rotocraft Hazards Aerodynamics ⟩ Principles of Flight ⟩ Forces Acting on Aircraft; Forces Acting on Rotor Wings; Hazards; Lift *8407, 8408, 8410, 8411, 8412, 8413, 8424, 8425, 8426, 8427, 8428, 9781*
PLT472	FAA-H-8083-21	Aerodynamics ⟩ Flight Characteristics ⟩ Abnormal Flight *8414, 8415, 8416, 9800*
PLT473	AC 65-15	Aerodynamics ⟩ Flight Controls ⟩ Secondary Flight Controls; Servos *8327, 8328, 8329, 8330, 8331, 8332, 8333, 8334, 8336, 8338, 8339, 8340*
PLT475	AC 00-6	Meteorology ⟩ Hazards ⟩ Definitions; Thunder Storms *9200, 9249, 9708, 9708-1*

Learning Statement Code	FAA Reference	Subject Description (or Topic ⟩ Content ⟩ Specific classification) Question Numbers
PLT477	ANA FAA-H-8083-25	Aerodynamics ⟩ Load Factor ⟩ Stall Speed Aerodynamics ⟩ Stall/Spins ⟩ Angle of Attack; Stall Warning Devices *8348, 9808*
PLT493	14 CFR 121 AC 00-6 AC 20-117 AC 135-17	Aerodynamics ⟩ Principles of Flight ⟩ Hazards Regulations ⟩ 14 CFR Part 121 ⟩ Icing Conditions Meteorology ⟩ Icing ⟩ Frost *8084, 8265, 9162, 9179, 9180, 9181, 9440, 9440-1, 9449, 9695, 9753, 9756*
PLT495	AC 00-6 AC 00-24	Meteorology ⟩ Hazardous ⟩ Arctic Flying; Thunderstorms Windshear/Turbulence ⟩ Clear Air Turbulence ⟩ Windshear *9196, 9197, 9198, 9199, 9201, 9202, 9203, 9204, 9205, 9211, 9212, 9233, 9706, 9835*
PLT497	AIM	Navigation ⟩ Avionics ⟩ Transponder Equipment *9051, 9052*
PLT498	49 CFR 830	Recall Transportation Security Regulations *8131, 8137, 9763*
PLT499	FAA-H-8083-25	Aerodynamics ⟩ Performance ⟩ Normal Flight Aerodynamics ⟩ Powerplant ⟩ Turbine *8394, 8974, 9058, 9060, 9768*
PLT500	FAA-H-8083-3	Aerodynamics ⟩ Powerplant ⟩ Turboprop *9070*
PLT501	AC 00-6 AC 00-30 AIM	Meteorology ⟩ High Altitude ⟩ Jet Stream Windshear/Turbulence ⟩ Clear Air Turbulence ⟩ Encountering; Reports; Windshear *9128, 9129, 9210, 9218, 9219, 9225, 9226, 9232, 9235, 9262, 9263, 9264, 9777, 9777-1*
PLT506	14 CFR 1	Regulations ⟩ 14 CFR Part 1 ⟩ General Definitions *8774*
PLT508	14 CFR 91	Regulations ⟩ 14 CFR Part 91 ⟩ Equipment/Instrument/Certificate Requirement *9375, 9376, 9377, 9404, 9405, 9406*
PLT509	AC 00-6 AIM	Aerodynamics ⟩ Principles of Flight ⟩ Forces Acting on Wing Windshear/Turbulence ⟩ Wake Turbulence ⟩ Turbulence Factors *9119, 9120, 9121, 9122, 9123, 9124, 9125, 9126, 9127, 9715, 9858*
PLT510	AC 00-6	Meteorology ⟩ Air Masses and Fronts ⟩ Winds Meteorology ⟩ Airflow ⟩ Temp Meteorology ⟩ Atmosphere ⟩ Haze *9152, 9156, 9176, 9208*
PLT511	AC 00-6	Meteorology ⟩ Air Masses and Fronts ⟩ Dry Line; Fronts Meteorology ⟩ Atmosphere ⟩ Pressure Meteorology ⟩ Hazardous ⟩ Thunderstorms *9160, 9191, 9192, 9213, 9214, 9215, 9215-1, 9216, 9217, 9228-1, 9228-2, 9259*
PLT512	AC 00-6	Meteorology ⟩ Atmosphere ⟩ Temperature Meteorology ⟩ Moisture ⟩ Change of State *8710, 9155, 9161, 9182, 9183, 9184, 9185, 9185-1, 9234, 9810*

Learning Statement Code	FAA Reference	Subject Description (or Topic 〉 Content 〉 Specific classification) Question Numbers
PLT514	AC 00-6	Meteorology 〉 Atmosphere 〉 Pressure *9305*
PLT515	AIM	National Weather Service (NWS) 〉 Functions 〉 Aeronautical Weather Forecasts; Aeronautical Weather Reports *9256, 9704, 9705, 9747, 9747-1, 9747-2*
PLT516	AC 00-6	Meteorology 〉 Air Masses and Fronts 〉 Winds *9158, 9177*
PLT517	AC 00-6	Meteorology 〉 Hazardous 〉 Tropic Storms *9178-1*
PLT518	AC 00-6 AC 00-54 AIM	Windshear/Turbulence 〉 Clear Air Turbulence 〉 Windshear Windshear/Turbulence 〉 Microbursts 〉 Loss of Airspeed Recovery; Windshear Windshear/Turbulence 〉 Windshear 〉 Characteristics; LLWAS *9054, 9133, 9134, 9135, 9135-1, 9136, 9137, 9138, 9139, 9141, 9142, 9166, 9220, 9236, 9252, 9283*
PLT524	FAA-H-8083-6	Navigation 〉 Avionics 〉 Primary Flight Displays (PFD) Navigation 〉 Radio 〉 Electronic Displays *8206, 9750, 9751, 9769, 9769-1, 9769-2*
PLT526	AIM	Recall near midair collision report *9836*

Professional aviation.

Written by the industry experts, these books provide insight for career pilots.
Rely on ASA authors for advice on how to get your foot in the door at the airlines, hone your interview skills, and operate effectively as a professional aviator.

Checklist for Success
by Cheryl Cage
Takes aspiring professional pilots step-by-step from preparing their resume and application, through to the interview itself. A must-have reference for all job seekers.

Mental Math for Pilots
by Ronald McElroy
Sharpen your math skills for the interview as well as for the cockpit with these great tips for figuring math problems in your head without paper or calculator — everything from fuel planning to temperature conversions to crosswind components.

Managing Risk: Best Practices for Pilots
by Dale Wilson and Gerald Binnema
This book provides viable strategies as well as "best-practice" countermeasures pilots can use to avoid or effectively manage risks during critical phases of flight. Students and pilots at all certificate levels will improve their risk management skills by learning the procedures described in this book.

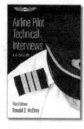

Airline Pilot Technical Interviews
by Ronald McElroy
Prepares you for the airlines' technical side of the interview process with real-world exercises. Aspiring professional pilots will be prepared to display their flying skills during the simulator ride, as well as their aeronautical knowledge during the face-to-face oral questioning.

Pilots in Command:
Your Best Trip, Every Trip
by Kristofer Pierson
This book goes beyond what is required by flight training curricula, into what is both a rarity and a necessity: solid advice from real pilots to student and professional aviators alike about how to be true leaders.

Job Hunting for Pilots
by Greg Brown
Covers all aspects of the job-hunting process and specifically focuses on how to get a resume hand-carried into flight departments. Not just another airline interview book — the author offers tips and techniques for job-seeking pilots at all levels of the industry, from commuter, corporate and airline pilots, to new CFIs and those flying helicopters. Second edition.

The Turbine Pilot's Flight Manual
by Greg Brown and Mark Holt
Whether you are a piston pilot preparing for turbine ground school, a military pilot transitioning to a corporate or airline job, or an old pro brushing up on turbine aircraft operations, this book is designed for you. Covers all major turboprop and jet systems, CRM, high-altitude weather, high-speed aerodynamics, and more. Also available as an eBook!

Air Carrier Operations
by Mark J. Holt and Phillip J. Poynor
Ideal for Air Carrier Flight Operations or Airline Operations courses, this book examines the regulations governing Part 121 air carriers. Includes Part 119 and relevant portions of Parts 135, 91 and 61 with emphasis on IFR operations.